lonely planet

P9-CRB-629

ADAM KARLIN
LISA DUNFORD

NEW ORLEANS
C I T Y   G U I D E

HIGHLIGHTS

FRENCH QUARTER

New Orleans is grounded in her history – the Quarter is a somewhat over-marketed version of that past. But for all the tourists, the narrative of this great US city is immediate and palpable in the flicker of gas lights on the Quarter's dark alleyways.

❶ Decatur Street
Hipster bars such as Molly's at the Market and goth punks accent this amble from the Quarter into the Creole suburb of the Marigny (p182)

❷ Mardi Gras
See the lines between civilized society and the realms of flight and fantasy shatter (p42)

❸ Royal Street
Creole architecture, salvaged antiques, outsider art – walk into a city's eccentric historical psyche along this lane (p76)

❹ Jackson Square
The green heart of the Old Town, and starting point for most New Orleans adventures (p68)

❶ Outsider Art
Find that perfect piece of outsider/folk art or salvaged beauty in shops like Simon of New Orleans (p196)

❷ Spirituality
See how Santeria and Voodoo are truly practiced in the 'Northernmost city in the Caribbean' at places such as Voodoo Spiritual Temple (p74)

❸ NOLA Vietnamese Community
Meet local Vietnamese, some of the city's hardest-working, most successful immigrants, over delicious bowls of pho (p167)

❹ Gay New Orleans
Wander the shotgun-shack lanes of Faubourg Marigny, one of the oldest gay neighborhoods in the American South, and drop into the namesake bookstore (p128)

THE PEOPLE

The food. The music. The art. The never-ending nightlife. These are all integral to New Orleans. But none of the above would exist were it not for the confluence of cultures and misfits who decided to make the mouth of the river home.

❶ Second Lines
What it means to be New Orleans: don't just witness, but participate in the city's spontaneous musical outbursts (p31)

❷ Preservation Hall
Join the crowds in this historic hall, a bona fide New Orleans trad jazz joint (p181)

❸ Vaughan's
Let Kermit Ruffins get your tail feather shaking during his live shows in Vaughan's (p183)

❹ Ogden Museum of Southern Art
Even the museums know how to party; try Ogden After Hours on a Thursday night (p89)

THE MUSIC

Straight up? This is the most musical city in the USA. It birthed blues, jazz and brass bands, and every pop movement that's been built on them. New Orleans seeks any excuse to groove and shuffle – join the dance.

DAY TRIPS

A city and its character are built from the countryside that surrounds them. For New Orleans, that's a beautiful, delicate bayou and waterscape inhabited by one of the most distinct regional cultures in the USA: the Cajuns. Bienvenue Louisiane, chère.

❶ Lafayette
The capital of Cajun Country is an anchor for local Francophone culture, and has good boudin to boot (p224)

❷ Down the Bayou
Explore the distinctive geography of this corner of America: the flooded forests of southern Louisiana (p231)

❸ Opelousas
One of America's great indigenous music styles, zydeco is accordion, washboards, guitars and lots of fun – and this town is the place to enjoy it (p229)

❹ St Francisville
Visit the antique-laden town where the nation's original conservationist made his famous bird sketches (p221)

EAT

Once you've eaten in New Orleans you'll see the rest of the world for the bland, flavorless wasteland it is. You'll spend your evenings dreaming of bacon candy and, if you're smart, you'll move here so you've got a permanent supply.

❶ Oysters
Take 'em fried, roasted or raw with a cold beer to be an honorary New Orleanian (p140)

❷ Po'boys
Fried oysters and shrimp? Roast beef debris with melted Swiss? All on French bread? Yeah, we got good sandwiches (p143)

❸ Crawfish
Nothing says celebrate like boiling up delicious mud bugs that outsiders would likely use a bottle of repellent on (p141)

❹ Cochon
Any restaurant that shows this much respect for the very best that pork has to offer has our undying love (p160)

CONTENTS

THE AUTHORS

Adam Karlin

On Adam's first trip to New Orleans, as a college freshman, he was that guy: the Bourbon St boozer who never leaves the French Quarter. To make up for this grievous error, for this book he threw himself into the Crescent City and a cast of chefs, bartenders, waiters, social workers, community organizers, lawyers, beer brewers, journalists, musicians, artists and every other funky thread of the New Orleans tapestry. New Orleans has struck Adam, an itinerant wanderer, as a city that could be home. And that's the highest compliment he could give any place he's written about for Lonely Planet.

Adam was coordinating author and wrote all chapters except Rebuilding New Orleans, Sleeping and Day Trips & Excursions.

ADAM'S TOP NEW ORLEANS DAY

First off, it's Thursday, in April, when it's green as hell but not as muggy, festivals are in season and girls are wearing summer dresses. My favorite day of the week (because it's a good gig night) during my favorite time of year in one of my favorite cities in the world.

I drive down Magazine St with the radio tuned to WWOZ or WTUL and the windows open to the spring air. Breakfast at Surrey's (p163), surely: think I'll go with whatever, because it's all good, washed down with fresh orange juice. Afterwards it's time for some café au lait and a little writing in Rue de la Course (p164). I like to laze around the Latter Library (p105) when I have off days, wandering the stacks and soaking up the sunlight. If my buddies are at their place around Bayou St John (p111) I might help them cut the grass in their front yard (it just gets so damn *lush* in spring) before we wander around the water. All that yard work makes us hungry, so best repair to Parkway Tavern (p171) for a po'boy. I'm thinking roast beef. Lotsa horseradish.

Me and my boys watch the sunset over the Bayou, hopefully with some crawfish at hand, then head to the Ogden Museum (p89) for its Thursday-evening concert. After the show we head to Bacchanal (p158) and get pleasantly drunk and full on wine and cheese, then repair to Vaughan's (p183) to watch the Kermit Ruffins show and shake a tail feather. We stumble out and cab it to R Bar (p182) for a few shots before finishing the night back in Uptown at St Joe's (p188), where the Strawberry Abita flows until I'm cheerfully kicked out, ready to face Friday, when we do it all again.

Lisa Dunford

Heeding the siren's call, Lisa first traveled to the Big Easy after moving to southeast Texas to be a newspaper editor, writer and restaurant reviewer in the early '90s. She's returned many times since, but it's the lilting French accent, upbeat two-step and delicious Cajun Country cuisine only a few hours from her home that call her back most often. Lisa is the author of the Sleeping and Day Trips & Excursions chapters.

New Orleans is an easy city for folks who operate by the seat of their pants. There's always some kind of concert on the horizon or festival about to erupt, and let's face it: folks here are very easygoing.

There's a lot of hospitality if you've arrived with no idea of what to do. On the other hand, this is a destination that rewards a bit of forward planning, especially if you want to see big events like Mardi Gras or Jazz Fest, when accommodation is hard to come by and restaurants are fully booked. For a US city you get a lot of bang for your buck in New Orleans: the cost of living is comparatively low, so you'll get meals of London and Paris quality (seriously) at a midrange US city price point.

Drinks are pretty cheap, especially if you've just been in a city like New York, and we've never seen a regular weekly cover charge top $10 (except, again, during events like Jazz Fest).

This town is easy for travelers – in some ways it's *made* for travelers. Tourism is the city's major money-maker. So as long as you can put up with maddening humidity in summer, lots of potholes in the roads, relatively slow but friendly service, great food, a never-say-die attitude and a penchant for parties, you and this city should fit together like crawfish and beer.

WHEN TO GO

The Gulf of Mexico provides New Orleans with plenty of moisture – the city receives about 60in of rainfall annually. No season is immune to rain.

From January to March the weather is quite variable, although rain is a given, but when spring arrives it brings long stretches of sunny, mild days that are perfect for the festivals.

Summer is hot and steamy; your clothes stick to your skin and you never feel properly dry. Brief afternoon showers, with thunder thrown in for dramatic effect, occur almost daily. On long summer days you can expect about eight or more hours of sunshine, out of a possible 14 hours. The months of September and October are the most likely to offer clear, temperate weather.

Winter temperatures average a comfortable 54°F, yet occasional drops in temperature, combined with the damp atmosphere, can chill you to the bone. Snow is rare in New Orleans. During December's short days, fog and rain conspire to allow only 4½ hours of sunshine a day. Localized river fog often forms from December to May.

FESTIVALS & EVENTS

New Orleanians are like kids when it comes to holidays: they'll take any excuse for a drink, a dance or a parade. The city has many holidays and festivals of its own, as well as all the federal holidays, and often does 'em better than anywhere else. Mardi Gras kicks into gear in February, making it the most festive time of year in New Orleans. The weather at this time sometimes has plans of its own, but figuratively speaking it rarely rains on the parade. Climate-wise, it doesn't get any better than April. With summer comes humidity and frequent showers; at this time locals

HURRICANE SEASON

Hurricanes – tropical cyclones in the Western Atlantic Ocean and the Gulf of Mexico – strike anytime from June 1 to November 30, with the greatest frequency in late summer and early autumn. In especially busy years, hurricanes can occur well into December, even January.

A developing hurricane passes through several stages. A tropical depression is the formative stage, and a tropical storm is a strengthened tropical depression, with wind speeds between 39mph and 73mph. A Category One hurricane brings winds between 74mph and 95mph. This can produce a storm surge, or large waves, which can flood coastal roads. The most intense is a Category Five hurricane, with sustained winds of 156mph or more.

Hurricanes are sighted well in advance, though their exact course can never be predicted. There are two distinct stages of alert: a Hurricane Watch, issued when a hurricane *may* strike in the area within the next 36 to 48 hours, and a Hurricane Warning, issued when a hurricane is likely to strike the area.

start vacationing and musicians often go on tour, but there's always another big event on the horizon.

January

SUGAR BOWL
Jan 1
☎ 828-2440
This football game, between two of the nation's top-ranking college teams, takes place on New Year's Day. It originated in 1935 and fills the Superdome to capacity every year.

BATTLE OF NEW ORLEANS CELEBRATION
☎ 589-4428
On the weekend closest to January 8, volunteers stage a re-creation of the decisive victory over the British in the War of 1812 at the original battleground in Chalmette National Historical Park. The highlight is the Saturday night tour, illuminated by lanterns, through battleground encampments. A noontime commemoration on Sunday in Jackson Sq features a military color guard in period dress.

MARTIN LUTHER KING JR DAY
3rd Mon in Jan
St Claude Ave
On this day, a charming midday parade, replete with brass bands, makes its way from the Bywater to the Tremé District, down St Claude Ave.

CARNIVAL SEASON
Early Carnival parades in January or February tend to be the most outlandish, such as the annual Krewe du Vieux parade that passes right through the French Quarter. Early in the Carnival season each year, the *Times-Picayune* runs a 'Carnival Central' section with maps of all the parades. See p46 for more information.

February

CARNIVAL SEASON
St Charles Ave & Canal St
The greatest free show on earth really heats up during the three weeks before Mardi Gras, culminating with multiple parades each day. Routes vary, but the largest krewes stage massive parades, with elaborate floats and marching bands, that run along sections of St Charles Ave and Canal St. None enter the French Quarter. See the Mardi Gras & Jazz Fest chapter for more information.

MARDI GRAS DAY
www.mardigrasneworleans.com
In February or early March, the outrageous activity reaches a crescendo as the French Quarter nearly bursts with costumed celebrants. It all ends at midnight with the beginning of Lent.

March

ST PATRICK'S DAY
Mar 17
Just when you thought the city would calm down, the festivities pick up again on St Pat's Day. At 6pm the annual Jim Monaghan parade, honoring the late owner of Molly's at the Market (p182), brings musicians and green-painted people together in the French Quarter. The parade ends up at Molly's. There's a simultaneous pub crawl disguised as a parade starting in the Bywater, at the corner of Burgundy and Piety Sts, and ending on Bourbon St in the Quarter. Even if these rowdy parades don't actually collide, you can easily jump the banks of one stream and find your way into the other. On the previous Sunday, the big Uptown/Irish Channel parade makes its way down Magazine St. Along the way, riders on the parade floats pelt bystanders with cabbages and potatoes. Follow them to Parasol's (p164), where a huge block party is a heel-kickin' good time.

INDIAN SUNDAY
Sun after Mar 19
www.mardigrasindians.com
St Joseph's Night, March 19, is a big masking event for black Indian gangs. After sunset, the Indians come out in their finery, and often their suits of feathers and beads are even more elaborate than they were on Mardi Gras. The confrontations between rival gangs can be intense, though rarely violent. If wandering the backstreets at night isn't your cup of tea, on the following Sunday, the Indians emerge for the last time for the Indian Sunday (also known as Super Sunday) parade. It's a much more relaxed and showy affair, which works to the audience's benefit. Bring a camera and get some amazing shots. The parade has no fixed route, but traditionally has gone through the heart of Mid-City. With the

neighborhood slow to recover from Hurricane Katrina, the event may undergo some changes; check the website for information.

TENNESSEE WILLIAMS LITERARY FESTIVAL
☎ 581-1144; www.tennesseewilliams.net
The end of March features a four-day fete in the playwright's honor. Tennessee Williams lived in the French Quarter early in his career, and thereafter called New Orleans his 'spiritual home.' Attendees of the event keep his spirit alive with a 'Stell-a-a-a!' shouting contest, along with colorful walking tours, theater events, film screenings, literary celebrity interviews and the usual quantities of food and alcohol. The festival runs through the last weekend of the month, with events held at theaters, restaurants and hotels in the French Quarter.

LOUISIANA CRAWFISH FESTIVAL
☎ 874-1921; 8200 W Judge Perez Dr, Chalmette
A huge crawfish feed qualifies as the epitome of southern Louisiana culture, and that's just what this is. It's fun for the entire family, with rides, games, live Cajun music and an array of dishes featuring crawfish. It's held in nearby Chalmette (drive down Claiborne Ave and you'll find yourself in Chalmette) in late March/early April.

April
FRENCH QUARTER FESTIVAL
☎ 522-5730; www.fqfi.org
One of New Orleans' finest music festivals, the French Quarter Fest no longer feels like a warm-up for Jazz Fest. It follows a similar formula of celebrating superb music and scrumptious food, but this one has the advantage of a smaller size, intimate Vieux Carré setting and free admission. But when we say 'smaller,' we don't mean puny. The festival's 15 stages spaced throughout the Quarter showcase jazz, funk, Latin rhythms, Cajun, brass bands, R&B and more over a period of three days. Dozens of the city's most popular restaurants operate food stalls in Jackson Sq and elsewhere in the Quarter. The French Quarter Festival is held over the second or third weekend of April.

JAZZ FEST
The Fair Grounds Race Track – and, at night, the whole town – reverberates with good

sounds, plus food and crafts, over two weekends in the latter part of April and early May. See p50 for details.

May
WINE & FOOD EXPERIENCE
☎ 529-9463; www.nowfe.com
Well, this is just an excuse to act all highbrow with strangers, but it's fun if you like wine and food. And who in New Orleans doesn't? You sign on (and pay a pretty penny) for various plans. 'Experiences' may include a vintner dinner, with wine-and-food pairings being the primary focus; an evening street fair on Royal St, made jolly by wine and song; and a whole host of tastings, seminars and brunches.

June
GREAT FRENCH MARKET CREOLE TOMATO FESTIVAL
☎ 636-1020; www.frenchquarter.com/events
Whether you say 'to-may-toe' or 'to-mah-toe,' you're sure to dig this celebration of the delta-bred red natives. If you're quickly tomatoed out, there's plenty of food and entertainment, and a gospel choir marches the Quarter singing the praises of the big tomato. It takes place in the French Market during the second weekend of the month.

July
INDEPENDENCE DAY   Jul 4
Food stalls and entertainment stages are set up on the riverfront, and fireworks light up the sky over the 'Old Man' – that's the Mississippi River, not Uncle Sam.

ESSENCE MUSIC FESTIVAL
☎ 800-274-9398; www.essence.com/essence/emf
Essence magazine sponsors a star-studded lineup of R&B, hip-hop, jazz and blues performances at the Superdome around the July 4 weekend. Started in 1995, the event regularly has big-name black recording artists, along with an array of stalls selling arts and crafts and delectable foods.

TALES OF THE COCKTAIL
☎ 948-0511; www.talesofthecocktail.com
Sure, Bourbon St seems to be holding a 24/7 festival of booze 365 days a year, but this three-day event, begun in 2003, sets its

sights a little higher. Appreciating the art of 'mixology' is the main point, and getting lit up is only an incidental part of the fun. If it sounds a little highbrow, well, it is. But that's no excuse for shying away from the free cocktail hour, which kicks off the event in the Hotel Monteleone (p202). This is also a literary event – perhaps in the same spirit in which *Playboy* is a literary magazine – for at some of the events you get to hear knowledgeable writers talk about booze and bartending, while you try interesting sorts of new drinks.

August & September

SATCHMO SUMMERFEST
Around Aug 4

☎ 636-1020; www.fqfi.org/satchmosummerfest
Louis Armstrong's birthday is celebrated with four days of music and food in the French Quarter. Three stages present local talents in 'trad' jazz, contemporary jazz and brass bands. The entertainment is free, and the food stalls offer festival staples such as po'boys, red beans and jambalaya at reasonable prices. At night the clubs hop, and throughout the fest seminars are conducted by notable jazz writers for serious music fans. It's tight like that.

SOUTHERN DECADENCE

☎ 522-8057; www.southerndecadence.com
Billing itself as the 'Gay Mardi Gras,' this five-day Labor Day weekend festival celebrates gay culture in the Lower Quarter. Expect music, food, dancing in the streets and a general boost in the city's gay population as thousands of visitors show up for the party. The Sunday parade is everything you'd expect from a city with a vital gay community, as well as rich traditions in masking and cross-dressing.

WHITE LINEN NIGHT

☎ 800-672-6124
Get decked out in your coolest white duds and wander about the Warehouse District, as galleries throw open their doors to art appreciators and lots of free-flowing drinks on the first Saturday in August.

October

VOODOO MUSIC EXPERIENCE
www.voodoomusicfest.com
In New Orleans rock 'n' roll tends to get overlooked, but not during Halloween

weekend, when the Voodoo Music Experience rocks City Park. Past acts have included the Foo Fighters, the Flaming Lips, Queens of the Stone Age, Billy Idol and Ryan Adams (all in one year!).

HALLOWEEN
Oct 31

Halloween is a holiday not taken lightly in New Orleans. Most of the fun is to be found in the giant costume party throughout the French Quarter. It's a big holiday for gay locals and tourists, with a lot of action centering on the Bourbon Pub & Parade Disco.

November

ALL SAINTS DAY
Nov 1

This being New Orleans, with its beautiful cities of the dead, you can expect to encounter memorable activities on this day. The cemeteries fill with people, some of them fairly eccentric, who come to pay their respects to ancestors and recently departed family and friends. It is by no means morbid or sad, as many people have picnics and parties. It wouldn't be out of line for a family to serve gumbo from a pot beside the family crypt. Interesting traditions are carried out, as many people spruce up the monuments and decorate them with creative memorials, some of which qualify as folk art. St Louis Cemetery No 1 (p112) and, around the corner, St Louis Cemetery No 2 are the easiest to drop in at,

ADVANCE PLANNING

Three Weeks Before You Go

Check online to see if any festivals are going down, and book tickets for any big name shows you may want to see at Tipitina's (p189) or Le Petit Théâtre du Vieux Carré (p196).

One Week Before You Go

Try to organize a car rental (p237). Make bookings at any high-end restaurants – such as Herbsaint (p160) or Bayona (p154) – that you don't want to miss out on.

One Day Before You Go

Read the Gambit (www.bestofneworleans.com) and check www.nolafunguide.com to see what's going on in the way of live music during your visit.

but pretty much any cemetery in town will have something going on.

BAYOU BACCHANAL
1st Sat in Nov

www.bayoubacchanal.com

This Caribbean festival features steel drums, carnival dancing, reggae, jerk chicken and a big ol' parade, which takes over Canal St before marching to Louis Armstrong Park.

CELEBRATION IN THE OAKS

www.celebrationintheoaks.com

If over-enthusiastic displays of holiday lights and decorations turn you on, you might want to check out the colorful constellations at City Park. It's a unique New Orleans take on the spirit of Christmas in America – a little bit Vegas, a little bit Disneyland, with 2 miles of the park's magnificent oak trees providing the superstructure. You can view it in its entirety from your car (turn off those headlamps) or in a horse-drawn carriage. A separate walking tour visits the botanical gardens and carousel area. The huge power cord is plugged into the socket every night after dark from the last week of November through to the first week in January. Admission is $10 per motor vehicle and $5 per person for the walking tour.

December

CHRISTMAS NEW ORLEANS STYLE
☎ 800-672-6124; www.fqfi.org

During December, St Charles Ave is a festival of light, as many of New Orleans' most posh homes are lavishly decorated and illuminated for the holidays. This is also a great time to tour historic homes. The lobby of the Fairmont Hotel in the CBD is transformed into a gaudy but charming Christmas grotto, its walls and ceiling concealed by shredded cotton. And, of course, the Celebration in the Oaks (above) continues all through the month. On Christmas Eve, St Louis Cathedral (p69) attracts a tremendous crowd for its midnight choral mass. Many restaurants offer réveillon dinners on Christmas Eve. French Quarter Festivals (www .fqfi.org) can provide a complete schedule of events, open homes and réveillon menus.

FEUX DE JOIE
☎ 524-0814

'Fires of joy' light the way along the Mississippi River levees above Orleans Parish

HOW MUCH?

Bottle of Abita beer $3

Po'boy $6-13

Gallon of gas $2.70

Tacky T-shirt $20

Bottled water $1.50

Frenchmen St show $5-10

Streetcar fare $1.25

Admission to the Ogden Museum $10

'Eye-opener' (morning cocktail) $5-8

Mardi Gras Beads $1-10, or your dignity

and below Baton Rouge in December and on Christmas Eve (December 24). To reach the giant bonfires you must either endure incredible traffic along the narrow River Rd, or drop a pretty penny to see the fires from a riverboat. Another option is to take I-10 to La Place (27 miles) or even Burnside (50 miles) to see the spectacle.

NEW YEAR'S EVE
Dec 31

Revelers – mostly drunk tourists – pack the French Quarter, especially around Jackson Brewery (p125), where the Baby New Year is dropped from the roof at midnight. Adding to the frenzy are thousands of college football fans, in town for the annual Sugar Bowl (p13).

COSTS & MONEY

Against all odds, including the aftermath of Katrina and the financial crisis at the end of the century's first decade, the New Orleans economy is doing pretty well. Ironically, partially thanks to Hurricane Katrina bringing the city into the international spotlight, tourism has been expanding at a good clip. American travelers have stayed at home to keep vacation costs down, and foreign travelers have rediscovered this great city, which is very good news for New Orleanians – after all, tourism dollars are what this city is built on.

With that said, New Orleans is still pretty cheap by American standards. You can find decent rooms for $100 , eat out very well for under $20 a meal, and enjoy the city's fabled nightlife at very reasonable rates. Of course, if you want to spend more, New Orleans will spoil you – we're just saying you don't have to.

Some ways to save money here include taking streetcars or buses instead of taxis, hitting up certain bars on specific nights when they're guaranteed to serve cheap or free food – many do red beans and rice for gratis on Mondays – and using the internet to suss out free concerts and such held in city parks and squares, which tends to be a weekly occurrence.

INTERNET RESOURCES

While you're planning your trip, get up to speed on local New Orleans news, culture and events by checking out the following websites.

Gambit (www.bestofneworleans.com)

Louisiana Weekly (www.louisianaweekly.com)

Offbeat (www.offbeat.com)

Times-Picayune (www.nola.com)

Following are other useful websites, many of which serve as gateways to an infinite number of interesting links.

Louisiana Music Factory (www.louisianamusicfactory.com)

New Orleans Jazz & Heritage Festival (www.nojazzfest .com)

Nola Fun Guide (www.nolafunguide.com)

WWOZ radio (www.wwoz.org)

BACKGROUND

HISTORY
THE RECENT PAST

There's a picture in the Tremé restaurant Dooky Chase, taken in the winter of 2009, of a newly inaugurated president Barack Obama about to tuck into some of the city's finest local soul food. The president looks happy, the staff look happy, and all in all the picture stands in complete contrast to another New Orleans image taken not four years earlier.

That is a shot of a family stranded on a flooded roof in the middle of Hurricane Katrina. The word 'help' has been written out several times, misspelled. This image spoke to the institutional failure that made the city so susceptible to disaster: not just of the levees that broke, but also of a neglected, poorly educated underclass that waited for days for rescue.

The Obama image suggested something different. Dooky Chase was a hang-out for members of the Civil Rights movement in the 1960s. The restaurant was devastated by the Storm but here it was, rebuilt and thriving, hosting the nation's first black president. Obama, who began his presidency by promising to reestablish something like the 1930s Works Progress Administration, a nationwide employment and civic improvement program that helped lift the nation from the Depression, made a specific point of visiting a city that, not much earlier, had felt abandoned by the country it had contributed so much to.

Pundits, geophysicists and even then–House Speaker Dennis Hastert (who claimed that rebuilding a city that lies below sea level 'doesn't make sense to me,' before backtracking) seriously debated writing off New Orleans as a lost cause. The city, they said, was – by dint of its geography – not worth rebuilding.

Native wags, such as journalist Chris Rose, a columnist for the *Times-Picayune* and author of post-Katrina memoir *1 Dead in Attic*, have suggested the USA has always distrusted this strange little city with a habit of marching to its own drummer (often enough, during a second line following a jazz funeral).

Yet millions of Americans and thousands of New Orleanians did rise to the challenge of rebuilding one of the greatest cities in the world. They waded into basements in 100-plus-degree weather and slopped out trash, rubble and corpses. They mowed lawns and planted gardens. They fixed each other's roofs, sometimes using discarded pieces of swept-away flooring. They celebrated small victories with what beer they could scrape together, and these impromptu parties became their own building blocks of reconstruction, the cultural component of rebirth in a city where enjoying life is as integral as cement.

Helping the locals were huge numbers of volunteers and professionals. Many were in their 20s and 30s, members of a transient generation that constantly moved between schools, jobs, Anywhere-America towns, MTV fads and online social networks. Always having some place to go, and never having some place like home. Talk to them in a bar, and many of these do-gooders will tell you how in New Orleans, city of misfits, great food, better music and a strange new thing – a historically established, distinctive sense of *place* – they were *making* a home. So they stayed

TIMELINE

Prior to European contact	1600s	1718
Today's Louisiana is populated by thousands of members of the First Nations, who fish, farm hunt and build large towns in the Gulf Coast region and northern prairies.	European explorers search for the entrance to the Mississippi River. Control of this access point would essentially provide command of the interior of the North American continent.	Bienville founds Nouvelle Orléans, which is populated by nuns, convicts, slaves and immigrants. The city is founded in its current location for its strategic position controlling the mouth of the Mississippi River.

in it. So many newcomers opted to stay that local academics suggested the term 'new New Orleanian' become an official demographic. Others just call these fresh neighbors YURPs: Young, Urban, Rebuilding Professionals. Very few seem to begrudge their presence.

The rebirth process has been slow, and some of the changes the Storm wrought on this town will be irreversible. It seems very unlikely New Orleans will regain its pre-Katrina African American population. As of this writing, almost four years after the Storm, city officials put the number of employees in the city's bus system down from a pre-Katrina 1400 to 400. Roughly 73% of pre-Katrina restaurants were back in business, but those that hadn't reopened could sadly be written off as lost causes. And only 61 out of 122 pre-Katrina public schools had reopened their doors. For more on the rebuilding process, see p56.

But for the purpose of the traveler, as a destination and as a city reintegrated into the great American conversation, New Orleans is back. And you should be, too. In April of 2009, political strategist James Carville determined New Orleanians have more civic pride than citizens of any other comparably sized US city. Folks here just aren't giving up on their home. It was a stunning statement of hope in a town still so obviously devastated by disaster.

FROM THE BEGINNING

Many aspects of New Orleans' culture today – street names, food, Mardi Gras – suggest a profound influence left behind by the French and Spanish, who took turns governing the waterlogged outpost before the USA absorbed it. It is equally significant that African culture, often with Caribbean influences, has always held a stronger sway here than elsewhere in the US. Of course, being a major capital of the South has determined many events in the city's history and contributes to its character today.

By North American standards, New Orleans is an old city, and the depth of its history has always been cherished by locals. An important part of post-Katrina rebuilding involves preserving the unique multicultural character that is very consciously rooted in the city's extraordinary history.

top picks

NEW ORLEANS HISTORY BOOKS

Aspects of New Orleans' fascinating history have been committed to paper by some mighty fine writers. Here is a selection of readable inroads into the Crescent City's past.

- Rising Tide: The Great Mississippi Flood of 1927 and How It Changed America (1998) An important and engrossing study of the politics of flood control in the lower Mississippi Valley by John M Barry. Especially pertinent in post-Katrina New Orleans.
- Storyville (1978) Al Rose takes a serious look at the city's notorious red-light district, but doesn't miss the intrigue and allure of the old 'hood.
- The Free People of Color of New Orleans (1994) Mary Gehman's engrossing overview of an integral ingredient of New Orleans' cultural gumbo.
- Frenchmen, Desire, Good Children & Other Streets of New Orleans (1949) Cartoonist John Churchill Chase sticks with the most colorful aspects of New Orleans' history and manages 260 pages of highly enjoyable reading.
- New Orleans: An Illustrated History (1981) An easy-to-digest, general history of the city by John R Kemp.
- Breach of Faith (2006) By Times-Picayune metro editor Jed Horne, this may be the definitive work on the human error inbuilt into New Orleans' levees, relief and infrastructure networks that evolved into one of the USA's worst disasters.
- Nine Lives (2009) Dan Baum's almost epic retelling of, well, nine lives and their fates before and following Hurricane Katrina.

BACKGROUND HISTORY

1750s	1762	1791
French Cajuns begin to arrive in southern Louisiana following the British conquest of Canada. The area they settle becomes known as (and is still referred to as) Acadiana.	France hands the Louisiana Territory, which has proven to be an unprofitable colony, over to Spain in exchange for allies in its wars in Europe. The Spanish add their architectural influence to the French Quarter.	Following a revolution in St Domingue (now Haiti), the arrival of French-speaking migrants, black and white, doubles New Orleans' population. The new arrivals add a veneer of Caribbean culture to the growing city.

Native Inhabitants

Louisiana was well settled and cultivated by the time of European arrival. Spanish explorers reported sighting hundreds of villages in southern Louisiana as early as the 16th century. Contrary to the myth of hunter-gatherers living in a state of harmony with the forest, local Native Americans significantly altered and impacted their environment with roads, trade networks and significant infrastructure. They were, however, susceptible to European diseases; the germs brought by early explorers wiped out thousands of Native Americans. Ironically, by the time the French arrived with the goal of colonization, the region had probably reverted to something like a state of nature due to the massive deaths caused by introduced diseases.

After 1700, Europeans documented numerous direct contacts with local tribes. A confederation known collectively as the Muskogeans lived north of Lake Pontchartrain and occasionally settled along the banks of the Mississippi River. The Houma nation thrived in isolated coastal bayous from Terrebonne to Lafourche up until the 1940s, when oil exploration began in southern Louisiana and disturbed their way of life.

Alliances between escaped African slaves and Native Americans were not uncommon. Early French settlers also sometimes married Native American women. Today, some 19,000 Louisianans identify themselves as American Indian; most are culturally and racially mixed.

European Exploration

Europeans probably first saw the mouth of the Mississippi River as early as 1519, when the Spanish explorer Alonso Alvarez de Pineda is believed to have come upon it. Word of such an entryway to the heart of North America reached Europe, and several explorers attempted to find it, but the Mississippi eluded ships on the Gulf until 1699, when Canadian-born Pierre Le Moyne, Sieur d'Iberville, and his younger brother Jean-Baptiste Le Moyne, Sieur de Bienville, located the muddy outflow. They encamped 40 miles downriver from present-day New Orleans on the eve of Mardi Gras and, knowing their countrymen would be celebrating the pre-Lenten holiday, christened the small spit of land Pointe de Mardi Gras. With a Native American guide, Iberville and Bienville sailed upstream, pausing to note the narrow portage to Lake Pontchartrain along Bayou St John in what would later become New Orleans.

French & Spanish New Orleans

Iberville died in 1706, but Bienville remained in Louisiana to found Nouvelle Orléans – named in honor of the Duc d'Orléans – in 1718. Bienville chose a patch of relatively high ground beside the Bayou St John, which connected the Mississippi to Lake Pontchartrain, thereby offering more direct access to the Gulf of Mexico. Factoring in the site's strategic position, Bienville's party decided to overlook the hazards of perennial flooding and mosquito-borne diseases. Engineer Adrien de Pauger's severe grid plan, drawn in 1722, still delineates the French Quarter today.

From the start, the objective was to populate Louisiana and make a productive commercial port, but Bienville's original group of 30 ex-convicts, six carpenters and four Canadians struggled against floods and yellow-fever epidemics. The colony, in the meantime, was promoted as heaven on earth to unsuspecting French, Germans and Swiss, who soon began arriving in New Orleans by the shipload. To augment these numbers, additional convicts and prostitutes were freed from French jails if they agreed to relocate to Louisiana.

1803	1808	1815
Napoleon reclaims Louisiana, then sells the entire territory (which encompasses almost the entire drainage area of the Mississippi River) to the US for $15 million. The transaction doubles the size of the USA.	As American settlers move into Creole New Orleans, the territorial legislature officially adopts elements of Spanish and French (ie civil instead of common) law to preserve its cultural identity.	General Andrew Jackson leads US troops in the battle of New Orleans and defeats the British in Chalmette, just outside of the city. The battle actually occurred after the War of 1812 had technically ended.

The colony was not a tremendous economic success, and women were in short supply. To increase the female population, the Ursuline nuns brought young, marriageable girls with them in 1728. They were known as 'casket girls' because they packed their belongings in casket-shaped boxes. New Orleans was already establishing itself as, and gaining a reputation for being, a loosely civilized outpost. Looking about her, one recently arrived nun commented that 'the devil here has a very large empire.'

In a secret treaty, one year before the Seven Years' War (1756–63) ended, France handed the unprofitable Louisiana Territory to King Charles III of Spain in return for an ally in its war against England. But the 'Frenchness' of New Orleans was little affected for the duration of Spain's control. Spain sent a small garrison and few financial resources. The main enduring impact left by the Spanish was the architecture of the Quarter. After fires decimated the French Quarter in 1788 and 1794, much of it was rebuilt by the Spanish. Consequently, the quaint Old Quarter with plastered facades we know today is not French, as its name would suggest, but predominantly Spanish in style.

The Spanish sensed they might eventually have to fight the expansion-minded Americans to retain control of the lower Mississippi. Hence, Spain jumped at Napoleon Bonaparte's offer to retake control of Louisiana in 1800.

Antebellum Prosperity

While Napoleon Bonaparte was waging war in Europe, the US was expanding westward into the Ohio River Valley. Napoleon needed cash to finance his wars, and US President Thomas Jefferson coveted control of the Mississippi River. US merchants were already playing a rapidly increasing role in the commerce of New Orleans. Nevertheless, the US minister in Paris, Robert Livingston, was astonished by Bonaparte's offer to sell the entire Louisiana Territory – an act that would double the USA's national domain – at a price of $15 million. On December 20, 1803, the US flag was raised.

Little cheer arose from the Creole community, who figured the Americans' Protestant beliefs, support for English common law and puritan work ethic jarred with the Catholic Creole way of life. In 1808 the territorial legislature sought to preserve Creole culture by adopting elements of Spanish and French law, a legacy that has uniquely persisted in Louisiana till today, to the persisting frustration of many a Tulane law student.

New Orleans grew quickly under US control, becoming the fourth-wealthiest city in the world and second-largest port in the USA in a matter of years. The city's population grew as well, and spilled beyond the borders of the French Quarter. In the 1830s Samuel Jarvis Peters bought plantation land upriver from the French Quarter to build a distinctly American section. That plot, beginning with today's CBD, was separated from the Creole Quarter by broad Canal St. Peters married into a Creole family and epitomized the American entrepreneur operating within the Creole host community.

Developers further transformed the 15 riverbank plantations into lush American suburbs. By 1835 the New Orleans & Carrollton Railroad began providing a horse-drawn streetcar service along St Charles Ave, linking the growing communities of Lafayette, Jefferson and Carrollton. Today, these one-time suburbs are all part of Uptown New Orleans. Creole families that benefited from the city's flourishing economy built their opulent homes along Esplanade Ave, from the Quarter all the way out to City Park.

1817	1820s	1828
Jean Lafitte – smuggler, slave trader, folk hero and pirate king – leaves for Texas after helping to defend New Orleans in the War of 1812. The cause of his eventual disappearance remains a mystery.	New Orleans becomes the second-largest immigrant hub in the USA, attracting migrants from all across Europe, particularly Germans and Irish. The latter largely settle in the area now known as the 'Irish Channel.'	The first synagogue in the city opens for services. New Orleans Jews are a mixture of Spanish, Alsation and Germanic groups, giving their community a unique cultural makeup.

Obviously, the wealthy chose the highest ground for their gorgeous enclaves. But the city also expanded into low-lying wetlands that had to be drained. Underprivileged immigrants and blacks settled the city's swampy periphery, including an area eventually called the Ninth Ward. These poor, flood-prone neighborhoods would be hardest hit in September 2005.

On a much lighter note, the late 1850s saw the revival of Carnival. The old Creole tradition, now propelled by Americans, hit the streets of New Orleans as a much grander affair than ever before. Americans also assumed control of the municipal government in 1852, further illustrating the erosion of Creole influence in New Orleans.

Slaves & Free People of Color

From the beginning, people of African descent were an important part of the city's population; many households in New Orleans included a few slaves. Equally significant, though, was the city's considerable number of blacks who were free in the antebellum period.

The French brought some 1300 African slaves to New Orleans in the city's first decade. In 1724, French Louisianans adopted the Code Noir (Black Code), a document that carefully restricted the social position of blacks, but also addressed some of the needs of slaves and accorded certain privileges to free persons of color. Under the Code Noir, abused slaves could legally sue their masters. The number of slaves in the city grew to thousands by the time of the Civil War. In the city slaves usually served in the household as cooks, maids, butlers and footmen.

Slaves in French and Spanish Louisiana were allowed to retain much more of their African culture than slaves in other parts of the USA. Drumming and dancing were permitted during nonworking hours, and since the 1740s free blacks and slaves were allowed to congregate at the huge produce market at Congo Sq (initially called Place des Negres), just beyond the city's ramparts. The Congo Sq market was a cultural brewing pot unlike anything else in the country, and immense crowds (including occasional tourists from the East Coast and Europe) showed up to witness complicated polyrhythmic drumming and dances, which, by stuffy European standards, were considered highly exotic and suggestive. Congo Sq today is a quiet corner of Louis Armstrong Park, on Rampart St.

Additionally, thousands more slaves were sold at public auctions held throughout the Vieux Carré. By the mid-19th century New Orleans had become the largest slave-trading center in the country. With the import of slaves outlawed, smugglers such as the 'pirate' 1 Lafitte (see boxed text, opposite) brought slaves into New Orleans by way of the state's bayous and swamps. As the price of slaves rose to $2000 or more, depending on their skill levels, slave numbers fell in the city. By the 1850s the influx of Irish laborers presented an inexpensive alternative, with very little cash commitment required on the part of the employer.

Long before the start of the Civil War, New Orleans had the South's largest population of free blacks. In Creole New Orleans they were known as *les gens de couleur libre* – free people of color. Throughout the 18th and 19th centuries, it was not altogether uncommon for slaves to be granted their freedom after years of loyal service. Sometimes the mixed offspring of slaves and owners were granted their freedom. Skilled slaves were often allowed to hire themselves out, working jobs on the side until they were able to earn enough money to buy their freedom. The Code Noir permitted free blacks to own property and conduct business. Many made a decent living as skilled carpenters and blacksmiths.

1830s	1840	1853
Marie Laveau becomes the Voodoo Queen of New Orleans. Although the religion has existed in diverse incarnations in the city since its founding, Laveau popularizes it amongst the upper and middle classes.	Antoine's opens for business. The restaurant is still open today, the oldest family restaurant in America, and its kitchen is supposedly responsible for dishes like oysters Rockefeller.	Yellow-fever epidemic claims the lives of almost 8000 citizens, or 10% of the city's population. Thousands more flee New Orleans. Eventually, the cause of the outbreak is traced back to mosquito-borne transmission.

A GENTLEMAN & A PIRATE (& A SLAVE TRADER)

Jean Lafitte, New Orleans' celebrated pirate, is a peculiar legend whose story frequently strays into the realm of mythology. Historical accounts seem overeager to stress his patriotism, while excusing some of his more suspect activities, which included raiding ships and slave running. His biographers typically emphasize his well-mannered, swaggering style while downplaying nasty little penchants for wreaking death and destruction. One thing's for sure: he's an alluring figure who fits right in with the New Orleans' mystique.

Lafitte's origins are hazy (he may have been from France, St Domingue or the Cajun Wetlands, and some scholars think he was a descendant of Spanish Jews), but by the time of the Louisiana Purchase he was already a highly public figure in New Orleans. He supplied stolen and smuggled goods to the remote, oft-deprived city. From his compound on the island of Grande Terre in Barataria Bay, about 40 miles south of New Orleans, Lafitte led a band of some 1000 pirates who plundered Spanish ships sailing in the Gulf of Mexico. (Technically, Lafitte could insist he was a 'privateer,' working on behalf of the state of Cartagena, which was battling Spain for its independence.) His brother Pierre kept a blacksmith shop in the city, where in fact he oversaw the wholesale and retail of the pirates' loot. Through the labyrinthine waterways of southern Louisiana, Lafitte's men transported clothes, spices and furnishings past US customs officials. In the city he sold his coveted merchandise at below-market prices. Obviously, he was a very popular outlaw, mixing with society's best (including Mayor Nicholas Girod), eating and drinking in the finest restaurants and having his pick of local women.

Louisiana officials tended to look the other way with regard to Lafitte's various activities. Most local politicians were supposedly the pirate's friends and customers. Governor WCC Claiborne, who took office in 1803, saw things differently and sought to put an end to Lafitte's reign. He put a price on the pirate's head, to the sum of $500. Lafitte countered by putting a price of $1000 on Claiborne's head, and hid out in the swamps, where Claiborne's bounty-hunters couldn't track him down. Thus, the French-speaking pirate wittily outfoxed US authorities, earning his way into the hearts of the Creole city forever. When Claiborne finally tracked Lafitte down and arrested him, Lafitte was sprung on bail, disappeared again to the swamps and flouted all orders to appear in court. The battle between these two men seems to have entertained New Orleanians for the better part of a decade.

When the Royal Navy threatened to invade New Orleans during the War of 1812, Lafitte offered to help block British passage from the Gulf. In return he asked that Claiborne stop hounding the pirates. Claiborne refused, but General Andrew Jackson arrived in town and agreed to Lafitte's terms. Whether Lafitte's pirates in fact helped much in the Battle of New Orleans (1815) is sometimes questioned, but for many it's a matter of faith that Lafitte proved himself a true patriot on behalf of the stars and stripes.

In any case, it doesn't appear that the USA held up its half of the bargain. In 1817 Lafitte was forced to leave Barataria. In Galveston, TX, he set up another small kingdom of pirates and outlaws. When the import and export of slaves in the USA was outlawed in 1818, Lafitte saw another money-making opportunity. Exploiting a loophole in this law, he was able to make a large and technically legal profit by capturing slave ships and selling the slaves at a discounted price to smugglers, who would turn the slaves over to customs officials. The same smuggler would often have a representative purchase the slaves from the customs auction (from which the smuggler would be given half the purchase price) and could then transport them legally to sell elsewhere in the USA.

Lafitte was rousted off the island by the US Navy four years later. He and his flotilla of ships disappeared in the night, never to be heard of again. Some historians think he may have ended up in Illinois or St Louis, which would be something like the worst anticlimax ever. Others simply surmise that Lafitte and his band of corsairs were wiped out in a hurricane. We'd like to think Lafitte rode out his days engaged in comical but highly dramatic adventures with Keira Knightley and Orlando Bloom, escaping ghost ships and sea monst... Oh. Been done.

1857	1862	1870s
The Mistick Krewe of Comus launches modern Mardi Gras with a torch-lit night parade. Eventually, hundreds of other 'krewes' (parading societies) will add their imprint to the city's most famous celebration.	New Orleans is taken by the Union and occupied for the duration of the Civil War. Many citizens resent the Northern presence, setting the stage for a difficult postwar Reconstruction period.	The 'White League' is formed in post–Civil War years as an often-violent backlash against the election of black politicians and the presence of Northern government officials.

The city's free blacks typically identified with Creole culture, speaking French and attending Mass on Sunday. Trained musicianship was prized among many families, and orchestras of free black musicians regularly performed at wealthy Creole balls. The free blacks of New Orleans were considered a highly cultured class who probably enjoyed a higher quality of life than blacks anywhere else in the US (and even many whites). They were often well educated, and some owned land and slaves of their own. But they didn't share all the rights and privileges of white Creoles and Americans. They were not entitled to vote or serve in juries, and while going about their business blacks were sometimes required to show identification in order to prove that they were not slaves.

Affairs between the races were socially accepted, but interracial marriages were not. The *plaçage* was a cultural institution whereby white Creole men 'kept' light-skinned black women, providing them with a handsome wardrobe and a cottage in the Vieux Carré, and supporting any resulting children. Subtle gradations of mixed color led to a complex class structure in which those with the least African blood tended to enjoy the greatest privileges (octoroons, for instance, who were in theory one-eighth black, rated higher than quadroons, who were one-quarter black).

The multiple classes of blacks in New Orleans greatly enhanced the cultural gumbo that made New Orleans such a unique and fascinating place. The city's cuisine, music, religion and holiday traditions were all enriched by the influence of Creole-African culture, and the city's persistent social divisions have its roots in this history as well.

A Demographic Gumbo

The multicultural stew was by no means limited to people of African descent, and European influences expanded well beyond the French. The Creoles could only loosely be defined as being of French descent. The progeny of unions between French Creoles and Native Americans and blacks also considered themselves Creole. Early German immigrants to the city frequently Gallicized their names, began to speak French and were soon blending into the soup.

When the French Acadians began to arrive in Louisiana in 1755, however, they did not assimilate into New Orleans' French-speaking society. The Cajuns, as they are now called, had been deported by the British from Nova Scotia in 1755 after refusing to pledge allegiance to England. Aboard unseaworthy ships they headed south, but the largely illiterate, Catholic peasants were unwanted in the American colonies. Francophile New Orleans seemed a more natural home for the Cajuns, but even here the citified Creoles regarded them as country trash. The Cajuns fanned out of the city into the upland prairies of western Louisiana, where they were able to resume their lifestyle of raising livestock. For three decades, wandering Acadians continued to arrive in Louisiana in the forced migration they called *le Grand Dérangement*.

Other former-French subjects soon arrived from St Domingue (now Haiti). The slave revolt there in 1791 established St Domingue as the second independent nation in the Americas and first black republic in the world. Following those revolts, thousands of slaveholders fled with their slaves to Louisiana, where they helped bolster French-speaking Creole traditions. During the following two decades, thousands of former slaves also relocated from St Domingue to New Orleans as free people of color. This influx doubled the city's population and injected an indelible trace of Caribbean culture that remains in evidence to this day. Their most obvious contribution was the practice of voodoo, which became popular in New Orleans during the 19th century.

1880s	1895–1905	1896
Mardi Gras Indians begin to appear. The 'Indians' are black New Orleanians who dress in stylized Native American costume, supposedly as a gesture of respect to those Indian tribes that resisted white conquest.	Buddy Bolden, who will eventually go insane and die in relative obscurity, reigns as the first 'King of Jazz.' His music ends up influencing generations of performers.	Homer Plessy, an octoroon (one-eighth black) resident of New Orleans, challenges the city's segregation laws. In the subsequent *Plessy v Ferguson* case, discrimination remains legal under the 'separate but equal' clause.

ANDREW JACKSON & THE WAR OF 1812

A month after Louisiana's admission to the Union as the 18th state in 1812, President James Madison declared war against the British. Madison's unpopular action barely registered with New Orleans' residents until a British force assembled in Jamaica.

General Andrew Jackson arrived in Louisiana in November 1814, but locals were suspicious of his intentions when he imposed martial law. Their distrust of Jackson lessened when the British landed on the Louisiana coast. Jackson convinced Jean Lafitte to side with US forces in exchange for amnesty, thereby gaining the help of the pirate's band of sharpshooters and his considerable arsenal of weapons. Jackson also enlisted free black battalions and Choctaws.

The Battle of New Orleans at Chalmette, just 4 miles from the French Quarter, was a one-sided victory for the Americans, with nearly 900 British losses versus only 13 US losses. Word soon reached New Orleans that the battle had actually begun after the USA and Britain agreed to end the war. But the decisive US victory clearly put a lid on British designs on the Louisiana Territory.

Antebellum New Orleans was the second-largest gateway, after New York, for a steady flow of immigrants entering the USA. As the Civil War approached, nearly half of the city's population was foreign born. Most were from Ireland, Germany or France. The Irish, in particular, were largely unskilled and took grueling, often hazardous, work building levees and digging canals. Their wages were low enough to justify hiring them rather than risk the lives of $2000 slaves. They settled the low-rent sector between the Garden District and the docks, still known as the Irish Channel.

Despite the Napoleonic Code's mandate for Jewish expulsion, and an anti-Semitic, Southern Christian culture, trade practices led to tolerance of Jewish merchants. Alsatian Jews augmented the small Jewish community in New Orleans, and by 1828 they had established a synagogue. Judah Touro, whose estate was valued at $4 million upon his death in 1854, funded orphanages and hospitals that would serve Jews and Christians alike.

Union Occupation

At the dawn of the Civil War, New Orleans was by far the most prosperous city south of the Mason-Dixon Line, and had commercial ties to the North and the rest of the world. But Louisiana was a slave state, and New Orleans was a slave city, and it was over this very issue that the nation hurtled toward civil war. On January 26, 1861, Louisiana became the sixth state to secede from the Union, and on March 21 the state joined the Confederacy – but not for very long. The Union captured New Orleans in April 1862 and held it till the end of the war.

New Orleanians, otherwise famous for their hospitality, didn't take too kindly to the occupation government or its leader, Major General Benjamin 'Beast' Butler. As his nickname suggests, Butler was not intent on winning hearts and minds. Soon after the US flag went up in front of the US Mint, a local man named William Mumford cut it down. Butler hung Mumford from the very same flagpole. Toilet bowls were soon being imprinted with Butler's visage.

On the other hand, Butler was also credited with giving the Quarter a much-needed clean-up, building orphanages, improving the school system and putting thousands of unemployed – both white and black – to work. But he didn't stay in New Orleans long enough to implement Lincoln's plans for 'reconstructing' the city. Those plans, blueprints for the Reconstruction of the South that followed the war, went into effect in December 1863, a year after Butler returned to the North.

1897	1901	1906
Storyville, New Orleans' infamous red-light district, is established. Some of the top-line brothels become architectural landmarks, and the music played in the best 'clubs' helps popularize jazz with out-of-town visitors (ie customers).	Louis Armstrong is born on August 4. He will eventually go on to reform school and a storied career in music, becoming perhaps New Orleans' most famous musical icon.	The muffuletta sandwich is invented at the Central Grocery. Along with gumbo, po'boys, jambalaya and red beans and rice, this will become one of the signature dishes of the city.

MUCH ADO ABOUT VOODOO

Voodoo has in no small way contributed to New Orleans' reputation as the 'least American city in America.' It is perceived as both a colorful spectacle and a frightening glimpse of the supernatural, and this has proved to be an irresistible combination. Scores of shops selling voodoo dolls, gris-gris (amulets) and other exotic items attest to the fact that visitors to New Orleans can't help but buy into the mystique of voodoo.

All the hype aside, voodoo has remained a vital form of spiritual expression for thousands of practitioners. It came to the New World via the French colony of St Domingue (now Haiti), where slaves from West Africa were able to continue their religious traditions. A hybrid voodoo developed on the island, as people from many different tribal communities contributed various spiritual practices – including animism, snake worship, ancestor worship and making sacrifices to deities, called *loas*.

Voodoo is no scarier or more compassionate than Christianity or any other major faith, and like many religions born of cultural intermixing, blends several religions (including Christianity) into one. The focus of worship is spirits tied to both the natural world and the paranormal.

See p74 for information about an existing voodoo temple and p73 for a voodoo museum. Also see the boxed text on p74. If you want to visit an authentic voodoo shop not aimed at tourists, stop by F&F Botanica (p133) in Mid-City.

A City Divided

The 'Free State of Louisiana,' which included only occupied parts of the state, was re-admitted to the Union in 1862. Slavery was abolished and the right to vote was soon extended to a few select blacks. But the road to equality would not be a smooth one, as it quickly became clear. The move to extend suffrage to all black men, in 1863, sparked a bloody riot, and after an exceedingly violent police response the melee ended with 36 casualties. All but two were black. It was a grim beginning for the Reconstruction period, foreshadowing an endless series of race-related struggles that would leave the people of New Orleans hardened, embittered and battered.

At the war's end Louisiana's state constitution was redrawn. Causing no small amount of resentment among white Southerners, full suffrage was granted to blacks, but the same rights were denied to former Confederate soldiers and rebel sympathizers. Emboldened, blacks began challenging discrimination laws, such as those forbidding them from riding 'white' streetcars, and racial skirmishes regularly flared up around town.

White-supremacist groups such as the Ku Klux Klan began to appear throughout the South. In New Orleans, organizations called the Knights of the White Camellia and the Crescent City Democratic Club initiated a reign of terror that targeted blacks and claimed several hundred lives during a particularly bloody few weeks in 1874. In the 1870s the White League was formed, with the twin purposes of ousting what it considered to be an 'Africanized' government (elected in part by newly enfranchised black voters) and ridding the state government of Northerners and Reconstructionists.

By all appearances, the White League was arming itself for an all-out war. Police and the state militia attempted to block a shipment of guns in 1874, and after an ensuing 'battle,' the Reconstructionist Governor William Pitt Kellogg was ousted from office for five days. Federal troops entered the city to restore order.

Although Reconstruction officially ended in 1877, New Orleans remained at war with itself for many decades after. Many of the civil liberties that blacks were supposed to have gained after

1927	1936	1955
During the Great Mississippi Flood, the levee is dynamited in St Bernard Parish, flooding poorer residents' homes to divert water and protect the wealthy in New Orleans.	Vieux Carré Commission founded to regulate moderations made to French Quarter exteriors. As a result, the Quarter remains to this day one of the oldest preserved neighborhoods in the USA.	Fats Domino records hit record 'Ain't that a Shame.' Along with Dave Bartholomew, Domino will help generate the distinctive groove – the 'New Orleans Sound' -- that defined the city's music in the mid-20th century.

the Civil War were reversed by what became known as Jim Crow law, which reinforced and in some ways increased segregation and inequality between blacks and whites.

With its educated class of black Creoles, New Orleans was a natural setting for the early Civil Rights movement. In 1896, a New Orleans man named Homer Plessy, whose one-eighth African lineage subjected him to Jim Crow restrictions, challenged Louisiana's segregation laws in the landmark *Plessy v Ferguson* case. Although Plessy's case exposed the arbitrary nature of Jim Crow law, the US Supreme Court interpreted the Constitution as providing for political, not social, equality and ruled to uphold 'separate but equal' statutes. Separate buses, water fountains, bathrooms, eating places and courtroom Bibles became fixtures of the segregated landscape. Louisiana law made it illegal to serve alcohol to whites and blacks under the same roof, even if the bar had a partition for segregation.

'Separate but equal' remained the law of the land until the Plessy case was overturned by *Brown v the Board of Education* in 1954. Congress passed the Civil Rights Act in 1964.

Into the 20th Century

As the 20th century dawned, manufacturing, shipping, trade and banking all resumed, but New Orleans would never again enjoy the prosperity of its antebellum period. The turn of the century was a formative period in which New Orleans became known as a very different sort of city.

Most important was the emergence of a new musical style brewing in the city. Called 'jass' and later jazz, the new music brought together black Creole musicianship and African American rhythms. It also benefited from a proliferation of brass and wind instruments that accompanied the emergence of marching bands during the war years. As jazz spread worldwide, the music became a signature of New Orleans much as impressionist painting had become synonymous with Paris.

New Orleans continued to escape the natural calamities that were always thought to be the city's destiny, but there was seemingly nothing to be done to offset human folly. The great Mississippi Flood of 1927, which inundated dozens of counties from Illinois down to Louisiana, generated natural fear in New Orleans. To the north, the great river broke its levees in 145 places and washed over 27,000 sq miles (70,000 sq km). Among the hardest hit areas was the Mississippi Delta, where thousands of destitute, black field hands, after struggling mightily to bolster the levees, were stranded for months afterward. The upriver levee breaks greatly reduced the threat to New Orleans but as a precaution city and state leaders arranged for the destruction of levees in St Bernard Parish, downriver from the city, deliberately flooding out some 10,000 residents' homes and livelihoods. (The residents were evacuated first, but this did little to make them any happier about the destruction of their neighborhoods.) This effort to protect the wealthier communities at the expense of poorer areas would not be forgotten – it fed conspiracy theories that ran rampant after Hurricane Katrina, as people observed a familiar pattern of devastation in poorer areas while wealthier zones such as the French Quarter and Garden District survived.

20th-Century Shifts

In the 1930s, oil companies began dredging canals and laying a massive pipe infrastructure throughout the bayou region to the southwest of New Orleans. This new industry contributed to erosion of Louisiana's coastal wetlands, and today the wetlands are disappearing at an

1960	1965	1970
Federal marshals escort black children into their classrooms as schools are desegregated. In the following years, 'white flight' into city suburbs will leave city schools largely bereft of white students.	Hurricane Betsy, the billion-dollar hurricane, batters the Big Easy. Improvements to the levee system made following the disaster will not prove sustainable enough to protect the city in 2005.	Jazz Fest is held for the first time, beginning its long history as a gathering of a few hundred fans celebrating the city's unique musical heritage.

YELLOW FEVER

New Orleans' reputation as an unhealthy place was widespread and well deserved during the 18th and 19th centuries, when its residents were ravaged not so much by wild living but yellow fever. Symptoms of the disease showed themselves suddenly, and death soon followed. An 1853 epidemic resulted in almost 8000 deaths; that was about 10% of the residents who remained in the city after some 30,000 fled.

Yellow fever's primary victims were male immigrants, children and laborers, many of whom lived and worked in squalid conditions. Yet no one was immune, and entire families were often lost.

Some of the supposed treatments only hastened death, including exorbitant bloodletting and large doses of calomel, a poisonous mercury compound, whose horrid effects mortified skin and bone, causing them to slough away. In 1836 one visiting physician commented, 'We have drawn enough blood to float a steamboat and given enough calomel to freight her.'

Morticians were overworked and underpaid during these epidemics. In the rush to entomb the dead, who were believed to be contagious, funeral services were often dispensed with. Cemeteries became putrid, fouled by the mass of bodies that could not be interred quickly enough.

In 1881, Dr Carlos J Finlay, a Cuban, revealed that the disease was spread by mosquitoes, and his findings were confirmed by Walter Reed in 1905. Health authorities in Louisiana urged people to screen their homes and eliminate mosquito-breeding grounds, but New Orleans suffered one last epidemic in 1905.

alarming rate (30 sq miles of coast every year). Some Cajun towns on Bayou Lafourche have already shrunk down to a smattering of buildings and trailers on wood pilings. Refineries crowd up along the Mississippi River between New Orleans and Baton Rouge. But gas and oil brought a new source of wealth to New Orleans' CBD, where national oil companies opened their offices. The State of Louisiana produces one-fifth of the nation's oil and one-fourth of the nation's natural gas today.

New Orleans was inundated with military troops and personnel during WWII. German U-boats sank many allied ships in the Gulf of Mexico, but New Orleans was never directly threatened. With war came manufacturing jobs. Airplane parts and Higgins boats, used for shuttling troops and supplies to the beach during the Normandy invasion, were built in New Orleans. For the duration of the war Mardi Gras was canceled.

The demographics of the city were changing. During the 'white flight' years, chiefly after WWII, black residents moved out of the rural South and into the cities of the North as well as Southern cities such as New Orleans. Most whites responded by relocating to suburbs such as Metairie. Desegregation laws finally brought an end to Jim Crow legislation, but traditions shaped by racism were not so easily reversed. In 1960, as schools were desegregated, federal marshals had to escort black schoolchildren to their classrooms to protect them from white protestors. The tragic irony is that as many whites moved their children into private schools, many formerly all-white public schools became nearly all-black.

New Orleans' quaint cityscape also changed during the postwar years. A new elevated freeway was constructed above Claiborne Ave. The neutral ground in the middle of the thoroughfare, once overgrown with trees, was paved for parking. Elevated freeways were also built along the uptown edge of the CBD, cutting immediately above Lee Circle. High-rise office buildings and hotels shot up around the CBD, and in the mid-1970s the Louisiana Superdome opened.

In 1978 New Orleans elected its first black mayor, Ernest 'Dutch' Morial, marking a major shift in the city's political history. Morial, a Democrat, appointed blacks and women to many city

1978	1987	2002
New Orleans' first black mayor, Ernest 'Dutch' Morial, is elected. Despite lingering racial tensions, a dynasty is established: his son, Marc Morial, will be elected mayor in 1994 and '98.	The Saints post their first winning season since joining the NFL in 1967; it will prove to be their last successful season for many years following.	Long-shot Ray Nagin becomes major of New Orleans. Nagin vows to clean up the city's corruption issues and flush out its old power networks, but his term in office will have its share of scandals.

posts during his two terms in office. Morial's tenure ended in 1986, and in 1994 his son, Marc Morial, was elected mayor and then reelected in 1998. In 2001 the younger Morial attempted to pass a referendum permitting him to run for a third term, but the city electorate turned him down. Another African American, businessman Ray Nagin, became mayor in 2002.

Preservation & Tourism

During the first few decades of the 20th century, the French Quarter was no longer a center for business, having been long overshadowed by the American sector and the CBD. It was an old and crumbling district, with almost all of its buildings dating from before the Civil War, and by this time it was heavily populated by large families of working-class immigrants and blacks. The Lower Quarter was largely populated by Sicilian immigrants, many of whom worked the port and the farmers market and opened Italian restaurants. It was a bustling, if decrepit, neighborhood.

The issue of preservation arose as prominent citizens began to recognize the architectural value of the French Quarter. The Vieux Carré Commission was founded in 1936 to regulate exterior modifications made to the historic buildings. Gentrification began to take its course as wealthy New Orleanians began to purchase property in the French Quarter, driving up the value of real estate and eventually nudging out the Quarter's poorer residents. A similar process took place in many other neighborhoods in the city, such as the Garden District and Faubourg Marigny.

As New Orleans accentuated its antiquity, tourism increased. Bourbon St became largely oriented toward the tourist trade, with souvenir shops and touristy bars opening up along the street. To accommodate the tourist influx, large-scale hotels were built in the heart of the French Quarter in the traditional architectural styles. As the oil boom of the 1970s went bust in the 1980s, tourism became the rock of the local economy. Conventioneers and vacationers regularly outnumbered locals on the weekend, spending cash and spilling beer, primarily in the French Quarter.

Tourist dollars meant job opportunities for locals, and also helped prop up some of the city's specialty industries, particularly the food scene. New Orleans effectively promoted its unique cuisine as reason enough to visit the city, and some restaurants propped up their chefs to celebrity status. In addition, the city became a magnate for ambitious Cajun chefs, such as Paul Prudhomme, who gained international renown while working at Commander's Palace (p162) in the Garden District and then his own K-Paul's (p154) in the French Quarter.

Since Katrina

For a detailed account of the impact of Hurricane Katrina and its aftermath, see p56. Since the Storm, Mayor Nagin has endured scandal after scandal involving racially loaded statements and allegations of favoritism, misappropriation of funds, conflict of interest cases and other controversies. As of 2009 his poll ratings were lurking near rock bottom, even among a relatively loyal black voting base.

In 2007, Republican Bobby Jindal was elected governor of Louisiana and embarked on a controversial relationship with the state's largest city. Democratic New Orleans has complained about significant cuts in state funding to city social services. Jindal, tipped as a potential Republican presidential candidate in 2012, has been criticized by the press and his own constituents

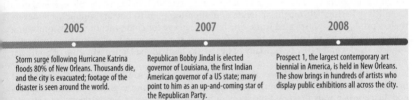

2005

Storm surge following Hurricane Katrina floods 80% of New Orleans. Thousands die, and the city is evacuated; footage of the disaster is seen around the world.

2007

Republican Bobby Jindal is elected governor of Louisiana, the first Indian American governor of a US state; many point to him as an up-and-coming star of the Republican Party.

2008

Prospect 1, the largest contemporary art biennial in America, is held in New Orleans. The show brings in hundreds of artists who display public exhibitions all across the city.

for spending too much time outside of his state, seemingly prepping for a presidential run. His decision to turn down federal bailout money following the 2008 financial crisis was widely criticized in New Orleans.

Yet in the face of these political difficulties, New Orleans is, in its way, thriving. Tourism is up and with it the economy. New restaurants and bars pop up with happy frequency, and the arts scene in particular seems to be turning this town into something of a Southern Left Bank for the 21st century. The city has learned to essentially rely on itself and the efforts of (and partnerships with) nonprofit agencies; the sense among many in the city is, if government – federal, state and local – can't help us, we'll help ourselves. This has resulted in such things as homegrown charter school programs, green rebuilding projects and an energetic arts council. While there are still many divisions in this city, there's also a great sense of community solidarity and a fierce, if measured, optimism.

ARTS

The arts of New Orleans go far beyond the proliferation of dabbers you'll meet around Jackson Sq, who can always eke out a living by hawking quaint scenes of the French Quarter. Over the centuries standouts in the Louisiana arts scene have produced truly brilliant work by turning sharp eyes on city and regional themes, or by departing entirely from the Vieux Carré aesthetic. The history of New Orleans is recorded in brilliant paintings left behind by the French and Spanish, haunting poetry, elegant architecture and, of course, music. But the city's art scene is not just rooted in history; New Orleans has taken on a muscular identity in the world of modern art, thanks to its hosting of the biennial Prospect 1 (see p198), the largest contemporary arts show in America.

Feeding much of the city's creativity is the intense appreciation of art held by the locals. Many of the city's Creole cottages and antebellum mansions are full of art. Tastes run the gamut, from traditional to envelope-pushing. Galleries were quick to reopen after Katrina, and today art purchases are a significant cash cow in the local tourism industry.

New Orleans is a city of good museums that are generally strong in local and regional art. Reputable galleries turn up in great numbers all over town. The city supports several distinct arts hubs. Royal St is the main stem of the mostly mainstream French Quarter arts scene, where savvy self-marketers have opened shop among the expensive antique shops. More down to earth (and lower in price) are the up-and-coming galleries along lower Decatur St. On the strength of the monthly Bywater Art Market (p195) and the New Orleans Center for Creative Arts (Nocca), an educational facility for young artists, the low-rent Bywater is a fertile artistic zone. More highbrow are the quality galleries of Julia Row in the Warehouse District. Upbeat Magazine St has several dispersed blocks of excellent galleries.

FOLK ART

The South has long been known for its rich folk-art traditions, now fashionably referred to as 'outsider' art, and New Orleans is a good place to seek out reasonably priced works for your collection back home. The very best paintings demonstrate highly individualistic techniques developed in complete isolation from the art world. Many great outsider works are in museums, but true gems can also be found in galleries and shops on Magazine St.

Clementine Hunter (1886–1988), an African American woman whose life spanned most of the 20th century, developed her wonderful painting style while living a quiet life in Louisiana's Cane River Parish. Self-taught, illiterate and often too poor to buy art supplies, she nevertheless produced sophisticated work. She had a keen eye for color, blending and combining hues with subtlety, and out of pure resourcefulness she occasionally substituted canvas with window shades and paper bags. Many of her works hang in the Ogden Museum of Southern Art (p89).

Roy Ferdinand (1959–2004) was another self-taught African American artist who specialized in what he termed 'urban realism.' His paintings capture life in the ghetto, with hip-hoppers and 'black urban warriors' amid the shotgun houses and fences of New Orleans' backstreets. Voodoo and Santeria images are frequent motifs in Ferdinand's finely detailed work. The Ogden Museum and the Barrister's Gallery (p194) both exhibit pieces by him.

RECOMMENDED READING

Don't just get bombed on Bourbon St. Get to know America's most interesting city by reading about it. Here's a short syllabus for your pretrip studies.

- *1 Dead in Attic* (2006) A collection of Chris Rose's compelling post-Katrina columns, which initially appeared in the *Times-Picayune*.
- *Why New Orleans Matters* (2005) Tom Piazza's an evocative, almost elegiac overview of New Orleans culture set in the context of the natural threats hovering in the city's future.
- *New Orleans, Mon Amour: Twenty Years of Writing from the City* (2006) Andrei Codrescu's book reads like a love letter tinged with sadness, but it's also filled with humor, irony and appreciation for a rare city.
- *Up from the Cradle of Jazz* (1986) A highly readable inroad to the city's musical heritage, from jazz to R&B and funk, by Jason Berry, Jonathan Foose and Tad Jones.
- *French Quarter Manual* (1997) An attractive, illustrated overview of architectural styles and features commonly found in the French Quarter, by Malcolm Heard.
- *New Orleans Cemeteries: Life in the Cities of the Dead* (2005) By self-proclaimed cemetery hound Rob Florence, this book delves into some of the more intriguing stories about New Orleans' fascinating bone yards.
- *Managing Ignatius: The Lunacy of Lucky Dogs and Life in the Quarter* (1999) The real-life account of Jerry E Strahan, who for 20 years managed the Lucky Dog company and a motley collection of vendors, some of whom served as inspiration for Ignatius J Reilly, main character in John Kennedy Toole's classic *A Confederacy of Dunces*.
- *Mardi Gras Indians* (1994) A full-color collection of photos and text by Michael P Smith that is both fascinating and beautiful.
- *Bayou Farewell* (2003) Mike Tidwell visits the disappearing Cajun Wetlands and uncovers a unique Cajun culture threatened by environmental changes.
- *Historical Atlas of Louisiana* (1995) By Charles Robert Goins and John Michael Caldwell, this is an engrossing, cartographic history of the state, with routes of Native American migration and colonial exploration, along with pages of maps and text specific to New Orleans.

Nilo Lanzas, a native Nicaraguan who moved to New Orleans in 1956, began painting late in life. He was self-taught, frequently applying his oils to wood. In his unique, accessible style, he has depicted such scenes as OJ Simpson, Saddam Hussein and Al Capone together in hell. The New Orleans Museum of Art (p110) owns some of his best work, but you can also visit Berta's & Mina's Antiquities (p196), a gallery operated by Lanzas' daughter, and buy something if it strikes you.

The local artist who calls himself 'Frenchy' has attracted attention with his exuberant style. The main attraction with his work, especially his series of live musical performances, is that it is created in the moment. It's spontaneous art that draws on the energy of dynamic human events.

Alabama artist Anton Haardt also owns a gallery on Magazine St (see p195), which generally features a handful of excellent outsider art from around the South.

MUSIC

Katrina scattered many of the city's musicians to the four winds, but the return of great talents and names from big-ticket cities such as New York speaks to the loyalty and solidarity many homegrown musicians feel for their town. In turn, projects like Musicians' Village, a Habitat for Humanity affordable housing neighborhood for musicians, are evidence of this town's affection for her musical talent.

Like never before, music is ingrained in this town's soul. This is a celebratory city. Parades happen nearly every day, and 'parade' in New Orleans means 'second line' – look for the marching brass band and file in after. There's your parade. Funerals, parties, brunches, festivals, fireworks, steamboat rides down the Mississippi – all are accompanied by music.

The city's history can be traced in its music. The French and their descendants, the Creoles, were mad about ballroom dancing and opera. New Orleans boasted two opera companies before any other US city had even one. Meanwhile, slaves and free persons of color preserved African music and dance at public markets such as Congo Sq. These European and African influences inevitably came together when French-speaking black Creoles, who prided themselves on their musicianship and training, began livening up traditional European dance tunes by adding African rhythms. From there, jazz was an inevitability.

The postwar influx of non-Creole blacks from elsewhere around the South was accompanied by a flourishing of blues, R&B, soul and funk music. And, as things will do, it all came full circle. All of these influences poured into the 1980s brass-band renewal that's going strong to this day.

Jazz

A proliferation of brass instruments after the Civil War led to a brass-band craze that spread throughout the South and the Midwest, and many musicians of the postwar generation learned how to play without learning how to read sheet music. These untrained musicians 'faked' their way through a song, playing by ear and by memory, often deviating from the written melody. Thus, improvisation became another way to breathe extra life into musical arrangements. The stage was set for jazz. New Orleans, as nearly everyone knows, was at the center of the birth of this American musical form.

JAZZ PIONEERS

One of the most problematic figures in jazz history is Charles 'Buddy' Bolden, New Orleans' first 'King of Jazz.' Very little is known about the cornetist's life or music, and no recordings survive. The details of this legend paint an attractive, larger-than-life man, indicating that he made a huge impression on those who saw him play. Some said Bolden 'broke his heart' when he performed, while others mused that he would 'blow his brains out' by playing so loud. One eyewitness account asserted that his cornet once exploded as he played it.

But the exaggeration veiling the actual truth about Bolden cannot cheapen his stature. For roughly a decade, between 1895 and 1906, he dominated a town already crowded with stellar musicians. People were drawn in by Bolden's expressive and energetic playing, and audiences deserted the halls where rival dance bands were performing when word spread that Bolden was playing somewhere else in town. Naturally, all the young musicians of New Orleans wanted to be just like him, and his influence was widely felt.

Sadly, Bolden went insane while still at the top of the New Orleans music scene. He was institutionalized for 25 years, oblivious to the fact that, after his abrupt departure from the scene, jazz had spread worldwide and developed into many new styles. When Bolden died, he was already long forgotten. Bolden is buried in an unmarked grave in Holt Cemetery.

After Bolden, New Orleans enjoyed a series of cornet-playing kings, including Freddie Keppard, Bunk Johnson and Joe 'King' Oliver. While Keppard's star passed over like a comet and Bunk languished in obscurity until he was rediscovered by 'trad' jazz enthusiasts in the 1940s, Oliver made a break for Chicago, where his Creole Jazz Band reached a much larger audience. Those who followed Oliver's career say his sudden fame was deserved but that he was past his prime when he reached Chicago. He was soon overshadowed by his protégé, Louis Armstrong, whom Oliver summoned from New Orleans in 1922. Together with Baby Dodds, Johnny Dodds and Lil Hardin (Armstrong's wife), Oliver and Armstrong made many seminal jazz recordings, including 'Dippermouth Blues.'

Pianist Jelly Roll Morton was a controversial character – he falsely claimed to have 'invented' jazz while performing in a Storyville bordello in 1902 – but he had uncommon talents in composition and arrangement. Kid Ory, who hailed from nearby La Place, LA, was also important in the development of jazz. His expressive 'tailgate' style on the trombone accompanied many of the first jazz

top picks

NEW ORLEANS TRACKS

- Na Na Na Theresa Andersson
- Ain't Got No Home Clarence 'Frogman' Henry
- Walkin' to New Orleans Fats Domino
- Right Place, Wrong Time Dr John
- Gimme My Money Back Tremé Brass Band
- Carnival Time Al Johnson
- Iko Iko The Dixie Cups
- Mother-in-Law Ernie K-Doe
- When the Saints Go Marching In Louis Armstrong
- La La La Lil' Wayne

OL' SATCHMO

Although he is sometimes referred to as 'King Louis,' in the world of jazz Louis Armstrong (1901–71) is really beyond royal sobriquets. The self-deprecating Armstrong is more widely remembered as 'Satchmo' (satchel-mouth), or 'Satch' for short.

Armstrong made his greatest contributions to music during the 1920s, when he began to modify the New Orleans sound. New Orleans jazz had always emphasized ensemble playing, but, to showcase his unique gifts, Armstrong shaped his arrangements specifically to support his own driving, improvised solos. With his cornet riding above the ensemble, songs such as 'Muskrat Ramble' and 'Yes! I'm in the Barrel' had an intensity not heard before. If the music sounds all too familiar today, it's because Armstrong's influence was so far-reaching.

As his popularity grew, Armstrong became the consummate showman, singing, jiving and mugging for his audience. His tours of Europe helped spread the popularity of jazz worldwide.

All of this, incredibly, was accomplished by the son of a prostitute. Armstrong grew up on the outskirts of New Orleans' notorious Storyville district, where he and fellow street urchins would sing on the streets for pennies. While residing in the Waifs' Home for troubled youth, he began to learn the trumpet, and, obviously, he was a natural talent. Armstrong's big break came in 1922, when King Oliver hired him to play in his band in Chicago. Satch never looked back. He only returned to New Orleans to play the occasional gig and, in 1949, to assume the role of King Zulu for Mardi Gras. He lived for several decades in a nondescript house in Queens, NY.

stars, including Louis Armstrong, and when Ory moved his band to Los Angeles in 1919, he introduced jazz to the West Coast.

Sidney Bechet was the first jazz musician to make his mark on the soprano saxophone, an instrument he played with vibrato and deep, often moody feeling. For 14 years clarinetist Barney Bigard was a key member of the Duke Ellington Orchestra. Henry 'Red' Allen was born across the river in Algiers, where he began playing in his father's marching band at age eight.

JAZZ RESURGENCE

When Wynton Marsalis released his first album in 1982, he was only 19 years old – and yet music critics proclaimed him a genius. Not since Louis Armstrong had a New Orleans jazz musician been so well received on the national scene. It was the start of good things to come. Soon, Wynton's older brother Branford Marsalis was also making waves, and other young musicians who were studying with Wynton and Branford's father, Ellis Marsalis, at the New Orleans Center for the Creative Arts, formed the nucleus of a New Orleans jazz revival. These included pianist-crooner Harry Connick Jr and trumpeters Terence Blanchard and Roy Hargrove. This wasn't another resuscitation of 'trad' jazz, though. The Young Turks of the '80s were clearly products of the post–Miles Davis and John Coltrane world.

Trumpeter Nicholas Payton began his career recording classic New Orleans standards with a modern musical approach. He joined forces with the ancient legend Buck Clayton in a Grammy-winning performance of 'Stardust.' More recently, Payton has experimented with blending jazz-psychedelic-funk fusion styles with hip-hop and digital effects. You can hear his groovy sound on the album *Sonic Trance*.

Trumpeter Kermit Ruffins is one of the most entertaining musicians in town. His shows at Vaughan's (p183) every Thursday night always pack the house and often attract other musicians, who come for the chance to play with Kermit's band, the Barbecue Swingers. Another trumpet player to watch is Irvin Mayfield, who, with legendary percussionist Bill Summers, has formed the popular outfit Los Hombres Calientes. They've got a good thing going with their intense concoction of wildly expressive and percussive Latin jazz, and they put on a great live show.

Donald Harrison Jr (namesake son of the late Mardi Gras Indian chief), an inspired contemporary jazz innovator on alto sax, made a name for himself in New York City before returning to his native New Orleans. He's followed his father's footsteps as a community leader and Mardi Gras Indian.

REBIRTH OF BRASS

It could reasonably be argued that modern New Orleans music began with marching brass bands. Mobile brass outfits parading through the city's backstreets for funerals and benevolent

EXPERIENCING NOLA MUSIC

You don't have to try very hard to catch music in New Orleans, because music is everywhere in the city. Much of what you'll hear as you walk through the French Quarter is either canned zydeco music (designed to lure free-spenders into shops) or cover bands rumbling out danceable grooves in Bourbon St bars. Rest assured, this is far from the bottom of the well. To really familiarize yourself with New Orleans music, take the following simple steps.

- Before your trip, tune into the WWOZ internet stream, which broadcasts local music round the clock. And if driving in the New Orleans area, keep your radio tuned to 90.7FM.
- Your first shopping stop should be the Louisiana Music Factory (p124). This excellent record store specializes in the music of Louisiana and has listening stations to sample recent releases and re-releases.
- In the afternoon, stroll through Jackson Square (p68), where you're likely to see local buskers working for tips.
- Catch weekly gigs (p183), such as Rebirth at the Maple Leaf Bar (p189) or Kermit at Vaughan's (p183).
- Don't miss the legendary club Tipitina's (p189), and while there pay your respects to Professor Longhair's statue.
- Visit the R&B hit maker Ernie K-Doe's Mother-in-Law Lounge (p190), opened before his death and lovingly maintained as an entertaining tribute.
- The New Orleans Jazz & Heritage Festival (p50) is a music-lover's smorgasbord packed into two weekends.

society 'second-line' parades during the late 19th century pretty much set the tone for things to come – Buddy Bolden, Freddie Keppard and even Louis Armstrong grew up idolizing the horn players, who frequently played along the streets where these future jazz innovators lived. While early-20th-century ensembles such as the Excelsior, Onward and Olympia Brass Bands never became nationally recognized, their tradition did not die. Many brass bands today, including the current generation of the Onward, Olympia and Tremé brass bands, still play very traditional New Orleans music, although surely they're jazzier than pre-20th-century bands were.

The brass band scene received a welcome infusion of new blood in the late 1970s with the emergence of the Dirty Dozen Brass Band. The Dirty Dozen was anything but traditional, fusing diverse styles of music from 'trad' jazz to funk, R&B and modern jazz. No longer a marching band, the Dirty Dozen continues to perform in clubs around town, and tours frequently. It paved the way for the much funkier and streetwise Rebirth Brass Band, formed in 1983. Original members of Rebirth, including trumpeter Kermit Ruffins, have moved on, but a younger crew of musicians has kept the band alive, and it remains one of the most popular groups in New Orleans, where Rebirth performs regular club gigs. Tremé Brass Band, headed by Uncle Lionel Batiste on the bass drum, is a nice mix of elder statesmen and young guns, mixing in traditional New Orleans jazz with original numbers with a little funk hitch to the beat.

Brass music has evolved in interesting ways, sometimes fusing with reggae and even hip-hop. Rappin' trombone player Coolbone is at the forefront of what he terms the 'brasshop' movement. The Soul Rebels also borrow freely from hip-hop for their innovative brass arrangements. Bonerama infuses the genre with the funk of the Meters and the loaded energy of Jimi Hendrix.

Blues

Despite its proximity to the Mississippi Delta, where the blues began, New Orleans never became a blues capital the way Chicago did, but it has been home to a few great blues guitarists, beginning with Mississippi native Eddie Jones, who preferred to be known as Guitar Slim. By the 1950s Guitar Slim was based in New Orleans, where he packed patrons into nightclubs such as the Dew Drop Inn. He wooed audiences with his anguished vocal style and agitated guitar licks. His biggest hit – a gift from the devil, he said – was 'The Things I Used to Do,' which sold a million copies. Other New Orleans blues guitarists include living legends Earl King, whose 'Trick Bag' and 'Come on Baby' are essential items on any New Orleans jukebox, and blind guitarist Snooks Eaglin.

R&B & Funk

Although New Orleans is still widely regarded as a jazz city, it is just as much an R&B and funk city. Since the 1950s and '60s the city has been churning out popular singers, drummers and piano players.

New Orleans owes its solid reputation as a breeding ground for piano players to Henry Roeland Byrd – otherwise known as Professor Longhair. His rhythmic rumba and boogie-woogie style of playing propelled him to local success with tunes such as 'Tipitina' (for which the legendary nightclub is named) and 'Go to the Mardi Gras.' He did not tour and his name soon faded away, but his style of playing lived on in younger pianists such as Huey 'Piano' Smith. In 1970, Professor Longhair was barely making a living sweeping floors when promoter Quint Davis tracked him down and booked him for that spring's Jazz Fest. His performance launched a decade of long-overdue recognition for one of New Orleans' great performers. He died in 1980.

While Professor Longhair was still mired in obscurity, some very unforgettable tunes came out of the Crescent City. 'Lawdy Miss Clawdy' was cut by Lloyd Price, with a backup band that included Dave Bartholomew and Fats Domino, a duo credited with shaping the 'New Orleans sound' after recording 'Blueberry Hill,' 'My Blue Heaven' and 'Ain't That a Shame.'

The familiar expression 'see you later, alligator' naturally resulted in a catchy New Orleans pop song, recorded by Bobby Charles in 1955. The often-covered 'Ooh Poo Pah Doo' is also a local creation, and was first sung by Jessie Hill. The late great Johnny Adams wooed the city with smooth, gut-wrenching ballads, and the dynamic pop duo Shirley and Lee's 'Let the Good Times Roll' became standard fare on radio playlists nationwide.

In the 1960s R&B in New Orleans and elsewhere fell under the spell of Allen Toussaint, a talented producer who exhibited a remarkable adaptability in molding songs to suit the talents of many of New Orleans' young artists. The formula worked for Ernie K-Doe, who hit pay dirt with the disgruntled but catchy 'Mother-In-Law,' a chart-topper in 1961, and the coy 'A Certain Girl.' Toussaint also wrote and produced the Lee Dorsey hit 'Working in the Coal Mine.'

Irma Thomas, the 'Soul Queen of New Orleans,' also frequently collaborated with Toussaint. The former waiter was discovered in a talent show and was soon recording hits such as 'Time Is on My Side' (later covered by the Rolling Stones) and the autobiographical 'Wish Someone Would Care.' A number of Toussaint-penned ballads, including 'It's Raining' and 'Ruler of My Heart,' lent definition to her body of work.

Aaron Neville, whose soulful falsetto hallmarks one of the most instantly recognizable voices in pop music, began working with Toussaint in 1960, when his first hit single, the menacing but pretty 'Over You' was recorded. The association later yielded the gorgeous 'Let's Live.' But 'Tell It Like It Is' (1967), recorded without Toussaint, was the biggest national hit of Neville's career.

Art Neville, a piano player from the Professor Longhair school, began performing with a group called the Hawkettes in the mid-1950s. In the late '60s he formed the group Art Neville & the New Orleans Sound with guitarist Leo Nocentelli, bassist George Porter Jr and drummer Zigaboo Modeliste, a group that would soon change its name to the Meters and define New Orleans funk music. The Meters later joined forces with George Landry, who, as Big Chief Jolly, was head of the Wild Tchoupitoulas Mardi Gras Indian gang (see boxed text, p45).

top picks

NOLA FILMS

Whether made on the streets of New Orleans or on a soundstage, some excellent flicks have drawn from the city's sultry, decadent and loony environment. These films capture the Big Easy in its multifarious guises.

- **A Streetcar Named Desire** (1951; Elia Kazan) New Orleans' seamy side, with some definitive casting: Brando as Stanley Kowalski and Vivienne Leigh as Blanche Dubois.

- **Down by Law** (1986; Jim Jarmusch) The opening shots, taken from a moving car panning past shotgun houses and housing projects, captures a side of New Orleans that we'll never know again.

- **King Creole** (1958; Michael Curtiz) One of Elvis' better films, with Michael Curtiz of *Casablanca* renown behind the camera. The King dominates, but New Orleans plays a key supporting role. Stagey, but has some great scenes of the French Quarter and seedy nightclubs.

- **New Orleans Exposed** (2005) Filmed just before Katrina wiped out much of the back-of-town area, this shoestring documentary delves into the housing projects where some of the city's biggest rap stars and most notorious criminals lived. It's a harrowing look at the flip side of the Big Easy.

- **Abbott & Costello Go to Mars** (1953) The old-school comic duo thinks they're going to Mars, but end up in New Orleans during Mardi Gras – the old chums never catch on to the fact they haven't left planet Earth.

Cajun & Zydeco

The traditional music of rural southern Louisiana began with dances – waltzes, quadrilles and two-steps. The 20th century brought innovations that led to two separate types of music. Cajun music is the music of the white Cajun people and zydeco is the music of French-speaking blacks who share the region.

The traditional Cajun ensemble comprised a fiddle, diatonic button accordion, guitar and triangle (the metal percussion instrument common to symphony orchestras and kindergarten music classes). Zydeco accordionists prefer the piano accordion, and the rhythm section usually includes a *frottoir*, a metal washboard-like instrument that's worn like armor and played with spoons.

Hip-Hop

It perhaps follows that a predominantly African American city widely known as the 'murder capital of America' should have had a thriving gangsta rap scene. The city's dangerous back-of-town neighborhoods and housing projects served as a petri dish for hustlers looking for alternative sources of income to drug dealing. The biggest rap star to come out of the Big Easy is Lil' Wayne, whose growling licks and almost stoned-sounding delivery have become the object of veritable idol worship among many teenage New Orleanians.

ARCHITECTURE

New Orleans' architectural strength is in its great quantity of 19th-century homes, and in the uncommon cohesion of so many of its historic neighborhoods. The city has no fewer than 17 historic districts on the National Register. Several, including Mid-City, Gentilly Terrace and Parkview, were devastated by floods after Hurricane Katrina. The French Quarter and the Garden District, which were spared flooding, have long been considered the two standouts. But, really, if you could relocate an entire neighborhood such as the Tremé, the Marigny or the Irish Channel to another city, these districts would stand out as architectural treasure troves. Such is the depth of New Orleans' historic housing stock.

The French Quarter and Garden District nicely illustrate the pronounced difference between the Creole and US influences that defined Old New Orleans. The Quarter and the Creole 'faubourgs' downriver from Canal St are densely packed with stuccoed brick structures built in various architectural styles and housing types rarely found in other US cities. The wide lots and luxuriant wooden houses of the Garden District, upriver from the French Quarter, more closely resemble upscale homes found throughout the South. Here we see a spectacular quantity and variety of architectural gems. Uptown, further upriver, the display intensifies to the point of near-gaudiness. New Orleans was an exceedingly wealthy city when this part of town was developed, in the decades preceding the Civil War, and these neighborhoods remain decidedly upmarket today.

FRENCH COLONIAL HOUSE

Surviving structures from the French period are extremely rare. New Orleans was a French colony only from its founding in 1718 until the Spanish took over in 1762, and it was really a small outpost at that time. Twice during the Spanish period fires destroyed much of the town. Only one French Quarter building, the Ursuline Convent (p72), remains from the French period. The convent was built in a style suitable to the climate of French Canada, but the French quickly recognized that the Caribbean styles were more appropriate in steamy New Orleans. A few houses built during the Spanish period and later have French-colonial trappings.

Madame John's Legacy, at 628 Dumaine St, dates to 1788 but in many ways reflects the French style. It is often described as a French plantation house. It's marked by a steep, hipped roof, casement windows and batten shutters. In common with French plantation houses in the Caribbean, it has galleries – covered porches – that help keep the house cool in summer. Galleries shaded rooms from direct light and from rainfall. Residents could ventilate the house by leaving windows and doors open during the day. This house has narrow open spaces around all four sides, indicating the streets of the town were not so tightly packed during the French period as they became during the Spanish period. Out on Bayou St John, the Pitot House (p111) also has signature French-colonial components.

Briquette *entre poteaux*, in which brick fills the spaces between vertical and diagonal posts, was common to French-colonial houses, and this style endured during the Spanish period. This structure is visible where stucco is cleared to expose the exterior walls of Lafitte's Blacksmith Shop (p178), and on the side of the Hotel St Pierre, at 911 Burgundy St. Neither of these buildings would otherwise be considered French colonial.

SPANISH COLONIAL HOUSE

During the town's Spanish period, adjacent buildings were designed to rub shoulders, with no space between, which created the continuous (though subtly varying) facade we now see along so many streets in the French Quarter. The signature type of home of this period is the two-story town house, with commercial space on the ground floor and residential quarters upstairs. The space between houses – the courtyard – represented a significant piece of well-shaded and private outdoor space. The courtyard was used like a family room. A covered space along the back of the house, the loggia, served as a sort of courtyard gallery, and within it a curved stairway led to the upstairs living spaces. A carriageway linked the courtyard to the street. Arches, tiled roofs and balconies with ornate wrought-iron railings became common. Often, servants quarters occupied part of the courtyard area.

The house at 729–733 Royal St was built in the Spanish era and retains much of its original character.

CREOLE TOWN HOUSE

Very few buildings survive from the Spanish-colonial period, and not all the survivors reflect the Spanish style. But the Creoles of New Orleans appreciated Spanish architecture and regularly applied its key elements (especially the courtyard, carriageway and loggia) to the town houses that are so common in the French Quarter still.

Most surviving examples date from the American period. An especially elaborate, three-story example of the Creole town house, with key Spanish elements, is Napoleon House (p178).

CREOLE COTTAGE

Free-standing cottages pop up all over the French Quarter and the Faubourg Marigny. The most common type of cottage is the Creole cottage, which, while simple, is not necessarily small. High-pitched gabled roofs are a signature quality, and dormers on some of the roofs indicate upstairs living spaces. The front of the house usually has two casement doors, sometimes four. Where there are two doors, the other two openings are windows. These openings are often shuttered to shield the interior space from sidewalk traffic, passing just inches away. An extension of the roof overhangs part of the sidewalk.

top picks

NOT-TO-MISS ARCHITECTURE

When roaming New Orleans' historic neighborhoods, keep your eyes peeled for these architectural gems.

- **St Louis Cathedral** (p69) New Orleans' most recognized building anchors Jackson Sq in the French Quarter.
- **Labranche Buildings** (p78) Stop and admire the great variety of cast-iron balcony rails that wrap around this block of buildings. You might also spot some wrought iron in the mix.
- **Napoleon House** (p178) Have a decadent cocktail in the rustic courtyard of this grand old Creole town house.
- **Lafitte's Blacksmith Shop** (p178) The pirate's humble cottage, listing slightly to one side, looks like a relic from the French outpost. It was actually built in the Spanish period.
- **Gallier Hall** (p88) The epitome of Greek revival pomp and circumstance, the hall overlooks Lafayette Sq.
- **Garden District** (p94) Nearly all the houses here deserve special mention – just stroll anywhere along Prytania St or St Charles Ave between First St and Louisiana Ave.
- **Ursuline Convent** (p72) In the French Quarter, this is the lone survivor from the French period.

CAGED BEAUTIES

Several components contribute to the unique appeal of the architecture of New Orleans, but perhaps none makes so instant an impression as the ironwork that adorns the city's many balconies and galleries.

Some beautiful wrought ironwork remains from the Spanish period. Wrought by hand, these railings have segmented geometric patterns, fine bars and forged arrows. Some have monograms. Have a look at the high-quality wrought-iron balcony rails on the Cabildo (p69) and the Presbytère (p72).

The innovation of casting iron made mass production possible. During the 1850s, after Madame Pontalba added the cast-iron railings to her prominent Pontalba Buildings (p68), the entire town went mad for ironwork. Cast iron made it possible to integrate complex patterns and shapely filigrees into designs. Decorative motifs such as flowers and ears of corn became not only possible, but popular.

You'll also find wrought- and cast-iron fences and gates around some of the crypts in St Louis Cemetery No 1 (p112).

The airy floor plan is as simple as can be, with four interconnected chambers, each with an opening (a door or window) to the side of the house. Ceilings are high. There is usually space on the sides of the house for exposed access to a back courtyard. At the back of the house there is a gallery, often with arched openings to the courtyard.

Simple Creole cottages probably started to appear during the Spanish period. Over time they became more stylish, reflecting Victorian tastes with intricate fanlights, ornately carved eve brackets and elaborately designed dormers. In some instances the form is expanded to include two full floors, plus dormers. But structurally, and in terms of floor plan, Creole cottages tended to vary little, for this style of house was well suited to the French Quarter's urban density and Louisiana's steamy climate. The house at 936 St Peter St is a Creole cottage, although the Corinthian pilasters that frame the facade are not at all typical. In the Marigny, the double cottage at 1809–11 Dauphine St is an even better example. Similar houses can be seen throughout the neighborhood.

SHOTGUN HOUSE

During the latter half of the 19th century, as New Orleans grew, the shotgun house became a more popular type of single-family dwelling than the Creole cottage. Shotgun houses were inexpensive homes that could be built on narrow property lots, and they were built in great numbers all over New Orleans. The name shotgun supposedly suggests that a bullet could be fired from front to back through the open doorways of all of the rooms, but in truth only the most basic shotgun has its doors lined up so perfectly. Walk along Orleans or St Anne Sts toward Rampart St and you'll see rows of shotguns with four-step stoops and finely trimmed eves.

The most basic 'single-shotgun' house is a row of rooms with doors leading from one to the next. As there is no hall, you have to pass through each room to get from the front to the back of the house. These houses are freestanding, with narrow spaces along either side of the house. Windows on both sides encourage cross-ventilation and keep the rooms cool. High ceilings also help with ventilation. The interiors are often comfortable and adorned with Victorian flourishes.

'Double-shotguns' are duplexes, with mirror-image halves traditionally forming two homes. Many double-shotguns have been converted into large single homes. Some shotguns, called 'camel-back shotguns,' have a 2nd floor above the back of the house.

AMERICAN TOWN HOUSE

The town house (see Spanish Colonial House, p37) was popular among Anglo-Americans, but the Americans had their own style. They replaced the open carriageway with a closed hall leading from the front to the back of the house. They also had no commercial space on the ground floor. Americans tended not to conduct their business at home.

You'll see American town houses throughout the Quarter, but some stand out. Gallier House (p73) is a landmark designed by James Gallier Jr and is open for tours. The house has both a carriageway and hallway, and for Gallier it was a conscious fusion of the two styles.

FEDERAL

Federal-style architecture, with its restrained grace and Classic Roman references, may not be representative of the New Orleans aesthetic. However, architect Benjamin Henry Latrobe's Louisiana State Bank (401 Royal St) is a local landmark that reflects the straightforward geometry, plain surfaces and fine detail of the Federal style. Note the elegant, slightly pitched beams over the second-story windows and the narrow arched dormers. Slender wrought-iron balconies extend just far enough to allow the parting of casement shutters to peek out and wave hello. The influence of this style can be observed in many town houses in the French Quarter. Simply patterned cornices commonly found on cottages often represent a Federal influence.

GREEK REVIVAL

Perhaps no other style symbolizes the wealth and showiness of mid-19th-century America than Greek revival architecture. The style, which is readily recognizable for its tall columns, was inspired by such classics as the Parthenon. Greek revival houses can be found in droves along St Charles Ave Uptown and in the Garden District. A nice example is the raised villa at 2127 Prytania St. In the French Quarter you'll see grand Greek revival entryways at 840 Conti St and 1303 Bourbon St.

New Orleans' best example of monumental Greek revival architecture, with its columned porticos and stolid structure, is Gallier Hall (p88).

FIVE-BAY CENTER HALL HOUSE

The 1½-story, center hall house became common with the arrival of more Anglo-Americans to New Orleans after the Louisiana Purchase in 1803. The raised center hall house, found in the Garden District and Uptown, became the most common type. It stands on a pier foundation 2ft to 8ft above ground, and its columned front gallery spans the entire width of the house. The front door leads directly into the center hall and is flanked by two windows to each side. The roof is gabled and usually has a dormer to illuminate an upstairs room. This type of house is clad in wood.

TWO-LEVEL GALLERY HOUSE

This type of home is most common in the Lower Garden and Garden Districts, although a few can be seen along lower Chartres St in the French Quarter and along Esplanade Ave, heading toward the lake. It's a two-story house, set back from the sidewalk, with front galleries on both levels. Each level has three or four openings, with doors usually to one side. Stately box columns are common.

ITALIANATE

The Italianate style gained popularity after the Civil War. Although the style originally drew its influence from the stately villas of Tuscany, you won't necessarily recognize the connection in New Orleans. You're more likely to identify certain details that mark the Italianate style, including wide roof overhangs with closely spaced brackets or double-brackets. Segmental arches, frequently used over doors and windows, and the ever-popular decorative box-like parapets over galleries are also commonly identified as Italianate features. You'll find such details on many different types of buildings in New Orleans. On the outskirts of the French Quarter, the town house at 547 Esplanade Ave has a graceful Italianate entrance and signature double-eve brackets.

BEAUX ARTS

The hefty beaux-arts style, with its grand scale and cold stone siding, is atypical of the more earthy architecture New Orleans is known for. In the heart of the French Quarter, the beaux-arts State Supreme Court Building (p79) dwarfs its neighbors, but nevertheless has an impressive beauty that defies its context. Opposite, the building at 410–414 Chartres St, which houses the research center of the Historic New Orleans Collection (p76), boasts staunch beaux-arts features on a relatively modest scale. The terracotta-clad Hotel Monteleone (p202) displays some of the finer, more decorative features of the style.

SECOND EMPIRE

The Second Empire style made its way to New Orleans from France via the East Coast during the Reconstruction period. It is marked by mansard roofs, prominent dormers and rounded moldings over the windows and doors. In New Orleans, where classical styles remained influential, the Second Empire style was more restrained than elsewhere. A good example is the house at 1437 Eighth St in the Garden District.

ENVIRONMENT & PLANNING

The damage wrought by Hurricane Katrina, though devastating for so much of the city, was not the cataclysmic event long foreseen by ecologists. Nature seems to have her own plans for southern Louisiana and, despite consistent human efforts to stave off the inevitable, New Orleans remains an enjoy-it-while-you-can sort of place.

THE LAND

The first important factor to consider is that New Orleans is surrounded by water. It stands between the Mississippi River, which curls like a devilish snake around much of the city, and Lake Pontchartrain, a large saltwater body connected to the Gulf of Mexico. Swamps and marshes cover much of the remaining area around the city.

The land the city stands on has been wrested from the Mississippi's natural floodplain. The oldest parts of town adhere to the high ground, which is, in fact, made up of natural levees created by the Mississippi depositing soil there during floods. The moniker 'Crescent City' comes from this old footprint on the natural levees, which got its shape by forming along the curve of the river. The high ground in New Orleans is just a few feet above sea level. Much of the rest of the city is below sea level, forming a bowl that obviously remains vulnerable to flooding, despite human-made levees. The city's elevation averages 2ft below sea level. And it is sinking.

Most of Louisiana and Mississippi was formed over millennia by the Mississippi, which spilled huge amounts of soil toward the gulf, forming sandbars and land. The river constantly shifted its course in search of shorter paths to the Gulf, forever fanning east then west and back, pushing the coast further south. The land it created was of a fine and loose soil, excellent for planting. It also gradually sinks under its own weight, in a process known as subsidence. Before the levees were put in place, flooding regularly replenished the soil and offset this subsidence. The 'bowl' that flooded after Hurricane Katrina is partly land that has subsided, and partly former swamp.

New Orleans is surrounded by 130 miles of levees. The US Army Corps of Engineers built and maintains these levees, which have kept the Mississippi River on a fixed course for more than a century. You'll see the levee from Jackson Sq, in the French Quarter, as it rises like an evenly graded hill and hides the river from view. You can also walk along the levee for an up-close look at it and one of the world's most powerful rivers.

The other important factor for New Orleans is its proximity to the Gulf of Mexico, and its vulnerability to the storm systems generated there. The Atlantic hurricane season lasts approximately half a year, from early summer to late fall. The 2005 hurricane season was particularly brutal, with a record 27 tropical

DEMOGRAPHIC SHIFT

Before Katrina, Orleans Parish was home to approximately 500,000 people. African Americans held a considerable majority, with 67% of the population, making New Orleans one of the 'blackest' cities in the USA. Whites comprised just over 30% and the remainder was mostly Hispanic and Vietnamese. These figures are changing as the population resettles. Some projections have suggested the future New Orleans will be a city of about 250,000 people, though it is easy to imagine this figure rising considerably once the city is actually rebuilt. New Orleans will likely continue to be very diverse, perhaps more than before. The percentage of blacks currently stands at around 59% and the Hispanic population is increasing.

storms spawning 15 hurricanes. Of the five to make landfall, two, Katrina and Rita, slammed southern Louisiana within a three-week period. Katrina was by far the most destructive, but Rita was actually stronger.

Neither Katrina nor Rita was a direct, cataclysmic hit on New Orleans. Had the eye of either storm passed over the city, damage from wind and flying debris may well have exceeded damage done by flooding. In such an event, neighborhoods on the higher ground would not have been spared. New Orleanians must continue to brace themselves for a disaster of that magnitude. With Hurricane Ivan having struck near the city in 2004, it seems Louisiana is experiencing major hurricanes with increased frequency.

Hurricanes cause floods by pushing in surging volumes of water from the Gulf. New Orleans is exposed to Gulf storm surges via Lake Pontchartrain, which is connected to the Gulf, and via the Industrial Canal, which links up with the Gulf, Lake Pontchartrain and the Mississippi River. Surging gulf waters can be far more difficult to predict than rising river tides. Storm surges rise up like tsunamis, lunging upward as they squeeze through narrow canals. River floods, by contrast, can be observed far upstream, often weeks in advance.

SAVING THE COAST

Some 30 sq miles of Louisiana coast – an area roughly equivalent to the size of Manhattan – is lost each year due in part to subsidence of the natural floodplains. Erosion is further enhanced by the extensive canal network dredged for oil production, and the wakes of shipping traffic wear away at the delicate edges of these canals. Quickly disappearing are miles of bird refuges, home to more than half of North America's bird species, as well as freshwater homes to Louisiana's treasured crawfish bounty. The Cajun fishers who have maintained their unique lifestyle for so many generations are facing the reality that their lifestyle and their homes are endangered. For New Orleans, the loss of these wetlands makes the city more vulnerable to hurricanes, as the diminishing land buffer enables hurricanes to maintain full strength nearer to the city. For similar reasons, New Orleans will become more vulnerable to storm surges such as the one that followed Hurricane Katrina. Mike Tidwell's book *Bayou Farewell* is a compelling look at what is lost in environmental and cultural terms.

A plan to offset coastal erosion, calling for some controlled flooding of the lower Mississippi and restoration of offshore islands, was drawn up in the early 1990s, but hasn't yet been implemented. In the meantime, Governor Jindal's administration has been criticized by environmentalists for tackling the issue of coastal reclamation far too slowly. At the time of writing, Governor Jindal's proposals to save the coast have focused on private-public partnership agreements.

One sliver of hope, on June 5, 2008, was the closing of the Mississippi River Gulf Outlet (MRGO), a canal dug to provide more direct access from the Gulf to the Port of New Orleans. Katrina made a decisive case for closing down the environmentally destructive outlet; levees all along the MRGO were breached, causing flooding to St Bernard Parish and leading to the Industrial Canal breach that decimated the Lower Ninth Ward. Questions remain as to whether the canal will simply be dammed or if storm gates will be added along its length.

MARDI GRAS & JAZZ FEST

In February or March each year New Orleans expands on the Fat Tuesday concept with a 10-day festival during which the fun steadily intensifies until the entire city is certifiably insane. That's Carnival, or Mardi Gras, for you. Then the city does it again for the New Orleans Jazz & Heritage Festival (commonly just 'Jazz Fest'), which also falls over a 10-day period. Both festivals flout the old showbiz adage of leaving 'em wanting more. These festivals deliver course after course until no one is left standing; you simply can't take any more. But many people will come back again next year, and year after year after that.

Mardi Gras is a deeply rooted tradition in New Orleans that goes all the way back to the city's origins as a French colony. In 1699 on Lundi Gras (Mardi Gras Eve), Pierre Le Moyne, Sieur d'Iberville, took possession of the Louisiana territory and named his first encampment Pointe de Mardi Gras. Since then, New Orleans' Mardi Gras has evolved into one of the greatest spectacles in the world.

Jazz Fest, while dating back only to 1970, is not to be outdone by Mardi Gras. By showcasing music, food and the arts, Jazz Fest celebrates the culture that is so integral to life in New Orleans. As a tourist attraction, Jazz Fest is on a par with Mardi Gras. In 2006, the post-Katrina comeback year, visitors pouring into New Orleans for Jazz Fest outnumbered those who came for Mardi Gras. It was the great show of faith the city so badly needed from out-of-town fanatics.

Both festivals are tremendous and unique events. If we had to pick, we'd still say to do both.

MARDI GRAS

Carnival is New Orleans' leviathan holiday – a beautiful, undulating, snakelike festival that first rears its head on January 6 (the Feast of the Epiphany) and weeks later unfolds in all its startling, fire-breathing glory to terrify and delight the millions who come to the city to worship it. (Mardi Gras, translating as 'Fat Tuesday,' is used here specifically to refer to the actual day, rather than to the entire season; Carnival refers to the season from January 6 to Fat Tuesday.)

In New Orleans, Carnival operates on the subconscious. It's the flame that burns in the city's soul, the elaborate overture that tells us what the city is all about. It's a baroque fantasy, a vibrant flower, a circus, a nightmare, a temptation from the devil. It permeates all levels of New Orleans society. Families of all classes and colors come out before each parade. All over the city imaginative people create theatrical costumes for seasonal masquerade parties.

> ### FUTURE MARDI GRAS DATES
>
> Mardi Gras can occur on any Tuesday between February 3 and March 9, depending on the date of Easter. Dates for the next five years:
>
> 2010 February 16
>
> 2011 March 8
>
> 2012 February 21
>
> 2013 February 12
>
> 2014 March 4

Above all, Mardi Gras is a hell of a party, and New Orleans, in its characteristic generosity, welcomes travelers from around the world to join in the revelry.

HISTORY

To understand and appreciate Mardi Gras it is helpful to first become familiar with its history, for many of the traditions that shape the holiday today actually acquired their significance decades, even centuries ago.

Pagan Rites

Carnival's pagan origins are not lost on anyone in New Orleans. Carnival can be traced all the way back to the ancient Greeks, who held pre-spring festivals that could be downright decadent.

The Romans took up the torch, and added oil to the flames, with their Lupercalia, which was celebrated in an atmosphere of characteristic debauchery. During Lupercalia, all social order broke down as citizens and slaves, men and women cavorted in masks and costumes and behaved in a totally lawless and licentious manner. Sadism, masochism and prostitution were the order of the day, followed by a period of recovery and introspection. An ox was sacrificed, and its blood was believed to wash away the sins of the people. Similar pagan rites were practiced by Druid priests in France, culminating in the sacrifice of a bull.

The early Catholic Church failed to appreciate these traditions, but after trying unsuccessfully to suppress them, the church eventually co-opted the spring rite and fit it into the Christian calendar. In Rome, it came to be known as *carnevale* (farewell to the flesh), referring to the fasting that began on Ash Wednesday. For many centuries the celebration, lasting several days, continued to be characterized by chaos and public lewdness, with a pervading sense of violence in the air.

In Venice by the 17th century, a sophisticated theatrical sensibility turned Carnival into a baroque masquerade in which citizens transformed themselves into characters of the *commedia dell'arte* and ran rampant on the city's streets. The festival continued to thumb its nose at social conventions, and a preponderance of satyr costumes indicated the holiday's pagan origins had not been forgotten. This theatrical form of Carnival became the custom in France, and variations of it spread to French outposts in the New World.

Creole Carnival

Early generations of Creoles loved to dance, and they celebrated the Carnival season with balls and a full calendar of music and theater. The Creoles also had a penchant for masking, and on Mardi Gras the people of the city would emerge from their homes wearing grotesque, sometimes diabolical, disguises.

From the beginning the spirit of Carnival appears to have crossed race lines and permeated every level of society. Early on, Creoles of color held Carnival balls to which slaves were sometimes invited. The popularity of masking among blacks was made evident by an ordinance, passed during Spanish rule, which prohibited blacks from masking. The fear was that blacks, effectively disguising their color, might easily invade elite white balls. Several times, masking was altogether outlawed by authorities who distrusted the way in which masks undermined the established social order. This didn't stop people from masking, though, and on Mardi Gras, the citizenry tended to blend into an unruly, desegregated mob.

Carnival remained primarily a Creole celebration for several decades after the Louisiana Purchase made New Orleans a US city, and Creoles continued to elaborate on the festivities. By the 1830s parades replete with ornamented carriages, musicians and masked equestrians had become an important part of the Mardi Gras celebration. But the public splendor was short-lived, and by the mid-19th century Creole Carnival revelers had begun withdrawing into their ballrooms. Many Creoles lamented that New Orleans had become too American, too practical-minded, to sustain such a fanciful holiday as Mardi Gras.

Carnival's Golden Age

Mardi Gras was saved not by Creoles, but by a secretive group of wealthy Anglos who resided in the Garden District. Calling themselves the Mistick Krewe of Comus, these men made their first public appearance after dark, their spectacular horse-drawn floats illuminated by flambeaux (torches) on Mardi Gras in 1857. On that night, the stage was set for Carnival as we know it today.

New clubs modeled themselves on the Comus, calling themselves 'krewes' (a deliberately quirky spelling of 'crews'). Rex first appeared in 1872, Momus a year later and Proteus in 1882. Pompous parades, presided over by a king, coursed through the streets at night, delighting audiences with elaborately decorated, torch-lit floats fashioned from horse-drawn carriages. Mythological and sometimes satirical themes defined the parades, making these processions coherent theatrical works on wheels. The parades would end at a theater or the opera house, where exclusive balls would close out the evening.

These old-line krewes were (and for the most part remain) highly secretive societies comprising the cities wealthiest, most powerful men. They are to New Orleans as the nobility is to Europe, and their parades are often cynically regarded as condescending gestures from the privileged class to the masses. Rex naturally anointed his annual king the 'King of Carnival,' and his krewe also contributed several lasting traditions. He contributed the official colors of Carnival – purple, green and gold, which New Orleanians continue to work into their Mardi Gras attire – and the anthem of Carnival, a corny tune called 'If I Ever Cease to Love.' Additionally, the Rex parade featured floats that depicted biting political satire, which would become a recurring motif shared by other krewes.

But Comus' king remained the true king of Carnival. Whereas the identity of Rex' king was generally known to the public, the Comus' true identity was a carefully guarded secret. On Mardi Gras, Rex paid his respects to Comus by visiting him at his ball. These odd traditions are steadfastly observed to this day.

Carnival rose to new heights during the years that followed the Civil War, and as New Orleans coped with the hardship and insult of 'carpetbag' rule, the importance of Mardi Gras as the cultural focal point of the year was cemented. At times, the seriousness with which Carnival was regarded in New Orleans was exhibited in rather extreme ways. In 1890 two parades, those of Comus and Proteus, reached the edge of the French Quarter at the same time. In a heated dispute over which krewe would enter the Quarter first, several krewe members appeared ready to draw swords, but the confrontation was resolved without violence.

Many enduring black traditions emerged around the turn of the 20th century. The spectacular Mardi Gras Indians began to appear in 1885 (see boxed text, opposite). The skull-and-bones gang (influenced, some think, by Mexican Day of the Dead artwork), wearing comical skeleton suits, chased frightened little kids around neighborhoods on Mardi Gras morning. Their purported 'purpose' was to put a little fear in the youngsters in order to make the kids behave.

A band of women calling themselves the Baby Dolls also began masking on Mardi Gras. Dressed in bloomers and bonnets, they danced from bar to bar, sometimes playing the part of innocent children, sometimes acting like prostitutes (and actually turning tricks). The Baby Dolls still march, subverting ideas about femininity while asserting their sisterhood in their unique costumes.

The black krewe of Zulu first appeared in 1909, with members initially calling themselves the Tramps and parading on foot. By 1916, when the Zulu Social Aid & Pleasure Club was incorporated, the krewe had floats, and its antics deliberately spoofed the pomposity of elite white krewes. Zulu members paraded in black face, and their dress was a wickedly absurd interpretation of African tribal culture, as if to say, 'Is this really how you see us?' Krewe hierarchy included a witch doctor, a mayor, the absurdly uppity Mr Big Shot and a phalanx of tribal warriors bearing shields and wearing grass skirts. In time, Zulu's members would include some of the city's more prominent black citizens. Jazz star Louis Armstrong reigned as King Zulu in 1949, and although his float broke into pieces during the parade (fortunately, in front of a bar), he had no complaints. As he summed up the experience, 'I always been a Zulu, but King, man, this is the stuff.'

Modern Carnival

The 20th century saw the coming and going of dozens of different krewes, each adding to the diversity and interest of Carnival. Iris, a women's krewe, was formed in 1917 and began parading in 1959. Gay krewes began forming in the late '50s, with Petronius, the oldest gay krewe still in existence, staging its first ball in 1962. (Petronius is not a parading krewe.)

Today's 'superkrewes' began forming in the 1960s. Endymion debuted as a modest neighborhood parade in 1967; now its parades and floats are the largest, with nearly 2000 riders and one of its immense floats measuring 240ft in length. Endymion is so big, its ball is held in the Louisiana Superdome. While Endymion was still fledgling, Bacchus, which began in 1969, shaped the trend for bigger things to come. From its start, Bacchus deliberately set out to break Carnival tradition, wowing its audiences by anointing celebrity monarchs (including Bob Hope, Jackie Gleason, Kirk Douglas and William Shatner) and opening its ball to the paid public. Orpheus, a superkrewe founded by musician Harry Connick Jr first appeared in the mid-1990s.

Tradition was dealt a blow when the old-line krewes Comus, Proteus and Momus stopped parading in the early 1990s. City council member Dorothy Mae Taylor challenged these

MEET THE BOYS ON THE BATTLEFRONT

The most significant African American tradition of Carnival began in 1885 when a Mardi Gras Indian gang, calling itself the Creole Wild West, paraded the city's backstreets on Mardi Gras. Their elaborately beaded and feathered suits and headdresses made a huge impression, and many more black Indian gangs soon followed – the Wild Tchoupitoulas, Yellow Pocahontas and Golden Eagles, among many others. The new tradition, some say, signified respect for Native Americans who constantly fought US expansion in the New World. A canon of black Indian songs was passed down from generation to generation, with lyrics often fusing English, Creole French, Choctaw and African words until their meaning was obscure.

From the beginning, 'masking Indian' was a serious proposition. Tribes became organized fighting units headed by a big chief, with spy boys, flag boys and wild men carrying out carefully defined roles. Tremendous pride was evident in the costly and expertly sewn suits, and when two gangs crossed paths, an intense confrontation would ensue as members of each tribe sized each other up. Often violence would break out. As is the case with many of Mardi Gras' strongest traditions, this was no mere amusement.

Big chiefs became pillars of communities, and some became legends – among them Big Chief Jolly of the Wild Tchoupitoulas and Tootie Montana of the Yellow Pocahontas. Chief Jolly, an uncle of the Neville Brothers, made his mark by recording black Indian classics backed by the Meters. Bo Dollis and the Wild Magnolias are one of the most dynamic Indian performers, and they appear at clubs in New Orleans and at Jazz Fest.

Over the years, black Indian suits gained recognition as extravagant works of folk art, and they are exhibited as such at the Backstreet Cultural Museum (p113), at the Presbytère (p72) and at Jazz Fest (p50). Layers of meaningful mosaics are designed and created in patterns of neatly stitched sequins. Multilayered feathered headdresses – particularly those of the big chiefs – are more elaborate and flamboyant than the headgear worn by Las Vegas show performers. The making of a new suit can take the better part of a year.

After Hurricane Katrina, the fate of the Mardi Gras Indians was in doubt. Most of the gangs hailed from the city's worst-hit neighborhoods, and the Indians had scattered across the country. Many were unable to sew new suits for Mardi Gras 2006, but an encouraging number came back and made their presence known on the streets. As Big Chief Victor Harris of the Spirit of Fi Yi Yi gang told *OffBeat* magazine, 'Even though it's sort of a ghost town, we have to bring the spirit out of the ghost.'

Visitors not in town for Mardi Gras are likely to have other opportunities to see the Indians at Jazz Fest, or occasionally performing in clubs such as Tipitina's (p189). They also parade annually on St Joseph's Night (roughly midway through the Lenten season) and on Indian Sunday (p13; also known as Super Sunday).

all-white krewes to integrate, and their response was to retreat from the streets, continuing their elite Carnival traditions in private. In recent years, a public shooting that kicked off the 2009 Mardi Gras prompted fears – that turned out to be unfounded – of a significant police crackdown on festivities.

Despite many changes, and although rambunctious tourists generally outnumber rowdy locals during Mardi Gras, the holiday continues to mark the zenith of New Orleans' festive annual calendar. And despite the grayish ooze of trash, spilled beer, piss and vomit that's ground into the city's gutters by thoughtless mobs, a hearty spirit manages to shine through, somehow linking today's Carnival to those of 18th-century France and even to the Lupercalia of ancient Rome. The masking tradition, carried out primarily in the French Quarter and Faubourg Marigny, upholds an ancient and enchanting Mardi Gras aesthetic. Night parades continue to haunt St Charles Ave and Canal St with surreal and terrifying floats, Mephistophelian masked riders and infernal flambeaux. The skull-and-bones gangs and black Indians continue to carry out their spontaneous rituals. When it comes right down to it, the good, the bad and the ugly are all parts of Mardi Gras tradition.

EXPERIENCING CARNIVAL

Carnival begins slowly, with related events, parties and parades becoming more frequent as Mardi Gras nears. During the final, culminating weekend, particularly on Lundi Gras and Mardi Gras, many things are scheduled to occur simultaneously, and you will have to make some decisions. Preplanning and prioritizing are definitely in order, as getting around town grows more difficult with each passing day (a bicycle will grant you the greatest mobility). Be prepared to improvise a little.

A GRAS LIKE NO OTHER

The parades were shorter, some of the floats looked a little ragged, crowds were smaller and people less rowdy than usual. But Mardi Gras 2006, taking place just six months after Hurricane Katrina, was loaded with significance. Not everyone approved of the decision – some thought the 2006 Mardi Gras was for the benefit of tourists as opposed to New Orleans itself. And to be sure, there was a touch of sadness about this Mardi Gras. As Andrei Codrescu wrote, 'Mardi Gras feels more like Dia de los Muertos.' Maybe so. Or perhaps it can be likened to the point in a jazz funeral when a somber procession turns into a more joyous second-line parade. The city needed to let go of its grief so that it could move forward. For that, Mardi Gras came just in time.

Parades

PARADING KREWES

The parade season is a 12-day period beginning two Fridays before Fat Tuesday. Most of the early parades are charming, almost neighborly, processions that whet your appetite for the later parades, which increase in size and grandeur by the day, until the awesome spectacles of the superkrewes emerge during the final weekend.

A popular preseason night procession, usually held three Saturdays before Fat Tuesday, is that of the Krewe du Vieux (see boxed text, opposite). By parading before the official parade season and forgoing motorized floats (nearly all krewe members are on foot), Krewe du Vieux is permitted to pass through the French Quarter. It's a throwback to the old days, before floats and crowds grew too large, when parading krewes typically traversed the Quarter while onlookers packed the sidewalks and balconies. The themes of this notoriously bawdy and satirical krewe clearly aim to offend puritanical types.

Krewes that traditionally parade during the first weekend are Pontchartrain, with a Mid-City promenade known for its stellar marching-band contests; the Knights of Sparta, with an Uptown night parade that features traditional touches such as flambeaux carriers and a mule-drawn float; and Carrollton, an 80-year-old krewe that rolls down St Charles Ave on Sunday afternoon.

In some years, parades are held every night of the subsequent week, getting larger as the final weekend gets near. Toward the end of the week, the highly secretive Knights of Babylon presents its attractive traditional parade, replete with flambeaux and riding lieutenants (eerily reminiscent of hooded Klansmen); it follows the Uptown route, but continues toward the lake on Canal St and down Basin St for a few blocks. On the Friday night before Mardi Gras, Uptown is the domain of Hermes, with its beautiful nighttime spectacle maintaining the aloof mystery of 19th-century Carnival processions. Hermes is followed directly by Le Krewe d'Etat, whose name is a clever, satirical pun: d'Etat is ruled by a dictator, rather than a king. However menacing this modern krewe may be, d'Etat's floats and costumes reflect fairly traditional standards of beauty.

Mardi Gras weekend is lit up by the entrance of the superkrewes, with their monstrous floats and endless processions of celebrities, marching bands, Shriner buggies, military units and police officers. The superkrewes always take the 'bigger is better' approach to the fullest allowable extent, and are as flashy as a Vegas revue. The crowds of spectators also grow larger by the day, and that comfortable corner you'd staked out for yourself earlier in the week is now likely to be overrun by tourists. All of these considerations aside, if you've been in town all week, you'll be ready for something bigger by this time. (A few nonsuperkrewes parade on the weekend as well.)

The all-women's krewe, Iris, parades down St Charles Ave with more than 30 floats and 750 krewe members. Iris is usually followed by Tucks (see boxed text, opposite), an irreverent krewe with the inspired alliterative motto of 'Booze, Beer, Bourbon, Broads.'

On Saturday night the megakrewe Endymion stages its spectacular parade and Extravaganza, as it calls its ball in the Superdome. With about 1900 riders on nearly 30 enormous, luminescent floats rolling down Canal St from Mid-City, the Endymion parade is one of the season's most electrifying events. Endymion always has celebrity marshals, and the krewe's massive 240ft steamboat float is the biggest in New Orleans.

On Sunday night the Bacchus superkrewe wows an enraptured crowd along St Charles Ave with its celebrity monarch (Val Kilmer in 2009) and a gorgeous fleet of crowd-pleasing floats.

Monday night is parade night for Proteus, one of the oldest krewes to have a parade. Proteus' parade is an old-school affair, replete with riding lieutenants, flambeaux and lovely hand-painted floats. The main event of the evening is staged by Orpheus, a spirited and stylish superkrewe founded by Harry Connick Jr (who hails from New Orleans). Connick rides annually, and he always enlists a handful of movie stars and musicians to join his 1200-member krewe. Orpheus is such a huge parade, you may have to wait several hours before seeing the famous 140ft Leviathan float. It's a spectacular float, and most people are glad they waited.

On Mardi Gras morning Zulu rolls its loosely themed and slightly run-down floats along Jackson Ave, where the atmosphere is very different from the standard parade routes. Folks set up their barbecues on the sidewalk and krewe members distribute their prized hand-painted coconuts to a lucky few in the crowd. When Zulu reaches St Charles Ave, it follows the Uptown route toward Gallier Hall (p88) for a spell, before ending up on Orleans St and in the Tremé District.

Zulu typically runs blithely behind schedule while the 'King of Carnival,' Rex, waits further Uptown for clearance on St Charles Ave. Rex' parade is, naturally, a much more restrained and haughty affair, with the monarch himself looking like he's been plucked from a deck of cards, as he smiles benignly upon his subjects. Rex' floats are beautifully constructed and hand-painted, but certain loot-hungry spectators note Rex' stinginess in terms of throws.

On Mardi Gras afternoon you can continue to watch parades. The populist spirit of the truck parades (haphazardly decorated semis loaded up with people line-dancing and throwing beads) is sociologically interesting but minimally entertaining. If you've been in town all weekend you'll be paraded-out by this time and there's plenty going on elsewhere around town.

PARADE ROUTES

There are two primary Carnival parade routes in Orleans Parish. The Uptown parade route typically follows St Charles Ave from Napoleon St to Canal St (where these parades actually begin and end can vary, but this stretch is fairly constant). The Zulu parade departs from this course by rolling down Jackson Ave until it reaches St Charles Ave, at which point it follows the standard

WISE-CRACKING CARNIVAL KREWES

New Orleans' old-line Carnival krewes enjoy a bit of satire, but mostly just create an aura of pompous mystery with their secret kings and queens and their exclusive balls. No doubt they enjoy themselves and their own exquisiteness. But for we common folk, the most fun to be had during Mardi Gras is with the smart-asses. For many, the whole point of Carnival is to crack wise about pretty much anything. And while they're taking the piss out of authority figures and the most vaunted traditions of Carnival itself, they manage to have as much fun as anyone anywhere.

The Krewe of Mystic Orphans and Misfits (aka MOMs) does a commendable job of mocking the elites. MOMs' titular heads are King Quasimodo the Megamillion and Queen Inertia the Inumerable. MOMs has some serious fun at its raging masquerade ball, held annually at Blaine Kern's Mardi Gras World, amid the grand floats of bigger krewes. The ball is not exclusive, but it is by invitation only. Make friends in town and you might find your way in.

More accessible are the marching krewes, such as the bawdy Krewe du Vieux (www.kreweduvieux.org), whose rocking walking parade through the French Quarter two weeks before Mardi Gras weekend is reason enough to do Mardi Gras earlier than the rest of the tourists. The krewe's annual themes tend to challenge accepted notions of good taste, and awful puns are de rigueur. The 2006 theme was 'C'est Levee.' The 2009 theme was 'Krewe du Vieux's Stimulus Package.' In spite of itself, Krewe du Vieux has become a cherished tradition, with the only float parade going through the French Quarter. After the parade, its ball, the raucous Krewe du Vieux Doo, is open to the public (admission $20). See the krewe's website for information.

For mockery that's even less gracefully articulated, don't miss the parade of the Krewe of Tucks (www.kreweoftucks .com), which got its name from an old bar and celebrates the frat-boy virtues of beer, broads and beads. Its parade is the only one that spectators are allowed to throw things at, although you're really only supposed to toss unwanted beads into the giant toilet on one of its floats. Anyone can join this most undiscriminating of krewes, ride in its parade and party at its ball. See the krewe's website for information.

Not anyone can join the Krewe of Barkus, however, as it's strictly for dogs. Founded in 1993 (by humans on behalf of their dogs), this canine krewe has a king and queen. On Sunday before Mardi Gras, some 1500 costumed pooches sniff the streets and piss on fire hydrants in a parade with floats and marching bands.

NOBLESSE OBLIGE

Parading Carnival krewes don't just aim to entertain the masses – they come bearing gifts. Krewe members aboard floats toss trinkets, called 'throws,' to eager mobs clamoring for free booty.

It is important to impress upon Carnival virgins that getting your share is not passive work. Regardless of how cheap or garish the throws are, people want 'em. You have to plea for the sympathy of krewe members, and once a throw is airborne you often have to fend off aggressive rivals. It's all in good fun, of course, but it helps to have a little competitive drive.

The traditional plea 'Throw me something, mister!' is a holdover from the days when all krewe members were men. You'll still hear people say it, but if you're addressing a woman, a simple 'Throw me something!' will suffice.

The standard item tossed from Carnival floats is a string of plastic beads. By the end of Mardi Gras, aggressive throw-catchers can proudly drape several pounds of beads around their necks.

Quantity isn't the only issue. Creative throws, such as Zulu's famous hand-painted coconuts, are among Carnival's highest prizes. 'Medallion beads' (or 'krewe beads') bearing an emblem representing the krewe are also highly sought after. Doubloons (minted aluminum coins bearing krewe insignia and themes) are popular collectors' items. Other things you may acquire along a parade route range from plastic cups to bags of potato chips.

The smaller, common plastic beads coveted by spectators a generation ago have come to be called 'tree beads,' for their ignominious fate is to be tossed into the branches of the live oaks along St Charles Ave, where some actually hang on long enough to see the following year's Carnival. They can also be strung together to make elegant Christmas tree ornaments.

A word of caution: when a throw lands on the street, claim it by stepping on it, then pick it up. If you try to pick it up without first stepping on it, someone else will surely step on your fingers – and then insist that the object is by rights theirs!

---

route toward Canal St. The Mid-City parade route begins near City Park and follows Orleans Ave to Carrollton Ave and then onto Canal St, down toward the French Quarter, hooking into the Central Business District (CBD) in order to pass the grandstands at Gallier Hall.

These lengthy routes, which can take several hours for some of the larger krewes to traverse, obviously afford many vantage points from which to see the parades. But your choice is fairly straightforward: either head away from the crowded Quarter to get a more 'neighborhood' feel, or stick close to the corner of Canal St and St Charles Ave, where the crowds are thickest and a raucous, sometimes bawdy party atmosphere prevails. Grandstands (with paid admission of varying prices) are set up along St Charles Ave in the area between Lee Circle and Gallier Hall, and parading krewe members tend to go into a bead-tossing frenzy through this corridor.

If catching throws is of highest priority, here's a tip: near the end of parade routes, krewe members often discover they've been too conservative early on, and they tend to let loose. However, by this time the excitement level of the parade may already have passed its crescendo.

WALKING PARADES

On Mardi Gras there are many 'unofficial' walking parades that are worth seeking out and, in some cases, even joining.

The Jefferson City Buzzards, a walking club that has been moseying from bar to bar on Mardi Gras morn since 1890, starts out at 6:45am at Laurel St near Audubon Park. If you're into drinking early, you are likely to run into them at drinking establishments between there and the French Quarter. Since 1961, jazzman Pete Fountain's Half-Fast Walking Club has been making similar bar-hopping rounds, starting out from Commander's Palace (p162) at around 8am.

Downtown has its own morning activities, the biggest event being the parade of the Society of St Anne. This is a gloriously creative costume pageant – krewe members, clad in elaborate hats, capes, makeup and masks or, in some cases, in very little at all, march through the Bywater, Faubourg Marigny and the Quarter to the jazzy rhythms of the Storyville Stompers. The parade starts around 10am in the Bywater, and the colorful procession, which strives to re-create scenes from 19th-century oil paintings of French Mardi Gras, flows down Royal St all the way to Canal St, where it sometimes arrives in time to run into the Rex parade.

Another costume-oriented downtown walking parade is that of the Krewe of Cosmic Debris, which convenes at around noon in Marigny. The krewe's wandering musical voyage through the Quarter is largely determined by which bars it elects to patronize along the way.

Costume Contests

Mardi Gras is a citywide costume party, and many New Orleanians take a dim view of visitors who crash their party without a costume. Needless to say, they take costumes seriously. On Fat Tuesday, exquisitely attired maskers, human beasts and exhibitionists mingle, and a spirit unique to Mardi Gras animates the streets; this is all-ages material, folks.

This unbound creativity is distilled into two costume contests – a high-proof one for adults and a watered-down one for the entire family. The notorious Bourbon St Awards, attracting a large number of gay contestants, is staged not on Bourbon St (as it once was) but in front of the Rawhide Bar at Burgundy and St Ann Sts; it begins at noon. The cleaner Mardi Gras Maskathon is held in front of the Meridien Hotel on Canal St, after the Rex parade concludes.

MARDI GRAS MASK MARKET

The main point of Mardi Gras is to wear a mask. If you're unprepared for this, never fear, for an astounding selection of high-quality handmade masks is available at the outdoor Mask Market. Artisans from around the country show their wares in stalls set up in Dutch Alley, behind the French Market, Sunday through Monday leading up to Mardi Gras. A live music stage is set up there, too.

Balls

You can't expect to roll into town on Friday night and on Fat Tuesday gain admittance to one of the invitation-only society functions that typify the Carnival ball season. You can, however, buy your way into a party put on by one of the more modern krewes, including Orpheus (☎ 822-7211), Tucks (☎ 288-2481), Bacchus (www.kreweofbacchus.org) and Endymion (☎ 736-0160; www.endymion.org). Gay krewes include Petronius (☎ 525-4498) and the Lords of Leather (☎ 347-0659).

Information

The glossy magazine Arthur Hardy's Mardi Gras Guide (www.mardigrasneworleans.com; Mardi Gras Guide, 602 Metairie Rd, Metairie, LA 70005; $9) is an indispensable source of information and a worthwhile souvenir. Published by an obsessive Carnival aficionado, the annual publication appears in bookstores each year before Twelfth Night (January 6). It includes parade schedules, route maps and loads of history and commentaries that give an in-depth understanding of the entire culture of

DOING FAT TUESDAY

There is a lot going on throughout the day on Mardi Gras, and it ain't all pretty. Your day can turn into a dog's breakfast if you don't have a plan. Take stock of what you want to check out, and figure out the where and when of it. We have our own rotund agenda for a Fat Tuesday that takes in Mardi Gras Indians, the big Zulu and Rex parades, some key walking parades and enough time for partying in the French Quarter and Faubourg Marigny.

Firstly, know that Mardi Gras is an all-day affair, and it's going to feel like you're going full throttle the entire way. Fortunately, fun and excitement on this scale will spur you to superhuman feats. For some, this means drinking booze from dawn till dissolution. Scarf some food wherever you can. Pace yourself, and you'll avoid the crash-and-vomit phase. But don't be a wet blanket. Approach the day as a migratory bird approaches flight over a large body of water.

Some things happen early. Mardi Gras Indians don't operate on a schedule, but often congregate at the Backstreet Cultural Museum (p113) in the early morning. Drop by around 10am, when the museum starts its 'open house.' If you don't spot any Indians in this vicinity, you might try Congo Sq in Louis Armstrong Park (p113).

On Rampart St you can catch Zulu as it reaches the end of its route. Then make your way back into the French Quarter to see the Society of St Anne walking parade, which reaches the Quarter around 11am or so. If you're in costume, you can just file in, joining the revelry as it makes its way to Canal St. Here, you'll meet up with the Rex parade.

The afternoon is a good time to hang out in the Quarter, which by now is a big masquerade party. Back at the Backstreet Cultural Museum, a cool party might be in full swing (you'll know about it if you stopped by earlier). Keep an eye out for the Krewe of Cosmic Debris, a fun krewe that usually hits a bunch of bars in the Quarter before ending up on Frenchmen St for a big musical street party that lasts on into the evening. At the R Bar (p182), also in the Marigny, another raging party spills out onto Royal St.

THE LAW OF MARDI GRAS

New Orleans has fostered a reputation as a permissive city, and Mardi Gras is obviously a time of unbridled debauchery. But don't come expecting utter lawlessness. Overall, the New Orleans Police Department does a commendable job maintaining order, despite immense, spirited crowds consuming unbelievable quantities of liquor. Along parade routes and in the French Quarter, cops are everywhere. If their ranks appear to have swelled, it's because the entire force is working long shifts, with little time for rest in between. Rule No 1 is don't push your luck with tired cops!

Surprisingly, the presence of so many overworked cops does not interfere with the general merriment of Carnival. The attitude of the police during Carnival is to let people have their fun, but officers draw the line at potentially dangerous behavior. If a cop tells you to watch what you're doing, don't try to argue. If you start with the 'Aw, but ossiffer...' routine, you're likely to end up in the slammer until Ash Wednesday.

Many special laws go into effect during Carnival. Here are a few that visitors ought to bear in mind:

- Do not park your car along a parade route within two hours of the start of a parade – it's guaranteed that your car will be towed.
- Do not cross police barriers unless permitted to do so by an officer.
- During parades, do not cross the street if it means stepping between members of marching bands or in front of moving floats.
- It is against the law to throw anything at the floats (except for Tucks' toilet float).
- Police tend to look the other way (figuratively, anyway) while women expose their breasts in the French Quarter. But don't expect the same tolerance elsewhere.
- It isn't true that it's OK to have sex in public.

Carnival. Similar information is offered by the *Gambit Weekly* (www.bestofneworleans.com), which publishes a Carnival edition during February or March, depending on the date of Mardi Gras. *OffBeat* (www.offbeat.com), a music magazine, offers invaluable information on Mardi Gras–related events.

NEW ORLEANS JAZZ & HERITAGE FESTIVAL

Jazz Fest sums up everything that would be lost if the world were to lose New Orleans. Much more than Mardi Gras, with its secret balls and sparkly trinkets, Jazz Fest reflects the tremendous generosity of New Orleans. It's a big-hearted, open-armed party that welcomes the world to share in the city's bounty. Jazz Fest celebrates the exotic and the fun, and the crowds, while huge, are civilized and appreciative.

Of course the Fest is first and foremost about music, but it isn't just about jazz. The multitude of stages and tents feature everything that pours in and out of jazz – blues, gospel, Afro-Caribbean, folk, country, zydeco, Cajun, funky brass, and on and on. The music shares the marquee with the unique and varied food of southern Louisiana, served up in great portions during the festival. Second-line parades – a uniquely New Orleanian phenomenon wherein a crowd dances behind a street parade, funeral, wedding etc – part crowds and pull people along with them. The astonishing spectacle of the Mardi Gras Indians always has a show-stopping effect. But the show doesn't stop – not until the sun starts to go down on the second Sunday.

Indeed, Jazz Fest is more than just a festival. Ordinarily New Orleans entertains itself like no other city in the US, but during Jazz Fest some of the city's most loyal fans from around the world pour into the little city, and New Orleans kicks everything up a notch. For 10 or 11 days the city rocks round the clock. Clubs and restaurants are packed to the gills, and jazzy beats and bluesy grooves keep the rafters shaking till dawn most nights. The town's full of musicians and artists and characters. Don't just sit there. Join 'em.

HISTORY

Jazz Fest began in 1970, and, of course, the idea of staging a big music festival in New Orleans couldn't have been more natural. George Wein had already organized the well-established Newport Jazz Festival, so he was brought to New Orleans to launch a similar tradition. Wein hired Quint Davis to help in the promotion of the project. Both men are still in charge of organizing the event each year.

The first festival, held in Louis Armstrong Park (p113), featured a remarkable lineup of legendary artists, including Duke Ellington, Mahalia Jackson, Clifton Chenier, Fats Domino and The Meters. Mardi Gras Indians performed, and every now and then a second-line parade swept through the audience. The ingredients were already in place for a major cultural event with a genuine regional significance. Outside talent, such as Ellington, complemented the local talent as well as beefed up the event's exposure.

Only 350 people attended that first Jazz Fest. It's startling to think there was so little interest. Most likely, the low numbers were due to poor promotion outside of New Orleans. Out-of-towners arrived in much greater numbers for the '71 Fest, and with them came a far stronger local response. To accommodate another anticipated jump in attendance, the Fest was moved to the far larger Fair Grounds Race Track (p111) a year later, and Jazz Fest really hasn't looked back since. By the late 1970s the festival had grown from one weekend to two, with already many legendary moments solidifying the event's cultural importance. Mesmerizing performances by the likes of James Booker, the Neville Brothers and Professor Longhair have been recorded for all posterity. The musical lineup soon expanded to include big-time national acts, such as Lenny Kravitz, Kings of Leon and Bon Jovi, as well as international acts from South America, the Caribbean and Africa.

The festival may have peaked in 2001, when some 650,000 people attended and 12 stages featured nearly every kind of music with the possible exception of Goth. The years since have seen some much-needed slimming down of numbers, but the festival remains immense, with all the high-profile talent and new discoveries you'd expect, and it continues to draw die-hard regulars who come to New Orleans year after year.

The 2006 Fest drew impressive crowds, though the number of stages was reduced to nine. With Jazz Fest providing the first real boost for local tourism since Hurricane Katrina, it was a case of a cultural event really coming through for its city. In 2009 the Fest hit a post-Katrina attendance record with some 400,000 attendees – not the crowds of 2001, but still more than the city's population.

EXPERIENCING JAZZ FEST

Some people choose to do Jazz Fest over and over again, year after year, so obviously there's something addictive about the experience. It doesn't hurt that there are umpteen ways to approach this gargantuan feast of music, food and culture. It hosts three three-ring circuses and a city of concessionaires crammed into a single horse track, so get oriented, sort out your priorities, confer with your pals, and head to the Fair Grounds.

Setting the Stage

The first thing to decide is whether or not to go to New Orleans during Jazz Fest instead of at a different time of year. It's not a difficult decision to make. If you don't mind spending your days at a race track without being able to bet on horses, and you are an unabashed lover of music and New Orleans culture, this is absolutely your party. All you need to ask yourself is: one weekend or two? And if one's enough, then which one?

No one will laugh if you choose one weekend. The drawback is you may have to pick your dates before the Fest schedule is announced. Some early planners book their hotel room a year

---

BIG BONES FOR BIG SHOTS

Jazz Fest ticket prices cost $50 per day or $150 for a full weekend. It's a bargain, when you consider how much entertainment is packed into the eight-hour days. Tickets entitle you entry to the Fair Grounds, and then you're on your own to shuffle through the crowd from tent to stage. Occasionally, if you arrive late for a popular act, you might be refused entry to a full tent. Tickets can be purchased at the gate, or in advance through the Jazz Fest (www.nojazzfest.com) website. Ticketmaster (www.ticketmaster.com) also sells Jazz Fest tickets.

For an added advantage, the Big Chief VIP Experience ($500 for a weekend) is a privilege pass that entitles you to be ushered to seating near the front of each stage. And you'll always get in. An extra $100 gets you a parking place. Purchase your Big Chief pass in advance through the Jazz Fest website or Ticketmaster.

FEST SURVIVAL KIT

Eight hours in the sun in New Orleans, even on a day so exhilarating as a day at Jazz Fest, is always to some degree an endurance test. Throw in booze and the chance of rain and, well it ain't exactly Verdun, but you'll want to be properly equipped. Here's a quick checklist.

Essentials

- sunscreen
- hat
- shades
- bottled water
- *OffBeat* magazine or a copy of *Gambit*
- camera
- rain poncho (if you don't like the look of that sky)
- Cajun shrimp boots (again, if rain and muddy grounds are likely)

Nonessentials

- folding chair (the kind of portable seats GCI and Crazy Creek make for hike-in campers)
- blanket to sit on
- goofy get-up

in advance – for some, this year's room was secured with a deposit when they checked out after last year's Fest. The schedule isn't announced until early February at the earliest. However, there's a statistical logic to making blindfolded decisions in this way, as both weekends are always packed equally with big-name show-stoppers and unheard-of talents from the nearby swamps and faubourgs. Sometimes you'll miss out on a personal favorite if you're not attending every day of the Fest, but in the end something along the way will make up for the loss.

For those who make their Jazz Fest plans late – that's to say, after February – there's the advantage of knowing the schedule and the disadvantage of not having your pick of hotel rooms. Free-spenders are still likely to find a pricey suite of rooms in the French Quarter at this point, but thrifty types with particular tastes might be a little frustrated if they've waited this long to make up their minds to go to the Fest. Our advice for novices is make your plans and reserve your rooms in November or December.

Of course, planning ahead to do both weekends removes the doubts and uncertainties and doubles your pleasure. If you decide to do both weekends, you'll have four days for bopping around town, or maybe driving out to Cajun Country. No matter what, be prepared for an overcrowded city full of people who share your passion for music, food and nightclubbing. It's a competitive but jovial crowd.

Once your dates and rooms are secured and the schedule is released, you can begin to plot out your days at the Fair Grounds.

You can also begin to assemble your get-up. Your threads, babe. For the most spirited attendees, Jazz Fest is another excuse to don a costume in New Orleans. The snazzier/sillier/louder, the better. Having your duds in order is the surest way to make friends and influence people at Jazz Fest. It's another aspect of the show.

Once in New Orleans, get your hands on the latest *OffBeat* magazine. Grab two – one as a keeper, the other to tear out essentials like the Fair Grounds map and the Fest schedule. Study these, fold 'em up, keep 'em in your pocket at all times. You'll want to know the who/what/where.

At the Fair Grounds

It takes a well-bred racehorse about two minutes to circumnavigate the Fair Grounds track, but the average human will require up to 10 minutes to get from one stage to the next. The only way to get from stage to stage is to walk or half-jog through dense crowds and all kinds of tempting food stalls and vendors.

On entering through the Sauvage St gate, for some, Life's Reward is already found. The Gospel Tent, while no longer a well-kept festival secret, remains a cherished chapel of earth-shaking musical performances. Chances are, for all but the most devout gospel music enthusiasts, nearly all of the talent here will be new to you – and maybe later you won't remember the names of half the southern church choirs and quartets you've stomped your feet with. But you'll never forget the exhilarating experience of live gospel music. This is one of the reasons why Jazz Fest has so many repeat visitors.

Also on the sidewalk near the Sauvage St gate is the Jazz Tent. The lineup here leans more toward the contemporary side of things. You might see Irvin Mayfield, Terence Blanchard, Astral Project, Donald Harrison Jr, Ellis Marsalis or Nicholas Payton on this stage.

To take in the infield stages, follow the track in a counterclockwise direction, as the ponies do. The Jazz & Heritage Stage is a smaller stage where brass bands and the Mardi Gras Indians perform. Suitably enough, the Backstreet Cultural Museum (p113) has an exhibit in the next little tent over.

The Economy Hall Tent is where all those buck-jumpin', parasol-twirlin' Fest-goers end up. You'll stomp your feet to 'trad' jazz with the likes of the Preservation Hall Jazz Band, Walter Payton, the Dukes of Disneyland, the Young Tuxedo Brass Band, the Tremé Brass Band and Pete Fountain. These elder statesmen are strong as oxen, so expect to see 'em doing there thing for many years to come. Dozens of food stalls (see Food & Drink, p54) line up behind Economy Hall.

Turn into a corridor midway along the grandstand to reach the Winners' Circle, which during Jazz Fest is transformed into the Lagniappe Stage. Here the entertainment is varied. The stage's isolation from the rest of the fairgrounds makes it ideal for intimate performances by singers and small ensembles – the type of acts that do well in clubs but don't always translate to outdoor festivals. Lounge singers might follow acoustic blues performers on this stage. This is also where interviews are done; local writers chat with music legends.

Up in the grandstand, in the glassed-in areas where big shots wait for their ponies to run, take a look at the photo and art exhibits.

From the grandstand, get back on track. The Kids' Tent (below) is next, with playful troubadours and nonstop puppet shows that make a special plea to the young at heart. Heading around the track's curve gets you to the Blues Tent. Traditionally, this stage was next to the Gospel Tent, but it was moved here in 2006. Maybe it'll get moved back. Either way, this is where you are likely to catch blues, R&B and funk acts such as Snooks Eaglin, Etta James and The Meters. The Blues Tent also integrates rock acts like the Radiators and Cowboy Mouth. Sometimes popular funky brass bands such as Rebirth end up here.

Cajun and zydeco music is the emphasis at the Fais Do-Do Stage. If CJ Chenier, DL Menard, Geno Delafose, Rosie Ledet and BeauSoleil are at Jazz Fest this year – and they almost always are – then you'll find 'em here. Sometimes local roots rockers such as the Iguanas also take the Fais Do-Do Stage.

Following the direction of the ponies once again gets you to Congo Sq, a legendary Jazz Fest stage. It's a big stage with an expansive patch of grass to accommodate huge crowds. The stage has become the venue for world acts from Africa and Latin America. The lineup tends to be completely different each year, and there's often a buzz about performers who are making rare appearances in the US. Past performers have included Los Van Van from Cuba and King Sunny Adé from Nigeria. Congo Sq is not so easily defined, however, as rapper Juvenile has also worked the stage here, as have countless brass bands and some of the bigger Mardi Gras Indian gangs.

By far the biggest stage in the infield is the Acura Stage, where the biggest names appear. The audience here stretches clear across the infield, with a giant, high-resolution video screen beaming the performances to those so far from the stage they can only hear the performances. A lot of people plant picnic blankets in front of the stage first thing in the morning and stay there all day. If you're buzzing around the infield like a hummingbird, chances are you won't reach the front row here (unless you have a Big Chief VIP pass). The headliners vary from year to year, and many of them have little or no connection to New Orleans or the culture that this festival professes to celebrate. But who's to complain about a live performance by Bruce Springsteen? Earlier in the day the stage is often taken over by the locals, such as Irma Thomas or Big Chief Bo Dollis and the Wild Magnolias.

Jazz Fest for Kids

There is plenty of fun for the young 'uns at Jazz Fest, most of it concentrated in the Children's Cultural Village, Storytellers Pavilion and Kids' Tent. Dancing, sing-alongs, captivating stories, puppet shows and hands-on arts and crafts are happening all day long. The talent is usually worth catching even if you're not a kid. Local living legends David and Roselyn often appear; they have that authentic traveling troubadour style and a deep well of timeless tunes to draw on. Off campus, Big Top Gallery and Three Ring Circus (p98) stages 'Kids' Fest' between the weekends, with family-oriented entertainment.

SURPRISE ATTACKS

The Jazz Fest schedule inevitably lists a healthy mix of musicians everyone has heard of and some that nobody outside of New Orleans knows about. Keep your ear to the ground, and some of the unknowns will soon become familiar names to you. Each year Jazz Fest delivers surprise discoveries that everyone talks about.

In 2009, for example, Theresa Andersson, a Louisianan of Swedish extraction (of course) burned her name into Jazz Fest history by essentially upstaging every other act that followed her on the day she performed. Andersson's act – wherein she loops vocals and instrumental riffs in real time, creating a one-woman band phenomenon – wowed visitors and made hometown fans prouder than punch.

You're bound to discover dozens of comparable Jazz Fest moments. This thing isn't scripted; each year promises its own set of surprises.

Food & Drink

Among the crowds at the Fair Grounds there are always scores of people holding plates of food and looking very satisfied. At some point you're sure to be one of these people. Fest food vendors cook up some fine vittles, much of it reflecting regional tastes. Many stalls seem to have a cult following and return to the Fest year after year. Lines can be long, but this is Louisiana. People are patient and friendly, which makes the wait bearable.

There are usually two concentrated food areas, plus scattered stalls around the Fair Grounds. Most of the vendors' signs are basically menus – what the sign says is what they sell, so it's not difficult to find what you're hankering for. The food is not dirt cheap, but considering they have a captive, hungry audience the vendors could probably gouge prices. To their credit, they don't.

Some of the more popular Fest foods are fried soft-shell crab, Crawfish Monica (cream crawfish sauce over fusilli pasta), crawfish bread, *cochon de lait* (roast suckling pig), po'boys, spinach and artichoke casserole, Cuban sandwiches and Palmer's Jamaican chicken. Of course, you'll also find great jambalaya, red beans and fried catfish. Second-liners always recommend the 'ya ka mein,' an Asian noodle soup that's commonly sold along parade routes. The beer selection's limited to MGD and Fosters, but what the hell – finely crafted microbrews don't really go with the climate or this kind of food. You can also refresh yourself with rose-mint iced tea, mango freezes (like a smoothie) or a syrupy snowball (see p171).

Shopping at the Fest

Shopping and having to carry a lot of stuff around a music festival might not sound like something a sane person would do, but some of the vendors at the Fair Grounds have desirable stuff for sale: posters, photographs, paintings, jewelry, African drums, CDs and DVDs. Even if you're deaf to the vendors' siren song, check out such shops as the one operated by accordion-maker Clarence 'Junior' Martin. Admire lovely handcrafted button accordions of the sort played by zydeco sweetheart Rosie Ledet (the best advertisement the squeezebox ever had). Hamacher Woodworks & Engraving has a nice stall packed with finely crafted bowls made from pecan and other regional hardwoods. Very nice stuff. Jazz Fest Live sells recordings of performances you saw maybe two hours ago, so you can relive the experience at home.

Off-Campus Highlights

When the last band has finished its set at the Fair Grounds, take a victory lap around the track and catch a cab to your favorite restaurant. You might want to have a copy of *OffBeat* in hand. While waiting for your cab and then your table, you can consider your evening plans. Hopefully you still have a little gas in the tank, because there's a lot going on in the clubs around town. All the clubs will have stacked the deck for every night during the festival – including all the off-nights between the two weekends.

Aside from standout gigs and jam sessions raising the rafters in the clubs, several annual events accompany Jazz Fest. Piano Night is a tradition where the hottest piano players take turns at the ivories and basically try to out-play each other. Don't expect routine performances from anyone who takes the House of Blues (p181) stage during this event. It's usually on the Monday after the first weekend.

All day every day during the Fest – that's on the two weekends and the weekdays in between – the Louisiana Music Factory (p124) has free shows. There's something in the air during Jazz Fest, so the performances are charged with an energy you wouldn't expect to find at a free show in an overcrowded record shop.

In 2006, percussionist Washboard Chaz inaugurated Chaz Fest. It's a one-day music festival held on the Thursday between the two weekends from noon to 10pm; see the Chaz Fest (www .chazfestival.com) website for info. Since 2006, Chaz Fest has turned into a sort of Bywater community party, bringing that entire neighborhood together into a day-long block party.

It's also worth poking around the web to see what sorts of smaller one-off events are going on. Some musicians host parties, barbecues and crawfish boils in their backyards or favorite bars and invite the public to join them. That's the kind of people New Orleans are.

REBUILDING A CITY *Sean Mussenden*

In the days after Hurricane Katrina swamped New Orleans in August 2005, predictions of the city's future ran the gamut from pessimistic to downright gloomy. Some advocated the unprecedented abandonment of a major US city, saying it would never recover from the mass flooding. Even those who loved New Orleans and longed for its swift return surveyed the damage and concluded recovery would take several decades, even with an unparalleled campaign of taxpayer assistance.

Years after the Storm, it appears that the pessimists – some would say realists – called it just about right. The slow, steady, and frequently frustrating reconstruction of New Orleans began in earnest the moment the floodwaters receded, a month after Katrina hit. The city's residents were determined to bring their city back to life, and with substantial help from the US public they have partly achieved that goal – but only in certain quarters.

In neighborhoods on higher ground, almost all traces of Katrina's wrath have vanished, replaced by a new vibrancy and civic energy that followed the Storm. But in areas that suffered the worst flooding, only a hollowed-out shell of once-populated poorer neighborhoods remain, its residents unable or unwilling to return. Rehabitation of these areas will likely take the predicted decades, if it happens at all.

The fallout has transformed the city into a smaller, more concentrated being. It now stands about two-thirds of its pre-flood size, with an altered demographic face that has the potential to impact the city's essential character in the years ahead, in both positive and negative ways. Positive and Katrina are two words not often associated. But then, every crisis presents opportunity for positive change. Katrina was no exception, as it gave the city the chance to address pervasive problems that predated the Storm in a comprehensive way.

Hurricane Katrina passed over the city in under a day. The floodwaters remained for a month. The rebuilding – and the ongoing debate over the city's future – will take much, much longer.

A DEADLY STORM

Occupying a low-lying, drained swamp that sits in one of the most hurricane-prone spots in the world, New Orleans has long lived in fear of the one powerful storm that could wipe out the city. On the morning of Saturday August 28, 2005, Hurricane Katrina prepared to lay claim to that title. The Storm had just cut a path of destruction across Florida – killing seven people – when it spilled into the warm Gulf of Mexico waters. It quickly recharged from its trip across land, and morphed from a dangerous Category Three storm into a Category Five monster, the deadliest designation on the Saffir-Simpson Scale of hurricane strength. Computer models predicted a direct hit on New Orleans.

Mayor Ray Nagin ordered a mandatory evacuation, the first in the city's history. Four out of five residents left the greater New Orleans metropolitan area. Nearly 200,000 stayed behind. The holdouts included those who could not find transportation, people who thought the predictions too dire, and those who wanted to protect their homes and stores from looters. They boarded up windows, hunkered down in their houses or trekked to an emergency shelter set up at the Louisiana Superdome.

The winds increased as night fell and pelting rain bombarded the city. A bit of good news came first. The Storm weakened to a Category Three and jogged east before making landfall near the Louisiana–Mississippi line just before midnight. Entire beachside towns to the east were swept out to sea with the rising tide. But like Hurricane Camille in 1969, a deadly storm that passed just east of the city, and Hurricane Andrew, which passed to the west in 1992, Katrina proved yet another close call. As the sun rose Monday morning, it was clear that Katrina's winds had caused extensive damage – blowing out windows, tearing large sections of the Superdome's roof, and knocking over trees and telephone poles. Yet a sense that it could have been much worse prevailed, a sense that seemed reinforced by cable news journalists reporting from the relatively unscathed French Quarter.

NEW PROTECTIONS

Two years after Katrina, the US Army Corps of Engineers, the agency that built the flood control system, produced a report admitting that a series of decisions – based on scheduling, politics and money – unintentionally left the city with weaker hurricane protection than originally envisioned.

Floodwaters breached approximately 50 walls, spilling into protected areas. Surging water that overtopped the floodwalls and eroded the earthen levees that supported the walls created most of the breaches. Four of the most damaging breaches appeared in the outfall canals that drain the city into Lake Pontchartrain after major rainfalls. The storm surge in the lake sent water rushing into the outfall canals. That put stress on the floodwall, pushed it out, creating a gap between the wall and the earthen levee that supported it. Water rushed into the gap, widened it, and collapsed the wall. Breaches along the 17th St and London Ave outfall canals flooded the Lakeview and Gentilly neighborhoods.

To prevent a similar catastrophe in the future, the Army Corps is spending $14 billion to repair the breaches, strengthen the levees and floodwalls, and make other improvements. The Army Corps says the changes will guarantee the city protection from a storm that appears on average once a century. But critics of the plan say that level of protection is inadequate, and have called for protection from the sort of super hurricane that appears once every 500 years.

House-flattening winds are the most celebrated feature of hurricanes. But often the most deadly aspect is the storm surge, the rising tide of water driven inland by the gales. Katrina's winds pushed water from the Gulf of Mexico up the Mississippi River, into Lake Pontchartrain, and through the canals that lace the city. The levees built to protect the city did not hold. Reports started coming in that the walls across the city had been breached. In the Lower Ninth Ward, residents heard a loud boom as massive sections of the walls of the Industrial Canal levee crumbled. A torrent of water rushed in, freeing houses from their foundations, leaving only a concrete pad behind. In neighborhoods like Lakeview and Gentilly to the north, houses were submerged when the 17th St Canal and London Ave canal gave way.

In all, four-fifths of the city was submerged in a toxic soup of salt and fresh water, gasoline, chemicals, human waste and floating bodies. The city was built on stolen swamp land and, given the opportunity, the swamp quickly reclaimed the low ground. The massive pumps that clear the city after rainy days couldn't process the volume of water. The water rose as high as 15ft in parts of the city, and remained for weeks. Stranded residents found little time to escape the rising water. They moved from the 1st floor to the 2nd floor, then the attic. Some drowned there; those lucky enough to find tools to hack through the roof got out, some using spare cans of paint to dash out crude appeals for help.

A HORRIFYING SCENE

The older, more well-to-do sections of New Orleans on higher ground near the Mississippi River were largely spared Katrina's floodwaters. But almost everywhere else, the environment and many distressed residents reverted to a Hobbesian state of nature. Looters broke into stores, taking necessities such as food and medication, along with luxuries like DVDs and flat-screen TVs. Houses burned to the ground, some intentionally set ablaze by arsonists, and emergency crews were too preoccupied rescuing survivors to douse the flames.

Around 26,000 people took shelter at the Superdome, in increasingly squalid conditions, while other too ad-hoc shelter in the Convention Center. Some attempted to walk out of the city across a bridge into neighboring Jefferson Parish only to find their way blocked by police. Officials stated that evacuees were not being allowed out of the city because the neighboring areas didn't have sufficient facilities to aid them, but also claimed they feared the lawlessness taking hold in New Orleans would accompany the refugees.

Engineers attempted to stop the rising water by filling levee gaps with sandbags. The Coast Guard and a 'Cajun Navy' of local emergency responders piloted the floodwaters to rescue those stranded by the Storm. Those who could wait no longer for rescue turned flotsam into makeshift canoes – air mattresses, closet doors, tires – and slowly made their way to safety. The agency tasked with coordinating the response to major disasters of this kind, the Federal Emergency Management Agency (FEMA), was widely and intensely criticized for its seemingly slow reactions to the increasingly desperate situation on the ground. (Indeed, a House of Representatives committee

GEOGRAPHY, POVERTY & RACE

As the federal response to Hurricane Katrina unfolded on TV, it was difficult to ignore the demographic makeup of the crowds stranded on rooftops and the Superdome. Overwhelmingly poor. Overwhelming black. Many saw the response in racial terms, claiming that the government wouldn't have let citizens endure such harsh conditions if they were a white-majority community. At a televised Hurricane Katrina relief concert a few days after the Storm, Rapper Kanye West controversially lent voice to this belief, declaring 'George Bush doesn't care about black people.'

Katrina destroyed poor black neighborhoods like the Lower Ninth Ward right along with middle-class neighborhoods such as Gentilly and upper-middle-class ones such as Lakeview. At the same time, it exposed the racial and economic divide that has long existed in New Orleans. The effects of the Storm fell disproportionately on blacks.

In New Orleans blacks tended to be poorer than whites. Poorer people tended to concentrate in areas of lower elevation, and thus were more likely to be flooded out. They also were much less likely to own cars, and thus had a harder time getting out of the city before the Storm.

Though New Orleans remains a majority black city, the African American population slipped from 67% the year before the Storm to 58% the year after. A much smaller percentage of blacks has returned to the city than whites. The city lost 57% of its black population between 2005 and 2006, compared with 36% of whites.

At a Martin Luther King Jr Day celebration in 2006, Mayor Ray Nagin announced his intention to make the city 'chocolate again,' a remark that brought much mocking. T-shirts portraying Nagin as Willy Wonka sold briskly in the city. In a radio interview in 2009, Mayor Nagin discussed the social effects of the hurricane: 'Katrina exposed the soft underbelly of America; issues of race, class and poverty… It allowed America to reflect upon itself.'

that investigated the issue found FEMA's eroded state caused its inadequate response to Katrina to be 'all but inevitable.') New Orleans has had many nicknames over the years, and one sobriquet that had fallen out of fashion suddenly seemed relevant: 'The City That Care Forgot.'

FEMA head Michael Brown, who became the poster child for the government response (or lack thereof), said he was not aware of the Convention Center survivors until Thursday, September 1. When food and other supplies arrived, fights broke out as survivors struggled to secure their share. It took until September 4 for both the Convention Center and the Superdome to be completely evacuated.

RESTORING ORDER & MORE FLOODING

On Friday and Saturday, a semblance of order was restored to the city when 28,000 National Guard troops entered the city. The occupying force would remain in the city for almost four years. The troops set up military checkpoints that blocked residents from returning to their homes for the first two weeks, even in the relatively undamaged high-ground neighborhoods near the river, while cleanup crews began to clear debris, restore power and repair damaged pumps.

Just as residents began to return in mid-September, another Category Five storm, Hurricane Rita, appeared in the gulf and forecasters put it on a path to New Orleans. Some took it as a sign that God wanted to completely wipe out a city that ranked second only to Las Vegas in the annals of American sin. New Orleans was again evacuated, this time completely. Like Katrina, Hurricane Rita weakened before making landfall. It moved west to the Texas–Louisiana line to make landfall. Again, the city was spared a direct hit, but it brought another round of flooding.

REBUILDING BEGINS

In Louisiana and Washington, the debate about the future of New Orleans was already underway. Some suggested that Katrina had dealt the city a death blow. It would never recover. Moreover, they said, it was foolish to waste tens of billions of taxpayers' dollars rebuilding then fortifying a below-sea-level city. Another hurricane could hit next year, or the year after that, and rising sea levels from global warming would only make the problem worse. But these arguments failed to win over the decision makers. New Orleans would be rebuilt – how quickly, in what form and at what expense to taxpayers remained open questions.

Almost immediately, the city began to recover in measurable ways, defying those who had written its hasty obituary. Residents began trickling back into the city on September 30. The floodwaters had largely receded, replaced by a dark line on buildings that marked the high water line. For three years, New Orleans' tattoo provided a simple shorthand to track the flooding in each neighborhood. The hardest hit neighborhoods – those with second-story or rooftop tattoos – were unrecognizable. Mountains of debris shed by hollowed-out homes crowded the streets. Neighborhoods with foundation-level tattoos or, luckier, no line at all, saw the swiftest return of residents. By November, an estimated 60,000 people were living in the city, down from 450,000 in the month before the Storm.

They had returned to a once joyous city that now had a dramatically different feel. The city fell into near-total darkness at night. Heavily armed troops and police patrolled the streets, enforcing a strict curfew that dropped crime levels to near zero. Recovery crews began to pour into the city, and their numbers seemed to dwarf the residential population. New Orleans had always taken pride in its laid-back lifestyle, but circumstances had changed dramatically. Everyone got to work.

The areas most familiar to tourists, the wealthier parts of town like the French Quarter and Garden District, began to recover quickly. Dozens of restaurants reopened each week, though they had problems getting waiters and line cooks because of the lack of housing. The reopened restaurants served the army of recovery workers alongside residents, who ate out with a passion to keep the city's legendary restaurant scene alive.

Though it seemed an impossible hope in September, Mardi Gras went on as planned in February 2006, followed by Jazz Fest in April. More residents returned to the city every day, and a year after the Storm, 100,000 people were living in New Orleans. The city was still tiny by pre-Katrina standards, but it was progressing.

BRIGHT SPOTS

For all the dark clouds associated with Katrina, the scale of the destruction fueled several positive developments that few noticed in the early rebuilding stages. It sparked an unprecedented level of civic involvement at all levels. From the small – neighborhood associations reseeding devastated community gardens and bike-rack construction – to the big. When the city needed it the most, the remaining New Orleanians stepped up to take ownership of their city.

The most pressing question, naturally, was how to rebuild. The city established a commission, Bring Back New Orleans, to wrestle with those thorny details. In early 2006, a group of urban planners contracted by the commission recommended constructing new urbanist town centers in high-ground neighborhoods, while restricting construction in flood-prone areas. The restrictions were ultimately rejected by Mayor Nagin after a public outcry complained that it would disproportionately prevent poor blacks from moving back into their neighborhood. In essence, the city gave residents permission to rebuild in their old neighborhoods, whatever the risks.

Citizens also set to work to preserve institutions threatened by Katrina. The Storm had destroyed the homes of many of the city's most talented blues and jazz musicians. Harry Connick Jr and Branford Marsalis worked with Habitat for Humanity to raise funds to build Musicians' Village (see p82) in the Upper Ninth Ward.

Aficionados of the city's legendary food culture also came together to preserve two institutional restaurants flooded out by the Storm in the Tremé: Willie Mae's Scotch House (p172) and Dooky Chase (p171). Their fans raised hundreds of thousands of dollars to rebuild the two restaurants better than new.

The can-do spirit that gripped the city after Katrina not only resurrected local institutions, it spurred the creation of new enterprises. New Orleans once hosted a dozen regional beer brewers. By the time Hurricane Katrina hit, only one brewer – Dixie, creator of the celebrated Blackened Voodoo Lager – was still pumping out suds in the city. The Storm flooded the company's Mid-City brewery, and looters made off with much of the brewing equipment. The company shut it down, and now contracts with a Wisconsin firm to produce its beer. That left the city without a brewery for the first time in living memory. Kirk Coco, a New Orleans native and Navy officer, was on deployment in the Arabian Gulf when the Storm hit. Like many former residents of the city, he was driven to return home and help the city reestablish itself anyway he could. He joined forces with Peter Caddoo, an ex-Dixie brewmaster, and began making beer under the flag of NOLA Brewing Co. It quickly found its way to taps across the city.

The city has always attracted transplants, people drawn to the city's easygoing style and its unique culinary and music scenes. These people still make pilgrimages to New Orleans, but after Katrina they've been joined by eager young professionals drawn to the city because of its

KATRINA GRAFFITI

Emergency response crews tagged thousands of houses with a spray painted 'X' to inform other crews that a house had been searched, and plenty of houses across the city still feature them. Most are unoccupied, but some homeowners have left theirs up after returning as a reminder of the Storm.

Each X tells a powerful story about the fate of the occupants in less than a dozen characters. At the top of the X the crew wrote the date of arrival. (In some cases, houses weren't searched for more than a month after the Storm.) On the right side of the X the crews dashed out the number of occupants and their condition. A '0' meant crews found no one, '2' meant two alive, '2D' meant crews found two dead. On the bottom of the X the crews frequently listed the number of animals in the house. On the left of the X the crews listed their home state – emergency responders came from all over the country. Even the location of the Xs fills out the story, offering a rough approximation of the water level when the emergency crew visited the house. The crews also sometimes dashed out other details, noting a hole in the roof homeowners busted through to escape rising floodwaters.

unparalleled need for do-gooders. The city now attracts idealistic young Ivy Leaguers for the same reasons that Washington, DC, always has. It offers an easy way to make a difference. And the food, music and atmosphere crushes DC's.

OLD PROBLEMS, NEW OPPORTUNITIES

Katrina also provided an unexpected opportunity to attack longstanding problems that had nothing to do with the Storm. The city's public school system serves as the best example. Students generally ranked near the bottom of national reading and math achievement tests. After the Storm, a state takeover of the school system opened the door to a wave of innovative educators to establish charter schools. The schools are public, but operators are free to establish a curriculum as they see fit. Less than 2% of students attended charter schools in 2005. By 2008, 57% did, the highest concentration in the USA. The change has brought about small but measurable improvement on standardized tests. Certain schools, like those run by Knowledge Is Power Program (KIPP), a nationwide network of charters, have doubled or tripled math and reading scores.

GREEN SOLUTIONS

The destruction of vast numbers of homes created serious challenges for the city. For green building advocates, it also created an opportunity to push for environmentally friendly building practices on a wide scale. The advocacy effort has thus far produced only small-scale success, such as the innovative Make It Right project, fronted by Brad Pitt, to build some of the city's most environmentally friendly homes in the Lower Ninth Ward. The Make It Right project aims to build 150 energy efficient homes for residents of this poor neighborhood. At the time of writing, eight homes had been built, with enough money raised to construct another 83. It's a start.

Make It Right linked up with several internationally known architectural firms and a handful of local ones to design the green houses. Concrete pilings set the homes more than five feet off the ground to protect from rising floodwaters, and are equipped with roof escape hatches. They draw energy from solar panels and harvest rainwater, and use energy efficient appliances, tankless water heaters and dual-flush toilets and low-flow shower heads. Energy efficient LEDs light parts of the homes, which were built with nontoxic, environmentally friendly materials. The eight homes constructed by spring 2009 stick out because they are surrounded by block after block of empty lot. But then, they would stick out in any neighborhood in the city, because of the ultra-modernist designs. The roofs are pitched at odd angles – one home has a flat one – and they employ bright colors of shades not often seen in the city. Critics of the design complain that they are out of character with the standard shotgun house common in the neighborhood, but the new homeowners seem to love them.

The project sells the homes for $150,000 to displaced residents of the neighborhood it has selected through an application process. The homes cost more than that to build, but the price is kept low through donated material and labor. The residents use a combination of insurance payouts and money from the Road Home program, and make up any shortfall with a mortgage at extremely favorable terms from the foundation.

Beyond project such as this, the steeper upfront costs of energy-savings practices (though they generally pay for themselves in the long run) have turned off some homeowners operating with a tight pool of rebuilding capital.

LONG ROAD TO RECOVERY

The influx of outsiders and the exodus of poorer residents has tweaked the demographic face of the city. New Orleans is now younger, better educated, whiter and less likely to have kids than it was three years ago. And they have had a real influence in certain clusters of the city, bringing an indie, occasionally Northeastern, sensibility.

After years of slow but steady rebuilding, the pace began to intensify in the last half of 2008 and the beginning of 2009. The city's survival of the first serious test of the repaired flood protection system since 2005 – Hurricane Gustav in August 2008 – helped convince more to return. And long-delayed insurance payments and grants from federal programs like the Road Home initiative provided more people the money to rebuild. Road Home, a $9.4 billion program, gave an average of $62,748 to homeowners to rebuild or sell and move elsewhere. In July 2008, the Census Bureau said 312,000 people had returned to New Orleans, about 70% of the pre-Katrina population.

The recovery has not been equal in all corners. In higher-elevation areas, there are few lingering reminders of the Storm. But in lower-elevation neighborhoods such as the Lower Ninth Ward, Lakeview and Gentilly, block after block of gutted houses or empty concrete pads still testify to the Storm's destruction. The returning population has flocked disproportionately to higher ground. Slightly more people call the French Quarter home than before the Storm, while only 20% of the Lower Ninth Ward's population has returned. In Lakeview and Gentilly, slightly more than half have come back. An army of volunteer workers is helping to speed up the pace of rebuilding, but the progress has been slow.

For poorer residents, steep financial and logistical obstacles have delayed easy return. Plans to rebuild public-housing projects were repeatedly delayed. Katrina reduced the supply of available houses and apartments. The average monthly rent for a one-bedroom apartment in the metro area jumped from $578 in 2005 to $881 in 2008, well above the affordable range for most blue-collar workers. For those who cannot afford cars, delays in the rehabilitation of the city's public transportation system has added to list of woes. Less than half of the pre-Katrina routes are in service at the time of writing, and a third as many buses are in operation.

CREATIVITY FROM PAIN

New Orleans has long served as a muse for artists, boasting a funky energy that powers exceptional creativity. The city is best known for its jazzy contribution to American music, but it also has a strong underground visual arts scene. After Hurricane Katrina, the scene blossomed anew as photographers, sculptors, painters and performance artists turned to the destruction of the Storm for both subject and canvas. Their work helped the city channel its rage, sadness and hopefulness, capturing the evolution of the city's spirit while providing powerful social commentary on the flaws exposed by the Storm.

Perhaps the most creative use of the wrecked city as canvas can be found in St Roch, where artists have transformed abandoned, gutted houses into living works of art. At one such house, titled SAFEHOUSE (2641 N Villere St), the artist Mel Chin replaced the front facade with a 10ft circular bank vault door. Inside, the walls are lined with fake hundred-dollar bills hand colored by school children. In one of the poorest neighborhoods in the city, the presence of the giant vault is striking. A series of posters educates visitors of the city's health problems exacerbated by Katrina, especially damage done by lead contamination. The artists are trying to convince Congress to spend $300 million to fix the problems.

The interior of another gutted house on the block was lined with sod, and the exterior almost completely covered with lush greenery. The house evokes the manner in which Katrina allowed nature to reclaim large parts of the city.

The houses were hosted and sponsored by KKProjects (p82), which maintains a gallery hosting work by local and international artists. Prospect 1, which bills itself as the largest biennial contemporary art event in the United States, ran for three months between November 2008 and January 2009 (see boxed text, p198).

Beyond the high-concept, Katrina also infected the work of local artists creating more approachable work, using their creativity as a vehicle to help the city make sense of the Storm. The artists at T-shirt shop Dirty Coast created one of the city's most iconic post-Katrina images – a woodcut-style homage to Grant Wood's 'American Gothic.' It features a black couple outfitted in dust masks in front of a damaged home. Instead of a pitchfork, the man holds a paintbrush.

GUILT-FREE DISASTER TOURISM

There are several ways to witness Hurricane Katrina's destruction, each carrying their own moral baggage. Guided tour bus tours may leave you feeling like a voyeur of human suffering. A car trip is less invasive and allows for more individual interaction, but how can you help beyond bearing witness? Visitors planning to venture into destroyed neighborhoods may feel better with a purpose beyond observation. Nonprofit rebuilding organizations are your guilt-free ticket in.

Dozens of groups need volunteers to gut old houses, build new ones and clear debris. The rebuilding of New Orleans will take decades, and this is how it works – slowly, one house at a time. The groups are generally looking for volunteers to work a day or longer. For budget travelers, some offer discounted accommodations. Though people with construction experience are appreciated, groups generally do not require such expertise.

The volunteer labor offers a nice side benefit. The work will likely offer the chance to talk with those benefiting from your labor about their experiences before and after Katrina. It sure beats staring at people through the window of an air-conditioned bus.

Groups seeking volunteers include the following:

HandsOn New Orleans (www.handsonneworleans.org) Rebuilding of schools, homes and parks; offers housing for 50 out-of-town volunteers in a hostel setting.

New Orleans Area Habitat for Humanity (www.habitat-nola.org) New home construction.

Phoenix of New Orleans (www.pnola.org) Construction and renovation of homes in the lower Mid-City neighborhood.

Preservation Resource Center of New Orleans (http://prcno.org/programs/rebuildingtogether) Rebuilding of homes for low-income elderly and disabled.

St Bernard Project (www.stbernardproject.org) Construction and renovation of homes in St Bernard Parish, adjacent to New Orleans.

THE FUTURE

The future for New Orleans looks bright. As a deep recession gripped the United States and the world towards the end of the new millennium's first decade, the city's economy kept right on humming, driven by the massive rebuilding effort. Unemployment remained low by historic standards, and the city actually added jobs as the rest of the country shed them.

But the city still has far to go, especially in the tourism sector on which the economy has historically depended. Hotel sales tax revenues, the number of passengers arriving at Louis Armstrong International Airport and the number of restaurants in the city have rebounded to about three-quarters of pre-Storm levels.

The pace of the rebound has surprised some urban planners. Even the city's Katrina tattoo – the watermark – turned out to be a temporary one. Where it wasn't painted over, the sun bleached it to an unnoticeable hue across the city by the time Jazz Fest opened in 2009. It can be found by those looking for it, but it no longer dominates.

Katrina remains a defining event here, much in the way September 11 will always be a defining event in New York. But with each passing day, with each rebuilt house, with each returning resident, the dominance of the Storm in daily affairs lessens.

As a guide for one of the city's 'disaster tours' through the city's troubled neighborhoods put it, 'every day, more and more of my props disappear. And that's a good thing.'

Despite the progress, it will likely be decades before the city regains its former strength, if ever. At the end of 2008, more than 63,000 ruined houses – or the lots on which houses once stood – blighted the landscape. The plan for remedying this situation is unclear.

And the question of what the city should look like five, 10, 20 years from now remains a hotly contested one. Important questions are unanswerable at this stage. Has the population exodus robbed New Orleans' DNA of something vital? Will the influx of new residents change the city for better or for worse?

It is clear that New Orleans walks a different path than it would had Katrina not flooded the city. The city hopes to retain its essential character as it charts a new course. But will it keep its independent, fun-loving, funky, jazzy, take-it-easy soul, its essential 'New Orleansness'?

NEIGHBORHOODS

top picks

What's your recommendation? lonelyplanet.com/new-orleans

NEIGHBORHOODS

We'd like to open this chapter with a nod to those New Orleans neighborhoods – huge swathes of the city at the time of writing – still recovering from Katrina's floodwaters. These 'hoods aren't covered as destinations here per se as they're largely still abandoned, but travelers interested in seeing the Dead Zones and helping rebuilding efforts (many locals recommend you combine exploration and aide to avoid being labeled a disaster voyeur) should check our driving tour of some of the city's worst hit areas (p116). This includes information on places to volunteer and contribute money to sustainable restoration.

Beyond these areas, the parts of New Orleans you'll likely spend time in are those areas largely unaffected by the storm (or rebuilt since). Much of this landscape constitutes the 'New' New Orleans – not in the sense that the buildings are fresh, but rather many of their inhabitants are. Katrina not only sent thousands of New Orleanians into exile; it also drew in thousands of individuals intent on rebuilding a great American city.

Most visitors begin exploring in the French Quarter, also known as Vieux Carré (voo car-*ray*; Old Quarter), the original city as planned by the French in the early 18th century. Here lays the infamous Bourbon St, but of more interest (unless you happen to be in a bachelor/bachelorette party) is an elegantly aged grid of shop fronts, iron lamps and courtyard gardens. North of the Quarter are the Creole faubourgs (literally 'suburbs,' although neighborhood is a more accurate translation in spirit, as these areas are still very much within the city) of the Marigny, Bywater and the Tremé. The first two are the edge of gentrification, where cheap rents and an atmosphere of experimen-

> 'Neighborhoods are the backbone of this city'

tation attract artists, ambitious chefs, good bars, plenty of hipsters and much of the city's gay and lesbian population. When we say this is the edge, we mean it; Bywater in particular still straddles the ghetto line.

The Tremé is the oldest African American neighborhood in the country, a cluster of low-slung architecture and residential blocks, some middle class, some rotted by poverty. This historic area essentially runs on its west side into Mid-City, a semi-amorphous district that includes long lanes of shotgun houses, elegant mansions, dilapidated shacks, the gorgeous green spaces of City Park and the slow laze of Bayou St John.

Canal Street is the 'great divide' that splits the French Quarter from the Central Business District (CBD) and Warehouse District. Between offices and municipal spinach are some of the city's best museums, most posh restaurants, an eyesore of a casino and excellent art galleries.

Proceeding south along the Mississippi, following the curve of a 'U,' the streets become tree-lined and the houses considerably grander; this is the Garden and Lower Garden Districts, where American settlers decided to prove to the original French inhabitants they could be as tasteful and wealthy as any old-world aristocrat.

Heading west, you come to Magazine St, probably the coolest (detractors may say overly gentrified) strip of restaurants and shopping outlets in town. Eventually the 'U' curves north again along the river's bend into Riverbend, popular with Tulane students, glitterati and literati.

Neighborhoods are the backbone of this city; unlike so many US metropolises, you can practically traverse all of New Orleans by residential road without ever hopping onto the highway. Getting stuck into the side streets and lazing in the shade of magnolias or shotgun awnings is more than enjoyable: it's the beginning of feeling what it means to live in – and love – New Orleans.

Lower Ninth Ward

Mississippi River

Orleans Parish
Jefferson Parish

FAUBOURG MARIGNY & BYWATER (p81)

Bywater

Algiers

Gretna

Harvey

Faubourg Marigny

The Tremé

FRENCH QUARTER (pp70-1)

French Quarter

CBD

CBD & WAREHOUSE DISTRICT (pp86-7)

Warehouse District

Gentilly

Lower Garden District

GARDEN, LOWER GARDEN & CENTRAL CITY (pp96-7)

Garden District

Esplanade Ridge

Bayou St John

MID-CITY & THE TREMÉ (pp108-9)

Mid-City

City Park

Uptown

UPTOWN & RIVERBEND (pp102-3)

Riverbend

West End

Bonnabel Place

Metairie

Jefferson Parish
Orleans Parish

Bridge City

Westwego

Mississippi River

Jefferson

2 miles
4 km

ITINERARY BUILDER

New Orleans is compact, but because of class gaps between different parts of the city, physical distances can seem exaggerated. The best of New Orleans is inside her neighborhoods, so make sure you have enough time to explore outside of the French Quarter – but give the Quarter some time, too.

ACTIVITIES	Sights & Activities	Eating
French Quarter	Jackson Square (p68)	Bayona (p154)
	Historic New Orleans Collection (p76)	Fiorella's (p151)
	Cabildo (p69)	Port of Call (p150)
Faubourg Marigny & Bywater	Musicians' Village (p82)	Bacchanal (p158)
	St Roch Cemetery (p83)	The Joint (p158)
		Elizabeth's (p158)
CBD & Warehouse District	Aquarium of the Americas (p90)	Cochon (p160)
	National World War II Museum (p89)	Café Adelaide (p160)
	Ogden Museum of Southern Art (p89)	Restaurant August (p159)
Garden, Lower Garden District & Central City	Goodrich-Stanley House (p97)	Commander's Palace (p162)
	Lafayette Cemetery No 1 (p95)	Surrey's Juice Bar (p163)
	Grace King House (p97)	Stein's Deli (p163)
Uptown & Riverbend	Audubon Zoological Gardens (p101)	Mat & Naddie's (p166)
	Latter Memorial Library (p105)	Domilise's Po-Boys (p168)
	St Charles Avenue Streetcar (p105)	Boucherie (p167)
Mid-City & the Tremé	Backstreet Cultural Museum (p113)	Parkway Tavern (p171)
	Bayou St John (p111)	Lola's (p170)
	City Park (p107)	Dooky Chase (p171)

AREA

HOW TO USE THIS TABLE

The table below allows you to plan a day's worth of activities in any area of the city. Simply select which area you wish to explore, and then mix and match from the corresponding listings to build your day. The first item in each cell represents a well-known highlight of the area, while the other items are more off-the-beaten-track gems.

Drinking & Nightlife	Museums & the Arts	Shopping
Tonique (p182)	Michalopoulos Gallery (p194)	Faulkner House Bookstore (p126)
Molly's at the Market (p182)	Dutch Alley (p193)	Maskarade (p124)
Napoleon House (p178)	Greg's Antiques (p193)	Save Nola (p123)
Vaughan's (p183)	KKProjects (p82)	Dr Bob's Studio (p127)
Snug Harbor (p184)	New Orleans Center for Creative Arts (p80)	Faubourg Marigny Bookstore (p128)
Saturn Bar (p183)	Bywater Art Market (p195)	The Green Project (p128)
Circle Bar (p185)	Arthur Roger Gallery (p194)	Meyer the Hatter (p128)
Le Chat Noir (p185)	Louisiana Artworks (p91)	International Vintage Guitars (p128)
Le Phare Bar (p186)	Contemporary Arts (p196)	New Orleans School of Glassworks (p128)
Saint Bar & Lounge (p187)	Zeitgeist (p198)	House of Lounge (p129)
Bridge Lounge (p186)	Ashe Cultural Arts Center (p98)	Style Lab for Men (p130)
Bulldog (p186)	Anton Haardt Gallery (p195)	New Orleans Music Exchange (p131)
St Joe's Bar (p188)	Cole Pratt Gallery (p196)	Dirty Coast (p132)
Cooter Brown's Tavern & Oyster Bar (p187)	Lupin Theatre (p196)	Maple Street Bookstore (p131)
Cure (p187)	Prytania Theatre (p198)	Yvonne La Fleur (p132)
K-Doe's Mother-in-Law Lounge (p190)	New Orleans Museum of Art (p110)	F&F Botanica (p133)
Mid-City Rock & Bowl (p190)	Sydney & Walda Besthoff Sculpture Garden (p111)	
Mid-City Yacht Club (p189)		

FRENCH QUARTER

Drinking & Nightlife p177, Eating p149, Shopping p120, Sleeping p201

Every city has a district that it sells itself with; an exaggerated version of what defines the town. Think Times Sq (flashier than NYC's usual neon), Hollywood (more glam than glimmering LA) and South Beach (over-sexy compared to sizzling Miami). The Quarter is New Orleans' hyperbolic vision of itself. We're not saying it's not authentic – some of the city's best architecture, most picturesque urban landscapes and loveliest gardens are the norm in the Quarter – but it's also the heart of the tourism scene. Bourbon St, a sort of caricature of a Girls Gone Wild video, generates a loutish membrane that sometimes makes the rest of the Quarter difficult to appreciate.

Look past said silliness. The Vieux Carré (Old Quarter; laid out in 1722) is the focal point of much of this city's culture. In New Orleans' early days this *was* the city – in the quieter lanes and alleyways there's a rich sense of faded time shaken and stirred with joie de vivre. The French Quarter, which in many ways is a Spanish manor (much of the original district was destroyed by fire and rebuilt by Spaniards in the late 18th century), retains the hallmarks of its parent cultures: Gallic and Iberian buildings, a pedestrian-friendly layout and flat-fronted homes buttressed by balconies creating a median space between the public avenue and the home inside.

Behind said homes are gardens plucked from an olde-Empire dream, as if you were in a Caribbean courtyard instead of the heart of a great US city. This Euro-Caribbean sensibility is, in many ways, the unique contribution the Quarter makes to the city – while other areas may offer such visuals, nowhere are they packed in such density. In turn, this attitude and its complicated relationship with American energy is what New Orleans offers the world.

Boozy silliness and T-shirt stands haven't yet overwhelmed the Creole character, whose romantic edges are evident throughout: wrought-iron lamp posts flickering with gas flames, horse-head parking posts, Creole town houses, shotgun cottages and a capillary of cobblestone and concrete that helps peel back the layers that ensconce and enhance this historical heart of the city, as well as some of the best restaurants and bars in a town that takes its pleasures seriously.

Start your visit in Jackson Sq, heart of the heart, a public green surrounded by everything that makes New Orleans what she is: artists, performers, restaurants and the historic buildings that house Louisiana's state museums, where the legacy of this place is realized in a well-executed narrative that can take the better part of the day to explore. Have a beignet or a muffuletta and wander into the streets. As you amble, look out for remnants of the past and those mad details – a vampire-couture shop or outsider art gallery – that are the new face of the Vieux.

A compact grid of six blocks by 13, the Quarter is bounded by the Mississippi River levee, Canal St, Rampart St and Esplanade Ave. Jackson Sq is perfectly centered on the river side of the Quarter. The upper Quarter (located further south – welcome to New Orleans), nearest Canal St, is most touristy. That said, around Orleans Ave things quiet down again, and most of the buildings are private residences with the odd corner shop or guesthouse thrown in.

Metered parking is available on most streets, but pay close attention to restrictions. Street parking is easier in the Lower Quarter. Many parking lots and garages are overpriced. No bus cuts through the middle of the neighborhood. Buses 55 and 5 run down the east edge (along Decatur St and N Peters, respectively). Bus 11 runs the entire length of Magazine St to Canal St, 42 runs on Canal St through Mid-City, and 88 runs from Rampart St to Bywater.

Riverfront streetcar 2 edges the levee side of the Quarter from Esplanade Ave to the Convention Center (in the Warehouse District). When it's operating, the St Charles Ave streetcar runs from Canal St along St Charles Ave through the CBD, the Garden District and Uptown. Streetcar 45 runs on Canal St from the river through Mid-City.

The Canal St Ferry crosses the Mississippi to Algiers Point. It docks near the foot of Canal St.

LOWER QUARTER

The Lower Quarter is actually the Quarter's northern end: in New Orleans, 'up' and 'down' are determined by the flow of the Mississippi rather than the cardinal compass points. This is the quieter, more residential end of the Vieux Carré, filled with museums and historical houses.

JACKSON SQUARE Map pp70–1

Sprinkled with lazing loungers, surrounded by fortune tellers, sketch artists and traveling performers, and overlooked by cathedrals, offices and shops plucked from a Parisian fantasy, Jackson Sq is one of America's great green spaces. It manages both to anchor the French Quarter and beat out the heart-rhythm of this corner of town. Whatever happens in the Quarter usually begins here. The identical, block-long Pontalba Buildings overlook the square, and the near-identical Cabildo and Presbytère structures flank St Louis Cathedral, the square's centerpiece.

The square was part of Adrien de Pauger's original city plans and began life as a military parade ground called Place d'Armes. Madame Micaëla Pontalba transformed the muddy marching grounds into a trimmed garden and renamed the square to honor Andrew Jackson (see boxed text, p25).

In the middle of the park stands the Jackson monument – Clark Mills' bronze equestrian statue of Jackson, unveiled in 1856. The inscription, 'The Union Must and Shall be Preserved,' was added by General Benjamin Butler, Union military governor of New Orleans during the Civil War, ostensibly to rub it into the occupied city's face. (It worked.)

ST LOUIS CATHEDRAL Map pp70–1
☎ 525-9585; Jackson Sq; donations accepted; ⏲ 9am-5pm Mon-Sat, from 1pm Sun
One of the best examples of French architecture in the country is the triple-spire cathedral of St Louis, King of France, an innocuous bit of Gallic heritage in the heart of old New Orleans. Still used for services, the structure is packed on Christmas Eve midnight mass and is one of the most important (and beautiful) churches serving black – or any, really – Catholics in the USA today. Besides hosting black, white and Creole congregants, St Louis has also attracted those who, in the best new Orleanian tradition, mix their influences, such as voodoo queen Marie Laveau, who practiced a hybrid voodoo-Catholicism and worshiped here during the height of her influence in the mid-19th century.

In 1722 a hurricane destroyed the first of three churches built here by the St Louis Parish. Architect Don Gilberto Guillemard dedicated the present cathedral on Christmas Eve in 1794. Extensive remodeling from 1849 to 1851 was designed by French-trained architect JNB DePouilly. In

1850 the cathedral was designated as the metropolitan church of the Archdiocese of New Orleans. Pope Paul VI awarded it the rank of minor basilica in 1964.

Buried in the cathedral is its Spanish benefactor, Don Andrés Almonaster y Roxas, who also financed the Cabildo and the initial construction of the Presbytère.

CABILDO Map pp70–1
☎ 568-6968; http://lsm.crt.state.la.us; 701 Chartres St; adult/child/senior & student $6/free/5; ⏲ 9am-5pm Tue-Sun
The former seat of power in colonial Louisiana serves as the gateway for exploring the history of the state, and New Orleans in particular. It's also a fairly magnificent building on its own merits; the Cabildo, a Spanish term for a city council, leads visitors into airy halls reminiscent of Spanish colonial design and a mansard roof (the narrow, steep-sided roofs commonly found in Europe) added in the French style.

The exhibits, from Native American tools on the 1st floor to wanted posters for escaped slaves on the 3rd, do a good job of reaffirming the role the building and surrounding region has played in history. This was the site of the Louisiana Purchase ceremonies, city-council hall of New Orleans up till the 1850s, and the courtroom for *Plessy v Ferguson,* the 1896 case that legalized segregation under the 'separate but equal' doctrine. The Cabildo, destroyed or damaged by fire twice, looks small from the outside but conceals a deceptively large interior, which includes the magnificent Sala Capitular (Capitol Room), a council room fronted by enormous windows and sweeping views onto Jackson Sq. Give yourself at least two hours to explore. Friends of the Cabildo does one

FRENCH QUARTER

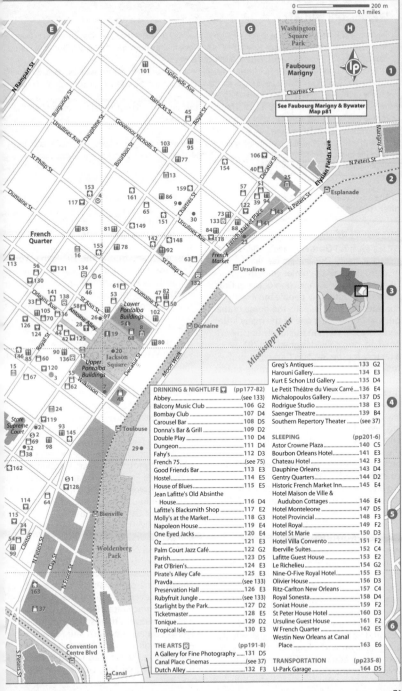

71

WHERE ARE YOU AT?

The Mississippi River serves as a false compass in New Orleans. While it's true that the river flows from north to south, it curves *under* New Orleans and thus is actually flowing from west to east where it passes the French Quarter. So, when locals give directions, they rarely indicate north, south, east or west.

Directions upriver or downriver are relative to the water flow, which bends to all points of the compass – fore example, the Convention Center is upriver from (or above) the French Quarter, even though a compass would show that the Convention Center is south-southwest (ie below).

In addition, the river and Lake Pontchartrain serve as landmarks in 'riverside' or 'lakeside' directions: 'You'll find Louis Armstrong Park on the lakeside of the French Quarter – head toward the lake and you'll find it,' and 'Preservation Hall is on St Peter St toward the river from Bourbon St.'

Canal St divides uptown from downtown. However, to add confusion, a large part of the city, from the Garden District to the Riverbend, is commonly referred to as Uptown. Because of the vagaries of the river, Uptown streets are labeled 'south' and downtown streets are 'north.'

---

of the best walking tours of the city on offer (see p242).

PRESBYTÈRE Map pp70–1

☎ 568-6968; 751 Chartres St; adult/child/senior & student $6/free/5; ☼ 9am-5pm Tue-Sun
It seems like half the major cities in the USA throw their own version of Mardi Gras these days, but many people incorrectly consider the New Orleans the home of the original festival: just one of the many little lessons you'll learn in the lovely Presbytère building, originally designed in 1791 as a rectory for the St Louis Cathedral, and today serving as New Orleans' more-or-less official Mardi Gras museum. Here you'll find there's more to the city's most famous celebration than wonton debauchery – or at least you'll learn the many levels of meaning behind the debauchery. There's a whole encyclopedia's worth of material inside on the krewes, secret societies, costumes and racial histories that are the threads of the complex Mardi Gras tapestry. It's illuminating and easy to follow; we particularly like the exhibit on the 'Courir' Cajun Mardi Gras held in rural Louisiana.

FRENCH MARKET Map pp70–1

Within the shopping arcades of forgettable souvenirs, mediocre art and overrated food, it's easy to forget that for centuries this was the great bazaar and pulsing commercial heart of much of New Orleans. Today the French Market is a bit sanitized, a safari through a tourist jungle of curios, flea markets and harmless, shiny tat that all equals great family-friendly fun. Occasionally you'll spot some genuinely fascinating and/or unique arts and craftwork.

The Spanish built the first meat-and-produce market here in 1791, which was destroyed by hurricane and fire. In 1813 the replacement Halle des Boucheries (Meat Market), at 900 Decatur St, was designed, and during the 1930s the Works Progress Administration (WPA) extensively renovated (and in some respects, remodeled) the city-managed French Market from St Ann to Barracks Sts. The cupolas atop the old Meat Market were added at this time, as was the sturdy colonnade that runs the length of the market. Radio station WWOZ currently airs from a French Market building.

URSULINE CONVENT Map pp70–1

☎ 529-2651; 1112 Chartres St; adult/under 8yr/child/senior $5/free/2/4; ☼ tours hourly 10am-3pm Tue-Fri, 11:15am, 1pm & 2pm Sat & Sun
One of the few surviving examples of French-colonial architecture in New Orleans (though it probably reflects a design more common to French Canada), this lovely convent is worth a tour for its architectural virtues, although it also houses a small museum of Catholic bric-a-brac.

After a five-month voyage from Rouen, France, 12 Ursuline nuns arrived in New Orleans in 1727 to provide care at the French garrison's miserable little hospital and to educate the women of the colony. The Ursuline order had a missionary bent, but it achieved its goals through advancing the literacy rate of women of all races and social levels; their school admitted French, Native American and African American girls, and free persons of color and slaves alike were educated in these halls. By the mid-18th century the literacy rate among women in the colony was an astounding 71% – higher than for men at the time.

GALLIER HOUSE MUSEUM Map pp70–1

☎ 525-5661; www.hgghh.org; 1118 Royal St; adult/child/student & senior $10/free/8, combined Hermann-Grima House adult/student & senior $18/15; ☺ tours hourly 10am-3pm Mon-Fri

Walking down the road of New Orleans' history, take note of the buildings along the way: physical evidence of the city's evolution. Many of those buildings owe their existence, either directly or in terms of design, to James Gallier Sr and Jr, who added Greek-revivalist, British and American accents to the French/Spanish/Creole architectural mélange evident in so much of the Quarter. In 1857 Gallier Jr began work on this impressive town house, which incorporated all of the above plus the latest in then-contemporary amenities, such as copper interior plumbing, skylights and ceiling vents. The period furniture is lovely; not so much are the intact slave quarters out back – once you see these, you'll recognize them throughout the Quarter.

BEAUREGARD-KEYES HOUSE
Map pp70–1

☎ 523-7257; www.neworleansmuseums.com; 1113 Chartres St; tours adult/child/student/$5/2/4; ☺ tours hourly from 10am-3pm

This attractive 1826 Greek-revival house is named for its two most famous previous inhabitants. Confederate General Pierre Gustave Toutant Beauregard, a native of Louisiana, commanded the artillery battery that fired the first shots at Fort Sumter in Charleston, SC (starting the Civil War); he lived here for 18 months after the war ended. Author Francis Parkinson Keyes, who wrote 51 novels, many of which were set in New Orleans (and one, the 1962 *Madame Castel's Lodger*, which was set in this house), stayed longer: from 1942 until her death in 1970. Her collection of some 200 dolls and folk costumes are also on display. Entry via tours only.

1850 HOUSE MUSEUM Map pp70–1

☎ 568-6968; 523 St Ann St; adult/child/senior & student $3/free/2; ☺ 9am-5pm Tue-Sun

The 1850 House is one of the apartments in the lower Pontalba Building. Madame

Micaëla Pontalba, daughter of Don Andrés Almonaster y Roxas, built the long rows of red-brick apartments flanking the upper and lower portions of Jackson Sq. Initial plans for the apartments were drawn by the noted architect James Gallier Sr. In 1927, the lower Pontalba Building was bequeathed by William Ratcliffe Irby to the Louisiana State Museum, and three years later the city acquired the upper Pontalba Building, where Micaëla once lived.

Today, knowledgeable volunteers from the Friends of the Cabildo give tours of the apartment (every 45 minutes or so), which includes the central court and servants' quarters, with period furnishings throughout. Innovations include the use of bricks imported from the East Coast, extended porches to create covered walkways, and the upstairs galleries, which have cast-iron railings in place of wrought iron. Repeated along the railings are the initials AP, signifying the union of the Almonaster and Pontalba wealth.

When guides are not available, visitors can roam the house at their leisure.

NEW ORLEANS JAZZ NATIONAL HISTORIC PARK Map pp70–1

☎ 589-4806; www.nps.gov/jazz; 916 N Peters St; admission free; ☺ 9am-5pm

The headquarters of the Jazz National Historic Park has educational music programs on most days of the week. Many of the park rangers are musicians and knowledgeable lecturers, and their presentations discuss musical developments, cultural changes, regional styles, myths, legends and musical techniques in relation to the broad subject of jazz. A nearby 'Jazz Walk of Fame' ambles by lamp posts dedicated to jazz greats. You can also pick up a self-guided audio walking tour of jazz sites in the Quarter at this office – the tour can be downloaded as MP3s or listened to on your phone. At some point (there have been several delays so far), the center is supposed to relocate to a permanent headquarters in Louis Armstrong Park.

HISTORIC VOODOO MUSEUM
Map pp70–1

☎ 680-0128; 724 Dumaine St; adult/child $7/3.50; ☺ 11am-5pm

Of the (many) voodoo museums in the French Quarter, this one is probably our favorite. The narrow corridors and dark rooms, stuffed with statues, dolls and paintings, are something approaching spooky, and the information placards, which seem to have been written by an anthropology dissertation student with too much time of their hands, are genuinely informative (if a little dry).

HULA MAE'S LAUNDRY Map pp70–1

☎ 522-1336; 840 N Rampart St; ۞ 10am-9pm

Cossimo Matassa's J&M Music shop was the place where New Orleans musicians recorded some of the biggest R&B hits in the 1950s. It closed down years ago, but the site, now a busy Laundromat, preserves some fine musical heritage. The pebbly J&M sign is still inlaid on the front threshold; inside, one wall is dedicated to a photo-and-history exhibit. It was in this building that Fats Domino and Dave Bartholomew established the 'New Orleans Sound.' Countless oldies but goodies, including Lloyd Price's 'Lawdy Miss Clawdy,' were recorded right there by that box of Tide.

VOODOO SPIRITUAL TEMPLE

Map pp70–1

☎ 522-9627; www.voodoospiritualtemple.org; 828 N Rampart St; donations accepted; ۞ 10:30am-5pm Mon-Fri, sometimes Sat

Priestess Miriam Williams keeps her Voodoo Spiritual Temple stocked with religious paraphernalia from…damn, is that a Mexican crucifix next to a Nigerian Eshu statue? Under a Tibetan mandala? Above a Balinese Garuda? You get the idea. Miriam's temple feels as New Age as it does voodoo, or maybe that's just her interpretation of voodoo, or…whatever. The temple is big on the tour-group circuit and it's often entertaining as hell to watch Miriam give her lectures on life, the universe and everything. In a back room, a snake relaxes in its vivarium and on the odd occasion, with a transfixed countenance, Miriam will take it out and lift it up, the snake appearing to move its body according to her will. There is, of course, an adjacent gift shop doing a brisk trade in candles, cards and gris-gris (amulets or spell bags).

VOODOO QUEEN

Voodoo became wildly popular in New Orleans after it was introduced by black émigrés from St Domingue (now Haiti) at the beginning of the 19th century, but very little is known with certainty about the legendary 19th-century Voodoo Queen Marie Laveau, who gained fame and fortune by shrewdly exploiting voodoo's mystique. Though details of her life are shrouded in myth and misconception, what has been passed down from generation to generation makes for a fascinating story.

She was born in 1794, a French-speaking Catholic of mixed black and white ancestry. Invariably described as beautiful and charismatic, at age 25 she married a man named Paris. He died a few years later, and Marie became known as the Widow Paris. She had 15 children with another man, Glapion, who is believed to have migrated from St Domingue, and may have been Marie Laveau's first connection to voodoo.

In the 1830s she established herself as the city's preeminent voodoo queen, and her influence crossed racial lines. Mostly she reeled in stray husbands and helped people avenge wrongs done to them. According to legend, she earned her house on St Anne St as payment for ensuring a young man's acquittal in a rape or murder trial.

Marie apparently had some tricks up her sleeve. She is said to have worked as a hairdresser in the homes of upper-class white women, and it was not uncommon for these women to share society gossip while having their hair done. In this way, Laveau gained a thorough familiarity with the vagaries of the elite, and she astutely perceived the value of such information. At the peak of her reign as voodoo queen, she employed a network of spies, most of them household servants in upper-class homes.

Reports on Laveau's activities suggest that there was much more to her practice than nonpractitioners were permitted to witness – which probably makes these reports suspect. However, part of the Laveau legend involves rituals she presided over in the countryside around New Orleans. According to sensational accounts related after her death, Laveau's followers danced naked around bonfires, drinking blood and slithering on the ground like snakes before engaging in all-out orgies.

A brothel out by Lake Pontchartrain called Maison Blanche was reputedly operated by Marie Laveau, but it is uncertain if this was the same Marie Laveau – there were two people known as Marie Laveau, the second being the daughter of the original Marie Laveau. It is unclear where the influence of one gave over to the other. The elder Marie Laveau died in 1881 and is believed to be buried in St Louis Cemetery No 1. The younger lived into the early 20th century.

THE BIG MUDDY

The Mississippi River is more than the defining geographical landmark of New Orleans. It is its soul, its center and its reason for being. 'Why was New Orleans built below sea level?' folks ask. First off, only half the city is below sea level, but the reason is that this spot commands the entrance to the most important river in North America. All the trade, conquest and exploration of this continent is wrapped up in the Mississippi and her moods. It would be criminal to come here and not catch a glimpse of the Mother of Waters.

It can be difficult to appreciate just where the river is from the streets. Some of our favorite spots for river watching include numerous benches along the levee opposite Jackson Sq and the Moon Walk, a boardwalk built by and named for former mayor Moon Landrieu (not the dance).

The Mississippi is no lazy river. Through New Orleans, the river's depth averages about 200ft. Its immense volume of water and sand roils with tremendous, turbulent force, whirling and eddying and scouring at the banks of snakelike curves. It runs some 2400 miles from Minnesota to the Gulf of Mexico, and its drainage basin extends from the Rockies to the Alleghenies, covering 40% of the continental USA. The rain that falls in this vast area ultimately ends up in the Gulf, and most of it is carried there by the Mississippi. The Platte, the Missouri, the Ohio, the Cumberland and the Arkansas – mighty rivers themselves – all feed into the Mississippi, which carries their waters past New Orleans. It drains more water than the Nile, and only the Amazon and the Congo carry a greater volume of water to the sea.

It also moves up to several million tons of sediment into the Gulf every day. Thus, the river has shifted more than 1000 cubic miles of earth from north to south, depositing soil into the Gulf and spreading it to the east and west as the river changed its course. The land that is Louisiana and much of the states of Mississippi and Alabama was created by the river.

The river's name is a corruption of the old Ojibwe *Misi-ziibi* (great river). For early European settlers to the Mississippi Valley, the river initially proved too unruly to serve as a viable route inland until the advent of the steamboat in 1807. During the early part of the 19th century New Orleans' population mushroomed, largely as a result of river traffic and trade.

It is natural for deltaic rivers to flood regularly and periodically change course, and preventing the Mississippi from flooding is no simple engineering feat. The river has proven more than mere levees can handle on several occasions, most notoriously in 1927, when the river breached levees in 145 places. That spring, some 27,000 sq miles of farmland, from Illinois to southern Louisiana, turned into a raging sea, up to 30ft deep in places, that flowed steadily down to the Gulf. Entire towns were washed away and a million people were driven from their homes. It took several months for the flooding to recede back to within the river's banks. New Orleans, however, remained high and dry, as north of the city the floodwaters chose the Atchafalaya River's shorter path to the Gulf.

CHEZ VODUN Map pp70–1

☎ 558-0653; 822 N Rampart St; ☼ 10am-6pm
Screw welcome mats; this place has an aroused Legba statue giving the nod (as it were) to tourists looking for an introduction to the voodoo religion. Within are the Temple of Pythons, an active place of worship; the requisite gift shop selling voodoo art and artifacts; a hookah parlor; and a bar that serves voodoo martinis. Presiding over Saturday-night ceremonies is Dr Sharon Caulder, a scholar, author and voodoo chief who conducts healing rites for members of the audience. Visitors are welcome.

OLD US MINT Map pp70–1

☎ 568-6968; http://lsm.crt.state.la.us; 400 Esplanade Ave
The Mint, housed in a somewhat blocky Greek-revival building, was the only one in the USA to have printed both US and Confederate currency. Its roof was badly damaged during Hurricane Katrina and the majority of displays housed here remained closed at the time of writing. There's a small exhibition in the interior hall on the currency that has been printed here.

When they've been reopened, the jazz exhibit is worth a visit to see dented horns, busted snare drums and homemade gut-stringed bass fiddles played by some of the Crescent City's most cherished artists, and the Houma Arts exhibit is an impressive and often humorous collection of colorful wood carvings depicting men and animals – many of them life-sized.

UPPER QUARTER

South of Jackson Sq is where you'll find most of the booziness and souvenir stands that most tourists associate with the Old Quarter.

BOURBON STREET Map pp70–1

'That street just T-shirts and tit bars,' says one local, and he's not far off. Bourbon St, like the Vegas strip and Cancun, is where the great id of the repressed American psyche is let loose into a seething mass of karaoke, strip clubs and (it seems) every bachelorette party ever. It's sold as New Orleans squared; ironically, it's actually negative New Orleans, a far cry from what the city truly is. Locals don't tend to unleash their need for sin in such concentrated bursts; there is a grace to their debauchery (usually). But Bourbon St can be fun for a sliver of an evening, when you need to remind yourself that this is indeed what happens when buttoned-down mankind decides to chuck all the rules of acceptable behavior out the window and revert back to a *Lord of the Flies*–like stage of primal instinct.

ROYAL STREET Map pp70–1

Walk over a little ways from Bourbon St and sober up; this is where you go to engage in the more acceptable vacation behavior of culinary and consumer indulgence rather than party-till-unconscious excess. Royal St, with its rows of high end antique shops, block after block of galleries and potted ferns hanging from cast-iron balconies, is the elegant yin to Bourbon's Sodom-and-Gomorrah yang. Stroll past the beauty and its sense of patina-ed grace, have a chat with a local as they lounge on their porch, and get a sense of the fun with a dash of the…well…not reserve, but dignity that is the true soul of Vieux Carré.

HISTORIC NEW ORLEANS COLLECTION Map pp70–1

☎ 523-4662; www.hnoc.org; 533 Royal St; admission free, tours $5; ☽ 9:30am-4:30pm Tue-Sat, from 10:30am Sun

A combination of preserved buildings, museums and research centers all rolled into a short introduction to the city's history, the Historic New Orleans Collection has an equal pull on visitors, local researchers and foreign scholars.

The complex is anchored by Merieult House and a series of regularly rotating exhibits in the Williams Gallery (admission free; ☽ 9:30m-4:30pm Tue-Sat). Past displays have included photo essays, oral histories and videos that document the enormous influence émigrés from St Domingue (now Haiti) had on New Orleans at the beginning of the 19th century.

Upstairs, the meticulously researched Merieult History Tour dives into 11 galleries' worth of New Orleans' history – it's slightly overwhelming (the original Jazz Fest poster, transfer documents of the Louisiana Purchase, 1849 broadside advertising '24 Head of Slaves' [individual children for $500 or entire families for $2400]) and imminently rewarding. The building itself has served as private residence, storehouse and hotel, and is a rare survivor of the 1794 fire that gutted the Quarter.

The Williams family was always considered eccentric, and their Residence, purchased in 1938 in what was then considered a dowdy neighborhood, is stuffed full of art and furniture collected in their world travels. Tours are given Tuesday to Saturday at 10am, 11am, 2pm and 3pm for $5.

Dedicated travelers and history heads should pop into the Williams Research Center (☎ 523-4662; 410 Chartres St; ☽ 10am-4:30pm Tue-Sat); if you have specific queries about almost anything New Orleans, the staff here can help. The archives contain over 350,000 images and some 2 miles of manuscripts.

NEW ORLEANS PHARMACY MUSEUM Map pp70–1

☎ 565-8027; www.pharmacymuseum.org; 514 Chartres St; adult/child $5/4; ☽ 10am-2pm Tue & Thu, to 5pm Wed, Fri & Sat

This beautifully preserved little shop is all a-groaning with ancient display cases filled with intriguing little bottles. Established in 1816 by Louis J Dufilho at a time when the pharmaceutical arts were – shall we say – in their infancy, the museum claims Dufilho was the nation's first licensed pharmacist,

top picks

IT'S FREE

- Magazine St (p131) Top place for window shopping.
- Bayou St John (p111) Give your toes a dip.
- Tulane University (p104) Relive those student days.
- Jackson Sq (p68) A great place for free concerts.
- Metairie Cemetery (p112) and St Louis Cemetery No 1 (p112) Just two of the many town's cemeteries worth strolling through.

CASKET GIRLS & WORKING GIRLS

During the early days of their work, the Ursuline nuns (see p72), having quickly observed that an unusually high propor- tion of the colony's women were working the world's oldest profession, decided to call in marriageable teenage girls from France (generally recruited from orphanages or convents). The girls arrived in New Orleans, Biloxi and Mobile with their clothes packed in coffin-like trunks, and thus became known as the 'casket girls.' Educated by the nuns, the girls were brought up to make proper wives for the French men of New Orleans. Over the centuries, the casket-girl legacy became more sensational as some in New Orleans surmised the wood boxes may have contained French vampires.

Of course, prostitution never lost its luster in this steamy port. New Orleans' fabled bordellos are one of the earliest foundations upon which the city's reputation as a spot for sin and fun are built. The most famous 'sporting' houses were elegant mansions, reputedly decorated with some of the finest art and furnishings of their era and staffed with, this being New Orleans, a multiracial cast of employees ranging from white to Creole to black. Around the turn of the 20th century, famously puritan city alderman (councilor) Sidney Story wrote an ordinance that moved the bordellos out of the city's posh residential neighborhoods and into that side of the French Quarter that borders the Tremé. Never ones to pass up good irony, New Orleanians dubbed their red-light district 'Storyville' in honor of Sidney.

Although there were no Lonely Planet books around at the time, visitors could explore Storyville with the help of the 'Blue Book,' a guide to the area's…attractions. Each book was imprinted with the passage: 'Order of the Garter: *Honi Soit Qui Mal Y Pense*' (Shame to Him Who Evil Thinks). Jazz was largely popularized by visitors listening to music in Storyville's storied pleasure houses. One of the most famous, the Arlington, operated at 225 North Basin Street (look for the onion-domed cupola, all that's left of the demolished bordello).

Storyville was shut down in 1917 by the federal government. At the time Mayor Martin Behrman lamented that while authorities could make prostitution illegal, 'you can't make it unpopular.'

although his practices would be suspect today (gold-coated pills to the wealthy; opium, alcohol and cannabis to those who needed to feel better for less money).

INSECTARIUM Map pp70–1

☎ 410-2847; www.auduboninstitute.org; 423 Canal St; adult/child/senior$14/9/11; ☯ 10am-5pm Tue-Sun

The newest jewel in the Audubon Insti- tute crown is this supremely kid-friendly learning center that's a joy for budding etymologists, or really anyone with a bit of interest in biology. Exhibits are pretty fun: an 'underground' den where the floor feels like soil and a giant worm burrows through the walls; a typical New Orleanian cupboard overflowing with cockroaches (the accompanying history of the city from a 'roach's point of view is pretty hilarious); and a lovely Japanese garden dotted with whispering butterflies. Although it's a little weird that many of the exhibit's sponsors seem to be pest control companies, this is a worthy addition to the Audubon Institute's animal education lineup.

MUSÉE CONTI HISTORICAL WAX MUSEUM Map pp70–1

☎ 581-1993; www.neworleanswaxmuseum.com; 917 Conti St; adult/child/senior $6.75/5.75/6.25; ☯ 10am-4pm

This place sells itself as one of New Orle- ans' 'best kept secrets,' which is like saying po'boys are undiscovered culinary gems. It's a wax museum that's kitschy and en- tertaining in the way wax museums should be: local historical figures include Andrew Jackson, Huey Long, Louis Armstrong and Napoleon Bonaparte (caught in the bathtub for some reason), then Franken- stein's monster (chained down, for your protection) and Swamp Thing (unchained!).

MASPERO'S EXCHANGE Map pp70–1

☎ 524-8900; 440 Chartres St

Now Original Pierre Maspero's (a fairly mid- dling restaurant), this was once La Bourse de Maspero: a cafe-cum-slave-auctioneer- ing house where the city's elite sipped au lait while human chattel were traded in Exchange Alley (now Exchange Place). Note the entresol (a mezzanine floor with a low ceiling visible from the exterior through the arched windows); this cramped little room was only reached through a ceiling door from the bottom floor, and is where slaves are said to have been imprisoned while awaiting their sale. This room now serves as a dining room. In 1814, the building was the headquarters for the local Committee of Public Safety, charged with marshaling citizens to fight under General Andrew Jackson.

HERMANN-GRIMA HOUSE Map pp70–1

☎ 525-5661; www.hgghh.org; 820 St Louis St; tours adult/senior $6/5; ⏱ tours 10am, 11am, noon, 2pm & 3pm Mon-Fri

Samuel Hermann, a Jewish merchant who married a Catholic woman, introduced the American-style Federal design to the Quarter in 1831. Hermann sold the house in 1844 to Judge Grima, a slaveholder, after he reportedly lost $2 million during the national financial panic of 1837. Cooking demonstrations in the open-hearth kitchen are a special treat on Thursdays from October to May.

SOBER STROLL
Walking Tour

This walk explores the French Quarter's two main drags: Bourbon St and Royal St. Goofus and Gallant, if you will. Think of this as a quick introduction to the Quarter. Every block is worth a stroll if you're really into the architecture and atmosphere of this beautifully preserved historic district. This tour just samples a bit of the Quarter's architecture and some of its intriguing lore, and closes out with a relaxing courtyard lunch.

1 St Anthony's Garden Begin at Pirate's Alley, an inviting walkway that cuts through the shadow of St Louis Cathedral. The alley is supposedly where the pirate Jean Lafitte hawked goods plundered from Spanish ships. However, some city records indicate the alley did not open until 1831, long after Lafitte and his gang were gone. To the right is gated St Anthony's Garden, which lost some of its lushness in the hurricanes of 2005 but nevertheless remains a peaceful pocket in the bustling Quarter.

2 Faulkner House Bookstore Halfway up the alley, stop in at the small but charming Faulkner House Bookstore (p126). It opened in 1990 and very quickly became a focal point for New Orleans literary circles. It's named William Faulkner's brief 1925 stay in the house.

3 Labranche Buildings Much of the alley is occupied by these buildings, built by Jean Baptiste Labranche, a Creole sugar planter, which wrap around Royal St to St Peter St. Slow down to admire the attractive cast-iron and wrought-iron balconies. Turn right at

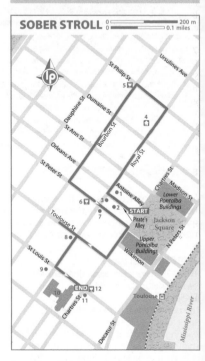

Royal St, which takes the cake for classic New Orleans postcard images. Take it slow and appreciate the details.

4 Cornstalk Hotel This hotel stands behind one of the most frequently photographed fences anywhere. The 1859 cornstalk-motif fence has seen many coats of paint over the years but is looking pretty good. Turn the corner at St Philip St and head towards Bourbon St (p76).

5 Lafitte's Blacksmith Shop A ramshackle structure on the corner of St Philip St, Lafitte's Blacksmith Shop (p178) is, according to legend, where pirate Jean Lafitte ran a blacksmith shop with his brother, Pierre, as a front for their trade in stolen and smuggled goods. The little relic looks like the real deal and indeed it

78

is old enough. Have a drink to brace yourself for Bourbon St. We'll just stroll down it for a few blocks.

6 Pat O'Brien's Turn left down St Peter St towards the river and you'll come to Pat O'Brien's (p179), a bar famous for its syrupy signature beverage, the 'Hurricane.' You can walk through Pat's large scenic courtyard and reemerge on Bourbon St. Loop back around to St Peter St, and head in the direction of Royal St.

7 LeMonnier Mansion At the corner of Royal, take a look at LeMonnier Mansion (640 Royal St), commonly known to be New Orleans' first skyscraper. Begun in 1795, the structure grew to three stories tall by 1811 (a 4th floor was added in 1876). Until that time, building was generally limited to two floors for fear that the swampy soil couldn't support taller structures.

8 Court of Two Lions Pass the Avart-Peretti House (632 St Peter St) where Williams wrote *A Streetcar Named Desire* and turn left on Chartres St. Walk a block past a pretty row of antique shops to Toulouse St and turn right. At the corner of Royal and Toulouse Sts stand a pair of houses built in the 1790s. The corner house, the Court of Two Lions (541 Royal St), has a well-known gate on the Toulouse St side, flanked by marble lions atop the entry posts.

9 Peychaud's Apothecary Past the Historic New Orleans Collection (p76), continue down Royal St to St Louis St. On this corner, in what is now James H Cohen & Sons antique gun shop, the cocktail was supposedly invented. The premises were occupied at the beginning of the 19th century by Peychaud's Apothecary. Old Peychaud is said to have dabbled in the chemistry of drinkable spirits, and served his mixtures to the public. Whether he was the first to do so is, of course, widely disputed.

10 State Supreme Court Building Turn left and walk a block of St Louis St, back to Chartres. All the while, it's impossible not to notice this building. Opened in 1909, the white-marble and terra-cotta facade stands in jarring yet attractive contrast with the rest of the Quarter. Scenes from the movie *JFK* were shot in and around the building.

11 Maspero's Exchange The intersection of St Louis and Chartres is flanked by two noteworthy buildings. First there's the sobering history of Maspero's Exchange (p77), a restaurant that once was known as La Bourse de Maspero. It was a slave-trading house and coffee shop operated by Pierre Maspero.

12 Napoleon House Just across from Maspero's Exchange is Napoleon House (p178), where we'll end our tour over a bowl of gumbo and a beer in the beautiful courtyard.

FAUBOURG MARIGNY & BYWATER

Drinking & Nightlife p182, Eating p156, Shopping p127, Sleeping p206

We love this 'hood, but it's a sort of urban example of the law of diminishing returns as applied to coolness. Edgy…artsy…height of hip…damn – gentrified.

OK, not quite. Faubourg (old French for 'suburb') Marigny (mare-*eh*-knyee), a gorgeous cluster of cozy 19th-century houses and some of the city's best nightlife, is still a neighborhood with plenty of awesome edges: in terms of the arts, its music, its gay community (the biggest in the city and one of the largest, and oldest, in the South), the racially mixed population, Creole residences and still generally bohemian vibe. In many ways the Marigny is what the French Quarter could be minus the Bourbon St mobs – still tons of fun, and infused with the same architectural and historic heritage, but a bit more mature, a Manhattan sipped at a jazz concert as opposed to a Jaeger bomb slammed to Bon Jovi. (This is still New Orleans, so let's say *a lot* of Manhattans sipped over the course of the night but…well, you get the idea.) Frenchmen St, which runs through the heart of the Marigny, is one of the best live music strips in the country, and while more and more tourists are finding their way north of Decatur, most of the folks you meet will still be from down the block.

That said, those Marigny-ers (-ites?) may have only been down the block for a few years. Here's some New Orleans trivia: this neighborhood has the greatest concentration of historic buildings in the city. Now guess which 'hood has the most new New Orleanians, population-wise?

From the Quarter, cross Esplanade Ave and you're in Faubourg Marigny. Bywater is the next neighborhood down. Both are wedged between the river and St Claude Ave. The two neighborhoods are divided by the railroad tracks along Press St. Bywater ends at Poland St, opposite the naval base, more than a mile below Esplanade Ave. Frenchmen St is the cultural hub of the Marigny and within walking distance of the French Quarter. Bywater is more spread out and less walkable. Some of the bigger sites are actually just north of the region described here, but don't let that fool you into thinking the Marigny and Bywater aren't worth the trip in themselves.

The slight gentrification of the Marigny followed Katrina, when many of the volunteers, artists and do-gooders intent on rebuilding New Orleans poured into the neighborhood. Said transplants brought a lot of great energy, but on their heels came higher real-estate prices and the inevitable accompanying bland. Many of the most hip, as well as one of the most demographically mixed muddles of humanity we can imagine, stepped east across the tracks into Bywater.

If the Marigny's moment has come, Bywater's is waiting, but to be honest, we'd hate to see this area lose its character as the city's thin red line. Red line between what, you ask? About anything you can think of: income brackets, working and creative classes, black and white, even geography. It's called Bywater for a reason – both the Mississippi and some of its most important canals are adjacent to this area. In Bywater, many of New Orleans' still-often-segregated communities exist side by side, and if they're not living in perfect harmony, there is at least a tough sense of community. You feel like you're about to stumble upon some outsider art gallery half the time – but there are also moments when you'll want to keep a hand on your wallet. This isn't the safest part of town, which can be hard to forget as you stroll past rows of beautifully painted double shotgun shacks, groves of palm decked with papier-mâché sculptures and some of the coolest restaurants and dives in the city. Just across St Claude Ave are rough projects – watch where you step at night.

Bus 5 runs down on Dauphine and back up Royal St through the Marigny and Bywater, and extends through the Quarter. Bus 55 runs on Elysian Fields Ave and down Decatur St through the Quarter, and the 88 runs along the lakeside of Bywater and the Marigny, on St Claude Ave, continuing along Rampart St. The riverfront streetcar 2 starts from Esplanade Ave (near the Faubourg Marigny) and edges the Quarter and the Warehouse District. If you're driving, street parking, while not always easy to find, is all there is.

NEW ORLEANS CENTER FOR CREATIVE ARTS Map p81
Nocca; ☎ 800-201-4836; www.nocca.com; 2800 Chartres St

New Orleans, like few American cities of its size, lives and dies off its arts scene. This is a city unapologetically in love with (and largely built on) the work of its musicians, painters and writers, and many of the next generation of such artists are educated at Nocca. Admission to this prestigious center, one of the best arts schools in the USA, is

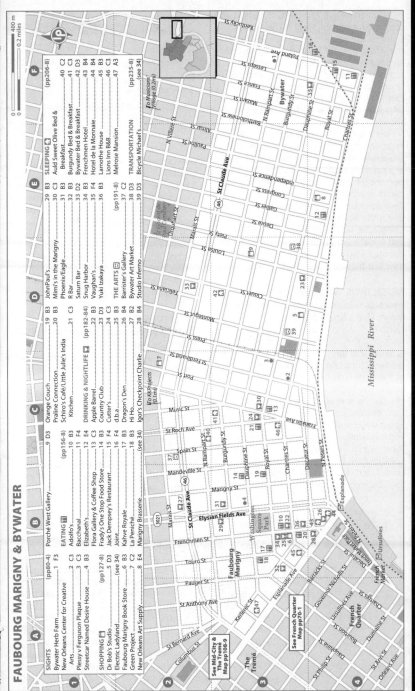

FAUBOURG MARIGNY & BYWATER

SIGHTS (pp80–4)
Bywater Herb Farm...........................1 F3
New Orleans Center for Creative
  Arts..2 C3
Plessy v Ferguson Plaque................3 C3
Streetcar Named Desire House.........4 B3

SHOPPING 🛍 (pp127–8)
Dr Bob's Studio...............................5 D3
Electric Ladyland............................6 B3
Faubourg Marigny Book Store..........7 C2
Green Project..................................8 E4
New Orleans Art Supply.......(see 34)

Orange Couch.................................9 D3
Porché West Gallery.......................10 B3

EATING 🍴 (pp156–8)
Adolfo's..10 B3
Bacchanal......................................11 F4
Elizabeth's....................................12 E4
Flora Gallery & Coffee Shop...........13 C3
Frady's One Stop Food Store..........14 B3
Jack Dempsey's Restaurant............15 F4
Joint...16 F4
Kahve Royale................................17 B3
La Peniché....................................18 B3
Marigny Brasserie.................(see 34)

Schiro's Café/Little Julie's India
  Kitchen......................................21 C3

DRINKING & NIGHTLIFE 🍸 (pp182–84)
Apple Barrel..................................22 B3
Country Club.................................23 D3
Cutter's...24 C3
d.b.a..25 B3
Dragon's Den................................26 B4
Hi Ho...27 B2
Igor's Checkpoint Charlie...............28 B4

JohnPaul's....................................19 B3
Mimi's in the Marigny...................20 B3
Phoenix/Eagle...............................31 B3
R Bar..32 B3
Saturn Bar.....................................33 D2
Snug Harbor.................................34 B3
Vaughan's.....................................35 F4
Yuki Izakaya..................................36 B3

THE ARTS 🎭 (pp191–8)
Barrister's Gallery..........................37 C2
Bywater Art Market.......................38 D3
Studio Inferno...............................39 D3

SLEEPING 🛏 (pp206–8)
Auld Sweet Olive Bed &
  Breakfast....................................40 C2
Burgundy Bed & Breakfast.............41 C3
Bywater Bed & Breakfast...............42 D3
Frenchmen Hotel............................43 B4
Hotel de la Monnaie......................44 B4
Lamothe House..............................45 B3
Lions Inn B&B...............................46 C3
Melrose Mansion............................47 A3

TRANSPORTATION (pp235–8)
Bicycle Michael's...................(see 34)

To Musicians'
Village (0.2mi)

Mississippi River

See Mid-City &
The Tremé
Map pp108–9

See French Quarter
Map pp70–1

81

by audition only. If accepted, students (who are concurrently enrolled in their normal schools) specialize in fields ranging from the visual arts and creative writing to dance and cooking, instructed by artists at the top of their craft. As it is indeed a school, Nocca understandably isn't open to visitors 24/7, but check the website for details on upcoming public performances, gallery shows, and the like.

Just a little ways north at the corner of Press and Royal Sts is a plaque marking the site where African American Homer Plessy, in a carefully orchestrated act of civil disobedience, tried to board a whites-only train car. That action led to the 1896 *Plessy vs Ferguson* trial, which legalized segregation under the 'separate but equal' rationale. The plaque was unveiled by Keith Plessy and Phoebe Ferguson, the descendants of the opposing parties in the original trial, now fast friends.

MUSICIANS' VILLAGE off Map p81
www.nolamusiciansvillage.com; bounded by North Roman, Alvar & North Johnson Sts
North of Bywater, one of the most prominent post-Katrina reconstruction projects is this 8-acre tract of some 81 houses, built primarily for musicians, a vital component of the city's cultural and economic landscape. The brightly painted homes look like skittles scattered over the cityscape; their brilliant colors, when combined with appealingly modest design, both blend in with and enliven this corner of the Upper Ninth Ward. The village came about via collaboration between Branford Marsalis, Harry Connick Jr, Habitat for Humanity, and the volunteer efforts of hundreds of con-

NEIGHBORHOOD ASSOCIATIONS

Bywater Neighborhood Association (www .bywaterneighbors.com)

Faubourg Marigny Improvement Association (www.faubourgmarigny.org)

Faubourg St Roch Improvement Association (www.fsria.org)

struction workers and local residents. While mainly intended for musicians, it is not exclusively inhabited by them – nonmusicians live here as well. Still, the centerpiece of the Village is decidedly music-oriented: the Ellis Marsalis Center for Music, where cultural events and seminars are held.

If you visit, please bear in mind this is a living neighborhood inhabited by real people; folks can get understandably tetchy if you take pictures of them or their property without asking permission or even getting out of your car.

KKPROJECTS off Map p81
☎ 218-8701; www.kkprojects.org; 2448 N Villere St; ☺ 10am-4pm Sat & Sun & by appointment
Dum-dee-dum, here we are driving through the hard end of St Roch (the neighborhood north of the Marigny that runs into the Upper Ninth Ward), looking at homes – some inhabited, some gutted – and a giant ubermodern house-sized bank vault and…

Hold up.

You, intrepid traveler, have just stumbled upon KKProjects, one of the more innovative galleries/arts missions in the city. KK has taken six abandoned homes (at the time of writing) and, with the input

NEIGHBORHOODS FAUBOURG MARIGNY & BYWATER

CREOLE ORIGINALS

Faubourg Marigny was the first Creole suburb of the old city when it was laid out in 1806 on the plantation of Bernard Xavier Philippe de Marigny de Mandeville. Monsieur Marigny, an unpredictable character, was the first to introduce the game of craps to New Orleans after acquiring a taste for the dice on a visit to London. Marigny gambled away much of his fortune, but managed to survive some 27 duels. He chose whimsical names for the streets of his development, though many were changed decades ago. Originally, Burgundy St in the Marigny was called Rue de Craps. Other street names in the district included Poets, Music, Love and Good Children.

Early inhabitants of the neighborhood included whites and free persons of color. By the 1840s, some 40% of the homes in the Marigny were owned by the black mistresses of white Creoles. Marriages between the races were not legal, but unions, called *plaçages*, were relatively common. Sometimes these mixed-race couples lived together, but more often the men bought property for the women and supported the children, who were considered legitimate offspring. Many of these children were schooled in France where they learned classical music; upon returning to New Orleans they combined their talents with that of African American musicians, laying the early groundwork for jazz.

of the local community, turned them into studios/galleries/structures/works of art in their own right that feel both a little out of place and refreshingly welcome in this hard-up corner of town. Examples include the afore-mentioned giant safe/bank vault, where visitors can color-in fake money to be sent to Congress to petition for lead removal in New Orleans; a house floored and roofed with sod and turf that looks like a hobbit hole in the middle of the ghetto; and community gardens and greenhouses. Due in part to distance and in part to safety concerns, you'll want to drive or cab out here.

ST ROCH CEMETERY Map p81

☎ 945-5961; cnr St Roch Ave & N Roman St;
⏰ 9am-4pm

One of New Orleans' more interesting cemeteries, and arguably the most eccentric chapel, is but a few blocks toward the lake from Faubourg Marigny (driving is still recommended). Named for St Roch ('rock'), a semilegendary figure whose prayers averted the Black Death, the site became popular with New Orleans Catholics during the city's frequent outbreaks of yellow fever.

The main reason to schlep out here is to walk through the necropolis and see the 'relic room,' a great example of the old Catholic practice of offering fake body parts up to the healing power of a sacred site. You'll see all sorts of ceramic body parts (ankles, heads, breasts), prosthetics, leg braces, crutches and false teeth that hang from the walls and coverings; these are *ex-votos*, testaments to the healing power of St Roch. Marble floor tiles are inscribed with the words 'thanks' and '*merci*.' The chapel has been appropriated by syncretic voodoo worshippers as well. If you take a picture inside, floating orbs may appear in your photo, which could be spirits of the dead, manifestations of saintly healing power, or bits of dust.

NEW NOIR-LEANS
Walking & Driving Tour

In contrast to our sober French Quarter stroll, this walk highlights some of the city's best bars and live music joints, as well as some gothic edges of the city that truly come alive under the mad light of a Louisiana moon. Needless to say, this tour needs to be done after dark.

1 Bacchanal Start at Bacchanal (p158), on the corner of Poland Ave and Chartres St, one of the most inviting, innovative restaurants in town. Pick up a cheese plate and gorge yourself into a *fromage* state of bliss in the overgrown back garden while flipping through a book on the local arts scene.

2 Vaughan's Follow Poland Ave up and turn right onto Dauphine St, admiring the cute little shotguns in the area, until you come to Vaughan's (p183). If it's Thursday night, you may just want to end the tour right now, as local legend Kermit Ruffin will be tearing down the house. Otherwise, enjoy this cozy, authentic

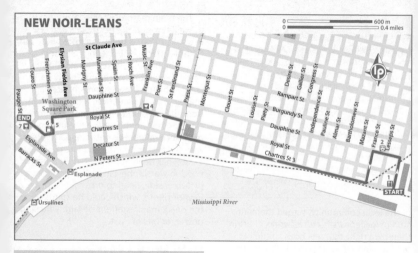

NEW NOIR-LEANS

WALK FACTS

Start Bacchanal
End R Bar
Distance 2.5 miles
Duration Could go all night...
Fuel Stop All over the place

Bywater bar and get into your car for a small drive.

3 Chartres St Follow Frances St back to Chartres St, which, for the record, is pronounced 'Charters' or 'Charts' in New Orleans French. Driving along this (not particularly pedestrian-friendly) road, which runs by the water (hidden by brick embankments) and blocks of homes, warehouses and train tracks, feels particularly post-industrial and beautiful in a rusty, bombed out way, especially at night.

4 Mimi's Tapas time! Hang a right on Press St and a left onto Royal, park the car, and hand someone the keys, because you'll likely not want to get back into a car (unless it's a taxi) after the rest of this tour. The walking/pub crawl portion of our evening begins in Mimi's in the Marigny (p182), which – besides serving good beer in a neighborhood-but-hip setting – has a fine tapas menu. Those small plates provide some fuel without slowing the tour

down. If you're off the booze, just across the street is Flora's (p159), a hip coffee shop that meets every criterion of Bohemian-chic you can think of.

5 Frenchman St Cross over Elysian Fields Ave and by Washington Square Park and begin the stumble down Frenchman St. Sure, our tour only covers one block, but there are plenty of bars and jazz joints packed into a small area that's easy to navigate on foot. We're loathe to recommend just one; follow your ears to the best sounds. If you insist, we can practically guarantee there'll be something great going on in Snug Harbor (p184), another spot that might tempt you to abandon the rest of the tour.

6 Faubourg Marigny Book Store We do insist you stop in at this bookstore (p128; open till 10pm). Besides being a great spot to browse some text, it's the oldest gay bookstore in the South and one of the oldest of the genre in the country; it's also located at the center of Frenchmen St's live-music scene.

7 More Bars End the night by wheeling your way over to the R Bar (p182), or, if you can find a taxi, heading up to the Saturn Bar (p183). These are both kind of dives; Saturn has hit-and-miss shows but is always good for the leopard-skin-meets-asylum decor, while the R Bar is almost always good for a bit of dancing and lots of drinking.

CBD & WAREHOUSE DISTRICT

Drinking & Nightlife p184, Eating p159, Shopping p128, Sleeping p208

There are very few Central Business Districts (CBDs) in the USA that immediately seize the imagination – New Orleans' CBD, anchored by Canal St, is no exception. The high-rise buildings and municipal office blocks around here feel worlds removed from the Crescent City's green streets and faded shacks. But New Orleans' spirit is too subversive to be skyscrapered over. The city's quirks liven up the CBD at its concrete and glass edges, reminding you, in the midst of corporate Americana, where you really are.

Here – an old hat shop passed down through the same Jewish family for generations. There – a police officer wiping a gravy dribble from a po'boy from Mother's. Around the way – a burlesque show at Le Chat Noir attended by seersucker-suited Tulane frat boys and their cocktail-dressed girlfriends. Amid it all are the city's grandest museums – all of which deserve some of your time – and dozens of restaurants defying the convention that downtown dining must be bland.

The energy of the area is also sparked by the city's decision to place its official arts district here. Peppered along the CBD and neighboring Warehouse District are galleries and studios that make wandering past the office parks pretty enjoyable. Artists get a very public platform for their work at this unlikely intersection – the buttoned-down business world and conceptual sculpture – but this is a city that embraces the unlikely. There are also some good bars and clubs, and most of the city's best (or at least, most posh) superhotels, all within easy walking distance of the French Quarter. And there are some nice shopping safaris to be had in this concrete jungle, although it's a mallish sort of remedy for those needing retail therapy.

Downtown New Orleans was once a quiet neighborhood known as Faubourg St Mary. Then came the Louisiana Purchase. New American arrivals streamed into an essentially French city and, seeing as the Quarter was kind of full, established their businesses in what would become the CBD (and their homes in the future Garden District). Faubourg St Mary became the American sector, a nexus of offices, banks, warehouses and government buildings clustered around Lafayette Sq.

Herein was the beginning of Canal St playing the part of the great divide, at the time not so much in terms of distance as separating old-world elites from nouveau riche *Americains*. The wide median down the middle of Canal St was neither of the French or American sector and came to be called the 'neutral ground'; in time, all medians in the city would be referred to as such.

Toward the lake, extending to Claiborne Ave, is the modern City Hall, the Superdome and new office buildings and convention hotels. Most of this area was formerly part of the back o' town, primarily inhabited by African Americans. The official CBD is just above Canal St. It more-or-less extends out to S Claiborne Ave and to the elevated I-90. Poydras St runs through the heart of the district, from the river on past the Superdome. Above Poydras St, the riverside of the CBD is the Warehouse District, extending out to Magazine St or St Charles Ave, depending on who you ask. Julia St runs from the river past St Charles Ave and is known as 'Gallery Row' – the heart of the arts district. Lafayette Sq, the center of the old American sector, is on St Charles Ave. Riverwalk Mall is on the levee and the Convention Center is adjacent to it.

Bus 11 runs from Canal St along the entire length of Magazine St, to Audubon Park. Bus 42 runs on Canal St through Mid-City all the way to City Park, and bus 10 runs on Tchoupitoulas St to Audubon Park. Riverfront streetcar 2 runs along the river from the Convention Center and along the entire length of the French Quarter. When operating, the St Charles Ave streetcar runs from Canal St along St Charles Ave through the CBD, the Garden District and Uptown. The 45 streetcar runs on Canal St from the river through Mid-City. There are public lots on nearly every block, with convenient parking at the Riverwalk Mall and near the Contemporary Arts Center on Camp St. Metered parking is available on most streets.

CBD

The CBD, New Orleans' modern skyscraper zone, has its share of bland buildings. The area immediately surrounding Lafayette Sq is the heart of the former Faubourg St Mary, and has some places of historic interest.

LOUISIANA SUPERDOME Map pp86–7

☎ 587-3663; www.superdome.com; Sugar Bowl Dr
Hovering like a giant, bronze-tinted hubcap amid the CBD skyscrapers and the elevated I-10 freeway, the Superdome is one of New Orleans' most easily recognized structures. The immense indoor stadium,

INFORMATION
Accent on Children's
  Arrangements 1 D3
Downtown Refund Center .... (see 33)
French Consulate 2 C3
Hibernia National Bank 3 E2
Immigration & Naturalization
  Service 4 C4
Kinko's FedEx Office Center 5 E4
Main Post Office 6 C3
Post Office 7 E3
Post Office 8 G3
Tulane University Medical Center ... 9 D1
UK Honorary Consul 10 E3
Whitney National Bank 11 E2

SIGHTS (pp85–93)
Aquarium of the Americas 12 G3
Blaine Kern's Mardi Gras World 13 G6
Canal Street Ferry 14 G3
Civil War Museum 15 E5
Cookin' Cajun 16 G4
Creole Queen 17 G3
Factors Row 18 E3
Gallier Hall 19 E3
Harrah's Casino 20 F3
K&B Plaza 21 D5
Lee Circle 22 E5
Louisiana Artworks 23 D4
Louisiana Children's Museum 24 F4
Louisiana Superdome 25 B3
National World War II Museum 26 E5
New Orleans Cotton Exchange 27 E2
New Orleans Public Library 28 D2
Ogden Museum of Southern Art 29 E4
Preservation Resource Center 30 F5
Robert E Lee Monument 31 D5
Scrap House 32 F5
Southern Food & Beverage
  Museum 33 G4
United Fruit Company 34 E3

SHOPPING (p128)
International Vintage Guitars 35 F4
Meyer the Hatter 36 E2
New Orleans Centre 37 C3
New Orleans School of
  Glassworks .... (see 63)

EATING (pp159–62)
Bon Ton Café 38 E3
Café Adelaide .... (see 76)
Cochon 39 F5
Crescent City Farmers Market 40 F4
Cuvée 41 F3
Drago's Seafood Restaurant 42 G3
Emeril's 43 F4
Herbsaint 44 E4
Liborio Cuban Restaurant 45 F3
Luke .... (see 34)
Mother's 46 F3
Nola Grocery 47 F5
Red Eye Grill 48 F4
Restaurant August 49 F3
Rio Mar 50 F4
Wine Institute of New Orleans 51 F3

DRINKING & NIGHTLIFE (pp184–6)
Howlin' Wolf 52 F5
Le Chat Noir 53 E4
Le Phare Bar .... (see 77)
Loa .... (see 72)
Lucy's Retired Surfers Bar .... (see 35)
Polo Lounge .... (see 83)
Republic New Orleans 54 F4
Swizzle Stick Bar .... (see 76)
Vic's Kangaroo Cafe 55 F4
Whiskey Blue .... (see 82)

THE ARTS (pp191–8)
Arthur Roger Gallery 56 E4
Bergeron Studio & Gallery 57 F3
Contemporary Arts Center 58 E4
Entergy IMAX Theater .... (see 12)
George Schmidt Gallery 59 E4
Heriard-Cimino Gallery 60 E4
Jean Bragg Gallery of Southern
  Art 61 E4
Lemieux Galleries 62 E4
New Orleans Glasswork &
  Printmaking Studios 63 E4
Orpheum Theatre 64 D2
Soren Christensen Gallery 65 F4
UNO Downtown Theatre 66 D3

SLEEPING (pp208–10)
Circle Bar 67 D5
Doubletree Hotel New Orleans 68 F3
Embassy Suites Hotel 69 F4
Hampton Inn New Orleans
  Downtown 70 E2
Harrah's New Orleans 71 F3
International House 72 E2
La Quinta Inn & Suites
  Downtown 73 E3
Lafayette Hotel 74 E3
Le Pavillon 75 D3
Loews New Orleans Hotel 76 F3
Loft 523 .... 77 E3
Queen & Crescent Hotel 78 E3
Roosevelt Hotel 79 E2
Sheraton New Orleans 80 E3
St James Hotel 81 F3
W New Orleans 82 F3
Windsor Court Hotel 83 F3

TRANSPORTATION (pp235–8)
American Airlines Office .... (see 79)
Delta Queen Dock .... (see 13)
Hertz 84 F5
New Orleans Union Passenger
  Terminal 85 C4

Tulane Ave
Gravier St
CBD
Poydras Ave
Sugarbowl Dr
Poydras St
Perdido St
Union St
Girod St
New
Orleans
Arena
Lafayette St
Girod St
Julia St
Earhart Blvd
Clio St
Simon Bolivar St
Howard Ave
Pontchartrain Expwy
Erato St
Clio St
Canal St
Tulane Ave
S Claiborne Ave
S Robertson St
S Villere St
Cleveland St
Saratoga St
S Liberty St
Loyola Ave
S Rampart St
Penn St
Baronne St
O'Keefe Ave
Loyola Ave
Carondelet St
St Charles Ave Streetcar
Oretha Castle Haley Blvd
Camp St
S Roman St
S Villere St
La Salle St
S Prieur St

See Mid-City & The Tremé Map (pp108–9)

See Garden, Lower Garden & Central City Map (pp96–7)

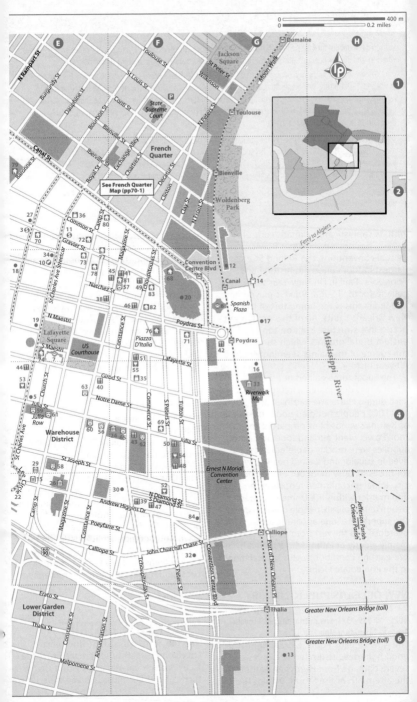

CBD LANDMARKS

Scattered throughout the CBD are historic buildings where some of the city's biggest (and, in some cases, most notorious) wheelers and dealers operated. Keep an eye out for them when wandering through the neighborhood.

New Orleans Cotton Exchange (Map pp86–7; 231 Carondelet St) Some would say New Orleans was built on cotton. In the mid-19th century, when one-third of all cotton produced in the USA was routed through New Orleans, the receiving docks on the levee were perpetually covered by tall stacks of cotton bales ready to be shipped out. The Cotton Exchange was founded in 1871 to regulate trade and prices. The building here, dating from the 1920s, is the third Cotton Exchange to occupy this site.

United Fruit Company (Map pp86–7; 321 St Charles Ave) A cornucopia of tropical produce graces the entrance to this building. The United Fruit Company, infamous for controversial neocolonial practices in Central America, was based here from the 1930s until the 1970s. For many decades, the company held a virtual monopoly on the banana trade throughout much of the world. It's now part of Chiquita Brands International, based in Cincinnati, OH.

Factors Row (Map pp86–7; 806 Perdido St) Edgar Degas painted *The Cotton Market in New Orleans* while visiting his uncle's office in this building in 1873.

---

with its sophisticated climate-control system, has hosted six Super Bowls, presidential conventions, the Rolling Stones (largest indoor concert in history) and Pope John Paul II. On New Year's Day the college-football Sugar Bowl is played here, and in fall this is the home turf of the New Orleans Saints. All of this excitement occurs in a structure built on top of an ancient burial ground, which some say is the source of the Saints seemingly cursed 40-year history.

The Superdome gained notoriety in 2005 when it was designated a 'refuge of last resort' during Hurricane Katrina. Some 20,000 to 30,000 people huddled under the dome as Katrina's winds blew off part of the roof. Power went out and food and water supplies were quickly depleted as people lived in squalor and waited nearly a week for buses to carry them out of the flooded city. Initial unconfirmed reports of rape, riot and murder within the Dome have been debunked. In all, six people died inside the superdome (one apparent suicide, one overdose and the rest from natural causes, mainly elderly or infirm who suffered from pre-existing conditions), plus several more in the immediate vicinity.

NEW ORLEANS PUBLIC LIBRARY
Map pp86–7

NOPL; ☎ 529-7323; ww.nutrias.org; 219 Loyola Ave; 🕙 11am-4pm Mon-Fri; 🖵
The New Orleans Public Library fights the good fight despite limited resources and severe damage from Hurricane Katrina. In the aftermath of the Storm, 90% of NOPL

employees were laid off, leaving a staff of 19 for the entire NOPL system. At the time of writing three of 14 branches are served by temporary structures, five are closed indefinitely and six, including the main headquarters listed here, have been reopened. The library is worth visiting just for the sake of supporting its good works, although it is a lovely building in its own right. The Louisiana Room, on the 3rd floor, is a good resource of regional history, while the computer room is handy for getting online for free.

GALLIER HALL Map pp86–7

☎ 658-3623; www.gallierhall.com; 545 St Charles Ave
Architect James Gallier Sr designed this monumental Greek-revival structure, which was dedicated in 1853. It served as New Orleans' city hall until the 1950s, and far outclasses the city's current city hall (a few blocks away). Today the building is used for private functions and VIP funerals (both Confederate president Jefferson Davis and homegrown R&B legend Ernie K-Doe have lain in state here – only in New Orleans) and is a focal point for Mardi Gras parades, most of which promenade past the grandstand that is put up along St Charles Ave.

WAREHOUSE DISTRICT

The old warehouses that line most of the streets in this part of town have proved perfectly suitable for the arts district that now thrives here. The museums and galleries are

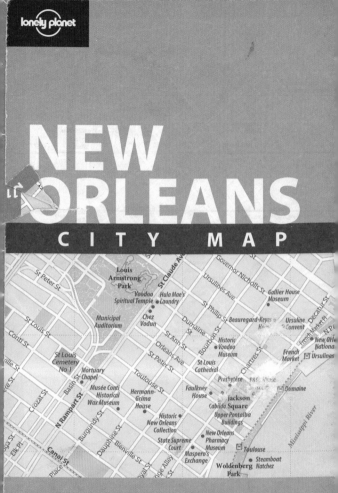

NEW ORLEANS
CITY MAP

USEFUL INFORMATION

BUSINESS HOURS

Banks	9am–5pm Mon–Sat
Bars	5pm–2am or 3am
Businesses	9am–5pm Mon–Fri
Restaurants	10am–11pm
Shops	10am–10pm

Exceptions are noted in specific listings.

TELEPHONE

Area code	☎ 504
Country code	☎ 1
International dialing code	☎ 00 + country
Directory assistance	☎ 0

Emergency	☎ 911
New Orleans Tourism	☎ 800-672-6124
Weather	☎ 522-7330

TRANSPORTATION

Louis Armstrong Airport info	☎ 464-0831
RTA information	☎ 248-3900
United Cabs	☎ 522-9771
White Fleet Rollins Cab Co	☎ 822-3800

Taxis can often be flagged on the streets in the French Quarter. Elsewhere in town you'll generally need to call for a cab. Fares start at $2.50 but quickly rise.

joined by some of the city's finest restaurants (see p159).

OGDEN MUSEUM OF SOUTHERN ART Map pp86–7

☎ 539-9600; www.ogdenmuseum.org; 925 Camp St; adult/child $10/6; ☻ 10am-5pm Mon-Sat, also 6-8pm Thu

One of our favorite museums in the city manages to be beautiful, educational and unpretentious all at once. New Orleans entrepreneur Roger Houston Ogden has assembled one of the finest collections of Southern art anywhere – far too large to keep to himself – which includes huge galleries ranging from impressionist landscapes and outsider folk-art quirkiness to contemporary installation work. In addition, the Ogden is affiliated with the Smithsonian Institute in Washington, DC, giving it access to that bottomless collection. Make sure to visit on Thursday nights for Ogden After Hours, when you can listen to great concerts and pop an Abita with a fun loving, arts obsessed crowd in the midst of the masterpieces.

NATIONAL WORLD WAR II MUSEUM Map pp86–7

☎ 527-6012; www.nationalww2museum.org; 945 Magazine St; adult/child/senior $14/6/8; ☻ 9am-5pm Tue-Sat

This grand facility should satisfy the historical curiosity of anyone who possesses even a passing interest in WWII. The museum is well designed, physically and thematically, and presents an admirably nuanced and always-thorough analysis. Of particular note is the D-Day exhibition, arguably the most in-depth of its type in the country. The oral-history sections are fascinating, and the Academy Award–winning film *D-Day Remembered* is screened daily – don't miss it.

The museum, already enormous, is only going to get larger in coming years, with a gaggle of planned expansions that include a USO-style theater, pavilions dedicated to

FROM THE MEKONG TO THE MISSISSIPPI

Following the Vietnam War, thousands of South Vietnamese fled to America, settling in Southern California, Boston, the Washington, DC, area and New Orleans. If the last choice seems odd, remember that many of these refugees were Catholic and the New Orleans Catholic community – one of the largest in the country – was helping to direct refugee resettlement. In addition, the subtropical climate, rice fields and flat wetlands must have been geographically reassuring. For a Southeast Asian far from home, the Mississippi delta may have borne at least a superficial resemblance to the Mekong delta.

Most Vietnamese in Louisiana settled in New Orleans' newer suburbs: New Orleans East, Versailles, Algiers and Gretna (some also moved to rural parishes in south Louisiana). Their work ethic was legendary, their presence revitalized many formerly crumbling neighborhoods and their story is as American Dream–like as a bald eagle hatching from apple pie. The first generation of Vietnamese worked in Laundromats, nail shops, restaurants and shrimp boats; the second became doctors, lawyers and engineers. Following Hurricane Katrina, the New Orleans Vietnamese community gained the reputation as being the first back in the city, quickly rebuilding their homes and businesses.

To see where New Orleans Vietnamese work and play, you need to drive a little ways out of the city proper. Although many Vietnamese refugees were Catholic, Vietnamese religion has always been pretty syncretic, and there were many Buddhists among the boat people. In New Orleans East, the Trung Tam Phat Giao Van Hanh temple (☎ 254-6031; 13152 Chef Menteur Highway) suffered severe damage during the storm but was rapidly rebuilt by its congregation; further south, the Chua Bo De temple (☎ 733-6634; Hwy 996) is about 25 minutes outside of the city near English Turn golf course. Both temples are typically Vietnamese Buddhist structures, filled with Chinese-style bodhisattvas (Buddhist saints), photos of and offerings to dead ancestors, and lots of red and gold in the color scheme. You don't have to call ahead before visiting, but it may be polite to do so (plus, you can check if the temples are open).

Probably the most pleasant way to experience local Vietnamese culture is by eating its delicious food; to this end we've put together a list of our favorite Vietnamese restaurants, most of which are in Gretna, in the Eating chapter (see boxed text, p167). Try not to miss the local markets either; the Hong Kong Food Market (☎ 394-7075; 925 Behrman Highway; ☻ 8am-9pm) is a general Asian grocery store that serves plenty of Chinese and Filipinos, but the main customer base is Vietnamese. The closest you'll come to witnessing Saigon on a Saturday morning (by the way, lots of local Vietnamese, being southern refugees, still call it 'Saigon') is the Vietnamese Farmers' Market (☎ 394-7075; 14401 Alcee Fortier Blvd; ☻ 6am-9am), also known as the 'squat market' thanks to the ladies in *non la* (conical straw hats) squatting over their fresh, wonderful-smelling produce.

every major campaign the USA participated in during the war and other materials that will essentially quadruple the size of the museum.

AQUARIUM OF THE AMERICAS
Map pp86–7

☎ 581-4629; www.auduboninstitute.org; Canal St; adult/child/senior $18/11/14; ☼ 9:30am-5pm

Part of the Audubon Institute (which includes the Audubon Zoological Gardens and the Insectarium), the immense Aquarium of the Americas is one of the country's best. The emphasis is loosely regional, with exhibits that delve beneath the surface of the Mississippi River, Gulf of Mexico, Caribbean Sea and far-off Amazon rainforest.

One highlight is Spots, a rare white alligator who usually draws a large crowd around the Mississippi River Gallery where he suns himself. The Caribbean Reef has a 30ft-long glass tunnel that runs under a 130,000-gallon tank, and the sea-horse gallery and penguin colony are perennially popular. Some 10,000 fish were lost when Hurricane Katrina wiped out the aquarium's filtration and temperature control systems, but the aquarium reopened the following year and continues to restock its tanks.

CONTEMPORARY ARTS CENTER
Map pp86–7

CAC; ☎ 528-3805; www.cacno.org; 900 Camp St; admission varies; ☼ 11am-4pm Tue-Sun

The grand modernist entrance to the CAC, a soaring ceiling vault of airy space and

top picks

MUSEUMS

- New Orleans Museum of Art (p110) The largest arts museum in the city.
- Backstreet Cultural Museum (p113) Get a view of the city's culture from the street level.
- Historic New Orleans Collection (p76) The best short intro into New Orleans' history.
- National World War II Museum (p89) Perhaps the best museum on WWII in the country.
- Ogden Museum of Southern Art (p89) One of the finest collections of Southern art anywhere.

NEIGHBORHOOD ASSOCIATIONS

Downtown Development District (www.new orleansdowntown.com)

New Orleans Arts District (www.neworleans artsdistrict.com)

conceptual metal and wooden accents, is almost reason enough to step into this converted warehouse. Almost. The best reason for visiting is a good crop of rotating exhibitions by local artists, plus a packed events calendar that includes plays, skits, dance and concerts that draw names as big as Death Cab for Cutie.

PRESERVATION RESOURCE CENTER
Map pp86–7

☎ 581-7032; www.prcno.org; 923 Tchoupitoulas St; admission free; ☼ 9am-5pm Mon-Fri

For anyone with a special interest in the architecture of New Orleans, this is a great place to stop and get a sense for the lay of the land. Its headquarters, in the expansive Leeds-Davis building, has a street-level museum. The display is modest but manages to impart key information in a very straightforward manner. The best reason for visiting is grabbing some of the dozens of free pamphlets with walking-tour maps and information on virtually every part of town. Engaging staff provide information on everything from cycling routes to securing low-interest loans to buy and restore your dream shotgun house. Upstairs, a library contains volumes on local history and architecture.

CIVIL WAR MUSEUM Map pp86–7

☎ 523-4522; www.confederatemuseum.com; 929 Camp St; adult/child & senior $7/2; ☼ 10am-4pm Mon-Sat

Once known (and still often referred to) as the Confederate Museum, this is Louisiana's oldest operating museum. It's a smallish space centered on the Confederate Memorial Hall, a chamber of dark wood, exposed cypress ceiling beams and a decidedly stately vibe. The museum used to be a center of Confederate apologia; today it's been largely politically corrected, although there's a lack of material relating to slavery, perhaps because of the paucity of material possessions slaves could have left behind, and this really is a collection of *things* as opposed to a contemporary, interpretation-driven educational museum.

The permanent exhibition includes the second-largest compilation of Confederate artifacts in the world, including lots of swords, guns, buttons, flags and uniforms, which goes some way towards humanizing the conflict and its combatants. The newer and temporary exhibits are to be commended; the section on the Creole black regiments that fought for the Confederacy (many free blacks in New Orleans owned slaves) is particularly fascinating.

LOUISIANA CHILDREN'S MUSEUM
Map pp86–7

☎ 523-1357; www.lcm.org; 420 Julia St; admission $7.50; ☯ 9:30am-4:30pm Tue-Sat & noon-4:30pm Sun

Probably the most kid-friendly site in the city, this educational museum is like a high-tech kindergarten where the wee ones can play in interactive bliss till nap time. Lots of corporate sponsorship equals lots of hands-on exhibits like a stocked supermarket and a TV-news studio. Children under 16 must be accompanied by an adult. During the summer (June to August) the museum is open till 5pm, and till 8pm on Thursday nights.

BLAINE KERN'S MARDI GRAS WORLD
Map pp86–7

☎ 361-7821; www.mardigrasworld.com; 1380 Port of New Orleans Pl; adult/child $18/11; ☯ 8:30am-5pm

We dare say that Mardi Gras World is one of the happiest places in New Orleans by day – but at night it must turn into one of the most terrifying funhouses this side of Hell. It's all those *faces*, man, the dragons, clowns, kings and fairies, all leering and dead-eyed…sorry. Maybe it's just us.

That said, we love Mardi Gras World, the studio, as it were, of Blaine Kern – 'Mr Mardi Gras' – who has been making parade floats since 1947. Kern learned the trade from his father and passed it down to his sons, who now help run the business. The best floats in the city are made here, and you can see them being built or on display any time of the year.

LOUISIANA ARTWORKS Map pp86–7

☎ 565-8998; www.louisianaartworks.org; 725 Howard Ave; admission $7; ☯ 10am-5pm Tue-Sat, noon-5pm Sun

This 90,000-sq-ft space was established by the Arts Council of New Orleans to bring working artists and lovers of art together. By providing artists with affordable studio spaces, the project hopes to foster a continuation of the city's growing arts scene, even as rents go up around town. The Arts Council hopes to promote the local arts by keeping the facility open to the public, thus giving visitors the opportunity to witness art being created. Tourists who appreciate art are the obvious target audience here. It's an interesting idea, and a positive step for the city as it attempts to rebuild its tour-

MISSISSIPPI RIVERBOATS

New Orleans' current fleet of steamboats are theme-park copies of the old glories that plied the Mississippi River in Mark Twain's day. Gone are the hoop-skirted ladies, wax-mustachioed gents, round-the-clock crap games and bawdy tinkling on off-tune pianos. In their place are pudgy tourists clad in white shorts, Bourbon St T-shirts and tennis shoes, content to rest their plump bottoms on plastic stadium seats. The evenings are given over to urbane jazz cruises, and while the calliope organ survives, even this unique musical instrument loses some of its panache when applied to modern schmaltz like 'Tie a Yellow Ribbon on the Old Oak Tree.' Alas.

Still, few visitors to New Orleans can resist the opportunity to get out on the Mississippi and watch the old paddle wheel propel them upriver and back down for a spell. It's a relaxing pastime that the entire family can enjoy.

Creole Queen (☎ 524-0814, 800-445-4109; www.creolequeen.com) Runs a two-hour dinner-and-jazz cruise (adult/3-5yr/6-12yr $64/10/30, without dinner $40/free/15), featuring a live Dixieland jazz combo, boarding nightly at 7pm and departing at 8pm. Three-hour cruises to Mardi Gras World (above) board at 1:30pm daily (adult/child/senior $36/21/30). For all cruises, passengers board at the Canal St Wharf.

Steamboat Natchez (Map pp70–1; ☎ 586-8777, 800-233-2628; www.steamboatnatchez.com) The closest thing to an authentic steamboat running out of New Orleans today, the *Natchez* is steam-powered and has a bona fide calliope on board. The evening dinner-and-jazz cruise (adult/child/teen $64.50/12.25/32.25, without dinner adult/child $40/20) takes off at 7pm nightly. The *Natchez* boards behind the Jackson Brewery.

ist-based economy without going down the Mickey Mouse route.

CANAL ST FERRY Map pp86–7
Canal St Wharf; trips free; ⊗ 6am–midnight
A short ferry ride from the foot of Canal St to Algiers Point is the easiest way to get out on the Mississippi River and admire New Orleans from the traditional river approach (mmm, smells like mud, poo and petroleum). Ride on the lower deck next to the water, and you're likely to see the state bird, the brown pelican. The state-run ferry leaves Canal St on the hour and half-hour, and returns from Algiers on the quarter-hour.

SOUTHERN FOOD & BEVERAGE MUSEUM Map pp86–7
☎ 569-0405; www.southernfood.org; Riverwalk Mall; admission $5; ⊗ 10am-6pm Mon-Sat

top picks

ONLY IN NEW ORLEANS

An expression often heard here is 'Only in New Orleans.' Even native-born denizens of the city are moved from time to time to utter these words while shaking their heads in wonder. Every day the city will confound you, make you laugh, move you to tears and get beneath your skin.

- Mid-City Rock & Bowl (p190) Dance to zydeco, bowl a few frames, beer, repeat.
- Parkway Tavern (p171) Feel the gravy drip down your arm on a roast beef po'boy.
- K-Doe's Mother-in-Law Lounge (p190) Party with a lifelike statue of local legend Ernie K-Doe.
- Kermit Ruffin's barbeque at Vaughan's (p183) Listen to one of the best brass bands in the city, then let the leader dish you some of his home-cooked 'que.
- Faulkner House Bookstore (p126) Buy a book by Faulkner in his old house.
- Praline Bacon at Elizabeth's (p158) That's right. 'Praline Bacon.' Praline-Freaking-Bacon!
- 'I got Bourbon-faced on Shit Street' T-shirt (p76) After much research, we have conclusively decided this is the tackiest thing you can buy in the city.
- Second lines Join the second line at a jazz funeral or second-line parade, easiest to come across in Mid-City or the Tremé.

Sitting as it does in the commercial crassness of Riverwalk Mall, the Southern Food & Beverage Museum isn't immediately appealing – from the outside it looks more like a gift shop than anything else. Don't judge this book by that cover. There's actually a pretty fascinating, well-executed exhibit behind the fronting shop that includes more information than you'll probably ever need on the food staples and dishes of the South, and New Orleans and Louisiana in particular. The attached Museum of the American Cocktail isn't much more than a small gallery hall, but admission is free with the food museum and, hey, how often do you get to see 19th-century ads for Sazerac?

SCRAP HOUSE Map pp86–7
Convention Center Blvd, near John Churchill Chase St
Artist Sally Heller designed this sculpture, built entirely out of found and recycled material, and dedicated it to the victims of Hurricane Katrina. A ruined shack that resembles Dorothy's house blown off-track sits in a tree constructed from pieces of oil drums. Inside, a light shines for those seeking to return home. It's a powerful piece of work that sits in an appropriate setting – across from the Convention Center, where so many refugees were displaced in the aftermath of the Storm.

LEE CIRCLE Map pp86–7
Called Place du Tivoli until it was renamed to honor Confederate General Robert E Lee after the Civil War, Lee Circle is a tragic example of an urban junction planned horribly wrong. The presence of a nearby elevated freeway and two gas stations mars what should be a pleasant roundabout. Oh well; the Robert E Lee monument at its center, dedicated in 1884, is attractive, and still refuses to turn its back on the North.

Also on Lee Circle, K&B Plaza (1055 St Charles Ave; ⊗ 8:30am-4:30pm Mon-Fri) is a modish office tower dating to 1963 with an indoor-outdoor sculpture gallery. The outdoor sculptures, featuring Isamu Noguchi's *The Mississippi*, can be viewed anytime.

HARRAH'S CASINO Map pp86–7
☎ 533-6000; www.harrahsneworleans.com; 4 Canal St; ⊗ 24hr

You'd think all manner of vice would be welcome in the Big Easy, but Harrah's, near the foot of Canal St, doesn't get much local love. In spite of its best efforts to fit in – there's a perfunctory Mardi Gras parade every night – Harrah's still manages to make guests feel like they're in Sparks, Nevada. It's a big ol' casino that's part of a national chain, and it pretty much feels exactly like that. Nevertheless, people do trickle in for the casino gambling, buffet dining, free parking and hotel discounts.

GARDEN, LOWER GARDEN & CENTRAL CITY

Drinking & Nightlife p186, Eating p162, Shopping p128, Sleeping p211

New Orleans has a reputation as one of the most European of US cities. But this is still a US city, and the earliest evolution of that Yankee character was born in the Garden District, a section of town that's every bit as pretty as her title suggests. And we do mean Yankee: this is the Deep South in geography – and a sticky, sensory embrace of jasmine, magnolia and bougainvillea soak warm Garden District nights in spicy-sweet romance – but the enormous houses that give the neighborhood its architectural cachet were largely built by English-speaking Protestants.

Many of these transplants arrived from New York and New England in the 1850s and found themselves aliens in their own country, immigrants and interlopers largely looked down upon by the 'native' French and Creole elite. In the grand tradition of moneyed America, the new arrivals built enormous mansions to mark their entrance to the New Orleans scene.

The Garden District is not sight heavy, but it is worth a slow day of driving or, better, strolling, soaking up the mixture of tropical fecund beauty and white-columned old-money elegance. There's something about walking past a mansion Scarlett O'Hara would have envied on sidewalks bursting with Banyan roots that imparts a very unique sense of place.

Closer to the CBD, the Lower Garden District ('lower' due to its position along the Mississippi) is somewhat like the Garden District but not quite as posh. Here the houses are pleasant, not palatial; the green accents the streets rather than overflowing into them. There's a student vibe about, and plenty of bars and restaurants for those with university-stunted wallets and university-sized appetites for fun.

Note the streets named for classical gods, goddesses, nymphs and muses, an embellishment to the Greek-revival style houses. The Greek-crazy 1830s and surveyor Barthélémy Lafon envisioned a posh and sophisticated suburb that would be the envy of other classical-minded contemporary planners. The city's elite built their mansions here, paying their own homage to the toga-and-sandal days with columned galleries looking out over gardens burgeoning with pecan trees, bananas and fish ponds. New Orleans' craze for cast-iron struck the denizens of the Lower Garden District, who adorned and fenced their homes with ornate metallic designs, today lending the area a rustic grace.

Later, the wealthy moved further uptown to the newer, more fashionable Garden District. Lots of the larger residences of the Lower Garden District were divided into rental units to accommodate immigrants from Germany and Ireland, many of whom were employed on the docks. Low-income projects cropped up and remain near the river, while closer to Magazine St the Lower Garden is far more yuppie-ish and student- and shopper-friendly.

Central City, which lays between the CBD and Lower Garden District, is very much in transition. While there are large stretches of blight here, there is also a wonderful concentration of community activist organizations that are trying to rebuild what was once one of the most important African American neighborhoods in the city.

The Garden District is a rectangular grid bounded by St Charles Ave, Jackson Ave, Magazine St and Louisiana Ave. Magazine St and St Charles Ave are the main commercial thoroughfares, Prytania St is the most scenic. The Lower Garden District is upriver (in this case, south) from the CBD. Magazine St is the main thoroughfare.

Bus 11 runs along Magazine St from Canal St to Audubon Park; bus 10 runs on Tchoupitoulas St, past Tipitina's nightclub, to Audubon Park. When it's operating, the St Charles Ave streetcar runs from Canal St along St Charles Ave through the CBD, the Garden District and Uptown. Metered parking is available on Magazine Street and St Charles Ave. Free parking can be found on side streets.

GARDEN & LOWER GARDEN DISTRICTS

Leafy, lovely and very walkable, the Garden and Lower Garden districts are good places to walk around and soak up 19th-century architecture and the green, lush vibe that gives this city its distinct, subtropical character. Magazine St is good for window shopping and restaurant and bar hopping.

LAFAYETTE CEMETERY NO 1

Map pp96–7

Washington Ave at Prytania St; ⊗ **9am-2:30pm**
Another excellent addition to the New Orleans cemetery scene, this necropolis was established in 1833 by the former City of Lafayette. Sitting as it does just across from Commander's Palace (p162) and shaded by magnificent groves of lush greenery, the cemetery has a strong sense of Southern subtropical gothic about it. The layout is divided by two intersecting footpaths that form a cross. As you walk about, look out for the constructs built by fraternal organizations such as the Jefferson Fire Company No 22, which took care of their members and their families in large shared crypts. Some of the wealthier family tombs were built of marble, with elaborate detail rivaling the finest architecture in the district, but most tombs were constructed simply of inexpensive plastered brick. You'll notice many German and Irish names on the aboveground graves, testifying that immigrants were devastated by 19th-century yellow-fever epidemics. Not far from the entrance is a tomb containing the remains of an entire family that died of yellow fever.

The cemetery was filled to capacity within decades of its opening, and before the surrounding neighborhood reached its greatest affluence. By 1872, the prestigious Metairie Cemetery had already opened and its opulent grounds appealed to those with truly extravagant and flamboyant tastes.

In July 1995, author Anne Rice staged her own funeral here. She hired a horse-drawn hearse and a brass band to play dirges, and wore an antique wedding dress as she laid down in a coffin. (It wasn't pure frivolity – the event coincided with the release of one of Rice's novels.)

IRISH CHANNEL Map pp96–7

The name Irish Channel is a bit of a misnomer; although this historic neighborhood was settled by poor Irish immigrants fleeing the potato famine in the 1840s, it's also been the home of many German and black residents living together in a truly multiculti gumbo. Still, 'Irish Channel' sounds better than 'Mixed-ethnicity/nationality Channel,' right? Paradoxically, wage-earning Irish were widely regarded as more economical than slaves, particularly for dangerous assignments, since it cost nothing to replace an Irish laborer who died on the job. This is still a working-class cluster of shotgun houses and you may not want to walk around alone at night, but in general it's pleasant for ambling. Come St Patty's day (p138), the biggest block party around takes over Constance St in front of Parasol's Bar (p164).

HOUSE OF BROEL Map pp96–7

☎ 522-2220; www.houseofbroel.com; 2220 St Charles Ave; adult/child $10/5; ⊗ 10am-5pm Mon-Sat
Built in the 1850s, this is an excellent example of the sort of elegant architecture

FROM MYTHS TO THE MOVEMENT

Dryades St, named for legendary Greek tree spirits, is still known as such in much of town, but the official new name of this road is Oretha Castle-Haley Blvd (often shortened to OC Haley). The road is named for a local legend and Civil Rights activist who was a founding member of the Congress of Racial Equality, one of the leading organizations in the 1960s Civil Rights movement. Castle-Haley organized boycotts of segregated businesses and was one of the main leaders of local civil-disobedience and direct-action campaigns. Ironically, Castle-Haley's successful battle for integration helped hasten the decline of the street eventually named for her. When African Americans could shop anywhere they wanted, they began moving away from the traditionally black businesses clustered around Dryades, while simultaneously white flight contributed to an economic downturn across the city.

This part of town was once a major center for African American health care. The (now defunct) Keystone Insurance Company was one of the few of its kind that would fund pensions, funerals and, of course, medical treatment for black citizens. Said individuals may have been treated at Flint Goodridge Hospital (at Louisiana and Freret Sts); up until the 1950s, this was the only facility in the city where black doctors could legally practice medicine. First African Baptist Church of New Orleans, at 2216 3rd St, was founded in 1817 and is the oldest continually operating black church in Louisiana.

In testament to this area's contribution to the Civil Rights struggle, there is a statue of Martin Luther King at the corner of Martin Luther King Blvd and S Claiborne Ave.

GARDEN, LOWER GARDEN & CENTRAL CITY

INFORMATION
ATM	1 D3
New Orleans General Hospital	2 E5

SIGHTS (pp94–100)
Ashe Cultural Arts Center	3 C2
Big Top Gallery & Three Ring Circus	4 E1
God's Vineyard	5 E4
Goodrich-Stanley House	6 E3
Grace King House	7 E3
House of Broel	8 C3
Irish Channel	9 C5
Lafayette Cemetery No 1	10 B5
McKenna Museum of African American Art	11 C3
St Vincent's Infant Asylum	12 E3

SHOPPING (pp128–31)
Aidan Gill For Men	13 E4
Belladonna Day Spa	14 B6
Big Fisherman Seafood	15 B6
Dark Room	16 E4
Funky Monkey	17 B6
Garden District Bookshop	(see 22)
House of Lounge	18 E4
Jim Russell's Records	19 E4
Magazine Antique Mall	20 B6
New Orleans Music Exchange	21 B6
Rink	22 B4
Southern Fossil & Mineral Exchange	23 D4
Style Lab for Men	(see 21)
Thomas Mann Gallery I/O	24 E4
Trashy Diva	25 E4
Winky's	(see 18)

EATING (pp162–4)
Blue Plate Café	26 E2
Café Reconcile	27 C2
Commander's Palace	28 B5
Coquette	29 C5
Joey K's	30 B6
Juan's Flying Burrito	31 E4
Parasol's	32 C5
Rue de la Course	33 B6
Sake Café II	34 C5
Slice	35 D2
Slim Goodie's Diner	36 B6
Stein's Deli	37 D5
Sucré	38 B6
Surrey's Juice Bar	39 E3
Trolley Stop	40 D3

DRINKING & NIGHTLIFE (pp186–7)
Balcony Bar	41 B6
Bridge Lounge	42 F2
Bulldog	43 B6
Half Moon	44 E4
Igor's Lounge	45 C3
Rendezvous	46 B6
Saint Bar & Lounge	47 E4

THE ARTS (pp191–8)
Anton Haardt Gallery	48 C6
Simon of New Orleans	49 D4
Zeitgeist	50 C2

SLEEPING (pp211–13)
Avenue Garden Hotel	51 D2
Garden District B&B	52 D5
Green House Inn	53 F2
Henry Howard House	54 D3
Magnolia Mansion	55 D4
Maison St Charles	56 E2
Marquette House Hostel	57 C3
Prytania Park Hotel	58 E2
Sully Mansion B&B	59 B4
Terrell House	60 E3

Central City

Lower Garden District

Garden District

Irish Channel

See Uptown & Riverbend Map pp102-3

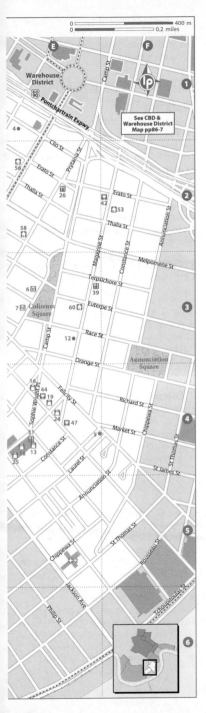

that makes the Garden District so darn pretty. Look out for the black marble fireplace and original mirror framed by carved tobacco leaves, plus a dollhouse museum that will appeal primarily to those with frilly tastes. Besides these exhibits, the house mainly hosts weddings and other events.

ST VINCENT'S INFANT ASYLUM
Map pp96–7
1507 Magazine St
This large, red-brick orphanage was built in 1864 with assistance from federal troops occupying the city. It helped relieve the overcrowded orphanages filled with youngsters of all races who lost their parents to epidemics. The orphanage is now a hotel, but a sign from orphanage days still hangs from the finely styled cast-iron gallery in front. Not open to the public.

GOODRICH-STANLEY HOUSE
Map pp96–7
1729 Coliseum St
This historic home was built in 1837 by jeweler William M Goodrich. Goodrich sold the house to the British-born merchant Henry Hope Stanley, whose adopted son, Henry Morton Stanley, went on to gain fame for finding the missing Scottish missionary, Dr David Livingstone, and uttering the legendary question, 'Dr Livingston, I presume?' He was subsequently knighted and founded the Congo Free States. The house originally stood a few blocks away, at 904 Orange St, and was moved to its current spot in 1981. Not open to the public.

GRACE KING HOUSE Map pp96–7
1749 Coliseum St
Behind a handsome wrought-iron fence, this papaya-hued house was named for the Louisiana historian and author who lived here from 1905 to 1932. It was built in 1847 by banker Frederick Rodewald and features both Greek Ionic columns on the lower floor and Corinthian columns above. Not open to the public.

CENTRAL CITY
Some areas here can get dodgy after dark. For the three sites listed here, check websites or call ahead to get information on their respectively packed events calendars.

MCKENNA MUSEUM OF AFRICAN AMERICAN ART Map pp96–7

☎ 524-1697; www.themckennamuseum.com; 2003 Carondelet St; adult/child/student & senior/$5/2/3; ⏰ 11am-4pm Thu-Sat, by appt Tue & Wed

The permanent exhibition of this beautiful little institution represents the amassed effort of some 30 years of collecting by Dr Dwight McKenna. Although the displayed work comes from all over the African diaspora, most of it is created by local New Orleans artists. Temporary exhibitions tend to be the real standout; such as photo-portrait essays on black intellectuals Romare Bearden, Ralph Ellison and Albert Murray.

ASHE CULTURAL ARTS CENTER
Map pp96–7

☎ 569-9070; www.ashecac.org; 1712 Oretha Castle-Haley Blvd

An important anchor for the local African American community, Ashe (from a Yoruba word that could loosely be translated as 'Amen') regularly showcases performances, art exhibitions, photographs and lectures with an African/African America/Caribbean focus. The on-site collection of African art is definitely worth a gander.

BIG TOP GALLERY & THREE RING CIRCUS Map pp96–7

☎ 569-2700; www.3rcp.com; 1638 Clio St

Just bordering downtown, this arts and education center is essentially a very funky cross between an art gallery (2pm to 6pm Thursday and Friday, noon to 5pm Satur-

day), studio space and something like a circus of dreams. There's a small main stage that occasionally hosts some great live performances.

GREEN, GREEN NEW ORLEANS
Walking Tour

This tour is all about experiencing the green of New Orleans on every level of the color: from the historic, magnolia-shaded streets of the Garden District to the Emerald Island heritage of the Irish Channel and the community gardens and neighborhood arts spaces of Central City. We've even thrown in a bit of window shopping along Magazine St – sure, it's not particularly 'green' by any real measure but we love it, OK? We recommend starting this tour early in the morning.

1 Commander's Palace & Lafayette Cemetery We start with two of the Garden District's most recognizable landmarks. Commander's Palace (p162) is the elegant crown jewel of the Brennan restaurateur empire and one of the best restaurants in the USA, period. Pop in for a 25-cent martini if it's lunchtime, although you may not want to in warm months, as shorts aren't allowed. Across the street is Lafayette Cemetery No 1 (p95), one of the city's oldest.

2 Colonel Robert Short's House Just around the corner is Robert Short's House (1448 Fourth St), also known as the Short-Favrot Villa. The home of a Confederate officer, the house was designed by architect Henry Howard, who is renowned in these parts. It's an exem-

---

GARDENS OUTSIDE THE DISTRICT

New Orleans has always been a green city, at least in terms of color and hue. The climate and the Caribbean-colonial planning philosophy of the city is the cause behind a lush overgrowth effect that is noticeable even in poorer parts of the city. Indeed, the Lower Ninth Ward, which was wiped out by floodwaters, presently looks more like a wilderness than a ghetto. Nature works fast here, and is always sprouting through walls and foundations.

The trick of many New Orleanian plant lovers is channeling this awesome fecundity into plots that are both attractive and utilitarian. Enter Parkway Partners (☎ 620-2224; www.parkwaypartnersnola.org; 1137 Baronne St), one of the best NGOs operating in New Orleans at the time of writing. Besides funding urban tree-planting projects and similar programs, Parkway is looking to expand, with local contribution, its series of community gardens.

At the time of writing there were almost 30 such gardens scattered across the city, each one a lovely example of community partnerships and grass-roots beautification efforts. All are undoubtedly pretty, but some gardens also serve a functional role as a source of fresh veggies and produce for local tables, and all help to leech lead out of the local soil (New Orleans has unusually high levels of lead contamination in its soil). There's a full list of active community gardens at www.parkwaypartnersnola.org/gardenlist.html; some of our other favorites include Le Jardin du Soleil (Map pp102–3; 3458 Annunciation St), Bywater Herb Farm (Map p81; 4327 N Rampart St) and God's Vineyard (Map pp96–7; 928 Felicity St).

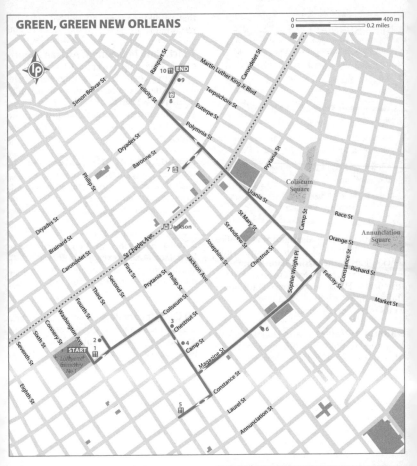

plary double-gallery home with fine cast-iron details, further distinguished by a cornstalk cast-iron fence, identical to the more famous one on the French Quarter walking tour.

3 Joseph Carroll House Amble along the tree-lined corridor of Coliseum St to the Joseph Carroll House (1315 First St), a beautiful center-hall house with double galleries laced with cast-iron filaments. The house was designed by architect Samuel Jamison. Peer towards the back of the lot to see the similarly impressive carriage house.

4 Anne Rice's House Just a little ways down First St is Rosegate (1239 First St), former home of author Anne Rice. The vampire-tale spinner lived here for many years, and regularly invited fans to tour her home. Which, by the

> **WALK FACTS**
>
> Start Commander's Palace
> End Café Reconcile
> Distance 2 miles
> Duration Half-day
> Fuel Stop Po'boys and/or beer at Parasol's; optional final meal at Café Reconcile

way, is beautiful but disappointingly free of bats, organ music, pale women in neck-and-cleavage exposing bustiers or even Tom Cruise prancing about in a frilly jacket (but then, we visited during the day). No longer open to the public.

5 Parasol's New Orleans neighborhoods change character with breathtaking quickness;

walk south of First past Magazine and notice how quickly the villages become shotgun shacks. This is the Irish Channel, home to working-class Irish, Germans and African Americans. Hook a right onto Third Street and pop into Parasol's (p164), a quintessential New Orleans neighborhood bar.

6 Simon of New Orleans Double back to Magazine St, the prime boutique-shopping strip of the city. Head into Simon of New Orleans (p196), the shop of a groovy local painter known for his hand-painted folk-art signs

that are all the rage in a lot of New Orleans restaurants.

7 McKenna Museum of African American Art Head up to Central City by walking up pretty Felicity St. It's a little over a half-mile to the next stop – grab a cab if you're tired. The McKenna Museum of African American Art (p98), an intimate, beautiful addition to the New Orleans museum scene (call ahead for hours).

8 Ashe Cultural Arts Center A host of community organizations are working to re-vitalize Central City, including Ashe Cultural Arts Center (p98), which focuses on promoting the creativity and heritage of the city's Caribbean and African American populations.

9 Zeitgeist Further up Oretha Castle-Haley Blvd (see boxed text, p95) is Zeitgeist (p198), another arts and community center with a more contemporary (but no less activist) bent.

10 Café Reconcile Sit down at Café Reconcile (p164), which employs at-risk youth to both prepare and serve excellent soul food. Just up the street is Haley's Harvest (1603 Oretha Castle-Haley Blvd), one of the many community gardens sprouting up in this area.

UPTOWN & RIVERBEND

Drinking & Nightlife p187, Eating p164, Shopping p131, Sleeping p213

Uptown has arrived.

OK, that's not exactly accurate. Uptown has been around for a while – at least since the late 19th century, as the outlaying American Protestant suburbs of Lafayette, Jefferson and Carrollton, and the grounds of several plantations were absorbed by the city. But Uptown's current incarnation as the seat of New Orleans' best shopping and preppy cool is as recent as any neighborhood developments in this city. Give credit (or blame) to Whole Foods, titan of upscale grocery stores. The company took a bus depot on Magazine St, turned it into an enormous link in their corporate chain, and ta-da: novelty cupcake shops, stores specializing in smelly paper and indie fashion boutiques soon flooded in.

But it's unfair to characterize this area as only upper crust. Uptown, as defined in this book, is a large entity that includes, along with the architectural extravagance near Magazine St and Audubon Park, the more middle- and working-class neighborhoods of West Riverside, Black Pearl and Broadmoor. Riverbend and Carrollton are adjacent to Tulane and Loyala universities, and while there are plenty of tropical mansions here that denote the wealth of business-minded 19th-century Americans, the general vibe is one of a sometimes raucous, sometimes retail-obsessed but ultimately inclusive college town.

As economically disparate as these districts may be, physically they very much run into each other, and culturally their populations mix on a relatively regular basis in po'boy shops and corner bars. Everyone who lives here does so under the pleasant shade of tree-lined lanes that run past some 8000 buildings listed on the National Historic Register.

Closer to the main commercial corridor of Magazine St, Uptown is where recent graduates and young families like to have a good time, but with a fine meal, coffee sipped on sidewalk cafes, a bit of self-indulgent shopping, and…well, this is still New Orleans. There are some great, very popular bars down here. And yes, we mean down. The 'Up' in Uptown refers to 'upriver'; geographically, this is one of the southernmost points of the city.

A lot of Uptown's idiosyncrasies came on the heels of transplanted new New Orleanians. The Storm magnetized thousands of individuals intent on raising the phoenix from Katrina's sodden ashes, and while many volunteer and grass-roots types settled in the Marigny and Bywater, a good glut of professionals and more-established artists opted for the safer (if still strange enough) blocks ensconced in, as some locals call it, 'the Magazine St bubble.' Ultimately, this neighborhood feels both oddly posh and nonconformist. It's a great place to get a sense of city life away from the Quarter's tourist traps, but also removed from the Crescent City's edgier 'hoods.

Maps of New Orleans rarely agree on the area's extents, but for the purposes of this book we'll say Uptown includes everything west of Louisiana Ave, between Magnolia and the river, including the Universities and Audubon Park. St Charles Ave, Magazine St and Tchoupitoulas St are the main routes that more or less follow the contours of the river. The Riverbend is the area where the campuses and Audubon Park. Where St Charles Ave meets S Carrollton Ave is the nexus of the area. Maple St and Oak St are narrow shopping strips that have some interesting restaurants and bars.

Bus 11 runs along Magazine St from Canal St to Audubon Park; bus 12 runs the length of St Charles Ave; and bus 10 runs the length of Tchoupitoulas St. When operating, the St Charles Ave streetcar runs from Canal St along St Charles Ave from the Riverbend all the way to Canal St at the edge of the French Quarter. Metered parking is available on Magazine St and St Charles Ave. Free parking can be found on side streets.

AUDUBON ZOOLOGICAL GARDENS

Map pp102–3

☎ 581-4629; www.auduboninstitute.org; adult/child/senior $12/7/9; 6500 Magazine St; ☽ 9am-5pm

Long acknowledged as one of the country's best zoos, this garden-like enclosure is the heart of the Audubon Institute. At the time of writing, the newest stars were two cuddly (really) red rover hogs, Matthew and Isabel.

The zoo is divided into distinct sections, and while it is international in focus, its spirit feels very much like a part of the Louisiana landscape, best exemplified by the Louisiana Swamp. The Cajun setting details

Mississippi River

how Spanish moss is used as furniture stuffing, while an authentic fishing camp displays shrimp trawls, crawfish traps and an oyster dredge. Alligators laze on the muddy banks; bobcats, red foxes and endangered Louisiana black bears lope through the swamp scrub; and a 200lb alligator snapping turtle *(Macroclemys temminicki)* wiggles its pink tongue as bait for…hey, it found Nemo! Human intrusions into the swamp environment are poignantly represented with a *traânasee* cutter, used by fish and game trappers to create access across shallow swamps.

The Reptile Encounter displays representatives of the largest snakes in the world – from the king cobra that grows to over 18ft in length to the green anaconda that reaches 38ft. Many local species of snake are also on display.

There are all sorts of rides inside the zoo that are great fun for kids (or kids at heart). A Swamp Train ($5) departs on lazy grounds tours every 30 minutes from the Carousel train depot; a rock climbing wall ($5) is available; the Safari Simulator ($5) is a moving movie theater based on NASA simulators and, of course, there's a carousel ($2), where you can ride traditional horses and, in an eco-educational nod, endangered species.

The zoo is located inside Audubon Park. The park is in itself a lovely spot for sitting under trees, enjoying a snow cone in the summer swelter and generally lazing about. All along the park edges are the gorgeous

top picks

FOR KIDS

- Audubon Zoo (p101)
- Aquarium of the Americas (p90)
- Insectarium (p77)
- Blaine Kern's Mardi Gras World (p91)
- City Park (p107)
- Historic Voodoo Museum (p73)
- Louisiana Children's Museum (p91)
- Musée Conti Wax Museum (p77)
- Southern Fossil & Mineral Exchange (p130)
- House of Broel (p95)
- Storyland (p110)
- St Charles Avenue Streetcar (opposite)
- Bourbon Street – Just kidding

NEIGHBORHOOD ASSOCIATIONS

Carrollton-Riverbend Neighborhood Association (www.crna-nola.org)

Central Carrollton Association (www.central carrolltonassociation.org)

Claiborne-University Neighborhood Association (www.cuna-nola.org)

Magazine Street Merchants Association (www .magazinestreet.com)

Maple Area Residents (www.maplearea residents.net)

Upper Audubon Association (www.upper audubon.org)

Uptown Freret Community (www.freret street.com)

mansions of some of the city's wealthiest residents.

TULANE UNIVERSITY Map pp102–3

☎ 865-4000; www.tulane.edu; 6823 St Charles Ave
A premier Southern university, Tulane has an interesting origin as a yellow-fever buster. In 1834 the Medical College of Louisiana was founded in an attempt to control repeated cholera and yellow-fever epidemics. By 1847 the University of Louisiana merged with the school, and in 1883, Paul Tulane gave the school a $1 million donation that initiated significant expansion and slapped his name on the entire institution. Today the school sprawls across an attractive cluster of greens, red-brick buildings and quads above Audubon Park – this is one of the prettiest colleges in the country, and well worth a stroll for anyone wanting to reclaim a sense of school days (or daze).

Tulane boasts 22,000 students in 11 colleges and schools, including a law school whose entire student body seems to fill up Magazine St cafes during exam time, and the highly regarded medical school, since relocated downtown. Big-name alumni include former French president Jacques Chirac, Newt Gingrich, Jerry Springer and a very long list of Louisiana governors, judges and assorted politicos.

The University Center is a typical student union, sporting a box office (☎ 861-5105 ext 2) that sells tickets for sporting and special events. *Hullabaloo,* the campus newspaper, is a good source for school listings.

The Amistad Research Center (☎ 865-3222; www .amistadresearchcenter.org; Tilton Memorial Hall; ⏲ 9am-4:30pm Mon-Sat) is one of the nation's largest repositories of African American history. The rotating exhibits offer insight on ethnic heritage you're not likely to get from any other source. The displayed works of art from the Aaron Douglas Collection are another reason to drop by.

Jazz heads, and really anyone interested in New Orleans music, should pop into the Hogan Jazz Archive (☎ 865-5688; 3rd fl, Joseph Merrick Jones Hall, 304 Freret St; ⏲ 9am-4:45pm Mon-Fri); most of its great wealth of material is not on exhibit; the librarian will retrieve items from the stacks for you. That collection includes stacks of 78rpm recordings like early sides by the Original Dixieland Jazz Band in 1917. More casual visitors may enjoy the Storyville Room, with its emphasis on Jelly Roll Morton (who played piano in the district's bordellos during the early 20th century).

Flanked by beautiful Tiffany stained-glass triptychs, the Newcomb Art Gallery (☎ 865-5328; Woldenberg Art Center; admission free; ⏲ 10am-5pm Mon-Fri, noon-5pm Sat & Sun) is a great spot to soak up some art; just outside is a pretty green where students sunbathe, toss Frisbees and generally recede into the happiest rhythms of American higher ed.

ST CHARLES AVENUE STREETCAR
Map pp102–3

fare $1.25; ⏲ 6am-11pm
A buck twenty-five gets you on the St Charles Avenue Streetcar, which plies the oldest continuously operating street railway system in the world. New Orleanians are justifiably proud of this moving monument, which began life as the nation's second horse-drawn streetcar line, the New Orleans & Carrollton Railroad, in 1835. In 893 the line was among the first systems to be electrified. Now it is one of the few streetcars in the USA to have survived the automobile era. The fleet of antique cars survived the hurricanes of 2005 and today full service has been restored all the way to South Carrollton Ave.

TOURO SYNAGOGUE Map pp102–3

☎ 895-4843; www.tourosynagogue.com; 4238 St Charles Ave

Despite the fact that Jews were officially banned from New Orleans under the Code Noir (Black Code), they have been calling the Crescent City home since the 18th century. Founded in 1828, Touro is the city's oldest synagogue (and the oldest in the country outside of the original 13 colonies). The synagogue bears a slight resemblance to a red-brick Byzantine temple, with squat buttresses and bubbly domes. The local congregation began as an amalgamation between local Spanish-descended Jews and German Jewish immigrants, a relatively rare mixed lineage in American Judaism. Today, this is a pretty progressive Reform congregation that's famous for holding 'jazz Shabbat' near Jazz Fest.

LATTER MEMORIAL LIBRARY
Map pp102–3

☎ 596-2625; www.nutrias.org; 5120 St Charles Ave; ⏲ 9am-8pm Mon & Wed, to 6pm Tue & Thu, 10am-5pm Sat, 1-5pm Sun
Poised elegantly above shady strands of palm on St Charles Ave, the Latter Memorial Library was once a private mansion residence, passed along from the Isaac family (owners 1907–12), who installed Flemish-style caved woodwork, Dutch murals and French frescoed ceilings, to aviator Harry Williams and his silent-film–star wife, Marguerite Clark (1912–39), to a local horse racer named Robert S Eddy, then finally, in 1948, to the Latters. The latter (sorry) converted the mansion into its current form as a library. The bottom floor and the entire exterior facade remain as stately as ever.

LEVEE PARK Map pp102–3

The levee space that follows the curve of the Mississippi River has been turned into a public right of way that runs all the way from Audubon Park to Jefferson Parish. It's a nice spot for walking, jogging or biking joggers, but views onto the river are occasionally only so-so and there aren't enough paths connecting the levee to the street below (if you try to cross off the path, you may get ankle deep in Mississippi mud). Still, it's a good little green space.

MID-CITY & THE TREMÉ

Drinking & Nightlife p189, Eating p169, Shopping p133, Sleeping p214

New Orleanians speak of the great divide, the line that separates the French Quarter and her Creole faubourgs from the green lanes of the Garden District and Uptown. But is the divide an idea, or a living place with a character of its own?

Laying between the poles of the Crescent City's most famous neighborhoods is the middle ground of Mid-City, a buffer zone that's difficult to define, both physically and culturally. This was once swamp that stood between a city and its hinterlands; today its clusters of shotgun houses huddled near cozy taverns and cafes, blots of highway strip-mall blah, one of America's great city parks and – why not? – a Bayou fringed by some of the most elegant historical structures in the city.

This is a neighborhood made for slow exploration and aimless saunters, especially along the stately, tree-lined Esplanade Ridge. Here you'll find houses plucked from Tennessee Williams' most romantic dreams, a glut of great restaurants and the digs where Edgar Degas shacked up during his time in New Orleans. On good days it's not hard to see how the muddy, liquid light that filters through the leaves of this corner of town might have inspired the impressionist master to new levels of genius.

You'll need a car to really appreciate Mid-City's charms. That's partly because the area is so large, partly because neighborhoods here run from cute to criminal in the space of a block, and partly because public transportation links are pretty poor. Starting from the southwest, near Banks St, there's a mix of commercial lots and residential blocks. Northeast is the juncture of Mid-City: Bayou St John, ringed about with historic houses, and the great green stretches of City Park. Southeast from is Esplanade St, which runs past Creole mansions into the next great neighborhood in this part of town.

Bus 91 runs down Esplanade Ave from City Park to Rampart St, where it skirts the French Quarter. Bus 27 goes to City Park from the Garden District primarily via Louisiana and Washington Aves. Street parking is generally easy to find, but beware of the two-hour residential restrictions, especially during Jazz Fest, when the city loves to ticket and tow.

Although technically part of Mid-City, and in some ways geographically linked to the French Quarter, the Tremé is in many ways its own island. This is the oldest free black neighborhood in the USA, although what constitutes 'black' has been a subject of historical debate for years. Creoles, light skinned, mixed race and several other shades have all made this neighborhood more complicated than 'black,' even as it has become synonymous with that element of New Orleanian identity. In fact, for most of its history the Tremé has been populated predominantly by mixed-race Creoles; African Americans from elsewhere in the South are relatively recent arrivals. Although the latter dominate much of the neighborhood today, you'll also find businessmen here with coffee skin, gray eyes, a Jewish middle name from some distant Polish immigrant ancestor and a cousin who might have played backup to Ernie K-Doe.

The neighborhood, already on hard times by 2005, was hit hard by Katrina (her winds instead of her flood waters), and there are still swathes of this area that look Third World. Yet the historic importance of the Tremé, the arrival of an eponymous TV show and the attentions of savvy real estate types will probably bring a bit of a facelift – whether it retains its unique character remains to be seen. In the meantime, check out essential sites such as Louis Armstrong Park and St Louis Cemetery No 1. Be careful (but not paranoid), as it can get rough at night.

The actual residential neighborhood is bound by Rampart St, Louis Armstrong Park, Claiborne Ave and Esplanade Ave. Bus 88 runs along Rampart St between the Tremé and the French Quarter, and connects to the Bywater along St Claude Ave. Street parking is generally easy to come by.

MID-CITY

The Mid-City region we refer to here includes the area comprising City Park, Esplanade Ridge and Bayou St John – the center of what most New Orleanians would classify as classical 'Mid-City.'

CITY PARK Map pp108–9

☎ 482-4888; www.neworleanscitypark.com

Three miles long, 1 mile wide, stroked by weeping willows and Spanish moss, and dotted with museums, gardens, waterways, bridges, birds and the occasional alligator,

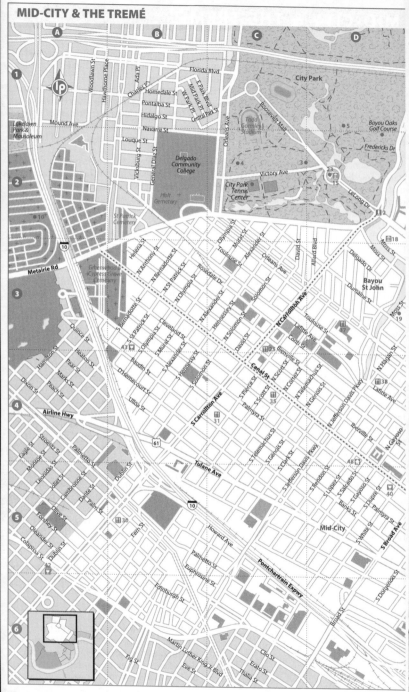

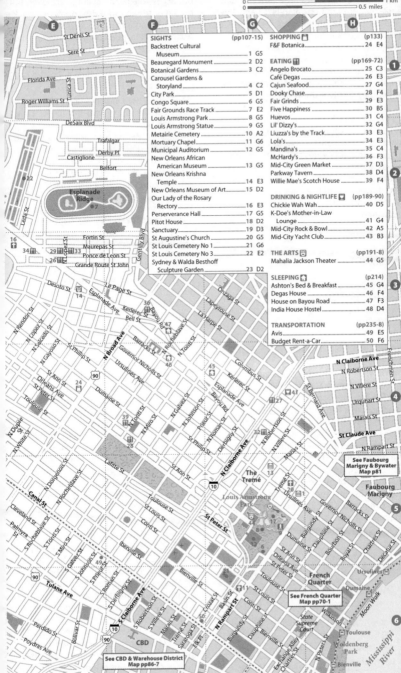

SIGHTS	(pp107-15)
Backstreet Cultural	
Museum	1 G5
Beauregard Monument	2 D2
Botanical Gardens	3 C2
Carousel Gardens &	
Storyland	4 C2
City Park	5 D1
Congo Square	6 G5
Fair Grounds Race Track	7 E2
Louis Armstrong Park	8 G5
Louis Armstrong Statue	9 G5
Metairie Cemetery	10 A2
Mortuary Chapel	11 G6
Municipal Auditorium	12 G5
New Orleans African	
American Museum	13 G5
New Orleans Krishna	
Temple	14 E3
New Orleans Museum of Art	15 D2
Our Lady of the Rosary	
Rectory	16 E3
Perserverance Hall	17 G5
Pitot House	18 D2
Sanctuary	19 D3
St Augustine's Church	20 G5
St Louis Cemetery No 1	21 G6
St Louis Cemetery No 3	22 E2
Sydney & Walda Besthoff	
Sculpture Garden	23 D2

SHOPPING	(p133)
F&F Botanica	24 E4

EATING	(pp169-72)
Angelo Brocato	25 C3
Café Degas	26 E3
Cajun Seafood	27 E3
Dooky Chase	28 F4
Fair Grinds	29 E3
Five Happiness	30 B5
Huevos	31 C4
Lil' Dizzy's	32 G4
Liuzza's by the Track	33 E3
Lola's	34 E3
Mandina's	35 C4
McHardy's	36 F3
Mid-City Green Market	37 D3
Parkway Tavern	38 D3
Willie Mae's Scotch House	39 F4

DRINKING & NIGHTLIFE	(pp189-90)
Chickie Wah Wah	40 D5
K-Doe's Mother-in-Law	
Lounge	41 G4
Mid-City Rock & Bowl	42 A5
Mid-City Yacht Club	43 B3

THE ARTS	(pp191-8)
Mahalia Jackson Theater	44 G5

SLEEPING	(p214)
Ashton's Bed & Breakfast	45 G4
Degas House	46 F4
House on Bayou Road	47 F3
India House Hostel	48 D4

TRANSPORTATION	(pp235-8)
Avis	49 E5
Budget Rent-a-Car	50 F6

City Park is the nation's fifth-largest urban park (bigger than Central in NYC) and New Orleans' prettiest green lung. It's a perfect expression of a local 'park,' in the sense that it is an only slightly tamed expression of the Louisiana wetlands and forest that are the natural backdrop of the city. It's always open, but for safety reasons we recommend only visiting during daylight hours.

The arboreal life here is magnificent: dense groves of mature live oaks – thousands of them, some as old as 600 years – along with bald cypresses, Southern magnolias and other species. During Hurricane Katrina nearby canals flooded and inundated over 90% of the park in up to 8ft of salt water, but the ground seems to have recovered, although many priceless trees were lost. The land feels particularly bare at the entrance to the museum of art, once framed by a natural arcade of beautiful old growth oak trees that were lost in the Storm.

Tad Gormley Stadium, located inside the park, isn't particularly impressive on its own, but the art-deco sculptures of athletes on the outer gates are beautiful.

NEW ORLEANS MUSEUM OF ART
Map pp108–9

☎ 658-4100; www.noma.org; 1 Collins Diboll Circle; adult/child/senior & student $8/4/7; ☻ 10am-5pm Thu-Tue, noon-8pm Wed

Looking like a vague cross between a library, Lenin's tomb and a Greek temple, this is one of the finest museums in the city and one of the best art museums in the entire South. There's strong representation from regional and American artists, but the work of masters who have passed through the city, such as Edgar Degas, is also prominent. The European presence is generally quite strong, also. Temporary exhibitions have consistently been daring

NEIGHBORHOOD ASSOCIATIONS

Bayou St John Conservation Alliance (www .savebayoustjohn.org)

Mid-City Neighborhood Organization (www .mcno.org)

Treme Neighborhood Association (http://historic treme.wordpress.com)

but accessible to the average art lover, but our favorite section is the top floor, chockablock with a fantastic collection of African, Asian, Oceanic, pre-Columbian and Native American art.

CAROUSEL GARDENS & STORYLAND
Map pp108–9

☎ 483-9382; www.neworleanscitypark.com; City Park; admission $3; ☻ 10am-3pm Tue-Fri, 11am-6pm Sat & Sun

We reckon anyone who doesn't like these charmingly dated theme parks probably has a cold heart of stone; how sad. The centerpiece of Carousel Gardens is a restored antique carousel, housed in a 1906 structure with a stained-glass cupola. In the 1980s, residents raised $1.2 million to restore the broken animals, fix the squeaky merry-go-round and replace the Wurlitzer organ. The results are spectacular in a tweedy, tinkly kind of way. You can board the tiny City Park Railroad here as well, which just throws the entire cuteness factor into 'kittens playing with cotton candy string' territory. Rides at Carousel Gardens cost an additional $1 each, however an $8 pass will allow you unlimited rides for the whole day.

Storyland has no rides, but the fairytale statuary is plenty of fuel for young imaginations. Children can play with – and climb upon – the Jabberwocky from Alice in Wonderland, or enter the mouth of the whale from Pinocchio. If these characters seem strangely similar to Mardi Gras floats, it's because they were created by master float-builder Blaine Kern. During the Christmas season, it's lit up like a Christmas tree; it's a good thing it rarely snows here, because the entire experience would be so magic your head might explode with fairy dust.

BOTANICAL GARDENS Map pp108–9

☎ 482-4888; www.neworleanscitypark.com; adult/child $6/3; ☻ 10am-4:30pm Tue-Sun

Katrina utterly wiped out these beautiful 12-acre gardens, flooding the delicate plants in salt water and blacking out the electricity that regulated temperatures in the greenhouses. But it only took six months and the work and donations of a lot of volunteers and do-gooders before the gardens reopened. They're not what they once were, but the plant life is grow-

NEW ORLEANS: BORN ON THE BAYOU

You wouldn't guess it today, seeing as it's not much more than a pleasant if occasionally stinky little creek popular with canoers and kayakers, but Bayou St John is the reason this city exists. Originally used by Native Americans as a wet highway to the relatively high ground of Esplanade Ridge, French explorers realized the waterway was the shortest route between the Mississippi River – and by extent the Gulf of Mexico – and Lake Pontchartrain. It was essentially for this reason New Orleans was built in its commanding position at the mouth of the Mississippi. Eventually a canal built by Governor Carondelet extended the bayou to the edge of the French Quarter, and the bayou acted as the city's chief commercial harbor. Life in the area thrived; beautiful houses lined the bayou (many are still here today), and Voodoo Queen Marie Laveau and followers supposedly conducted rituals on the waterfront.

The era of steamboats made direct navigation up and down the Mississippi easier, and the bayou began to be eclipsed. Navigation ended with the filling of the canal in 1927, but the bayou remained an important geographic point of reference. Since 2005 it has also become a bone of contention between local residents and the Army Corps of Engineers. The Corps insists St John is a dangerous potential source of floodwater and have proposed sealing it off from Pontchartrain. Some local residents say opening sector gates on the bayou's pump houses could facilitate the natural flow of water, which would in turn freshen up the bayou (which can grow darkly stagnant), improve water quality and reintroduce important flora and fauna to the bayou bank.

The issue is still being fought. In the meantime, come out here to stroll along the bayou (stagnant or not, it is scenic), enjoy a po'boy from the Parkway (p171), catch one of the many concerts played on the median that runs through the bayou and gape at the gorgeous residences. You're only allowed to enter one: Pitot House (Map pp108–9; ☎ 482-0312; www.pitothouse.org; 1440 Moss St; adult/child & senior $7/5; ☺ 10am-3pm Wed-Sat), a restored mansion with a lovely set of gardens in the back.

ing and visitors are increasing – be one of them, and help bring back a city gem. On weekends and special events, pop into the New Orleans Historic Train Garden, a neat replica of old New Orleans intersected by G-gauge streetcars.

SYDNEY & WALDA BESTHOFF SCULPTURE GARDEN Map pp108–9
☎ 488-2631; www.noma.org; 1 Collins Diboll Circle; ☺ Fri-Sun

Just outside the New Orleans Museum of Art, the Besthoff Sculpture Garden opened in 2003 with some 45 pieces from the world-renowned Besthoff collection. The growing collection includes mostly contemporary works by such artists as Antoine Bourdelle, Henry Moore and Louis Bourgeois.

OUR LADY OF THE ROSARY RECTORY Map pp108–9
1342 Moss St

Built around1834 as the home of Evariste Blanc, Our Lady of the Rosary Rectory exhibits a combination of styles characteristic of the region. The high-hipped roof and wraparound gallery seem reminiscent of West Indies houses but were actually the preferred styles of the French Canadians who originally settled Bayou St John. However, it's the house's neoclassic details that

make it obvious that this building is from a later period.

ST LOUIS CEMETERY NO 3 Map pp108–9
☎ 482-5065; 3421 Esplanade Ave; ☺ till dark

This relatively tiny cemetery was established in 1854 at the site of the old Bayou Cemetery and is worth strolling through for a few minutes (longer if you're a cemetery enthusiast). Of particular note is the striking monument James Gallier Jr designed for his mother and father, who were lost at sea. The cemetery's wrought-iron entrance gate is a beauty.

SANCTUARY Map pp108–9
924 Moss St

This historic house was built by Evariste Blanc, from 1816 to 1822, on land originally granted in 1720–1 to French Canadians. The once-swampy property was later transferred to Don Andrés Almonaster y Roxas, the real-estate speculator who commissioned St Louis Cathedral on Jackson Sq in the French Quarter.

FAIR GROUNDS RACE TRACK
Map pp108–9
☎ 944-5515; www.fairgroundsracecourse.com; 1751 Gentilly Blvd

The Union Race Course was laid out on this spot in 1852, and New Orleanians have been betting on the ponies ever since. Today the Churchill Downs Company, which also hosts the Kentucky Derby, operates the track, and rechristened the Fair Grounds in 1863 during the Union occupation.

This is the third-oldest track in the nation. During the Civil War, in addition to horse races, you could catch a bear fight down this way. Today, besides horse races, the Fair Grounds is the site of the annual Louisiana Derby (in March) and the New Orleans Jazz & Heritage Festival (p50).

The Fair Grounds' handsome gatehouse entryway was designed by James Gallier Jr in 1859 for an agricultural fair, and the stands were rebuilt following a disastrous fire in 1993. Buried in the infield are derby winners from an era when New Orleans was one of the premier tracks in the country. The racing season runs from November to March on Wednesday through Sunday, with a 1:30pm post time.

NEW ORLEANS KRISHNA TEMPLE
Map pp108–9

☎ 304-0032; www.myspace.com/iskcon_nola; 2936 Esplanade Ave

We've mentioned lots of churches, voodoo temples and even a synagogue in this city, and we're not leaving the International Society of Krishna Consciousness – you probably know them as Hare Krishnas – out of the loop. The Krishnas worship in a rather gorgeous house plopped right on Esplanade, and have regular veggie buffets, *pujas* (prayer ceremonies) and lectures; in addition, the interior of the temple is as colorfully close to India as you'll get in the Big Easy. Check their MySpace page or call ahead for details on when the temple is open to the public.

METAIRIE CEMETERY Map pp108–9

☎ 486-6331; 5100 Pontchartrain Blvd

Visiting other New Orleans cemeteries doesn't quite prepare you for the architectural splendor and over-the-top extravagance of Metairie Cemetery. Established in 1872 on a former race track (the grounds, you'll notice, still follow the oval layout), this is the most American of New Orleans' cities of the dead and, like the houses of the Garden District, its tombs appear to be attempts at one-upmanship.

This is the final resting place for many of New Orleans' most prominent citizens. Wil-

liam Charles Cole Claiborne, Louisiana's first American governor, rests here, as does Confederate General PGT Beauregard. Jefferson Davis was originally interred here, only to be moved to Richmond, VA, two years later. But the real highlight is the architecture. Many of the family tombs and monuments mix stone, bronze and stained glass, and the statuary is, in turns, elegant, touchingly sad and even sensual. Highlights include the Brunswig mausoleum, a pyramid guarded by a sphinx statue; the Moriarty monument, the reputed 'tallest privately owned monument' in the country; and the Estelle Theleman Hyams monument, with a stained glass casting a somber blue light over a slumped, despondent angel.

Visitors can drop by the funeral home on the grounds and select either the 'Soldier, Statesmen, Patriots, Rebels' or 'Great Families and Captains of Commerce' self-guided tours. You will be given a map and loaned a recorded cassette and tape player (no charge).

Seeing everything on the 150-acre grounds is most easily accomplished by car. Tape tours take about an hour, but stretching this out by getting out of the car for a closer look is highly recommended.

THE TREMÉ

The oldest free black neighborhood in the USA is experiencing something of a rebirth. This is the likeliest spot in the city to spot a second line or a jazz funeral (although the latter is still pretty rare).

ST LOUIS CEMETERY NO 1 Map pp108–9

1300 St Louis St; ⏰ 8am-3pm

New Orleans is something of a city of cemeteries. Influenced by the massive mausoleum building cultures of the Spanish and French, large above-ground necropolises were once all the rage here. The most famous example of the genre is St Louis Cemetery No 1, opened in 1789 and today stuffed with tombs, graves and tourists.

The supposed crypt of voodoo queen Marie Laveau (see p74), where people leave offerings and candles, and folks scratch 'XXX's onto a family tomb bearing the names Glapion, Laveau and Paris (all branches of Marie Laveau's family) is the big drawcard. Debates over *which* Marie Laveau – mother or daughter, if either – was actually buried here, will never be resolved, but what is known is that living members of the Glapion family consider the 'X' marks to be vandalism. There is no spiritual significance to these chicken scratches, and visitors are strongly discouraged from desecrating this or any other tomb (doing so is also technically illegal.

In the adjacent family tomb rests Ernest 'Dutch' Morial, New Orleans' first black mayor. Civil-rights figure Homer Plessy also rests in the cemetery, as do real-estate speculator Bernard de Marigny, architect Henry Latrobe and countless others.

The Italian Mutual Benevolent Society Tomb is responsible for the tallest monument in the cemetery. Like a lot of immigrant groups in New Orleans, the Italians formed a benevolent association to pool funds and assist in covering burial costs. That fund pool got Olympic sized – the benevolent society tomb is big enough to hold the remains of thousands. In 1969, to the obvious shock of the families who own tombs here, a demented rape scene in the movie *Easy Rider* was filmed here. Take note of the headless statue called *Charity* on the Italian Society tomb – urban myth maintains that actor Dennis Hopper, who starred in the film, was responsible for tearing the head off.

It can be hard to find all of the noteworthy sights, but a good organized walking tour, such as those offered by Haunted History Tours (☎ 861-2727; www.hauntedhistorytours .com), will help you see them all.

LOUIS ARMSTRONG PARK Map pp108–9

The entrance to this massive park has got to be one of the greatest gateways in the USA; a picturesque arch that ought rightfully be the final set piece in some period drama about Jazz Age New Orleans.

We wonder how Satchmo would feel about the park dedicated in his name. Parts of it, particularly the walkways over little rivers and streams, are gorgeous, and the original Congo Sq (see below) is here. On the other hand the park is surrounded by imposing, unfriendly walls; parts of it remain undeveloped and rough looking, and overall this isn't a good place to walk around at night. Too bad – a public space with a jazzy name on this particular spot really ought to be a cultural focal point for New Orleans.

While you're inside, check out the Louis Armstrong statue and the bust of Sidney Bechet. The Mahalia Jackson Theater has been done up with a $22 million renovation and now hosts opera and Broadway productions, but next door the more historic Municipal Auditorium remains in a state of rot.

In the future, the New Orleans Jazz National Historic Park (☎ 589-4806) will be based at the park's Perseverance Hall, but this process has been ongoing for years with little evidence of resolution. Tune in to WWOZ Radio (www.wwoz.org) and other cultural media to learn about concerts and parades sponsored by the National Park Service.

BACKSTREET CULTURAL MUSEUM
Map pp108–9

☎ 287-5224; www.backstreetmuseum.org; 1116 St Claude Ave; donations accepted; ☒ 10am-5pm Tue-Sat, call ahead

If you measure 'culture' by passed down traditions, rituals, celebrations and their

CLOSING THE CONGO SQUARE CIRCLE

Near the main entrance to Louis Armstrong Park is one of the most important spots, arguably, in the development of modern music: Congo Sq. Once known as Place de Negres, this area was once just outside the city's walls (Rampart St, as the name suggests, was the town limit). Under the French colonial law, slaves were allowed to gather here on Sundays. The period of rest became one of both celebration and preservation of West African rituals, which largely revolve around song and dance. Sundays became a way of letting off steam and channeling latent discontent, and it must have been, at the time, the largest celebration of traditional African culture in continental North America – slaves were forbidden from practicing traditional culture in the American colonies.

The practice was shut down when US settlers took over New Orleans, but it was alive long enough to imprint its musical traces into the city's cultural substrate. By the late 19th century, brass bands were blending African rhythms with classical music imported by European settlers and French-educated old New Orleanians. These bands played on a weekly basis in Congo Sq, and their sound eventually evolved, especially near the bordellos of nearby Storyville, into jazz – itself a foundation for the variations of pop music (R&B, rock 'n' roll, even hip-hop) the USA would give the world in the 20th century.

HBO'S NEW DAY FOR THE TREMÉ

A pretty convincing critical consensus agreed *The Wire* (2002–8), created by David Simon and shown on HBO, was one of the best shows on US TV during its run. A police procedural based in Baltimore, the show evolved into a sort of TV novel on the state of the American city and the nature of institutional rot. Now Simon has turned his attention to post-Katrina New Orleans with a new show, *Treme*, (yet to be released at the time of writing, but not far off) focusing on local musicians from the iconic title neighborhood.

The Wire was known as one of the most unapologetically gritty shows of its day. But it also brought a lot of cachet and brand to Baltimore, and was largely embraced by locals for its authentic portrayal of their city. By the same extant, New Orleanians who have worked with *Treme* (including Gentilly native and *Wire* veteran Wendell Pierce) say Simon is bringing the same level of attention to his portrayal of the Crescent City. An apparent sleeper star of the show, according to those behind the scenes, is local son and brass band leader Kermit Ruffin, famous for his shows at Vaughan's in the Bywater (see p183).

physical evidence (yeah, we took a couple of anthropology classes), this town may have the most distinctive local culture in the USA. This is the place to see how one facet of said customs – its African American side – is expressed in daily life.

The museum isn't terribly big – it's the former Blandin's Funeral Home, itself a converted house – but if you have any interest in Mardi Gras Indian suits, second lines and the activities of social aid and pleasure clubs (the local black community version of civic associations), you need to stop by. Particularly jarring are funeral T-shirts imprinted with the departed one's face, 'sunrise' (date of birth) and 'sunset' (date of death). Curator Silvester Francis is a collector and self-taught documentarian whose personal involvement in the community gives him access to a spectacular array of artifacts and archival footage. His guided tours are usually great, but sometimes they feel rushed, so be sure to ask lots of questions as he (or his wife) guides you from room to room.

NEW ORLEANS AFRICAN AMERICAN MUSEUM Map pp108–9

☎ 566-1136; www.noaam.info; 1418 Governor Nicholls St; adult/child/senior & student $5/2/3; ☽ 11am-4pm Wed-Sat

This small museum has no permanent displays, and its temporary exhibitions can feel hastily cobbled together. Still, it's an interesting spot for those interested in local African American history, if just by dint of its location: the Meilleur-Goldthwaite House, also known as the Tremé Villa. This pretty house was the site of the city's first brick yard and is an exemplar of the Creole architecture style, with an airy center and

low-slung but lushly attractive facade. In the back are restored shotgun houses and slave quarters that house supplemental exhibitions and office space.

MORTUARY CHAPEL Map pp108–9

☎ 525-1551; 411 N Rampart St; donations accepted; ☽ 7am-6pm

An unfounded fear of yellow-fever contagion led the city to forbid funerals for fever victims at the St Louis Cathedral. Built in 1826 near St Louis Cemetery No 1, the Mortuary Chapel offered hasty services for victims, as its bell tolled constantly during epidemics. In 1931 it was renamed Our Lady of Guadeloupe Church. Inside the chapel is a statue of St Jude, patron saint of impossible cases, and a curious statue of St Expedite, a saint who may have never existed (legend says his name comes from a box of saint statues being stamped with the order 'Expedite').

ST AUGUSTINE'S CHURCH Map pp108–9

☎ 525-5934; www.staugustinecatholicchurch -neworleans.org; 1210 Governor Nicholls St

In a town that suffered so many casualties from Hurricane Katrina, it's nice to stumble across a success story every now and then. St Aug's, the second-oldest African American Catholic church in the country, is a place where slaves once prayed prior to the Emancipation Proclamation. Its continued existence is thanks to the work of countless community activists, parishioners, grants from the National Trust for Historic Preservation and even a 2007 documentary *(Shake the Devil Off)*. Designed by JNB DePouilly, who later rebuilt St Louis Cathedral, St Augustine's opened in 1841. It was where Creoles, émigrés from St Domingue and free persons of color could worship shoulder to shoulder, but separate pews were also designated for slaves.

The future of the church remains in question, so try to pay a visit; more tourists increase the chance of ensuring this historic landmark stay with us. Call ahead to see if it's possible to arrange a visit. One of St Augustine's stained-glass panels depicts the Sisters of the Holy Family, the order of black Creole nuns founded in 1842 by Henriette Delille and Archbishop Antoine Blanc. There is also a Tomb of the Unknown Slave fashioned to resemble a grim cross assembled from chain links.

DRIVING TOURS

DO YOU KNOW WHAT IT MEANS TO REBUILD NEW ORLEANS?

If you've stuck to the neighborhoods we've described in this book, you may leave New Orleans thinking the city has entirely recovered from Hurricane Katrina. It hasn't. There are still huge swathes of town that remain devastated, and the population hovers around 80% of pre-hurricane levels. We hope this driving tour of the damaged heart of New Orleans allows you to bear witness and contribute to the resurrection of one of the greatest cities in the world. While exploring, please do not take pictures of people without asking their permission, and try to get out of your car so you can interact with the real communities that are still struggling to live a normal life years after the fact. We list several aide and volunteer organizations in this tour; contact details for all of them are included at the end. See also the Rebuilding a City chapter. Grab a New Orleans street map, available in any gas station, for this tour.

1 Mid-City Yacht Club We start at the Mid-City Yacht Club, (p189), a pleasant neighborhood pub on a quiet residential lane. The bar, which is nowhere near a body of water, gets its name partly from the fact its owner sailed around rescuing local residents when this part of Mid-City flooded after the storm. The interior wood on the ceiling and windows comes from debris found scattered about after the hurricane. As food stops are few and far between on this tour, you may want to order some sandwiches to go before heading out.

2 Lakeview Turn right onto Bernadotte St, then left onto Canal St and head north through St Patrick, Firemen and Greenwood Cemeteries. Continue north along Canal Blvd. You're now in Lakeview, a middle- to upper-middle-class, largely white neighborhood that

was badly flooded after Katrina. While most residents were able to flee the city, there were dead bodies found in attics here. Detour off Canal onto a side street like Lane St or Filmore Ave to see the current state of the neighborhood: some homes are rebuilt, some remain gutted and there's lots of new construction as many people here found it economical to scrap their old homes completely.

3 Metairie Canal Breach Head west on Robert E Lee Blvd until it becomes the Hammond Hwy, then left (south) onto Bellaire Dr or west over the Hammond Highway Bridge. This bridge crosses the Metaire Canal; Bellaire Dr and Stafford Pl was where the canal levee breached, flooding neighborhoods like Lakeview and West End.

4 Lakeshore & Lake Vista Double back and go east on Robert E Lee Blvd; alternatively you can drive along Lake Pontchartrain by using Lakeshore Dr. Either road takes you through Lakeshore and Lake Vista, one of the wealthiest residential neighborhoods in the city. The slightly increased elevation of the land here and the strength of the lakeside levees spared these beautiful homes from destruction. At 1200 Robert E Lee Blvd, just before you cross over Bayou St John, you'll spot the domed Greek Orthodox Cathedral of the Holy Trinity, one of the oldest Greek Orthodox churches in the country.

5 London Canal Breach You are now east of City Park in Gentilly; west of this area is predominately white, while these neighborhoods are mixed and African American. At Robert E Lee Blvd and the London Canal you may be able to see the discolored portion of the levee wall that marks the site of the London Canal breach, which flooded out much of the surrounding neighborhood. Prior to Hurricane Katrina, these areas had some of the highest home-ownership ratings in the city. Barnes & Noble–founder Leonard Riggio's Project Home Again is working to repopulate this once-thriving area. The project has built new homes in the neighborhood; Gentilly homeowners who lost their houses can trade in their old deeds in for a Project Home Again property.

6 Milneburg Continue east on Robert E Lee Blvd, then right (south) on Elysian Fields Ave and left (east) on Prentiss Ave. You're

DRIVE FACTS

Start Mid-City Yacht Club
End Duany Houses
Distance 20 miles
Duration Half-day
Fuel Stop End with a meal at The Joint

now in Milneburg, once one of New Orleans most vibrant middle-class African American neighborhoods; as of 2009, four years after the Storm, it looks like Fallujah on a bad day. Lots are abandoned, homes lie in rubble and the streets are like a giant pot hole (particularly if you head down side streets). While the majority of media attention on the storm focused on damage in the low-income Lower Ninth Ward, this area was just as devastated.

7 Gentilly Terrace Go east on Prentiss Ave, then right (south) onto Franklin Ave. The Milne Boys Home at 5420 Franklin Avenue, a community center for wayward boys, was where Louis Armstrong learned to play the trumpet. Continue south into Gentilly Terrace, another hard-hit area that is in the process of rebuilding.

8 KKProjects Take Franklin Ave south for about 5 miles until you reach N Villere St; hang a right (west). See the house modeled like a big bank vault and the house roofed with sod and turf? This is the neighbor to KKProjects (p82), a collection of studios, galleries and arts projects that works on community projects in the surrounding low-income St Roch and St Claude neighborhoods.

9 Musicians' Village Go a block north, than right (east) on N Robertson St for a mile. Bang a left (north) onto Bartholomew St until you hit N Roman St. You're in the Upper Ninth Ward, in the area known as Musicians' Village (p82). The brightly colored houses here have been built for New Orleans musicians who previously lived in inadequate housing. The homes are not handouts; residents of the village pay interest-free mortgages, must contribute 350 hours of home building 'sweat equity' and have to maintain clean credit and debt records.

10 The Lower Ninth Head east on N Roman and south on Poland Ave, then left (east) onto N Robertson across the Industrial Canal into the Lower Ninth Ward. This was the poster neighborhood for Hurricane Katrina devastation. If you have an image of a flooded New Orleans from 2005 in your mind, it probably corresponds to the Lower Ninth. Go right (south) on Tennessee St, then turn around on N Robertson back towards the levee. Since rebuilt, many residents say the wall was previously barely taller than a grown man. A discolored area marks the spot where the barge ING 4727 was swept into, and eventually through, the levee.

11 Common Ground & Make It Right Head north along the closest road to the levee (Jourdan Ave), then right at N Roman St. At the corner of Roma and Deslonde (1800 Deslonde) is the headquarters for Common Ground Relief, a community-rebuilding volunteer organization that provides a free legal clinic, job training and works on wetland reclamation projects in this area. Just across from the headquarters is one of the ubermodern houses built by Brad Pitt's Make It Right foundation. The homes are green, affordable and sustainable, and many are being occupied by returning residents. But they have also been criticized as too modern for this neighborhood, their vaguely cubist design clashing with the traditional architecture. That said, the folks who live in the Make It Right houses

RELIEF ORGANIZATIONS

Bush-Clinton Katrina Fund (www.bushclintonkatrinafund.org)

Common Ground Relief (☎ 304-9097; www.commongroundrelief.org; 1800 Deslonde St)

Make It Right (www.makeitrightnola.org)

New Orleans Area Habitat for Humanity (☎ 861-4121; www.habitat-nola.org; 7100 St Charles Ave)

Parkway Partners (☎ 620-2224; www.parkwayparntersnola.org; 1137 Barronne St) Focuses on green space, community gardens and tree planting.

Project Home Again (www.projecthomeagain.net; PO Box 851008, New Orleans, LA 70185)

Websites www.hurricanekatrinarelief.com and www.katrinarelief.org are good information clearinghouses on relief efforts. Check out www.nola.com/katrina/graphics/flashflood.swf for an excellent graphic on the evolution of the flood in the city, and see p62 for more on how you, as a visitor, can contribute to the rebuilding effort.

seem to love them, and Pitt's presence (he often makes public appearances at Make It Right houses when he's in town) brings a lot of media attention to the area.

12 Wetland restoration Head north on Deslonde. 'Devastated' doesn't really sum up this part of the Lower Ninth; at the time of writing it was simply wilderness. Abandoned lots can be claimed by the city, but if locals maintain lots through yard work and cleaning up, they will gain ownership of the land. Many streets remained unsigned, or signed by homemade planks. Take Deslonde to its end, then go right (east) on Florida Ave to the unfortunately named Flood St. By the water, you'll notice a platform that looks out over a wetland restoration project maintained by Common Ground. The bald cypress poking through the water aren't just pretty; they provide a natural line of defense against future flooding and erosion.

13 The House of Dance and Feathers Take Caffin Ave right (south) for a little less than a mile, then hang a left (east) onto Claiborne Ave and a right (south) onto Tupelo St. Here, further back from the water, houses are occupied and life seems fairly back to normal. At Tupelo and Urquhart St visit the House of Dance and Feathers (p83), a community museum

that focuses on the culture of the Lower Ninth Ward, but make sure you call ahead.

14 The Joint Take Tupelo south to St Claude Ave, then head right (west). At St Claude and Caffin you'll see the Sankofa Marketplace, open every second Saturday from 10am to 3pm, where you can buy fresh local produce and listen to live music – it's a great day out. If it's not a market day, continue west on St Claude over Industrial Canal. You're now back in the Bywater. Assuming you're hungry, hang a left (south) onto Poland Ave and grab some barbeque at the Joint (p158).

15 Duany houses Before you go home, head south on Poland and right (west) on Chartres St, then right (north) on Gallier St to the intersection of Gallier and Dauphine St. See those new homes? No? Exactly: the four double shotgun shacks here, designed as affordable post-Katrina housing by Miami architect Andres Duany, were modeled to perfectly fit into the surrounding neighborhood. They retain the usual characteristics of a shotgun house, with one exception: instead of sharing a double central wall, the houses are linked by a conjoined 'L' that facilitates cooling breezes. These homes aren't as grand as the Brad Pitt houses but seem a much better match for the surrounding neighborhood.

NEIGHBORHOODS DRIVING TOURS

SHOPPING

top picks

- Dirty Coast (p132)
- Meyer the Hatter (p128)
- Retroactive (p133)
- Faubourg Marigny Book Store (p128)
- Maskarade (p124)
- New Orleans Music Exchange (p131)
- F&F Botanica (p133)
- Green Project (p128)
- Trashy Diva (p130)
- Yvonne La Fleur (p132)

SHOPPING

It's not obvious at first, but there is more to shopping in New Orleans than terrible tackiness. A recent drive among city marketing types to promote 'shop local' campaigns, plus a wariness of the weather and a large number of strictly zoned historical districts, has kept the city relatively free of chain-store blah. We want to stress that you contribute to the rebirth of a great city when you opt to patronize local businesses. Check out www.staylocal.org for details.

On to the fun! Yes, there's more than awful souvenirs, but there are some really *great* awful souvenirs, especially T-shirts. Other cheesy favorites include Mardi Gras masks, stripper outfits, voodoo paraphernalia, French Quarter–style street signs and, of course, beads, beads, beads. Besides the unintentional kitsch is quite a bit of the intentional, of the light-up religious icons and hurricane memorabilia school. This is a city that has a healthy sense of humor.

Music makes New Orleans go round, and this is a fantastic town for buying original CDs, vinyl and the like, plus some very high-quality instruments. A large literary scene has resulted in a good number of independent bookshops, some of which have evolved into unofficial anchors of their respective communities. And visual artists will find no shortage of stores selling supplies for their work.

Antiques are a big business here, and sometimes it feels like you can't walk past parts of Royal, Chartres, lower Decatur and Magazine Sts without tripping on some backyard, warehouse or studio space exhibiting beautiful examples of found furniture. Pieces tend to be relatively cheap compared to the antique action in similarly sized metropolises, and the genre goes beyond chairs and armoires to lots of old maps, watches, prints, books and similar doodads.

If you've ever been to a costume party in America, you likely have this town and its long tradition of 'masking' to thank for the privilege. Beyond the mask and wig shops in the Quarter are some very fine costume and vintage shops in areas such as Uptown, Riverbend and the Lower Garden District. The city's costume shops really get going as Mardi Gras approaches, although Halloween is also, as you might guess, huge.

Probably the most distinct face of the local shopping scene is the innumerable boutiques and vintage shops that are sprouting up all along Magazine St and in the vicinity of Riverbend. The post-Katrina arrival of artists, students and save-the-city types added a lot of funky sprinkles to an already pretty hip fashion sundae. A distinctive New Orleans style that is starting to evolve takes the preppy formality of a Southern garden party and wilds it up a little. Examples include linen shirts and light-colored pants for guys with smart straw fedoras and cloth flat caps; flowing but daring summer frocks for girls set off by 1920s- and '40s-style earrings and bangles; and the use of lots of little 'organic' elements in local jewelry design (feathers, flowers and the like). This isn't a city that has a lot of time for the cold, modern school of design or fashion. Locals have opted to live in a place that drips history, and when it comes to personal style, be it interior decor or exterior fashion, they like to reference older eras set off with their own individualistic accents.

Common shop hours are Tuesday through Saturday from 10am or 11am until 5pm or 6pm. Independently owned shops can keep odd hours. For instance, a shopkeeper might not feel any compunction about arriving an hour late to open. Some might even stay closed on the odd day or two each week. Many bookstores are open daily, and some keep later hours in the evening.

FRENCH QUARTER

The Quarter is lined with great strips that are well suited to window shopping. Many regard Royal St as the 'Main St' of the French Quarter. Portions of it are closed to automobiles during daytime shopping hours. Between Iberville and St Ann Sts are a number of distinguished galleries and shops selling antiques and collectibles, housed in buildings that have been prominent commercial addresses since before the Louisiana Purchase.

In shopping terms, Chartres St is Royal's equal. It's lined with small interesting stores dealing in antiques, art and expensive curiosities. Recently clothing boutiques and other small shops have extended the Royal St shopping area into the Lower Quarter to St Philip St. Lower Decatur St, below Governor Nicholls St, is lined with interesting antique and junk shops, boutiques and some good bars. Upper Decatur is where all the T-shirts and cheap tourist bric-a-brac are sold.

ARCADIAN BOOKS & ART PRINTS

Map pp70–1   Antiquarian & Used Books

☎ 523-4138; 714 Orleans Ave; ☷ 10am-6pm

Arcadian is a small, crowded little shop that's filled with Southern literature and history, as well as many volumes in French. Owner Russell Desmond speaks French fluently and is a wonderful, if cynical, ambassador for New Orleans.

BECKHAM'S BOOKSTORE

Map pp70–1   Antiquarian & Used Books

☎ 522-9875; 228 Decatur St; ☷ 10am-5pm

Across the street from House of Blues, this large, neatly organized store has two floors of used books, and also sells used classical LPs. It's definitely worth a browse.

LIBRAIRIE BOOKS

Map pp70–1   Antiquarian & Used Books

☎ 525-4837; 823 Chartres St; ☷ 10am-6pm

A jam-packed little shop of delights for the avid bookworm and collector. The emphasis here is squarely on very old (and sometimes dusty) volumes. You might dig up an ancient copy of Herbert Asbury's *The French Quarter,* or other tales of old New Orleans. And there are scholarly texts and ample material of more general interest as well.

CENTURIES Map pp70–1   Antique Prints & Maps

☎ 568-9491; 408 Chartres St; ☷ 10am-6pm

OK, it's a little on the stodgy side, with its selection of 19th-century lithographs and old maps. But flip through the inventory (all of it well organized by theme, date or locale) and you just might find yourself slowing down to look things over. Particularly interesting are the Civil War and Black History sections. If you're at all interested in this stuff, you're sure to be absorbed by the ancient maps here, beautifully drawn with outdated demarcations and occasional glaring cartographic errors – why yes, Asia is apparently half the size of Europe.

COLLECTIBLE ANTIQUES

Map pp70–1   Antiques

☎ 566-0399; 1232 Decatur St; ☷ 10:30am-6pm

You never know what you'll find between the piles of old furniture stacked along the walls of this large, garagelike emporium of tantalizing junk. Perhaps you collect old photographic portraits from long defunct studios. You might find everything you need for that tiki bar you're slapping together in the basement. Or maybe you're just after an art-deco martini shaker, an old dented trumpet, a Pewee Herman doll, a heavy army-surplus coat or some silverware. Remarkably, the entire assemblage is not just a heaping mess. Every piece is lovingly contextualized to add interest. Browsing through the wares here is somewhat like a visit to a grab-bag museum.

LUCULLUS Map pp70–1   Antiques

☎ 528-9620; 610 Chartres St; ☷ 9:30am-5pm Mon-Sat

Peeking in the window, you'll see a battery of ancient copper pots that appear to have generations of dents tinkered out of their bottoms. Owner Patrick Dunne is an advocate of using, not merely collecting, culinary antiques. Follow his advice and add more ritual and elegance to your life with an antique café au lait bowl or an absinthe spoon for creating your evening cocktails. Don't just pop open your champagne and pour it; chill it in a silver bucket. You get the idea. A visit to this shop can turn an ordinary dinner party into the classiest, most exotic to-do.

MOSS ANTIQUES Map pp70–1   Antiques

☎ 522-3981; www.mossantiques.com; 411 Royal St; ☷ 10am-5pm, closed Sun

Watch your head when you enter this gallery of low-hanging chandeliers. Oof! Too late! Moss is a Royal St institution in the local antiques trade. Only the finest quality antiques and *objets d'art* are sold here. You'll find the perfect thing for your Garden District mansion. Or perhaps you can take home the busted chandelier they made you pay for.

MS RAU ANTIQUES Map pp70–1   Antiques

☎ 523-5660; www.rauantiques.com; 630 Royal St; ☷ 9am-5pm Mon-Sat

With a massive 30,000-sq-ft showroom (you'd never know it passing by on Royal St), and after nearly a century of doing business, MS Rau ranks among New Orleans' most venerated dealers of antiques. It's a bit serious – these are the sort of frosty antiques that require their own insurance

TAXES & REFUNDS

There is a 9% sales tax on goods sold in the city. International visitors can get refunds on sales taxes from Louisiana Tax Free Shopping (LTFS) stores; look for the sign in the window. You must show participating merchants a valid passport (Canadians may show a birth certificate or driver's license) to get a tax-refund voucher. To get your refund at the refund center in the Louis Armstrong New Orleans International Airport present the vouchers, sales receipts, your passport and round-trip international ticket indicating less than 90 days' stay. Refunds under $500 are made in cash; otherwise, a check will be mailed to your home.

Check out www.louisianataxfree.com for a directory of businesses participating in the LTFS program.

policies – but it's a family business and the professional salespeople are quite approachable. You'll find fine art, jewelry, music boxes, clocks, Judaica, 19th-century globes – all in impeccable condition and unbelievably expensive. Nothing's keeping you from just having a look, though.

JAMES H COHEN & SONS
Map pp70–1   Antiques & Memorabilia
☎ 522-3305; www.cohenantiques.com; 437 Royal St; ☽ 10am-6pm

From the sidewalk windows, you might be inclined to pass this one by if you're not interested in guns. Cohen & Sons does sell antique guns for people who like to play cowboys and Indians with authentic hardware. The choice of firearms here includes some remarkable specimens of flintlocks, colts, Winchester '73s and even a French musket or two. Beyond weaponry, the place is a repository of relics and historical curiosities, with many fascinating artifacts on view in glass display cases. Duck in for a look at the ancient coins from Celtic and Hellenic cultures worn smooth by human hands millennia ago. Or disturbing slave documents and notarized bills of sale for the transfer of human chattel. The store's unique selection of campaign buttons for US presidential elections spans back to the 1900 contest.

DAVID'S Map pp70–1   Antiques & Used Goods
☎ 568-1197; 1319 Decatur St; ☽ 9am-7pm Mon-Sat, noon-6pm Sun

Squeezed in among the numerous antique stores and clothing boutiques along lower

Decatur is this small rummage shop filled with found objects, collectibles, funky lamps, swanky duds, bar accoutrements, jewelry and other odds and ends.

LE GARAGE Map pp70–1   Antiques & Used Goods
☎ 522-6639; 1234 Decatur St; ☽ 10am-6pm

Got to admit, we liked the name better when it was simply 'The Garage.' But why quibble over a little ironic Frenchness? The place is still a garage loaded with interesting stuff to paw through. Things for sale here include odd items of clothing, hats, army surplus, curtains, yellowed pool balls, tattered Mardi Gras costumes from yesteryear, knitted Coors-can caps, furniture, and oodles of objects d'art to ogle or even buy. Treasures galore, we tell you. Dive in.

QUARTER PAST TIME
Map pp70–1   Antiques & Used Goods
☎ 410-0010; 606 Chartres St; ☽ 6am-6pm, closed Wed

This quiet little shop carries a selection of beautiful timekeepers. We didn't see any grandfather clocks, but they seemed to have everything else covered – wristwatches, pocket watches, wall-mounted clocks etc. Also, some nifty old radios of Jack Benny and the Brooklyn Dodgers vintage. You can buy, sell or trade here, and if your watch ain't winding properly they'll fix it for you.

PHOTO WORKS
Map pp70–1   Art & Photography
☎ 593-9090; www.photoworksneworleans.com; 839 Chartres St; ☽ 10am-5pm Thu-Mon

This is a polished showroom for the accomplished photographer Louis Sahuc (sigh-ook), who has been shooting New Orleans for years and years. Sahuc's beautiful prints capture timeless images of the city. They are vantages upon which even Hurricane Katrina failed to impose change.

STONE & PRESS
Map pp70–1   Art & Photography
☎ 561-8555; www.stoneandpress.com; 238 Chartres St; ☽ 9am-5pm

A cool shop for enthusiasts of fine-art mezzotints, lithographs, wood engravings and etchings by modern American artists. Mezzotints are the emphasis here, and flipping through the huge collection (filed away in bins like records in a record store) is a good way to gain an appreciation for a largely underappreciated art form. Most of the artists featured are contemporary, and some are clearly pushing the envelope, exploring new possibilities and techniques. A startling range in texture, tone and definition is achieved in black and white and sepia hues. All works are original and printed in limited editions.

SANTA'S QUARTERS
Map pp70–1   Christmas Decorations
☎ 581-5820; www.santasquarters.com; 1025 Decatur St; ☽ 10am-6pm
This place keeps the Christmas spirit alive year-round, with ornaments, lights and every festive trinket imaginable. Now, you have to wonder about people who might be tempted to purchase Christmas ornaments on one of August's most sultry days. And what about the zero-receipt days this shop surely endures for much of the year. So is it a front for something more sinister? Or is it simply a vanity concern for St Nick? And, if so, why is it New Orleans? Or is the fat man indulging a local filly he's keeping on the side? Anyway, on with your shopping…

TABASCO COUNTRY STORE
Map pp70–1   Condiments & Gifts
☎ 539-7900; www.neworleanscajunstore.com; 537 St Ann St; ☽ 10am-6pm
Bet you thought Tabasco was either red or green and always hot, right? Guess again: there's Tabasco ketchup, mayonnaise, cookbooks, plenty of souvenirs and a fairly incredible range of hot (and not so hot) sauces. Don't you need a 500-count pack of mini-Tabasco bottles?

JAVA HOUSE IMPORTS Map pp70–1   Gifts
☎ 581-1288; www.javahouseimports.com; 913 Decatur St; ☽ 10am-7pm, from 9am Fri & Sun, 9am-8pm Sat
There are, indeed, cool imports and statues from Java here, as well as Balinese and West African masks, Indian-style Buddhas, lacquer-work from Lombok and all the other items that prove what a savvy traveler you are.

SAVE NOLA Map pp70–1   Gifts
☎ 558-1951; www.savenolanow.com; 600 Decatur St; ☽ 10am-6pm
The Save NOLA store, located inside the Jackson Brewery, sells handbags, souvenirs,

shirts and such; proceeds go towards the group of the same name and are invested in community rebuilding projects like Habitat for Humanity. The sort of store where your need for retail therapy is a good deed.

BOUTIQUE DU VAMPYRE
Map pp70–1   Gothic Gifts
☎ 561-8267; www.feelthebite.com; 712 Orleans Ave; ☽ 10am-7pm
Dark candles and gothic gargoyles look down on you, promising a curse of blood and terror and the undead on those who only browse but do not buy! Mwa ha ha! Or…not. All kinds of vampire- and voodoo-themed gifts stock this cool, dungeon-esque store; our favorite item was a deck of tarot cards with truly surreal, somewhat disturbing artwork.

CENTRAL GROCERY Map pp70–1   Groceries
☎ 523-1620; 923 Decatur St; ☽ 9am-5pm Tue-Sat
A hyper-busy store offering many of the cooking ingredients typically found in Louisiana kitchens: Zatarain's Creole Seasoning and Crab Boil, McIlhenny Tabasco or Crystal hot sauce, chicory coffee and filé for making gumbo. While you're here, grab a jar of Central Gro Co's famous olive relish, the not-so-secret weapon of the muffuletta sandwich.

FLORA SAVAGE Map pp70–1   Florist
☎ 581-4728; www.florasavage.com; 1301 Royal St; ☽ 11am-6pm Mon-Sat
In town for an anniversary? Met someone you want to impress in a hurry? Take care of your floral needs here. You'll soon be festooning your hotel room with romantic aromas and colors, and your sweetheart will be swooning with romantic feelings for you.

top picks

SHOPPING STRIPS

- Magazine St (p130)
- S Carrollton Ave, riverside (p131)
- Royal St (p120)
- Chartres St (p120)
- Decatur St (p120)

FRENCH MARKET

Truth be told, from a shopping standpoint, the French Market is a bit of a disappointment. It no longer plays a vital role in French Quarter life, and locals don't rely on it as they once did for their foodstuffs. For the most part, it now caters to tourism. Still, it's an atmospheric old market with a range of shops and vendors, and is a hive of activity most days, but especially on weekends.

The market is split into two sections – the Farmer's Market and Flea Market – and neither is particularly special. In a pinch, the French Market will supply the visitor with cheap gimcracks to give away back home, but for quality shopping you'll have to look elsewhere.

Shoppers can pick up some unique southern Louisiana products at the Flea Market any day of the week. There is a motley assortment of T-shirt and sunglasses vendors, as well as African art (mass-produced), inexpensive silver jewelry, chintzy Mardi Gras masks and dolls, music tapes and CDs of dubious origin, and enough preserved alligator heads to populate a polyurethane swamp. Most prices at the Flea Market are negotiable. Officially the Flea Market is open 24 hours, but most vendors keep their own hours and are open from 9am to 5pm.

Only a vestige of former market activity remains at the Farmer's Market, where large freezer trucks have replaced the small trucks of farmers. Still, you might occasionally see an old pickup truck on sagging springs heading from the market to sell a load of fresh produce on an Uptown street.

Merchants in the Farmer's Market offer fresh fruit and vegetables, such as green beans, mangos, papayas, bananas, plantains, peaches, strawberries, watermelons, apples and pecans, as well as cold drinks. In addition, there are lots of kitchen supplies, spices and condiments (including a large selection of hot sauces), garlic and chili strings, and cookbooks for the tourist trade. The Farmer's Market opens up early every morning and gradually peters out in the afternoon.

FLEUR DE PARIS Map pp70–1   Haute Couture
☎ 525-1899; www.fleurdeparis.net; 712 Royal St; ☽ 10am-6pm, from noon Sun

Some stores in New Orleans exist to indulge the most eccentric and particular interests a person can possibly have. This boutique in the Labranche Building is a case in point. The woman who wants to appear ready for the 1904 St Louis World's Fair need look no further. The custom hats are bouquets of plumage, fur felt, lace and, here and there, a snatch of black netting. The evening gowns are devastating showstoppers guaranteed to make a dapper Dan in spats swoon. The store's website suggests wearing one to the Academy Awards. Failing that, you'll want to promenade around a city park or at least have your picture taken.

MASKARADE Map pp70–1   Masks & Gifts
☎ 568-1018; www.themaskstore.com; 630 St Ann St; ☽ 10am-7pm

This shop deals in high-quality masks by local and international artisans, and the selection includes everything from classic *commedia dell'arte* masks from Venice to more way-out designs for your wigged-out end-of–Mardi Gras state of mind. If your nose is too small, many of the selections here can correct the problem. Maskarade also sells beguiling handcrafted gifts as

well. How about a little demon paperweight for your office mate?

SWORD & PEN
Map pp70–1   Military Memorabilia
☎ 523-7741; 528 Royal St; ☽ 10am-5:30pm

Military memorabilia nerds, rejoice. There are armies of miniature soldiers here marching past Confederate kitsch, WWII posters, recruitment buttons from every conflict of the 20th century (apparently) and anything else that could fulfill a little kid, or grown travel writer's, most lurid toysoldier fantasies.

LOUISIANA MUSIC FACTORY
Map pp70–1   Music
☎ 586-1094; www.louisianamusicfactory.com; 210 Decatur St; ☽ 10am-7pm Mon-Sat, noon-6pm Sun

Here's your first stop if you're looking for music. The selection of new and used CDs delves deep into New Orleans and Louisiana musical culture, with recordings from the 1900s to this week. Get your jazz here, from King Oliver and Jellyroll to the Marsalises and Los Hombres Calientes. Get your R&B from Fess and K-Doe to the Meters and John Boutté. Get your Cajun and zydeco here, from the Hackberry Ramblers and Boozoo to Clifton Chenier and Buckwheat. Brass bands? Get 'em here. The listening stations are a great way to familiarize yourself with local artists. There's also a nice selection of cool T-shirts that you won't find elsewhere, along with books, DVDs and posters. Live performances on Saturday afternoons rock the joint.

HOVÉ PARFUMEUR Map pp70–1 Perfume

☎ 525-7827; www.hoveparfumeur.com; 824 Royal St; ☷ 10am-5pm Mon-Sat

Grassy vetiver, bittersweet orange blossoms, spicy ginger – New Orleans' exotic flora has graciously lent its scents to Hové's house-made perfumes for over 70 years. A brief sniffing visit will leave your head swirling with images of the Vieux Carré's magnificent past. Thus intoxicated, you can ask staff to custom mix a fragrance for you.

LEAH'S PRALINES Map pp70–1 Pralines

☎ 523-5662; www.leahspralines.com; 714 St Louis St; ☷ noon-6pm Mon-Sat

In the heart of the French Quarter, this old candy shop specializes in that special Creole confection, the praline. Here you'll get some of the very best in town. If you've already tried pralines elsewhere and decided that you don't care for them, we suggest you try some at Leah's before making up your mind completely. The creamy pralines are deadly. Try one with rum in it if you don't mind a nice extra zing. Grab a box and have it expressed to your friends back home. Throw in some of the pecan brittle or rum pecans while you're at it.

BOURBON STRIP TEASE
Map pp70–1 Risqué Clothing

☎ 581-6633; 205 Bourbon St; ☷ 10am-8pm

If you've just asked to be excused while you 'slip into something more comfortable,' but haven't actually packed anything 'comfortable,' sneak down to this shop. It has all manner of dainty things to put on before you take 'em off, starting with lacy lingerie and progressing to edible undies and sleazy toys. *Very* comfortable stuff.

CANAL PLACE Map pp70–1 Shopping Mall

☎ 522-9200; www.theshopsatcanalplace.com; 333 Canal St; ☷ 10am-7pm Mon-Sat, noon-6pm Sun; Ⓟ

A standard-issue shopping mall right at the edge of the French Quarter? That's right,

but as it's just below the towering Wyndham New Orleans Hotel you'd hardly notice it if you weren't looking for it. This is where you'll want to go if your shoe suddenly implodes or if your only suit has to be shipped off to the cleaners after a gin-fizz mishap. The upscale mall is anchored by a Saks Fifth Ave store; supporting roles are played by Kenneth Cole, Ann Taylor, Laura Ashley, Brooks Brothers and Banana Republic. A multiplex cinema (p197) and the Southern Repertory Theater (p197) are on the 3rd floor. The mall parking lot is convenient and has reasonable rates.

JACKSON BREWERY
Map pp70–1 Shopping Mall

☎ 566-7245; www.jacksonbrewery.com; 600 Decatur St; ☷ 10am-7pm; Ⓟ

This site really was a brewery once but, despite its proximity to boozy Bourbon St, the company failed, and the old brick structure was converted into a shopping mall. Jax has dozens of shops and eateries, most of them singing siren songs to unwary tourists. Proceed with caution or your next credit card statement will include charges for such items as Cajun golf clothing (?!), novelty ties, old-time photographic portraits and the like. However, if you're looking for a crawfish T-shirt for your cool niece or a new pair of sunglasses, or are just in need of a bathroom break, come on by. There's an ATM on the sidewalk.

top picks

PLACES FOR SOUVENIRS

- Simon of New Orleans (p196) A hand-painted sign or some Zulu coconuts.
- Centuries (p121) A 19th-century lithograph.
- Maskarade (opposite) Carnival masks.
- Electric Ladyland (p128) Tattoos.
- Louisiana Music Factory (opposite) Local music.
- Zombie's House of Voodoo (p126) Plaster-of-Paris bust of Louis Armstrong.
- Faulkner House Bookstore (p126) *The Sound and the Fury*.
- Meyer the Hatter (p128) Fedora.
- Big Fisherman Seafood (p131) Trash bag full of crawfish.
- Trashy Diva (p130) Bustier.

FAULKNER HOUSE BOOKSTORE

Map pp70–1   Specialty Books

☎ 524-2940; www.faulknerhousebooks.net; 624 Pirate's Alley; ⏰ 10am-5:30pm

Like many authors, William Faulkner did a New Orleans stint, briefly renting an apartment in a town house on Pirate's Alley in 1925. While living in the city he described as a 'courtesan, not old and yet no longer young,' Faulkner worked for the *Times-Picayune,* contributed to literary magazine *Double Dealer* and consorted with local literati. Now a business and a bona-fide literary attraction, Faulkner House is an essential stop for any book lover. It's a pleasant space, with beautifully crafted shelves packed floor to ceiling, lending the dignified atmosphere of a private library. It's not a large store – if there are more than five or six customers at a time, it starts to feel crowded – but it offers a commendable mix of new titles and first editions. The selection of books by local and Southern authors is particularly strong, and naturally William Faulkner is a staple. The shop is something of a literary hub, and local authors (Richard Ford, Andrei Codrescu etc) regularly stop by.

HUMIDITY SKATE STORE

Map pp70–1   Sporting Goods

☎ 529-6822; www.humidityskatestores.com; 515 Dumaine St; ⏰ 11am-7pm

Graffiti chic, Vans shoes, Element, Darkstar and Organika decks, grip tape, Krux trucks and Zero wheels – if any of that made sense to you, make your way up to Dumaine St. If not, you may want to avoid this store.

SOUTHERN CANDY MAKERS

Map pp70–1   Sweets

☎ 523-5544; www.southerncandymakers.com; 334 Decatur St; ⏰ 10am-7pm

Sweet-smelling confections with a Southern accent are created in this neat little

shop. A visit is guaranteed to put a big ol' Dolly Parton smile on your face. The toffee is divine and the pralines are to die for. The shop does special candies for every holiday (fat Santas for Christmas, fat bunnies for Easter, chocolate hearts for Valentines) and you can have something sent off to loved ones around the country.

MARY JANE'S EMPORIUM

Map pp70–1   Tobacco & Pipes

☎ 525-8004; www.maryjanesemporium.com; 1229 Decatur St; ⏰ 11am-7pm Sun-Thu, 10am-10pm Fri & Sat

By 'Mary Jane,' they're not referring to shoes. This is an essential stop for smokers of legal tobacco products, including finer brands of cigarettes not sold at your basic corner store. Also, a variety of apparatus for the smoking of unsanctioned herbal products and such is sold here. All right, it's basically a head shop.

STARLING BOOKS & CRAFTS

Map pp70–1   Voodoo & Occult

☎ 595-6777; www.starlingmagickal.org; 1022 Royal St; ⏰ noon-7pm

This place is about the serious side of the occult, lest we've got the idea the whole thing's been cooked up for our own amusement. This scholarly shop sells books concerning voodoo and the occult, and also has a few shelves of potions and voodoo dolls. The staff are knowledgeable, so fire away with questions if you're genuinely interested. Otherwise, walk on by.

ZOMBIE'S HOUSE OF VOODOO

Map pp70–1   Voodoo & Occult

☎ 486-6366; 725 St Peter St; ⏰ 10am-6pm

Just around the corner from Bourbon St, this voodoo shop gamely makes its pitch amid the drunken hordes. Step inside and it's plain to see this is one religious store that's not bent on snuffing out the party. There's an altar at the entry with a serious note not to disrespectfully take photos, and then there is the truly splendiferous display of plaster-of-Paris statuettes imported from the Santeria realms of Brazil. All of them are fun and charming, and many are simply beautiful. Works of folk art are mass produced. They laugh at death, celebrate sex and honor great figures in history. Some make great gifts to take back home – such as the smiling bust of Louis Armstrong. You can

---

ESSENTIAL NEW ORLEANS FASHION ITEMS

- 'Defend New Orleans' T-shirt
- Unique vintage jewelry
- Seersucker suit or shorts for guys
- Sun dress for girls
- 'y@t' sticker or similar 'Only in New Orleans' in-joke accessory

THE GIFT OF FOOD

Customs won't always allow you to take sacks of groceries back home with you, but New Orleans does offer the gourmand many tempting and unique edibles that make nice gifts for the loved ones back home. (By the way, local parlance for grocery shopping is 'making groceries.')

Pralines are a local confection that never really caught on anywhere else in the country. Freshness really counts, though, so buy a box on your last day in New Orleans and don't wait a week to unpack. Good places to buy pralines are Leah's Pralines (p125) and Southern Candy Makers (opposite).

Crawfish are another delicacy underappreciated everywhere outside of Louisiana. Though the tasty little crustaceans thrive throughout the US, they're often hard to find. You can buy them at Big Fisherman Seafood (p131) and have them shipped back home. (Out-of-state crawfish fiends do this all the time.)

Louisiana hot sauces – Tabasco, Crystal etc – are available in grocery stores throughout America, but judging by the great number of souvenir shops selling these products there must be places in the world where you can't get this stuff. If you live in such a place, grab a few bottles at the French Market (p124) and your condiments shelf will have a new zing.

also choose your pick of potions and browse the selection of books on the occult. If you don't find what you're looking for here, try Marie Laveau's House of Voodoo (Map pp70–1; ☎ 581-3751; 739 Bourbon St), which carries similar stock. Shipping is available from either store.

VIEUX CARRÉ WINE & SPIRITS

Map pp70–1   Wine

☎ 568-9463; 422 Chartres St; ☺ 10am-9pm

This is a densely stocked shop run by two Italian-born brothers who can often be found socializing at a table near the front door. It has an impressive selection of wines from California, Australia, France and Italy, and a commendable choice of international beers. If you're really serious about wine and willing to pay good money for it, ask to see the back room, where the rare vintages are kept.

FAUBOURG MARIGNY & BYWATER

As fun and creative as the Marigny is, there's surprisingly little in the way of shopping around here. Most of what you'll find is along Frenchmen St, among the clubs and restaurants. There are galleries and art-related shops scattered throughout Bywater.

PORCHÉ WEST GALLERY

Map p81   Art & Photography

☎ 947-3880; www.porche-west.com; cnr Burgundy & Louise Sts; ☺ call ahead

In Bywater, this is the rustic shop and studio of photographer Christopher Porché West. Pathos defines Porché West's black-and-white images of the people of New Orleans, and his photos of the Mardi Gras Indians are among the best. Call for an appointment.

DR BOB'S STUDIO

Map p81   Art

☎ 945-2225; www.myspace.com/drbobart; 3027 Chartres St; ☺ call ahead

Self-taught outdoors artist Dr Bob is a fixture in the Bywater, and you're sure to recognize his signature work – the 'Be Nice or Leave' signs that appear in restaurants and bars around town. Dr Bob's work also turns up in the House of Blues (p181) and museums throughout the South. In addition to the signs, he's known for his alligator carvings and sculptures of assembled found objects. Garbage-can lids, bottle caps, pieces of junked musical instruments and essentially anything that strikes Dr Bob's weird sensibility is turned into art. His gallery is really a fascinating junkyard of art, with a sculpture garden comprising spray-painted lawn ornaments. The man himself is a bit ornery (ironic, considering his signs, but no matter) and not always in – call ahead.

NEW ORLEANS ART SUPPLY

Map p81   Art Supplies

☎ 949-1525; www.art-restoration.com; 3620 Royal St; ☺ 10am-5pm Mon-Fri

If you're one who likes to sketch while traveling, here's a good place to go for a fresh supply of pencils and pads. Surprisingly, it's the most central art store in New Orleans, and it's not a bad one. The selection isn't huge, but it's high quality. The shop is an annex of the New Orleans Conservation Guild.

FAUBOURG MARIGNY BOOK STORE
Map p81   Specialty Books
☎ 947-3700; 600 Frenchmen St; ☾ noon-10pm
The South's oldest gay bookstore is a ramshackle, intellectual spot, and a good place to pick up local 'zines and catch up on the New Orleans scene, gay or otherwise. Look for the subtle (enormous) rainbow flag.

GREEN PROJECT Map p81   Sustainable Goods
☎ 945-0240; 2831 Marais St; ☾ 9am-5pm
You probably don't need a large panel door or gallons of paint or heaps of salvaged building materials if you're just visiting New Orleans, but you should still stop by this wonderful store to see what a good business can do for its community. The Green Project sells salvaged building material at extremely cut-rate costs to New Orleanians, providing cheap housing supplies that also preserve the unique architectural facade of the city. It also runs a recycling center, donates paints and art supplies to schools and artists, plants community gardens, runs garden workshops and does outreach in the surrounding neighborhoods. Basically, it's businesses like this that make us love New Orleans over and over again.

ELECTRIC LADYLAND Map p81   Tattoos
☎ 947-8286; 610 Frenchmen St; ☾ noon-midnight, 1-9pm Sun
New Orleans is an old port filled with bars, right? Then a tattoo is just about the coolest souvenir you can get here (if they're your thing). Day or night you'll spot people whose florid and lurid body art indicates business is not at all bad at Electric Ladyland. It's a clean, brightly lit spot where young tattoo artists can set you up with a classic set of dice ('born to lose'), a growling wolf or a naked woman sashaying beneath a coconut palm. Customized designs can also be arranged.

CBD & WAREHOUSE DISTRICT
This part of town is chiefly concerned with business and art. It's not good for window shopping, but if you know what you're looking for you may find yourself zeroing in on that perfect little specialty shop. The main drag for galleries is Julia St, between Commerce and Baronne Sts. Drop by the Con-temporary Art Center (p196) or any gallery to pick up a comprehensive guide to the area's art dealers.

NEW ORLEANS SCHOOL OF GLASSWORKS Map pp86–7   Art
☎ 529-7277; 727 Magazine St; ☾ 11am-5pm Mon-Fri
This school and gallery impressively fills 25,000 sq ft of an old brick warehouse. Glassworks is the sister school of the Louvre Museum of Decorative Arts, and excellent pieces are sold here. On Saturday afternoon you'll usually see artists at work, and glass blowing is always worth seeing. Artists also specialize in stained glass, fine silver alchemy, copper enameling, printmaking, paper sculpture and bookbinding.

MEYER THE HATTER Map pp86–7   Hats
☎ 525-1048; 120 St Charles Ave; ☾ 10am-5:45pm
A cluttered asylum for lovers of hats. (If that doesn't include you, we'll have you know that New Orleans is a hat town, and hats are good.) This shop, just a half block from Canal St, has a truly astounding inventory of world-class headwear. Biltmore, Dobbs, Stetson and Borsalino are just a few of the classy milliners represented. Fur felts dominate in fall and winter, and flimsy straw hats take over in spring and summer. The clerks shoo away interlopers who come looking for the wrong type of hat at the wrong time of year.

INTERNATIONAL VINTAGE GUITARS
Map pp86–7   Musical Instruments
☎ 524-4557; 646 Tchoupitoulas St; ☾ noon-6pm
In the Warehouse District, this is a small shop specializing in used guitars and amps. The collection usually features a few showpieces, but its stock generally consists of new Fenders, Epiphones and a few Gibsons. It's a convenient place to grab new strings if you busted yours while busking in the Quarter.

GARDEN, LOWER GARDEN & CENTRAL CITY
Magazine St is by far New Orleans' best shopping strip, and as a center for commercial activity it begins in the Lower Garden District,

near its intersection with Felicity St. From here you can follow Magazine west all the way to Audubon park and essentially shop or window browse in antique stores, boutiques etc almost the entire way.

LOWER GARDEN DISTRICT

Magazine St gets cooking in the Lower Garden District. There is a heady concentration of galleries, boutiques, restaurants and other shops between St Mary St and Jackson Ave.

WINKY'S Map pp96–7 · Clothing & Gifts

☎ 568-1020; 2038 Magazine St; ☒ 10am-6pm
Retro toys and clothing for childish adults – we mean that in the best possible way, of course. Fun stuff sold here includes tiki paraphernalia, tools of the cocktail hour and actual toys. The swinging casual duds for men and women and even children are worth trying on.

THOMAS MANN GALLERY I/O

Map pp96–7 · Jewelry

☎ 581-2113; www.thomasmann.com; 1812 Magazine St; ☒ call ahead
The 'I/O' in the name stands for 'insightful objects.' Local craftsman Thomas Mann specializes in jewelry and sculpture. His gallery is a smorgasbord of glass and metal; the necklaces and bracelets make nice gifts.

AIDAN GILL FOR MEN

Map pp96–7 · Men's Coiffure & Gifts

☎ 587-9090; www.aidangillformen.com; 2026 Magazine St; ☒ 10am-6pm Mon-Fri, 9am-5pm Sat
Smartly dressed mobsters of the Prohibition era would have felt at home in the clubby environs of this metrosexual headquarters for Orleans Parish. It's all about looking neat and stylish, in a well-heeled, masculine sort of way. High-end shaving gear, smart cufflinks and colorful silk ties are sold in front, and there's a popular barber shop ($35 for a trim, $40 for a shave; reserve a week ahead) in back.

JIM RUSSELL'S RECORDS

Map pp96–7 · Music

☎ 522-2602; www.jimrussellrecords.com; 1837 Magazine St; ☒ 11am-5pm Mon-Sat
A dense emporium of used 45s, with some highly rare, collectable and expensive disks featuring all the blues, R&B and soul stars of the past. (Collecting Johnny Adams' sin-

gles? This is the place.) The used LPs have mostly given way to CDs, with an uneven selection available. Turntables make it possible to assess the quality of your purchases before you lay down some greenbacks.

DARK ROOM Map pp96–7 · Photo Processing

☎ 522-3211; www.neworleansdarkroom.com; 1927 Sophie Wright Pl; ☒ 10am-6pm Mon-Sat
New Orleans is photogenic, and home to hundreds of photographers, so it stands to reason there would be a place to get some very high-quality print work done. Dark Room is a center for the photographic arts, and you can take classes in photography and printing too, if you're interested.

HOUSE OF LOUNGE

Map pp96–7 · Risqué Clothing

☎ 671-8300; www.houseoflounge.com; 2044 Magazine St; ☒ 11am-6pm, noon-5pm Sun
Its name doesn't exactly have a svelte ring to it, but House of Lounge has its

CLOTHING SIZES

Women's clothing

Aus/UK	8	10	12	14	16	18
Europe	36	38	40	42	44	46
Japan	5	7	9	11	13	15
USA	6	8	10	12	14	16

Women's shoes

Aus/USA	5	6	7	8	9	10
Europe	35	36	37	38	39	40
France only	35	36	38	39	40	42
Japan	22	23	24	25	26	27
UK	3½	4½	5½	6½	7½	8½

Men's clothing

Aus	92	96	100	104	108	112
Europe	46	48	50	52	54	56
Japan	S		M	M		L
UK/USA	35	36	37	38	39	40

Men's shirts (collar sizes)

Aus/Japan	38	39	40	41	42	43
Europe	38	39	40	41	42	43
UK/USA	15	15½	16	16½	17	17½

Men's shoes

Aus/UK	7	8	9	10	11	12
Europe	41	42	43	44½	46	47
Japan	26	27	27½	28	29	30
USA	7½	8½	9½	10½	11½	12½

Measurements approximate only; try before you buy

big vampish heart in the right place. The shop sells just about everything you would need to turn your foreplay into a classy burlesque review. The lingerie is sexy and shameless, the 'baby doll' assemblages are cute as all get-out (and gettin' out's the idea) and the feather fans will keep everything coyly covered. For the femme fatale who really knows how, the shop also sells cigarette holders and flasks, and – if all of the above fail to induce intimacy – there's a good stock of vibrators on offer, too.

TRASHY DIVA Map pp96–7 Risqué Clothing
☎ 299-8777; www.trashydiva.com; 2048 Magazine St; ⏰ 1-6pm Mon-Sat
It isn't really as scandalous as the name suggests, except by Victorian standards. Diva's specialty is sassy 1940s- and '50s-style cinched, hourglass dresses and Belle Epoque undergarments – lots of corsets, lace and such. The shop also features Kabuki-inspired dresses with embroidered dragons, and retro tops, skirts and shawls reflecting styles plucked from just about every era.

SOUTHERN FOSSIL & MINERAL EXCHANGE Map pp96–7 Used Goods
☎ 523-5525; 2049 Magazine St; ⏰ 10:30am-5pm
This store – something like a curiosity museum where most everything's got a price tag on it – can induce bone-rattling nightmares. If you're impressed by the selection of skulls from all creatures great and small, you can take some home with you. More subdued are the rocks on which ancient life forms have imprinted images of themselves. Pretty cool, even if it just ends up as a paperweight. A selection of animal puppets is just the thing to appease terrified children.

MAGAZINE ST
For the true-blue shopper, New Orleans doesn't get any better than Magazine St. For some 6 miles the street courses through the Warehouse District and along the riverside edge of the Garden District and Uptown, lined nearly the entire way with small shops that sell antiques, art, contemporary fashions, vintage clothing and other odds and ends. The street hits its peak in the Lower Garden District (near Jackson Ave), the Garden District (between 1st and 7th Sts) and Uptown (from Antonine St to Napoleon Ave).

GARDEN DISTRICT

On Magazine St, where it forms the riverside extent of the Garden District, you'll find another intriguing pack of shops. Rink (Map pp96–7), opposite Lafayette Cemetery No 1 at Prytania St and Washington Ave, houses a small group of upscale shops including a bookstore and coffee shop.

MAGAZINE ANTIQUE MALL
Map pp96–7 Antiques & Used Goods
☎ 896-9994; www.magazineantiquemall.com; 3017 Magazine St; ⏰ 10:30am-5:30pm, from noon Sun
Hard-core rummagers are likely to score items of interest in the dozen or so stalls here, where independent dealers peddle an intriguing and varied range of antique bric-a-brac. Bargain hunters aren't likely to have much luck, though.

GARDEN DISTRICT BOOKSHOP
Map pp96–7 Books
☎ 895-2266; www.gardendistrictbookshop.com; 2727 Prytania St; ⏰ 10am-6pm, to 4pm Sun
In the Rink, this place offers a select collection of 1st-edition works. It also stocks mostly new books about the region and hosts book signings with local authors, who have a habit of dropping in every now and then.

BELLADONNA DAY SPA
Map pp96–7 Day Spa & Homewares
☎ 891-4393; www.belladonnadayspa.com; 2900 Magazine St; ⏰ 9am-6pm, to 8pm Wed & Thu
After a few hard days of getting stuffed with rich Creole food and sloshed on gallons of Abita, it's time to treat yourself to a little cleansing experience at Belladonna. When you're done cleansing and spoiling yourself, take home some hip homewares and cleansing products so you can engage in some homegrown renewal.

STYLE LAB FOR MEN
Map pp96–7 Men's Fashion
☎ 304-5072; www.stylelabformen.com; 3641 Magazine St; ⏰ 11:30am-6pm Mon-Fri, 10:30am-5pm Sat, noon-5pm Sun
Let's be honest: the idea of a men's clothing store run by two women is a little off-putting. Shouldn't a guy have some input on what men should wear? But then Style Lab's resident Great Dane, a dog

INTERESTING JUNK

New Orleans rewards the shopper who appreciates that a surprising number of things just get better with age, including lamps, ashtrays, toys and the kind of bric-a-brac that once was considered worthless. The best parts of town to go looking for these sorts of treasures are on lower Decatur St in the French Quarter and along Magazine St in the Garden District and Uptown. You could easily spend an entire afternoon browsing the Decatur St shops, or an entire day on Magazine St.

the size of a small dinosaur, comes out to sniff around, and you realize these ladies have a man's sensibility about certain things: dogs, and definitely duds. No less an authority than *GQ* has declared this shop as the place where the well-dressed New Orleanian male gets outfitted, in Ben Sherman, Diesel, Trovata and similar such labels.

NEW ORLEANS MUSIC EXCHANGE
Map pp96–7　　　　　　　Musical Instruments
☎ 891-7670; www.dkclay-nola.com/neworleans musicexchange; 3342 Magazine St; ✆ 10:30-6pm, 1-5pm Sun
It's high time you learned how to play trumpet. This large shop, specializing mostly in secondhand instruments, is the place to go for a nice used horn. There's an entire room of brass and woodwinds, all priced fairly. But to find it, you must weave through a maze of guitar and bass amps. It also sells guitars, guitar strings and all that other stuff. But really, you ought to go for the trumpet.

BIG FISHERMAN SEAFOOD
Map pp96–7　　　　　　　　　　　Seafood
☎ 897-9907; www.bigfishermanseafood.com; 3301 Magazine St; ✆ varies with season
If you're here in the spring, when it's crawfish season, you may develop a taste for the little mudbugs. But you haven't really had the full-on crawfish experience unless you've been invited to a crawfish boil in someone's backyard. If that hasn't happened, send some crawfish back home and invite your friends over. This busy little shop will pack and ship crawfish to anywhere in the USA. The price fluctuates widely from season to season, so call ahead for prices.

FUNKY MONKEY
Map pp96–7　　　　　　　　Vintage Clothing
☎ 899-5587; 3127 Magazine St; ✆ 11am-6pm, noon-5pm Sun
Vintage attire for club-hoppers is on sale in this funhouse of frippery, as well as wigs, shades and jewelry. It's annoyingly turned into one of those vintage shops where the secondhand stuff is as expensive as new clothes from a big brand name, but the clothes are admittedly very hip-to-trip.

UPTOWN & RIVERBEND

Magazine St is the city's best shopping strip. You can take a good multimile window-shopping hike stretching from Audubon Park to Louisiana Ave. The area around Maple St up in Riverbend is another hopping carnival of consumption.

Fashionable shops and restaurants front a small square on Dublin St near S Carrollton Ave, where it meets St Charles Ave. To get here, take the St Charles Ave streetcar (or bus 12) to the Riverbend near Camellia Grill.

On the riverside of S Carrollton, Oak St is an older neighborhood commercial zone intersecting with the streetcar line. It's reasonably compact for strolling and offers a few interesting businesses, along with a few restaurants and the stellar Maple Leaf Bar.

MAPLE STREET BOOKSTORE
Map pp102–3　　　　　　　　　　　　Books
☎ 866-4916; www.maplestreetbookshop.com; 7523 Maple St; ✆ 9am-7pm, Sun 11am-5pm
Shopkeeper Rhonda Kellog Faust advocates for antiracism group Erace and is a storehouse of local knowledge. The business, which includes a children's bookstore, was founded by her mother and aunt more than 30 years ago and is one of the most politically progressive, well-stocked bookshops in the city.

C COLLECTION Map pp102–3　Boutique Fashion
☎ 866-4916; www.ccollcectionnola.com; 8141 Maple St; ✆ 10am-6pm Mon-Sat
This converted house-cum-boutique does its best to keep the female population of Tulane University (and women of Riverbend region in general) fashionable and smiling with its range of cute dresses, chunky belts, skinny pants and hip-hugging shorts.

SWEET PEA & TULIP
Map pp102–3   Boutique Fashion
☎ 899-4044; 802 Nashville Ave; ⏰ 10am-6pm
Mon-Sat, 11am-5pm Sun
Sweet Pea & Tulip – jeez, the name alone –
is almost painfully cute. You can be too if
you deck yourself out in the frocky and fun
contemporary goodness and retro-inspired
outfits that stack these shelves. It comes
across as the fashion equivalent of a small
dog wearing a tight pink dress, but there
are some good finds here.

PIED NU
Map pp102–3   Boutique Fashion & Homewares
☎ 899-4118; www.piednuneworleans.com; 5521
Magazine St; ⏰ 10am-5pm Mon-Sat
If you need a hand-poured candle that lasts
60 hours, try one of the sweet-smelling
Diptyques on sale here. As you soak up that
vanilla-scented goodness, browse elephant-
printed cotton T-shirt dresses, cinched-poet
dresses and low-joe sneakers. Set it all off
with tiny leaf earrings – you'll make yourself
almost as endearing as this precious shop.

YVONNE LA FLEUR
Map pp102–3   Classic Clothing
☎ 866-9666; www.yvonnelafleur.com; 8131
Hampson St; ⏰ 10am-6pm Mon-Sat, to 8pm Thu

top picks

COSTUMES & MASKS
Mardi Gras and Halloween give New Orleanians two
excuses to disguise themselves, but the preponderance
of shops specializing in duds for such occasions suggests
that the locals are playing dress up more often than
that. Out-of-towners can get with the program right
quickly in a fun-filled shopping excursion that ought to
include some or all of the following shops.
■ Uptown Costume & Dancewear (right) In a pinch,
  this place can address all your needs.
■ Le Garage (p122) Frumpy old MG costumes, hats,
  army surplus.
■ Maskarade (p124) Great selection of high-quality
  Mardi Gras masks.
■ Mardi Gras Mask Market (p49) On Mardi Gras
  weekend vendors and artisans from around the
  country converge on the French Market for what
  basically amounts to the Olympics of handmade
  masquerade wear.

They just don't make them like this any-
more – neither the clothes, millinery or
lingerie for sale in Yvonne La Fleur, nor
Yvonne herself, the definition of steel in
silk. She's an amazing businesswoman who
has outfitted generations of local ladies for
their weddings, debuts and race days. She
makes her own perfumes and gorgeous
hats overflowing with silk flowers that
seem to belong to another era.

DIRTY COAST Map pp102–3   Clothing
☎ 324-3745; www.dirtycoast.com; 5704 Magazine
St; ⏰ 9am-6pm
You're not a cool new New Orleanian if you
haven't picked up one of the clever T-shirts
or bumper stickers ('Make Wetlands, Not
War'), all related to local issues, inside jokes
and neighborhood happenings, in this
ridiculously cool store.

UPTOWN COSTUME & DANCEWEAR
Map pp102–3   Costumes & Masks
☎ 895-7969; 4326 Magazine St; ⏰ noon-6pm
Tue-Fri, 10am-5pm Sat
A one-stop emergency shop for anyone
caught completely unprepared for Mardi
Gras, Halloween or any other occasion that
calls for an utterly frivolous disguise. It's
an emporium of goofy get-ups, packed to
the rafters with boas, tiaras, masks, Elvis
capes, ballerina tutus and a truly astounding selection of cheap-ass wigs. Guaranteed
to keep you from blending into the woodwork, and fun stuff for the entire family.

HAZELNUT Map pp102–3   Homewares
☎ 891-2424; www.hazelnutneworleans.com; 5155
Magazine St; ⏰ 10am-6pm Mon-Sat
It's hard to be a cool Uptowner if you
haven't brought home some of the gilded
glassware, post-modern ceramic, classically
cool toile, gorgeous tableau that looks like
it should decorate a fairy-tale palace, or
other interior-decor must-haves that overflow Hazelnut's showroom.

MUSICA LATINA DISCOTECA
Map pp102–3   Music
☎ 895-4227; 4714 Magazine St; ⏰ 10am-6pm
With a growing Spanish-speaking population and well-established cultural ties to
the Caribbean, it makes sense that New
Orleanians would have an appreciation for
the music of Latin America. That's all this
jam-packed, one-room shop sells. Every-

thing's covered, from the musical traditions of Cuba to Argentina. The mambo greats are thoroughly stocked and there's a smattering of mariachi and salsa artists from the ages.

SHOEFTY Map pp102–3 — Shoes & Accessories

☎ 896-9737; 6010 Magazine St; ✆ 10am-6pm Mon-Sat

This charming little shoe store has a lot for women, and there's no doubt girls will be in footwear heaven here amid the strappy, the pumpy, the chunky and the tottering-heely. But metrosexual men (or dragged along boyfriends) will also find some cool kicks that may convince the most male among us that, perhaps, it's acceptable to own more footwear then one pair of sneakers.

RETROACTIVE Map pp102–3 — Vintage Jewelry

☎ 895-5054; 5414 Magazine St; ✆ 10am-6pm

This little glad-rag grotto spills over with eye-catching treasures. Duck in through the vintage handbags and crazy hats that literally hang from the ceiling then slow down to inspect the jaw-dropping selection of costume jewelry. Beautiful glass and Bakelite pieces plucked from the middle of the 20th century cost anywhere from $20 to $500. You're sure to find a snazzy little something to pin to your sweater.

MID-CITY & THE TREMÉ

These neighborhoods aren't packed with shopping strips per se, unless you're interested in picking up some hardware or groceries. On that note, there are some interesting corner stores that serve local residents, bucking the big-box shopping trend you see in so many other US cities, although the Tremé especially could do with some more retail. Otherwise, we'd direct tourists out here for, of course, spell components.

F&F BOTANICA Map pp108–9 — Santeria & Voodoo

☎ 289-2304; www.orleanscandleco.com/ff/htm/home; 801 N Broad St; ✆ 10am-6:30pm Tue-Sat

Forget all the fake voodoo shops in the French Quarter; this is a genuine Puerto Rican botanica that sells candles, gris-gris (spell bags) and spell components for use in voodoo and Santeria (the latter is a Puerto Rican religion related to voodoo). No tourist-oriented Hollywood-style dolls here; real worshippers drop in to deal with real issues, which, according to the spell lists, seem to mainly be related to heartache, immigration issues and the law.

EATING

top picks

- **Casamento's** (p168)
- **Bacchanal** (p158)
- **Cochon** (p160)
- **Domilise's** (p168)
- **Bayona** (p154)
- **Cooter Brown's** (p168)
- **Dick & Jenny's** (p165)
- **Kim Son** (p167)
- **The Joint** (p158)
- **Mat & Naddie's** (p166)

What's your recommendation? lonelyplanet.com/new-orleans

EATING

In what other American city do people celebrate the harvest season of sewage-dwelling, feces-eating crustaceans? The crawfish boil, when Louisianans joyfully share corn and craws with strangers, crack beers and generally live life like God was laughing through them, exemplifies New Orleans' relationship with food: unconditional love.

Food here is inextricably tied up in sense of place, and few cities in America emanate such a distinctive sense of place as New Orleans. This city finds itself in its food; meals are both expression of identity and bridges between white and black and brown and native and transplant and rich and poor. We're not exaggerating: chances are high a family in a mansion on Audubon Park are enjoying red beans and rice on Monday night, same as tenants in a shotgun shack in the Tremé. To balance the loud demands of pride and tradition, the settlers of this city – Acadians, Germans, Irish, Jews, Africans and Vietnamese – have added their ingredients to (yes, we'll say it, cliché it may be) the New Orleans gumbo. Said soup takes new influences in and spits them out, if not gentrified, at least Creole-ed up. *Banh mi* sandwiches are sold as 'Vietnamese po'boys,' while a local may slather Srichacha chili sauce instead of Tabasco on their fried oysters.

This city's natural impulse for indulgence is best realized in its homegrown cuisine. Meals here are unapologetically over the top: goat cheese and prawn crepes; roasted beef 'debris' on hollandaise and poached eggs; pork cracklin' and cane syrup; rabbit livers on toast with pepper jelly; chicken fried in duck fat; gumbo, gumbo, gumbo. New Orleans food is as rich as a tycoon and as dangerous, in its way, as a hurricane. Make friends with someone in food service here and you'll notice how chefs promise their friends, 'Come over for dinner and I will *kill* you.'

Making friends with chefs in this town is, by the way, pretty easy. Young, hungry talents with sharp knives and sharper ambitions are flocking here from around the world, attracted by a restaurant scene that includes some of the best scenery in America's culinary landscape. The locals' love of food is a draw, as is the playing field: New Orleans lacks much of the competition of a city such as New York. The kitchens of this city are like the Wild West, every young blade eager to carve a name, and some pork belly while they're at it.

Beyond sit-down dining are the culinary traditions that make New Orleans city of, as some say, a thousand restaurants and three dishes. This isn't entirely true – there are better and better international options popping up here, although it's still certainly a city where the homegrown, distinctive cuisine (Cajun and Creole) is what's best. The food writer's credo of great food from humble origins is overused these days, but that is the essence of this city's gastronomical scene. Gumbo: culled from leftovers into God's own soup. The hot, simple filling satisfaction of good jambalaya. The name alone: po'boy. Damn. Let's eat already.

HISTORY

Two French settlers fresh off the boat from Marseilles arrive in 18th-century Louisiana.

Pierre: Ugh. This *pais* is *tres calor.*
Claude: *Oui.*
Pierre: Have we some bread?
Claude: *Non.*
Pierre: Cheese?
Claude: *Non.*
Pierre: Wine?
Claude: *Non.*
Pierre: What the hell is here?
Claude: *Insecte de boue et lezard.*
Pierre: Mud insects and lizards?!
Claude: *Oui.*
Pierre: *Merde.*

We're not just having fun with French stereotypes: letters home from early French colonists fairly busted with nostalgia for Old World food. Bread was a particular source of longing – unsurprising, as it would have been the staple of most settlers from Europe. But cheer up, *mes amis!* What seemed like an inhospitable swamp is, in its unique way, heaven's own pantry. Local Native Americans knew it: there were oysters, crawfish, crabs, shrimp, turtle, speckled trout, catfish, hogs, pigeons, rabbits, doves, squirrels, duck, deer, greens, onions, berries, beans, pumpkins, squash, watermelon, peaches and corn in them thar bayous (tributaries).

Folks learned to love the produce and game harvested out of their backyard, but the land kept a dagger hidden in that bountiful smile:

a flood-prone basin that bred disease like rabbits in a fertile hutch. New Orleanians have always drank, ate and made merry partly because, for much of their history, tomorrow they may well have died.

Once Pierre, Claude and company realized rice was a tasty staple and got the hang of pounding sassafras leaves into a powder the natives called filé (*fee*-lay), the early *mise en place* of a great cuisine was laid out. Waves of new settlers all added their ingredients to the set up. Germans brought the sacred arts of sausage making and meat curing; the Spanish, their spices and love of rice; African slaves threw in okra and oily cooking; the Louisiana purchase opened the state to American commerce and foodstuffs; and the French, bless them, kept the kitchen well stocked with lots of butter. The hybrid cuisine that developed was given the name of its mixed-up population base: Creole. Today, the newest chefs in the Louisiana kitchen are Latino and Vietnamese, whose foodstuffs are integrating easily into local palettes.

New Orleanians probably regarded the rise of foodie culture in the rest of America around the late 20th and early 21st century with some bemusement. Food has always been a topic of passion here – we'd argue this is the 'humblest' food town in the country, in the sense that the eating obsession here truly exists across racial and class lines. But there's a negative side to New Orleans possessing one of the only genuinely homegrown great American cuisines: menus here can lack international variety, and we'd love to see, say, an Ethiopian or Malaysian place open up on Magazine St.

In another corner of the state, the 18th-century arrival of the Cajuns led to another regional cuisine. Although New Orleans had a few Cajun restaurants, it really wasn't until chef Paul Prudhomme rose to fame that the city became known as a mecca for Cajun cuisine.

CELEBRATING WITH FOOD

The city's biggest holiday is 'Fat Tuesday,' right? Celebrations here mean indulgence, or at least more indulgence than usual…

Home Cooking

It is always an honor to be invited to someone's home for dinner while traveling, and as New Orleanians are a hospitable people, they consider having a guest an occasion; however,

don't expect a seven-course Creole meal. New Orleanians generally dine out when the occasion calls for an extravagant spread. Many home cooks have a personal gumbo recipe and can whip up some fine local seafood and meat. Generally, expect American and Southern standards with a dash of Creole and Cajun flavor.

Some New Orleanians with backyards have adopted the Cajun tradition of holding crawfish boils during the late spring. If you are invited to a crawfish boil, expect a large cross-generational crowd of extended family and friends. It's a boisterous, informal affair, with lots of beer and piles of crawfish. If you're squeamish about biting into crustaceans you're not going to make many friends, so come hungry and ready to put away a few pounds of the little critters.

Special Events

The local calendar seems to have more holidays than regular work days (see p12). On some of these special days it's all about the food.

CARNIVAL

Carnival season in New Orleans means a flurry of private celebrations and gatherings that tailgate parades, balls or other seasonal parties. Food can range from chill-chasing chicken sauce *piquante* to fancy hors d'oeuvres or delicate finger sandwiches filled with ham salad and cheesy artichoke dip. For devout Catholics, Mardi Gras is the last day of feasting before somber Lent begins on the morrow. Although the number of people partaking in Lenten vows may have dropped, the tradition of meat-feasting on 'Fat Tuesday' continues, and tables – both private and commercial – overflow with New Orleans favorites such as steak, ribs, roasts and baked hams. For more information about Mardi Gras, see p42.

JAZZ FEST

People show up hungry for this one. Over two weekends from the end of April, Jazz Fest is a nonstop flurry of amazing live music and an opportunity to sample *a lot* of food. Some Jazz Fest booths enjoy a unique level of celebrity (shrimp flautas at the Taqueria Corona stand…mmm…) equal to the musical acts that grace the major stages. Die-hard fans and repeat customers invariably have food factored into their festival routine. As

UNDERSTANDING THE MENU

For those not from the US, the typical American restaurant meal is divided into three sections: the appetizer (starting course), entrée (main course) and dessert. Most restaurants will present a printed menu and have the daily specials recited by the waiters. At country restaurants that serve plate lunches, the menu might be completely verbal, so pay attention if you don't see a blackboard or printed menus.

You may also encounter specialized restaurants that only serve one item cooked in a particular way, for example fried catfish or boiled crawfish. In this case, all you have to do is say how much you want, as the food will be sold by the plate, pound or piece.

an added bonus, the festival coincides with the peak seasons for crawfish and soft-shell crab. Each night for the duration of the festival, expect long lines outside nearly every restaurant in town. See p54 for further details on Jazz Fest.

THANKSGIVING

Louisiana's contributions to the American Thanksgiving tradition are the deep-fried turkey and the turducken. The deep-frying technique requires a standard oversized crawfish pot and a high-output propane burner. The bird is rubbed down with Cajun spices and, with a comically large syringe, injected with pepper sauce before it is submerged into the hot oil. Once cooked, the meat is moist and flavorful (with an added zing from the injected marinade) without the slightest trace of oil. The skin is crispy and spicy with a little caramelized sweetness.

If you could give form to the American penchant for excess food, it'd probably resemble the turducken, a chicken stuffed into a duck stuffed into a turkey. Yeah, you right.

CHRISTMAS SEASON

Sugar-dusted cookies, sticky homemade candies, moist cakes and special group cocktails (such as eggnog) make a yearly appearance around the holidays. A gumbo made from the Thanksgiving turkey may be the centerpiece of a pre-Christmas meal. During the cold months of December and January, Gulf oysters are at their plumpest, so the versatile shellfish shows up on party tables as stew, soup and gumbo.

On Christmas morning a huge breakfast is served and tables are piled high with fluffy biscuits, *pain perdu* ('lost bread,' a baguette-based version of eggy French toast), and salty bacon or the New Orleans classic grits and grillades (grilled beef braised in tomato sauce).

ST PATRICK'S DAY

In a city looking for any excuse to revel, an event celebrating Ireland's patron saint is not to be missed. Crowds follow a festive parade from the French Quarter into the Irish Channel. Along the way the participants make regular stops at various bars to enjoy that most American (and disgusting) of St Paddy specialties, beer dyed green with food coloring. Not the most flavorful of traditions, but in the end, a party's a party. Of course, corned beef and cabbage appear on tables and in bars all over the city.

THE FEAST OF ST JOSEPH

Every March 19, two days after the Irish celebrate their favorite saint, the Sicilian community honors their patron, St Joseph, with feasts and elaborate rituals. At church services the altars heave with food arranged to represent crosses, crowns of thorns, sacred hearts, palm leaves, chalices and St Joseph's staff. After mass, all are welcome to dig in. Check the newspaper for churches holding services that day.

CAJUN FAIS DO-DO

Originally referring to any organized Cajun dance (be it at home or in the community), the term *fais do-do* (fay-do-do) now refers mainly to outdoor street dances that take place during local festivals. What hasn't changed is the basic scene: young and old dancing to fiddles and accordions et al. The basic Cajun step is a flowing partner dance with waltz, two-step and more complex jitterbug variations. Some clubs in New Orleans may hold the occasional *fais do-do,* but the best place to experience one is out in the country.

The dancing traditionally begins after dinner and replenishment is usually required by midnight. During the interlude, you might dig into a chicken gumbo, rich beef stew cooked with onions and thyme, or links of boudin (p141), then down another beer to cool your sweat.

The name *fais do-do* comes from the French sweet nothings that mothers whisper to their babies to send them off to sleep. In the old days, mothers would coo their children to sleep (do do, *bebe,* do do) in a quiet room attached to the dance hall.

SPECIALTIES

When we speak of contemporary New Orleans food, we're actually speaking of the unique mixing of three dominant cooking styles – Creole, Cajun and soul food (see below) – commonly associated with both the city and the state of Louisiana. The first two are native to predominantly French southern Louisiana, while soul food is popular throughout the American South.

Buttery-rich, refined and sophisticated, Creole cuisine is the food of the city and the delicious legacy of its French heritage. Dishes such as the delicate *poisson en papillote* (fish cooked in parchment paper) and shrimp rémoulade (p140) are prime examples of how the chefs of New Orleans reflect the city's French roots, while using local ingredients and incorporating contributions of the other cultures that have passed through the port city. On the whole, Creole cuisine is smooth and rich, with a tip of the hat to the sauces and formal presentations of the French motherland.

Rustic, flavorful and bold, Cajun food is the food of the country – in this case, the southern Louisiana marshes, bayous and prairies west of New Orleans proper. Often mistakenly attributed to New Orleans, Cajun food has its physical and cultural roots with rural settlers from British Maritime Canada. When the French Acadians arrived in Louisiana they brought their unique frontier cuisine and adapted it to the remote areas of what is now alternately called Acadiana, Acadian Louisiana or Cajun Country. The long-simmering single-pot dishes (such as crawfish étouffée, shrimp jambalaya and roux-based gumbo) reflect the survival-oriented frontier traditions of the Acadians – simple foods based on the varied bounty of the land.

Broadly speaking, soul food – as well as its closely related cousin, southern country-style food – is derived from British cuisine adapted with indigenous ingredients and the cooking techniques of African slaves and African American hired cooks. The often-blurred distinction between the southern cooking of blacks and whites is the quality of the raw ingredients. As a general rule, southern country-style cooking starts with the pick of the crop or carcass, and soul food stews up the rest. Crispy fried chicken, okra smothered with tomatoes, collard greens cooked with salt pork, hearty yellow cornbread and fluffy raised biscuits are common to both styles of cooking. Soul food includes such delicacies as turkey neck stew, pigs' feet and chitterlings (tripe).

Some of the staples available in southern Louisiana can be found almost anywhere there is immediate access to abundant seawater and freshwater life, wild game, and common grains and vegetables. But by and large what the cooks of New Orleans do with these foodstuffs is unparalleled elsewhere.

Seafood

Many staple dishes of Louisiana cuisine feature creatures yanked from the state's intricate wetlands – saltwater, freshwater and brackish marshes. The local joke in these parts is that there are four seasons in Louisiana: crawfish, shrimp, oyster and crab.

FISH

Local fish such as snapper, speckled trout, pompano and flounder are all used in straightforward Creole preparations, usually with copious amounts of butter. Trout and catfish meunière is fillets of fish lightly dusted in flour, pan-fried in butter and topped with

---

SOUL FOOD Charmaine O'Brien

In early days, African slaves may have been preparing meals for wealthy white families, but they certainly weren't eating the same food. The white families ate the hams of the pig and the slaves made do with the ribs, offal, feet and skin. The white folks ate vegetables such as turnips and the slaves got the green tops. Slaves were given molasses (used as a flavoring), cornmeal and whatever else was left over or considered second-rate.

Slaves were usually permitted to keep their own small patch of herbs and vegetables as well as a few chickens, and out of this they created their own family meals. Food was often deep-fried in pig fat, which was readily available. They stewed poor-quality meat for hours to tenderize it and develop its flavor. While the slaves had little choice in the foods they ate, they came to develop a rich, hearty, delicious cuisine – including greens, chitterlings (tripe), cornbread and ham hocks – we now know as soul food.

Soul food is not indigenous to southern Louisiana like Creole and Cajun food, and while you will find soul food all over the southern US, the version you eat in Louisiana will have more pepper, spice and garlic.

CATFISH

Until recent years, the catfish had a bit of an image problem. With its natural freshwater habitat in muddy rivers and ponds, the bottom-feeding catfish *(Ictalurus furcatus)* vacuums the watery floors for tasty morsels. Unfortunately, this means it also ingests a fair amount of sludge, pesticide and post-industrial goop. Consequently, the catfish has traditionally been the food for poor folks.

But if you've grown up on the stuff, you know there's no better finned friend. Thanks to modern farming techniques (and, we reckon, the arrival of the Vietnamese, who treated the catfish with the respect it deserved), the whiskered wonder has risen to new levels of acceptance. The taste of the fish was transformed when it was farmed in clean ponds and fed compressed grain pellets. For aqua farmers, catfish are an attractive proposition since they are easy to breed and grow quickly.

lemon butter sauce; almandine means the fish is also crusted with almonds. A simple grilled pompano is transformed into pompano Pontchartrain with a topping of sautéed lump crabmeat (below). Cajun cooks turn redfish or snapper into flavorful dishes such as court-bouillon (a spicy tomato-based dish rich with peppers and spices). Coated in cornmeal and deep-fried, the catfish is a stalwart of the soul food pantheon.

CRABS

Maryland sees itself as the blue crab king of the country, but the dirty secret is this: many 'Maryland' crabs are now harvested in Louisiana. During the lengthy crab season (April to October), these delicious shellfish are available fresh-boiled at informal restaurants and boiling points across the state. The rest of the year, sweet chunks of peeled meat (usually described as 'lump' crabmeat) make flavorful fillings for stuffed eggplant and are the basis for crunchy crab cakes (fried patties of crab, breadcrumbs and seasonings). You'll also find it in seafood gumbos. Scraping the meat out of a crab is an art all its own.

Travelers lucky enough to visit during the earlier part of crab season can indulge in a prized delicacy – the soft-shell crab. As part of its molting process, the blue crab sheds its shell three or four times a year for the first few years of its life. If caught more or less in their birthday suit, they can be eaten whole, shell and all. Soft-shelled crabs are usually pan-fried with browned butter sauce or stuffed with various seafood mixtures. They are, with no exaggeration, abso-freakin'-lutely delicious.

Patrons of the New Orleans Jazz & Heritage Festival (p50) can enjoy soft-shelled crab in its popular po'boy incarnation. Once fried, the crabs are cut in half and inserted into a crusty sandwich roll in the legs-up position for easy snacking on the crispy appendages. Jokingly referred

to as the 'bug po'boy' or 'spider sandwich,' it's a great way to taste the season's best in between stages.

SHRIMP

Culled from the nearby Gulf of Mexico (and, increasingly, from farms), these little critters feature on just about every menu in southern Louisiana. Shrimp is the star attraction in Cajun shrimp étouffée (shrimp smothered in gravy), fried in an overflowing shrimp loaf (po'boy) and chilled in a shrimp rémoulade.

The barbecued shrimp featured on many local menus is misleadingly named. The shrimp aren't grilled at all, but rather pan-fried in their shells (heads on) with butter, olive oil, garlic, Worcestershire sauce, black pepper and other spices. Even in upmarket establishments, patrons who order this dish are given a paper bib to minimize splatter-related dry-cleaning bills.

OYSTERS

These salty bivalves can be found in coastal waters throughout the Northern Hemisphere, but in New Orleans, oysters, even in the simplest form, are considered high art. That said they're also reasonably priced – a round dozen

ERSTER WARNING

You're likely to see elaborately worded disclaimers on signs and menus of oyster bars. They commonly read as follows: 'There may be a risk associated with consuming raw shellfish as is the case with other raw protein products. If you suffer from chronic illness of the liver, stomach or blood, or have other immune disorders, you should eat these products fully cooked.'

The lawyers have spoken. Now belly up for a 'dozen raw and a beer' and slurp away.

rarely runs you over $10 unless you're in a high-end joint. In oyster bars all over town, patrons watch with reverence as the oysters are ritualistically shucked – by the dozen or half-dozen – and served raw on the half-shell. Just add a dash of horseradish and a squirt of lemon, and slurp it down whole.

Farmed 'ersters,' as they're called in the local 'Yat' dialect, are available year round, but are best in the colder months (the months that have an 'r' in their names) when they're plump and salty.

Oysters also make their way into many Creole and Cajun specialties, including oyster soup, oyster casserole, gumbos and rice dressing (p144). They are also commonly coated in seasoned cornmeal and deep-fried for a classic po'boy filling. Old-line Creole establishments typically feature elaborate dishes such as oysters Rockefeller (named after John D because they're so rich), which are baked in the shell with a mixture of chopped spinach, breadcrumbs and aromatic vegetables. Back in the day, fried oysters stuffed in a loaf of bread were known as a 'peace maker' or *médiatrice* (mediator or peacemaker), supposedly brought home to angry wives by sheepish husbands who'd been out all night.

CRAWFISH

If caricatures of this crustacean on souvenir T-shirts, billboards and brochures are any indication, the crawfish is king of Louisiana. During springtime it features on just about every menu in the state. If you leave Louisiana without once tasting crawfish, book a ticket back.

Resembling tiny lobsters, crawfish can either be served fresh-boiled or in the form of pre-peeled tail meat. When crawfish are in season – from early December to mid-July, but best from mid-February – the most popular way to enjoy them is boiled. You can try boiled crawfish at a no-nonsense seafood restaurant called a 'boiling point,' where crawfish are served on aluminum beer trays. Being only a few inches in length, you need to eat a lot to make a meal, and about 4lb to 5lb (2kg to 2½kg) of the little creatures per person is usual.

Crawfish also form the foundation for well-known Cajun dishes such as crawfish étouffée (crawfish smothered in gravy), crawfish boulettes (fried stuffing balls), crawfish jambalaya (p144) and the labor-intensive crawfish bisque. In this classic Cajun delicacy, boiled crawfish heads are filled with a sausagelike stuffing

THE CRAWFISH LEGEND

When the Acadians were forced to leave Nova Scotia, the local lobsters (very loyal shellfish, indeed) decided to follow their adopted humans to Louisiana. During the arduous marathon swim, the crustaceans lost a lot of weight and most of their size. By the time the lobsters reached the bayous and swamps of southern Louisiana to reunite with their beloved proto-Cajuns, they had transformed into the Acadian's smaller, and now-totemic, crawfish.

made of crawfish tails. They're then simmered in a rich roux-based crawfish soup, and served over white rice.

Huh? How do you eat a crawfish? That's an easy one: pinch de' tail and suck de' head, as the overused advice goes. That basically means rip the tail off, squeeze the meat out (it can be tricky, and may require a little tail-peeling), then suck the juices out of the head. This author takes it a step further and scoops out the yummy, mustard-y brains, which has resulted in no shortage of funny looks. If the little dude has claws, go ahead and crack those open too.

Meats
PORK, SAUSAGE & HAM

Pork is popular throughout the South, where every part of the animal can be prepared in countless ways. While ham and pork chops are as popular here as anywhere else, Louisiana naturally has a few porcine specialties of its own. Most popular is andouille (ahn-*doo*-wee), a spicy smoked sausage that turns up in gumbo and jambalaya.

Boudin is a tasty Cajun sausage made with pork, pork liver, cooked rice and spices. Boudin blanc (white boudin) is a popular quick bite, sold by the link in ready-to-eat form in groceries, meat markets and gas stations all over Acadiana. To eat one, cut a link in half, insert an open end into your mouth, and slowly squeeze the filling out (eating the elastic casing is considered questionable). The hard-to-find boudin rouge (red boudin) contains the blood of the freshly slaughtered pig. Boudin rouge can't be sold commercially due to health regulations governing the use of blood in products, but it is still made by families and some butchers on the side.

Gratons (called 'cracklings' elsewhere in the South) are made by cooking down pork skin until most of the fat is rendered and the skin

THE POPULARITY OF POPEYE'S

Ask a New Orleanian where the best fried chicken in town is and they'll probably tell you to try Willie Mae's (p172) or Fiorella's (p151). Now ask them where *they* eat fried chicken, and they'll very likely reply, 'Popeye's.' The chain was voted by locals 'best fried chicken in the city' in the 2008 'Best Of' issue of *Gambit*.

Fried chicken is popular here, as in the rest of the South, although perhaps not as much so. You can thank the plethora of other dishes on offer for that reduced status. Nonetheless, folks take their fried bird seriously here, which is why we find it all the more amusing that so many locals swear by a chain restaurant that largely markets a lousy caricature of the city outside of its limits.

But hey – we trust any New Orleanian native's take on food. The Popeye's here is pretty good (folks say it tastes better than in other states, and to be honest, it just might), and it's cheap, too. We'll never tell you to pass up a local business in favor of Popeye's, but if there's nothing else around…well, we're just sayin'.

itself is golden and crisp. It's a popular snack throughout the region.

Tasso is another highly prized butcher-shop specialty. It's basically a lean chunk of ham, cured with filé (crushed sassafras leaves) and other seasonings, and then smoked until it reaches the tough consistency of beef jerky. Small portions add flavor to soups, sauces and beans.

The bits that are usually discarded elsewhere are used in inventive ways in the Deep South, where you can order pickled pigs' feet, chitterlings (also known as 'chitlins') or smoked ham hocks.

POULTRY

How you like that chicken, hon'? Stuffed, fried, roasted, barbecued, stewed, fricasseed? Swimming with gooey dumplings? We got you covered.

Turkey has made a jump from the Thanksgiving table to become a more workaday dish. Some enterprising Cajun cooks put their crawfish boiling rigs to use in wintertime for deep-frying whole turkeys. For a really fowl feast, look out for the turducken.

Duck is all the rage now, and you'll find it in as humble a form as sandwiched between some po'boy loaves, served in a lovely, rich brown gumbo or stuffed with all sorts of rich goodness in high-end establishments.

BEEF & WILD GAME

Though not as popular as seafood or pork, beef does find its way into countless dishes in its ground form – as in rice dressings, stuffed bell peppers and Creole-Italian meat sauces. Younger milky veal is used in more refined Creole dishes, such as tender veal scallops topped with mushrooms bordelaise.

The fertile wetlands and dense northern forests of Louisiana provide habitats for a wide variety of furred and feathered creatures, such as deer, duck, geese and quail. Being an adaptive bunch, the inhabitants of the state have cultivated a taste for all of them. Even alligator and turtle meat turn up in a variety of Cajun soups and dishes.

BARBECUE

Barbecue isn't the spiritual issue it is in nearby Texas or Memphis, but there are small joints in the city and countryside, and it's becoming increasingly common at big catering events. When you get hold of good barbecue it can be anything from pork ribs to chicken, mutton and hot links, accompanied by soft white bread, coleslaw, potato salad, pinto beans and plenty of beer or sweet soda. Dig in *mano a mano,* as true barbecue is a no-utensils affair.

Roux

Very few meals begin life in Louisiana without a roux (pronounced roo) base. Simply put, a roux is flour slowly cooked with oil or butter. Over time, the product will evolve from a light-colored and flavored 'white' roux into a smokier, thicker 'dark' roux. The final product is used as a thickening and flavoring agent. While deceptively simple, many local cooks insist their dishes live or die based on the foundation roux.

Gumbo

Ladies and gentlemen, please rise for the culinary ambassador of New Orleans: gumbo. This spicy, full-bodied soup/stew is more than a representative dish – with its combination of catch-all components and the *impratur* of individuality from every gumbo cook out there, it's sort of Louisiana, food-ified. No cook (and sometimes, it seems, citizen) in the city is without a personal recipe for it. The ingredients – which can include products from the sea, land and air – vary from chef to chef, but gumbo is almost always served over starchy steamed rice. Close to the coast, you can find gumbos teeming with all manner of seafood (oysters, jumbo shrimp, half-shelled crabs), while prairie-bred Cajuns turn to their barnyard and smokehouse traditions for inspiration. Creole cooks in New Orleans often add tomato to their gumbos, adding a sweeter cast to the finished product.

The distinctively thick texture that separates gumbo from the broth-based soup family comes from the use of various thickening agents: dark roux, okra or the late addition of filé.

Breads & Sandwiches

As you might expect from a Franco-centric culture, New Orleans enjoys its daily bread, whether it be a hot loaf wrapped in restaurant linen or the omnipresent po'boy. The trademark bread of the Crescent City is an oblong French loaf, with a feather-light interior and crispy crust, although not too crispy – New Orleanians have never liked the sharp flakes that snap off a traditional French baguette. The local loaf is wider than a baguette as well, well suited for sopping up sauces and soups. The most famous purveyor of the New Orleans loaf is Leidenheimer's Bakery; according to some, it ain't a po'boy if it comes on any other kind of bread.

PO'BOYS

Maybe you call it a submarine, grinder or hoagie. You are wrong. This is New Orleans, son, and you are about to bite into a po'boy – and you are going to *enjoy* it. We've had variations of 'sandwich' across the world, and this, friends, is the best.

Simply put, a po'boy is an overstuffed bit of Louisiana loaf dripping with whatever, although the most popular fillings are roast beef, fried shrimp and/or fried oysters, and 'debris' – the bits of roast beef that fall into the gravy and get all soft and lovely and…oh yeaahhh. Alligator, sausage, roast duck, French fries, crawfish and *cochon de lait* (slow-roasted pig) also make appearances. Somewhere out there we are sure there is a tofu po'boy merchant, huddling in terrified fear of being found out by vengeful local food purists. The fast food of Louisiana is served everywhere, from neighborhood groceries to interstate gas stations.

What's in a name? Well, back in the early 20th century, brothers Bennie and Clovis Martin opened a coffee shop in the French Market after working jobs as streetcar operators. In 1929, when the street railway union went on strike, Bennie and Clovis did right and served up free sandwiches for their former union brothers. 'Our meal is free to any members of Division 194 [the union],' the Martins wrote in a letter. 'We are with you until hell freezes, and when it does, we will furnish blankets to keep you warm.' Later, Bennie recalled, 'whenever we saw one of the striking men coming, one of us would say, "Here comes another poor boy."' The legend was born.

You may consider the po'boy enormous. It is. A half loaf ought to satisfy most folks. They used to be pretty cheap, but unfortunately, many of the better po'boys in town are more like 'middle-class boys' ($14 for a foot long? Seriously!?).

When you order a po'boy, your server will ask if you want it 'dressed,' meaning with mayonnaise, shredded iceberg lettuce and tomato slices. Just say yes.

MUFFULETTAS

It's only a slight exaggeration to say that New Orleans muffulettas are the size of manhole covers. Named for a round sesame-crusted loaf, muffulettas are layered with various selections from the local Sicilian deli tradition, including Genoa salami, shaved ham, mortadella and sliced provolone cheese. The signature spread – a salty olive salad with pickled vegetables, herbs, garlic and olive oil – is what defines the sandwich, though. It's a flavorful, greasy mess.

Muffulettas are a great option for frustrated vegetarians traveling in New Orleans, as they can easily be made without meat.

Rice & Beans

When a poor man's meal in French Louisiana doesn't come wrapped in a crunchy po'boy roll, odds are that it's served on a bed of white rice. Louisiana rice consumption is considerably higher than that of the rest of the nation, and even rivals some Asian countries. Rice is the staple grain of both Creole and Cajun cuisines.

Rice fields dominate the marshy lands of the Cajun prairie. The texture is somewhere between glutinous Japanese sushi and fluffier American long-grain – if you've grown up on Asian rice it may not impress, but for these

LOUISIANA CHICKEN & OKRA GUMBO

Here's a gumbo you can make almost anywhere.

Ingredients

2 chickens, quartered (for meat and 6 cups chicken stock)

3 garlic cloves, crushed

1 small onion, peeled

2/3 cup neutral-flavored oil

2/3 cup flour

1 large red bell pepper, diced

1 large green bell pepper, diced

2 onions, diced

2 stalks celery, diced

10oz (300g) tomatoes, diced

5 tbsp Worcestershire sauce

2 tbsp Tabasco sauce

2 tbsp tomato paste

1 bay leaf

2 tsp dried thyme leaves

2 tsp dried oregano leaves

1 tsp ground cayenne pepper

1 tsp ground white pepper

2 cups fresh okra, sliced

sea salt to taste

freshly ground pepper to taste

pepper sauce to taste

filé powder

Simmer the chicken in eight cups (2L) of water with the garlic cloves and the small onion for about an hour. Remove the chicken from the pot and discard the garlic and onion. Skim all the fat from the chicken stock. If you have time, the easiest way to do this is to put it in the refrigerator overnight and skim off the solidified fat in the morning. When the chicken has cooled, remove the meat from the bones and discard the bones and skin.

In a heavy soup pot that will hold at least eight quarts (8L), make a dark brown roux with the oil and flour.

When the roux is the desired color, turn off the heat and add the peppers, onion and celery, sautéing until the vegetables are soft (about five minutes). Add the tomatoes, Worcestershire, Tabasco, tomato paste, bay leaf, thyme, oregano, cayenne and white pepper. Stir thoroughly. Slowly whisk in the skimmed chicken stock a little at a time, making sure there are no lumps. Cook over a medium heat for 20 minutes. Add the okra and chicken meat and continue cooking for another 30 minutes. Season with salt and pepper as required. Remember, the gumbo should be fairly thick.

To serve, mound half a cup of steamed rice in a bowl. Ladle gumbo around the rice. Serve with pepper sauce and filé powder. Makes 12 servings.

parts it's pretty good stuff. The starchy texture helps the rice keep its integrity whether it's covered in a pool of shrimp étouffée or acting as sausage filler in links of hot Cajun boudin. The drier, more discrete grains of long-grain rice are more common in dishes from the Anglo-influenced soul food traditions of northern Louisiana, such as hoppin' John (rice and black-eyed peas).

As an inexpensive and easily prepared source of protein, beans have played an integral role in the culinary history of New Orleans, as well as in the rest of Louisiana.

JAMBALAYA

Hearty, rice-based jambalaya (johm-buh-*lie*-uh) is a Louisiana classic. It is loosely based on Spain's paella, although in practical terms it's probably closer to *arroz con pollo* (chicken and rice). Jambalaya can include just about any combination of fowl, shellfish or meat, but usually includes ham, hence the dish's name (derived from the French *jambon* or the Spanish *jamón*). The meaty ingredients are sautéed with onions, pepper and celery, and cooked with raw rice and water into a flavorful mix of textures. You'll find jambalaya at restaurants and food stalls during music, food or cultural festivals.

RICE DRESSING

It's a regional call whether you refer to this chicken, pork and rice mélange as rice dressing (the traditional Cajun name) or dirty rice (a Deep South slang variant). Either way, it's a tasty way to use the giblets from a roast chicken or holiday turkey, and any leftover rice.

RED BEANS & RICE

A poor man's meal rich in smoky flavor, the combination of red beans and rice is a lunch tradition synonymous with Mondays throughout the state, especially in New Orleans. Monday was traditionally wash day, and in the days before large household appliances it took all day to hand-wash the family laundry. So a pot of red beans would go on the stove along with the ham bone left over from Sunday dinner; the longer it cooked, the better it tasted. By the time the washing was finished, supper was ready.

In the absence of red beans, larger maroon kidney beans are often used. The flavoring meat can also be spicy andouille sausage (p141) or chunks of pork *tasso* (p141); the latter is particularly delicious.

Black-eyed peas, a hearty soul food staple, are creamy beige with a single dark spot (the eye) near the center. They're traditionally cooked with a flavoring meat (ham hocks and salt pork are common).

No matter what type of beans are on the table, locals typically reach for a trusted pepper sauce (below) before digging in.

Grits & Cornbread

Corn, introduced to European settlers by the Native Americans, is a keystone staple of American cuisine. Around wet New Orleans, where wheat doesn't grow well, corn is used in a variety of breads and other dishes. Dried corn, when ground into a coarse meal, is suitable for coating oysters and catfish before deep-frying.

Dried hominy grits are prepared as a porridge (similar in texture to polenta) and are served as a breakfast side option at any Southern diner. On their own grits can be bland, but add a chunk of butter, a shake of black pepper and (if you like) a few squirts of hot sauce and they become an addictive morning ritual.

Cornbread is the simple, everyday bread most often seen on southern country-style and soul food menus. It comes in a lot of variations, including muffins, corn sticks (cornbread baked in corn-shaped moulds), crackling bread (cornbread with cracklings added) and hush puppies (balls of deep-fried cornbread batter).

Herbs, Spices & Seasonings

The trademark herbs and spices of Louisiana cooking illustrate how the state's culinary traditions melded the bold flavors of European traditions with indigenous ingredients (filé, bay leaves). The emphasis in the Creole cooking of New Orleans is on balanced flavors, rather than spices that overwhelm the palate, while Cajun dishes are generally hotter. Cajun cooks usually use a blend of salt, peppers, spices and dried herbs; similar mixes can be purchased commercially, but buyer beware, as some companies go heavy with cayenne at the expense of a balanced flavor. That said, it's a fallacy that Louisiana food is searing hot – it's more flavorful than anything else, and if you're used to Indian curries, Cajun and Creole food is cake.

A small bottle of hot sauce, usually Tabasco and Crystal, can be found on every table in New Orleans. Usually a fermented mix of pepper pods, salt and vinegar, pepper sauces have departed from the standard red-pepper variety in recent years. Avery Island's McIlhenny dynasty, the manufacturers of the omnipresent Tabasco sauce, has recently expanded its line to include other peppery bases such as green jalapeño, mild garlic and the painful habanero chili.

Brownish Creole mustard, more rustic and flavorful than its yellow American counterpart, is similar to a European whole-grain mustard except that the mustard seeds are marinated in vinegar during preparation. It's a vital ingredient in shrimp rémoulade and goes well with every sandwich ever.

Parsley and green onions are important finishing herbs in Cajun cuisine. Usually minced and added at the last stage of cooking, they provide a distinctly 'green' flavor to gumbos, jambalayas and other classic dishes. Whole bay leaves are commonly used to flavor many savory dishes, particularly long-cooked beans.

A seafood boil, also known as crab and shrimp boil, can contain a blend of bay leaves, mustard seeds, cayenne pepper, peppercorns, cloves and allspice.

Sauces

Another French hand-me-down, highly refined sauces add flavor and warmth to many Creole dishes. The New Orleans take on rémoulade is a spicy sauce that greatly differs from the French mayonnaise-based classic. New Orleans recipes for this sauce sometimes call for a base of tomato ketchup spiked with horseradish, red pepper and Creole mustard. You're likely to find it on chilled shrimp as shrimp rémoulade.

THE HOLY TRINITY

The combination of three vegetables – white onion, sweet green bell pepper and celery – is popular enough in Cajun and Creole cooking to warrant the nickname 'The Holy Trinity.' Local dishes such as gumbo, red beans, court bouillon and sauce *piquante* (spicy tomato-based stew) all require this flavorful trio to be sautéed in the initial stages of the cooking process. Their collective importance is similar to the *mirepoix* (base of onion, celery and carrot) in continental French cuisine. In many dishes, garlic is also added, but that messes up the Biblical metaphor. The sweet bell pepper sometimes goes it alone as a dinner course, filled with meat and bread stuffing.

Mayonnaise in Louisiana is considered a relative of the French original, rather than your standard American bland white sandwich spread. In many homes and restaurants, you'll find a pale yellow version of this continental classic in dishes or on salads such as potato salad and coleslaw. Hollandaise sauce, rich with eggs and butter, is an important ingredient in more upscale brunch offerings, such as eggs Benedict, eggs Sardou (poached eggs with creamed spinach, artichoke bottoms and hollandaise sauce) and trout *marguery* (trout in a hollandaise sauce mixed with crabmeat, oysters, shrimp, paprika and lemon juice). Béarnaise sauce is a common variant on hollandaise that includes a mixture of herbs, shallots and vinegar.

Cocktail sauce makes regular appearances at oyster bars and crawfish boils. It's a simple concoction with ketchup, prepared horseradish, pepper sauce and lemon.

Vegetables

With its long growing season and rich soil, the land around New Orleans yields a wide range of farm fresh vegetables. Whether they're brought in for sale at the French Market (p72) or purchased from roadside vendors, the products of Louisiana gardens are an essential part of the local culinary tradition.

Okra came with the African slaves and made a distinct culinary impression on the Deep South. It has a significant amount of mucilage (also known as 'goo'), and is used as the primary thickener in traditional Creole gumbo. It can also be served as crispy pickled pods, or breaded and deep-fried until crunchy.

Significant native vegetables include a variety of squash that choke the markets during the summer season and a sweet potato known as 'Louisiana yam.' (If you see yams on a menu, you can safely assume it's sweet potato.) Actual yams are also widely available. Candied yams are a popular side dish served with roasted meats.

Turnips, mustard and collard greens – individually or in combination – are soul food regulars. The greens are usually cooked with a chunk of flavoring meat (usually some sort of pork, and hopefully *tasso*), sprinkled with a bit of pepper sauce, and served with cornbread.

Italian cooks in the city like to transform the eggplant into eggplant parmigiana, which is cooked with red gravy (spiced tomato sauce). Similar preparations await the mirliton, a vegetable squash eaten throughout Latin America, where it is known as 'chayote.'

The home gardens of Louisiana produce their fair share of green beans. The French *les haricots* is said to have morphed into the term 'zydeco,' appellation for the music of the rural blacks in Cajun Country.

Fruits

While most fruit is shipped in from someplace else, some tasty specialties are grown locally. Ponchatoula, northwest of New Orleans, produces strawberries that are tangy and sweet and, come spring, refined by Abita into excellent strawberry beer. Along roadsides and fencerows throughout the state, sweet and tart dewberries grow in sticky brambles. When the summer berries turn deep purple, intrepid pickers hit the bushes, braving sharp thorns and possible snakebites for a bucket load. Another roadside sign to look for in southern Louisiana is one advertising Ruston peaches, a popular summer fruit eaten fresh, or baked into dessert pies.

The homegrown Creole tomato can be integrated into a wide variety of dishes. Creole cooks are likely to add it to their gumbo and jambalaya recipes. Cajuns like to smother okra or summer squash with a tomato or two. But at peak tomato season, you only need to slice them up, sprinkle a little salt and serve.

Watermelons grow well in the semitropical conditions and are commonly purchased from roadside truck stands during summer. Oranges grow around Port Sulphur, south of New Orleans; the Washington orange is its specialty.

Sweet Treats

Collectively, New Orleanians have a famously sweet tooth. The desserts of the region give ample incentive to save a little room, which is not easy to do, considering the predominance of tasty and filling starters and main courses.

PECANS & PRALINES

Though the peanut rules many other southern states, the pecan is Louisiana's nut of choice. It's indigenous to the region and was often used in cooking by the Native Americans. While driving the backroads in the north of the region you'll see deep shady groves of huge pecan trees. Pecans are used mostly in sweet dishes and are a common ingredient in stuffing for poultry and vegetables. Pecan pralines (*praw*-leens in Louisiana) are an extremely popular sweet treat.

BEIGNETS

Not so much a dessert as a round-the-clock breakfast specialty akin to the common doughnut, beignets are flat squares of dough flash-fried to a golden, puffy glory, dusted liberally with powdered (confectioner's, or icing) sugar, and served scorching hot. They're good any time of day (even after a big meal) with a cup of rich café au lait. Ground zero for this treat is Café du Monde (p152) in the French Quarter.

BREAD PUDDING

A specialty in New Orleans and Acadiana, this custardy creation is a good use for leftover bread. Variations in New Orleans generally involve copious amounts of butter, eggs and cream and will usually come topped with a bourbon-spiked sugar sauce. In recent years cooks have taken to adding white chocolate and other ingredients to spice up this simple fare.

PIES

The Deep South's traditional dessert is usually available in a variety of flavors and served with a cup of steaming hot coffee. The baking process is relatively simple and the fillings are infinitely variable – a crust can be filled with fresh berries, gooey pecans, coconut cream, apples, rhubarb, custard or lemon curd topped with mile-high meringue.

Fried pies, similar to the Central American empanada, are a popular convenience dessert. A flaky crust is wrapped around fruit or custard fillings and deep-fried in fat or lard.

BANANAS FOSTER

This now infamous dish of sliced bananas, brown sugar, spices, butter and various liqueurs was made famous at Brennan's Restaurant (p152) in the French Quarter, and is now a New Orleans dessert standard. The bananas are sautéed (usually tableside) in a flood of butter and sugar, reduced to a thick sauce, and then flamed with strong rum and a well-placed match. This preparation is served over rich vanilla ice cream.

VEGETARIANS & VEGANS

Things are getting better for vegetarians in this town. We credit the rise of tourism and the waves of post-Katrina do-gooders, many of whom were of, shall we say, a leftist, veggie-friendly bent. This website may be your best guide to eating meat-free in the Crescent

---

KING CAKES

Of all Mardi Gras traditions, none is more kitschy than the king cake. Every year, on Twelfth Night (January 6), the first king cakes emerge from bakeries all over New Orleans and soon appear in offices – including the mayor's – and at Twelfth Night parties throughout the city.

The king cake is an oval, spongy Danish pastry with gooey icing and purple, green and gold sugar on top. More importantly, it always contains an inedible peanut-size plastic baby somewhere inside. The baby is the key – it's what perpetuates the king cake tradition. The rule is, whoever is served the piece of cake with the baby inside (don't swallow that baby!) has to buy the next cake. Some office workers eat king cake five days a week between Twelfth Night and Mardi Gras.

The king cake originated in 1870, when the Twelfth Night Revelers used it to select a queen for the 'Lord of Misrule,' and a Carnival tradition was born. Early king cakes contained an uncooked golden bean instead of a baby, and the recipient of the bean was crowned king or queen of a Carnival krewe. That ritual is still maintained by some krewes, but such important matters are no longer left to chance. The bean, or baby, is always planted in the piece of cake served to a preselected king or queen. It seems the king cake has lost some of its clout.

Nevertheless, these cakes are big business in this city. One local bakery chain claims they sell 30,000 king cakes a day during Carnival season. According to local statisticians, 750,000 king cakes are consumed every year in the New Orleans metropolitan area.

SUNDAY BRUNCH

In New Orleans, Sunday brunch is an important family tradition. The concept was originally shaped by the demands of the Catholic Church, which required the faithful to fast from midnight Saturday until after mass on Sunday.

By the time you left church, not only were you spiritually refreshed but also mighty peckish. But it was too late for breakfast and too early for lunch, so brunch was devised as an in-between sort of meal and popularized by such old-line Creole restaurants as Brennan's (p152) and Commander's Palace (p162). Grillades and grits (grilled beef or veal slices braised in tomato sauce and served with a cooked mush of coarse-grained hominy) is a classic New Orleans brunch dish. Jazz bands were added to the mix, and the tradition of the 'Jazz Brunch' is now a common Sunday morning repast.

New Orleans may not be the devout Catholic city it once was, but brunch remains a very popular meal among tourists who can afford the pricey egg dishes and morning cocktails referred to as 'eye-openers.'

City: www.pakupaku.info/neworleans/eating nola.shtml.

The cooking techniques that make Louisiana food so flavorful can also make mealtime challenging for the vegetarian traveler. The common use of 'flavoring meats' and meat-based stocks means many apparently flesh-free vegetable dishes may well include a bit of ham, sausage or seafood. It's not that the cooks of Louisiana are out to persecute the herbivorous diner, it's just that they come from a thoroughly omnivorous heritage.

And yet there are restaurants catering exclusively to vegetarians, and most upscale places will be able to assemble something, even if they don't have vegetarian dishes on the menu. Italian restaurants, with their pastas and tomato-based red gravy dishes, are good bets.

With some planning, you will be able to enjoy the regional cuisine without compromise or despair. Firstly, if you can make an exception for seafood, close this book and go eat. Seafood is one of the region's culinary strengths, although you should double-check with staff whether sausage and ham have been added, particularly in seafood gumbo.

Gumbo z'herbes, a green gumbo made with a hearty variety of turnip, collard, spinach and other greens, is a meatless Lenten staple that many Creole restaurants offer year round. Just ask whether the roux was made with butter or oil, and if there are any pork products used in the cooking process. Neighborhood joints shouldn't provide any difficulty as they will invariably have bean-and-vegetable side dishes, which you can combine to make a substantial meal. While vegetables and beans used to be cooked in pigs' fat, these days most places use vegetable oil, although you should check first. A muffuletta (p143) without the Italian meats (cheeses and olive salad only) is a good way to sample a reasonable meatless facsimile of the local sandwich specialty.

It will be easier to find vegetarian infrastructure in New Orleans, but if you're out in Cajun Country don't overlook local diners, which will have a wide selection of vegetable dishes for the choosing. Vegans should steer clear of cornbread, since it's usually prepared with a batter that includes eggs and milk.

Slim Goodie's Diner (p163), Angeli on Decatur (p151) and Bennachin (p150) have vegetarian standards on their menus, and every high-end restaurant includes a vegetarian option these days. Japanese, Latin and Indian restaurants are, as ever, reliable sources of veg fare.

PRACTICALITIES

Opening Hours

Most places that serve breakfast are open from 7am or 8am until 10am or 11am. Some of these establishments also serve lunch, with breakfast and lunch menus available until 2pm or so. Brunch is available on Sundays from around 11am until 2pm or 3pm, though some places that stake their reputations on brunch keep it going all week. Dinner hours are generally 6pm to 9pm or 10pm. There are a few late-night eateries out there (see boxed text, p151) – some, but not all, are bars.

How Much?

New Orleans is generally not as expensive as most other US cities, but it's becoming something of a foodie mecca. As a result, prices are climbing at both high-end places and neighborhood joints that have been discovered by the Travel Channel, Food Network and, well, folks like us. Sorry.

Booking Tables

Some of New Orleans' restaurants are just too popular. Where reservations are really necessary, we'll say so in our listings in this chapter.

But many restaurants have no-booking policies; Galatoire's (p155) and K-Paul's (p154) are two notable examples. This means that instead of calling ahead, you can expect to wait out on the sidewalk for a table to open up.

Keep in mind many of the city's best restaurants are small, family-run establishments that aren't set to handle large groups unannounced. A quick way to cop a dirty look from a host is to roll 11-deep into a neighborhood joint and expect immediate seating and service. In this case, while reservations may not be accepted, it's a good idea to call ahead and announce your arrival.

If no tables are available in your favorite restaurant (there's always the small chance that the maître d' could make a table turn up with the right incentive, but the Big Easy might turn out not to be *that* easy), take heart – this city has a *lot* of excellent restaurants!

Tipping

Tipping is not optional in sit-down restaurants. An adequate tip is 15%, but here, where so many people work in the service industry, folks tend to be generous; a 20% tip (generous in most of the USA) is almost standard. That said, you're fine with 15%, but if the service is good, go a little higher.

Most over-the-counter establishments will have a tip jar with a note telling you it's bad karma not to tip. That may be so, but you're not obliged to. And if you feel like tipping a dude for pouring coffee into a paper cup for you, a little spare change will do. That little jangle in the jar will make them eternally grateful to you. Delis and po'boy shops operate on a similar basis. Some places will charge an automatic 18% gratuity for large groups (usually of six or more people).

FRENCH QUARTER

This is the beating heart of the New Orleans tourism industry, and many of those tourists are in town to eat. The chefs of the French Quarter do not disappoint: here you'll find the most classic old-line Creole standbys as well as many spots slicing along the cutting edge of nouveau Louisiana cuisine. In between are plenty of diners and cafes. Standards vary enormously – there are more than a few spots here living off a name or a good location on the tourism track, so if you want the best this city can offer, do a little homework before visiting the Vieux Carré.

LOWER QUARTER

The Lower Quarter features the best cheap eating options around, but there are a few decent high-end places here as well.

TUJAGUE'S Map pp70–1   Creole $$$
☎ 525-8676; www.tujaguesrestaurant.com; 823 Decatur St; 6-course dinners $30-40; 5-10pm
Tujague's has been holding down its corner since 1856, making it the second-oldest eatery in New Orleans. Dinner is a traditional six-course affair that highlights the joint's signature items: a piquant shrimp rémoulade and tender beef brisket with a simple Creole sauce for dipping. Diners can select from four mains based on choice offerings from the butcher and the fishmonger. Sometimes this set meal is fantastic, but part of Tujague's staying power comes from its position on several organized group tours of New Orleans, so the kitchen can get rushed. The atmosphere is classy but far more casual than institutions such as Antoine's (p153). Patrons enter the small dining room via a narrow bar, where you can envisage a past century's mustached, jauntily hatted crowd – try a Bloody Mary.

WOLFE'S
Map pp70–1   Modern American $$$
☎ 593-9535; www.wolfesrestaurant.com; 1041 Dumaine St; mains $17-35; 6pm-9:30pm Tue-Thu & Sat, 11:30am-1:30pm & 6-9:30pm Fri
Formerly Peristyle's, Wolfe's is now named for its chef, Tom Wolfe, an alumnus of Emeril's kitchens and popular stalwart of the New Orleans eating scene. The space is wonderful, all warm lighting and cozy accents, and has served as a restaurant space in one form or another for over 130 years. The food's great, too; the lamb T-bones with lavender demi-glace are gorgeous, and while the menu isn't as adventurous as we might have hoped, this is a dependable place for a sumptuous meal. If you want to push the limit of the kitchen's skill, we recommend opting for the tasting menu (from $35 for three courses).

MURIEL'S Map pp70–1   Modern Creole $$
☎ 568-1885; www.muriels.com; 801 Chartres St; mains $17-35; 5:30-10pm Mon-Sat, 11:30am-2:30pm & 5-10pm Sun
Good food, sultry atmosphere and location, location, location make Muriel's hard to

PRICE GUIDE

$$$	over $30 a meal
$$	$15-30 a meal
$	under $15 a meal

pass up. You have your choice of settings: the main dining room evokes the lurid pomp of Storyville, with deep-red walls and chandeliers; in the eclectic bistro, 19th-century art hangs from exposed brick walls; the courtyard bar exemplifies traditional tropical decadence with potted palms and marble-topped cafe tables; while the balcony seating affords an elevated view of Jackson Sq's motley krewe of musicians, magicians, painters and tarot readers. The kitchen tinkers with the Creole ethos enough to steer clear of stodginess without alienating the average patron. It's also a good spot for a steak.

CAFÉ AMELIE Map pp70–1 — French $$
☎ 412-8965; 912 Royal St; mains $8-32; ⏰ 11am-3pm & 6-9pm Wed-Sat, 10am-4pm Sun
We've waxed rhapsodic over the Quarter's beautiful backyard gardens, but Amelie's takes the cake. This may be the most romantic dining spot in the city, an alfresco restaurant that's practically as cute as the movie of the same name, tucked behind an old carriage house and surrounded by high brick walls and lush shade trees. Fresh seafood and local produce are the basis of a modest, ever-changing menu. Lunch is lovely, when you can nibble sandwiches amid the green, but an evening dinner under starlight while feasting on shrimp and mushroom linguine is just as magic.

IRENE'S CUISINE Map pp70–1 — Italian $$
☎ 529-8811; 539 St Philip St; mains $16-20; ⏰ 5:30-10pm Mon-Sat
Irene's may be in the Quarter, but its in a corner generally missed by tourists – not that that's easy to do given the overwhelming(ly good) scent of garlic emanating from this cavern of Italian intimacy. It's Italian-French, really: you can pick from seasoned rosemary chicken, seared chops, pan-sautéed fish fillets and great pasta, but leave room for the decadent pecan-praline bread pudding. Reservations are not accepted and long waits are the norm.

PORT OF CALL Map pp70–1 — Grill $$
☎ 523-0120; 838 Esplanade Ave; mains $7-21; ⏰ 11am-late
The Port of Call burger is, simply put, one of the best we've had, anywhere. The meat is unadulterated and, well, meaty – when you bite into a POC burger, you *know* you are eating cow, not some preprocessed, chemically treated imitation. The sensation of beef infuses your entire being, and the burger is enormous – a half pound that easily looks the size, and we mean this, of your face. Then there's the baked potato on the side, buckling under the weight of sour cream, butter and baco-bits. It's all served in a 1960s-ish Polynesian tiki bar, dim and hot-pink lit and kitschy as hell. There are a lot of other menu items, but we can't get enough of that burger-y heaven, and neither can locals, who willingly wait outside in long lines for a seat (no reservations).

BENNACHIN Map pp70–1 — West African $
☎ 522-1230; 1212 Royal; St; mains $8-16; ⏰ 11am-11pm; Ⓥ
This is about as foreign as flavors get in the French Quarter, although West African cuisine (specifically Cameroonian and Gambian) doesn't pose too many challenges to the conservative palette. In some ways it's more meat and potatoes than meat and potatoes; the main dish is a meat, often served in a stew form (spicy upon request) with some kind of starch used as a scooping accompaniment. Bennachin admirably makes full use of American ingredients to keep flavors stronger and more colorful than they tend to be in Africa; couscous in yogurt sauce and coconut rice are good examples. The heavy use of okra reminds you how much this cuisine has influenced Louisiana. All in all, this is a great ethnic eatery in a city that can lack in the genre.

COOP'S PLACE Map pp70–1 — Cajun $
☎ 525-9053; 1109 Decatur St; mains $8-17.50; ⏰ 11am-3am; 🛜
Coop's gets all credit for maintaining high standards in the midst of the Quarter, where restaurants know they can get away with serving tourists pap. This could almost be an authentic Cajun dive, but more rocked out. Make no mistake: it's a grotty chaotic place, and the layout is annoying

(be ready for an elbow in your back at some point in the night). But it's worth it for the food: rabbit jambalaya, chicken with shrimp and *tasso* (in a cream sauce – there's no such thing as 'too heavy' in New Orleans). This is rural, rustic and rich food served at an honest price.

FIORELLA'S Map pp70–1   Italian & Louisianan $

☎ 523-2155; 1136 Decatur St; mains $7-15; ✆ 11am-midnight Sun-Thu, to 2am Fri & Sat

If you need to eat right in the Quarter for under $20 a head, Fiorella's and nearby Coop's (opposite) are as good as it gets. Where Coop's is a Cajun Country shack hipstered up, Fiorella's is a Sicilian cafe, all red-checkered cloth, but run through the same punk-rock wringer. Don't get the wrong idea – it's bright and cozy, but this is more neighborhood spot than tourist trap, and said 'hood is the slightly grungy north end of Decatur St. The food is quintessential Italian New Orleans: pastas, pizzas, veal cutlets and, arguably, the best fried chicken in town. Some find the latter too salty; we say it's just right, especially with a bit of hot sauce.

ANGELI ON DECATUR

Map pp70–1   Upscale Diner $

☎ 566-0077; 1141 Decatur St; mains $6-18; ✆ 11am-2am Sun-Thu, to 4am Fri & Sat; Ⓥ

Great philosophers have long debated one of the most pressing of human questions: what makes a late-night place great? We humbly submit: the food tastes as good sober as when you're trashed at 3am. Enter Angeli: decked out with hipster art and patrons, the food here is wonderful no matter your state of mind/inebriation/ whatever. It serves burger, pasta and pizza fare, but it's top-of-the-line stuff, especially if you need to layer your tummy after a long night out. Early music sets by solid live acts are a good way to launch your evening, but bring cash – credit cards are not accepted. Good range of vegetarian dishes.

LOUISIANA PIZZA KITCHEN

Map pp70–1   Pizza $

☎ 522-9500; www.louisianapizzakitchen.com; 95 French Market Place; mains $8-16; ✆ noon-9pm Wed-Sun

Opposite the Old US Mint, this is a popular local chain offering wood-fired, individual pizza crusts that resemble toasted pita bread as opposed to Domino's style cheesiness. Sometimes you just need a pizza, and this place provides.

MONA LISA Map pp70–1   Italian $

☎ 522-6746; 1212 Royal St; mains $9-14; ✆ 11am-11pm

An informal, quiet local spot in the Lower Quarter, dim and dark and candlelit romantic in its quirky way. Kooky renditions of da Vinci's familiar subject hang on the walls. In hair curlers, 50lb heavier or in the form of a cow, she stares impassively at diners munching on pizzas, pastas and spinach salads.

CENTRAL GROCERY

Map pp70–1   Italian Deli $

☎ 523-1620; 923 Decatur St; sandwiches $7-10; ✆ 9am-5pm Tue-Sat

There are a few New Orleans names inextricably linked to a certain dish – Café du Monde (p152) for beignets, for example – and Central Grocery is the word-association winner for the muffuletta (see p143). That's pronounced 'muffa-lotta,' and that about sums it up: your mouth will be muffled by a hell of a lotta sandwich, stuffed with meat, cheese and great, sharp olive salad. This is a real grocery by the way, one of the last neighborhood vestiges of the New Orleans Sicilian community, and the fresh Italian produce is a draw on its own.

top picks

LATE-NIGHT EATS

New Orleans' bars can stay open round the clock, which makes it possible to completely rearrange your schedule to whatever suits your night-owl soul. Only problem is, most restaurants close at 10pm. If you're likely to experience an undeniable hunger sometime past midnight, it's a good idea to commit the following late-night eateries to memory.

- Clover Grill (p152)
- Coop's Place (opposite)
- Angeli on Decatur (left)
- Alibi (p156)
- Cooter Brown's (p168)
- Trolley Stop (p163)
- Camellia Grill (p169)
- Delachaise (p167)

VERTI MARTE Map pp70–1 Deli $
☎ 525-4767; www.vertimarte.com; 1201 Royal St; meals $3.50-8.50; ☯ 24hr
Sometimes you just wanna wander the Quarter with a good burger or seafood sandwich in hand. If that's the case, get ye to Verti, a reliable deli with a take-out stand that's got a menu as long as a hot New Orleans summer day. If you're in your hotel room at 3am and craving some ribs (with two sides!), rejoice, for Verti delivers free anywhere in the French Quarter and Faubourg Marigny.

CLOVER GRILL Map pp70–1 Gay Grill $
☎ 598-1010; www.clovergrill.com; 900 Bourbon St; dishes $3-8; ☯ 24hr
Our subhead for this spot is a bit of a misnomer – you don't have to be gay to eat or work here. Indeed, much of the clientele base is loyal straight folk who live around the corner. But there is a big gay customer base thanks to nearby gay bars and a fair bit of gay vibe among employees. It's all slightly surreal, given this place otherwise totally resembles a '50s diner, but nothing adds to the Americana like a prima donna–ish argument between an out-of-makeup drag queen and a drunk club kid, all likely set to blaring disco music. The food isn't anything special, but it's dependable diner fare and good for a hangover, or those who can see the hangover approaching.

CROISSANT D'OR PATISSERIE
Map pp70–1 Cafe $
☎ 524-4663; 617 Ursulines Ave; meals $3-5; ☯ 7am-5pm
On the quieter side of the Quarter, this ancient and spotlessly clean pastry shop is where many Quarter locals start their day. Bring a paper, order coffee and a savory or sweet stuffed croissant and bliss out. On your way in, check out the tiled sign on the threshold that says 'ladies entrance' – a holdover from prefeminist days.

CC'S COFFEE HOUSE Map pp70–1 Cafe $
☎ 581-6996; 941 Royal St; pastries $2; ☯ 7am-late
Community Coffee has been a staple in most Louisiana homes since 1919. This corner cafe is its French Quarter outpost, and it's a good spot for perching, caffeine sipping, net surfing and the rest. Its very sweet ice-coffee blends are a treat on hot days.

CAFÉ DU MONDE Map pp70–1 Cafe $
☎ 800-772-2927; www.cafedumonde.com; 800 Decatur St; beignets $2; ☯ 24hr
Let us out with it: du Monde – a major icon in the city – is a bit overrated. The coffee is decent, particularly the café au lait, while the beignets are inconsistent. Coffee and beignets, folks, that's all they got. The main problem is, sorry to say, the tourists – this place is so crammed you rarely feel as if you're having anything like a romantic street-side shot o' caffeine and pastry. At least it's open 24 hours – you might be able to capture some measure of noir-ish cool as the drunks stumble past in the Edward Hopper–esque wee hours.

UPPER QUARTER
The Upper Quarter (south of Jackson Sq) is where the French Quarter's best high-end dining is to be found. Unfortunately there are a lot of pale imitators that want to break your bank, so read on closely…

BRENNAN'S RESTAURANT
Map pp70–1 Creole $$$
☎ 525-9713; www.brennansneworleans.com; 417 Royal St; 3-course breakfasts $36, 4-course dinners $40; ☯ 9am-1pm & 6-9pm Mon-Thu & Sun, 9am-2pm & 6-9pm Fri & Sat
Brennan's is many things: upscale Creole, French Quarter cornerstone, yada, yada, yada. But mainly, we give it credit for re-inventing the concept of 'poached eggs on bread with hollandaise.' In its quest to create the city's most extravagant breakfast, there's a dozen variations on the above eggs on offer – with andouille, wine sauce, trout, you name it. You'll have your not-so *petit déjeuner* in one of the restaurant's 12 elegant dining rooms or its lovely courtyard, and if you're big enough, you'll start the day with an 'eye-opener' (if you can imagine downing a Sazerac before breakfast). Bananas Foster is the recommended dessert, as it's a Brennan's original. The dinner menu emphasizes Creole seafood and, while not quite as decadent, is still pretty damn indulgent.

DICKIE BRENNAN'S
Map pp70–1 Steakhouse $$$
☎ 522-2467; www.dickiebrennanssteakhouse.com; 716 Iberville St; mains $23-44; ☯ 11:30am-2:30pm & 5:30-10pm Wed-Fri, 5:30-10pm Sat-Tue

New Orleans, a city of seafood and spices culled from swamps, isn't well known as a steak town. And yet the best steakhouse in the city is also considered one of the greatest in the country. Steaks, after all, are about indulgence, and indulgence is a key component of New Orleans. There's not a lot we can say about this place, which is essentially a good thing: it does steak and it does it incredibly well. The beef is of exceedingly high quality, comes with beautifully crafted traditional sauces (béarnaise, hollandaise and the like) and, if you like, can be topped with local oysters or shrimp. The sides are also gorgeous (key in any good steakhouse), particularly the Pontalba potatoes, done up with garlic, mushrooms and ham.

ARNAUD'S Map pp70–1 Creole $$$
☎ 523-5433; www.arnauds.com; 813 Bienville St; mains $24-40; ⏱ 6-10pm Mon-Sat, 10am-2:30pm & 6-10pm Sun

Back in 1918 'Count' Arnaud Cazenave, a French immigrant with some extravagant tastes, took roughly a city block's worth of buildings and turned them into a restaurant that's been serving fine upscale Creole cuisine ever since. The main dining room is much admired for its stately old-world elegance (which, in New Orleans, means hex-tile floors and cast-iron posts supporting the ceiling). Keep your eye peeled for the specialties, which appear in red type on the menu – shrimp Arnaud (shrimp in a rémoulade sauce), oysters Bienville (an original dish, with mushrooms and a white-wine sauce), speckled trout meunière (saved by a rich, gravy-like sauce) and steak stuffed with oysters. Bring it on. Show up early for a mint julep at the excellent bar, and men, bring that jacket.

ANTOINE'S Map pp70–1 Creole $$$
☎ 581-4422; www.antoines.com; 713 St Louis St; dinner mains $22-43; ⏱ 11:30am-2pm & 5:30-9:30pm

A California native once commented to us, regarding the tuxedo-ed formal service staff at Antoine's, 'What's with the waiters here? Dude, you're just a waiter.' To which we say: have some respect for history. Antoine's is the oldest of old-line New Orleans restaurants, and the oldest family restaurant in America (established

1840). Kitchen and floor jobs are held for decades and passed down between family members, which ispractically unheard of in this country. 'Class' is an understated description of the atmosphere, where the rooms all look like first-class lounges on the *Orient Express* and are named for Mardi Gras krewes. That said, the food is admittedly good but not great – lots of heavy sauces and sizzling butter over trout, crabs, lamb and the like. Even the great dishes this restaurant *invented,* such as oysters Rockefeller, aren't the best in town, but hey, you're eating history. Nowhere else will you feel as if you've stepped into a Rex Ball attended by Jay Gatsby. We suggest asking your waiter what's fresh and following suit. Jackets required; denim prohibited.

MR B'S BISTRO
Map pp70–1 Modern Louisianan $$$
☎ 523-2078; www.mrbsbistro.com; 201 Royal St; mains $24-42; ⏱ 11:30am-3pm & 5:30-10pm Mon-Sat, 10:30am-3pm & 5:30-10pm Sun

Really, we're not shilling for the Brennan family, but this is yet another one of their contributions to the local eating scene. Mr B's is a clubby, attractively designed restaurant that, in Brennan style, adds a bit of rocket fuel to push local Louisiana food into the future. The barbecue shrimp is the stuff of legend, and very arguably the best take on the stuff in the city. If water bugs aren't your thing, may we direct you to the rabbit braised in apple cider?

NOLA Map pp70–1 Modern American $$$
☎ 522-6652; 534 St Louis St; mains $26-38; ⏱ 6-10pm Mon-Thu, 11:30am-2pm & 6-10pm Fri-Sun

It migh seem   easy to deride Emeril Lagasse, still the most famous celebrity chef in America. The cynic in you wants to think he's overrated. But come visit NOLA, his French Quarter outpost, and your palette will say, 'Hey, this is damn good.' Of course, Emeril's not in the kitchen 'Bam!'-ing your food up, but whoever is does a great job with blackberry stout glazed ribs, buttermilk cornbread pudding and other sexed-up contemporary executions. This is one of the few top-end New Orleans restaurants that successfully whips some California-style fusion hip into Louisiana classics, but the top draw may be the waiters, who are enthusiastic and friendly as hell.

IRON CHEF NEW ORLEANS

New Orleanian foodies don't suffer pretension lightly and don't like to think of themselves as being as chef name-obsessed as their counterparts in, say, New York. It's all an act though! Names mean something here and folks *do* put a lot of stock in who's cooking their food. They should, too – getting an overpriced meal from an overrated chef, in a word, sucks.

During the course of our research, three names were eating up the attention in the New Orleans food scene. First: John Besh. A native southern Louisianan, Besh operates some of the biggest high-end names in the city, including Luke (p160) and August (p159). He's big on local ingredients and cooking them with a bit of a European kick – refined French classical in August and more roll-up-your-sleeves brasserie fare in Luke. The man is also, according to employees we've talked with, a total workaholic with an eye for expansion. He's won about every award you can imagine, including the James Beard award for Best Chef of the Southeast in 2006.

Donald Link was raised in Cajun Country and, after a long stint in San Francisco, came to New Orleans to basically blow the lid off its culinary scene. Like all the chefs in this list, he's a local sourcer, bringing in game, fish, fowl and wildlife from across the South and overseeing his own in-house *boucherie* (butchery). The cured meats here stock the kitchen in Cochon (p160), which currently serves the epitome of Link-style cuisine: food from his childhood with a decided emphasis on pork, done up rich but surprisingly light (well, as light as andouille and sweet potato pie can be). Link was the Beard award winner for Best Chef in the South in 2007.

Link rocketed onto the scene here in 2000, when he co-opened Herbsaint (p160) with Susan Spicer, who he worked under at Bayona (below). Of all the chefs we talked with in New Orleans – at least a dozen – during the course of researching this book, almost all seemed to reserve their greatest respect for Spicer. Born in Florida but for all intents raised in New Orleans, local chefs who've worked for her describe Spicer as obsessed with her craft and dismissive of celebrity. She's kept her empire relatively small and still apparently maintains a regular presence in Bayona's kitchen. More pertinently, Spicer's 'alumni' have gone on to open some of the city's finest restaurants, including Patois (p165) and Lilette (p165), whose own John Harris was a 2009 nominee for the Beard's Best in South award.

Of course, there's plenty more talent circulating around this city. Sue Zemanick of Gautreau's (p164) was a 2009 Beard nominee for Rising Star Chef. The Brennan family, who operate, among other places, Brennan's (p152) and Commander's Palace (p162), is as storied a dynasty as the Ming (if the Mings were south Louisiana cooks). Paul Prudhomme arguably started the modern Cajun cuisine movement and still operates the excellent K-Paul's (below). And, of course, there's the big ol' 'Bam!'-ing teddy bear himself, Emeril Lagasse, now operating three restaurants in New Orleans.

K-PAUL'S LOUISIANA KITCHEN
Map pp70–1   Cajun $$$
☎ 596-2530; www.kpauls.com; 416 Chartres St; mains $27-36; ⏲ 5:30-10pm Mon-Wed, 11am-2pm & 5:30-10pm Thu-Sat

This place has only been around since the 1980s, but in its way, K-Paul's is just as historic as Antoine's (p153). This is the home base of chef Paul Prudhomme, who is essentially responsible for putting modern Louisiana cooking on the map. Prudhomme isn't cooking here anymore, but the kitchen's still cranking out quality: blackened twin beef tenders, a signature dish, come with an incredibly rich 'debris' gravy that's been slowly cooked over a two-day period. The gumbo comes with hot andouille sausages made on site, while the jambalaya is simmered for hours with jalapeños – also pleasantly hot. Despite its popularity, K-Paul's retains a no-reservations policy downstairs, but takes reservations for its upstairs tables. For weekday lunches, you might be seated on arrival.

GW FINS Map pp70–1   Seafood $$$
☎ 581-3467; www.gwfins.com; 808 Bienville St; mains $22-35; ⏲ 5-10pm Sun-Thu, to 10:30pm Fri & Sat

The description 'best seafood in town' doesn't get lightly thrown around in this city, but we've heard it used by a fair few locals in reference to GW Fins. Maybe 'best upscale seafood' is more accurate, as this certainly isn't a crawfish-boil kind of joint. Fins focuses, almost entirely, on fish: fresh caught and prepped so the flavor of the sea is always accented and never overwhelmed. For New Orleans this is light, almost delicate dining – you'll still find the crabmeat stuffing and *tasso* toppings, but Fins also knows how to serve a rare yellowtail with a bit of air-fine sticky rice. It's a refreshing breath of salty air if you're getting jambalaya-ed out.

BAYONA Map pp70–1   Modern Louisianan $$
☎ 525-4455; 430 Dauphine St; mains $24-30; ⏲ 11:30am-2pm & 6-10pm Mon-Thu, 11:30am-2pm & 6-11pm Fri, 6-11pm Sat

Bayona is, for our money, the best splurge in the Quarter. It's rich but not overwhelming, classy but unpretentious, innovative without being precocious and all around just a very fine spot for a meal. Thank chef Susan Spicer and her army of line cooks – they all seem to have a genuine love of what they do and commitment to their craft. This is a white-linen spot, but you can tell camaraderie and love of food are the things most important to the folks staffing Bayona; you get the sense people *like* working here. The menu changes regularly, but expect fish, fowl and game done up in what we'd describe as 'surprisingly pleasant' style – the tastes make you raise an eyebrow, then smile like you've discovered comfort food gone classy.

PALACE CAFÉ Map pp70–1 Creole $$

☎ 523-1661; www.palacecafe.com; 605 Canal St; mains $18-34; ☼ 11:30am-2:30pm & 5:30-10pm Mon-Sat, 10:30am-2:30pm & 5:30-10pm Sun
This outpost of the Brennan family, one of the great houses of New Orleans cooking, straddles the undefined space that marks entry into the French Quarter. One of the best things the Palace has going for it is its space: occupying a former music store, the building's original tile floors and interior columns have been retained and a corkscrew staircase sets off the posh affair with a bit of idiosyncrasy. Businesspeople, conventioneers and office workers rule the roost here, eating off a menu that takes a generally nonexperimental but very good approach to classic Creole standards.

COURT OF TWO SISTERS
Map pp70–1 Creole $$
☎ 522-7261; www.courtoftwosisters.com; 613 Royal St; mains $18-32; ☼ 9am-3pm & 5.30-10pm
The court regularly makes at least top five in 'best place for brunch in New Orleans' lists, a standing that's as attributable to its setting as its food. The latter is a circus of Creole omelets, Cajun pasta salads, grillades, grits, fresh fruits, carved meats and fruity cocktails; the former is a simply enchanting Creole garden filled with sugar-scented warm air and a soft jazz backdrop. Outside of brunch, the quality of the Court drops a bit.

GALATOIRE'S Map pp70–1 Creole $$
☎ 525-2021; 209 Bourbon St; mains $17-32; ☼ 11:30am-10pm Tue-Sat, noon-10pm Sun

We're in a bit of a pickle here. We want to tell you the best time to come to this revered institution, whose interior resembles a debutante's ball, is Friday lunch. That's when a brand of New Orleanian you may not have known existed – ladies in big hats and gloves and men with names like 'Chet' – buys copious bottles of champagne, gossips to high hell, gets called honey or darlin' or just their first name by the waiters, and generally lives life in an unapologetic aristocratic rhythm. But if you arrive at this time you may not get a table and will probably feel like an outsider, so maybe you should come some other time, when Galatoire's feels like all outsiders. Unfortunately, grand dame as she is, this place is on Bourbon St, and can't quite escape the latter's tackiness. Ask a tuxedoed waiter for what's fresh, don a jacket if you're a guy and treat yourself to the old-line masterpieces and mainstays: pompano meunière, liver with bacon and onions, and the signature chicken *clemenceau*.

BACCO Map pp70–1 Italian $$
☎ 522-2426; www.bacco.com; 310 Chartres St; mains $17-30; ☼ 11:30am-2:30pm & 6-10pm
You shouldn't reduce our review of Bacco to three words, but these are three very important words: 10-(freakin')-cent martinis. That's what's going on for lunch here, and as a result, we can happily say Bacco does a very fun lunch. It also does good dinners, come to think of it; it's all of the upscale Italian school plopped into New Orleans. Fresh basil accents a pesto served with shrimp and bow-tie pasta, while Louisiana asserts itself in hickory-grilled redfish topped by lump crabmeat. And you know what makes it all better? Ten-cent martinis.

OLIVIER'S Map pp70–1 Creole $$
☎ 525-7734; www.olivierscreole.com; 204 Decatur St; mains $15-21; ☼ 5-10pm
Olivier's is run by an African American–Creole family that's been in the restaurant business for five generations, passing down and refining recipes over the decades. That should make for some of the best Creole dining in town, but we've found the food can be hit or miss, although when it does hit, it's great stuff. Go for the gumbo sampler to get an education in local cuisine before digging into specialties such as Creole rabbit, crab cakes and broiled catfish. Save room for bourbon-pecan pie.

GUMBO SHOP Map pp70–1 Louisianan $$

☎ 525-1486; 630 St Peter St; mains $8-24;
🕙 11am-11pm

For an unabashed tourist trap, Gumbo Shop (a) does pretty good gumbo, and (b) gets a fair amount of respect from locals, although we've never seen a local inside here (unless they're taking orders). The decor is actually quite lovely, all frescoed out with scenes of old New Orleans. We reckon the Shop, like most heavy-turnover food factories (for that is what this is), suffers from inconsistency in the food quality, though it's never below mediocre.

ACME OYSTER & SEAFOOD HOUSE
Map pp70–1 Seafood $$

☎ 522-5973; www.acmeoyster.com; 724 Iberville St; mains $7-21; 🕙 11am-late

They still shuck oysters to order here, which is a beautiful thing, but when Acme gets busy – which is fairly often – it serves them up pre-shucked. This heresy encapsulates the dance with quality Acme engages in: trying to stay true to its roots as one of the Quarter's oldest operating seafood joints, but within dangerous proximity of the undiscerning crowds from nearby chain resorts. It'll even serve gumbo in a bread bowl – nice if you're from California, but pure madness to local food purists. That said, when Acme is on, it's on; for midrange solid seafood this is good stuff, but don't expect the authentic Louisiana bounty of the Gulf you may have been promised.

YO MAMA'S Map pp70–1 American $

☎ 522-1125; www.yomamasbarandgrill.com; 727 St Peters St; mains $7-14; 🕙 11am-3am

'Where we eatin' tonight?' 'Yo Mama's.' Chortle, chortle, chortle. Now that *that's* out of the way, let's lay it on the line: peanut butter and bacon burger. Yep: looks like a cheese burger, but that ain't melted cheddar on top, it's Jif, baby (or Skippy, or Peter Pan…actually, we're not sure). Honestly, it's great. Somehow the stickiness of the peanut butter complements the char-grilled edge of the meat and, if you've got the backbone, a heaping mound of sour cream, butter and baco-bits on the accompanying baked potato.

CAFÉ BEIGNET Map pp70–1 Cafe $

☎ 524-5530; 334B Royal St; meals $6-8;
🕙 7am-5pm

In a shaded patio setting with a view of Royal St, this intimate cafe serves small meals over the counter. French-style omelets stuffed with ham, Belgian waffles and beignets are all a good start to the day, while quiches and sandwiches make up the simple lunch fare. There's a low-level war among foodies over who does the better beignet, here or Café du Monde (p152), with the general consensus being the former uses less powdered sugar as a topping. Whether this makes Café Beignet beignets better is all down to your sweet tooth and tolerance for mess making.

ALIBI Map pp70–1 Diner $

☎ 522-9187; www.alibineworleans.com; 811 Iberville St; mains $5-10; 🕙 24hr

Alibi is more bar than restaurant, but we're including it here because it's one of the better 24-hour joints in the Quarter (popular wisdom holds that local strippers head here after their shifts). The grub (definitely 'grub') is decidedly greasy, unhealthy and perfect after a long night of doing whatever it was you were doing on Bourbon St a few minutes ago – yes you, bleary eyes. Alibi does burgers and po'boys and fried stuff, largely, although salads are on the menu and, rumor has it, occasionally emerge from the kitchen.

JOHNNY'S PO-BOYS
Map pp70–1 Po'boys $

☎ 524-8129; www.johnnyspoboy.com; 511 St Louis St; dishes $4-10; 🕙 8am-3pm Mon-Fri, to 4:30pm Sat & Sun

We don't generally like to grab our po'boys in the tourist-y Quarter, but we make an exception for Johnny's. A local favorite since 1950, it's the only traditional po'boy joint around, all checkered tablecloths, hustle, bustle and good food served by good folks. Breakfast here is simple and delicious.

FAUBOURG MARIGNY & BYWATER

The food cachet of the Marigny is increasing by the month, thanks to the settlement of all those YURPs (young, urban rebuilding professionals) and the increasing presence of tourists drifting north from the Quarter. Frenchmen St, as always, remains the center of action. Over in the Bywater, there's no foodie strip per se, but some of our favorite restau-

HOW YA LIKE DEM ERSTERS?

Hard-core New Orleans oyster bars, such as Casamento's (p168), can be a little intimidating for neophytes. There's a certain cultishness in the way experienced patrons stand before a cold marble bar as half a dozen oysters (which some locals pronounce 'ersters') are shucked and laid out on the half shell. With restrained anticipation, often disguised by an air of ritualism, these oyster fiends dash lemon and a spot of hot sauce or a bit of horseradish onto the first of the oysters. They then slurp down the addictive bivalve, pausing to savor that first oyster's saltiness and to summon up a renewed sense of anticipation before turning their attention to the second one, and this behavioral pattern repeats itself until all six half shells lie empty on the counter. For many New Orleanians, this entire ritual is completed in about the length of time it takes to fill a tank of gas.

Naturally, people who hold oysters in such high esteem have come to attribute certain health-promoting qualities to them. According to one popular myth, eating oysters can increase a person's sex drive and enhance their sexual prowess.

Oysters also have a variety of ways of insinuating themselves into a leisurely classic New Orleans meal. In some people's minds, seafood gumbo must include oysters or be called something else. And the list of appetizers on many of the city's menus generally includes several baked-oyster dishes. The most famous local oyster dish, served with a devilish little fork, is oysters Rockefeller, an Antoine's (p153) creation that owes its success as much to an irresistible secret spinach sauce as it does to the well-hidden oysters.

Then, of course, oysters make the classic po'boy (see p143 for the whole story). In some traditional quarters of the city you can still order an oyster loaf. The loaf comprises oysters dipped in cornmeal, then deep fried and served on white toast.

rants in the city are dotted like delicious candy (bacon candy to be exact; see Elizabeth's, p158) over the shotgun shack landscape. The general bohemian vibe in this part of town makes for a plethora of good cheap eats.

MARIGNY BRASSERIE
Map p81 — American $$$

☎ 945-4472; www.marignybrasserie.com; 640 Frenchmen St; mains $22-32; ⏱ 11:30am-9:30pm Mon-Thu, to 10:30pm Fri & Sat, 11am-9pm Sun
Marigny Brasserie is as chic as the Marigny gets, which is to say, not too chic. Don't get us wrong, it's a very nice place, all white linens and ninja-clad waiters, and the food is modern-American style with a bit of a Louisiana kick: think blackened drum with wild rice and orange cardamom chutney, and roasted lamb with garlic grits. But the whole vibe is quite friendly, even laid-back, which sometimes shows in the varying quality of product being carted out of the kitchen to your table.

JACK DEMPSEY'S RESTAURANT
Map p81 — Seafood $$

☎ 943-9914; www.jackdempseysllc.com; 738 Poland Ave; mains $15-32; ⏱ 11am-2pm Tue, to 6pm Wed & Thu, to 8:30pm Fri, noon-8:30pm Sat
The old school of American seafood cookery believes in the following: fry it, then serve with a lemon wedge. That sounds a little simplistic, we know, but believe us: when chefs perfect the art of batter-frying there are few better ways to consume

something from the sea. The cooks at Jack Dempsey's are in that hallowed, great fry-and-broil fraternity. You may not think there's a lot of art or pretty edges to a catfish platter and fries, but bite into that firm flesh overflowing with salty, delicious grease and you'll realize this kitchen is working in its own rarefied air.

PRALINE CONNECTION
Map p81 — Soul Food $$

☎ 943-3934; www.pralineconnection.com; 542 Frenchmen St; mains $13-20; ⏱ 11am-10:30pm Sun-Thu, to midnight Fri & Sat
If you've never had soul food before, the PC might blow you away, but connoisseurs of the genre may find this popular tour-group stop middling. The food is pretty good, in a mom's-kitchen kind of way – standbys are of the meat loaf, fried chicken and fish topped with étouffée school of cooking – but this restaurant hovers in that frustrating space between 'meh' and 'wow.' The service is cool; besides being friendly, the waiters dress like the Blues Brothers, which we're always down with.

ADOLFO'S Map p81 — Italian $$
☎ 948-3800; 611 Frenchmen St; mains $8-20; ⏱ 6-11pm Mon-Sat
If you take a date to this intimate Italian cubby squeezed on top of a jazz club (the Apple Barrel; see p184) and get nowhere afterwards, they were too hard to please.

Adolfo's, which possibly sits around 30, is pretty much as romantic as New Orleans gets, atmosphere wise. It doesn't miss on food either, all working-class Italian-Americano fare with some requisite New Orleans zing. Pastas with Creole tomato sauces, chicken parmigiana and cheap reds by the carafe emerge from the kitchen and raise a diner's spirits, and if they don't, go back to your little black book.

ELIZABETH'S Map p81 American $$
☎ 944-9272; www.elizabeths-restaurant.com; 601 Gallier St; mains $11-25; ☽ 11am-2:30pm & 6-10pm Tue-Fri, 6-10pm Sat, 8am-2:30pm Sun
Elizabeth's in the Bywater is deceptively divey. It looks like – hell, it *is* – a neighborhood joint. But its food's as good as the best New Orleans chefs can offer. In a way, this is a quintessential New Orleans restaurant in a quintessential New Orleans neighborhood, all friendliness, smiling sass, weird artistic edges and overindulgence on the food front (but not, thankfully, your wallet). Dinners go from as humble as beer-barbecued oysters to as refined as seared duck with port sherry. But brunch and breakfast are the top draws. Whatever you get (it's all good, but the shrimp, grits and *tasso* 'hangover cure' is tops), be sure to order some praline bacon on the side. That's bacon fried up in brown sugar and, far as we can tell, God's own cooking oil. It's probably an utter sin to consume, but y'know what? Consider us happily banished from the Garden.

BACCHANAL Map p81 Wine & Cheese $$
☎ 948-9111; www.bacchanalwine.com; 600 Poland Ave; sandwiches $11, cheeses per piece from $5; ☽ 11am-9pm; Ⓥ
You may be surprised to hear one of the best wine and cheese selections in New Orleans sits just across the water from the Lower Ninth Ward. Enter Bacchanal: one of our favorite gems in a city full of diamonds in the rough. From the outside, it looks like a leaning Bywater shack of uncommonly large size; inside, there are fridges full of wine, a full deli counter and sexily stinky cheese sold at just above retail price. Order what you want, but we recommend an assemble-your-own cheese plate. Let the folks behind the counter prep that *fromage* into a work of art, which is then devoured in a backyard of overgrown garden green, scattered with rusted-out lawn chairs and tatty foldouts. It's

unspeakably fun and romantic, especially on warm nights. On chef Sundays, cooks from around the city are invited to guest star in Bacchanal's kitchen and let loose with whatever their talented hearts desire.

THE JOINT Map p81 Barbecue $
☎ 949-3232; www.alwayssmokin.com; 801 Poland Ave; mains $7-17; ☽ 11:30am-2:30pm Mon & Tue, to 9pm Wed-Sat
The Joint is seriously the joint (sorry non-Americans; that's slang for…well, really good). In a city that's not terribly big on barbecue, this is the best we got going, but the Joint is no second-rate effort. Its smoked pork has the olfactory effect of the Sirens' sweet song, pulling you, the proverbial traveling sailor, off course from your Ithaca into the gnashing rocks of a savory meat-induced blissful death (classical Greek epic analogies ending *now*). Knock some ribs or pulled pork or brisket (or all of the above – try the 'W special' for a good sampler) back with some sweet tea in the backyard garden and learn to love life (speaking of which, the Joint does a mean peanut butter pie for dessert). Poland Ave is a quiet little lane, but the presence of this spot, Bacchanal (left) and Jack Dempsey's (p157) make this one of our favorite eat streets in the city.

LA PENICHÉ Map p81 American $
☎ 943-1460; 1940 Dauphine St; mains $6-14; ☽ 24hr Thu-Tue
In the lazy twilight hour, La Peniché qualifies as an unassuming corner restaurant, a few blocks from the Frenchmen St scene. But it's open 24 hours, and tends to get interesting later on when night owls, club-hoppers, drag queens and insomniacs (you know, interesting folks) file through its doors. The waiters are incredibly friendly; we'd gladly eat their seafood platters, fried chicken, steaks, chops and po'boys – none of it exceptional, all of it reasonably priced – off the floor if they asked. Alright, maybe not.

SCHIRO'S CAFÉ/LITTLE JULIE'S INDIA KITCHEN Map p81 Diner & Indian $
☎ 944-6666; www.schiroscafe.com; 2483 Royal St; mains $5-16; ☽ 9am-10pm Mon-Sat; Ⓥ
Yes, you read it right: diner *and* Indian. One menu at Schiro's is typical New Orleanian greasy spoon, offering po'boys, blackened catfish, hushpuppies and gumbo; the other serves *saag paneer* (spinach curry with un-

BEST EATING STREETS

Decatur St (French Quarter)

Magazine St (Uptown & Riverbend)

Carrollton Ave, riverside (southwestern) end (Uptown & Riverbend)

Poland Ave (Faubourg Marigny & Bywater)

Dauphine St (French Quarter)

aged cheese), *tikka masala* and vindaloo. Oh, and the other part of the business? A launderette. Schizophrenic Schiro's is set in a lovely grand dame of a Marigny mansion, perfect for a cheap meal and repose under the eaves. This is a good choice for vegetarians.

FRADY'S ONE STOP FOOD STORE

Map p81   American $

☎ 949-9688; 3231 Dauphine St; po'boys around $8; 7:30am-5pm Mon-Fri, 9am-3pm Sat

This grocery store has inconvenient hours (look Frady's, we like to shop *after* we get off work), but it makes up for it with good produce and some very fine po'boys at the deli counter.

FLORA GALLERY & COFFEE SHOP

Map p81   Cafe $

☎ 947-8358; 2600 Royal St; coffees & pastries $3-5; 6:30am-midnight; V

Flora is almost the perfect New Orleans cafe. If you could smoke inside, as in the old days, it'd be 10 out of 10. No offense nonsmokers, but this is just the sort of place – madcap art, antique store furniture, a vibe that jukes between folk and punk rock, lush gardens and a perfect Parisian bohemian atmosphere – that demands the accompaniment of clouds of tobacco smoke. Alas, the latter isn't there, but for the majority of you readers, that only makes the great Flora better.

KAHVE ROYALE Map p81   Cafe $

2001 Royal St; coffees & pastries $3; 7am-8pm

Kahve is a bit more lo-fi than other Marigny cafes. It's cash only and the entire place feels a bit like it was assembled on a shoestring. This, of course, is the romance of the place, the most rustically charming caffeine haven in the neighborhood. The friendly service obviously doesn't hurt.

ORANGE COUCH Map p81   Cafe $

☎ 267-7327; 2339 Royal St; coffees & pastries $3; 7am-10pm; V

This is an icebox-cool cafe, all Ikea-esque furniture, polished stone flooring, pierced types behind the counter, local artwork and photography on the walls, graffitied up restrooms and, yes, an orange leather couch in the midst of it all. It's very much Marigny, the sort of place where a tattooed attorney with dyed-black hair takes out a Mac and a book on tort law and cracks away at work for hours.

CBD & WAREHOUSE DISTRICT

New Orleans' downtown isn't great for cheap eats (with a few exceptions), but as fine dining goes, you've hit the mother lode. Most of the city's big-name chefs have opened posh outposts downtown. That said, even the high-end restaurants here have affordable lunchtime menus if you want fine food without burning a hole in your wallet.

RESTAURANT AUGUST

Map pp86–7   Modern Creole $$$

☎ 299-9777; www.restaurantaugust.com; 301 Tchoupitoulas St; mains $24-45; 5-9pm Tue, Wed, Thu & Sat, 11am-2pm & 5-9pm Fri

In a city full of dining rooms plucked from a gilded age grand ball, we may give August's converted 19th-century tobacco warehouse the nod for most aristocratic dining room in New Orleans. Candles flicker and warm the soft shades over a meal that will, quite likely, blow your mind to another level of gastronomic perception. *Pied de cochon* (stuffed pig trotters) with black truffles, pork belly stuffed with crawfish and blood oranges, and a 10-course, three-hour degustation (tasting) menu that local foodies weep over mean this book's contents are actually more beautiful than its substantially attractive cover.

EMERIL'S Map pp86–7   Modern Creole $$$

☎ 528-9393; www.emerils.com; 800 Tchoupitoulas St; mains $27-39; 6-10pm Mon-Thu & Sat, 11:30am-2pm & 6-10pm Fri

In a converted warehouse in the Warehouse District, this is the flagship of chef Emeril Lagasse's restaurant empire. The noise level can be deafening, but Emeril's remains one of New Orleans' finest dining establishments. The kitchen's strengths are best appreciated by ordering the daily specials, although you can't go wrong with mainstays such as grilled *filet mignon au poivre* (poor man's steak; steak encrusted with peppercorns), which sounds like a contradiction but, of course, tastes wonderful. The full-on Emeril experience includes partaking of the cheese board with a selection from the restaurant's eclectic wine list.

CUVÉE Map pp86–7   Modern Louisianan $$$
☎ 587-9001; www.restaurantcuvee.com; 322 Magazine St; mains $24-44; ⌚ 6-9:30pm Mon & Tue, 11:30am-2:30pm & 6-9:30pm Wed & Thu, 11:30am-2:30pm & 6-10:30pm Fri & Sat

Cuvée is a high-class joint in a stylishly converted warehouse space. Its thoughtful, descriptive menu projects an understandable pride in fine ingredients and cooking methods. Influences range freely between Cajun, Creole and French cuisines for exotic originals that are to be admired and savored bite by bite. The dinner menu might include grilled redfish over andouille hash, mustard and herb-coated salmon, and seared sea scallops with toasted pearl pasta and truffle shellfish fumet.

BON TON CAFÉ Map pp86–7   Cajun $$$
☎ 524-3386; 401 Magazine St; mains $17-38; ⌚ 11am-2pm & 5-9pm Mon-Fri

Bon Ton looks classy and feels sassy, like a posh dinner party about to break into mass revelry. It's an old-style Cajun restaurant from New Orleans culinary history BPP (before Paul Prudhomme) that's been open for half a century. We give Bon Ton a very respectful nod for maintaining an old-school menu of red fish, rice, steak and lots of butter. Don't pass on the rum-soaked bread pudding at the end of dinner.

CAFÉ ADELAIDE
Map pp86–7   Quirky Creole $$$
☎ 595-3305; www.cafeadelaide.com; 300 Poydras St; mains $24-32; ⌚ 7am-2pm & 6-9pm Mon-Thu, 7am-2:30pm & 6-9:30pm Fri, 7am-12:30pm & 6-9:30pm Sat, 7am-12:30pm & 6-9pm Sun

The Brennan family tribute to their endearingly eccentric aunt Adelaide is as funky as you like; try dining in the 'Turtle Room,' where two shelled lovers dance a reptilian pas de deux on the wall. The motto here is the namesake's own: 'Eat, drink and carry on,' a philosophy realized by haute Creole cuisine cooked, apparently, by a pleasantly insane jester. Examples? Steak with brie mashed potatoes, a truffled crab-claw 'cake' and a brilliant take on biscuits and gravy, where the 'biscuit' is duck cracklin' and confit, and the 'gravy' is foie gras mustard. It's all as good as it sounds, and the attached Swizzle Stick (p185) is one of downtown's better bars.

HERBSAINT
Map pp86–7   Modern Louisianan $$
☎ 524-4114; www.herbsaint.com; 701 St Charles Ave; mains $22-27; ⌚ 11:30am-10pm Mon-Fri, from 5:30pm Sat

We'll make a claim that may cause a riot, but Herbsaint's duck and andouille gumbo might be the best restaurant gumbo in town. The rest of the food ain't too bad either – it's very much modern bistro fare with dibs and dabs of Louisiana influence, courtesy of owner Donald Link. Kurobuta pork belly comes with a local white-bean sauce, while frog legs hop off the pan (sorry, couldn't resist) with a fine herb dusting. The dining room, warmly lit by windows, is especially pleasant for lunch, or during the 1:30pm to 5:30pm limited bistro menu. Reservations are a good idea if you're coming for dinner.

LUKE Map pp86–7   European Bistro $$
☎ 378-2840; www.lukeneworleans.com; 333 St Charles Ave; mains $16-28; ⌚ 7am-11pm

James Beard–award-winning Luke is both John Besh's letter of love to the working person's bistro and his successful effort at refining the genre. The elegantly simple, tiled interior and warm staff support a kitchen that will make you reconsider the limits of what can be done in the realm of Louisiana-French fusion. With that said, don't come here looking for Creole food – while Louisiana influences the menu, its primary muse is the smoky, rich cuisine of Alsace, near the French–German border. Vanilla-scented duck with lavender honey, a white-bean cassoulet slow cooked to smoky new heights of flavor, and an admirable nod to German meats such as *bockwurst* all give us the pleasurable shudders.

COCHON Map pp86–7   Modern Cajun $$
☎ 588-2123; www.cochonrestaurant.com; 930 Tchoupitoulas St; mains $14-24; ⌚ 11am-10pm Mon-Fri, from 5:30pm Sat

YOU WINO

Topping our list of cute New Orleans acronyms is WINO – the Wine Institute of New Orleans (Map pp86–7; ☎ 324-8000; www.winoschool.com; 610 Tchoupitoulas St). The 'institute' runs classes on wine tasting, food pairing and the like, aimed at both amateur enthusiasts and folks looking to get professionally employed in the wine and spirit industry. The casual classes run $35 to $40 (some, such as a foie gras course, run a bit more), whereas professional certification classes will cost you $625.

But we're going to assume that beyond the classes, you just want to try some very good wines. Aren't you in luck? Pop by WINO and sample some 80 different types of vino, plus a fair bit of beer and pâté, cheese, chocolate and charcuterie plates. Call ahead for hours, find a designated driver and get ready to bliss out, fermented-grape style.

Chef Donald Link's homage to his Cajun culinary roots is deeply rooted in pig parts, from pork cheeks stuffed with goat cheese, to pig cracklin' with cane syrup, to local pig stuffed with cracklin', turnips and cabbage. There are plenty of other meats on offer, including some excellent rabbit livers on toast, fantastic oysters and a whole restaurant-servicing 'Cochon Butchery' next door. The food could be overtly rich, but ends up being just hearty and smoky enough without being totally coma-inducing. Lots of publications have deemed Cochon the best restaurant in the city. We won't go that far, but we do respect the kitchen's love of and talent for getting meat done right.

RIO MAR Map pp86–7 — Spanish $$

☎ 525-3474; www.riomarseafood.com; 800 S Peters St; tapas $4-8, mains $19-24; 🕑 11:30am-2pm & 6-10pm Mon-Fri, 6-10pm Sat

New Orleans is a city that hasn't embraced the tapas trend with the fervor of other American foodie towns, perhaps in part due to the excellence of homegrown cuisine. Rio Mar bucks this trend with a good selection of simply done but satisfying small plates; salt cod cakes, garlic oysters and white anchovies in vinegar top out a menu slanted toward but not limited to seafood. Lunch or dinner, we say opt for the tapas over the mains.

LIBORIO CUBAN RESTAURANT

Map pp86–7 — Cuban $$

☎ 581-9680; www.liboriocuban.com; 321 Magazine St; mains $9-28; 🕑 11am-2:30pm Mon, 11am-2:30pm & 5:30-9pm Tue-Sat

Cuban food is one of those gems of the American culinary scene that is often done better here than in the homeland (thanks, access to nonrationed ingredients). It's exceedingly easy on the most timid palette: flavorful meat and pork, strong but not spicy, usually served with some variation on rice and beans or sweet plantains. Liborio is a solid performer in the genre; we'd opt for the cheaper sandwiches over the somewhat overpriced mains.

DRAGO'S SEAFOOD RESTAURANT

Map pp86–7 — Seafood $$

☎ 584-3911; www.dragosrestaurant.com; 2 Poydras St; mains around $15; 🕑 11am-10pm Mon-Sat

You used to have to truck out to Metairie to enjoy the oyster creations of Drago Cvitanovich, one of the many Croatian immigrants who brought a heady knowledge of shellfish from the Dalmatian to the Gulf Coast. Now Drago's has an outpost in the downtown Riverside Hilton. The surf-and-turf menu is alright (we like the 'Shuckee Duckee' – a duck breast topped with oysters), but the real draw are the charbroiled oysters, dripping with butter, garlic, parmesan and their own juices after kissing an open fire. It's one of the better business lunches around, by dint of taste and price.

MOTHER'S Map pp86–7 — Southern Deli $

☎ 523-9656; www.mothersrestaurant.net; 401 Poydras St; meals $8-15; 🕑 8am-8pm

Like a lot of discovered New Orleans restaurants, the quality isn't what it was in the storied past (it doesn't help that it's located right in the conventioneer hotel heartland). There's a lot of history here: Mother's invented the 'debris' po'boy and serves the justifiably famous 'Ferdi Special,' a po'boy loaded up with ham, roast beef and debris. But in general its sandwiches don't pass muster compared with other city stalwarts. Breakfast is your best bet – it's standard meat-and-eggs stuff, but brilliantly done and served in ponderously enormous portions. Getting in requires waiting in occasionally miserably long lines; once you reach the counter, order without hesitation.

RED EYE GRILL Map pp86–7 Grill $
☎ 593-9393; 852 S Peters St; meals $5-8;
🕙 11am-late
A grungy bar in the Warehouse District
for those 21 years and up, the Red Eye is
strictly for greasy burgers and fries. It's
convenient if you're seeing a show at one
of the nearby clubs.

NOLA GROCERY Map pp86–7 Deli $
☎ 302-9928; www.nolagrocery.com; 351 Andrew
Higgins Dr; meals $2-8; 🕙 7am-10pm
One of our favorite hidden-in-plain-sight
gems in the city is this tiny deli. The friendly
dudes behind the counter make their boudin on site, do up some mean po'boys and
generally provide the best feed for under
$10 you'll likely find in the CBD.

GARDEN, LOWER GARDEN & CENTRAL CITY

Foodies here can pick and choose from stu-
dent-y Mexican burrito shops, to old-line
Creole cafes, to some truly excellent breakfast
nooks and lunchtime diners. With a high student population, there's a decidedly young, hip
and economical bent to the food on offer in the
Lower Garden. There's not as much variety of
eating in the Garden District – just one of the
most storied restaurants in the country.

COMMANDER'S PALACE
Map pp96–7 Creole $$$
☎ 899-8221; www.commanderspalace.com; 1403
Washington Ave; mains $29-42; 🕙 11:30am-2pm
& 6:30-10pm Mon-Fri, 11:30am-1pm & 6:30-10pm
Sat, 10:30am-1:30pm Sun
As elegant as the Garden District she looms
over, Commander's is one of the USA's
great restaurants. Owner Ella Brennan takes
pride in her ability to promote her chefs
to stardom; Paul Prudhomme and Emeril
Lagasse are among her alumni, and we met
more than one chef during our research
thanking their lucky stars for the chance
to work the Commander's line. The reputa-
tion is real; the nouveau Creole menu runs
from fig and foie gras beignets to quail
with apples stuffed with local blue crab
– decadence all around, ya heard? By the
way, don't say anything like 'ya heard' in
the dining room, where jackets are pre-

ferred for dinner and the general sense is
that you are in a *very* nice place. Of course,
some of that stiff upper lip is put on; the
lunch special, after all, is the 25¢ martini.
Reservations are required.

COQUETTE Map pp96–7 Modern French $$
☎ 265-0421; 2800 Magazine St; mains $15-25;
🕙 11:30am-10pm
A bright and beautiful addition to the
crowded Magazine St eating scene, Co-
quette mixes up wine bar ambience with
friendly service and a bit of white linen;
the combined result is a candlelit place
you don't feel bad getting a little trashed
in. Don't just focus on the respectable
wine menu, though – there's some great
French-inspired Louisiana-sourced food
served here, such as a succulent red snapper on pillow-y risotto. The small plates are
eclectic and highly recommended.

SAKE CAFÉ II Map pp96–7 Japanese $$
☎ 894-0033; www.sakecafeuptown.com; 2830
Magazine St; sushi & mains $10-22; 🕙 11:30am-
9:30pm
Believe it or not, fish in this town doesn't
have to come fried, swimming in a thick
sauce or stuffed with bacon/crawfish/
crabmeat/whatever. Sake II (the original
is in Metairie) serves decent sushi that's
popular with the younger, yuppier types
that populate the Lower Garden District
and around.

SLICE Map pp96–7 Pizza $
☎ 525-7437; www.slicepizzeria.com; 1513 St
Charles Ave; pizzas $12-15.50; 🕙 11am-11pm Mon-
Sat, noon-10pm Sun
Our favorite pizza in New Orleans is thin
crust and as artisanal or run-of-the-mill as
you like: you can opt for something as out
there as goat cheese, pesto and anchovies, or good ol' pepperoni. Take a snobby
buddy from New York and let 'em know
this part of the world delivers a damn decent pie. Order by the slice (imagine that!)
starting at just $2.15.

JOEY K'S Map pp96–7 Diner $
☎ 891-0997; www.joeyksrestaurant.com; 3001
Magazine St; mains $9-17; 🕙 11am-3pm & 5-
8:30pm Mon-Wed, 11am-3pm & 5-9pm Thu & Fri,
11am-4pm & 5-9pm Sat
'No sushi,' reads the sign, which gives us
a good chuckle. Indeed, this is good local

diner fare with a great menu of daily specials. We'll personally vouch that the cheese fries should be patented, while specialties such as fried pork chops and white beans, and turkey with stuffing, yams and green beans are as satisfying a meal as you'll find for under $20 in the Lower Garden.

SURREY'S JUICE BAR

Map pp96–7   American $

☎ 524-3828; www.surreyscafeandjuicebar.com; 1418 Magazine St; mains $6.25-12.50; 🕒 8am-3pm
Ready? Ready?! Here comes the controversial assessment: Surrey's does the best cheap breakfast in New Orleans, perhaps even the best breakfast, period. Boudin biscuits, biscuits swimming in salty sausage gravy, eggs scrambled with salmon, and a shrimp-and-grits-and-bacon dish that should be illegal – you won't go wrong. And the juice, as you might guess, is blessedly fresh. This, friends, is how a champion (or a hungover tourist) starts their day.

SUCRÉ Map pp96–7   Chocolate $

☎ 520-8311; www.shopsucre.com; 3025 Magazine St; 6 chocolates from $12; 🕒 7:30am-11pm
You pay to make someone happy (including yourself) by shopping at Sucré, but this is, by very wide consensus, the best chocolate in town. It's the sort of chocolate you'd think was hidden behind secret government titanium vaults – dollops of single espresso beans encased in bittersweet darkness like a silk kiss and all that other food porn adjective-heavy verbiage, but seriously, the cocoa here is that freaking good. It better be, considering some of its 21-piece boxes will run you $68.

TROLLEY STOP Map pp96–7   American $

☎ 523-0090; 1923 St Charles Ave; meals $5-12; 🕒 24hr
When last we stopped in at this 24-hour diner – in the wee hours, of course – we were called about every variation of 'baby,' 'darling,' 'sweetie,' 'honeychile' and 'sugar' out there. We only regret we didn't propose to that waiter after our meal, which was a very hefty mushroom-and-Swiss burger. This sort of food isn't particularly original (although it is very good), but hey sweetie-honeychile-sugarplum-darlin'-gooeycheeks, who's complaining when the service is this friendly?

top picks

BREAKFAST SPOTS

- Surrey's Juice Bar (left)
- Huevos (p171)
- Dante's (p166)
- Elizabeth's (p158)
- Brennan's (p152)

JUAN'S FLYING BURRITO

Map pp96–7   Mexican $

☎ 569-0000; www.juansflyingburrito.com; 2018 Magazine St; mains $5-11.50; 🕒 11am-10pm Mon-Thu, to 11pm Fri & Sat, noon-10pm Sun
The answer to that perennial question, 'What happens when you cross a bunch of skinny jean–clad hipsters with a tortilla?' is, ta da, Juan's. The food is about as authentically Mexican as Ontario, but that doesn't mean it's not good; the hefty burritos pack a satisfying punch against your hunger. Plus, the margaritas are tasty and it does a quesadilla with ground beef, bacon and blue cheese – yes, please.

STEIN'S DELI Map pp96–7   Deli $

☎ 527-0771; www.steinsdeli.net; 2207 Magazine St; sandwiches $5-11; 🕒 7am-7pm Tue-Fri, 9am-5pm Sat & Sun
How good is Stein's? Well, it's arguably more of a center for the city's Jewish population than any one synagogue, and every Jew or half-Jew we've met in New Orleans swears by it. If lunch, for you, rests on quality sandwiches, cheese and cold cuts, this is as good as the city gets. Owner Dan Stein is a fanatic about keeping his deli stocked with great Italian and Jewish meats and cheeses, and some very fine boutique beers; the man even hosts his own beer-brewing classes. We tip our hats to you, sir.

SLIM GOODIE'S DINER

Map pp96–7   Diner $

☎ 891-3447; 3322 Magazine St; mains $2.50-10.50; 🕒 9am-3pm; V
This hip retro diner, all overlaid with some punk-rock sensibility, was among the first restaurants to reopen after Hurricane Katrina, so it deserves a hell of a lot of credit just for that substantial accomplishment. Burgers, shakes, all-American breakfasts and

other short-order standards round out the menu; it's good, if not exactly awe-inspiring stuff. Vegetarians are well treated here, thanks to the presence of items such as latkes and black-bean nachos on the menu.

BLUE PLATE CAFÉ Map pp96–7 Diner $
☎ 309-9500; 1300 Prytania St; mains $7-13; 7:30am-3pm Mon-Sat

Cheap and cheerful and colorful, too, the Blue Plate does some solid servings of breakfast and lunch stuff that's firmly of the Louisiana diner genre. The three-egg omelets are a satisfying treat. It gets packed on Saturday mornings, and justifiably so – this is one of the city's better cheap breakfast options.

CAFÉ RECONCILE Map pp96–7 Diner $
☎ 568-1157; www.cafereconcile.com; 1631 Oretha Castle-Haley Blvd; mains $5-9; 11am-2:30pm Mon-Fri

Café Reconcile fights the good fight. By recruiting at-risk youth to work as kitchen and floor staff, the restaurant is training a generation of New Orleanians to realize their best potential. The food, which consists of daily specials, is simple and, frankly, really good. It's very much of the humble New Orleans school of home cookery: red beans and rice, fried chicken, shrimp Creole and the like. In summary: good food, good service and by eating at Reconcile you're doing a good thing for the city. Get over here already.

PARASOL'S Map pp96–7 Po'boys $
☎ 899-2054; 2533 Constance St; po'boys $8; 11am-10pm

Parasol's isn't just on the Irish Channel; it sort of *is* the Irish Channel, serving as community center, nexus of gossip and, natch, watering hole. Because yes, this is, first and foremost, a bar. But there is a little seating area in the back where you can order some of the best po'boys in town (although this largely depends on who's working the kitchen). That big ol' sandwich will help to layer against the copious amounts of booze you may very well be tempted to drink here. There's a mad cast of characters both behind and ordering from the bar, but don't ever feel threatened; all in all this is one of the friendliest neighborhood spots in New Orleans. This place is St Paddy's Day headquarters, when a huge block party happens on the street.

RUE DE LA COURSE Map pp96–7 Cafe $
☎ 899-0242; 3121 Magazine St; pastries $2-4; 7:30am-11pm

Why do we love this cafe? Well, for one we're literally typing these words as we sit in it. To be honest, this spacious coffee shop is constantly filled with folks on computers banging away on that next term paper, screenplay, email, Facebook post and, er, guidebook. It's friendly, the coffee is good and, crucially, there are lots of power outlets for our – sorry, your – laptop. Cash only.

UPTOWN & RIVERBEND

Uptown and Riverbend are arguably the hottest food corridors in the city. There's no shortage of options, including shotgun shack diners, po'boy slinging bars and cute garden cottages hiding some of the best Creole fine dining in town. Even the upper-crust restaurants here tend to be refreshingly informal. While the atmosphere is refined, service is always friendly and warm – customers are often neighbors, and tourists are a relative rarity.

BRIGTSEN'S RESTAURANT
Map pp102–3 Modern Cajun $$$
☎ 861-7610; www.brigtsens.com; 723 Dante St; mains $26-38; 5:30-10pm Tue-Sat

Despite all the critical acclaim that has been heaped upon chef Frank Brigtsen, the restaurant that bears his name remains a decidedly unpretentious place. Set in a converted double-shotgun house, the restaurant feels homey and inviting, with service that's attentive but never oppressive. Brigtsen terms his cooking 'modern Louisiana cuisine,' and those in search of haute Cajun cuisine will not be disappointed. Rabbit and duck are among his specialties. Look for the roast duck with cornbread dressing and honey-pecan gravy, or beef tournedos in a *tasso* wine sauce.

GAUTREAU'S
Map pp102–3 Modern American $$$
☎ 899-7397; 1728 Soniat St; mains $22-35; 6-10pm Mon-Sat

Sometimes it feels as though chef Sue Zemanick has won every award a rising young star can garner in American culinary circles – and then another honor passes her way (said recognition includes 'Top

10 Best New Chef' in *Food & Wine* magazine and 'Chef of the Year' in *New Orleans* magazine, among others). Her restaurant is supremely elegant and romantic, unsigned and tucked away in a residential neighborhood. Inside, savvy diners, many of them New Orleanian food aficionados, dine on fresh, modern American fare – gnocchi with truffled parmesan cheese and grouper in a salsa *verde*, to name some examples – content they're enjoying a known but, as regards tourists, undiscovered treasure of the local culinary landscape.

DICK & JENNY'S

Map pp102–3   Modern Creole $$$

☎ 894-9880; www.dickandjennys.com; 4501 Tchoupitoulas St; mains $20-34; 🕑 5:30-10pm Tue-Sat

You could easily accuse New Orleans of doing the contemporary Creole thing to death, but Dick and Jenny (a real couple) have breathed life into this overdone genre. Hidden away in what looks like grandma's shack by the river is a warm dining room packed with artsy accents, laughing locals, families out for a good night and couples on romantic dates. The food is a good example of what can be done when a profound respect for local ingredients meets a talent that goes beyond craft into art; the last time we visited, a roasted duck seemed to melt off the plate onto a bed of pecan risotto. We wanted to sleep a happy nap right there and then, and that's the essence of D&J's – food and atmosphere that go beyond good into uncannily cozy territory.

MARTINIQUE BISTRO

Map pp102–3   French-Caribbean $$$

☎ 891-8495; 5908 Magazine St; mains $17-32; 🕑 5:30-10pm Tue-Thu, 11:30am-2pm & 5:30-10pm Fri & Sat, 11:30am-2pm Sun

French cuisine with a squeeze of lime from the island of Martinique. In pleasant twilight, when the doors to the lush courtyard are flung open, the atmosphere at this converted cottage is both exotic and convivial. The cooking has an accomplished simplicity. Hawaiian sunfish glazed with a Tabasco beurre blanc, sesame-crusted salmon fillet drizzled with a cilantro-ginger-soy vinaigrette, curry Gulf shrimp – it all comes together perfectly. Make reservations.

JACQUES-IMO'S CAFÉ

Map pp102–3   Louisianan $$

☎ 861-0886; www.jacquesimoscafe.com; 8324 Oak St; mains $15-30; 🕑 5:30-10pm Mon-Sat

If cornbread muffins swimming in butter aren't rich enough, how about steak smothered in *bleu*-cheese sauce and bacon? Or the insane yet wickedly brilliant alligator sausage cheesecake? That's the whole attitude at Jack Leonardi's exceedingly popular restaurant: die, happily, with butter and heavy sauces sweating out of your pores. Just a few doors from the famous Maple Leaf Bar (p189), many people make an evening out of these two spots, but you don't need an excuse to dine at this dive-cum-haute-cuisine outpost. We mean that – it looks like a local's cluttered house (it helps that the owner can often be seen in the kitchen cooking in his boxer shorts), but the food is a knockout blow of excess and decadence. In fairness, the kitchen does send out duds from time to time. Blame the slamming stock in trade – this restaurant has gotten hugely popular in the past decade. On busy nights expect long waits to get in (reservations are not accepted).

PATOIS Map pp102–3   French-Creole $$

☎ 895-9441; www.patoisnola.com; 6078 Laurel St; mains $21-29; 🕑 5:30-10pm Wed, Thu & Sat, from 11:30am Fri, 10:30am-2pm Sun

Head chef Aaron Burgau went through the paces of New Orleans' top restaurants, including Bayona (p154) and Commander's Palace (p162), on the path to opening Patois. The man learned well in those years; this Uptown restaurant is one of the hottest names on local foodies' lips. The menu is French haute with New Orleans accents (or 'patois'); roasted pheasant in foie gras emulsions, saddle of rabbit, and new twists on surf and turf, such as pork belly with scallops, pop up on an ever-shifting, always-excellent menu. The setting is relatively casual; customers, largely locals, are here for a fine meal in an old house, so you feel more like you're at a friend's dinner party than a stuffy restaurant.

LILETTE Map pp102–3   French $$

☎ 895-1636; www.liletterestaurant.com; 3637 Magazine St; lunch mains $21-28; 🕑 11:30am-2pm & 5:30-9:30pm Tue-Thu, 11:30am-2pm & 5:30-10:30pm Fri & Sat

Lilette is a lively little bistro with a very traditional European vibe, although tradition is not an obsession, as chef John Harris works wonders with familiar dishes, making them subtly new. Lunch here is a nice way to pass a Magazine St afternoon; the pulled pork sandwich in its own gravy is gorgeous. Dinner's nice, too; start your meal with the white-truffle parmigiana toast with wild mushrooms, then pick from a solid lineup of mains, such as grilled hanger steak, which comes with fries and marrowed bordelaise sauce.

DANTE'S KITCHEN

Map pp102–3   Modern Louisianan $$

☎ 861-3121; www.danteskitchen.com; 736 Dante St; mains $19-26, brunch $9-12.50; 🕑 5:30-10pm Wed-Mon, 10:30am-2pm Sat & Sun

Dante's, which sits in a pretty patio/country cottage on the Mississippi levee, does some imaginative cuisine that is, by turns, basic and refined, and melds French, American and Louisiana traditions: pork shoulder with red boudin dirty rice and maple-glazed chicken with potato-bacon hash cake are good examples. But it's the Sunday brunch we enjoy most – it's one of the best in a city filled with famous brunch destinations. Debris and poached eggs on a caramelized onion biscuit, topped with a demi-glacé hollandaise sauce is a pretty unbelievable way to start your day, unless, of course, you decide to opt for the bread-pudding French toast.

LA PETITE GROCERY

Map pp102–3   French $$

☎ 891-3377; www.lapetitegrocery.com; 4238 Magazine St; mains $18-25; 🕑 11:30am-2:30pm & 5:30-10pm Tue-Sat

La Petite is one of the many cozy bistros squeezed into the crowded Uptown dining scene. The dinners are good but not great for the price, consisting of bistro mainstays such as braised lamb shanks. We prefer the lunches, which consist of some very fine sandwiches and salads, including sweet pepper and eggplant with goat cheese and aioli.

MAT & NADDIE'S

Map pp102–3   Modern Southern $$

☎ 861-9600; www.matandnaddies.com; 937 Leonidas St; mains $17-29; 🕑 11am-2pm & 5:30-9:30pm Mon, Thu & Fri, 11am-2pm Tue & Wed, 5:30-9:30pm Sat

If our friends were coming to New Orleans and we had one restaurant to take them to,

it would be Mat & Naddie's. We can think of no higher praise in this town of great eateries, but everything just comes together here. Set in a beautiful riverfront shotgun house with a Christmas light–bedecked patio in the back, it offers rich, innovative, even amusing food, such as duck-fat-fried chicken with waffles and pecan sweet-potato pie (all crazy delicious), and just damn friendly staff and service. It's kind of weird, it's high quality topped with quirkiness, and honestly, it's one of our favorite splurges in the city.

LA CREPE NANOU   Map pp102–3   French $$

☎ 899-2670; www.lacrepenanou.com; 1410 Robert St; crepes $10-15, mains $19-23.50; 🕑 6-10:30pm Mon-Thu, to 11pm Fri & Sat

New Orleans is a city that loves its bistros, but it all too often Creole-izes steak *frites* standbys. That's understandable, but sometimes you want your sweetbreads simple and unadorned by crawfish. Crepe Nanou feels your pain; it stays true to classically French form, slinging mussels, steaks, excellent *frites* and, of course, some very fine crepes. The latter is the one thing they've Louisiana-ed up, and that's fine by us: crabmeat in Mornay sauce is what we like in our thin pancakes.

PASCAL'S MANALE

Map pp102–3   Italian & Louisianan $$

☎ 895-4877; 1838 Napoleon Ave; mains $12.25-26; 🕑 11:30am-10pm Mon-Fri, 4-10pm Sat, 4-9pm Sun Sep-May

Pascal's Manale is an Uptown tradition, established in 1913, with walls bedecked with black-and-white photos of staff, patrons and the odd celebrity. It claims to have invented the local take on barbecue shrimp that requires no grill (it's sautéed in a garlicky sauce). Specialties are mostly Italian standards – lots of veal, seafood and steaks – enjoyed with a lot of gusto by a crowd that look like they could moonlight on weekends in a Mario Puzo novel.

KYOTO   Map pp102–3   Japanese $$

☎ 891-3644; 4920 Prytania St; mains $10-20; 🕑 11am-3pm & 5:30-9pm Mon-Fri, 5:30-9pm Sat

Sporting a blonde-wood interior, friendly hipster staff and, most importantly, chefs who truly care about doing some fine raw fish, Kyoto is our favorite sushi bet in the

CHÚC NGON MIÊNG (BON APPETIT)!

There are all kinds of great Vietnamese restaurants in New Orleans, but a lot of them are across the river in either Gretna or New Orleans East. While the atmosphere at all of these places is pretty locally 'Vietnamese,' there's usually a fair crowd of white, black and Latino diners as well, so don't expect to feel like an interloper. Prices are at the top end of the 'budget' category – unless you're really hungry, it's hard to spend more than $20 a head at any of these spots. Call ahead for hours, as these can be subject to some shifting.

Dong Phuong Oriental Bakery (☎ 254-0296; 14207 Chef Menteur Hwy, New Orleans East) For the best *banh mi* (Vietnamese sandwiches of sliced pork, cucumber, cilantro and other lovelies, locally called a 'Vietnamese po'boy') around and some very fine durian cake.

Kim Son (☎ 366-2489; 349 Whitney Ave, Gretna) Our favorite Vietnamese spot; its rice-paper rolls and marinated beef are off the freaking charts. The best argument for moving to Gretna we've experienced.

9 Roses (Hoa Hong 9; ☎ 366-7665; 1100 Stephens St, Gretna) One of the oldest Vietnamese restaurants in the area, famous for its seafood soups.

Pho Tau Bay (☎ 368-9846; 113 Westbank Expressway, Gretna) Great *pho* and very solid executions of every other Vietnamese main we can remember.

Tan Dinh (☎ 361-8008; 2005 Belle Chasse Hwy, Gretna) Some local Vietnamese say Tan Dinh has dipped a bit in quality, but others still swear by it. Where else can you find jellyfish salad? Contends with Pho Tau Bay for best *pho* in town.

city. The menu offers all the tuna/eel/yellowtail favorites plus some local specialties such as crawfish rolls. It's popular with students, young families and the smattering of Japanese expats we spoke with in the city, which may be the highest praise of all.

DELACHAISE   Map pp102–3   Wine & Cheese $$
☎ 895-0858; www.thedelachaise.com; 3442 St Charles Ave; small plates $7-18; ⏱ 5pm-late Mon-Sat, 6pm-late Sun

The winner of the wine-and-cheese war in New Orleans comes down to this spot versus the Bywater's Bacchanal (p158). We won't declare a victor, but we will say Delachaise is a lot more suave and open a fair bit later. Plus, you gotta love its cheese menu – the pictograms that explain 'stinky,' 'strong' etc are very cute. The small plates are all wonderful in their own indulgent way, especially the ridiculously over-the-top grilled cheese sandwich, apparently assembled from truffled bread and foie gras–infused cheese (that's a joke, but the thing really tastes that rich). If it's late at night, you're hungry and you need something a little more refined than a burger, head here.

BOUCHERIE   Map pp102–3   Modern American $
☎ 862-5514; www.boucherie-nola.com; 8115 Jeannette St; small plates $6-12, mains $11-15; ⏱ 11am-3pm & 5:30-9pm Tue-Sat

We didn't think you could improve on Krispe Kreme doughnuts, but along comes Boucherie's signature dessert: Krispy Kreme bread pudding. That heavy bread pudding becomes airy yet drool-tastically fattening when married with a honey glaze, drowning in syrup. Boucherie is the permanent outpost of the Purple Truck, New Orleans' most famous mobile restaurant, and it may be the best midrange dining in the city, spinning its unique menu into wacky new levels of delicious-ness. Barbecued shrimp and grits cakes are darkly sweet and savory; garlic parmesan fries are gloriously stinky, gooey and just oily enough; and duck confit with a truffled baby salad is both magically hearty and refined.

MAPLE STREET CAFÉ
Map pp102–3   Mediterranean $
☎ 314-9003; 7623 Maple St; mains $10-15; ⏱ 11am-10pm Mon-Thu, to 11pm Sat & Sun

While this city excels in the food stakes, it can admittedly be a little light on, well, light fare. Maple Street Café tries to remedy this situation with a menu of airy pastas and salads. The funny thing is, just as a New Orleans restaurant in your town may be good for your area but so-so by this city's measure, the Maple Street is great for its relative novelty but fairly middling by modern Mediterranean standards. Still, it's not bad, and sometimes you just need some pesto and pine nuts.

ST JAMES CHEESE CO

Map pp102–3   Cheese Deli $

☎ 899-4737; www.stjamescheese.com; 5004 Prytania St; mains $9-15; ⏱ 11am-6pm Mon-Thu, to 8pm Fri & Sat, to 4pm Sun

Founded by an Englishman obsessed over all the right things (namely, meat and fermented milk products), St James is the best cheese shop in the city. We won't exhaust all the details of what's available, but rest assured there's a veritable atlas worth of cheese in this shop. Premade sandwiches make for an excellent lunch; we opt for the mozzarella with basil pesto and salami. Hosts frequent cheese tastings.

IGNATIUS Map pp102–3   Creole $

☎ 896-2225; 4200 Magazine St; mains $8-15; ⏱ 9am-9pm

One of the better small neighborhood joints in a city that excels in the genre, Ignatius does old standbys such as alligator po'boys and red beans and rice very well, if not exceptionally. The brunches here are the main draw; there's a pretty deep menu on offer, and the omelets groaning under crab meat and crawfish étouffée are some of the finest around.

DOMILISE'S PO-BOYS

Map pp102–3   Po'boys $

☎ 899-9126; 5240 Annunciation St; po'boys $8-13; ⏱ 11am-7pm Mon-Sat

Domilise's is everything that makes New Orleans great: a dilapidated white shack by the river serving Dixie beer, staffed by folks who've worked here for decades, and prepping, if not the best po'boys in the city, at least the best seafood sandwich. Straight up; we haven't had a better oyster sandwich anywhere. Locals tell us to opt for the half-and-half (oysters and shrimp) with gravy and cheese, but honestly, we think the oyster, dressed but otherwise on its own, is the height of the po'boy maker's craft. Belly up to the bar, get us another Dixie and welcome home. Cash only.

CRABBY JACK'S

off Map pp102–3   Cajun & Creole $

☎ 833-2722; 428 Jefferson Hwy; mains $8-13; ⏱ 11am-3pm Mon-Sat

Jack's, about two miles west of Riverbend, is owned by the folks who own Jaques-Imo's (p165) and generates the atmosphere of the latter before it became one of the most popular restaurants in town. It's humble but eccentric Creole and Cajun fair, with dark, strongly spiced gumbo, mouthwatering duck po'boys and kooky art all over the walls. The staff sass you playfully while they dance to Bubba Sparxxx, and all in all this is an excellent local's joint. Located just outside of town on the way to Jefferson. To drive here (and you will need wheels, as it's off the highway) head west along S Claiborne Ave until the road becomes a highway, and Jack's is on your left.

CASAMENTO'S Map pp102–3   Seafood $

☎ 895-9761; www.casamentosrestaurant.com; 4330 Magazine St; mains $7-13; ⏱ 11am-2pm & 5:30-9pm Tue-Sat Sep–mid-May

This is as good as oysters get in NOLA. That's why you come here: to walk through the 1949 soda-shop-esque sparkling interior, across the tiled floors to a marble-top counter, trade a joke with the person shucking shells and get some raw boys with a beer. If the shucker respects the way you down your 'erster,' they might even give you a fist bump on your way out the door. If you can't take 'em raw, the thick gumbo with Creole tomatoes and oyster loaf (a sandwich of breaded and fried oysters) are suitably incredible. They keep it old school here in terms of friendly service, seasonal opening times (it's closed during the summer) and trading only in cash.

TAQUERIA CORONA Map pp102–3   Mexican $

☎ 897-3974; 5932 Magazine St; mains $6-13; ⏱ 11:30am-2pm & 5-9:30pm

Corona serves the best Mexican food in town. It's a friendly, neighborhood/student spot that gets jam packed with families, young Uptown professionals and Tulane kids chowing down on some excellent burritos (we like the bean), tacos (go for the fish or chorizo) and flautas (mmm, the shrimp) every evening. The food fills you up without sitting like a brick in your stomach, making this a great choice for a quality budget feed.

COOTER BROWN'S TAVERN & OYSTER BAR Map pp102–3   Seafood & Grill $

☎ 866-9104; www.cooterbrowns.com; 509 S Carrollton Ave; mains $5-13; ⏱ 11am-1am; 🛜
Cooter's is open late, does mean cheese fries, whips out a killer chili cheese dog and has one of the best beer selections in the city (see p187 for details on Cooter's virtues

as a bar). But our long, lingering romance with Mr C Brown is attributable to his oyster bar. The boys are shucked to order here, plump and cold, and at $8 for a dozen are an absolute steal.

FRANKY & JOHNNY'S Map pp102–3 Cajun $
☎ 899-9146; 321 Arabella St; mains $4-14; ⏲ 11am-9pm
If you took a New Jersey Italian diner's decor, plopped it by the Mississippi River and replaced the pizza with red beans and rice and some of the finest crawfish off the bayou, there, friends, would be Franky & Johnny's. It's a locals' favorite for casual Cajun food; opt for the daily specials and enjoy some very fine food at very reasonable prices.

REFUEL Map pp102–3 Cafe $
☎ 872-0187; www.refuelcafe.com; 8124 Hampson St; mains $8-10; ⏲ 7am-3pm Mon-Fri, from 8:30am Sat & Sun
New Orleans has no shortage of coffee shops, but most of them are more cute and cozy as opposed to cool. This hip cafe adds a bit of much-needed chic to the local coffee culture scene, but it's hardly pretentious; service here is some of the friendliest in town. The staff serve fresh food such as Baja omelets with avocado, but New Orleans mainstays like grits keep the kitchen rooted, as it should be, in the South.

GUY'S Map pp102–3 Po'boys $
☎ 891-5025; 5259 Magazine St; po'boys under $10; ⏲ 11am-4pm Mon-Sat
It's very simple: Guy's is basically a one-man operation that does some of the best po'boys in town. The owner is also the cashier, head shopper, chef and prep staff. Ergo your sandwich is made fresh and to order, with a level of attention you don't get anywhere else in the city. Even when the line is out the door – and it often is – each po'boy is painstakingly crafted. So yes, that loaf will take a while, but *damn* is it worth it.

ZARA'S Map pp102–3 Deli $
☎ 895-0581; 4838 Prytania St; po'boys under $10; ⏲ 9am-8pm
This local grocery store has some good produce and a solid deli that cranks out very decent po'boys, plus other variations on salads and sandwiches.

TEE-EVA'S CREOLE SOUL FOOD
Map pp102–3 Soul Food & Creole $
☎ 899-8350; 4430 Magazine St; snacks $1.50-3, mains $4-8; ⏲ 11am-6pm Mon-Sat, noon-5pm Sun
Just search out the little yellow shack with the singing lady painted on the side. That's Tee-Eva, who once sang backup to the late, great local legend Ernie K-Doe. Now she whips out snowballs and pralines and some fine hot lunches, such as baked chicken, plates of red beans and rice, and some very fine Louisiana sweet and savory pies.

CAMELLIA GRILL Map pp102–3 Grill & Diner $
☎ 309-2679; www.camelliagrill.net; 626 S Carrollton Ave; mains $3-8; ⏲ 9am-1am Mon-Thu, 9am-3am Fri, 8am-3am Sat, 8am-1am Sun
One of our favorite New Orleans stories: apparently a woman walked into Camellia and asked if it served low-fat dessert. The line cook's response? Dip a slice of pecan pie in melted butter and throw it on the grill. That's what you get! The other great thing about this spot, besides its great diner burger-chili-Reuben fare, is that it's the sort of place where the staff look like 50 Cent or The Ramones, and they all call each other – and you – 'baby.' All the time. Plus, they dress in tux shirts and black bow-ties, as if this place couldn't be any wonderfully weirder.

HANSEN'S SNO-BLIZ
Map pp102–3 Snowballs $
☎ 891-9788; www.snobliz.com; 4801 Tchoupitoulas St; snowballs $1.50-3.50; ⏲ 1-7pm Tue-Sun
The humble snowball (shaved ice with flavored syrup) is New Orleans' favorite dessert (see p171). Citywide consensus is that Hansen's, which has been in business since 1939, does the best ball in town. Even Zagat gave this little stand a 29 out of 30. Founder Ernest Hansen, who passed away after Hurricane Katrina, actually patented the shaved ice machine. Now his granddaughter, Ashley, runs the family business, doling out shaved ice under everything from root-beer syrup to cream of nectar.

MID-CITY & THE TREMÉ

As befits the most diverse neighborhood in the city, the food scene here runs from very fine upscale (but generally comfy and eclectic, and not hugely pricey) dining to some down-at-heel but still tasty-as-hell corner spots.

MID-CITY

Mid-City hosts a wide variety of restaurants, befitting one of the most diverse neighborhoods in the city. You'll find plenty of cheap and cheerful spots, but there are also a few formal, sit-down dining establishments for those seeking a more intimate evening. The variety of cuisines, from local Louisiana to Iberian peninsula, is commendable.

CAFÉ DEGAS   Map pp108–9   French $$
☎ 945-5635; www.cafedegas.com; 3127 Esplanade Ave; mains $18-23; ☽ 11am-2:30pm & 6-10pm Wed-Sat, 10:30am-3pm & 6-10pm Sun
A full-grown pecan tree thrusts through the floor and ceiling of the enclosed deck that serves as Café Degas' congenial dining room. This is a rustic and romantic little spot that warms the heart with first-rate, very reasonably priced French fare. The casual atmosphere is accentuated by eccentric, exceedingly polite waiters. Meals that sound familiar on the menu – steak frites au poivre, parmesan-crusted veal medallions, seared duck breast with mushroom spaetzle – are arranged with extraordinary beauty on their plates. You might feel guilty for disturbing art like this, but it's a crime for which you will be amply rewarded.

LOLA'S   Map pp108–9   Spanish $$
☎ 488-6946; 3312 Esplanade Ave; mains $7-18; ☽ 5:30-9:30pm Sun-Thu, to 10pm Fri & Sat
You gotta wait for the best Spanish food in the city, but that's alright. Pop outside into that warm Esplanade air and enjoy some wine and conversation with the clouds of Mid-City locals who swear by Lola's paellas and fideuas (an angel-hair pasta variation on the former). Once you get inside, it's all elbows and crowds and buzz of conversation, and, incidentally, some very good grub. This

top picks

PO'BOYS

- Domilise's (p168)
- Parkway Tavern (opposite)
- Guy's (p169)
- Zara's (p169)
- Crabby Jack's (p168)

isn't haute Barcelona cuisine; it's the sort of Spanish peasant fare Hemingway wrote chapters about, all rabbit and meats and hams and fresh seafood and olive oil and lots and lots of delicious garlic – vampires need not apply. Bring your cash.

MANDINA'S   Map pp108–9   Italian $$
☎ 482-9179; www.mandinasrestaurant.com; 3800 Canal St; mains $10-15; ☽ 11am-9:30pm Mon-Thu, to 10pm Fri & Sat, noon-9pm Sun
In the Italian-American New Orleans community, funerals were followed by a visit to this institution for the turtle soup. That's just the way it was and that's what Mandina's is: the way it was. The menu may be conservative, but hey: when you've been around for over 100 years you stick to what you know. In this case that's Sicilian-Louisiana food done well, if not exceptionally so: trout almandine, red beans and rice with veal cutlets, and bell peppers stuffed with macaroni and meat. The family-style dining room, in its way, is as historic as any building in the city and just as crucial to its culture. Cash only.

LIUZZA'S BY THE TRACK
Map pp108–9   Diner $
☎ 218-7888; 1518 N Lopez St; mains $6-14; ☽ 11am-7pm Mon-Sat
This quintessential Mid-City neighborhood joint does some of the best gumbo in town, a barbecue shrimp po'boy to die for and legendary deep-fried garlic oysters. Always start your visit with a beer and an inspection of the daily specials (red beans and rice, pork chops and the like), which are always up to scratch. All that said, the real reason to come is the atmosphere: we've seen a former city judge and a stripper dining out together in this spot, which is as 'Only in New Orleans' an experience as they come. Liuzza's is nearly impossible to squeeze into during Jazz Fest, natch.

FIVE HAPPINESS   Map pp108–9   Chinese $
☎ 482-3935; www.fivehappiness.com; 3605 S Carrollton Ave; mains $7-12; ☽ 11am-10pm Mon-Thu & Sun, to 11pm Fri & Sat
We very much doubt you came to New Orleans for the Chinese food, let alone the Chinese food served on the highway strip stretches of this corner of Carrollton Ave. But we couldn't let you leave without recommending Five Happiness. It's every

YELLOW SNOW (OTHER COLORS AVAILABLE)

Called snow cones elsewhere in the country, but more popular here than anywhere else, snowballs are a blast of winter on a steamy midsummer afternoon in New Orleans. Shaved ice in a paper cup doused liberally with flavored syrup, they're a simple pleasure that appeals to children and adults alike. During the hot months, bare-bones shacks and portable trailers magically appear on the streets. You'll see 'em on Magazine St and Tchoupitoulas St Uptown, and elsewhere around the city. It's an impulse buy you won't regret.

local's favorite Chinese place. It serves up the oily standards such as pepper steak and sweet-and-sour everything you expect in any Chinese restaurant anywhere (besides China). Five Happiness may not be gastronomically thrilling, but with three decades of history behind it, it's very much a beloved landmark on the culinary scene; locals love it with the same passion they have for the great Creole and Cajun grand dames.

HUEVOS Map pp108–9 Diner $
☎ 482-6264; 4408 Banks St; mains $5-12; 7am-3pm
Huevos is Spanish for eggs. Don't you love a restaurant that knows what it's good at? Really: it's eggs and eggs only, thrown into one of the most incredible, enormous breakfast sandwiches in the city, poached on hash with sausage and bacon, and ranchero-ed out with black beans. The chicory coffee is locally sourced and strong as hell, the service is friendly and, well, do you really need any other reason to start your day here?

PARKWAY TAVERN Map pp108–9 Po'boys $
☎ 482-3047; www.parkwaybakeryandtavernnola.com; 538 Hagan Ave; po'boys under $10; 11am-10pm Tue-Sat
Let's face it: no one is going to settle the 'best po'boy in New Orleans' argument anytime soon. But tell a local you think the top sandwich comes from the Parkway and you will get, at the least, a nod of respect. The roast beef in particular, an art some would say is dying among the great po'boy makers, is messy as hell and twice as good; take one down to nearby Bayou St John, feel the wind on the water and munch that sandwich in the shade. Louisiana bliss.

ANGELO BROCATO Map pp108–9 Ice Cream $
☎ 486-1465; www.angelobrocatoicecream.com; 214 N Carrollton Ave; desserts $2-5; 11am-5pm Tue-Sat
When an ice-cream parlor passes the 100-year mark, you gotta just step back and say, 'Alright. Clearly, they're doing something right.' Opened in 1905 by Signor Brocato himself, a Sicilian immigrant who scraped together his savings from working on a sugar plantation, this is the oldest ice-cream shop in New Orleans. We'd come for the beautiful copper espresso machine alone, but then there's the marble-top counter, silky gelatos, perfect cannoli, crispy biscotti and an irreplaceable sense of history. Molto bene.

FAIR GRINDS Map pp108–9 Cafe $
☎ 913-9072; www.fairgrinds.com; 3133 Ponce de Leon St; pastries $2-4; 6:30am-10pm
While Mid-City has good representatives of practically every dining genre out there, this seems to be its only cafe. But what a cafe. It's simultaneously airy and comfy and hip and unpretentious, and the coffee's good to boot. It showcases local art and generally acts as the beating heart of Mid-City's bohemian scene; plus, it supports any number of community development associations. A perfect spot for a shot (of espresso).

THE TREMÉ

It's all neighborhood restaurants in the Tremé; perhaps because it is a rough neighborhood, local restaurants, affordable as they are, work hard to provide polite, white-tablecloth service and a sense of class. Just because the surrounds look like the ghetto doesn't mean the restaurant has to feel like one (this is in contrast to cheap places in rich areas such as Uptown, which often consciously try to come across as dive-y).

DOOKY CHASE
Map pp108–9 Soul Food & Creole $
☎ 821-0600; 2301 Orleans Ave; mains $6-15; 11am-2:30pm Tue-Fri; V
Ray Charles wrote 'Early in the Morning' about Dooky's, local civil rights leaders used the spot as an informal headquarters in the 1960s, and Barack Obama ate here when he visited New Orleans after his inauguration. Leah Chase's labor of love

FINDING YOUR FARMERS MARKET

New Orleans makes up for its small number of huge supermarkets with a surfeit of farmers markets. Here's a list of some of our favorites.

Crescent City Farmers Market (Map pp86–7; www.crescentcityfarmersmarket.org; 700 Magazine St ⊗ 8am-noon Sat) There's also a Tuesday market (Map pp102–3; ⊗ 9am-1pm) held at 200 Broadway St.

German Coast Farmers Market East Bank, Ormond Plantation (13786 River Rd, Destrehan; ⊗ 8am-noon Wed); West Bank (13969 River Rd, Lulin; ⊗ 3-7pm Wed)

Gretna Farmers Market (Huey P Long Ave, btwn 3rd & 4th Aves; ⊗ 8:30am-12:30pm Sat)

Harrison Ave Marketplace (801 Harrison Ave, Lakeview; ⊗ 5-8pm every 2nd Sat)

Mid-City Green Market (Map pp108–9; 3700 Orleans Ave; ⊗ 3-7pm Thu)

Sankofa Marketplace (cnr Caffin St & Claude Ave, Lower Ninth Ward; ⊗ 10am-3pm every 2nd Sat)

Upper Ninth Ward Market (St Claude Ave & Gallier St; ⊗ 1-4pm Sat)

is a backbone of the Tremé, and the city as a whole celebrated when she finally reopened after Katrina. Good if not great grillades, fried chicken and other standards stock the menu, but the absolute standout, and perhaps the best meal for any vegetarian visiting New Orleans, is the gumbo z'herbes. Served on Thursdays during Lent, this is the great New Orleans dish done green and gorgeous with mustards, beet tops, spinach, kale collards and Leah knows what else; even committed carnivores should give it a try.

WILLIE MAE'S SCOTCH HOUSE
Map pp108–9   Soul Food $

☎ 822-9503; 2401 St Ann St; mains $6-13; ⊗ 11am-3pm Mon-Fri

We're going to commit a heresy, but here goes: the fried chicken at Willie Mae's is good. Very good. But it's not the best in the world, despite having built that reputation. Here's the story: the Scotch House (it used to double as a bar, hence the name) was named an 'American classic' by the James Beard foundation in 2005, eight weeks before it was swamped by Katrina. A subsequent huge community effort went into reopening the restaurant, and the narrative was irresistible. Folk from California, Canada and New York come wanting to take part in this story, and we don't begrudge them, but we'd score the fried chicken here seven out of 10. Fussy chicken eaters aside, we

still recommend dropping by here to soak up the community spirit.

LIL' DIZZY'S Map pp108–9   Soul Food $

☎ 569-8997; 1500 Esplanade Ave; mains $6-10; ⊗ 7am-2:30pm Mon-Fri, to 2pm Sat

One of the city's great lunch spots, Dizzy's does mean soul food specials in a historic shack owned by the Baquet family, who have forever been part of the culinary backbone of New Orleans. The fried chicken is excellent, the hot sausages may be better and the bread pudding is divine. Our one gripe is against the gumbo, which was more like thin brown water.

MCHARDY'S Map pp108–9   Fried Chicken $

☎ 949-0000; 1458 N Broad St; chicken pieces per box $5; ⊗ 11am-6:30pm Mon-Sat, to 3pm Sun

Strictly take-out and cheap as it gets, McHardy's does great fried chicken, period. You get five pieces in a normal box, which, when washed down with fruit punch, is as close to summer bliss as you'll likely experience in this town.

CAJUN SEAFOOD Map pp108–9   Take-away $

☎ 948-6000; 1479 N Claiborne Ave; take-out meals $3-5; ⊗ 10:30am-9pm

The name says it all: this is a grocery store/take-out that's one of the best budget options in town for raw seafood and cooked hot plates, such as fried chicken, boudin, fish plates and the like.

DRINKING & NIGHTLIFE

top picks

- Circle Bar (p185)
- Mimi's in the Marigny (p182)
- Cure (p187)
- Vaughan's (p183)
- Saint Bar & Lounge (p187)
- Tonique (p182)
- Le Bon Temps Roulé (p188)
- K-Doe's Mother-in-Law Lounge (p190)
- Columns Hotel (p187)
- St Joe's Bar (p188)

Ready?

Right: Zydepunks are burning it down early at the Hi Ho and then we gotta get a burger at Port of Call. What? Of course the burger's gonna make you tired – it's a half freaking pound! But a Red Turtle from the bar – like fruit punch and tequila but better – gets the energy going again, and they serve them in go cups. So: take the drink to Frenchmen St and don't forget to pop in for the plum sake at Yuki Izakaya; that stuff not only tastes good, it'll clear *anything* out of your system. Now, the Wild Magnolias – you know, the Mardi Gras Indian tribe – might practice across the way, and last time they played, chief Bo Dillis Jr said they were ready to show off some new chants. Watching that should give you time to work the hunger back up; good, because Kermit Ruffins is the lead act at Vaughan's tonight and you know he'll be serving red beans and rice in the back. That *should* tide things over till the cab gets here so you can swing to Uptown for Soul Rebels at the Bon Temps…

Well. You get the idea. New Orleans doesn't rest for much. But we don't want to give you the idea the city is just some alcoholic lush. In point of fact, you'll notice the above description of a typical New Orleans night out (oh yeah, that's typical) factors in just as much food and music as booze. Here they feast on the senses, every one: your ear for a brass band, your tongue for rich food that layers against your whetted thirst for another beer and shot…

This approach to nightlife is not, in fact, restricted to the night; it's just the New Orleans way. Not so much hedonism, it's rolling like a happy dog in the big backyard that is life's great palette – the visual, the auditory and the gustatory. That said, the fun faucet is not, as you might assume, constantly cranked to full blast. New Orleanians do work plenty of enjoyment into their routine (if they can be said to have a routine), but it's like London rain: spread out in a fine continuum throughout the day. The monsoon, on the other hand, is Bourbon St, where tourists who don't let loose enough simply explode. Few New Orleanians can be accused of winding up till they are so tight a few drinks have them stripping off their shirts for the sake of some cheap plastic beads. In fact, we say stay off Bourbon as much as you can, and opt for the local, live and lovely scenes on Frenchmen St, near Riverbend, out in Mid-City, on Magazine, in secret spots along Carrollton and Claiborne, in Lower Garden District dives – hell, anywhere but Bourbon.

OK, have a Hurricane at Pat O'Brien's. Maybe a Hand Grenade, too, if you buy us one.

There's a good gay scene here, too, one of the best in the American South, but it's not all that isolated from the rest of New Orleans' nightlife. This is probably a good thing; the city is so tolerant and accepting, the local gay and lesbian population hasn't been forced to segregate itself. Some do by choice, however, and this exclusively gay scene tends to be concentrated in the French Quarter and Faubourg Marigny. See p180 for details. New Orleans also lacks big, multistage bass-pumping nightclubs, but no one seems to complain about this state of affairs, least of all us.

One more thing: we're not trying to name drop like twits in that first paragraph. The fact is, a dedicated lover of the night can become very quickly acquainted with the local music and bar scene here in a short span of time. New Orleans is, at the end of the day, an intimate town made up of more intimate neighborhoods, and even recent transplants soon learn where the best of the bacchanals is going down.

SPECIALTIES

New Orleans has an enviable international reputation for debauchery. From the intimacy of neighborly beer joints to the over-the-top extravaganza of the Carnival season, the city has a gloriously excessive drinking culture. The party is fueled by beverages, ranging from watery beer to sophisticated cocktails, but they're not all alcoholic. When in Orleans, be sure to sober up with a pot of chicory coffee and soften things up at lunchtime with some lemonade or iced tea (or both mixed together – an Arnold Palmer or Half-and-Half).

Alcoholic Drinks

In the same way that gourmands attempt to eat their way across the city, hard-drinking

ABSINTHE & HERBSAINT

When absinthe, the once insanely popular licorice-flavored liqueur, was outlawed in the early 20th century for its extreme addictive and psychoactive potential, addicts and purveyors of the drink tried to find a substitute for the bitter liquor. The French developed pastis and Pernod as safer alternatives to the wormwood-based absinthe. Not to be outdone, a New Orleans company developed its own wormwood-free absinthe with star anise replacing the forbidden herb. The resulting yellowish-green Herbsaint replaced absinthe in cocktails and culinary preparations alike. Plenty of local specialties use Herbsaint as a primary ingredient or subtle flavoring, including local versions of oysters Rockefeller and New Orleans signature cocktails such as the Sazerac and Absinthe Suissesse. Some people find Herbsaint to be pretty foul stuff, considering it tastes a lot like absinthe and doesn't even give you a good hallucination.

pilgrims often try to sample the countless (and often near-flammable) specialty drinks of New Orleans. In a town where barrooms never seem to close, and even breakfast has a cocktail course, you can expect bottle-based indulgences to be plentiful and varied. Whether you prefer your poison on the rocks, on draft, in a snifter, or in a go cup, there will always be a range of 'adult beverages' within easy reach.

EYE-OPENERS

Cocktails in the morning hours are a bit decadent, even in New Orleans. But decadence is acceptable here. If you require the hair of the dog that bit you, New Orleans can accommodate no matter what the hour – it's a bit of an Uptown tradition to greet the sunrise at Ms Mae's (p188) with a Dixie.

Brunch wouldn't be popular without beverages with a little kick. The Absinthe Suissesse, a tame holdover from New Orleans' absinthe binge (prior to it being outlawed in the early 20th century), is a rich, licorice-flavored concoction that's more cream than booze. The subtle mix of Herbsaint, heavy cream and orgeat (primarily almond) syrup makes for a smooth start to any New Orleans morning after.

The Ramos Gin Fizz, named for 19th-century New Orleans bartender Henry Ramos, is a rich, frothy blend of gin, cream, egg whites, extra-fine sugar, fizzy water and a splash of orange-flower water.

The Mint Julep is more popular in other parts of the South, particularly in Louisville, KY, where it is traditionally drunk in great quantities on Derby Day. But most self-respecting barkeeps in New Orleans know how to properly mix bourbon, sugar and muddled mint. It makes an ideal afternoon refreshment on hot days.

Lately, the Aviation has become all the rage among local drinkers. It's a pretty old-school cocktail that's attained a level of modern hip, as these things are wont to do. Try it on a hot day: gin, maraschino liqueur and lemon juice, plus some other trade secrets depending on which bar you're at. They're very refreshing.

CLASSIC NEW ORLEANS COCKTAILS

Local classics such as the Sazerac, Pimm's Cup and Cafe Brulot represent the best of old-school New Orleans cocktail culture. Though each of these drinks have internationally known counterparts, drinking one here requires a slightly adventurous palate and a sense of local history. It used to be you had to find a bartender who was at least 70 years old to make any of these properly, but there's a new generation of very dedicated young mixers out there prepping some mean classics. To hit the point home, our favorite cocktails, classic or otherwise, are made at relatively young bars, such as Cure (p187) and Tonique (p182).

Sazerac is a potent whiskey drink that uses either rye or bourbon as its primary ingredient, with aromatic bitters (including the locally produced Peychaud's), a bit of sugar and a swish of Herbsaint.

Pimm's Cup is a summer refresher traditionally associated with the infamous French Quarter bar, Napoleon House (p178). It's a simple mix of the British gin-based liqueur (Pimm's No 1) topped with soda or ginger ale.

Cafe Brulot is more of an after-dinner experience than a cocktail. On your table, spices, sugar and brandy are heated to flaming point and ignited for dramatic effect; strong brewed coffee is then added.

TOURIST DRINKS

The bars on Bourbon St feature many beverages that have a local New Orleans cachet, such as the Hurricane and the Hand Grenade. These drinks are standards for those hell-bent on a French Quarter party experience. Much-imitated, and often more festive than

COCKTAIL COCKAMAMIE

It should come as no surprise that New Orleans claims to have invented the whole concept of having a drink for the hell of it – that is, a cocktail. As always, the Crescent City backs up the claim with a good story that may well explain the origin of the word.

The story begins with a man named Peychaud, who settled in New Orleans after fleeing the 18th-century slave uprisings in St Domingue (now Haiti). He opened an apothecary on Royal St, where, we are told, he developed a penchant for drinking brandy from an eggcup. The concept appealed to the people of New Orleans, and Peychaud began serving drinks in this fashion at his shop. (One might wonder why people were so willing to drink from an eggcup, but read on...)

The eggcup, of course, was not called an eggcup in French-speaking New Orleans. It was called a *coquetier*...or at least it was called that until Peychaud's inebriated patrons began mispronouncing it. The term evolved – much as the word Acadian turned into Cajun – from 'coquetier' to 'cock-tay' to 'cocktail.' In time, the eggcup was disposed of in favor of a regular glass, and other liquor came to be more popular than brandy, but the name stuck.

Whatever the truth of the story, it is well documented that the Sazerac is one of the earliest, if not *the* earliest, cocktails in existence.

substantial, these libations have contributed to many tales of blurry Mardi Gras mayhem.

The Hurricane was made famous by the French Quarter bar Pat O'Brien's (p179). It's a towering rum drink that gets its bright-pink hue from the healthy portion of passion fruit juice. The Hand Grenade, sold at Tropical Isle (p179), is a mix of melon liqueur, grain alcohol, rum, vodka and God knows what else. Suffice to say, two or more will destroy you. Frozen daiquiris, by New Orleans' definition, are a class of alcoholic Slurpees that come in all the brightest colors of the rainbow. You can pick them up, sometimes by the gallon (yeah you right!), from, yes, drive-thru take-outs.

BEER

Following Hurricane Katrina there were (gasp!) no breweries left in Orleans Parish, but this situation changed with the arrival of Nola Brewing Co. At the time of research, it was putting out two beers that were both pretty excellent: a blonde and a brown ale. It's planning on releasing new seasonal varieties in the future. Here's to its motto: *Laissez la bonne bière verser!* (Let the good beer pour!).

The biggest microbrew around is Abita Brewery (p234). From its standard amber ale to more ambitious Mardi Gras bock and seasonal Jockimo stout, Abita beers provide a welcome local alternative to the usual corporate lagers. It does good 'fruity' beers, such as the raspberry Purple Haze and its seasonal (spring) strawberry beer.

Founded in 1907, Dixie Beer used to be the beer everyone associated with New Orleans. Then Katrina happened. The copper brew kettles were looted from the brewery and operations were shipped north to, of course, Wisconsin. You can still get a Dixie here, but don't think you're getting a locally produced southern drink.

WINE

Wine is and ever has been popular in Louisiana thanks to a strong French cultural influence, but the homegrown industry is small; this state is too humid for viticulture. Restaurants such as Delachaise (p167), Bacchanal (p158) and the Wine Institute of New Orleans (WINO; p161) are all good spots to pick up some fermented grape juice.

Nonalcoholic Drinks
COFFEE & CHICORY

American readers: you may not know this, but most foreigners rip on us for having bad coffee. Foreign readers: stop doing that, come to New Orleans and have a cup of our stuff. American readers: you too.

Coffee here is traditionally mixed with chicory, a roasted herb root, in a Creole coffee or New Orleans blend. Originally used to 'extend' scarce coffee beans during hard times, chicory continues to be added for a fuller-bodied flavor. It gives local coffee a slightly bitter, much stronger taste than the brown water you get in other parts of the country. We like it served best as café au lait, which is empathically *not* a latte. Instead, it's coffee with chicory mixed with scalded (not steamed) milk poured from two cups.

ICED TEA

In hot and humid Louisiana, iced tea is more than just a drink – it's a form of air-con in a tall, sweaty glass. Preparation of the common beverage couldn't be simpler – it's simply chilled regular tea poured over ice and garnished with a lemon wedge or mint leaves. No milk, please, but some (especially black New Orleanians and folks from other parts of the South) like it with enough sugar to keep an army of dentists employed.

When you order iced tea at a restaurant, it is usually a bottomless cup and will be regularly refilled. If you want a proper English cup of tea, specify 'hot tea' or you'll get a tall, ice-filled glass instead of a steaming mug.

PRACTICALITIES
Opening Hours
Most dedicated bars open around 5pm, although some places serve drinks during lunch, and the wonderful Ms Mae's (p188), plus a few others, are open 24 hours. Closing time at local bars is an ill-defined thing; officially it's around 2am or 3am, but in reality it tends to be whenever the last customer stumbles out the door.

How Much?
This is a cheap town for nighthawks. You'll rarely pay more than $4 for a beer. Sometimes domestics will go for under $2. Cocktails rarely top $5, unless you're at a higher-end lounge, shots of hard spirits go for around $3 to $5 (more for top-shelf stuff), and everything is cheaper during happy hour. Wine can be expensive at wine bars, but is generally of very high quality. The only time prices go up to annoyingly high levels is during big events such as Mardi Gras and Jazz Fest.

Tipping
To our non-US readers: in America, it's common to leave a tip for your bartender, even if they just pop the cap off a bottle of beer. Leaving under a dollar is pretty insulting. You don't have to tip for every drink, especially if you're just getting a couple of beers, but the general rule is to leave a couple of bucks extra for every hour spent at the bar. Many New Orleanians have worked in bars or know someone who does, and tend to be generous with their drink tips.

LIVE MUSIC
New Orleans can shake, rattle and roll with the best of cities. At times, it seems musicians have everyone else outnumbered. But the Big Easy does things its own way. Where else can you dance to the funky grooves laid down by a tuba player? Live performances by Mardi Gras Indians and in jazz, R&B, rock, country, Cajun, zydeco, funk, soul and genre-defying experimentation are on every night of the week.

Tickets & Reservations
You generally won't need to purchase tickets in advance to see live music in a New Orleans club, but there are a few exceptions. When big names such as Dr John play at places like Tipitina's (p189), for instance, you'll want to buy ahead of time.

Ticketmaster (Map pp70–1; ☎ 522-5555; www.ticketmaster.com; 408 N Peters St) has information on, and sells tickets to, just about any major event in the city, including big music shows and sports events. This is a good option if you're purchasing tickets from home before you go to New Orleans.

FRENCH QUARTER
There's a lot going on in the Old Quarter, from boozy Bourbon St to quiet Pirate's Alley. Head down to lower Decatur St for a collection of interesting dives and locals' pubs, which lead in a boozy trail all the way to the fun on Frenchman St. We haven't reviewed the majority of cheese-ball Bourbon St action – these megabars are a dime a dozen and barely qualify as being in New Orleans.

CAROUSEL BAR Map pp70–1   Bar
☎ 523-3341; 214 Royal St; ☽ 11am-late
At this smart-looking hotel bar, inside the historic Monteleone (p202), everyone's a comic until they realize the barkeeps have heard 'em all before. No, you don't get to sit on a painted horse. Hey, how come the stools don't go up and down? What? No

GO CUPS
Guy walks into a bar and orders a drink. Bartender asks, 'Zat for here or to go?' True story. It is legal to walk the streets of New Orleans with a drink in your hand, as long as the drink is in a plastic 'go cup.' Wandering drinkers are prone to losing their grip on their drinks, leaving shattered glass on the sidewalk, so drinking from a real glass or bottle is strictly forbidden.

blaring mechanical orchestra?! The circular bar does revolve and it is canopied by the top hat of the 1904 World's Fair carousel with running lights, hand-painted figures and gilded mirrors. Wednesday night is Louis Prima Night, with John Autin and Julie Jules standing in for Louis and Keely Smith. It takes 15 minutes for the bar to complete a revolution. If it's spinning too fast for you, then you really ought to ease up on the sauce, pal. Careful on your way out.

FAHY'S Map pp70–1   Bar
☎ 586-9806; 540 Burgundy St; ☾ 1pm-late
One of the surest signs of a good bar is its popularity with chefs, who generally demand a high-quality drink after a long day in the kitchen. Fahy's is very popular with French Quarter service staff getting off their shifts, which is as high a praise as any local bar could hope for. Dogs are welcome and generally in abundance (another sign of a friendly spot), and the pool tables clack until the wee hours.

FRENCH 75 Map pp70–1   Bar
☎ 523-5433; 813 Bienville St; ☾ 5pm-late
The bar at Arnaud's (p153) is one of the better restaurant bars in the city. It's all wood and patrician accents, but staff are friendly and down to earth while still able to mix high-quality drinks that will make you feel (a) like the star of your own Tennessee Williams play about decadent Southern aristocracy and (b) drunk.

JEAN LAFITTE'S OLD ABSINTHE HOUSE Map pp70–1   Bar
☎ 523-3181; 240 Bourbon St; ☾ 10am-4am
The Old Absinthe House is rightfully a place you should come to check out the

historic bar, rather than drink at it, as the customer base is of the bottom-shelf Bourbon St sort. Here's the skinny: this historic spot was opened in 1807. A number of bars in New Orleans, including this one, served absinthe before it was outlawed in 1914. The mysterious beverage had a psychotropic allure – wormwood was the active ingredient – but it allegedly sent enthusiasts to the loony bin. Today, Herbsaint, a locally produced anisette, is a relatively safe stand-in for old absinthe-based drinks.

LAFITTE'S BLACKSMITH SHOP
Map pp70–1   Bar
☎ 523-0066; 941 Bourbon St; ☾ noon-late
This gutted brick cottage is one of the most atmospheric in the Quarter; it's a bit of a crying shame it feels like a frat boy hangout half the time. Rumors hold that this was once the workshop of the smuggler Jean Lafitte and his brother Pierre. Whether that tasty bit of lore is true or not (historical records suggest 'not'), the ancient house did go up in the 18th century and endured the fires that destroyed most of the French Quarter during the Spanish era. This is the oldest bar in the Quarter, but that sense of history is thrown out the window at night (in a fun way), when drunk tourists gather round the back-room piano and sing along to Fats Domino and Otis Redding tunes.

NAPOLEON HOUSE Map pp70–1   Bar
☎ 524-9752; www.napoleonhouse.com; 500 Chartres St; ☾ 11am-late
Just as the best emperors are the deposed ones, the best bars are those that have seen better days. Having opened its doors in 1797, Napoleon House is a particularly attractive example of what Walker Percy termed 'vital decay.' By all appearances, its stuccoed walls haven't received so much as a dab of paint in over two centuries, and the diffuse glow pouring through the open doors and windows in the afternoon draws out the room's gorgeous patina. The back courtyard is also pleasant, day or night. As an added bonus, the place has a colorful connection to Bonaparte himself: after the emperor was banished to St Helena, a band of loyal New Orleanians reputedly plotted to snatch him up and set him up in this building's 3rd-floor digs. It didn't happen, but you can easily imagine Napoleon whiling

DRINKING & NIGHTLIFE FRENCH QUARTER

ROOT BEER OF CHOICE

The Native Americans made tea from the roots of the sassafras tree, and it is from this original usage that root beer owes its creation. These days, Louisianans drink twice as much root beer as the American average. This is largely credited to the local Barq's root beer, created by Ed Barq in 1898 at his home in nearby Biloxi, MS. This carbonated New Orleans institution goes well with the hot weather and full-flavored food. Barq's, widely available in cans and bottles, is the only local brand, although it was recently acquired by the Coca-Cola Company.

BARS VS LIVE MUSIC VS LOUNGES

In most cities there's a pretty clear delineation between bars, clubs, lounges and live-music venues. To a degree this is true in New Orleans – no one is going to mistake Le Chat Noir (p185), an intimate small concert venue, for a dive like the Saturn Bar (p183). But look again – that same band of hipsters that entertained a cocktail-sipping crowd at Le Chat may well grace the greasy stage of the Saturn the following night.

Many bars in New Orleans double as live-music venues, and many of the city's best gig venues play the part of bar several days of the week. This city is simply too musically inclined to suffer too many rigid distinctions between the genres. To that end we haven't divided our nightlife reviews between bars and live-music clubs, since one spot so often ends up wearing both hats. But we have tried to identify the main thrust of what goes on — booze or music or both — in our reviews.

Finally, while the lines between bars and gig venues blur here, there is a clear delineation between bars, dives, lounges and the like. We classify 'dives' as grungy, grotty and gruffly endearing; bars can refer to several levels of drinking establishment, from neighborhood pub to sleek hotel hot spot; and lounges represent the most posh examples of the drink-sipping scene.

away his last days in this pleasant spot, telling fishing stories about conquering Europe.

PAT O'BRIEN'S Map pp70–1 Bar
☎ 525-4823; www.patobriens.com; 718 St Peter St; ⏰ 10am-4am

For a tourist trap, Pat O'Brien's has genuine atmosphere and history, though the gift shop does lend a whiff of commercialism, and the Bourbon St boozeoisie has the run of the joint. Anyways, the bar could be in a barren white room and folks would still pack in for the trademark drink, the Hurricane, a lethal 29oz blend of rum, orange juice, pineapple juice and grenadine. 'Hey, this doesn't taste strong at all!' Thirty minutes later: 'Dude. I love you sho much. Whash yer name agin?' The back courtyard, lit by flaming fountains, has an obvious allure for anyone who remembers wanting to jump ship during the *Pirates of the Caribbean* ride at Disneyland.

PIRATE'S ALLEY CAFE Map pp70–1 Bar
☎ 524-9332; www.piratesalleycafe.com; 622 Pirate's Alley; ⏰ noon-late

The narrow pedestrian alley hidden in the shadow of St Louis Cathedral is a natural spot for a tiny little bar, and this nook fits the bill perfectly. It's owned by friendly folk and has the atmosphere of a little Montparnasse hideaway with no claim to fame. You can snag a stool at the bar and meet the regular characters who seem to drop by every few minutes, or claim a table out on the alley and soak up the atmosphere of the Old Quarter. There's lots of pirate-themed fun going on.

PRAVDA Map pp70–1 Bar
☎ 525-1818; 1113 Decatur St; ⏰ 5pm-late

If you couldn't guess from the name, Pravda trades in on a Soviet-chic theme. But while the lighting, all dark and red and sexy, would probably make a KGB officer happy, the vintage furniture and inked-up bar staff are distinctly New Orleans. The soft atmosphere belies a fun-loving clientele sipping (or shooting) off the best vodka and absinthe menu in the city; if strong spirits are your thing, this bar is a must-try.

TROPICAL ISLE Map pp70–1 Bar
☎ 529-4109; 721 Bourbon St; ⏰ 24hr

Everyone has a Tropical Isle memory. Usually, it's pretty fuzzy. This is an unabashed Bourbon St tourist bar that serves 'Hand Grenades'; you can tell thanks to a subtle marketing campaign wherein a guy in a hand-grenade suit stands outside the bar. Drinking more than two Hand Grenades is usually the kicker to a night that involves screaming the lyrics of 'Sweet Home Alabama'/'Sweet Child O' Mine'/Insert Other 'Sweet' Titled Song Here, table dancing, bead tossing, bead receiving, the random mashing of tongues down strangers' throats and the eventual gathering of the limp shreds of your dignity the next day. Woo!

ABBEY Map pp70–1 Dive
☎ 523-7150; 1123 Decatur St; ⏰ 24hr

The riffraff congregating in this atmospheric Decatur St dive tend to dress in black. The place has a faded and jaded port-of-call feel to it, with blasé bartenders, transient hipsters and shifty-looking characters. You needn't be pierced or tattooed to fit in, but a little Joe Strummer swagger won't hurt. The jukebox reflects these sensibilities, but also includes rocking sides by the original Man in Black. And if you're seeking Lee Hazelwood's brand of trouble, the juke here has that covered, too. At least stop by for a shot of Jack if you're prowling the Lower Quarter.

ONE EYED JACKS
Map pp70–1   Dive & Live Music
☎ 569-8361; www.oneeyedjacks.net; 615 Toulouse St; cover $5-15; ☽ noon-late
If you've been wandering the streets at night thinking, 'I could really use a night at a bar that feels like a 19th-century bordello managed by Johnny Rotten,' well, you're in

luck. Honestly, even if this thought hasn't crossed your mind, you should check out Jacks. It's a great venue to start at: as mentioned, there's a sense very dangerous women in corsets, men with Mohawks and an army of gypsies with bottles of absinthe could come charging out of the walls at any moment. And the acts, which consist of punk, post punk and the like, are consistently good and a nice option, if you're getting tired of brass and jazz.

DUNGEON Map pp70–1   Goth Club
☎ 523-5530; www.originaldungeon.com; 738 Toulouse St; cover $5; ☽ midnight-late
Got to admit, this place made us a little nervous at first. It doesn't open till the witching hour, and some of the bouncers

GAY NEW ORLEANS SCENE

While New Orleans is a pretty integrated city where gays and straights tend to mingle on a regular basis, there is a strong gay scene here, primarily centered on the French Quarter and Faubourg Marigny. Quarter bars and clubs tend to be much more wild than their Marigny counterparts, which attract an older, quieter crowd. That said, the Marigny's neighborhood gay bars certainly aren't all sedate; things can get as out of hand here as in the rest of the city. Here's our breakdown of some of the best gay bars and clubs in the city. The following are all open from around 5pm till, really, whenever; we've pointed out which clubs are open 24 hours.

Country Club (Map p81; ☎ 945-0742; www.thecountryclubneworleans.com; 634 Louisa St) Strong Key West vibe in this Bywater mansion with a clothing-optional pool and garden in the back.

Cutter's (Map p81; ☎ 948-4200; www.cuttersbar.biz; 706 Franklin Ave) A convivial, popular neighborhood gay/sports bar that hosts buffets, good tailgate parties before big games and excellent monthly arts shows that showcase lots of local talent. Center for the local bear scene.

Double Play (Map pp70–1; ☎ 523-4517; 439 Dauphine St) As bad as behavior gets, this is where every envelope in the post office gets pushed. Needs to be experienced to be believed.

Good Friends Bar (Map pp70–1; ☎ 566-7191; www.goodfriends.com; 740 Dauphine St) A quintessential Quarter gay bar, where the scene can go from casual drink to debauchery unleashed at the drop of a hat.

JohnPaul's (Map p81; ☎ 942-1345; www.johnpaulsbar.com; 940 Elysian Fields Ave) Western-themed neighborhood bar with one of the friendliest vibes in town. Country and line dancing every Tuesday.

Oz (Map pp70–1; ☎ 593-9491; www.ozneworleans.com; 800 Bourbon St; ☽ 24hr) Your traditional shirtless, all-night-party, loud-music, lots-of-dancing-boys bar, where there are bowls of condoms set out for the customers.

Phoenix/Eagle (Map p81; ☎ 945-9263; www.phoenixneworleans.com; 941 Elysian Fields Ave; ☽ 24hr) Where the leather-and-denim community meets to rub each other's stubble. Much more of a locals' scene than similar spots in the Quarter.

Rubyfruit Jungle (Map pp70–1; ☎ 373-5431; 1135 Decatur St) The only dedicated lesbian bar-club in the city is often busy and plays one of the best track lists in the Quarter.

Starlight by the Park (Map pp70–1; ☎ 561-8939; www.starlightbythepark.com; 834 N Rampart St; ☽ 24hr) With Sunday barbecues, drag-queen revues and lots of beads laying around, Starlight strikes up a good balance between Quarter over-the-top madness and neighborhood vibe.

Check out www.gayneworleans.com for more listings. If you're looking for megaclubs, stop, because there are not many here – you'll have to head to Metairie for that sort of scene. Then again, if Bourbon St's north end doesn't satisfy your need for cheesy dance-off fun, what will?

have filed their teeth into pointy vampire fangs. Then we observed the words 'Ye Olde' in small type on the sign out front. So this is really just 'Ye Olde Dungeon,' which doesn't sound so threatening after all. Having descended into the club's basement chambers, we found Goths outnumbered by yuppies and bikers. DJs keep things throbbing until dawn's early light (egads! sunlight!) and several barkeeps serve up ghoulish cocktails (with creepy names like the Witches Brew and the Dragon's Blood), which the bar promises will help you 'leave your troubles behind.' Such caring, warm-hearted sentiments! Dungeon, we had you all wrong!

BALCONY MUSIC CLUB
Map pp70–1   Live Music
☎ 559-7770; 1331 Decatur St; ⏰ 5pm-late
Balcony is all about the acts; if there's a dud band playing you can pass it up, but on good nights it forms a very convenient crux in the French Quarter–Faubourg Marigny Decatur St stumble o' fun. The 1920s flapper nights, held on a semi-regular basis, are the best; if you've ever seen the 1996 movie *Swingers,* it's kind of exactly like the scene in the Brown Derby. If that cultural reference soared past, imagine walking into a speakeasy circa the Al Capone days and you've got an idea of what's going on.

DONNA'S BAR & GRILL
Map pp70–1   Live Music
☎ 596-6914; www.donnasbarandgrill.com; 800 N Rampart St; cover $5-10; ⏰ shows 10pm-late
Walk down St Ann St toward the lighted arches of Louis Armstrong Park and you'll end up at this humble little sweatbox. Everyone knows Donna's. It is the premier brass-band club in the city, with a nonstop lineup of top jazz and funky second-line outfits playing weekly gigs. The cats who aren't on the bill – someone who copped a gig with a touring band, say – frequently drop in to jam, which always ups the ante.

HOUSE OF BLUES   Map pp70–1   Live Music
☎ 529-2583; www.hob.com; 225 Decatur St; tickets $7-25; ⏰ 8pm-2am Mon-Sat, 9:30am-4pm & 8pm-2am Sun
While venue-wise it's only a little above average, in terms of acts, HOB may be the best place in the city for rock, alt-rock and alt-country. A full calendar of headliner acts, from the hottest local talent to major touring bands, makes this space a winner just about every night of the week. On Sunday morning HOB's gospel brunch will fortify your soul. A few doors down, a small auxiliary club, the Parish (Map pp70–1; ☎ 529-2583; 229 Decatur St), features mostly local acts.

PALM COURT JAZZ CAFÉ
Map pp70–1   Live Music
☎ 525-0200; www.palmcourtjazzcafe.com; 1204 Decatur St; cover around $5; ⏰ 7-11pm Wed-Sun
Fans of trad jazz who want to hang out with a mature crowd should head to this supper club alternative to Preservation Hall (below). Palm Court is a roomy venue that has a very consistently good lineup of local legends; you really can't go wrong if you're a jazz fan. Shows start at 8pm.

PRESERVATION HALL
Map pp70–1   Live Music
☎ 522-2841; www.preservationhall.com; 726 St Peter St; cover $5; ⏰ 8pm-midnight
The large crowds that file into this historic kitty club are always fully satisfied with the traditional New Orleans jazz performances. White-haired grandpas on tubas, trombones and cornets raise the roof every night – it's worth the discomfort of sitting on the floor for an entire set. 'When the Saints Go Marching In' is always a memorable moment. Barbara Reid and Grayson 'Ken' Mills formed the Society for the Preservation of New Orleans Jazz in 1961, at a time when Louis Armstrong's generation was already getting on in years. Get in line early to snag a good seat. When it's warm enough to leave the window shutters open, those not fortunate enough to get in can join the crowd on the sidewalk to listen to the sets. No booze or snacks are served in the club.

BOMBAY CLUB   Map pp70–1   Lounge
☎ 586-0972; 830 Conti St; ⏰ 5pm-late
'Why yes Lord Snarkypants, I did indubitably have a very fine martini in the colonies.' 'Surely you jest, Sir Tweedybottom! Wherever did you find one?' Right here, guys. In complete defiance of the Bourbon St jungle, Bombay is a study in Raj-era refinement, all overstuffed armchairs and candlelit tables. It's about sipping and savoring, rather than guzzling by the gallon, although a few of these bad boys will

get you as wild as anyone who's detonated a Hand Grenade (see p179). The list of over 100 martini cocktails, bound in leather, includes all those deadly vodka concoctions that veil the alcohol in frivolous fruity flavors. Of course, you can also order a stiff Churchill model (gin with just a whiff of vermouth). It's a friendly enough place, and cigar smoking is permitted and even encouraged. Live jazz combos perform most nights.

HOSTEL Map pp70–1 — Lounge

☎ 587-0036; www.hostelnola.com; 329 Decatur St;
☺ 5pm-late Tue-Sat

The Hostel is a hip little space with a smooth slate bar, a modern American food menu and attractive staff serving up just a little more than a Miller. Instead, they mix some fine cocktails and keep a good stock of wine behind the bar, serving the above to a well-heeled, well-dressed crowd of tourists and locals who demand a little more out of their night than Jägermeister and beads. Not that you can't find Jägermeister or beads here.

TONIQUE Map pp70–1 — Lounge

☎ 324-6045; 820 N Rampart St; ☺ 5pm-late

Tonique is one of those places in-the-know New Orleanians might give us flack for including in this book, a French Quarter gem as yet undiscovered by the unwashed masses. But it seems very unlikely this bar would ever attract the worst behavior off Bourbon St. First of all, it's too far away from that scene. And second, it's pretty dark, intimate and classy. Which is not to say that it's boring – on any given night, off-shift service-industry folks flock here like boozy leopards to a watering hole (and by 'water,' we mean 'gin'). They smoke and joke with bartenders they know from previous jobs (it's a small service fraternity) and drink some of the best-mixed, strongest cocktails in town – the Sazerac comes highly recommended.

MOLLY'S AT THE MARKET

Map pp70–1 — Pub

☎ 525-5169; www.mollysatthemarket.net; 1107 Decatur St; ☺ 10am-6am

We've favorably mentioned bars that are popular with service-industry regulars. Now it's time to highlight a waterhole patronized by another form of lush: journalists. Molly's

is the *Times-Picayune* bar, and much more. It's also popular with cops, firefighters and Irish Americans; home of a fat cat that stares stonily at its booze-sodden kingdom; heart of Irish activities in the Quarter (ie St Patty's Day fun); and provider of shelf space for the urn containing the ashes of its founder.

FAUBOURG MARIGNY & BYWATER

Tourists in the French Quarter, locals on Frenchmen – street that is. That's the general rule of thumb in Faubourg Marigny, although plenty of savvy travelers make it up here to wander possibly the best live-music lane in the city. The strip's proximity to the lower (northern) Quarter is another boon, making it possible to work your way from here back to lower Decatur in a fun-filled evening.

MIMI'S IN THE MARIGNY Map p81 — Bar

☎ 872-9868; www.mimisinthemarigny.com; 2601 Royal St; ☺ 5pm-late

The name of this neighborhood bar could justifiably change to Mimi's *is* the Marigny; we can't imagine the neighborhood without this institution, and we don't think its army of loyal patrons would ever want to consider such a horrifying possibility. Mimi's is as attractively disheveled as Brad Pitt on a good day, all comfy furniture, pool tables, an upstairs dance hall decorated like a Creole mansion gone punk, and dim, brown lighting like a fantasy in sepia. Everyone knows your name, and very likely what your next drink will be.

R BAR Map p81 — Bar

☎ 948-7499; www.royalstreetinn.com; 1431 Royal St; ☺ 3pm-late

'Look man,' an R Bar customer explains, 'I seen one guy get kicked out here. One guy. After 14 years of living in this city: one guy. I mean, you could get up on that bar and go to the bathroom and these cats would probably let you stay. Probably.' But why would one ever try to get kicked out of the illustrious bar named for R (Royal St, that is)? Why, when a beer and a shot runs you only a few bucks, when there's free crawfish on Friday nights when the bugs are in season, when the pool tables constantly crack and the music is great and, all in all, we're lounging in neighborhood-bar bliss?

WEEKLY GIGS

Some musicians in New Orleans are regular as clockwork, showing up at that same party time in the same party place every week. There's a great vibe at these shows, which feel like parties with a regular crowd of friendly people – and musicians here do not entertain friends lightly. Note that the following gigs are not set in stone – sometimes bands tour, after all – but these schedules were accurate as of research time. Incidentally, lots of these bars have great cheap weekly food specials as well.

Sunday Bruce Daigrepont and the Cajun Fais Do-Do at Tipitina's (p189).

Monday Mark Braud Jazz Jam at Donna's Bar & Grill (p181) with red beans, rice and fried chicken; bluegrass night at Hi Ho (below) with $1 red beans and rice.

Tuesday Rebirth Brass Band at Maple Leaf Bar (p189); New Orleans Jazz Vipers at d.b.a. (p184).

Wednesday Tin Men with Washboard Chaz, and Walter 'Wolfman' Washington, both at d.b.a. (p184).

Thursday Kermit Ruffins at Vaughan's (below) with free jambalaya; Soul Rebels at Le Bon Temps Roulé (p188).

Friday Joe Krown at Le Bon Temps Roulé (p188), plus free oysters; Ellis Marsalis at Snug Harbor (p184).

Saturday John Boutté at d.b.a. (p184); DJ Soul Sister at Mimi's (opposite).

VAUGHAN'S Map p81 — Bar
☎ 947-5562; 800 Lesseps St; cover $7-10;
🕑 11am-3am daily, shows 11pm Thu

On most nights of the week this is pretty much a Bywater dive of the best sort (old pictures on the wall, shotgun architecture, the occasional roach). Come here whenever, but you must stop by on a Thursday: that's when Kermit Ruffins, one of the trumpet-playing kings of New Orleans, brings the house, the neighborhood and likely a surrounding 10-mile radius *down*. The Ruffins show has to be one of the best regular live acts in the city, if not the country – everyone dances, laughs and loves in a scene so New Orleans it deserves its own Mardi Gras. On some nights Wynton Marsalis might drop in, and when pianist Henry Butler shows up, the bar's poor little upright piano darn near explodes. The crowds spill out onto the street, and between sets Kerm himself dishes out food and jokes.

HI HO Map p81 — Dive
☎ 945-4446; 2239 St Claude Ave; 🕑 5pm-late

The Hi Ho is a perfect Bywater bar, the sort of place where you're as likely to compare tattoos with the guy sitting next to you as witness a local second-line after party. Costume parties and punk concerts seem to take place with comparable frequency, and the atmosphere is reminiscent of a barnyard decorated by a farm full of Jimi Hendrix roadies. This is the best bar in town on Monday nights, when a very friendly bluegrass jam session goes from 8pm to 10pm; some mandolin music and the $1

red beans and rice are the ingredients of New Orleans nirvana.

DRAGON'S DEN Map p81 — Dive & Live Music
☎ 945-7744; www.myspace.com/dragonsdennola;
435 Esplanade Ave; cover $5-10; 🕑 shows start around 9pm

When it comes to rock, ska, punk, drum-and-bass and hip-hop, the Den consistently hosts some of the best acts in New Orleans. It's a decent, two-story venue that can get overcrowded, but when the attendance is just right it feels close enough to be intimate and big enough for you to bust some moves – which you'll inevitably want to do, as the music here, including the rock, tends to be stuff you can get down to.

IGOR'S CHECKPOINT CHARLIE
Map p81 — Dive & Live Music
☎ 281-4847; 501 Esplanade Ave; 🕑 24hr

Igor's is so grungy it could start a band in early '90s Seattle. It serves greasy food, good beer and a pleasant minimum of attitude (for some reason it feels like the sort of place where the bartenders should be jerks, but they're actually pretty cool). Acts you've likely never heard of constantly tromp through the stage, and many of them are surprisingly very good.

SATURN BAR Map p81 — Dive & Live Music
☎ 949-7532; 3067 St Claude Ave; 🕑 3pm-midnight

In the solar system of New Orleans bars, Saturn is planet punk, and yet much more so. Originally, it was simply a very eclectic neighborhood bar, where a working-class crew of regulars appreciated, in an unironic way, the outsider art, leopard-skin furniture and a general, genuinely unique aesthetic. Then the hipsters started moving into the Bywater and the navies of the skinny-jean empire began the colonization process. Today the Bywater community, punk scene and hipster enclaves are learning to live together in peace and camaraderie (by and large), united by neon-lighting fixtures, flashy gambling machines and great live music, primarily of the rock/punk school.

APPLE BARREL Map p81   Live Music

☎ 949-9399; 609 Frenchmen St; ☽ 5pm-late
The Barrel may be called as such because that's what it's roughly the size of: you can maybe fit a dozen customers in here without going elbow to elbow. It fits in musicians, too, who tend to play some very fine jazz, blues and folk. Usually it's someone reliving Dylan's acoustic period. Upstairs is the casual Italian eatery Adolfo's (p157), a good spot for a drink before dinner.

D.B.A. Map p81   Live Music

☎ 942-3731; 618 Frenchmen St; ☽ 5pm-4am; ☞
It's hard to pick any one great aspect of d.b.a. There's the booze menu, which is extensive enough to double as a draft of *Crime and Punishment*. How about the regular and invited music acts? Listening to John Boutté's sweet tenor, which sounds like birds making love on the Mississippi, is one of the best beginnings to a Saturday night in New Orleans. Then there are Wednesdays with Washboard Chaz, a man who demonstrates how a breastplate and two spoons can be the groundwork for Mozart-level musical genius. Great live music, great drinks – seriously d.b.a., you win.

SNUG HARBOR Map p81   Live Music

☎ 949-0696; www.snugjazz.com; 626 Frenchmen St; cover $5-25; ☽ 5pm-late
Local jazz aficionados will let you know: there might be bigger venues, but overall, Snug Harbor is the best jazz club in the city. That's partly because it usually hosts doubleheaders, giving you a good dose of musical variety, and partly because the talent is kept to an admirable mix of reliable legends and hot up-and-comers; in

the course of one night you'll likely witness both. Plus, the acoustics and sight lines in this spot are superb. Ellis Marsalis (Wynton and Branford's dad), R&B singer Charmaine Neville (of *that* Neville family) and touring jazz acts usually play here when in New Orleans, a testament to the loyalty Snug Harbor has built with both musicians and patrons.

YUKI IZAKAYA Map p81   Lounge

☎ 943-1122; 525 Frenchmen St; ☽ 5pm-3am
New Orleans is a city where folks like to get silly on the sauce; if you're into that sort of thing but want a clean feeling in the morning, we recommend ordering off the extensive sake menu at Yuki. It's a little pricier than your average New Orleans libation, but if you're going to get destroyed, this is like the difference between being blown up in an alcohol explosion and getting honorably executed by a samurai. As you sip your rice wine, chill out to a house/lounge DJ and achieve hipster Zen by watching the subtitled Japanese art-house flicks projected onto the walls.

CBD & WAREHOUSE DISTRICT

Downtown may look like a nightlife wasteland, but there's some great live music peppered about the office blocks. More pertinently, New Orleans, while home to many great dives, can lack in the hip lounge stakes; the CBD works to remedy this situation.

LUCY'S RETIRED SURFERS BAR
Map pp86–7   Bar
☎ 523-8995; www.lucysretiredsurfers.com; 701 Tchoupitoulas St; ☽ 11am-late
Can't you hear the Jack Johnson? Or maybe it's Jimmy Buffet? Oh well, either way this is a beach-bum kinda spot oddly plopped in the middle of downtown. It's decent for an after-work drink and some laid-back tropical times. Have something colorful and cold and we'll see you at the next bar.

POLO LOUNGE Map pp86–7   Bar

☎ 523-6000; 300 Gravier St; ☽ 11:30am-midnight Mon-Thu, to 1am Fri & Sat
You probably didn't come to New Orleans to fox hunt, but if the spirit to do so ever moved you, this bar, in the Windsor Court

(p208), would be a good place for psyching yourself up. The overstuffed chairs, tweedy bookshelves, nightly jazz and soft clink of hushed merry-making is meant to evoke aristocratic Olde England. In this sense the Polo Lounge goes way over the top, but hey, have a glass of sherry and enjoy it for what it is.

SWIZZLE STICK BAR Map pp86–7   Bar
☎ 595-3305; 300 Poydras St; ⏱ 7am-11pm
The bar at Café Adelaide (p160) is very much the boozy natural outgrowth of its parent restaurant. A dash of adult fun massaged with heavy levels of quirkiness, it's a good spot for an after-work drink or a pre- or post-convention tipple. Or if you need to get the night going already, order a Trouble Tree, which comes with a little bit of everything, including the potential for a very fun evening.

VIC'S KANGAROO CAFÉ Map pp86–7   Bar
☎ 524-4329; www.vicskangaroocafe.com; 636 Tchoupitoulas St; ⏱ 11am-2am Mon-Sat
Here's a little something to make Australians either sick or prone to bust out the Anzac Day regalia: Vic's phone number is, no joke, 524-GDAY. There are all kinds of other Australia-themed tat here, and while we admittedly haven't met any diggers at the bar, there must be some around. There's a kangaroo with boxing gloves on the sign, right? Well, if there aren't any Australians here, there certainly are plenty of service staff from downtown's restaurants, who pour into Vic's when they get off their shifts and generally turn it upside down under (heh).

LE CHAT NOIR Map pp86–7   Cabaret
☎ 581-5812; www.cabaretlechatnoir.com; 715 St Charles Ave; cover free-$20; ⏱ 4pm-2am Tue-Sat, shows 8pm
At this smartly accoutered bar and cabaret the beverage of choice is the martini and the entertainment ranges from Edith Piaf reincarnations to comic stage productions. CBD office workers prevail during 'happy hour' (4pm to 8pm), and a well-heeled mature audience turns out for the evening shows.

CIRCLE BAR Map pp86–7   Dive & Live Music
☎ 588-2616; www.circlebarnola.com; 1032 St Charles Ave; ⏱ 4pm-late, shows 11pm

MUSEUM GIGS

The Ogden Museum of Southern Art (p89) hosts Ogden After Hours, a Thursday-night happy hour with live music amid some fine Southern art. The entertainment is always top-notch and starts at 6pm. Check out the O's calendar online if you want to know what's planned while you're in town. The Contemporary Arts Center (CAC; p196) hosts the more formal Made In New Orleans, a music series on Saturday night. Again, some stellar acts, often from out of town, perform in the CAC's theater.

If Anne Rice's Lestat ever became an alcoholic, we imagine his pad would evolve into something resembling the Circle Bar: a sort of Victorian mansion gone disheveled and punk. It's the sort of bar where the tender doesn't even ask his or her customers what they want or if they want a refill; knowledge is simply and safely assumed and institutionalized. Live acts, ranging from the folk to the rock to the indie (all of varying quality), often occupy the central space, where a little fireplace and a lot of grime speak to the coziness of one of New Orleans' great dives.

HOWLIN' WOLF Map pp86–7   Live Music
☎ 522-9653; www.howlin-wolf.com; 907 S Peters St; cover $5-15; ⏱ 3pm-late Mon-Fri
One of New Orleans' best venues for live blues, alt-rock, jazz and roots music, the Howlin' Wolf always draws a lively crowd. It started out booking local progressive bands, but has become a regular stop for big-name touring acts such as the Smithereens and Hank Williams III.

REPUBLIC NEW ORLEANS
Map pp86–7   Live Music
☎ 528-8282; 828 S Peters St; cover $5-15; ⏱ 3pm-late Mon-Fri
Republic showcases some pretty awesome live acts, including George Clinton and other good funk and blues talent, but it's also the kind of place where teenagers from the 'burbs come to behave very badly. There's your conundrum: your night may consist of a potentially great show, but there's a very good chance it will also include greasy guys, screeching girls, lots of jostling and the person next to you being sick all over the sidewalk.

LE PHARE BAR Map pp86–7 Lounge

☎ 636-1891; www.lepharenola.com; 523 Gravier St; ⏲ 5pm-late Tue-Fri, from 9pm Sat

You know that guy in the skinny jeans, aviators, tight T-shirt, spray-painted Converse and pink kaffiyeh? He's here, talking to the girl with the fringe wearing the black dress, bright tights and ballerina flats. They're chatting each other up in a posh, candlelit, stone-floored, Scandinavia-style bar that sits above the Loft 523 (p209) boutique hotel. If everything we've just described made you pause as you twitter and think, 'Hey, that couple sounds *hot*,' hurry up and get to Le Phare, which is as much of the above genre as this town ever gets. Although you're still in New Orleans: brass bands have been known to tromp through, and all that chic fashionista-ism hasn't translated into anything resembling snobbery.

LOA Map pp86–7 Lounge

☎ 553-9550; 221 Camp St; ⏲ 5pm-late

Off the lobby of the fashionable International House (p209) hotel, Loa is a great place to grab a daytime drink. Huge windows overlook the CBD's streetscape of dedicated worker bees, and watching them while getting drunk is a pleasure akin to munching on doughnuts among people sweating it out at the gym. In the evening, live music runs the gamut of world beats, and everyone looks good bathed in candlelight. If you practice voodoo, or you're after a full-coverage religious plan, you can leave an offering at the voodoo altar on your way out.

WHISKEY BLUE Map pp86–7 Lounge

☎ 207-5016; www.gerberbars.com; 333 Poydras St; ⏲ noon-2am Mon, from 5pm Tue-Thu, 4pm-4am Fri & Sat, 5pm-midnight Sun

Whiskey Blue almost feels scarily out of place in this city: a sleek, sexy bar where people get dressed up like extras in *The Matrix* and sip what very clearly isn't a bottle of Dixie. But you know what? Not all bars must be dives or neighborhood joints where brass bands get the party started. Downtown is a neighborhood, too, albeit an increasingly modern and manicured one, and Whiskey Blue, located in the W Hotel (natch; p208) reflects those tastes. If you're missing Manhattan or Miami Beach, Whiskey Blue's waiting for you.

GARDEN, LOWER GARDEN & CENTRAL CITY

Bars in this part of New Orleans tend to attract a youngish student and post-student crowd. Magazine St is, in its way, as much fun as Bourbon or Frenchmen Sts. It's wild without being ridiculous or idiotic (unlike Bourbon St) and while it lacks the live-music scene of Frenchmen, it makes up for that with a better variety of bars, many of them filled with beautiful (and not-so-beautiful) people.

BALCONY BAR Map pp96–7 Bar

☎ 894-8888; 3201 Magazine St; ⏲ noon-late Mon, 4pm-late Tue-Sat, 4pm-midnight Sun

This student-centric neighborhood bar is a good place for pizza, carousing and sitting on the eponymous balcony while watching the Magazine St parade march by on balmy nights.

BRIDGE LOUNGE Map pp96–7 Bar

☎ 299-1888; www.bridgeloungenola.com; 1201 Magazine St; ⏲ 4pm-late Mon-Fri, from 6pm Sat & Sun

We respect any bar that has dedicated dog nights – Tuesday in the case of Bridge Lounge, which also posts some of the cutest black-and-white doggie photography ever on its walls. The Bridge also hosts lots of free crawfish boil nights and is a center for the local singles scene, due in no small part to friendly bar staff who mix a mean cocktail – the Mint Julep is a paragon of the genre.

BULLDOG Map pp96–7 Bar

☎ 891-1516; www.draftfreak.com; 3236 Magazine St; ⏲ 2pm-close Mon-Thu, from noon Fri-Sun

The Bulldog keeps a very respectable menu of microbrews served draft, which demands some respect. The best place to sink a pint or a pitcher is in the courtyard, which gets fairly packed with the young and the beautiful almost every evening when the weather is warm enough.

IGOR'S LOUNGE Map pp96–7 Bar

☎ 522-2145; 2133 St Charles Ave; ⏲ 24hr

A good old neighborhood joint with a greasy grill, pool tables and washing machines. Igor's constant rotation of characters makes it a good place to drop in if you're making your way up or down St Charles Ave. Or make this your terminus if you're staying nearby.

RENDEZVOUS Map pp96–7 Bar
☎ 891-1777; 3101 Magazine St; 2pm-late Sun-Thu, from 4pm Fri & Sat
Very much a locals' hang-out, the Rendezvous is pretty much made for just that, with a good group of friends. The pool tables and Golden Tee arcade game keep the collegiate crowd happy, while yuppie types stumble toward their favorite bartenders for another beer and late-night banter.

HALF MOON Map pp96–7 Dive
☎ 522-7313; 1125 St Mary St; 11am-4am
On an interesting corner, just half a block from Magazine St, the Half Moon beckons with a cool neighborhood vibe. The place is good for a beer, short-order meal or an evening shooting stick.

SAINT BAR & LOUNGE Map pp96–7 Dive
☎ 523-0500; www.thesaintneworleans.com; 961 St Mary St; 6pm-close
The Saint? Of what? How about a great backyard beer garden enclosed in duck blinds, tattooed young professionals, Tulane students, good shots, good beers, good times and a photo booth that you will inevitably end up in before the night is through. In fact, it may be a Louisiana law that visitors are not allowed to leave New Orleans without having one stupid series of pictures taken in the Saint's photo booth, preferably of you and all your buddies doing something obscene/silly/whatever. It's not the cleanest bar (nickname: the Taint), but it sure is a fun one.

UPTOWN & RIVERBEND

There's not much difference between this drinking scene and the fun going on in the Lower Garden District; Magazine St maintains a generally young, hip, neighborhood-y vibe throughout. Bars in Riverbend attract more of a student crowd, although the Maple Leaf keeps this mixed thanks to its music lineups. You can walk to bars in the Uptown end of Magazine St from the Garden and Lower Garden Districts, but it's a bit of a hike.

BOOT Map pp102–3 Bar
☎ 866-9008; 1039 Broadway St; 11am-late
Considering the Boot is almost located within Tulane's campus, it's not surprising this college bar practically doubles as student housing for that university. If you're within the vicinity of 21 years, this place is a lot of fun; otherwise, you might think you've accidentally stumbled into Athens, what with all the Greek System types (ie frat boys and sorority girls) about.

COLUMNS HOTEL Map pp102–3 Bar
☎ 899-9308; www.thecolumns.com; 3811 St Charles Ave; 3pm-midnight Sun-Thu, to 2am Fri & Sat
The Columns looks like a set piece from *Gone With the Wind*, as do a lot of its patrons. But it's not as aristocratic as all that; it's more a place where college students and just-graduates act the part of the Southern upper crust. This hotel bar is a great place to come and sit back with a cool glass of gin while fanning yourself and wiping the sweat off your white jacket, panama hat and loafers, all while perfecting that Foghorn Leghorn accent. The crowd is multiracial enough to make this scene not as potentially disturbing as it sounds.

COOTER BROWN'S TAVERN & OYSTER BAR Map pp102–3 Bar
☎ 866-9104; www.cooterbrowns.com; 509 S Carrollton Ave; 11am-late
Cooter's is a Riverbend local that takes its beer seriously, serving over 40 draft brews and hundreds of international bottled brews. College kids, local characters and Uptown swells drop in for a few brews and freshly shucked oysters, or to shoot pool or watch sports on TV. While you're joining them in any of these activities, pause to appreciate the tavern's 'Beersoleum & Hall of Foam' – a gallery of 100 plaster bas-relief statuettes of everybody from Liberace to Chairman Mao, each holding a bottle of beer (Albert Einstein, Mother Theresa and Andy Warhol also appear). This curious, still-growing exhibit is the work of the uniquely talented Scott Conary.

CURE Map pp102–3 Bar
☎ 302-2357; www.curenola.com; 4905 Freret St; 5pm-midnight Sun-Thu, to 2am Fri & Sat
It's so rare that a genuinely innovative bar comes along, so hooray for Cure. Set in

a smooth and polished space of modern banquettes, anatomic art and a Zen garden outdoor area, this is where you come for a well-mixed drink, period. The bar operates on the premise that a good cocktail is the height of the bartender's craft, and takes its mixology *very* seriously. Drinks are neither too sweet nor too bitter, never fruity and always strong as an ox; try the appropriately dubbed Howitzer (bourbon, bitters, lemon juice and magic), which will pretty much blow your sobriety to smithereens. In the evening you need to come correct: no shorts and sandals for guys, guys.

DOS JEFES UPTOWN CIGAR BAR
Map pp102–3   Bar

☎ 891-8500; www.dosjefescigarbar.com; 5535 Tchoupitoulas St; cover free-$10; ☽ 5pm-late Mon-Sat, to midnight Sun

Long touted as one of New Orleans' better venues for modern jazz, Dos Jefes is also a great spot for a smoke. Patrons can select from a list of 40 fine cigars, light up and puff plumes of sweet-smelling smoke into the room. There's a ridiculously addictive game outside where you try and hook a ring on a string to a series of hooks; if aliens ever wanted to catch the male population of New Orleans off guard, they need only install this toy in every one of the city's backyards.

F&M PATIO BAR Map pp102–3   Bar
☎ 895-6784; www.fandmpatiobar.com; 4841 Tchoupitoulas St; ☽ 24hr

If you're not decorating your apartment with empty liquor bottles or are a year into paying off your student loans or have a real driver's license, you may want to give F&M a pass on weekends, when every college student in Louisiana tests the structural integrity of the bar's leopard-print pool tables by dancing on them. For the rest of the week this is a really nice place, with good pool going (on the aforementioned tables), a nice grill slinging some killer cheese fries, and a semi-outdoor area that's well-suited for a cold beer under the hot sun.

MONKEY HILL BAR Map pp102–3   Bar
☎ 899-4800; www.monkeyhillbar.com; 6100 Magazine St; ☽ 3pm-late

Toward the quiet end of Magazine St, Monkey Hill looks and feels like a neighborhood bar, which it basically is. But it's one of the best happy-hour (3pm to 8pm week nights) spots in this part of town and hosts some good live music on a monthly basis. If you're getting off work and near Audubon Park, there's no reason not to stop on in.

ST JOE'S BAR Map pp102–3   Bar
☎ 899-3744; 5535 Magazine St; ☽ 5pm-late

Joe's is one of the better neighborhood bars in the city (it is, admittedly, this author's local). Its mojitos have been voted the best in town by New Orleanians several times over the past few years, and the jukebox is well stocked with jazz, rock and blues. Patrons are in their 20s and 30s, friendly and chatty, as are the staff. The main draw is the layout, which, while narrow in the front, leads past a series of faux-Catholic shrines into a spacious backyard that feels like a cross between an Indonesian island and a Thai temple – a good spot for one of those aforementioned mojitos.

LE BON TEMPS ROULÉ
Map pp102–3   Bar & Live Music

☎ 897-3448; 4801 Magazine St; ☽ 11am-3am

A neighborhood bar – a very good one at that – with a mostly college and postcollege crowd drawn in by two pool tables and a commendable beer selection. Late at night, high-caliber blues, zydeco or jazz rocks the joint's little back room. It's the sort of bar where a lesbian punches a guy for trying to steal her girlfriend's Abita, and then they all three laugh about the incident afterwards.

MS MAE'S Map pp102–3   Dive
☎ 895-9401; 4336 Magazine St; ☽ 24hr

Calling Ms Mae's a dive is like calling the Pacific Ocean a body of water; it's technically true, but kind of misses the greater spirit of the thing. This 24-hour den of all that is sinful and fun, right across from a police precinct, is one of the toughest bars in the city. In the meantime, every thread of the human tapestry gets woven into this great grotty hole. You'll probably end up doing something very embarrassing; there's even a website dedicated to the stupid behavior folks inevitably engage in here (http://msmaeswallofshame.blogspot.com). Ms Mae herself manages the bar, and she looks the part. Be nice and she might do a shot with you.

SNAKE & JAKES Map pp102–3   Dive

☎ 861-2802; www.snakeandjakes.com; 7612 Oak St; ☻ 24hr

When you've seen the gray light of dawn creep under the door and heard the birds chirp their infuriating morning songs of happiness while you blearily grab at your twelfth bottle of beer in Snake & Jakes, pat yourself on the back: you, my friend, are now a fully-fledged honorary New Orleanian. It's unsigned, decked out in Christmas lights and located in what looks like someone's toolshed. And if you end up here any time before 3am, it's probably too early. When you're out with your buddies and someone says, 'Let's go to Snakes,' that's a sure sign the night is either going to get much better or immeasurably worse.

CARROLLTON STATION

Map pp102–3   Live Music

☎ 865-9190; www.carrolltonstation.com; 8140 Willow St; cover $5-10; ☻ noon-late

An old stalwart on the Riverbend club scene, Carrollton Station has the tumble-down exterior you'd expect from a Mississippi Delta juke joint. The club's musical offerings don't really deliver on that promise, unfortunately. You'll generally encounter a very young, white crowd shakin' it to bluesy bar bands. Just a good co-ed party atmosphere.

MAPLE LEAF BAR Map pp102–3   Live Music

☎ 866-9359; 8316 Oak St; cover $5-10, Mon free; ☻ 3pm-4am

The premier nighttime destination in the Riverbend area, the legendary Maple Leaf's dimly lit, pressed-tin caverns are the kind of environs you'd expect from a New Orleans juke joint. Scenes from the film *Angel Heart,* in which the late, great blues man Brownie McGhee starred, were shot here. You can regularly catch performances by local stars such as Walter 'Wolfman' Washington, zydeco squeezebox virtuoso Rockin' Dopsie Jr and the funky Rebirth Brass Band. Slide guitarist John Mooney also plays here often, and on Monday night a traditional piano player sets the tone. You can choose to work up a sweat on the small dance floor directly in front of the stage or relax at the bar in the next room. There's also a nice back patio in which to cool your heels.

TIPITINA'S Map pp102–3   Live Music

☎ 895-8477, concert line 897-3943; www.tipitinas .com; 501 Napoleon Ave; cover $8-25; ☻ 5pm-late

'Tips,' as locals call it, is one of New Orleans' great musical meccas. The legendary nightclub, which takes its name from Professor Longhair's 1953 hit single, is the site of some of the city's most memorable shows, particularly when big names such as Dr John comes home to roost. Outstanding music from the local talent pool still packs 'em in year-round, and this is one of the few non–French Quarter bars tourists regularly trek out to. The joint really jumps in the weeks prior to Mardi Gras and during Jazz Fest, when Dr John and a bevy of Fess-inspired piano players takes over.

RIVERSHACK TAVERN

off Map pp102–3   Roadhouse

☎ 834-4938; 3449 River Rd; ☻ 11am-midnight Mon-Thu, to 3am Fri & Sat

In Jefferson, upstream from Riverbend beside the levee, is an advertisement-adorned roadhouse that probably hit its prime in the 1940s. It's packed with students, older bikers and hospital staff (hopefully not heading back to the surgery room). It has a good selection of beers on tap. If you're hungry, the lunch specials are pretty good.

MID-CITY & THE TREMÉ

There are some pretty good bars out this way, but they tend to be neighborhood places you may not want to drive all the way out here for. With a few exceptions… In general the scene is lively, local and happy to share a beer and a story with a stranger. Plus, there's a bowling alley, concert hall and a bar with a mannequin calling himself emperor of the universe. Just sayin'.

MID-CITY YACHT CLUB Map pp108–9   Bar

☎ 483-2517; www.midcityyachtclub.com; 440 S St Patrick St; ☻ 5pm-late

Sitting across, as it does, from a softball field, Mid-City is a very post-softball kind of bar; players come in after games and buy rounds for the opposing team. What we're saying is this is a very neighborhood kind of place. It's so much a part of the neighborhood that one of the owners took his boat out to save flooded Katrina victims after the storm (hence the name of the bar, which isn't anywhere near a lake or ocean).

And it's so much a part of the neighborhood that the neighborhood is literally a part of it: the bar is actually made from local wood salvaged from storm debris.

CHICKIE WAH WAH
Map pp108–9   Live Music

☎ 304-4714; www.chickiewahwah.com; 2828 Canal St; ☾ shows start around 8pm

Despite the fact it lies on one of the most unremarkable stretches of Canal St as you please, Chickie Wah Wah is a great jazz club. It hosts some good names such as John Mooney, Jolly House and Papa Mali in a cozy little setting where the French Quarter feels several universes away.

MID-CITY ROCK & BOWL
Map pp108–9   Live Music

☎ 861-1700; www.rockandbowl.com; 3000 S Carrollton Ave; ☾ 5pm-late

A night at the Rock & Bowl is a quintessential New Orleans experience but, following its change of location, we were unable to check out Rock & Bowl's new digs at 3000 S Carrollton. Friends who have checked it out say the scene and the shows are the same as ever: a strange, wonderful combination of bowling alley, deli and

huge live-music and dance venue, where patrons get down to New Orleans roots music while trying to avoid that 7-10 split.

K-DOE'S MOTHER-IN-LAW LOUNGE
Map pp108–9   Lounge

☎ 947-1078; www.k-doe.com/lounge; 1500 N Claiborne Ave; ☾ 5pm-late

Local son Ernie K-Doe was famous for writing the song 'Mother-in-Law' and frequently proclaiming himself 'Emperor of the Universe.' Here was a man known for his humility. The Mother-in-Law lounge was a labor of love of his wife Antoinette, a bedrock of the New Orleans scene who was well known for her hospitality and gumbo. Antoinette's 'sunset' (death) was on Mardi Gras day in 2009, when the entire city seemed to mourn. But the Mother-in-Law lounge carries on, filled with life-sized statues of the Emperor of the Universe, touching pictures of his empress and lots of loyal customers. Note the hearse out front: Antoinette bought it before Katrina (because hey, a hearse has storage space, right?) and staff apparently used the car to sneak back into the flooded city several times (because who's going to stop a hearse?).

THE ARTS

top picks

THE ARTS

The arts in New Orleans are in the midst of something of a transition phase. On the one hand, painters, musicians, authors and similar folk were among the thousands who fled the city following Hurricane Katrina, and some among their number did not come home. But the creative class by its nature bucks convention, and by and large many of the city's artists were among the first back when the floodwaters receded.

They didn't come back to town alone. A large chunk of new New Orleanians are aspiring and established artists, drawn by – excuse the expression – a perfect storm of conditions that makes post-Katrina New Orleans an almost ideal city for the aesthetically inclined. By the measurements of cost, exposure and reputation, this simply is a very good city for the arts.

Let's take the example of exposure. A silver lining to Katrina's storm clouds was the way the hurricane put the city in the public eye like few other events could. Many of the people who have donated to or participated in rebuilding efforts are of the professional class that, incidentally, very much likes to patronize the arts. Thus, a lot of art-world attention was turned, perhaps indirectly at first, toward the Gulf of Mexico following the storm. Those eyes settled on a city where rents and competition, especially when compared with cities such as New York, Miami, Los Angeles and San Francisco, are relatively quite low.

But maybe more important is the fact New Orleans has always been an island for outcasts, especially in the relatively conservative American South. We're not saying all artists are eccentrics, but it's safe to say members of the arts community often march to the beat of their own drum, and there's no city of comparable size in America that bops to a more unique drum than New Orleans. Hell, this town will probably play said drum at its own jazz funeral…

In addition, artists have always thrived among artist communities where there are extensive networks of mutual support. The increased sense of civic engagement and responsibility in post-Katrina New Orleans has really reinforced this sense of solidarity, and sometimes it feels like you can't walk in parts of the Marigny or Bywater without tripping on an artist co-op. Finally, the tourism draw of this city and the backbone of its economy is its culture. Without writing an anthropological dissertation, it's safe to say most visitors to town consider New Orleans culture best represented by its food, nightlife, history and arts.

The New Orleans arts scene isn't all accommodating, though. Understaffing and underfunding at all levels of municipal government has impacted the arts population heavily. In a city where there are still urgent needs for affordable housing, road repairs, increased law enforcement and improved public education, arts funding has sometimes been characterized as a low priority. In reaction, artists have taken it upon themselves to self-fund, provide mutual support and generally operate on whatever shoestring fate has currently handed them.

This is a city whose aesthetic seems to shift between the very fresh and hip, the classic and old school and the slightly mad outsider. Modern and contemporary art thrives across town, particularly in the Warehouse District. An early-20th- and late-19th-century (and sometimes earlier reference points) sense of taste and visual values is evident in parts of the French Quarter and Uptown. And the inspired, colorful and hard-to-classify work of 'outsider' artists is perhaps better represented here than any other city in America, with the possible exception of Baltimore.

But the schools of art here tend to share one important characteristic: creativity rarely seems to be done for its own sake. From the most respected museums to experimental studio spaces along St Claude Ave, there's a general sensibility that the work has a purpose: namely, keeping this weird and wonderful city alive so it can share its vision with and inspire future generations.

ART GALLERIES

Galleries of local celebrity painters are concentrated in the French Quarter. The Warehouse District, commonly called the arts district, has some of the city's most highly respected galleries on Julia St. There's a funky mix of galleries all along Magazine St, from the Lower Garden District up to Audubon Park.

FRENCH QUARTER

Galleries are all over the Quarter, particularly on Royal and Chartres Sts.

A GALLERY FOR FINE PHOTOGRAPHY Map pp70–1

☎ 568-1313; www.agallery.com; 241 Chartres St;
🕙 10am-6pm Thu-Sat, noon-4pm Sun & Mon

This impressive gallery usually has prints such as William Henry Jackson's early-20th-century views of New Orleans and EJ Bel-locq's rare images of Storyville prostitutes, made from the photographers' original glass plates. The gallery also regularly features Herman Leonard's shots of Duke Ellington and other jazz legends, as well as the occasional Cartier-Bresson enlargement (available at second-mortgage prices).

DUTCH ALLEY Map pp70–1

☎ 412-9220; www.dutchalleyonline.com; 912 N Peters St; 🕙 9am-8pm

An artists-managed and -operated co-op located in the French Market. You can see the work of some 20 artists here, meet the creators directly and occasionally listen to live blues and jazz concerts.

GREG'S ANTIQUES Map pp70–1

☎ 202-8577; www.gregsantiques.net; 1209 Decatur St; 🕙 noon-10pm Tue-Sun

Besides rooms full of salvaged furniture and antiques, Greg's regularly exhibits works by New Orleans underground and outsider artists, which can also take the form of found and folk art sourced from across the city.

HAROUNI GALLERY Map pp70–1

☎ 299-8900; www.harouni.com; 829 Royal St;
🕙 noon-5pm Thu-Sat

Artist David Harouni is a native of Iran who has lived and worked in New Orleans for several decades. He creates works of absorbing depth by painting and scraping multiple layers of medium; the finished product has a surreal eerie beauty.

KURT E SCHON LTD GALLERY Map pp70–1

☎ 524-5462; www.kurteschonltd.com; 510 St Louis St; 🕙 9am-5pm Mon-Fri, to 3pm Sat

For moneyed art collectors, and the rest of us who just like to look at great artwork, Kurt E Schon is an immense gallery and storehouse that purveys fine paintings from the 19th century. The gallery is like a small museum showcasing the works of the lesser-known contemporaries of the master

RECONSTRUCTING ART

How did Hurricane Katrina impact and change New Orleans' arts community? Hurricane Katrina undoubtedly changed the physical landscape of the city, but it also changed the perspective of its citizens. When you believe you have lost everything, you can either give up or you can pull yourself up. Moving forward, we have an entire community of people rebuilding their lives asking what's important, what's really worth it? Why will my life matter? For so many, this continues to be a catalyst to create art and pursue a career as an artist.

How would you describe the change in New Orleans art? Institutional-level and grassroots organizations alike have sprung up to aid in the city's cultural recovery. Artists are learning to take action and this spirit of entrepreneurship has been captured throughout the city in galleries, festivals, markets and public-art pieces that did not exist pre-Katrina. The newfound energy behind our local arts scene is building excitement behind the contemporary arts movement in New Orleans and is drawing internationally acclaimed artists to the city.

Why have the arts been an engine for regrowth in New Orleans? Art and culture mean business in New Orleans. We have managed to build a very organic and authentic arts community while utilizing arts and culture as an economic engine for the city. It's a tricky balance and also the reason our culture is known and appreciated worldwide, even by the most discerning arts organizations. Many who came to our aid after Katrina have discovered and fallen in love with New Orleans, resulting in new opportunities for local artists to thrive. The Joan Mitchell Foundation, the Ford Foundation and many others have done an amazing job of investing in the local arts community.

Why should visitors consider purchasing artwork while in New Orleans? Art is a solid investment and as New Orleans' prestige as an international art center grows, prices will increase. Many galleries and arts markets are located in a Cultural Products District, meaning that no tax will be charged for a piece of original or limited-edition art. But beyond the economics, art is about experience. One of the official Prospect 1 (see p198) artists came to the city and created no work for the biennial. It may seem odd that someone commissioned to create art brought no work to the city for the event, but his contribution to the biennial was experiencing New Orleans. We live in a sensory city. From the architecture, food, music, people and colors of the city, art is all around us. Living New Orleans is art and art is the best way to remember this city.

An interview with Lindsay Glatz, Director of Marketing and Communication, Arts Council of New Orleans (p196).

impressionists; most of the works on display are pieces of remarkable beauty.

MICHALOPOULOS GALLERY
Map pp70–1

☎ 558-0505; www.michalopoulos.com; 617 Bienville St

Michalopoulos has become one of New Orleans' most popular painters in recent years, in part on the strength of his best-selling Jazz Fest posters. His shop showcases his colorful and expressive architectural studies and paintings that look like van Gogh meets the Vieux Carré. The gallery holds frequent openings on Friday night. Check out the website or call ahead for hours and to check on specific events.

RODRIGUE STUDIO Map pp70–1

☎ 581-4244; www.georgerodrigue.com; 721 Royal St; ☽ noon-5pm Wed-Sun

Cajun artist George Rodrigue's gallery is the place to go to see examples of his unbelievably popular 'Blue Dog' paintings. He just keeps painting and painting that darn dog. Look for topical works, in which the dog quietly comments on post-Katrina issues.

FABOURG MARIGNY & BYWATER

More and more edgy art is cropping up in the Creole suburbs, although while many artists live here, much of their work is exhibited in other parts of town.

BARRISTER'S GALLERY Map p81

☎ 525-2767; www.barristersgallery.com; 2331 St Claude Ave; ☽ 11am-5pm Tue-Sat

A little ways beyond the Lower Garden District, this gallery has some edge to it. It has represented the works of Julie Crozat, who gained some notice for her lurid and visually stunning 'Deadly Sins' series. The gallery also specializes in works by African American and Haitian artists.

STUDIO INFERNO Map p81

☎ 945-1878; 3000 Royal St; ☽ 10am-4pm Mon-Sat

Primarily focuses on glass-related arts and crafts, although there's some amazing folk art and salvaged pieces of New Orleans history (think old signs) upstairs.

CBD & WAREHOUSE DISTRICT

With the most impressive concentration of serious galleries in New Orleans, Julia St is the core of New Orleans' Arts District. Nearby, the excellent Ogden Museum of Southern Art (p89) and the Contemporary Arts Center (p196) are easily worked into an afternoon of gallery hopping.

ARTHUR ROGER GALLERY Map pp86–7

☎ 522-1999; www.arthurrogergallery.com; 432 Julia St; ☽ 10am-5pm Mon-Sat

One of the district's most prominent galleries, Arthur Roger represents several dozen artists, including Simon Gunning, whose landscapes are haunting records of Louisiana's disappearing wetlands.

BERGERON STUDIO & GALLERY
Map pp86–7

☎ 522-7503; www.bergeronstudio.com; 406 Magazine St; ☽ 9am-5pm Mon-Fri, 11am-3pm Sat

This gallery has a superb collection of historic photographs by key artists who worked in New Orleans over the past century, from Pops Whitesell to Michael P Smith.

GEORGE SCHMIDT GALLERY
Map pp86–7

☎ 592-0206; www.georgeschmidt.com; 626 Julia St; ☽ 12:30-4pm Tue-Sat

New Orleans artist George Schmidt, a member of The New Leviathin Oriental FoxTrot Orchestra, describes himself as a 'historical' painter. Indeed, his canvases evoke the city's past, awash in a warm, romantic light. His Mardi Gras paintings are worth a look.

HERIARD-CIMINO GALLERY Map pp86–7

☎ 525-7300; www.heriardcimino.com; 440 Julia St; ☽ 10am-5pm Tue-Sat

Established contemporary artists from across the USA are represented in this elegant space. The emphasis is on abstract and figurative paintings, but you might also encounter photography and sculpture here.

JEAN BRAGG GALLERY OF SOUTHERN ART Map pp86–7

☎ 895-7375; www.jeanbragg.com; 600 Julia St; ☽ 10am-5pm Mon-Sat

This is a good source for the Arts and Crafts–style Newcomb Pottery, which

ART FOR EVERY WEEKEND

Every weekend in New Orleans offers a unique opportunity to discover local artwork and meet artists.

Art Market of New Orleans (www.artscouncilofneworleans.org; Palmer Park, cnr S Carrollton & S Claiborne Aves) This monthly market is held on the last Saturday of every month. Featuring 100 of the area's most creative local artists, it is juried for quality. With local food, music and kids' activities, the market makes a good day trip for visitors looking to experience New Orleans like a local. Off the typical tourist track, Palmer Park (just north of Riverbend) is accessible via the St Charles Ave streetcar.

Bywater Art Market (Map p81; www.art-restoration.com/bam; cnr Royal & Piety Sts) Known as New Orleans' original art market, this market takes pride in a strict jurying process and features original artist work. Held the third Saturday of the month from 9am to 4pm, it's located in the heart of the Bywater.

Freret Street Market (Map pp102–3; www.freretmarket.org; cnr Freret St & Napoleon Ave) A combination farmers, flea and art market, this gathering offers a great mix of local culture. Held the first Saturday of the month (except for July and August) from noon to 5pm, it features more than 75 vendors with fresh produce, prepared foods, gifts, art, live music and flea-market items. Managed by the Freret Street Business & Property Owners Association.

New Orleans Arts District Art Walk (www.neworleansartsdistrict.com) The first Saturday of each month beginning at 6pm until close (whenever, really), the fine-art galleries in New Orleans' arts district celebrate the opening night of month-long feature-artist exhibitions. These art walks often coincide with special street parties. Visitors can enjoy fine art, an evening stroll and mingling among the city's elite on Julia St.

St Claude Arts District Gallery Openings (www.scadnola.com) New Orleans' newest arts district, this growing collective of art exhibition spaces spans Faubourg Marigny and the Bywater, and is home to some of the city's more eclectic artists. Spend an evening viewing anything-goes art with local characters and mingle directly with the artists. Ask locals for weekend recommendations and you may be rewarded with a fire-eating display or impromptu collective installation at a secret, hidden art space.

With thanks to Lindsay Glatz.

originated at New Orleans' own Newcomb College. Bragg also deals in classic landscapes by Louisiana painters and every month she features the work of a contemporary artist.

LEMIEUX GALLERIES Map pp86–7

☎ 522-5988; www.lemieuxgalleries.com; 332 Julia St; ☽ 11am-5pm Mon, 10am-6pm Tue-Sat

Gulf Coast art is the emphasis in this nationally recognized gallery, and it's a good place to get a handle on the breadth of the regional arts scene. Paintings here include Kate Samworth's sardonic grotesqueries and Jon Langford's depictions of local musicians.

NEW ORLEANS GLASSWORK & PRINTMAKING STUDIOS Map pp86–7

☎ 529-7277; www.neworleansglassworks.com; 727 Magazine St; ☽ 11am-5pm Mon-Fri

In an immense 25,000-sq-ft brick building, New Orleans Glasswork & Printmaking Studios is a combination studio and gallery space primarily for glassblowers and stained-glass artisans. Not only can you admire and purchase works here, you

might also watch artists blow glass, which is pretty impressive.

SOREN CHRISTENSEN GALLERY Map pp86–7

☎ 569-9501; www.sorengallery.com; 400 Julia St; ☽ 10am-5:30pm Tue-Fri, 11am-5pm Sat

This impressive space showcases the work of nationally renowned painters and sculptors. The gallery is known for its nontraditional sensibility.

GARDEN, LOWER GARDEN & CENTRAL CITY

Magazine St gets into high gear in this part of town with some excellent art galleries. While you're here, you also ought to have a look in some of the shops, many of which specialize in creative clothing and jewelry (see p128 for more).

ANTON HAARDT GALLERY Map pp96–7

☎ 891-9080; www.antonart.com; 2858 Magazine St; ☽ noon-5pm Fri & Sat

Among the finest galleries anywhere to specialize in contemporary folk art from the Deep South. The gallery has featured the works of well-known artists such as Howard Finster and Clementine Hunter, but you are more likely to come across Lamar Sorrento's cool portraits of blues musicians or Jimmy Lee Sudduth's striking earth-tone figures. Alabama artist Haardt quietly mixes her own accomplished work into the gallery.

SIMON OF NEW ORLEANS Map pp96–7
☎ 561-0088; 2126 Magazine St; ⏱ 10am-5pm Mon-Sat

Local artist Simon Hardeveld has made a name for himself by painting groovy signs that are hung like artwork in restaurants all over New Orleans. You'll probably recognize the distinctive stars, dots and sparkles that fill the spaces between letters on colorfully painted signs such as 'Who Died & Made You Elvis?' The gallery is a ramshackle indoor-outdoor affair. Out back, a tabletop box contains hand-painted Zulu coconuts – collectors' items in these parts.

UPTOWN & RIVERBEND

Magazine St goes in spurts for miles. The blocks between Louisiana and Napoleon Aves are particularly strong on galleries.

BERTA'S & MINA'S ANTIQUITIES
Map pp102–3
☎ 895-6201; 4138 Magazine St; ⏱ 10am-6pm Mon-Sat, from 11am Sun

This cluttered gallery, with paintings seemingly tumbling out onto the sidewalk, specializes in regional folk art, especially the works of the late Nilo Lanzas, whose daughter operates the shop. Lanzas began painting at 63 and produced an impressive body of work, most of it of an outsider art/religious bent, up until his death. Museums and serious collectors have snatched up many of Lanzas' paintings already, but there are dozens of nice pieces, all very eye-catching and worthy of homes. Lanzas' work is, in fact, very easy to like. His daughter, Mina, also paints and her works show alongside her father's and a few other artists from the city and its surrounds.

COLE PRATT GALLERY Map pp102–3
☎ 891-6789; www.coleprattgallery.com; 3800 Magazine St; ⏱ 10am-5pm Tue-Sat

ARTS INFORMATION
- Arts Council of New Orleans (www.artscouncilofneworleans.com) The best site to begin exploring the local creative scene.
- New Orleans Arts District (www.neworleansartsdistrict.com) Gateway to the city's official arts neighborhood.
- Art New Orleans (www.artneworleansmag.com) A magazine that focuses on local arts happenings.
- Nola Rising (http://nolarising.blogspot.com) Nonprofit that works to increase arts access and encourage the spread of public art in the city.
- Nolaphile (www.nolaphile.com) One of the better New Orleans arts blogs.

Contemporary Southern artists are showcased in this fine-art gallery. Paintings here might include Lea Barton's earthy abstractions or Gustave Blanche's warmly rendered still-lifes.

THEATER

New Orleans has a strong theatrical bent; numerous local theater companies and a few large theatrical venues for touring productions frequently stage shows. Student plays are often performed at the UNO Downtown Theatre (Map pp86–7; ☎ 800-433-3243, 539-9580; 619 Carondelet St) and Tulane University's Lupin Theatre (Map pp102–3; ☎ 865-5106). Le Chat Noir (p185) is an intimate cabaret bar.

CONTEMPORARY ARTS CENTER
Map pp86–7
☎ 528-3805; www.cacno.org; 900 Camp St

The grand modernist entrance to the CAC, a soaring ceiling vault of airy space and conceptual metal and wooden accents, is almost reason enough to step into this converted warehouse. Almost. The best reason for visiting is a good crop of rotating exhibitions by local artists, plus a packed events calendar that includes plays, skits and dance. It also hosts concerts featuring bands as big as Death Cab for Cutie.

LE PETIT THÉÂTRE DU VIEUX CARRÉ
Map pp70–1
☎ 522-2081; www.lepetittheatre.com; 616 St Peter St

Going strong since 1916, Le Petit Théâtre is one of the oldest theater groups in the country. In its Jackson Sq home the troupe offers an interesting repertory, with a proclivity for Southern dramas and special children's programming. Shows are sometimes followed by an informal cabaret performance, with the cast, audience and a resident ghost (so we hear) mingling over drinks.

SAENGER THEATRE Map pp70–1
☎ 585-1310; 143 N Rampart St

Once New Orleans' premier site for major touring troupes, the Saenger's ornate 1927 interior is one of the best indoor spaces in the city. A round of renovations underway at the time of writing was due to keep this grand dame's doors closed till late 2010 or possibly 2011.

SOUTHERN REPERTORY THEATER
Map pp70–1

☎ 522-6545; www.southernrep.com; 333 Canal St

Though its home in a shopping mall isn't particularly reassuring, this company has established itself as one of the city's best. Founded in 1986, the company performs original works by Southern playwrights. There's not a bad seat in the 150-seat theater.

FILM

New Orleans has a few quality cinemas scattered about, but the city could really use a decent art house or two. Making up for this deficiency are sporadic screenings in some bars and clubs (check www.bestofneworleans.com or www.nolafunguide.com), which can be a fun way to take in a flick. But on the whole, New Orleans doesn't get independent movies until months after they've screened in major coastal cities, and many films never make it here at all.

CANAL PLACE CINEMAS Map pp70–1
☎ 525-1254; 3rd fl, 333 Canal St; adult/child $8/5.50

New Orleans' best all-around multiplex in a convenient downtown location. The cinema features first-run art and mainstream movies.

ENTERGY IMAX THEATER Map pp86–7
☎ 565-3020; www.auduboninstitute.org/imax.html; 1 Canal St; adult/child $8/5

Part of the Audubon Institute complex at the foot of Canal St. IMAX stands for 'image maximum' and its films are shown on a 74ft-by-54ft screen. It's all about the size of the image, and indeed cinematography

BANKSY VS THE GRAY GHOST

In the spring of 2008, Banksy, the famed British artist/vandal/genius/overrated hack (take your pick, but the man doesn't tend to inspire neutrality) came to New Orleans, leaving behind 12 works that primarily highlighted the city's slow pace of rebuilding. Whether you think Banksy's work clever, creative or crap, it's certainly noticeable, particularly an image of an older man waving an American flag under a pre-existing spray-painted 'No Loitering' sign, and a man chasing a windblown umbrella along a city levee. The work was hailed as art by many New Orleanians, but others, including Fred Radtke, also known as the Gray Ghost, considered it graffiti.

Radtke is one of New Orleans' most loved/scorned vigilantes/vandals – suffice to say he's another man who doesn't inspire neutrality. For years, he had taken it upon himself to paint over the city's graffiti with uniform swatches of gray paint. Some New Orleanians cheered him on; others said the gray paint, which rarely matched the wall beneath it, was just another example of egregious vandalism. What particularly enraged some New Orleanians was Radtke's habit of painting over 'legal graffiti,' works of art like murals (as opposed to gangster tags) that property owners allowed to be painted on their homes and businesses. Radtke claimed in local news media such individuals were breaking the law by allowing graffiti on their property. According to the *Times-Picayune*, Radtke has been supported (or at least conveniently ignored) by the New Orleans police in the past.

Banksy poked fun at Radtke in some of his pieces, depicting a faceless painter with a gray paint roller blotting out a nervous stick figure. The Ghost stuck to form, going after Banksy's work with his signature can of gray paint. This really boiled blood; no matter what you think of Banksy, he is one of the world's most buzzed-about pop artists, and his work can increase the value of a home by tens of thousands of dollars.

Radtke was finally arrested – by military police – after painting over a mural in the Bywater near that neighborhood's military base. On March 24, 2009, a city judge told the Gray Ghost he could no longer paint over graffiti on private property without the owner's permission.

To see images of Banksy's New Orleans work, check out www.banksy.co.uk/outdoors/horizontal_1.htm.

PUBLIC ART & PROSPECT 1

Public art is starting to take off in post-Katrina New Orleans, especially since 2009, when the 'Art in Public Places' project resulted in 19 artists being commissioned to create public art throughout the city. Standouts include No Place Like Nola in the Botanical Gardens (p110), a conglomeration of 14 birdhouses that references New Orleans architecture and historical structures, and Watermarks, 12 posts situated on Elysian Fields Ave that indicate the height of Katrina floodwaters. For a map and description of all works, see the Arts Council of New Orleans (www.artscouncilofnew orleans.org) website.

In 2008 New Orleans began hosting Prospect 1 (www.prospectneworleans.org), currently the largest biennial contemporary arts event in the USA. Artists from around the world (and New Orleans, of course) exhibited work for two months in venues scattered across the city as well as public spaces; in all, some 100,000 sq ft of gallery space was utilized. Obviously, Prospect 1 is rocketing the city to the top of the international art world's attention. If you're here in winter of 2010, you'll see New Orleans transform into one of the world's great urban-art spaces, so hurry up and book that plane ticket.

at this scale can be very impressive. Check the website to see what films are showing.

PRYTANIA THEATRE Map pp102–3
☎ 891-2787; www.theprytania.com; 5339 Prytania St; tickets $5.75
This old movie house has been around since the 1920s and screens independent and art films. Our favorite theater in the city.

ZEITGEIST Map pp96–7
☎ 352-1150; www.zeitgeistinc.net; 1618 Oretha Castle-Haley Blvd
This multidisciplinary arts center hosts independent film screenings on a fairly regular basis. The venue doesn't have a lot of character, but the quality of the movies makes up for that.

CLASSICAL MUSIC

New Orleans makes a deeper musical impression in its nightclubs than in its concert halls. But the city does have a philharmonic orchestra, an opera and a ballet. You might want to have a look at upcoming events to see if anything strikes your fancy.

The Louisiana Philharmonic Orchestra (☎ 523-6530; www.lpomusic.com) is the only musician-owned and managed professional symphony in the

USA. It lost its home, the Orpheum Theatre, which was badly damaged by Hurricane Katrina. Currently, it performs in various venues around town such as Roussell Hall at Loyola University (Map pp102–3), Dixon Hall at Tulane University (Map pp102–3) and at City Park (p107).

DANCE

The New Orleans Ballet Association (NOBA; ☎ 522-0996; www.nobadance.com; tickets $30-75) usually runs a few productions annually. The season is very short, and is fleshed out with presentations by visiting dance companies from around the world. Performances are primarily held at the Mahalia Jackson Theater (Map pp108–9; ☎ 525-1052; 801 N Rampart St) in Louis Armstrong Park and Dixon Hall at Tulane University (Map pp102–3).

For contemporary dance, see what's on at the New Orleans Center for Creative Arts (p80).

OPERA

The New Orleans Opera (☎ 529-2278; www.neworleans opera.org; tickets $30-125) rarely causes much of a stir, but remains an important part of the local culture. Productions are held at the Mahalia Jackson Theater (Map pp108–9; ☎ 525-1052; 801 N Rampart St).

SLEEPING

top picks

Audubon Cottages (p202)
Hotel Royal (p204)
Soniat House (p201)
Loft 523 (p209)
Columns Hotel (p213)
Sweet Olive Bed & Breakfast (p207)
The Chimes (p213)
Garden District B&B (p212)

SLEEPING

Where you stay in New Orleans depends largely on why you've come. Planning to play tl
whole time in the French Quarter? Shell out the few extra bucks to stay there. Especially
you're a first-timer, you can't beat having all the food and fun at your doorstep – and you ca
save the cost of taxi rides or a rental car. Small hotels and inns (with immensely varied roo
sizes) are the hallmark of this historic district. Choose a room with a streetside balcony ar
you can watch the revelry in your pajamas; courtyard views are a bit quieter. But the Quarte
is not all booze and Bourbon St; there are calmer residential corners to the northwest ar
northeast.

Looking for a more local experience? Northeast of Esplanade Ave, the Quarter morphs in
Faubourg Marigny, an arty, transitional neighborhood with kicked-back, quirky B&Bs and
great nightlife of its own. Farther afield, public transport puts the Garden District's (and tl
Lower Garden District's) B&Bs and moderate lodgings in easy reach. The leafy lanes here oo
a gentrified quiet, near the city's best shopping on Magazine St. Continue west along the
Charles Ave streetcar line to Uptown and Riverbend, where mansions host glorious inn-lil
guesthouses close to Tulane University.

Need to seal a deal? Mammoth business hotels and conference centers rise up forming car
yons in the CBD and Warehouse District. Prices here drop to surprising lows at the weeker
and when convention business is slow. The options around Canal St border the Quarter, bu
don't expect intimate accommodations or character-filled cottages here.

Those arriving for Jazz Fest should book at one of the few mansions-turned-B&B on E
planade Ridge in Mid-City. You'll need a cab to get to the Quarter, but you can hoof it to tl
soulful sounds.

ACCOMMODATION STYLES

New Orleans hotels come in all the standard
shapes and sizes. Most commonly you'll find
either large purpose-built properties or more
cozy lodgings in older buildings. Figuring out
which is which by an establishment's name
alone is impossible (an 'inn' here might have
five rooms or 500), so read reviews carefully.
There are surprisingly few boutique properties with design-driven rooms, and no
condo-hotels at all in this tourist town. In
fact, the ho-hum traditional floral bedspread
and quasi-Colonial furnishings are all too
common, even at top-end properties. On
the upside, a huge number of rooms in town
have been rehabbed post-Katrina, so at least
the sometimes-bland decor is brand-spankin'
new. (Note that old hotels often have exterior
access rooms and no elevators.)

For charm, you can't beat the Crescent
City's hundreds of B&Bs – housed in everything from colorful Creole cottages to stately
town houses and megamansions. Three obvious selling points are intimate surroundings, interesting architecture and, in many
cases, a peaceful courtyard in which to escape
the maddening crowds. The complimentary
morning meal at area B&Bs (and at the many

hotels that serve it) is almost always a cont
nental breakfast of homebaked breads an
yogurts. (Hot food requires a special license
If the options listed in this chapter are fu
consider seeking help from Bed & Breakfast I
(☎ 488-4640, 800-729-4640; www.historiclodging.com) •
Louisiana B&B Association (☎ 346-1857, 800-395-497
www.louisianabandb.com). Some places do not allo
children – this is noted in our reviews.

All accommodations listed here have
least some nonsmoking rooms. If you want
nonsmoking–only property (most B&Bs ar
some hotels), look for the ⊠ icon. Air-con
standard in all New Orleans lodgings; you'
melt in the summer without it.

CHECK-IN & CHECK-OUT TIMES

Officially you can usually check into your roo
by 3pm or 4pm, but if the room's available be
fore that, properties are good about letting yo
in. B&Bs often need to know when guests wi
be arriving in order to ensure staff are on han
to check them in. Check-out times range fro
10am to noon. If business is slow, you may b
able to negotiate a later time, especially if yo
belong to a hotel's loyalty program.

LONGER-TERM RENTALS

Even if you're just staying for a week or less, renting an apartment is an option in the French Quarter, Faubourg Marigny and the Garden districts. Live in the lap of luxury at corporate digs or keep costs down by buying groceries and using the full kitchens at more basic options. Independent owners list places for rent at Vacation Rentals by Owner (www.vrbo.com) and Vacation Rentals Online (www.vacationrentalsonline.com). Contrary to the name, New Orleans Bed & Breakfast (☎ 524-9918; www.neworleansbandb.com) manages unhosted properties around town.

RESERVATIONS

It's good policy to have room reservations before you arrive in New Orleans. Conventions can fill up the city any time and you'll almost always get a better rate by booking ahead. For Mardi Gras or Jazz Fest, reserve at least six months to a year in advance. Check out Lonely Planet's online booking service at lonelyplanet.com for more accommodation reviews and personal recommendations by authors. Hotel websites usually have some good deals, especially if you're willing to prepay. Reservation agents like Book It (www.bookit.com), Expedia (www.expedia.com) and Travelocity (www.travelocity.com) also have negotiated deals. For more on cheap, no-name reservations, see Bidding for a Bed (p204).

All that said, some hotels do turn over a portion of their last-day bookings, at reduced rates, to the New Orleans Welcome Center (Map pp70–1; ☎ 566-5031; 529 St Ann St; ⏰ 9am-5pm).

ROOM RATES

In general, lodgings in New Orleans charge by the room (ie the price is the same for one or two people staying in it). The city is peculiar in that it's busy during the shoulder seasons of spring and fall (February through May and September through November) and slow during the summer months (due to some seriously oppressive heat June through August). Most hectic and high-priced of all are Mardi Gras (February or March), Jazz Fest (late April to early May) and other holidays and festivals (see p12). Prices listed here are for the high spring and fall seasons, but note that rates depend entirely on occupancy: rooms may be available for up to 50% less on any day that business is super slow, especially during summer and nonholiday days in December and January.

Note that if you're staying in the Quarter or the CBD, parking can seriously add to your bottom line (an extra $17 to $33 per night). Stashing your car while staying in other neighborhoods is usually free. If having your car accessible in a dedicated, on-site lot is important to you, look for the Ⓟ icon in our reviews. Internet access via wi-fi or broadband (ie using your own laptop) is usually included in the room rate, but it might cost $5 to $10 extra. This type of access is indicated by the 🛜 icon; On-site internet-connected computers are indicated with the 🖥 icon.

FRENCH QUARTER

If you are looking for the historic flavor of the Old Quarter, a general rule of thumb is the further away you stay from the CBD, the better. As you probably know, Bourbon St is party central. The Lower Quarter is more residential, with guesthouses and smaller hotels, and staying down there is just as convenient. Large hotels with all the conveniences you would expect from high-end tourist accommodations, surrounded by T-shirt shops and take-out daiquiri bars, cluster around Iberville and Canal Sts.

SONIAT HOUSE Map pp70–1 Boutique Hotel $$$
☎ 522-0570, 800-544-8808; www.soniathouse.com; 1133 Chartres St; r from $240, ste from $425; ✂ 🛜
The three town houses that make up this hospitable hotel in the Lower Quarter epitomize Creole elegance at its unassuming best. The place is run with congenial efficiency. You enter via a cool loggia into a courtyard filled with ferns, palmettos and a trickling fountain. Some rooms open up onto the courtyard, while winding stairways lead to the elegant upstairs quarters. Singular attention has been paid to the art and antiques throughout. This is a genuinely romantic spot (children under 12 are not permitted). Switch on a balcony

PRICE GUIDE

$$$	double more than $200
$$	double $100 to $200
$	double under $100

ceiling fan and relax with a glass of wine or a splash of whiskey while mules clip-clop lazily by outside.

HOTEL MONTELEONE Map pp70–1 Hotel $$$
☎ 523-3341, 800-535-9595; www.hotelmontel eone.com; 214 Royal St; r from $250; **P** 🖳
Perhaps the city's most venerable old hotel, the Monteleone is also the French Quarter's largest. (Not long after the Monteleone was built, preservationists put a stop to building on this scale below Iberville St.) Since its inception in 1866, the hotel has been the local lodging of choice for writers, including luminaries like William Faulkner, Truman Capote and Rebecca Wells. The Carousel Bar – a New Orleans classic – has appeared in numerous films and TV shows. Rooms throughout exude an old-world appeal with French toile and chandeliers. Some guests liked it so much, they never left (see boxed text, opposite).

HOTEL MAISON DE VILLE & AUDUBON COTTAGES Map pp70–1 Hotel $$$
☎ 561-5858; www.hotelmaisondeville.com; 727 Toulouse St; ste from $230; 🛜
The one- and two-bedroom Audubon Cottage suites (where artist John J Audubon stayed and painted while in town) overflow with elegant touches: goose down feather-erbeds, Gilchrist & Soames bath products and Egyptian cotton robes are just a few. These suites surround a lushly landscaped courtyard; the pool is rumored to be the oldest in the Quarter (from the late 1700s). At the time of writing, the sumptuous 19th-century main town-house hotel was being renovated – check for updates when you travel.

RITZ-CARLTON NEW ORLEANS
Map pp70–1 Hotel $$$
☎ 524-1331, 800-542-8680; www.ritzcarlton.com; 921 Canal St; r from $220; **P** 🖳

BOOKING SERVICES

The number of online booking services is staggering. Here are a few worth checking.
Hotel Discounts (www.hoteldiscounts.com)
Last Minute Travel (www.lastminutetravel.com)
Lonely Planet (lonelyplanet.com)
Places to Stay (www.placestostay.com)

Sip tea surrounded by neoclassical antiques and French fabrics, dip into a magnolia-scented aromatherapy bath at the spa or retire to the library cigar club: indulgence is the name of the game at the Ritz-Carlton. An ample number of smiling staff wait to attend, whether you're ready for turn-down service or need a complimentary shoe shine. If you think this is something, you should see the 'club-level' Maison Orleans. The solid wood floors, tall beds and brick fireplaces would fit right in at an English manor house. A romantic getaway if there ever was one.

LAFITTE GUEST HOUSE
Map pp70–1 Boutique Hotel $$
☎ 581-2678, 800-331-7971; www.lafitteguest house.com; 1003 Bourbon St; r incl breakfast from $190; 🛜
This elegant three-story 1849 Creole town house is at the quieter end of Bourbon St. Its 14 guest rooms are lavishly furnished in period style, though antique wash-basins and fireplaces seem an odd contrast to the flat-screen TVs. Many rooms have private balconies. Lafitte's Blacksmith Shop, one of the street's more welcoming (and some say haunted) drinking taverns, is on the opposite corner.

W FRENCH QUARTER Map pp70–1 Hotel $$
☎ 581-1200, 888-625-5144; www.whotels.com; 316 Chartres St; r from $180; **P** 🖳 🖾
Like all W hotels, this one wears its style on its trendy, businesslike sleeve. Whether it blends with the French Quarter is questionable, but this is the flashier, less residential side of the district so maybe it does. (The Bourbon St racket is two blocks away.) Rooms vary, but all have that contemporary sleekness. The best are airy spaces opening onto an inner patio. Ponder the pool's azure waters or just enjoy a breeze while checking your email or watching a large-screen TV. Bacco's (p155) classy Italian fare is served at the on-site dining room.

HOTEL PROVINCIAL Map pp70–1 Hotel $$
☎ 581-4995, 800-535-7922; www.hotelprovincial .com; 1024 Chartres St; r incl breakfast from $179; **P** 🛜 🖾
Behind its stately stucco facade, this hotel fills much of the block with a series of finely restored buildings and a large parking area. The best rooms have high ceilings and

HAUNTED HOTELS

An eerily cold 14th-floor hallway leads to a vision of children playing; the cafe doors open and shut on their own; despite the bar being locked, guests see a patron who isn't there… Andrea Thornton, Director of Sales & Marketing at the Hotel Monteleone (opposite) had heard dozens of first-hand accounts of supernatural sightings when she decided investigation was in order. In 2003 the hotel invited the International Society of Paranormal Research (ISPR) to come spend several days, during which they identified 12 disparate spirits on the property, one a former employee named 'Red'. And, indeed, hotel records showed that an engineer who went by the nickname Red worked at the hotel in the 1950s.

Hearing or seeing children is the most common of the mischievous-but-benign activities people experience in the historic hotel. Numerous guests have reported seeing a little boy in a striped suit (about age 3) in room 1462. Speculation is that it's Maurice, son of Josephine and Jacques Begere, looking for his parents. While Maurice was in the hotel being watched by a nanny, his father was thrown from a coach and died instantly; his mother passed a year later.

In a town with such a strife-torn history – slavery, war, fever, flood – hauntings (if they exist) are hardly a surprise. And the Monteleone is far from the only hotel in the Quarter to report sightings. Among others, ghostbusters might want to check out the following:

Bourbon Orleans Hotel (p205) Once an orphanage and an African American convent, children have been seen and heard playing on the 6th floor.

Dauphine Orleans (p204) Bottles appear rearranged at May Bailey's bar, site of a once-infamous brothel, and moans and sounds of beds moving go bump in the night.

Hotel Provincial (opposite) Building 5 was constructed on the site of a Civil War hospital; guests report sometimes gruesome visions of wounded soldiers and bloody sheets.

Lafitte Guest House (opposite) A little girl who died of yellow fever, 'Marie' is said to appear in the mirror outside in room 21, where her mother stayed.

Le Pavillon (p210) Apparitions materialize bedside in this 1907 hotel, where the ISPR identified at least four resident spirits.

open onto the interior courtyards (one with a pool). Others can be cramped and dark. Decor ranges from commercial standard to ornately historic. Check out a few rooms before booking. The excellent on-site restaurant, Stella!, is much calmer than Brando's hollering in *A Streetcar Named Desire*.

ROYAL SONESTA Map pp70–1 Hotel $$$
☎ 586-0300, 800-766-3782; www.royalsonestano.com; 300 Bourbon St; r from $169; P 🖥 🖾
Don't the boys look fancy as they open the grand doors for you in their blue royal-guard–look tux and tails? Most times of year this hotel exudes a gracious charm, but the location is ground zero for the tourist excesses during Mardi Gras (staff grease the pillars to keep revelers from climbing up to the balconies). Still, the nearly 500 rooms provide classy retreats from the strip clubs and lousy cover bands. The Mystic Den is a dignified old bar – perfect for a civilized gin and tonic.

HOTEL VILLA CONVENTO
Map pp70–1 Hotel $$
☎ 522-1793, 800-887-2817; www.villaconvento.com; 616 Ursuline Ave; r from $165; 🖾

Classic New Orleans in every sense, the Villa Convento occupies an 1833 town house in the residential part of the Lower Quarter, complete with a three-story red-brick facade and wrought-iron balconies. Out back in the annex (probably the former servants' quarters) there are more rooms. All rooms have traditional decor, from comfy quilts to lacy canopies. It's all very low-key here in this local-family–owned and cheerfully operated hotel. Free off-site parking, wi-fi in courtyard only. No children under 10. Prices for budget doubles fall to as little as $89 when demand dwindles.

ASTOR CROWNE PLAZA
Map pp70–1 Hotel $$
☎ 962-0500, 888-696-4806; www.astornew orleans.com; 739 Canal St; r from $160; 🖾
An $11 million renovation (completed in 2009) buys you some stylish design details. Look for stacked silver bubble lamps and tall-tufted headboards with pops of russet orange in a primarily neutral color scheme. Business is this 638-room hotel's primary pleasure, but tourists, too, will enjoy the grand lobby, pool terrace and Dickie Brennan's Seafood Bar.

BIDDING FOR A BED

When maximizing quality while minimizing price is your aim, websites like Hotwire (www.hotwire.com) and Priceline (www.priceline.com) are an excellent gamble to take. They don't let you see the property name before you commit to paying, but you can choose the neighborhood, star level and amenities before you either bid or buy at up to 50% off the advertised rate. The drawbacks: you can't change your mind (they're nonrefundable) and nonsmoking rooms can't be guaranteed. Still, if you're flexible, the system works. Testing the theory, we 'won' a room at an excellent four-star by Louis Armstrong International Airport for $60 a night.

Even splashing out can be affordable if you find a chi-chi package auction on Luxury Link (www.luxurylink .com). Occasionally there are 'mystery name' properties but quite often the hotels are identified and described (with gorgeous photos to ogle) so you know what you're gambling on. Hmm…maybe we should have tested one of those instead…

DAUPHINE ORLEANS Map pp70–1   Hotel $$
☎ 586-1800, 800-521-7111; www.dauphine orleans.com; 415 Dauphine St; r incl breakfast from $159; P 🛜 🖵

Judging from the outside of the block-long terra-cotta hotel, you'd never guess that through a courtyard lay 14 bright yellow Creole cottage-style exterior-access rooms (once part of a carriage house). Request one of those, or one of the nine rooms, with exposed cypress beams and brick, across the street in the merchant Herman Howard's former home. The other 100 main-building rooms all have less character, but similar appointments, including earthy color schemes and high thread-count sheets. May Bailey's, once an infamous brothel, is now the bar.

IBERVILLE SUITES Map pp70–1   Hotel $$
☎ 523-2400, 866-229-4351; www.ibervillesuites .com; 910 Iberville St; r from $150; P 🖵

Promotional rates can be a real bargain at this property that shares the back of the house with the Ritz-Carlton. You get to use the Ritz's 25,000-sq-ft spa and other white-glove amenities while paying Iberville prices. The trade off? You sleep in very traditional, nice-but-ho-hum surrounds. Each suite does have two rooms (and a pull-out couch), plus microwave and mini-fridge, so families can feel right at home.

HOTEL ROYAL Map pp70–1   Boutique Hotel $$
☎ 524-3900, 800-776-3901; www.melrosegroup .com; 1006 Royal St; r from $140

Lacy ironwork balconies, gas lanterns and decorative topiaries – everything an 1833 New Orleans home should be. Inside, renowned architect and designer Lee Ledbetter infused each of the 45 individually decorated guest quarters with subtle,

soft-contemporary touches. A modern dark-wood four-poster bed and chocolate linens contrast nicely with the rough, white-plaster walls and plantation shutters in the king suite. Other rooms have wood floors and exposed brick, and some have balcony access. Fragrant chicory coffee and pastries await on arrival in season (ie not summer). No internet access.

LE RICHELIEU Map pp70–1   Hotel $$
☎ 529-2492, 800-535-9653; www.lerichelieuhotel .com; 1234 Chartres St; r from $135; P 🛜 🖵

Le Richelieu's red-brick walls once housed a macaroni factory, but extensive reconstruction in the early 1960s converted it into a conservative hotel. Rooms are decorated with standard synthetic floral spreads, but the price includes parking (a big plus), and there is a pool. Having an on-site bar and a restaurant are other perks here on the quiet side of the Quarter. Prices drop precipitously (down to $89) when things are slow.

OLIVIER HOUSE Map pp70–1   Hotel $$
☎ 525-8456; www.olivierhouse.com; 828 Toulouse St; r from $135; 🛜 🖵

The main house was built in 1838 by Marie Anne Bienvenu Olivier, a wealthy planter's widow, and is an uncommon beauty with Greek-revival touches. Two elegant town houses expand the hotel's capacity. Rooms range from the small and relatively economical to the elaborate, with balconies and kitchens. Each has its own style, but most have furnishings evoking the early 19th century. Out back the main courtyard is lush with mature trees, thick vines and numerous flowers. A second courtyard has a small pool. The house is within a few minute's walk of darn near everything.

BOURBON ORLEANS HOTEL

Map pp70–1   Hotel $$

☎ 523-2222, 800-521-5338; www.bourbonorleans .com; 717 Orleans Ave; r from $134; P ✕ ⊗ ⊠

A polished-marble classic. The gray exteriors and white trim are almost as stately as the grand foyer. Combining several buildings, mostly dating from the early 1830s, the exterior hasn't made any unsightly bows to modernity. Most streetside rooms have access to the classic wrought-iron balconies. (Bourbon St, needless to say, can get noisy.) Traditional rooms feature especially comfortable beds and ergonomic desks. Note, however, that standard rooms set a new standard for smallness.

CHATEAU HOTEL Map pp70–1   Hotel $$

☎ 524-9636; www.chateauhotel.com; 1001 Chartres St; r from $130; ⊗ ⊠

Nothing is cookie-cutter here; rooms range in size and have varying floral motifs. Many feature wrought-iron beds, which echo the streetside balcony details. Though they're on the smallish side, we'd opt for the premium courtyard rooms, which are cool and peaceful and open up to a pool. The hotel is on a residential end of the Quarter, a block away Decatur St at its neighborly best. On-site restaurant; parking across the street.

HOTEL ST MARIE Map pp70–1   Hotel $$

☎ 561-8951, 800-366-2743; www.hotelstmarie .com; 827 Toulouse St; r incl breakfast from $130; ⊗ ⊠

The St Marie was built to look historic from the outside, but is up-to-date on the inside. Its best feature is the large and inviting courtyard, with a swimming pool and umbrella-covered tables amid lush plantings. The neocolonial guest rooms are somewhat lacking in authentic character, but are spacious and more than serviceable. Just around the corner, Bourbon St is at its most extreme.

WESTIN NEW ORLEANS AT CANAL PLACE Map pp70–1   Hotel $$

☎ 566-7006; www.westin.com; 100 Iberville St; r from $129; P ✕ ▯ ⊠

With 29 stories, the Westin has some of the city's best views of the Mississippi River. (Watching the parade of freighters, tankers and barges In the wee hours beats TV.) Rooms are rather bland, but large and modern, with good desks and signature 'heavenly beds,' as well as small sitting areas. There's a rooftop pool that, needless to say, has more good views.

NINE-O-FIVE ROYAL HOTEL

Map pp70–1   Hotel $$

☎ 523-0219; www.905royalhotel.com; 905 Royal St; s/d from $95/125; ⊗

On a particularly scenic block, the Nine-O-Five eschews much of the usual NOLA shtick and opts instead for the timeless comfort you'd expect to find if this house belonged to a dignified old aunt. Front rooms with balconies are the choice for those who want to survey the always entertaining Royal St scene, but for seclusion, get a room off the cute courtyard out back. All 13 rooms have private entrances and small kitchen areas.

GENTRY QUARTERS Map pp70–1   B&B $$

☎ 525-4433; www.gentryhouse.com; 1031 St Ann St; r incl breakfast from $115; ✕ ⊗

This charming old Creole house contains five homey rooms with kitchenettes. (Hot croissants are delivered to your door, and juice, milk and cereals are stocked in your room.) Modest but comfortable furnishings give the rooms a lived-in feel, while linens and towels are fresh and clean. Most rooms open onto a lush garden patio, where you might be visited by two friendly dachshunds. On the northern edge of the Quarter, away from the hubbub, the Gentry has loyal fans. Some guests stay a spell every

VOLUNTOURISM

Post–Hurricane Katrina recovery couldn't have taken place without the thousands of volunteers who journeyed here. Several hotels offer packages or discounts that help you do your part. At the Ritz-Carlton (p202) the 'Bring Back the Big Easy' room-rate includes a donation to plant new trees, or you can book a 'Crescent City Comeback' weekend that includes a bus ride to a Habitat for Humanity (www.habitat-nola.org) site (and a massage afterwards; hammering is hard work). All the Marriott Hotels (☎ 888-236-2427; www.marriott.com) in town have packages as well. If you plan to go it on your own, ask if your hotel has a special volunteer rate. For a list of volunteer opportunities, see the New Orleans Convention Bureau website, www.neworleanscvb.com. Also see boxed text, p62.

year, so book ahead. Two-night minimum. Some rooms are large enough for families.

HISTORIC FRENCH MARKET INN

Map pp70–1   Hotel $$

☎ 561-5621, 888-538-5651; www.neworleansfine hotels.com; 501 Decatur St; r from $100; P 🛜

You hardly have to stumble out of bed to get a souvenir T-shirt or daiquiri to-go on this busy block of Decatur St, not far from the Café du Monde's aromatic chicory coffee. A good budget choice, this fairly basic hotel has 95 functional rooms with crisp linens. Most are relatively small and get little daylight; think of it as a boon if you're only just getting home at daybreak. Hidden deep within the complex are a pleasant courtyards. Some dogs allowed.

URSULINE GUEST HOUSE

Map pp70–1   Hotel $

☎ 525-8509, 800-654-2351; 708 Ursuline Ave; r from $85; 🛜

Unadorned accommodations in the laid-back Lower Quarter. Rooms in these Spanish-era buildings have a friendly flophouse appeal. Those in front are just a short step up from the sidewalk, perhaps too close to the neighborhood's stream of yammering late-night pedestrians. Those in back are much quieter. Same-sex couples will feel welcome. No children; wi-fi in small office only.

ST PETER HOUSE HOTEL

Map pp70–1   Hotel $

☎ 523-5198, 800-535-7815; www.stpeterhouse .com; 1005 St Peter St; r from $79

Some of the 29 rooms in this small hotel are miniscule, but so are the prices. Each room has surprising individuality, with a carved bed or exposed brick, but not a whole lot else. Pastries are provided in the morning and you can hang out on the balconies or in the small courtyard. The St Peter is a little beyond where most of the tourists hang out, which has advantages (quiet) and disadvantages (you might want to take a cab home instead of facing the lonely walk north after a late night). No internet access.

FAUBOURG MARIGNY & BYWATER

Across Esplanade Ave from the Quarter, Faubourg Marigny's grid-defying street pattern is speckled with colorful old cottages and shotgun houses, many of which have been converted into homey, reasonable B&Bs. Savvy night owls feel the pull of the lively Frenchmen St scene. Adjacent Bywater also stays on the low-rent side of the spectrum. Same-sex couples are drawn to these neighborhoods by gay- and lesbian-owned accommodations. It's possible to walk from either to the Quarter. However, rather than making the long trek through emerging neighborhoods after dark, we recommend a taxi ride.

MELROSE MANSION Map p81   B&B $$

☎ 944-2255, 800-650-3323; www.melrose mansion.com; 937 Esplanade Ave; r from $100, ste from $185, all incl breakfast; P 🛜 🖳

An exquisite 1884 Victorian mansion, Melrose stands out even among its stately neighbors. This is a retreat for the well-heeled and for honeymooners. Rooms are luxurious, airy spaces, with high ceilings and large French windows. Fastidiously polished antique furnishings reflect impeccable taste, with four-poster beds, cast-iron lamps and comfortable reading chairs in every room. In season, fresh-baked breakfast pastries are accompanied by quiche, and nightly cocktails are mixed in the parlor. Full concierge service is available round the clock. Guests are pampered to death here, but it's an exquisite way to go.

HOTEL DE LA MONNAIE Map p81   Hotel $$

☎ 947-0009; www.hoteldelamonnaie.com; 405 Esplanade Ave; 1br ste from $140, 2br suite from $160; P 🛜

Traveling with a group or family? Staying in these suites, with kitchenettes and large rooms that sleep four to six, makes a lot of sense. Each room is stocked with cooking utensils and there's a ministore downstairs. The furnishings are nothing to write home about, but rooms on the top floor enjoy wonderful views of the mighty Mississippi. Across the street is the Riverfront Streetcar, which runs the length of the Quarter.

LIONS INN B&B Map p81   B&B $$

☎ 945-2339; www.lionsinn.com; 2517 Chartres St; d $110-120, s/d without bathroom $50/89, all incl breakfast; ☒ 🛜 🖳

On a quiet Marigny block, the Lions Inn is a bright and friendly place suitable for gays and straights. Nine simply furnished guest rooms have splashes of vibrant color and no fussy antiques. The choice space is the Sun Room, which can accommodate four and has a bank of windows overlooking the back courtyard. Jump into the swimming pool and Jacuzzi or use one of the free bicycles to peddle the five blocks to the edge of the Quarter.

BURGUNDY BED & BREAKFAST

Map p81   B&B $$

☎ 942-1463, 800-970-2513; www.theburgundy .com; 2513 Burgundy St; r incl breakfast from $100;

Cottage charm pervades this 1890s double-shotgun home decorated in a shabby chic style. The Chihuahua, Gizzy, welcomes you to the cheery front room. Through the six-panel door lies a guest kitchen with fridge, coffeemaker and microwave, next to a cozy dining room. No space is wasted in the four guest quarters, two of which have both a queen and a single bed. The courtyard outside is more roomy, and off to the side is a (clothing-optional) spa. Gay-owned-and-operated.

LAMOTHE HOUSE   Map p81   B&B $$

☎ 947-1161, 800-367-5858; www.new-orleans .org; 621 Esplanade Ave; r incl breakfast from $99;

Lovely, oak-shaded Esplanade Ave is a prime jumping-off point for prowling the nightlife of Frenchmen St and the Lower Quarter. Its charms are slightly faded, but Lamothe House doesn't lack for character. Guest rooms are furnished with antiques you won't feel guilty about bumping into, and thick curtains keep the sun out when you're sleeping off a big night. If you're determined to revive early, take a dip in the pool after the continental breakfast. The cheapest rooms are slender and open onto a long courtyard. More elaborately accoutred suites somehow suggest EJ Bellocq's beautiful Storyville photographs without being lurid or seedy.

AULD SWEET OLIVE BED &

BREAKFAST   Map p81   B&B $$

☎ 947-4332, 877-470-5323; www.sweetolive .com; 2460 N Rampart St; r incl breakfast from $99;

Mardi Gras lovers take note: the Krewe de Vieux parade goes right by this grand B&B. Even if you don't come during the pre-

top picks

GAY STAYS

Pretty much anywhere you stay in New Orleans is GLBT-friendly (what else would you expect in the Big Easy?) Corporate chain hotels provide staff sensitivity training, and oodles of gay-owned B&Bs are to be found in Faubourg Marigny. Some places go over the top showing their rainbow colors.

- **W Hotels (p202, p208)** Book a Pride 365 package and receive a *Passport* GLBT magazine subscription, Bliss spa facial products and two free cocktails.
- **Green House Inn (p211)** Don your Green House Inn robe and step out to the lush tropical gardens, patio, saltwater pool and hot tub – all clothing-optional. The long-time resident innkeeper provides extensive concierge services.
- **Magnolia Mansion (p211)** Book an event at this B&B and you can hire a celebrity impersonator to attend (the owner 'is' Tina Turner).
- **Bywater Bed & Breakfast (p208)** This lesbian-owned and -operated B&B is an arty oasis filled with authentic local folk art.

Lenten season, you can see parade regalia like the co-owner's King Endymion costume on display. The house itself is similarly theatrical, once owned by set designer and mural artist Stephen Auld. The large double parlor (filled with games, books, videos, TV, CD player, etc) resembles a banana-tree jungle; the soaking-tub room is painted to look like a night sky beneath branches. Individual rooms also have decorative touches – faux wood, or magnolia blooms – on a more refined scale. No room TVs.

FRENCHMEN HOTEL   Map p81   Hotel $

☎ 948-2166, 800-831-1781; www.french-quarter .org; 417 Frenchmen St; r incl breakfast from $89;

The three thoroughly refurbished 1850s houses that comprise this smart hotel are clustered around a courtyard with a swimming pool and Jacuzzi. High ceilings, balconies and some rustic exposed brick are remnant from the buildings' more elegant past. Mix-and-match furnishings have limited antique appeal. The real selling point is the hotel's proximity to some great Frenchman St bars and nightclubs. Concierge service is an upscale touch for a bargain hotel.

BYWATER BED & BREAKFAST

Map p81   B&B $

☎ 944-8438; www.bywaterbnb.com; 1026 Clouet St; r without bathroom $75; 🛜

An artsy B&B, Bywater is particularly popular with lesbians, and is about as homey and laid-back as it gets. It's a restored double-shotgun, very colorful, with a kitchen and parlors in which guests can cook or loiter. The walls double as gallery space, showcasing a collection of vibrant outsider and folk art. The four guest rooms are simple and comfortable with more cheery paint and art. The owners enjoy steering guests in the right direction, whether you're looking for a great po'boy, live music or gay bars. Two-night minimum usually required.

CBD & WAREHOUSE DISTRICT

The hotels in the CBD tend to be modern behemoths and posh high-rises catering to those with business-expense accounts. Even the Warehouse District, despite its artistic leanings, mostly accommodates the convention set. Prices at both plummet when occupancy is low. Reasons to stay in these parts include: proximity to the French Quarter; possible great deals; Mardi Gras parades pass through this part of town; and your employers are paying the bill and this is where they chose to put you. Note: there are far more big-name chain hotels in these neighborhoods than we could possibly mention, so if you have a loyalty-point fave, look it up online.

WINDSOR COURT HOTEL

Map pp86–7   Hotel $$$

☎ 523-6000, 888-596-0955; www.windsorcourt hotel.com; 300 Gravier St; r from $370; 🅿 🛜 🖭

The exterior is an architectural hangover from the 1980s, but it more than makes up for it inside. The public areas feature a long list of artworks and antiques; lavish floral displays add charm, while a harpist sets the tone. Service is superb, rooms large and comfy, and the bars and restaurants are local destinations. A large pool, Jacuzzi, health club, in-room massage services – these are the sorts of things you can expect from one of New Orleans' finer accommodations.

HARRAH'S NEW ORLEANS

Map pp86–7   Hotel $$$

☎ 533-6000, 800-427-7247; www.harrahs.com; 228 Poydras St; r from $299; 🅿 🛜 🖭

Twenty-six floors, 450 rooms, an 115,000-sq-ft casino, six restaurants, four blocks of retail space: some guests hardly even leave the property. Why would they, with swarms of white-gloved staff to wait on them? Silky purples and golds in the lobby make it seem like Mardi Gras all year round; rooms are similarly luxe. It's worth joining the Harrah's free loyalty program; even if you only gamble a little, you may get a suite upgrade.

ROOSEVELT HOTEL Map pp86–7   Hotel $$$

☎ 648-1200, 800-441-1414; www.therooseveltnew orleans.com; 123 Baronne St; r from $259; 🅿 🖭

With its majestic, block-long lobby, this was the city's elite establishment when it opened in 1893. By the 1930s, its swanky bar was frequented by governor Huey Long. After a meticulous $145 million renovation, the Roosevelt reopened its doors in June 2009 as part of the Waldorf-Astoria Collection. Swish rooms have classical details, but the full spa, a John Besh restaurant and the storied Sazerac Bar are at least half the reason to stay.

W NEW ORLEANS Map pp86–7   Hotel $$$

☎ 525-9444, 888-625-5144; www.whotels.com; 333 Poydras St; r from $209; 🅿 🛜 🖭

You have to hand it to W – this suave chain does things right. This incarnation is housed in a tower that was once a bland office building. After a wave of the magic Wand it became the modern hotel equivalent of Buddy Love: too cool for school, pops. The high standard of service here is called 'Whatever, Whenever'; they even offer to bring 'the city's best beignet directly to your bath.' Gather with friends in a private cabana at the rooftop pool for the ultimate in hipster cool.

LOEWS NEW ORLEANS HOTEL

Map pp86–7   Hotel $$

☎ 595-3300, 866-563-9792; www.loewshotels .com; 300 Poydras St; r from $189; 🅿 🛜 🖭

In a converted office building formerly occupied by a steamship company, Loews offers a boatload of amenities with a relaxed and unfussy style. The 285 rooms are larger than average and many have superb views. Rooms are decorated and furnished with understated yet elegant modernism. There's an indoor lap pool and health center, plus a noted spa. In Swizzle Sticks bar, off the lobby, live jazz is performed many nights. One of the most pet-friendly properties in the city.

LOFT 523 Map pp86–7 Boutique Hotel $$
☎ 200-6523; www.loft523.com; 523 Gravier St; r from $179; ✕ 🖵

Top design magazines have recognized the hip industrial-minimalist style of Loft 523's 16 lodgings. Whirligig-shaped fans circle over low-lying Mondo beds and polished concrete floors. Enjoy your freestanding half-egg shaped tub by ordering a milk-bath in-room spa service and listening to a mixed jazz CD in surround sound (or maybe just switching on the plasma screen). And since International House hotel is a sister property, you share their fitness center and Rambla room-service privileges.

INTERNATIONAL HOUSE
Map pp86–7 Boutique Hotel $$
☎ 553-9550; www.ihhotel.com; 221 Camp St; r from $169; ✕ 🖳

Lavish rooms in this boutique hotel offer an array of amenities like local wildflower arrangements, CD players with jazz CDs, ceiling fans (in addition to the air-con), and two-headed showers. Should the budget allow, go for the penthouse rooms and their sweeping terraces. One of New Orleans' most fashionable hang-outs is in the Loa bar (p186), amid soaring columns and plush tufted ottomans. There's even an iMac for those who want to check their email. Don't forgo a Castilian Spanish dinner at the similarly stylish Rambla restaurant.

SHERATON NEW ORLEANS
Map pp86–7 Hotel $$
☎ 525-2500, 800-325-3535; www.sheratonneworleans.com; 500 Canal St; r from $169; 🅿 🖳 🖭

To be sure, this 1100-room conventioneer hotel is a megamonster; the lobby feels bigger than the terminals at Louis Armstrong Airport. But it does have interesting art: George Rodriguez's famous Blue Dog appears everywhere, in sculpture, glass and paint. In the rooms you'll find nicely designed furniture and subtle color schemes

that are easy on the eyes. And needless to say, higher floors mean fabbo views. But we're digressing from the main point, which is that prices become very reasonable when there's no convention in town.

EMBASSY SUITES HOTEL
Map pp86–7 Hotel $$
☎ 525-1993, 800-362-2779; www.embassyneworleans.com; 315 Julia St; r incl breakfast from $159; 🅿 🛜 🖭

The architecture astonishes with vast size and a cacophony of angles, but the eccentric design grows on you. The soaring atrium is indeed impressive. Every room is a large, family-friendly suite, and no two are exactly the same. Most have balconies; higher floors have views of the city and the river. Adjoining historic loft-building rooms, in what was once a cotton warehouse, have tall ceilings and exposed brick walls. Just down the street at Mulate's you can eat crawfish and dance to Cajun tunes.

QUEEN & CRESCENT HOTEL
Map pp86–7 Hotel $$
☎ 587-9700, 800-455-3417; www.queenandcrescent.com; 344 Camp St; r from $159; 🛜

Two early 1900s commercial buildings make up this hotel, in a part of the CBD now dominated by midrange chains. The Q&C is not small (it has 196 rooms), and its gray-painted brick facade doesn't scream luxury, but the place manages to stand apart. The windows facing the street are wide, allowing maximum light inside. In the

top picks

PAMPERED PETS

- **Loews New Orleans Hotel** (opposite) Order vet-approved room-service meals from a lengthy menu designed for your coveted canine.
- **Hotel Monteleone** (p202) Upon check-in your four-legged friend gets their own mat, bowls and treats.
- **Westin New Orleans at Canal Place** (p205) A 'Heavenly Dog Bed' is provided free for Fluffy (dogs under 40lb only).
- **Green House Inn** (p211) Your dog or cat can make friends with Steuben, the resident German shepherd. Maximum two pets per room.

main building, many rooms above the 8th floor have interesting city views. All rooms have a certain European charm, but vary greatly. You might want to leave the bags in the lobby while you peruse.

HAMPTON INN NEW ORLEANS DOWNTOWN Map pp86–7 Hotel $$

☎ 529-5077, 800-292-0653; www.neworleans hamptoninns.com; 226 Carondelet St; r incl breakfast from $150; P 🛜

Despite occupying the Carondelet Building (considered the Crescent City's first skyscraper), the Hampton stays close to its modest chain roots by offering good-value accommodations. Per Hampton protocol, there's a complimentary breakfast buffet where you'll likely end up waffling over your choice of waffles, pancakes and more. On weeknights there's a free (!) happy hour, particularly beloved by business travelers. The central location is just two blocks from the Quarter and around the corner from a streetcar.

DOUBLETREE HOTEL NEW ORLEANS
Map pp86–7 Hotel $$

☎ 581-1300; www.neworleans.doubletree.com; 300 Canal St; r from $149; P 🛜 🐾

One of the better choices among the chain hotels on Canal St, the Doubletree manages to feel almost intimate with its 363 rooms (as opposed to nearby places with room totals in the four digits). Like most properties in this group, rooms are sizable if generic. The higher of the 17 floors have good views, especially rooms facing the river. Patrons range from package groups from Middle America to professionals from middle management.

LE PAVILLON Map pp86–7 Hotel $$

☎ 581-3111, 800-535-9095; www.lepavillon.com; 833 Poydras St; r from $145; P 🛜

Fluted columns support the porte cochere off the gleaming alabaster facade. The doorman wears white gloves and a top hat, and somehow doesn't look ridiculous. Both private and public spaces are redolent with historic portraits, magnificent chandeliers, marble floors, heavy drapery, blah blah etc. Get the picture? Le Pavillon may be a little too rich for some people's tastes. But just when you're getting the idea that this is some sort of asylum for deposed world conquerors, out comes the plate of peanut-

butter-and-jelly sandwiches – served at 10pm nightly in the lobby. Rates are unexpectedly low for a hotel of this quality. During slow periods Le Pavillon offers some astounding deals.

LAFAYETTE HOTEL Map pp86–7 Hotel $$

☎ 524-4441, 888-211-3447; www.neworleansfine hotels.com; 600 St Charles Ave; r from $105; 🛜

A small and luxurious 1916 hotel right on Lafayette Sq. The surrounding blocks have a classic feel that's generally lacking in most of the modern CBD. (Lafayette Sq was the center of the American St Mary neighborhood, developed after the Louisiana Purchase.) Its 44 rooms are furnished with dark woods, antiques and king-size beds. The walls are painted in rich, classic colors, and the bathrooms are roomy and finished in marble. Service is excellent and the hotel (unsurprisingly) has a loyal following. The Julia Row arts district is a short walk from here, as are numerous cutting-edge restaurants.

ST JAMES HOTEL Map pp86–7 Hotel $

☎ 304-4000, 888-856-4485; www.neworleansfine hotels.com; 330 Magazine St; r from $80; ✕ 🖳

Legend has it that a notorious Caribbean merchant haunted the original New Orleans St James Hotel in the Bank Arcade. An appropriately West Indian breeze blows through this namesake reincarnation down the street. Palms wave over the (teeny-tiny) courtyard pool and decorative old steamer trunks sit next to exposed beams. Expect tropical prints on the walls and bedspreads. Fourth-floor rooms shelter under slanted eaves (room 403 is especially large, with a private porch).

LA QUINTA INN & SUITES DOWNTOWN Map pp86–7 Hotel $

☎ 598-9977, 800-753-3757; www.lq.com; 301 Camp St; r incl breakfast from $80; P 🛜 🐾

Opened in 2009, a new-and-shiny high-rise is not necessarily what you expect from the La Quinta motel chain. Rooms are downright modern, with oversize graphic art and green throws on triple-sheeted beds. An outdoor pool, laundry facilities and continental breakfast all add to the value here, just a few blocks from the Quarter. Note that seniors and AAA motorclub members often get discount rates. Some pets allowed.

GARDEN, LOWER GARDEN & CENTRAL CITY

Wow, what amazing architecture. Suburbia in the 1800s was sure a lot prettier than today. Stately Greek-revival town houses front the leafy lanes in the lower district, and as you move northwest, the houses only get more elaborate. Both near-town historic Garden District neighborhoods are largely residential today, but you're in luck: there are a few hotels, B&Bs – and one hostel – to stay at here. Magazine St (with fun boutiques and eclectic eateries) is both neighborhoods' restrained commercial heart, connected by bus to Canal Street. The St Charles Ave Streetcar trundles along near the northern edge of the neighborhoods, connecting Riverbend mansions to the Quarter.

MAGNOLIA MANSION Map pp96–7 B&B $$$
☎ 412-9500; www.magnoliamansion.com; 2127 Prytania St; r incl breakfast from $195; P ⊠ 🛜

With its ornate white Corinthian columns, sky-blue veranda ceilings and elaborate dental moldings, the exterior of the Magnolia Mansion resembles nothing a huge wedding confection. The opulence continues inside with a bold red entryway filled with formal French antiques. Most guest rooms drip with crystal chandeliers, silk draperies and gilt mirrors. Choose the Vampire Lovers Lair and you'll sleep ensconced in a king-size bed that replicates the one used in the movie *Interview with a Vampire*. All the drama should come as no surprise given that the proprietor is Holy Vest, a famous Las Vegas impersonator, aka Tina Turner. No guests under 21.

HENRY HOWARD HOUSE
Map pp96–7 B&B $$
☎ 561-8550; www.henryhowardhouseinn.com; 2041 Prytania St; r incl breakfast $165-450; P ⊠ 🛜

Dappled light pours in through floor-to-ceiling windows in the parlor, lending it a conservatory feel that tall palms and a baby grand piano do nothing to dispel. It's no wonder the Henry Howard is such a favorite with bridal parties. But you don't have to be tying the knot to appreciate a stroll along the colonnade of this white, 1850s neoclassical mansion. Most of the 17 rooms in the B&B have a certain formality, with a restrained use of antiques, but one or two are done in wicker or pine. Relax on the roof garden before you ride the nearby St Charles Ave streetcar into the Quarter for the day's sight seeing.

TERRELL HOUSE Map pp96–7 B&B $$
☎ 247-0560, 866-261-9687; www.terrellhouse.com; 1441 Magazine St; r incl breakfast from $135; ⊠ 🛜

Impeccable. Architecture buffs and novices alike will appreciate the stately 1858 Georgian-revival house with cast-iron galleries, a spacious courtyard and exquisite details. Original art adds to the freshness of the simple but tasteful carriage-house rooms. Think high-thread-count linens, colorful spreads and clean-lined wood or iron beds. Suites in the main house are more antique in nature, with period furnishings, silk draperies and Oriental rugs; some even have marble fireplaces. Common rooms are galleries filled with art, antiques and potted plants. In addition to a full breakfast, complimentary cocktails are included. Other amenities include in-room minifridges stocked with soda and bottled water. No children under 12.

SULLY MANSION B&B Map pp96–7 B&B $$
☎ 891-0457, 800-364-2414; www.sullymansion.com; 2631 Prytania St; r incl breakfast from $135; 🛜

Surrounded by lush gardens and a cast-iron fence, the Sully Mansion pretty represents everything the Old South Garden District is cracked up to be. The seven guest rooms are elegant, each with a fireplace and antique four-poster beds. Curtains and art on the walls are oddly underwhelming. You'll want to spend some of your downtime in a wicker chair out on the mansion's curved porch.

GREEN HOUSE INN Map pp96–7 B&B $$
☎ 525-1333, 800-966-1303; www.thegreenhouseinn.com; 1212 Magazine St; r incl breakfast from $119; P ⊠ 🖳 🖲

Green it is – a tropical rubber-tree green, in fact. The house's striking color certainly stands out on the still-gentrifying end of Magazine St closest to downtown. Enter the landscaped pool garden (clothing-optional) and, surrounded by exotic blooms, the color starts to make more sense. Though named for flowers, guest rooms are more masculine and clean-lined than frilly and floral. Occasional complimentary weekend wine and cheese make for quite the gathering. Proud member of the International Gay & Lesbian Travel Association.

MAISON ST CHARLES Map pp96–7   Hotel $$
☎ 522-0187, 800-831-1783; www.maisonstcharles.com; 1319 St Charles Ave; r incl breakfast from $119; P 🛜 🚇

Garden-filled courtyards (one with a fine pool) connect the hodgepodge of historic and newer buildings that make up this hotel. Dramatic black-and-white checkered marble floors in the lobby are somewhat more interesting than the rooms. Thankfully, at the time of writing they were undergoing a makeover involving royal purple paint and elegant upholstered headboards. As with other, older multibuilding lodgings, you may want to look at more than one of the 130 rooms before making a selection. Note that this isn't the prettiest end of St Charles Ave, not far from the Hwy 90 overpass and Lee Circle (and next to a Wendy's).

AVENUE GARDEN HOTEL
Map pp96–7   Hotel $$
☎ 521-8000, 800-379-5322; www.avenuegardenhotel.com; 1509 St Charles Ave; r incl breakfast from $99; P ✗ 🖥

Ignore the uncharacteristically drab and treeless block of St Charles Ave; behind the

top picks

HOTEL BARS

When you're just tipsy enough to wonder about the way back to your hotel, you'll wish you were staying and drinking in one of these super cool establishments.

- **Carousel Bar** (p177) Hotel Monteleone's revolving bar sits beneath a carousel canopy, complete with lights and figurines.
- **Loa** (p186) A hip after-work crowd lounges on the swank ottomans in this International House bar.
- **Columns Hotel** (p187) A mint julep, or some other icy Southern cocktail, would be just the thing for sipping on the porch of a historic hotel.
- **Irvin Mayfield's Jazz Playhouse** (p203) Every Wednesday night Grammy-nominated Mayfield and his band jam bar in the Royal Sonesta . Headliners play other nights, too.

narrow facade, the cluster of buildings and rooms has been refreshed and repainted since a new owner took over in 2008. Homebaked treats wait on the hall table and rural art by the owner's mother, Myra Blanchard, graces the walls. All can enjoy the small courtyard in back. Some of the 30 rooms in this small, personal hotel are fancier than others; they vary greatly in size. (Room 47 has the only private balcony.)

GARDEN DISTRICT B&B Map pp96–7 B&B $$
☎ 895-4302; www.gardendistrictbedandbreakfast.com; 2418 Magazine St; ste incl breakfast from $90; 🖥

Staying in this small, private four-suite town house is like coming home to your own character-filled efficiency apartment. Each spacious room (most sleep three) has a separate entrance, kitchenette and table seating in addition to brick walls, tall ceilings and homey antiques such as a 1950s (nonworking) stove. Choose the Patio suite and get a wonderful little private courtyard. Fresh-made breads, muffins and fruits wrapped to go are set on the parlor table every morning and rooms are stocked with coffee, juice, yoghurt and cereals. The innkeeper provides loads of local restaurant info, and respects guests' privacy.

PRYTANIA PARK HOTEL Map pp96–7 Hotel $
☎ 524-0427, 800-862-1984; www.prytaniapark hotel.com; 1525 Prytania St; r incl breakfast from $89; P 🛜

The owners are always in the process of refreshing the exterior-access rooms spread across four older brick buildings. Updated rooms have painted furniture and light colors, but older ones can be dark and motel-traditional. A few suites have spiral staircases winding up to extra sleeping quarters and are well-suited to families. The oak-shaded location is one block from the streetcar line. This place is always worth checking for last-minute reservations. Sister properties the Queen Anne and Prytania Oaks have more character and quaintness.

MARQUETTE HOUSE HOSTEL
Map pp96–7   Hostel $
☎ 523-3014; www.neworleansinternationalhostel.com; 2253 Carondelet St; dm $25; P ✗ 🖥

The cheapest place around has limited amenities but is not a bad place to lay your head. The large facility consists of four buildings with 21 impressively clean and spare rooms. Dorms sleep eight to 10. Some have private bathrooms, others share. Picnic tables in the backyard are an ideal place to meet fellow travelers. Internet access is available in the lobby only, the kitchenette has no stove (there's a barbecue) and there's no on-site laundry (but there's one in a nearby bar). The hostel is around the block from St Charles Ave. To the north is a bit of a ragged area, but this block of Carondelet St is quiet.

UPTOWN & RIVERBEND

Uptown and Riverbend just ooze with wealth. Streetcars clank by the historic mansions, manicured gardens and parks that line leafy St Charles Ave. There are a handful of lovely places to stay in this part of town, and some up-and-coming restaurants. Closer to Magazine St (and the river), houses are slightly more modest but closer to quirky shops and eateries.

PARK VIEW GUEST HOUSE

Map pp102–3   B&B $$$
☎ 861-7564, 888-533-0746; www.parkviewguest house.com; 7004 St Charles Ave; r incl breakfast from $209; ✕ ⊠

Next to Audubon Park, this ornate wooden masterpiece was built in 1884 to impress people attending the World Cotton Exchange Exposition (and the size still turns heads today). The 21 rooms and guest lounge can feel a bit heavy with solid wood antiques, but from the wraparound veranda you can enjoy up-close views of stately oaks grizzled with Spanish beards in the park and on St Charles Ave. Tulane and Loyola Universities are just blocks away – many of the hotel's frequent guests are visiting parents. Extended-stay rates are available.

COLUMNS HOTEL

Map pp102–3   Boutique Hotel $$
☎ 899-9308, 800-445-9308; www.thecolumns.com; 3811 St Charles Ave; r incl breakfast from $160; ⊠

Built in 1883, this is one of New Orleans' truly great establishments. A bar-cafe starts on the columned front veranda and continues inside to two wood-paneled parlors. Guests lounge on Victorian settees while jazz bands play some evenings. A magnificent mahogany staircase leads to the 20 rooms on the 2nd and 3rd floors, ranging

from smallish doubles to the two-room Pretty Baby Suite (named for the Louis Malle film shot here in the 1970s). Elaborate marble fireplaces, richly carved armoires and claw-foot tubs are among the highlights. The public spaces are equally grand. To absorb the late-night revelry take, a front room on the 2nd floor (room 16 has a balcony overlooking the front entry and St Charles Ave). A lavish hot breakfast is included.

CHIMES

Map pp102–3   B&B $$
☎ 899-2621; www.chimesneworleans.com; 1145 Constantinople St; r incl breakfast from $140; ✕ ⊠

Five pleasant little rooms each have an outstanding individual touch or two – such as a floating staircase made from 4in-thick cypress slabs, or a sunken stone tub. All rooms are arranged around a lovely patio and gardens, creating a courtyard community of sorts. Breakfast consists of fresh-baked goods and local Community Coffee. It's located in a quiet residential neighborhood, but quite close to Magazine St. Note that the eight namesake chimes hang on the front porch of the main house, so all you hear is distant music among the birdsong.

LAGNIAPPE B&B

Map pp102–3   B&B $$
☎ 899-2120, 800-317-2120; www.lanyappe.com; 1925 Peniston St; r incl breakfast from $135; Ⓟ ⊠

This restored Creole house has very stylish rooms, all with high ceilings and private bathrooms. Furnishings are a mix of

AIRPORT ACCOMMODATIONS

Lots of flights out of New Orleans depart at the crack of dawn. Not an easy schedule if you've been tempted to make a full night of it in the French Quarter during your last hours in the Big Easy. Nervous, conscientious types might opt for staying as near to the tarmac as possible. Many airport chains have free shuttles that take just a few minutes to reach the terminals. These include the following:

Best Western (☎ 800-528-1238; www.best western.com)

Doubletree (☎ 800-222-8733; www.double tree.com)

Hilton (☎ 800-872-5914; www.hilton.com)

Sheraton (☎ 800-325-3535; www.sheraton.com)

antiques and well-made reproductions. The owners really know how to make their guests comfortable. Fresh fruit, fresh flowers, cold beer in the fridge, wine on the porch and a wonderful breakfast in the morning are just some of the ways. Concierge services are also available. The Lagniappe is in a transitional neighborhood, but only three blocks off St Charles Ave.

MID-CITY & THE TREMÉ

There's not a whole lot going on sleeping-wise in the remote, and sometimes gritty, Mid-City and Tremé neighborhoods. A few of the huge and beautiful old homes in Esplanade Ridge, near City Park, now accommodate guests looking for some Southern grandeur. It's an ideal area to stay in for Jazz Fest – the Fair Grounds are only a short walk away.

ASHTON'S BED & BREAKFAST
Map pp108–9   B&B $$

☎ 942-7048, 800-725-4131; www.ashtonsbb.com; 2023 Esplanade Ave; r incl breakfast from $149; ✄ 🛜

Looking at the detailed plaster ceilings, the ornate stained-glass and the crisp paint and trim, it's hard to imagine this mansion had a 60ft hole in the front after Hurricane Katrina. The owners have meticulously restored this restored 1861 Greek-revival and furnished it in a luxe style with half-tester canopy beds and claw-foot tubs. A hot Creole breakfast and complimentary refreshments throughout the day are included. The only drawback is the busy street and far-off location: unless you're heading to Jazz Fest, you'll need a taxi.

DEGAS HOUSE Map pp108–9   B&B $$

☎ 821-5009; www.degashouse.com; 2306 Esplanade Ave; r incl breakfast from $149; ✄ 🛜

Edgar Degas, the famed French impressionist, lived in this 1852 Italianate house when visiting his mother's family in the early 1870s. During his stay he produced the city's most famous painting, *The Cotton Exchange in New Orleans*. Rooms recall his time here with reproductions of his work and period furnishings. The suites have balconies and fireplaces, while the less expensive garret rooms are the cramped top-floor quarters that once housed the Degas family's servants. Weekend stays include a full hot breakfast; weekdays, fresh baked goods are served continental style.

HOUSE ON BAYOU ROAD
Map pp108–9   B&B $$

☎ 945-0992, 800-882-2968; www.houseonbayou road.com; 2275 Bayou Rd; r incl breakfast from $135; 🅿 🛜 🖭

The true gem of Esplanade Ridge is this 1798 Creole plantation house. It oozes sultry atmosphere, with wide galleries and French doors that open onto thick tropical gardens. Screened porches make it possible to enjoy the chirp of crickets at night without being slaughtered by mosquitoes, and a large swimming pool will keep you cool. Antiques in the three main-house rooms are splashed with natural light from tall windows. Four more rooms in the Kumquat House, also on the grounds, are in no way a compromise, maintaining the same quality atmosphere, style and comfort. For a really private and charming experience, a small Creole cottage with its own porch (and your own rocking chair) is also hidden away on the grounds.

INDIA HOUSE HOSTEL Map pp108–9 Hostel $

☎ 821-1904; www.indiahousehostel.com; 124 S Lopez St; dm $20, d $45; 🖳 🖭

Half a block off Canal St in Mid-City, this place has a free-spirited party atmosphere. A large above-ground pool and cabana-like patio add ambience to the three well-used old houses that serve as dorms. Bunk beds include linen and tax. For a unique experience, ask about the private Cajun shacks out back, which come with pet alligators. Guests can use the washer and dryer, and log onto the internet. Children not permitted.

DAY TRIPS & EXCURSIONS

Once you've had your fill of trout meunière and oysters Rockefeller, you might be ready to move on out of New Orleans and see what the rest of Louisiana tastes like. You'll notice a gradual change as you move west: plantation-filled River Road is still cultured and complex, like a good Creole dish, while Cajun Country is down-home and spicy. Day-trip opportunities include touring antebellum opulence, bird watching in forests that were once John James Audubon's stomping grounds, paddling a canoe through Barataria Preserve, coming face to face with a gator on a swamp tour and gambling on the Mississippi Gulf Coast. The Cajun heartland and prairies – where accordion music beckons in a pumped-up waltz, and peppery boiled crawfish promises to induce a healthy sweat – are an overnight excursion away. Why rush through such exotic country, where a strange French accent lingers in the air, and great food and a historic place to stay are just around the next bend?

A TASTE OF CAJUN COUNTRY

Traveling on your taste buds is one of the best ways to explore the area. Starting in the River Road area, make a reservation at Latil's Landing (p220) for a stunning seven-course meal, or drop into Grapevine Cafe (p220) for creamy sauced crawfish – just don't skip dessert. In the Cajun heartland, Cafe des Amis (p226), Cafe Blue Dog (p225), Prejean's (p225), Creole Lunch House (p225) and Poche's grocery store (p226) are among the gastronomic experiences not to be missed. If it's boiled crawfish you're after, even fruit stands sell the 'mudbugs' in season, but Crazy 'Bout Crawfish (p226) in Breaux Bridge and 1921 Seafood & Oyster Bar (p233) in Houma can surely fill you up. And don't forget the oysters in Abbeville (p227) and frog legs in Rayne (p225).

WHERE THE PAST IS PRESENT

The past is ever-present in the region around New Orleans. You can learn about the pre–Civil War, sugarcane-produced riches at any of the River Road plantation-house museums, but Shadows on the Teche (p228) in the Cajun heartland has the most well-documented history. At Laura Plantation (p218) the story is told from the point of view of the women, children and slaves who lived at the time. For more on the slave perspective, visit the River Road African American Museum (p219), and have a sobering look at some toppling slave quarters at the Laurel Valley Village (p232). Any of the three living-history parks and exhibits in Lafayette (p224) can shed light on the Acadian legacy and *le Grand Dérangement* that got them here. Years after the expulsion, star-crossed lovers eventually reconnected in St Martinville under the Evangeline Oak (p227) – at least according to one version. You may get to ask some of the spirits what exactly happened in times past if you stay at the reputedly haunted Myrtle's Plantation (p223) in St Francisville.

ALLONS DANCER

'A two-step partner and a Cajun beat; when it lifts me up I'm gonna find my feet…' At dance hall-restaurants and clubs across the region, you'll certainly hear all the toe-tapping Cajun favorites you know, *oh-me-oh-my-oh*. But here you also have the opportunity to listen to an extraordinary range of rhythms that has grown out of one French-speaking root. Search out soulful zydeco sounds (see p36)at either Slim's Y-Ki-Ki (p231) or the Zydeco Hall of Fame (p231) in Opelousas. Bop to swamp pop at the Atchafalaya Club (p227) in Henderson. And, if you're lucky, you'll hear the 'real French' old-timers croon on Saturday radio broadcasts at Fred's Lounge (p231) in Mamou and Liberty Theater (p231) in Eunice. When you just gotta 'dance to a band from a-Lou'sian tonight,' family-friendly Mulate's (p226) in Breaux Bridge and Randol's in Lafayette (p225) are excellent places to do just that – nightly. So, *allons dancer, Colinda; allons dancer…*

RIVER ROAD

Today River Road is a study in contrasts: graceful antebellum mansions and elaborate gardens alternate with industrial sites, shanties and sugarcane fields. You can hardly see the river past the tall levees the Army Corps of Engineers has built and rebuilt over the years. Still, peering down an alleyway of oaks, it's entirely possible to imagine times long past, making this a trip well worth taking.

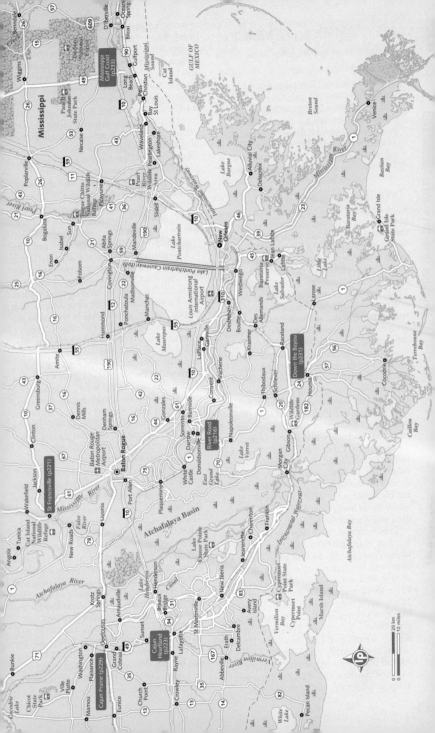

TRANSPORTATION: RIVER ROAD

Direction **100 miles northwest of New Orleans**

Travel Time **Six hours with stops**

Car **Take I-10 west to I-310, exit at Destrehan and follow River Road (alternately called Hwy 44) northwest from there. Don't despair if you're still on the road at 6pm and have 8pm dinner reservations in New Orleans. Even the distant upriver plantations are only a little over a one-hour drive from the city if you hop back on I-10. Note that crossings are not all that numerous on this part of the Mississippi River.**

This land was entirely agricultural back when it took two days to get from New Orleans to Baton Rouge by carriage, and the river was the main artery of trade. Plantation holdings lined both banks of the Mississippi, fanning out in triangles that narrowed at the river so that more properties gained precious river access. The first homes to be built, in the late 1700s and early 1800s, were relatively modest affairs – simple Franco-Creole raised cottages with large verandas and less than a thousand acres of land. Throughout the French colonial stewardship, rice and indigo were the principal plantation crops. In 1795 the introduction of the open-kettle process meant sugar could be reduced to easily transportable crystals. The USA absorbed the region in the 1803 Louisiana Purchase and sugarcane subsequently became king. Planters making oodles of money competed to build each over-the-top Greek-revival mansion more elaborate than the next. On the eve of the Civil War in 1861, Louisiana had 1200 plantations, many of which managed more than 100,000 acres. All were built and farmed on the back of slave labor. Out behind the big house were whole villages of cabins, where slaves lived, tended the fires, boiled the cane and worked the fields.

Things changed a bit after the war. Following the Confederate loss, less than 200 plantations remained. Blacks and whites alike left in droves, heading north and west in search of jobs. Restoration and conservation of the River Road mansions didn't start until the 1920s, but it hasn't abated since. Challenges like 2008's Hurricane Gustav have kept preservationists on their toes. Today you can visit a small sampling of what once was. Historic house tours usually take about an hour or so, and sometimes require reservations. You won't be able to see all the ones listed here in a day, so plan your timing accordingly.

Note that River Road is actually two roads lining the west and the east banks of the Mississippi River. Looking at a map, the east bank is the area above the river, the west bank is the area below the river. 'Downriver' means heading southeast, as the river flows toward New Orleans. 'Upriver' means northwest, against the river's flow toward Baton Rouge. River Road has various route names along the way, yet few of the towns you pass through will display any signage to indicate the change in route numbers. Sound confusing? It's not – just follow the sinuous levees.

Start your day at the oldest plantation home remaining in the lower Mississippi Valley, Destrehan Plantation (☎ 985-764-9315; www.destrehanplantation.org; 13034 Hwy 48, Destrehan; adult/child $15/5; ⌚ 9:30am-4pm), only 12 miles from New Orleans International Airport. Indigo was the principal crop in 1787 when Antoine Robert Robin DeLongy commissioned the original French colonial–style mansion, using *bousillage* (mud- and straw-filled) walls supported by cypress timbers. The house features a distinctive African-style hipped roof, no doubt a tip of the hat to the builder's ancestry. When DeLongy's daughter, Celeste, married Jean Noel Destrehan, they added the present Greek-revival facade. Costumed docents lead tours through the graceful home where the pirate Jean Lafitte was once a guest (no treasure found so far). On alternating days you can learn about making *bousillage*, cooking in a hearth and African American herbal remedies, but a highlight is seeing the historical-documents room that contains original Louisiana Purchase–era artifacts.

Destrehan looks plain-Jane in comparison to the next stop – the candy-colored 'steamboat Gothic-style' San Francisco Plantation (☎ 985-535-2341; www.sanfranciscoplantation.org; Hwy 44, Garyville; adult/student $15/7; ⌚ 9:30am-4pm), 21 miles upriver. The 1700-acre site was purchased in 1830 by Edmond B Marmillion from Elisee Rillieux, a free person of color. With $100,000 and 100 slaves, Marmillion's son, Valsin, built a grand sugar plantation. Today only the architectural confection of the 1856 house and metal-domed cisterns remain. Inside, the faux marbling and hand-painting techniques attest to the fact that no expense was spared.

West of Garyville (before Lutcher) you'll want to cross over the river bridge for the must-see Laura Plantation (☎ 225-265-7690; www.lauraplantation.com; 2247 Hwy 18, Vacherie; adult/student $15/5; ⌚ 10am-4pm) at Vacherie on the west bank. The West Indies–style plantation house was built in 1805 by Guillaume Duparc and named for his granddaughter, Laura Locoul. It stands apart not because of the simple, bright-yellow facade but because the historical tours are the best on the river. More than 5000 pages of plantation documents, including Laura's diary, were used to inform the tours that focus on the plantation life of women, children and slaves. More than 12 buildings – slave cabins, barns, sugar-processing stations and the like – still stand, making this one of the more complete plantations around. Tragically, a 2004 fire damaged a large portion of the main house, but it has been totally reconstructed and the story remains fascinating.

Hungry yet? You must be, after all that walking back in history. Good thing Oak Alley Plantation (☎ 225-265-2151; www.oakalleyplantation.com; 3645 Hwy 18, Vacherie; adult/student $15/7.50; ☽ 9am-5pm), just three miles upriver of Laura Plantation, has a breakfast and lunch restaurant (mains $5 to $15). A quarter-mile canopy of majestic live oaks makes for a dramatic approach to the house. The trees predate the house by 100 years. More symmetry awaits at the Greek-revival plantation house: 28 columns, each 8ft in diameter, frame the scene. Anne Rice fans will recognize this as Louis' home from the 1993 *Interview with a Vampire* movie. This property is more commercialized than most (costumed staff sells mint juleps from a souvenir table at the end of the tour), but you can spend the night here.

If you're not in a hurry, the tiny little town of Donaldsonville, 24 miles upriver, is an even better place for a meal. It's also home to the small River Road African American Museum (☎ 225-474-5553; www.africanamericanmuseum.org; 406 Charles St; admission $4; ☽ 10am-5pm Wed-Sat, 1-5pm Sun). Kathe Hambrick, a local African American woman, started the museum after visiting a plantation and deciding that someone needed to better tell the stories of the slaves. The growing exhibits detail the history of the rural blacks of Louisiana. The emphasis is not only on slavery, but also on the achievements of black doctors, artists and others throughout history. While in town, don't miss Rossie's Custom Framing (☎ 225-473-8536; www.alvinbatiste.com; 510 Railroad Ave; ☽ 9am-5pm Mon-Sat, 10am-3pm Sun), where the works of acclaimed folk artist Alvin Batiste are displayed and sold. His colorful interpretations of life in his hometown will take your breath away. Some afternoons he sets up his easel in the shop's window, watching the street life passing by.

Thirteen miles northwest of Donaldsonville, past White Castle, Nottoway Plantation (☎ 225-545-2730; www.nottoway.com; Hwy 1, White

RESTORING HISTORY

When Louisiana-born antique collector Marion Rundell bought the 7500-sq-ft Bocage Plantation (www.lebocage .com; Hwy 942) in 2008, it was a bit of a lark. He didn't necessarily think his bid of roughly half the asking price for the 110-acre property would be accepted. It was. And the work began. 'The first day I walked in, it was wet – wet. Water was dripping from the ceiling,' says Rundell. 'Is this what I was expecting? Are you kidding?'

Bocage first shows up on historical records in 1801, when Marius Pons Bringier bought the property and built a Creole cottage for his daughter, Francoise, and her husband, Christoph Colomb – a French descendent of Christopher Columbus. The house burnt and was rebuilt around 1835, but that's about all we know for sure. The plantation stood abandoned in the 1940s, when Anita Crozat and her husband, Dr Edwin Kohlsdorf, bought and salvaged it. By the time Rundell purchased the property, the house had again been uninhabited for a number of years. Many of the changes made mid-20th century had to be redone. But how do you go about faithfully restoring a home when you have no record to go by?

'We had the blueprints from what was there originally, but no furniture, no history, no nothing.' So Rundell and his consultants found clues where they could. A paint chip uncovered when stripping the facade lead to the yellow exterior. When the decorations on the rear doors resembled interior designs, they enclosed the loggia. 'You could probably make the call either way on that one, but at least now the porch is preserved.'

Speculation is that rather than remodeling the 1801 Creole cottage after the fire, the owners built an entirely new structure in front of it. Details of the existing Greek-revival structure are reminiscent of those architect James Dakin used in the Old State Capitol in Baton Rouge. Thus, Rundell chose to augment the plaster medallions and moldings that remained based on *Beauties of Modern Architecture* (1835), by Minard leFevre, a book that Dakin helped illustrate. As if to make up for the lack of historic record to-date, Rundell has documented even the smallest steps in the process. 'I may write a book about restoring a plantation someday,' he says. And what's his advice for anyone else thinking of undertaking such a project? 'Know what you're doing...'

At the time of writing, plans are to open Bocage Plantation for tours in the near future.

DETOUR: JOE'S DREYFUS STORE

Thirty miles west of Baton Rouge, the tiny town of Livonia has one claim to fame – people from all over Louisiana head there to eat at Joe's Dreyfus Store (☎ 225-637-2625; mains $8-15; ☻ 11am-2pm & 5-9pm Mon-Fri, to 10pm Sat, to 3pm Sun). You can still see the old display shelves and apothecary bottles from when the place was a mercantile store in the 1920s. Today customers sit beneath the slow-whirling fans and exposed beams enjoying sublime crab bisque and fresh bread. Even the salad dressings are homemade. Long-time staff members are part of the charm that keeps locals coming back.

Castle; adult/child $15/6; ☻ 9am-4pm) is known for its sheer size. The 64 rooms cover a whopping 53,000 sq ft that includes 22 columns and 200 windows. Renowned New Orleans architect Henry Howard designed the three-story Italianate–Greek-revival mansion for Virginian sugar planter John Hampton Randolph. Constructed from 1849 to 1859, it took four years to cut and dry the cypress framing timbers alone. The circular all-white ballroom, with impressively detailed plasterwork, is perhaps the finest room in the house (and quite in-demand as a wedding venue). After Hurricane Gustav, a multimillion-dollar renovation was completed in 2009. Guides don't wear costumes and don't deliver any drama, yet the tours are rich in the personal family history of the first owners. Stay overnight in one of the rooms within the mansion and you may get a more personal introduction to a Randolph family member: some guests have reported seeing a red-haired apparition that fits the description of the original owner's youngest daughter, Julia Marceline.

Unless the White Castle ferry (closed at this writing) reopens, you have to travel up-river 10 miles to Plaquemine to experience a traditional river crossing. The Louisiana Department of Transportation operates five Mississippi River ferries. The Plaquemine-Sunshine ferry (crossing $1, on the half-hour 5am to 9pm) can transport 35 cars, but historically they held far fewer.

In the 1940s members of the same Crozat family that salvaged Bocage Plantation (see boxed text, p219) also purchased Houmas House (☎ 225-473-9380; www.houmashouse.com; 40136 Hwy 942, Darrow; admission $20; ☻ 9am-5pm Mon & Tue, 9am-5pm Wed-Sun), 2 miles downriver. The original structure, built in the 1790s, now forms the back

end of the main Greek-revival house, built in 1840. In its heyday, this plantation controlled 150,000 acres of sugarcane, covering towns of today up to 8 miles away. Most of the furnishings are not original to the house, but the current owner (and resident), Kevin Kelly, has collected some fine period antiques to fill in. Check out the fascinating 1800s map of plantation plats found in the house. As you tour the wonderfully landscaped gardens, keep a look out for decedents of Princess Grace and King Sam Kelly, the yellow labs that were 'married' here in grand ceremony (and grander party) in 2003. A fine experience is to be had dining by candlelight in the 1790s rooms, now Latil's Landing (below) restaurant.

Before you head back to the city, stop at the rustic antique, craft and coffee shops of Cajun Village (☎ 225-675-5572; cnr Hwys 22 & 70, Sorrento; ☻ 9am-6pm Tue-Sun). The buildings are all old Creole shacks that have been moved here from around the region. Down the road you might notice the 1963 Sunshine Bridge, unexceptional except for the fact that it was named by Governor Jimmie Davis who rode to electoral success singing campaign songs he wrote. Ever heard 'You Are My Sunshine?'

Information

Ascension Parish Tourist Center (☎ 225-675-6550; cnr Hwys 22 & 70, Sorrento; ☻ 9am-5pm) Near I-10, off exit 182, this center has tons of info on River Road and beyond.

Eating & Drinking

In addition to Grapevine and LaFourche, Donaldsonville has a couple of small cafes on Railroad Ave.

Grapevine Cafe (☎ 225-473-8463; 211 Railroad Ave, Donaldsonville; mains $12-20; ☻ 11am-2:30pm & 5-9:30pm Tue-Fri, 11am-9:30pm Sat, 11am-2:30pm Sun) When the white-chocolate bread pudding tastes like a cloud, you have good reason to start with dessert first. But you shouldn't miss chef Cynthia Schneider's other dishes, like crawfish étouffée served in a pastry shell, or on top of polenta-like cornbread. Brunch is especially good.

Latil's Landing (☎ 225-473-9380; Houmas House, 40136 Hwy 942, Darrow; mains $26-36; ☻ 6-10pm Wed-Sat, 2-9pm Sun) This exquisite little eatery occupies rooms of the original 1700s home, where dishes like bisque of curried pumpkin and crawfish, and Creole lobster risotto are served on Limoges reproductions of the plantation's original china. You dine like a sugar baron could have only dreamed thanks to modern transport and fusion cooking. Chef Jeremy Langlois' seven-course tasting menu can be paired with selections from the plantation's historic cellars.

Cajun Village Coffee House (☎ 225-675-8068; cnr Hwys 22 & 70, Sorrento; mains $3-7; ❧ 6am-6pm) Sure they serve full Louisiana breakfasts and plate lunches, but it's the beignets filled with sweet and savory toppings that are the real highlight at this self-service cottage restaurant. Opt for strawberry-and-cream stuffing or spice it up with shrimp in the middle of your fried dough puff.

Cabin Restaurant (☎ 225-473-3007; cnr Hwys 44 & 22, Burnside; mains $8-16; ❧ 11am-9pm Tue-Sat, to 6pm Sun, to 3pm Mon) Two miles from River Road, this rustic old joint occupies a collection of slave dwellings and other dependencies rescued from the demolished Monroe, Welham and Helvetia plantations. The interior walls are papered with old newspapers in the same manner that slaves once insulated their rough-sawn cabin walls. Besides po'boys you can get dishes like red beans and rice with sausage. The restaurant is totally geared to serving tourist crowds, but the gumbo is pretty good.

Hymel's Seafood (☎ 225-562-7031; 8740 Hwy 44, Convent; mains $6-11; ❧ 11am-2:30pm Tue-Thu, to 10pm Fri & Sat, to 8pm Sun) A local favorite for more than 40 years, this former filling station packs in the patrons. A platter of soft-shell crab or turtle sauce piquant (a stew) might be among the weekday lunch specials. It's 4 miles downriver from the Sunshine Bridge.

Cafe LaFourche (☎ 225-473-7451; 817 Bayou Rd, Donaldsonville; mains $13-22; ❧ 10am-2pm & 5-10pm Tue-Fri, 4:30-10pm Sat, 11am-2pm Sun) Steaks, seafood and Cajun dishes are all part of the comprehensive menu offerings here. Out the window you can watch the bayou flow by, and hope you spot the restaurant's two 'friendly' alligator neighbors.

First & Last Chance Café (☎ 225-473-8236; 812 Railroad Ave, Donaldsonville; ❧ 9am-midnight Mon-Sat) This trackside joint was once the only place to grab a drink on the rail trip from New Orleans to Baton Rouge.

Sleeping

Nottoway Plantation (☎ 225-545-2730; www.nottoway .com; Hwy 1, White Castle; r $175-245, ste $295-310, all incl breakfast; ✗) Fifteen-foot ceilings and four-tier crown moldings are just some of the details to expect if you stay in one of the 2nd- or 3rd-floor mansion rooms. Whether you sleep

there, in the slightly less luxurious wing rooms or in the overseer's cottage, a welcome beverage and free house tour greet you on arrival. Note that if you opt for one of the mansion's two-room suites (some with original furnishings), you cannot check in until 5pm – your room is on the house tour.

Oak Alley Plantation (☎ 225-265-2151; www.oakalley plantation.com; 3645 Hwy 18, Vacherie; 1br cottages $130-165, 2br cottages $150-175, all incl breakfast; ✗) Lodgings at this plantation are not in the main house (tour extra) but in several 18th- and 19th-century cottages on the gorgeous grounds. Each combines well-heeled antiques with modern bathrooms and kitchens. Romance packages and pre-arranged dinner delivery available.

Bittersweet Plantation Bed & Breakfast (☎ 225-473-1232; www.jfolse.com/lafittes; 404 Claiborne Ave, Donaldsonville; r incl breakfast $250; ✗) Bittersweet was under renovation while we were writing. Whenever it reopens, staying in the antique-filled suites with whirlpool tubs come second to the opportunity to eat chef John Folse's sumptuous three-course breakfast. He literally wrote the book on Cajun and Creole cuisine (several of them, actually).

ST FRANCISVILLE

Tranquil St Francisville retains nearly 150 of its original 18th- and 19th-century houses and buildings. That includes the lodging place of the town's most famous (temporary) resident, John James Audubon, who lived a few months at Oakley Plantation. He returned frequently to sketch avian species in the surrounding woodlands for his *Birds of America*. For those interested in architecture, antiques, birding and B&Bs, St Francisville makes a fine trip. You could easily extend your River Road (p216) tour and overnight at a St Francisville B&B, 45 miles north of Plaquemine. Unless you need a cheap chain motel, there's not much reason to stop in Baton Rouge.

Right away you'll notice a difference in the bluff-and-forest ecosystem here compared to

TRANSPORTATION: ST FRANCISVILLE

Direction 113 miles northwest of New Orleans

Travel time Two hours

Car Follow I-10 west from town to Baton Rouge. Take US 110 and Hwy 61 north from there.

the swampy lowlands to the south. The Spanish Capuchin monks noted it in the 1700s, too. They found the highland to be a more suitable burial ground than the area around their home in Pointe Coupee Parish, and soon the area took on the name of the monks' patron saint, St Francis. Later, northern British loyalists settled here to escape the Revolutionary War, giving the area a decidedly Anglo (as opposed to French) influence. This area was not part of the 1803 Louisiana Purchase – it stayed with Spanish-controlled Florida territory until 1810. Cotton plantations sprang up from the 1800s into the early 1900s, followed by the town. Today the historic district buildings line up along Ferdinand St (Hwy 10), as well as Johnson, Prosperity and Fidelity Sts, all of which run perpendicular to Ferdinand as it heads to the river and the ferry dock. Pick up a walking-tour brochure at the information center (right). As long as you're wandering around, you might want to pop into some of the shops and galleries on Ferdinand St, and its extension, Commerce St.

Outside of town is Oakley Plantation & Audubon State Historic Site (☎ 225-342-8111; www.crt.state.la.us; 11788 Hwy 965; admission $2; ☼ 9am-5pm), where John James Audubon spent his tenure, arriving in 1821 to tutor the owner's daughter. Though his assignment lasted only four months (and his room was pretty darn spartan), he and his assistant finished 32 paintings of birds found in the plantation's surrounding forest. Furnishing of the small West Indies–influenced house (1806) include several original Audubon prints. Look for Gus the turkey wandering the 100-acre grounds, which include a lovely herb and vegetable garden, two slave cabins, a working kitchen and a barn. The ½-mile wooded Cardinal Trail is great for bird watching. Hundreds of species are visible throughout the year (pick up a bird list at the information center) but spring and fall are best for migrating song birds.

Every April, the Historic Site sponsors ecology exhibits in conjunction with the Audubon Country Birdfest (www.audubonbirdfest.com), which also includes birding tours to private properties. The Audubon Pilgrimage (www.audubonpilgrimage.info), the third weekend in March, is a townwide affair celebrating the artist's memory. Proceeds from the candlelight walking tours, private-home tours, receptions and dance benefit the historical society.

During the Pilgrimage, costumed docents guide special tours at Rosedown Plantation Historic Site (☎ 225-635-3332; www.crt.state.la.us; 12501 Hwy 10; adult/student $10/4; ☼ 9am-5pm), but you can also visit year-round. Daniel and Martha Turnbull's 1835 plantation house still contains many original mid-19th century furnishings. The formal gardens have been meticulously restored based on Margaret's garden diaries. Be warned: Rosedown is a major stop on the tour-bus circuit.

A little further off the beaten path, Butler Greenwood Plantation (☎ 225-635-6312; www.butler greenwood.com; 8345 Hwy 61; admission $5; ☼ 9am-5pm) offers a unique perspective in that it's never been sold out of the original family. Though still lived in, the formal Victorian parlor and its carved rosewood furniture are definitely museum quality. Fifty acres of gardens and grounds surround the main house, and small cottages off the pond are available for rent as B&B rooms (opposite).

If you enjoyed the alleys of oaks and manicured grounds at Butler Greenwood, you'll go gaga for the 250-acre Afton Villa Gardens (☎ 225-721-2269; www.aftonvilla.com; 9047 Hwy 61; adult/child $5/free; ☼ 9am-5pm Mar-Jun & Oct-Dec). The mansion itself burned down in 1963, but the ruins only add to the lush atmosphere. In springtime (especially April), the hundreds of azaleas lining the paths bloom brilliantly and the valley of daffodils becomes a sea of yellow.

Leaving town, you can head to New Orleans back the way you came or take the St Francisville ferry (crossing $1, 5am to 9pm) and drive south to I-10 with occasional river views through New Roads. At the time of writing, the ferry is one of five operating across the Mississippi River in Louisiana. Cruise while you can. Construction was underway on all 1583ft of the shiny new John James Audubon Bridge that will eventually replace the aging boat transport, expected to finish some time in late 2010.

Information

West Feliciana Historical Society Tourist Information (☎ 225-635-6330; www.stfrancisville.us; 11757 Ferdinand St; ☼ 9am-5pm) Information, gift shop and historical displays.

Eating & Drinking

Though there are a few places to eat, restaurants are not the highlight of the town.

Magnolia Cafe (☎ 225-635-6528; 5687 Commerce St; sandwiches $7-10, mains $12-20; ☼ 11am-4pm Sun-Wed,

DETOUR: CAT ISLAND

A little further than 7 miles northwest of St Francisville, you can stalk the largest North American bald cypress tree at Cat Island National Wildlife Refuge (☎ 601-442-6696; www.fws.gov/catisland; off Old Airport Rd; admission free; ☼ dawn-dusk) – so long as the Mississippi River is below 19-ft flood stage at Baton Rouge; the park is usually under water from January through June. This impressive tree stands 83ft tall with a circumference of 56ft, and may be about 1000 years old. It's hard to tell exactly, because as bald cypress age, their core hollows out. That's great for swampland creatures who need a new home, but not so helpful for scientists studying tree rings. 'Knees' of a cypress, the woody projections that jut up from the roots, usually rise a foot or two above the swamp floor – many of the ones here stand taller than a man, so it's definitely been around for a while.

to 9pm Thu-Sat) A colorful old house serves as the backdrop for fresh salads and sandwiches; try the spicy shrimp po'boy. Daily specials include Louisiana dishes. Live music some Friday and Saturday evenings.

Carriage House Restaurant (☎ 225-635-6278; Myrtles Plantation, 7747 Hwy 61; mains lunch $8-10, dinner $14-22; ☼ 11am-2pm & 5-9pm Wed-Sat & Mon, 11am-2pm Sun) Standard Louisiana fare is offered in a plantation setting. Eat out in the courtyard or in the Myrtle's former carriage house, which dresses up for dinner with white table cloths and starched napkins.

Birdman Coffee & Books (☎ 225-635-5446; 5695 Commerce St; ☼ 8am-6pm; ☎) Don't plan on lingering over homemade cookies and wi-fi first thing; this coffee shop is busy, busy in the morning. Come back in the afternoon and peruse the few used books at a more leisurely pace.

Wine Parlor (☎ 225-635-6502; 5720 Commerce St; ☼ 6:30-9pm) Enjoy any of 200 wines out in the courtyard or on the Victorian settees in the parlor of the St Francisville Inn.

Sleeping

St Francisville has a whole host of historic lodgings. If those listed here are occupied, check out www.stfrancisville.us.

3-V Tourist Court (☎ 225-635-5540; 5689 Commerce Street; r $75) Remember Model Ts and Bonnie & Clyde? No? Well, these 1920s motor court cabins might. Simple rooms with kitchenettes and small bathrooms are clean and well lit. Walk across the gravel drive and you're at Magnolia Cafe; the rest of the old town is just beyond.

Butler Greenwood Plantation (☎ 225-635-6312; www.butlergreenwood.com; 8345 Hwy 61; 1/2br ste incl breakfast $135/245; ☒ ☎) Stay in a 1796 plantation kitchen, in an enclosed hexagonal gazebo with stained-glass windows or in a three-story windmill. All eight of the one- and two-bedroom cottages on the grounds

of Butler Greenwood are unique. Each has a full kitchen and most have Jacuzzi tubs in addition to homey antiques and floral accents.

Myrtles Plantation B&B (☎ 225-635-6277; www.myrtlesplantation.com; 7747 Hwy 61; r incl breakfast $135-230) Many of the guests that come to stay at the Myrtles Plantation are looking for those who never left. Owners and docents alike perpetuate the idea that Myrtles is one of the 'most haunted houses in America.' (Mystery tours are offered Friday and Saturday evening.) Most of the B&B rooms are in the main house (c 1796) so you have a good chance of spotting a specter among the Carrera marble mantels and gold-leaf furnishings. Floating orbs have even been photographed in the Carriage House restaurant courtyard.

St Francisville Inn (☎ 225-635-6502, 800-488-6502; www.stfrancisvilleinn.com; 5720 Commerce St; s $90-105, d $100-115, all incl breakfast; ☒ ☎ ☒) The 1880s house that forms the core of St Francisville Inn is over-the-top Victorian, lacey gingerbread woodwork and all. The 10 guest rooms are a bit more subdued, but might still seem stuffy and old-fashioned to some. The attraction here is the lovely courtyard and pool, a sumptuous breakfast and an in-town, walking-distance-to-all location. Restaurant on-site.

CAJUN HEARTLAND

When you tire of silver service and rich Creole sauces and start to crave something spicier, head west from New Orleans and River Road. Oh sure, you get a hint of Cajun in the Big Easy, but it's here in the heartland around Lafayette that the down-to-earth culture really lives. This is the land of French-speaking farmers and fishers, of Cajun dance halls and crawfish boils. Here the roux are darker and more earthy, and much of the seafood is fried. Think of the Cajuns as the country cousins of their uptown New Orleans neighbors. Even if the setting is not as fancy, food is still serious business round here. Ask just about anyone for a restaurant recommendation, and not only will they have a strong opinion, they'll know the extended family history behind a place. Seven nights a week you have your choice of live bands at local eateries, and on weekends you can hop from one to the next without giving your twinkling toes a break. A Cajun music breakfast or brunch can be a highlight of any visit; don't skip it, even if you're staying at one of the area's wonderful B&Bs.

Cajun began because of *le Grand Dérangement*, the British expulsion of the rural French settlers from L'Acadie (now Nova Scotia) in 1755. A homeless population of Acadians searched for decades for a place to settle until seven boatloads of exiles arrived in New Orleans in 1785. The settlers spread out into the Louisiana countryside and mixed with early German peasant farmers, Isleños (Canary Islanders) and Americans. By the early 19th century some 3000 to 4000 Acadians, or Cajuns as they became known, lived in southern Louisiana. Some occupied the swamplands, where they eked out a living based on fishing and trapping, while others farmed rice.

Today Lafayette is the self-proclaimed capital of French Louisiana. (Though the patois they speak is sometimes hard to relate to the mother tongue, the region has the largest French-speaking minority in the USA.) Each of the little surrounding towns has its own claim to fame – Abbeville oysters, Breaux Bridge dance halls, New Iberia hot sauce… The heartland encompasses four parishes: Lafayette, St Martin, Iberia and Vermillion. Much of the area is beyond the reach of a traditional day trip, but the sights, sounds and smells of the region are plenty to draw you away from New Orleans for two or three days. You can find weekly live band listings for the region in the *Times of Acadiana* (www.timesofacadiana.com) newspaper and in the Patsy Report (www.thepatsyreport.arnb.org) online.

TRANSPORTATION: CAJUN HEARTLAND

Distance 175 miles northwest to Lafayette

Travel Time 2½ hours

Car Follow I-10 west all the way from New Orleans.

LAFAYETTE

By far the largest city in the region, sprawling Lafayette (population 259,000) is lacking in some of the quiet charm the neighboring towns and rural Cajun communities possess. There are a few interesting living-history parks here. And you'll not want for something to eat: the city has one of the highest concentrations of restaurants per capita in the nation. Lafayette is not known as the 'Hub City' for nothing – many towns in the region are indeed equidistant from here. You could certainly use this as your base for explorations (though we prefer Breaux Bridge, opposite). I-10 defines the north side of town; Hwy 90 (aka Evangeline Thruway) runs north–south bisecting it.

Part of the multisite Jean Lafitte National Park, the Acadian Cultural Center (☎ 337-232-0789; www.nps.gov; 501 Fisher Rd; admission free; ☺ 8am-5pm) is a good place to test the Cajun waters. Interpretive exhibits highlight the history and traditions of the Acadians (a highlight is the Cajun joke-telling booth). Rangers lead narrated boat rides describing the life of trappers and traders.

At Vermilionville (☎ 337-233-4077; www.vermilionville.org; 300 Fisher Rd; adult/student $8/6.50; ☺ 10am-4pm Tue-Sun) costumed guides attempt to bring that history to life by taking you through a 19th-century Cajun village. Among the 18 buildings are homes dating from 1795 to 1860. Bands perform in the barn, there are cooking demonstrations, and in spring and fall you can take boat tours on the bayou. It's all a bit corny, but entertaining. And the board behind the village is committed to preserving the cultural and natural resources of Bayou Vermilionville.

Less flashy is Acadian Village (☎ 337-981-2364; www.acadianvillage.org; 200 Greenleaf Dr; adult/student $7/4; ☺ 10am-4pm), where you follow a brick path around a rippling bayou to restored houses, craftsman barns and a church. If you're lucky enough to be there on a day when Mr Manville is minding the school house, be sure to sit a spell. The octogenarian shares stories of his childhood, plays a tune on his fiddle, tells a joke or two and kisses the ladies' hands – always the Cajun gentleman.

You could hit one, or all, of the historic sights in a day before you step out that night to dinner and dancing at Prejean's (opposite) or Blue Dog Cafe (opposite). The storefront Jefferson Street Market (☎ 337-233-2589; 538 Jefferson St; ☺ 10am-5pm Mon-Fri, 11am-4pm Sat), downtown, has arts and antiques vendors, as well as a health-food store and take-away.

DETOUR: FROG CAPITAL USA

The tourist board likes to say the little town of Rayne, 20 miles west of Lafayette, is the 'Frog Capital of the World.' What with a Frog Festival on Labor Day weekend (think frog-jumping contests) and a bevy of frog-themed murals around town, we'll concede it's at least the froggiest town in the USA. The wet rice fields around Rayne are ideal aquatic habitats. Locals started shipping the high-hopping amphibians to New Orleans restaurants in the 1890s; by 1946 they were being exported as far as France. Exports have since ceased, but you can still try fried frog legs at Chef Roy's Frog City Cafe (☎ 337-334-7913; 1131 Church Point Hwy; mains $12-16; ☷ 11am-10pm Tue-Sat, to 2pm Sun).

Information

Lafayette Visitor Center (☎ 318-232-3737, 800-346-1958; www.lafayette.travel; 1400 NW Evangeline Thruway; ☷ 8:30am-5pm Mon-Fri, from 9am Sat & Sun) Pick up one of the seasonal Bon Temps guides, which has up-to-date information on the whole Cajun heartland.

Eating

Entertainment almost always goes with eating in Lafayette, which is good for families especially; restaurant-dance halls are nonsmoking and all ages are welcome.

Prejean's Cajun Dining (☎ 337-896-3247; www.prejeans.com; 3480 I-49 N; dinner mains $11-20; ☷ 7am-10pm) Live music accompanies every dinner and weekend brunches (old-timer Gervais Matte is a regular), but food takes center stage here. Have crawfish omelets for breakfast, fried oyster salad for lunch, and lump crab and eggplant Abbeville (in a Worcestershire cream sauce) for dinner. Don't forget to say hi to Big Al, the 14ft stuffed alligator, on your way in.

Blue Dog Cafe (☎ 337-237-0005; 1211 W Pinhook Rd; www.bluedogcafe.com; mains lunch $8-12, dinner $12-22, brunch $23; ☷ 11am-2pm & 5-10pm Mon-Fri, 5-10pm Sat, 10:30am-2pm Sun) Make reservations if you hope to enjoy the live jazz and Cajun music brunch; any given Sunday, the line stretches out the door by 10:30am. Shrimp Rockefeller soup, pork grillades (thin, browned strips with gravy) and cornbread dressing are just some of the reasons why. Louisiana native artist (and restaurant co-owner) George Rodrigue displays more than 150 of his works here, including many incarnations of his Blue Dog. Live music Thursday through Saturday evenings.

Randol's (☎ 337-981-7080; 2320 Kaliste Saloom Rd; mains $13-21; ☷ 5-10pm Sun-Thu, to 11pm Fri & Sat) Dishes like crab cake au gratin are quite tasty, but the nightly live Cajun tunes are the why-go. Regulars are always here scooting around the floor; sit on the bench around the dance floor (separated from the tables by some awkward plexiglass) and you will be asked out onto the floor.

Old Tyme Grocery (☎ 337-235-8165; 218 W St Mary St; meals $5-9; ☷ 8am-10pm Mon-Fri, 9am-7pm Sat) For shrimp or roast-beef po'boys at lunch or dinner, this no-frills joint is heralded as the best in town. In summer, swing round the back for a refreshing ice-cream treat.

Creole Lunch House (☎ 337-232-9929; 713 12th St; mains $5-10; ☷ 11am-2pm Mon-Fri) Sausage-stuffed bread is what this little lunch house (literally, a house) is known for. Two slices make a meal, but you might also try the specials like chicken fricassee.

Sleeping

Chain motels and hotels crowd Hwy 90, south of the intersection with I-10.

T'Frere's B&B (☎ 337-984-9347, 800-984-9347; www.tfreres.com; 1905 E Verot School Rd; s/d incl breakfast $105/130; ☒) Maugie Pastor's family has been in the restaurant business for generations. You can tell by the dazzling Cajun Creole breakfasts that she serves (cookbooks available). Along with husband, Pat, and son, John, she runs the most welcoming B&B in the region. Sip a southern cocktail on the large veranda of the 1880 brick-and-cypress home before you retire to one of the six antique-and-lace guestrooms.

Juliet (☎ 337-261-2225; www.juliethotel.com; 800 Jefferson St, r from $140; ☷ ☒) Twenty upscale neutral rooms – with custom-made linens – occupy the former Le Parisienne department store in downtown Lafayette. Look for the lion's-head fountain gracing the curvaceous pool.

BREAUX BRIDGE

Nine miles east of Lafayette, the sign on the namesake drawbridge in downtown Breaux Bridge welcomes you to the 'Crawfish Capital,' a title bestowed on the town by the state legislature in 1959. Since then, the town of 7500 has hosted an annual Crawfish Festival

CAJUN COUNTRY CALENDAR

Central Louisiana's smaller towns seem to be in a constant state of celebration. A local festival – be it a church fair, a Christmas festival or a competitive gumbo cook-off – can provide great opportunities to rub shoulders with the locals and explore the state's regional specialties. For a full calendar with dates and details, check out the website of the Louisiana Association of Fairs & Festivals (www.laffnet.org).

February La Grande Boucherie, St Martinville; Courir de Mardi Gras, Mamou

March Crawfish Étouffée Cook-Off, Eunice

April Ponchatoula Strawberry Festival, Ponchatoula; Festival International de Louisiane, Lafayette

May Breaux Bridge Crawfish Festival, Breaux Bridge

July Greater Mandeville Seafood Festival, Mandeville; Catfish Festival, Des Allemands

August Delcambre Shrimp Festival, Delcambre

September Southwest Louisiana Zydeco Festival, Plaisance; Frog Festival, Lafayette; Louisiana Sugarcane Festival, New Iberia

October Andouille Festival, LaPlace; Yambilee, Opelousas; St Martinville Pepper Festival, St Martinville

(☎ 337-332-6655; www.bbcrawfest.com) each first complete weekend in May. Crawfish cook-offs, crawfish-eating contests (the record is 55.75lb in 45 minutes), crawfish royalty parades and even crawfish races fill the day. Cajun and zydeco bands play all day and well into the night. The rest of the year the town is fairly quiet, though on weekends the two main streets fill with treasure hunters and those walking off their brunch in the little old town. After you've seen the few art galleries and antique stores, there's not much to do here besides eat, listen to music, drink and eat some more before you head back to a cozy B&B or cabin. But what could be better?

La Poussiere (☎ 337-332-1721; 1301 Grandpoint Hwy; ☷ 7-11pm Sat, 3-7pm Sun) is one of the few Cajun clubs around here. It doesn't serve food, just drink and dance. Live bands play Saturday and Sunday – cover changes depending on who's playing.

Information

Bayou Teche Visitors Center (☎ 337-332-8500, 888-565-5939; 314 E Bridge St; ☷ 8am-4pm Mon-Fri, 10am-3pm Sat) Provides maps, B&B brochures and a lesson in listening to the local French patois from Miss Pris (pronounced pree). Mais of course, chère.

Eating

Cafe Des Amis (☎ 337-332-5273; 140 E Bridge St; breakfasts $4-11, mains $15-22; ☷ 11am-2pm Tue, 11am-9pm Wed & Thu, 7:30am-9pm Fri & Sat, 8:30am-2pm Sun) Well-known local restaurateur Dickie Breaux does things right at this long-time local fave in a 1920s

downtown storefront. The beignets are both crisp and light, and spicy barbecued shrimp never tasted so good. Friday mornings you can sit under the pressed-tin ceiling and hear French spoken by all the ol' boys who gather here. Saturday morning, the place is full to capacity for the zydeco breakfast featuring live bands.

Crazy 'Bout Crawfish (☎ 337-332-3071; 1905 Rees St; mains $8-18; ☷ 11am-9pm) A relative newcomer to the well-established scene, this wildly colored eatery is drawing raves from residents. Order your boiled mudbugs spiced a 'lil crazy' or 'X-crazy.' The fried fishes and crawfish maque choux (a sort of corn stew) are pretty good too.

Mulate's (☎ 337-332-4648; 325 Mills Ave; sandwiches $7-11, mains $13-18; ☷ 11am-10pm) Every night great Cajun bands draw dancers onto the much-used floor. Join in or just munch your fried seafood and watch. Sadly, owner 'Miss Goldie' passed in 2008 but her family carries on her welcoming tradition.

Poche's (☎ 337-332-2108; 3015-A Main Hwy; ☷ lunch counter 10am-2pm) This legendary local charcuterie (smoked-meat butcher) north of I-10 is a little hard to find, but that doesn't stop anyone. Poche's (po-shayz) specializes in boudin and cracklings, and serves daily cafeteria-style Cajun lunch specials. The grocery portion of the store opens from 6am to 6pm daily.

Sleeping

Maison Des Amis (☎ 337-332-5273; 140 E Bridge St; r incl breakfast $100-125; ☒ ☷) All four B&B rooms in this charming Creole cottage, which dates back to 1870, have their own private entrance. Antiques filling the rooms are tasteful and restrained (think comfy instead of stifling). The price includes breakfast at a downtown restaurant like Cafe Des Amis (no relation) and use of a guest kitchen. Owner off-site.

Bayou Cabins (☎ 337-332-6158; www.bayoucabins .com; 100 W Mills Ave; cabins $60-120; 🔊) Each of the 14 cabins on the Bayou Teche is completely individual. Cabin 1 has 1949 newspapers as wallpaper (aka insulation), cabin 7 has fine Victorian antiques and a claw-foot tub, and cabin 11 takes a retro look at the 1950s to '70s. Your full, hot breakfast is served at 9am and the on-site store sells homemade cracklings and boudin.

Isabelle Inn (☎ 337-412-0455; www.isabelleinn.com; 1130 Berard St; r incl breakfast $165; ✖ 🖥 🐾) Deep wall colors, fluffy robes and down featherbeds – plush is definitely the word for the expansive rooms in this 8000-sq-ft brick mansion. Relax on one of the porches or poolside in the garden. The grounds extend seven gorgeous acres on the bayou.

HENDERSON

On the Atchafalaya Basin, Henderson is the area's recreational resource for swamp tours, airboat rides and houseboat rentals. The basin water itself is out of sight unless you follow one of the business signs up from the levee road and over to a public landing to a restaurant or marina. Get information online and on the phone from **St Martin Parish Tourism** (☎ 888-565-5939; www.cajuncountry.org). The town itself, 8 miles east of Breaux Bridge, is not much to speak of. Keep going to the levee, 3 miles down off Hwy 352.

You can take a swamp tour, eat crawfish, listen to a jig and spend the night in a floating cabin at family-run **McGee's Landing** (☎ 337-228-2384; www.mcgeeslanding.com; 1337 Henderson Levee Rd; ⏰ 8am-10pm). Flat bottom boats leave daily at 10am, 1pm and 3pm for 1½-hour guided tours (adult/child $20/15) lead by local Cajun

characters. But this portion of the swamp – practically under the I-10 bridge – is hardly remote. You'll want to ask about the airboat tours (which go deeper, faster and noisier into the swamp) or the night trips. Saturday evening and Sunday noon live music plays in the cafe (mains $5 to $15). The rustic one-bedroom cabins are stationary houseboats of sorts, anchored to the dock on floating platforms. No room TVs or phones.

Pat's Fisherman's Wharf (☎ 337-228-7512; 1008 Henderson Levee Rd; sandwiches $7-10, mains $17-22; ⏰ 11am-9:30pm) has long been a reason people come to Henderson. Pat Huval (the town's first mayor) started selling crawfish from a shack in 1948 (at 40¢ a pound). Today the red-check-cloth tables of his family's restaurant parallel the water for a long way. Locals come to pile on the seafood, then shuffle the night away next door at the **Atchafalaya Club** (⏰ 8pm-late Fri & Sat, 6-10pm Sun). They host a great variety of Cajun bands; the Foret Tradition regularly belts out some mean swamp pop. At the end of the night you can waltz one more door down and check into **Pat's Edgewater Inn** (☎ 337-434-6182; r incl breakfast $65-90; 🔊). Rooms are pretty standard motel stuff, but the whole place is brand spankin' new, opened in 2009.

Houseboat Adventures (☎ 337-228-7484, 800-491-4662; www.houseboat-adventures.com; 1399 Henderson Levee Rd; two nights from $500) rents boats that sleep four to 10.

North of I-10, the humongous **Crawfish Town USA** (☎ 337-667-6148; 2815 Grandpoint Hwy; mains $13-21; ⏰ 11am-10pm), seating 300, is about as touristy as it gets, yet they consistently win awards for their crawfish.

ST MARTINVILLE

The little old town of St Martinville, 13 miles south of Breaux Bridge and 16 miles from Lafayette, is worthy of a couple of hours ambling about. The massive **Evangeline Oak**, poised along Bayou Teche just off Main St, has become a lodestar for those seeking a

---

DETOUR: ABBEVILLE

So close to Vermilion Bay and the Gulf, it's no wonder that Abbeville, 21 miles southwest of Lafayette, is known for oysters. Until recently, you could take your pick of three oyster-shucking restaurants within two blocks. At the time of writing, legendary Black's had been sold and remained empty. You can still suck 'em down in **Dupuy's Oyster House** (☎ 337-893-2336; 108 S Main St; sandwiches $7-9, mains $14-18; ⏰ 11am-2pm & 5-10pm Tue-Fri, 5-10pm Sat), first opened here in 1869, and at the newfangled **Shucks!** (☎ 337-898-3311; 701 W Port St; mains $9-17; ⏰ 11am-10pm Mon-Sat). Look up more information at the Vermilion Parish website: www.vermilion.org.

THE CAJUN BOUCHERIE

Before the advent of refrigeration, *boucheries* (communal pig butcherings) were regular events in the cooler months. As the fresh meat could not be kept for too long, families would gather together to slaughter a hog, prepare the meat and divide it up. Everyone pitched in – preparing seasonings, piping filling into the clean sausage casings, playing music and cooking the *gratons* (cracklings). The day ended with a plate of backbone stew, some fresh boudin rouge (blood sausage), music and an informal *fais do do* (house dance). Once a critical part of any Cajun community's culinary life, the Acadian *boucherie* is now less of a family affair than a large-scale festival. The most well-known celebration, La Grande Boucherie (www.cajuncountry.org), is held every February in the small town of St Martinville. The modern variation includes all the cooking, but otherwise resembles any area cultural festival. Most spectators just show up to eat, dance and toast a few beers to their friend the pig.

connection to the Acadians deposed during *le Grand Dérangement*. Thanks go in large part to Henry Wadsworth Longfellow's 1847 epic poem *Évangeline*, which recounts the story of star-crossed French lovers Evangeline and Gabriel. In 1907, local judge Felix Voorhees wrote *The True Story of Evangeline*, in which the lovers reunite under the fated tree. (Neither version is documented fact.)

To gain a deeper understanding of the events that compelled Longfellow to compose his ode and to grasp how African Americans have made this region their own, pay a visit to the Museum of the Acadian Memorial and the African American Museum, both inside the St Martinville Cultural Heritage Center (☎ 337-394-2258; 125 S New Market St; admission $3; ☼ 10am-4pm). The City of St Martinville Visitors Center (☎ 337-394-2233; www.stmartinville.org; 120 S Market St; ☼ 10:30am-4pm) offers guided and self-guided tours that take in these sights and the shady historic streets of the old town.

A mile north, Longfellow-Evangeline State Historical Site (☎ 337-394-3754; www.crt.state.la.us; 1200 N Main St; admission $2; ☼ 9am-5pm) contains further interpretive exhibits about the Acadians. Here you can tour a former sugar plantation, lush grounds with huge moss-draped trees, a narrow bayou's banks and a restored, raised Creole cottage (1815).

Every February the city celebrates its Cajun traditions at La Grande Boucherie (see boxed text, above).

NEW IBERIA

Settled by the Spanish in 1779, New Iberia prospered on the sugarcane of surrounding plantations. Today the town's best-known native son is mystery writer James Lee Burke, whose page-turning detective Dave Robicheaux novels take place in and around New Iberia. A stroll down Main St, past the

courthouse and Victor's Cafeteria, puts you squarely inside Robicheaux's world. You might even run into Burke, who still winters outside the town. Buy his works (signed copies often available) where the author kicks off book tours, at Books on the Teche (☎ 337-367-7621; 106 E Main St; ☼ 9:30am-5:30pm Mon-Sat). The tourist office (opposite) publishes a walking tour map (also online) of 'Dave's domain.'

Any walk around town should include a tour of Shadows on the Teche (☎ 337-365-5213; www .shadowsontheteche.org; 317 E Main St, New Iberia; adult/student $10/6.50; ☼ 9am-4:30pm Mon-Sat, noon-4pm Sun), a grand, Greek-revival plantation house set on the banks of the bayou. The home stayed in the Weeks family from construction in 1831 until it was willed to the National Society for Historic Preservation in 1958. More than 17,000 papers describing the most minute details of the house's history were left in the attic, making this one of the most well-documented historic plantations in Louisiana.

But New Iberia is not just for book worms and scholars. You can tour the oldest operating rice mill in the US and buy Cajun spice-and-rice packages at the Konriko Company Store & Conrad Rice Mill (☎ 337-367-6163; 309 Ann St; admission free; ☼ 9am-5pm). In a related vein, drive southwest of New Iberia along Hwy 329 through cane fields to Avery Island (admission $1), home of the McIlhenny Tabasco Factory (☎ 337-365-8173; www.tabasco .com; admission free; ☼ tours 9am-4pm) and a wildlife garden. The 'island' is actually a salt dome that extends 8 miles below the surface. The salt mined here goes into the sauce, as do locally grown peppers. The mixture ferments in oak barrels before it's mixed with vinegar, strained and bottled. At the factory gift shop, order a bag of the 'Tabasco dregs,' which are what remains from making the sauce, and you'll gain a fine seasoning mix and get a free tour to boot. The gift shop also has just about any Tabasco-imprinted item you can imagine.

In 1890 Tabasco founder EA McIlhenny also started a bird sanctuary on the island. At Jungle Gardens (☎ 337-365-8173; www.junglegarden.org; adult/child $6.25/4.50; ⏱ 9am-5pm) you can drive or walk through 250 acres of subtropical jungle flora and view an amazing array of water birds (especially snowy egrets, which nest here in astounding number), turtles and alligators. Watch for turtles and peacocks crossing the road.

Information

Iberia Parish Tourist Information (☎ 337-365-1540; www.iberiatravel.com; 2513 Hwy 14; ⏱ 9am-5pm) Website and tourist office have worthwhile coupons in addition to maps and info.

Eating

Lagniappe, Too (☎ 337-365-9419; 204 E Main St; mains $6-12; ⏱ 10am-2pm Mon-Thu, 10am-2pm & 6-9pm Fri, 6-9pm Sat) A historic Main St building, chalkboard specials, eyelet curtains – what a cute cafe. And yet there's nothing contrived about the food. These are the dishes a Cajun *grand-mère* might have made at home.

Victor's Cafeteria (☎ 337-369-9924; 109 E Main St; mains $5-14; ⏱ 6am-2pm Mon-Fri, to 10am Sat, 6:30am-2pm Sun) James Lee Burke's fictional detective Dave Robicheaux likes to drop by this place, and so do his fans. Line up at the counter to order favorites such as gumbo and fried shrimp, and home-style Cajun standards in this laid-back little landmark. Note the limited hours.

Yet more options:

Clementine Dining & Spirits (☎ 337-560-1007; 113 E Main St; mains $11-19; ⏱ 11am-2pm & 6-10pm Tue-Fri, 6-10pm Sat) Upscale Louisiana cooking and wine bar.

R&M Boiling Point (☎ 337-367-7596; 7413 Hwy 90; mains $6-17; ⏱ 10am-10pm Mon-Fri, 4-10pm Sat & Sun) All things Cajun – boiled and fried.

Sleeping

Estorage-Norton House (☎ 337-365-7603; www.estorge-nortonhouse.com; 446 E Main St; r incl breakfast $85-110; ⏱) In a historic district, this is a comfortable 100-plus-year-old bungalow home with four comfortable bedrooms. Two of them can sleep three or more. *Pain perdu* ('lost bread,' or French toast) topped with marmalade is a breakfast special.

Touch of Country B&B (☎ 337-367-5177; www.atouchofcountrynewiberia.com; 2517 Avery Island Rd; r incl breakfast from $100; ⏱) A sunny yellow color covers two complete cottages with king-size beds and full eat-in kitchens. But you don't have to cook if you don't feel like it; breakfast at Victor's Cafeteria is included with your stay.

CAJUN PRAIRIE

North of I-10 in central Louisiana the bayous and swamps give way to grasslands and prairies. Here animal husbandry and farming were the primary vocations of early Acadians. The region became known not for its seafood, but for braised beef, rice-and-pork boudin and various other smoked sausages and meats. The main attractions in these otherwise sleepy towns are music and more music. Too far away from New Orleans to be comfortable as a day trip, you'll need to overnight either here or in Lafayette (p224), the capital of the Cajun heartland.

Opelousas is the epicenter of Louisiana zydeco culture. You haven't heard the soul- and funk-mixed Acadian music till you've experienced it at Richard's Club, built in 1947 just west of town. Long a top venue in the state, Richard's reopened in 2008 (after a two-year, family-feud-driven hiatus) as the Zydeco Hall of Fame (p231). Although it might be best to call ahead, you can be assured that at 9pm Saturday night at least, this wood-frame building will be packed with Louisiana Creoles dancing to bands like Lil Nate and the Zydeco Big Timers. Mind the 'No parkin' on the dance floor' sign. Slim's Y-Ki-Ki (p231) is the other hotbed of zydeco activity in town. Listen for big names like Chris Ardoin and NuStep.

If you're keen to learn a bit more about zydeco, stop by the Opelousas Museum and Interpretive Center (☎ 337-948-2589; 315 N Main St, Opelousas; admission free; ⏱ 9am-5pm Mon-Fri, 10am-3pm Sat), home to a collection of recordings and the archives of the Louisiana Zydeco Festival (www.zydeco.org). The festival is held here and in nearby Plaisance every Labor Day weekend.

Can't get enough music? The best time to visit Eunice, 20 miles west of Opelousas, is on a Saturday. At 9am Savoy Music Center (☎ 337-

---

TRANSPORTATION: CAJUN PRAIRIE

Distance 155 miles northwest

Travel Time 2½ hours

Car Head west out of New Orleans on I-10; at Lafayette, turn north on I-49.

COURIR DE MARDI GRAS

In 1950, Mamou citizens revived the Cajun Mardi Gras tradition, where, instead of tossing beads from floats, celebrants mount horses and tear off through the countryside, often collecting the ingredients for a gumbo from nearby farmers. The garb worn (colorful suits, spooky wire-mesh masks) adds to the mystique. Mamou hosts a street party on the Monday night of Mardi Gras and sends its riders out at 7am on Tuesday morning, welcoming drunken celebrants back to Sixth St at around 3pm that afternoon.

457-9563; www.savoymusiccenter.com; Hwy 190, Eunice; 9am-5pm Tue-Fri, 9am-noon Sat), accordion factory and shop, hosts a Cajun-music jam session. Musician Marc Savoy and his guitarist wife, Ann, often join in. Look for the huge Savoy Music Company sign west of the Cajun Campground, 3 miles east of town.

Next, the Cajun Music Hall of Fame (337-457-6534; 240 S CC Duson Dr, Eunice; admission free; 8:30am-4pm Tue-Sat), showcasing Cajun instruments and other musical memorabilia, is worth a peek. And at 3pm there's a local Cajun music demonstration at the Prairie Acadian Cultural Center (337-457-8490; cnr Third St & Park Ave, Eunice; admission free; 8am-5pm Tue-Sat), which also has interpretive exhibits about the prairie Acadians. Read about the historic traditions before you hear today's musical stylings live next door at Liberty Theater (opposite). Built in 1924, the Liberty is known for its *Rendez-vous des Cajuns*, the live musical variety show broadcast on local radio stations every Saturday at 6pm.

The other local Cajun radio broadcast you can sit in on is in Mamou, 10 miles north of Eunice on Hwy 190. The main drag, Sixth St, is a ragtag collection of slow businesses and boarded storefronts. And yet, this little backwater attracts regulars from around the state to the Saturday morning jam fest at Fred's Lounge (opposite). Live, traditional Cajun bands play upbeat two-steps and accordion-filled waltzes for a jovial crowd getting awfully merry in the wee hours. The small brick saloon ain't much to look at, but it sure has hosted all the greats. In the 1950s, the Courir de Mardi Gras (above) started up again, and radio broadcasts begun here in 1967 helped fuel the Cajun revival.

A good way to round out your musical tour of the prairie is to stop by Floyd's Record Shop (337-363-2138; www.floydsrecordshop.com; 434 E Main St, Ville Platte; 8:30am-4:30pm Mon-Sat) in Ville

Platte, 14 miles northeast of Mamou. In 1957 Floyd Solieau left his DJ job to start both the record shop and Flat Tire Music. Through the years, under various label names, Floyd has waxed records for dozens of French-language Cajun and swamp pop legends. The shop, still in the family, is a cultural icon and an excellent resource for all things Cajun – CDs, instruments, books and souvenirs.

Information

Eunice Chamber of Commerce (337-457-2565, 800-222-2342; www.eunice-la.com; Hwy 13, Eunice; 9am-4pm Mon-Fri) Operates a visitors center downtown.

Evangeline Parish Tourist Commission (337-363-3687; www.evangelinetourism.com; 306 W Main St, Ville Platte; 9am-4pm) Tourist office covering Mamou, Ville Platte and Basile.

Opelousas City Website (www.cityofopelousas.com)

Eating

While you're on the prairie, keep your eye out for 'Slap ya Mama' seasonings. The hot sauces and pepper rubs produced in Ville Platte make tasty gifts.

Pig Stand (337-363-2883; 318 E Main St, Ville Platte; mains $4-10; 7am-10pm Tue-Sat, 11am-2pm Sun) doesn't get much more Southern than a place named the Pig Stand. This one-time hole-in-the-wall has received a spiffy makeover, but thankfully they haven't changed the amazing pulled-pork sandwiches. You'll want to take some of the mustard-based barbecue sauce home.

Palace Cafe (337-942-2142; 135 W Landry St, Opelousas; mains $5-14; 6am-9pm) Po'boys, roast duck and dressing, fried chicken, smothered okra – the Palace Cafe has been serving the tastes of Louisiana since it opened in 1927. It's still a local fave.

DI Restaurant & Dance Hall (337-432-5141; 6561 Evangeline Hwy, Basile; mains $10-17; 10am-1:30pm & 5-10pm Mon-Fri, 5-10pm Sat) Get your dancing shoes ready, because after you down piles of boiled crawfish at this Cajun eatery, you can twist and twirl it off on the dance floor. Live music six nights a week. Five miles west of Eunice.

Sleeping

Chicot State Park Cabins (337-363-2403, 888-677-2442; 3469 Chicot Park Rd, Ville Platte; cabins $90) Cathedral ceilings and exposed beams make the 'deluxe' cabins at Chicot park modern and airy. Two bedrooms sleep four in bunk beds and two in a queen. Full kitchens, screened porches and big living areas round out the amenities in these lakeside park lodgings. (Note that the old, 'standard' modular cabins are worth skipping.)

La Caboose Bed & Breakfast (☎ 337-662-5401; 145 S Budd St, Sunset; r incl breakfast $85-100; ⊠) The four rooms at this small B&B are in a real caboose, a 1900s train station depot and ticket office, and a mail car. The owner's homemade jam goes so well on the morning's baked goods.

Best Western Eunice (☎ 337-457-2800, 800-780-7234; 1531 W Laurel Ave, Eunice; r from $85; ⊠) It's a standard two-story chain motel, but at least it has rooms – there aren't a whole lot of places to stay on the prairie.

Entertainment

Zydeco Hall of Fame (☎ 512-447-5661; www.thezydeco halloffame.com; 11154 Hwy 190, Lawtell; ☯ 7pm-late Fri & Sat) Early days when Richard's (now the Hall of Fame) began, it was part of a circuit of clubs that welcomed African American musicians – such as Fats Domino – to play during pre-1960s segregation. Back then, owner Richard Eddie gave a start to many a 'French la-la' band, as he called the emerging zydeco sound. Today owner Michael DeClouet carries on the tradition. Tight crowds and oven-hot conditions just add to the attraction at this legendary club.

Slim's Y-Ki-Ki (☎ 337-942-6242; 182 N Main, Opelousas; ☯ 7pm-late Fri & Sat) Another down-and-dirty nightclub with low ceilings, a smoky atmosphere and some seriously hot Afro-Creole zydeco rhythms.

Fred's Lounge (☎ 337-468-5411; 420 6th St, Mamou; ☯ 8:15am-2pm Sat) Back in 1946 Alfred 'Fred' Tate purchased this bar and turned it into *the* Cajun gathering place. Today the lounge is only open during the Saturday morning concerts, but Fred's still packs them in. Doors open at 8:15am, but locals don't arrive till the broadcast starts at 9am. The white-haired gents and the ladies in their long prairie skirts and ballet-like dance slippers are the most fun to watch.

Liberty Theater (☎ 337-457-7389; cnr S Second St & Park Ave, Eunice; adult/child $5/3; ☯ ticket office 4-6pm Sat, shows 6-7:30pm Sat) It's kind of like the Cajun version of the *Grand Ole Opry* in Nashville. But at the Liberty Theatre locals dance in front of the stage where a variety of bands play for the Saturday-night radio broadcast.

DOWN THE BAYOU

The maze of bayous and swamps arching southwest of New Orleans, 'down the bayou' as locals say, is where the first Cajuns settled. Their traditional lifestyle is still in evidence in small part, though now it's mostly older folks who speak French and fish the waterways. The best way to experience what remains of the culture is to take a swamp tour and afterwards pull up a big plate of fresh-caught (not farm-raised) crawfish. Even as the culture fades away, the land itself is disappearing. Louisiana's coastal waterways are eroding, due in part to subsidence and hurricanes, and in part to flood management systems that prevent annual deposits of silt. The Army Corp of Engineers is at work on the problem, but an estimated 10 sq miles a year will be lost over the next 50 years according to the Coastal Wetlands Planning, Protection and Restoration Act. The region is hurting in these ecologically and economically tough times.

Below New Orleans, the Mississippi River flows 90 miles to the bird's-foot-shaped delta, where river pilots board ships entering from the Gulf. The 20,000-acre Barataria Preserve (☎ 504-589-2330; www.nps.gov; 6588 Barataria Blvd, Crown Point; ☯ visitor center 9am-5pm, trails dawn-dusk), a unit of southern Louisiana's Jean Lafitte National Historic Park, offers hiking and canoe trips into the swamp. It's a good introduction to the wetlands environment. Though not a pristine wilderness, as canals and other structures offer evidence of human activity, wild animals and plants are still abundant. Even a brief walk on the boardwalks

TRANSPORTATION: DOWN THE BAYOU

Direction 24 miles south to Barataria Preserve, 60 miles southwest to Houma, 110 miles southwest to Grand Isle

Travel time ½-hour, one hour, 2½ hours, respectively

Car To reach the Barataria Preserve take Business Hwy 90 across the Greater New Orleans Bridge to the Westbank Expressway and turn south on Barataria Blvd (Hwy 45) to Hwy 3134, which leads to the national park entrance. To get to Houma, take I-10 west to I-310, cross the Mississippi River and follow Hwy 90 south into town. Thibodaux is 20 miles northwest of Houma on Hwy 24. To Grand Isle, turn of Hwy 90 south at Hwy 1.

that wend their way through the swamp will yield sightings of gators and egrets. Ranger-led walks along the Bayou Coquille Trail are offered daily at 2pm. Other activities, which require reservations, include guided canoe treks on Saturday mornings and on evenings during a full moon. Bayou Barn (☎ 504-689-2663; 7145 Barataria Blvd, Crown Point; 2hr canoe rental $20; ☺ 9am-5pm Thu-Sun), a shack on the Bayou de Familles just outside the Barataria Preserve, has a large supply of canoes for hire. It's also a restaurant with a fun Sunday-afternoon Cajun dance.

After you cross the high-rise bridge and double back onto Hwy 45 heading south, you will first come to the little town of Jean Lafitte. Quaint and remote though it may be, it has nothing on the little fishing village of Lafitte, some 8 miles further down the road. Soon the road narrows and you can almost feel the swamplands closing in around you. Due to frequent flooding, even the mobile homes down this way are set on stilts, and the Spanish moss hangs heavy – like green streamers tossed pell-mell onto the boughs of the live oak trees. This was once the province of the pirate Jean Lafitte (see p23), and is now home to a hardy camp of commercial fishers. Around these parts, 90% of the locals still make their living from the waters, and daily life owes its design to the patterns of the seasons and the sea. Although there are no typical tourist attractions to visit, the abundant waterside accoutrements are interesting.

Another option for wetlands exploration is to head further west of New Orleans. Positioned at the confluence of Bayous Lafourche and Terrebonne, Thibodaux (ti-buh-dough; population 14,400) became the parish seat at a time when water travel was preeminent. The copper-domed courthouse (cnr 2nd & Green Sts)

was built in 1855 and remains a testament to Thibodaux's glory days, now long, long past. It's history that holds the interest for visitors here. Among the cane fields, Laurel Valley Village (☎ 985-446-7456; Hwy 308; admission by donation; ☺ 10am-3pm Tue-Fri, from 11am Sat & Sun), about 2 miles east of town on Hwy 308, is one of the best-preserved assemblages of sugar plantation slave structures in the state. Overall, some 60 structures (c 1755) survive here, including the old general store and a school house. Exhibits at the Wetlands Cajun Cultural Center (☎ 985-448-1375; 314 St Mary St; ☺ 9am-6pm Tue-Sun, to 7pm Mon) cover virtually every aspect of Cajun life in the wetlands, from music to the environmental impacts of trapping and oil exploration. Visitors learn about 'the time of shame,' from 1916 to 1968, when the Louisiana Board of Education discouraged the use of Cajun French. Cajun musicians jam at the center from 5pm to 7pm on Monday evenings.

Numerous bodies of water (Bayou Black, Little Bayou Black, the Intracoastal Waterway and Bayou Terrebonne) wend their way through the city center of Houma, a town of 30,000 people. The city itself offers little of interest to travelers, save functioning as a place for the swamp-tour bound to stop and eat. (Reservations are advised for all tours.)

The only company operating on a fixed schedule, Munson's Swamp Tours (☎ 985-851-3569; www.munsonswamptours.com; 979 Bull Run Rd, Houma; adult/under 12yr $20/10; ☺ tours 10:30am & 1:30pm) covers a privately owned area in the Chacahoula Swamp. Cruise the pristine waters beneath moss-draped oaks while your guides point out the area birds and beasts.

Looking for something more lively? Black Guidry entertains passengers with an accordion while piloting them through a scenic slice of Bayou Black on Cajun Man's Swamp Cruise (☎ 985-868-4625; www.cajunman.com; Hwy 182, off Hwy 90, Houma; adult/child $25/15). The launch is 10 miles west of downtown. Eight miles west of town, Annie Miller's Son's Swamp Tours (☎ 985-868-4758, 800-341-5441; www.annie-miller.com; 3718 Southdown Mandalay Rd, Houma; adult/child $15/10) is run by the son of a local story-telling legend. He, like his mom before him, has been feeding chicken drumsticks to the alligators for so long that the swamp critters rise from the muck to take a bite when they hear the motor. Captain Wendy Billiot's eco-oriented Wetland Tours (☎ 985-851-7578; www.wetlandtours.com; Janet Lynn Ln, Theriot; per person $30) cruise across a swampland lake near the coast (four-person minimum). She also hires out

DETOUR: WILDLIFE GARDENS

Alligator lovers shouldn't miss the opportunity to see babies to big 'uns up close at Wildlife Gardens (☎ 985-5306; N Bayou Black Dr, Gibson; admission $3; ☺ 9am-3pm), 20 miles northwest of Houma. The 30 acres of swamps, walking trails, an alligator farm, rescued animals and an old trapper's cabin have come a long way since Betty Provost Eschette started the place with her late first husband in the 1980s. You can rent one of four very rustic cabins ($95 including breakfast) in a quieter part of the swamp. They all have screened porches, but bring the mosquito spray anyway.

for angling charters, specializing in teaching women and children to fish (four hours $500). Twelve miles southwest of town.

The end of the road down bayou way is 70 miles southeast of Houma, in Grand Isle. The windswept barrier-island town took quite the beating from Hurricanes Katrina and Rita, but many businesses have reopened and the Old Fishing Bridge has been restored. In addition to seafood shacks and fishing camps, boat charters are the big business here. Bridge Side Marina (☎ 985-787-2419; www.swampweb.com/bridgeside; 1618 Hwy 1; ☉ 8am-6pm) can hook you up with rods, reels and guided boats. Watching the waves lap ashore at Grand Isle State Park (www.crt .state.la.us; Admiral Craik Dr; admission $1; ☉ 7am-10pm), it's easy to imagine the power of mother nature. Rent canoes ($20 per day) to explore the inland canals or just watch as the brown pelicans, the state bird, dive for fish offshore.

Information

Grand Isle Website (www.grand-isle.com)

Houma Visitor Center (☎ 985-868-2732; cnr Hwy 90 & St Charles St, Houma; ☉ 8am-4pm) West of the town limits, this large office has loads of info and helpful staff.

Lafourche Parish Tourist Office (☎ 985-537-5800; 4484 Hwy 1, Raceland; ☉ 9am-4pm Mon-Fri, 10am-3pm Sat) A few historic artifacts are on display next to the racks of brochures about attractions around the bayou region.

Thibodaux Visitor Center (☎ 985-446-1187; 318 E Bayou Rd, Thibodaux; ☉ 8:30am-4:30pm Mon-Fri) Stop by here for local event info.

Eating

Restaurant de Familles (☎ 689-7834; 7163 Barataria Blvd, Crown Point; mains $15-19; ☉ noon-8pm Wed-Thu, noon-10pm Fri & Sat, 10am-3pm Sun) Near the Barataria Preserve, de Familles offers upscale Creole cuisine in a dining room overlooking the bayou. The menu really shines when soft-shell crabs are in season. Reservations are a must for the five-course set-menu brunch ($28).

A-Bear's Café (☎ 985-872-6306; 809 Bayou Black Dr, Houma; meals $6-12; ☉ 7am-5pm Mon-Thu, to 10pm Fri, to 2pm Sat) With wood floors and walls (and red-checked tablecloths), the place looks and feels like an old country store. You'll see a good number of locals inside, tucking into plates of red beans and rice, po'boys and plate lunch specials – topped off with a slice of icebox pie. Expect a crowd on Friday nights when there's a live Cajun band and dancing.

1921 Seafood & Oyster Bar (☎ 985-868-7098; 1520 Barrow St, Houma; mains $8-15; ☉ 5-10pm) Don't let the fun neon signs and stuffed marlin on the shack's wall fool you: the seafood here is seriously stuff. In season (February through May) the boiled crawfish served are caught in area bayous, not in the region's fish farms. And the gulf shrimp are *huge*.

Gros Place (☎ 985-446-6623; 710 St Patrick St, Thibodaux; ☉ 9am-midnight) A popular spot set in an old service station where locals gather to shoot pool and quaff beer after beer. Stop by on a Friday evening and you're likely to get a chance to sample some deep-fried turkey, which the proprietor cooks for the crowd.

Rob's Donuts (☎ 985-447-4080; cnr St Mary & Tiger Sts, Thibodaux; sweets $0.50-4; ☉ 24hr) For breakfast, this is the place to try for praline-stuffed pastries oozing with pecans and syrup.

Sleeping

With New Orleans so close, there's no real reason to stay over here. Most of the swamp tours can also arrange cabin rentals if you want to, though; and Grand Isle has a whole host of cheap motels.

Victorian Inn (☎ 504-689-4757; www.victoriainn.com; 4707 Jean Lafitte Blvd, Lafitte; r incl breakfast $100-115; ✕) New Orleanians consider this a countryside break from the big city. The 14 B&B rooms in two raised West Indies–style plantation homes are surrounded by flower-filled gardens. Take a pirogue (Cajun canoe) out on the little lake or reserve ahead to enjoy high tea on fine china. The Creole restaurant is top notch, as are the extremely welcoming innkeepers.

MISSISSIPPI GULF COAST

In the backyard of New Orleans, the Gulf Coast of Mississippi is where Southern gamblers and beach bums go to play. Twenty-six

---

TRANSPORTATION: MISSISSIPPI GULF COAST

Directions 78 miles northeast to Gulfport, Mississippi

Travel time 1¼ hours

Car Follow I-10 east all the way.

DETOUR: ABITA SPRINGS

The waters once attracted visitors to Abita Springs, 45 miles north of New Orleans on the shore of Lake Pontchartrain; now beer does. Abita Brewery (☎ 985-893-3143; www.abita.com; 21084 Hwy 36; admission free; ☿ tours 2pm Wed-Fri, 11am, noon & 1pm Sat) produced its first microbrew (using spring water) in 1986. Its standard amber ale, more ambitious Mardi Gras bock and Jockimo stout all provide a welcome local alternative to corporate lagers. (The brewery also produces bottles of root beer sweetened with cane sugar.) Your tour begins and ends in the Tasting Room (166 Barbee Rd). You can try a larger quantity of the dark and malty TurboDog, or the raspberry-enhanced wheat beer, Purple Haze, in the nearby Abita Brew Pub (☎ 985-892-5837; 72011 Holly St; ☿ 11am-10pm Tue-Sun) — as well as at restaurants around the region.

miles of public-access sand stretches along the coast. The casinos are centered along and around Beach Blvd in Biloxi, which has been thoroughly rebuilt since Hurricane Katrina swept through. One Biloxi fisherman described the post-Storm scene as something out of a twisted Picasso painting: boats dangling like ornaments in tree branches, while slot machines from obliterated casinos floated down rivers that were once city streets. The nearby town of Gulfport was nearly obliterated. You can still see the scars, but businesses continue to open and it, too, is coming back. The beach and bar scenes are up and running – check on the openings of cultural and town attractions at Mississippi Gulf Coast Convention & Visitors Bureau (☎ 228-896-6699; www.gulfcoast.org; 11975 Seaway Rd, Gulfport; ☿ 9am-4:30pm Mon-Sat).

Long Beach, 5 miles west of Gulfport, is primarily a residential area, so the sun-bathing stretches of sand are nice and quiet. Though beach services are limited, charter fishing boats operate from the town's marina. You can see how far Gulfport has come since the Storm at the Hurricane Katrina Exhibit (Hancock Bank Bldg; 2510 14th St, Gulfport; admission free; ☿ 9:30am-4:30pm Mon-Fri), which is filled with photos and artwork from the hurricane's aftermath. Thirteen miles east in Biloxi, there are eight – count 'em, *eight* – giant casino-resorts. The rebuilt Beau Rivage (☎ 228-386-7111, 888-567-6667; www.beaurivage.com; 875 Beach Blvd, Biloxi; r from $139; ☎ ☒) has long been the king of the strip, a glittering gold behemoth that is to Biloxi what Bellagio is to Vegas. Guests party the nights away drinking 'Category 5 Hurricanes' at the numerous Hard Rock Hotel & Casino (☎ 228-386-7111, 888-567-6667; www.beaurivage.com; 777 Beach Blvd, Biloxi; r from $129; ☎ ☒) bars and nightclubs.

TRANSPORTATION

The compact and level nature of the French Quarter and downtown riverfront areas make walking and bicycling the preferred ways to get around for most visitors. As in other cities throughout the USA, public transit in New Orleans has deteriorated as transportation funds have been diverted to subsidize motorists. Hurricane Katrina was of course a blow to the city's transit systems. Nevertheless, visitors will find the buses, streetcars and ferries generally serve the most popular attractions. In fact, the streetcars and ferries themselves serve as attractions.

AIR

New Orleans is not a major airline hub and it is not a big center for national commerce, so direct flights are not always available, even from major travel centers like the Bay Area. International travelers will almost certainly need to change flights somewhere else within the USA before connecting to flights to New Orleans (and the connection may require an additional stopover en route).

The cheapest flights can often be found on the web. Sites worth checking include the following:

Cheap Tickets (www.cheaptickets.com)

Expedia (www.expedia.com)

Kayak (www.kayak.com)

Vayama (www.vayama.com)

Airport

Louis Armstrong New Orleans International Airport (MSY; ☎ 464-0831; www.flymsy.com) is in the suburb of Kenner, 11 miles (about a 20-minute drive) west of the city along the I-10 freeway. In the aftermath of Hurricane Katrina, the airport remained dry and its concourses served as an impromptu triage center. It's a small airport with only one terminal, so it's pretty easy to get around.

BICYCLE

On the positive side of the ledger for riders, New Orleans is flat and relatively compact. On the negative side are heavy traffic, potholes and bad neighborhoods, which make fat tires a near necessity. Oppressive summer heat and humidity also discourage a lot of bicyclists.

All state-operated ferries offer free transportation for bikes. Bicyclists board ahead of cars by walking down the left lane of the ramp to the swinging gate. You must wait for the cars to exit before leaving.

The Regional Transit Authority (RTA; ☎ 248-3900; www.norta.com) doesn't allow bikes on buses or streetcars.

CLIMATE CHANGE & TRAVEL

Climate change is a serious threat to the ecosystems that humans rely upon, and air travel is the fastest-growing contributor to the problem. Lonely Planet regards travel, overall, as a global benefit, but believes we all have a responsibility to limit our personal impact on global warming.

Flying & Climate Change

Pretty much every form of motor transport generates CO_2 (the main cause of human-induced climate change) but planes are far and away the worst offenders, not just because of the sheer distances they allow us to travel, but because they release greenhouse gases high into the atmosphere. The statistics are frightening: two people taking a return flight between Europe and the US will contribute as much to climate change as an average household's gas and electricity consumption over a whole year.

Carbon Offset Schemes

Climatecare.org and other websites use 'carbon calculators' that allow jetsetters to offset the greenhouse gases they are responsible for with contributions to energy-saving projects and other climate-friendly initiatives in the developing world – including projects in India, Honduras, Kazakhstan and Uganda.

Lonely Planet, together with Rough Guides and other concerned partners in the travel industry, supports the carbon offset scheme run by climatecare.org. Lonely Planet offsets all of its staff and author travel.

For more information check out our website: lonelyplanet.com.

Rental

Bikes can be rented for around $25 a day at Bicycle Michael's (Map p81; ☎ 945-9505; www.bicycle michaels.com; 622 Frenchmen St, Marigny).

BOAT
Ferry

The cheapest way to cruise the Mississippi River is aboard one of the state-run ferries. The most popular line, the Canal St Ferry, operates between Canal St and the West Bank community of Algiers from 6am to midnight daily. Another ferry stops at Jackson Ave, near the Irish Channel, and leads to the suburb of Gretna. The ferries are free for pedestrians and cyclists, and just $1 for vehicles.

Riverboat

Visitors to New Orleans during Mark Twain's time arrived by boat via the Mississippi River, but for now, the days of paddle steamboats plying the Big Muddy are over. Majestic America, which operated paddleboat cruises for years on the historic *Delta Queen,* has ceased operations. Unless someone buys up the business, overnight cruises on the Mississippi are a thing of the past.

BUS
Local

The RTA offers bus and streetcar (see p238) services. Fares are $1.25, plus 25¢ for a transfer. Service is decent, but we wouldn't recommend relying solely on public transport during a New Orleans visit.

No buses run through the heart of the French Quarter, so most visitors only use them when venturing Uptown or out to City Park. Convenient bus routes are indicated for all parts of town in the introduction sections in the Neighborhoods chapter (p64).

Long-Distance

Greyhound (☎ 800-231-2222; www.greyhound.com) buses arrive and depart at New Orleans Union Passenger Terminal (Map pp86–7; 1001 Loyola Ave), which is also known as Union Station. It's seven blocks upriver from Canal St. Greyhound regularly connects to Lafayette, Opelousas and Baton Rouge, plus Clarksdale, MS, and Memphis, TN, en route to essentially every city in the USA.

CAR & MOTORCYCLE
Driving

A car is not a bad thing to have in New Orleans. Having one makes it *much* easier to fully experience the entire city, from Faubourg Marigny on up to Riverbend, and out along Esplanade Ave. If you are planning to spend most of your time in the French Quarter, though, don't bother with a car. You'll just end up wasting money on parking.

Drivers in New Orleans are not overly aggressive, although you can always expect the car behind you to get within a few feet of your rear bumper. It's just a herd impulse, though. Pause a few beats at a green light, and that same tailgater is likely to wait patiently for you to realize that the light has changed. On the other hand, drivers in New Orleans can't resist speeding up for a yellow light to make it through an intersection before the light turns red. More often than not, the light is red by the time they are zipping through, so don't rush into an intersection immediately after your light turns green.

Here are the main concerns to watch out for when driving in New Orleans. First: potholes. The city streets are in an atrocious state, and tires here have accordingly short life spans. Tricky left turns through very common four-way intersections, and the intersections themselves, can be a hazard. While stop signs are set out in residential areas, not everyone obeys them. New Orleanian friendliness can be annoying if people stop their cars in the middle of a narrow street to chat with someone – every New Orleans driver has a story about this incident. Finally, New Orleans drivers are terrible turn signalers. Try to keep your head from exploding the fifth time you get cut off.

Visitors from abroad may find it wise to back up their national driver's license with an International Driving Permit, available from their local automobile club.

Parking

Downtown on-street parking is typically for short-term use only. In some parts of town, look for the solar-powered parking meters. One meter often serves an entire block, so don't assume parking is free just because there's no meter on the curb immediately beside where you park. There are also all kinds of restrictions for street cleaning that limit when you can park on certain streets. Be sure to read all parking signs before leaving your car. Enforcement is particularly efficient in the French Quarter, the CBD and the Warehouse District.

Vehicles parked illegally are frequently towed in the Quarter. If you park your car in a driveway, within 20ft of a corner or crosswalk, within 15ft of a fire hydrant or on a street-sweeping day, you will need to pay about $75 to $100 (cash or credit card) to retrieve your car from the Auto Pound (☎ 658-7450; 1415 N Claiborne Ave).

Free street parking is available on many blocks in the Lower Quarter (or try along Esplanade Ave). For more central parking, you might have to pay. Try the U-Park Garage (Map pp70–1; ☎ 524-5994; 721 Iberville St), near the upper end of Bourbon St. Most hotels in the Quarter and the CBD have parking garages where you can park with in-out privileges for around $20 to $30 a day.

Outside of the Quarter and Downtown, parking is a cinch. There's plenty of street parking and not many restrictions. With that said, be careful of street parking during Mardi Gras and Jazz Fest, when cops are liable to ticket you for any loophole of an infraction.

Rental

Most of the big car-rental companies are found in New Orleans, particularly at the airport. Typically you must be at least 25 years

GETTING INTO TOWN

Louis Armstrong New Orleans International Airport is 11 miles west of the city center. Shuttles and cabs depart regularly from the curb outside the baggage claim area.

Bus

If your baggage is not too unwieldy and you're in no hurry, Jefferson Transit (☎ 818-1077; www.jeffersontransit .org) offers the cheapest ride downtown aboard its Airport Downtown Express ($1.60). At the airport the bus stops along the median on the second level, near the Delta counter. The ride to New Orleans follows city streets, pausing for stoplights every few minutes, and will only get you as far as the corner of Tulane St and Carrollton Ave. From here it's a cheap cab ride to the French Quarter, or you can transfer to a Regional Transit Authority (RTA; ☎ 248-3900; www. norta.com) bus. Bus 27 will get you to St Charles Ave in the Garden District; bus 39 follows Tulane Ave to Canal St, just outside the French Quarter.

Car

The quickest way to drive between the airport and downtown is to take I-10. If you're coming from downtown on I-10, take exit 223 for the airport; going to downtown, take exit 234, as the Louisiana Superdome looms before you. Traffic can get very clogged and slow near the Huey Long Bridge.

Shuttle

Most visitors take the Airport Shuttle (☎ 522-3500; www.airportshuttleneworleans.com) to and from the airport. It's a frequent service between the airport and downtown hotels for $15 per passenger each way. It's a cheap and courteous introduction to the city, although it can be time-consuming, especially if your hotel is the last stop. At the airport, buy tickets from agencies in the baggage-claim area. For your return to the airport, call a day ahead to arrange for a pickup, which you should schedule at least two hours prior to your flight's departure.

Taxi

A taxi ride from the airport costs a flat rate of $28 for one to two passengers. Each additional passenger costs another $12. No more than four passengers are allowed in a single cab.

of age and have a major credit card, as well as a valid driver's license, to rent a car.

Rates go up and availability lessens during special events or large conventions. A compact car typically costs $30 to $40 a day or $150 to $200 a week. On top of that, there is a 13.75% tax and an optional $9 to $15 a day loss/damage waiver (LDW; insurance). US citizens who already have auto insurance are probably covered, but should check with their insurance company first.

Agencies in or near the downtown area include the following:

Avis (Map pp108–9; ☎ 523-4317, 800-3311-1212; 2024 Canal St)

Budget Rent-a-Car (Map pp108–9; ☎ 565-5600; 1317 Canal St)

Hertz (Map pp86–7; ☎ 568-1645; 901 Convention Center Blvd)

STREETCAR

Streetcars (aka trolleys or trams) have made a comeback in New Orleans, with three lines serving key routes in the city. Fares range from $1.25 to $1.50.

Canal Streetcar Lines

Bright-red streetcars began running up and down Canal St in 2004 (they look old, but they're not). All are fully modern, air-conditioned light-rail cars custom designed and built locally.

Two slightly different lines follow Canal St to Mid-City. Both run from the French Market and up the levee before heading up Canal St. The 47 line goes all the way to City Park Ave. More useful for tourists is the 8 line, which heads up a spur on N Carrollton Ave, ending up at the Esplanade Ave entrance to City Park. The cars run from 6am to 11pm.

Riverfront Streetcar Line

In 1988 the wheelchair-accessible Riverfront streetcar line began operating vintage red cars on the old dockside rail corridor wedged between the levee and flood wall. The 2-mile route runs between the French Market, in the lower end of the French Quarter near Esplanade Ave, and the upriver Convention Center, crossing Canal St on the way. It operates from 6am to midnight.

St Charles Ave Streetcar Line

When the St Charles Ave route opened as the New Orleans & Carrollton Railroad in 1835, it was the nation's second horse-drawn streetcar line. The line was also among the first systems to be electrified when New Orleans adopted electric traction in 1893. Now it is one of the few streetcars in the US to have survived the automobile era.

The line's fleet of antique cars survived the hurricanes of 2005, but the tracks and power lines did not. For a time the cars were running on the Canal St tracks, but the St Charles Ave tracks have now been successfully restored.

The important thing is that you can still enjoy a ride on one of these extraordinary streetcars, which employ technology that's intriguingly out of date. There is no need to worry about breakdowns when you hear the intermittent thunka-thunka sound – it's just the air compressor. The brakes, doors and even the fare box operate on compressed air. Unfortunately, these old streetcars are not wheelchair accessible.

TAXI

If you're traveling alone or at night, taxis are highly recommended. United Cab (☎ 522-9771) is the biggest and most reliable company in New Orleans. You might have to call for a pickup, unless you are in a central part of the French Quarter, where it is relatively easy to flag down a passing cab.

Fares within the city start with a $2.50 flag-fall charge for one passenger (plus $1 for each additional passenger and a $2 fuel surcharge). From there it's $1.60 per mile. Practically speaking, this amounts to fares of around $11 from the French Quarter to the Bywater and $13 or more to the Garden District. Don't forget to tip your driver 10% to 15%.

TRAIN

Three Amtrak (☎ 800-872-7245) trains serve New Orleans at the New Orleans Union Passenger Terminal (Map pp86–7; ☎ 528-1610; 1001 Loyola Ave). The *City of New Orleans* train runs to Memphis, TN, Jackson, MS, and Chicago, IL. Alternatively, the *Crescent Route* serves Birmingham, AL, Atlanta, GA, Washington, DC, and New York City. The *Sunset Limited* route between Los Angeles, CA, and Miami, FL, also passes through New Orleans.

DIRECTORY

BUSINESS HOURS

New Orleans maintains business hours similar to much of the rest of the USA, except when it comes to bars. Stores tend to stay open from around 10am to 7pm or 8pm, and restaurant hours are generally from 10am or 11am to 11pm (sometimes with a break from 2pm to 5pm). Bars tend to open at around 5pm and stay open till the last customer leaves, although official closing times are something like 2am on weekdays and 3am or 4am on weekends.

CHILDREN

New Orleans is easy on kids. Stuffed as it is with zoos, museums, riverboat cruises and the like, wee ones should rarely feel left out of the fun that defines this town. See p104 for some top kid-friendly suggestions.

Babysitting

Most major hotels can offer on-site babysitting arrangements. Smaller hotels are also familiar with parents' needs and can usually provide the name of recommended child-minding services. It's worth inquiring about such arrangement when you make your hotel reservations.

Accent on Children's Arrangements (Map pp86–7; ☎ 524-1227; www.accentoca.com; Ste 303, 615 Baronne St) is a service that takes the kids off your hands and engages them in organized activities. This might include a child-oriented tour of the city or educational entertainment. They are able to customize services for varying age groups and to meet you and your children's personal needs.

CLIMATE

New Orleans' climate is fairly simple: it's hot and humid in the summer, and not so hot and humid the rest of the year. The humidity is enough to drive some locals out of town for lengthy summer vacations in more pleasant climes, and to keep tourists away. In December temperatures can fluctuate from 40°F to 70°F. Snowfall is extremely rare. The wettest months are July and August and the driest month is October.

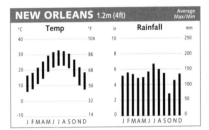

Hurricanes can come off the Gulf of Mexico anytime from June to December, though the peak season is in August and September.

COURSES

The New Orleans School of Cooking (Map pp70–1; ☎ 800-237-4841; www.neworleansschoolofcooking.com; 524 St Louis St) is a popular and pretty awesome way to learn the ins and outs of one of this city's great exports – its culinary tradition. There's a good variety of courses on offer, ranging from $27 short-cooking demonstrations to a $140 walk-through on creating your own four- or five-course menu.

CUSTOMS REGULATIONS

US Customs (www.customs.gov) allows each person over the age of 21 to bring 1L of liquor and 200 cigarettes duty-free into the USA. Non-US citizens are allowed to enter the USA with $100 worth of gifts from abroad. There are restrictions on bringing fresh fruit and flowers into the country and there is a strict quarantine on animals. If you are carrying more than $10,000 in US and foreign cash, traveler's checks, money orders or the like, you need to declare the excess amount. There is no legal restriction on the amount that may be imported, but undeclared sums in excess of $10,000 may be subject to confiscation.

ELECTRICITY

Electric current in the USA is 110-115V, 60Hz AC. Outlets may be suited for flat two-prong or three-prong grounded plugs. If your appliance is made for another electrical system, you will need a transformer or adapter; if you didn't bring one along, buy one at Radio Shack (which has several locations around town) or any consumer electronics store.

EMBASSIES

There aren't any embassies in New Orleans, but several countries have consulates and honorary consuls in town. Canada's nearest consulate is in Miami, FL.

French Consulate (Map pp86–7; ☎ 523-5772; www .consulfrance-nouvelleorleans.org; 1340 Poydras St)

UK Honorary Consul (Map pp86–7; ☎ 524-4180; 10th fl, 321 St Charles Ave)

EMERGENCY

Ambulance ☎ 911

Fire ☎ 911

Police (emergency) ☎ 911

Police (nonemergency) ☎ 821-2222

Rape Crisis Line ☎ 483-8888

GAY & LESBIAN TRAVELERS

The gay community in New Orleans is most visible in the French Quarter, to the lakeside of Bourbon St. While there is a strong gay scene in the city, as regards nightlife there is a lot of integration of the straight and gay worlds. This especially applies to live music shows, which are an integral component of going out in New Orleans. Gays are present but keep a lower profile in Faubourg Marigny, Bywater and elsewhere in town. For gay visitors, finding a place to stay, eat or party in New Orleans will not be a problem. See the Gay New Orleans Scene boxed text (p180) for listings.

Southern Decadence (p15) is a gay festival that draws a huge crowd to the Quarter in late August or early September. Halloween and Mardi Gras also have a strong gay component in New Orleans.

The Faubourg Marigny Book Store (Map p81; ☎ 943-9875; 600 Frenchmen St) is the South's oldest gay bookstore and is a good place to learn about the local scene. Several websites provide information geared toward the gay community in New Orleans, as well as gay travelers.

Ambush Mag (www.ambushmag.com)

Gay New Orleans (www.gaynewworleans.com)

HOLIDAYS

Note that when national holidays fall on a weekend, they are often celebrated on the nearest Friday or Monday so that everyone enjoys a three-day weekend. For further information on New Orleans' holidays and festivals see p12. The following are all national holidays.

New Year's Day January 1

Presidents' Day Third Monday in February

Memorial Day Last Monday in May

Independence Day July 4

Labor Day First Monday in September

Columbus Day Second Monday in October

Veterans Day November 11

Thanksgiving Fourth Thursday in November

INTERNET ACCESS

Many hotels offer internet access, but it's not yet something you can assume – be sure to confirm while making reservations. Wi-fi hot spots are becoming increasingly common in cafes.

Wi-fi hot spots include Coop's Place (p150), Cooter Brown's Tavern & Oyster Bar (p168) and d.b.a. (p184). With so many businesses adding wi-fi networks, if you're out in most major neighborhoods (outside of Mid-City and the Tremé) you're likely to be able to pick up a signal. If you're not traveling with your own laptop, try Bastille Computer Café (Map pp70–1; ☎ 581-1150; e@ netzero.net; 605 Toulouse St; ☺ 10am-11pm), located in the heart of the Quarter. The New Orleans Public Library (p88), near City Hall, has terminals for free web access.

LEGAL MATTERS

Although it may seem that anything goes, even New Orleans has its limits. Common tourist-related offenses include underage drinking, drinking outdoors from a bottle rather than a plastic go cup, teen curfew violations and, probably the most common, flaunting of private parts.

For people aged 21 years or more, the legal blood-alcohol limit in Louisiana is 0.08%, however you can be cited for driving while impaired even when your blood-alcohol content is lower.

The legal drinking age is 21. Anyone under the age of 18 on the streets after 11pm is violating the city's curfew. Most bars will offer your drink in a plastic cup, so accept it if you're going to wander off with your drink. Bourbon St flashers rarely get in serious trouble for exposing their private parts, but repeatedly doing so in front of the cops is asking for trouble. If you aren't flashing, be careful not to grope those who are. That's a no-no.

The legal age for gambling is also 21, and businesses with gaming devices (usually video poker machines) out in the open are closed to minors. Even cafes with gaming devices are off-limits to minors, unless the games are contained within private rooms or booths.

MEDICAL SERVICES

Excellent medical care is readily available, but the need for medical insurance when visiting anywhere in the USA cannot be overemphasized. Doctors often expect payment on the spot for services rendered, after which your insurance company may reimburse you. US citizens should check with their insurer before leaving home to see what conditions are covered in their policy.

If you need immediate medical attention and you are in your hotel, your first call should be to the front desk. Some of the larger hotels have agreements with on-call doctors who can make house calls if necessary. In really urgent situations, you can call an ambulance (☎ 911), which will deliver you to a hospital emergency room.

If you can get to an emergency room, your best bet is the Tulane University Medical Center (Map pp86–7; ☎ 988-5800; 1415 Tulane Ave; ☉ 24hr), located in the CBD.

Pharmacies

Nonprescription medications and contraceptives can be purchased in the pharmacy section of drugstores like Walgreens (Map pp70–1; ☎ 525-7263; 619 Decatur St) in the French Quarter. Pharmacies such as Rite-Aid and Woolworth are fairly common around the city.

MONEY

There are three straightforward ways to handle money in the USA: cash, US-dollar traveler's checks and credit or bank cards, which can be used to withdraw cash from the many automatic teller machines (ATMs) across the country. US dollars are the only accepted currency in New Orleans.

ATMs

With a Visa card, MasterCard or a bank card affiliated with the Plus or Cirrus networks you can easily obtain cash from ATMs all over New Orleans. The advantages of using ATMs are that you don't need to buy traveler's checks in advance, you don't have to pay the usual 1% commission on the checks and, if you're from a foreign country, you may actually receive a better exchange rate. However, most ATMs charge a $2 or $3 service charge for each withdrawal, so it doesn't make sense to grab $40 several times a day.

There are four ATMs at the airport: in the east lobby near Concourse B, next to the Whitney National Bank; and two in the baggage claim areas on the lower level.

Changing Money

Most major currencies and leading brands of traveler's checks are easily exchanged in New Orleans. You will also find various independent exchange bureaus. When you first arrive at the airport terminal you can change money at TravelEx America Business Center (☎ 465-9647; ☉ 6am-5pm), which you'll find in the ticket lobby. TravelEx charges a sliding service fee ($2 for amounts up to $20, $4 for greater amounts). It also offers travel insurance, photocopies, fax services, emergency cash and wire money transfers. The Money Gram section of the office closes at 4:30pm.

Nearby, Whitney National Bank (☎ 838-6492; ☉ 8:30am-3pm Mon-Thu, 8:30am-5:30pm Fri) also changes money, charging a flat $5 service fee. Other services offered here include cash advances on credit cards, traveler's checks, money orders and ATMs. Since the exchange counters are only feet apart, get quotes from both.

Better exchange rates are generally available at banks in the CBD. Typical opening hours are 10am to 5pm Monday to Thursday, 10am to 6pm Friday and 10am to 1pm Saturday. The Hibernia National Bank (Map pp86–7; ☎ 533-5712; 313 Carondelet St) and the main office of the Whitney National Bank (Map pp86–7; ☎ 586-7272; 228 St Charles Ave) both buy and sell foreign currency.

For exchange rates see the Quick Reference page inside the front cover.

Credit & Debit Cards

Major credit cards are widely accepted by car-rental agencies and most hotels, restaurants, gas stations, shops and larger grocery stores. Many recreational and tourist activities can also be paid for by credit card. The most commonly accepted cards are Visa, MasterCard and American Express. Discover and Diners Club cards are also accepted by a large number of businesses.

Traveler's Checks

ATMs and debit cards have nearly rendered traveler's checks obsolete, but if your bank isn't affiliated with one of the common bank networks such as Cirrus or Plus, the old-fashioned way can be pretty handy. Some younger waitstaff and shop clerks might be unsure how to react to them, though.

They're still virtually as good as cash in the USA, and they can still be replaced if lost or stolen. Both AmEx and Thomas Cook, two well-known issuers of traveler's checks, have efficient replacement policies.

You'll save yourself trouble and expense if you buy traveler's checks in US dollars.

ORGANIZED TOURS

Friends of the Cabildo (☎ 523-3939; www.friendsofthe cabildo.org) conducts excellent historical and cultural tours of the French Quarter (adult/child $15/10) leaving from Jackson Sq. For a more hokey if harrowing experience, Haunted History Tours (☎ 861-2727; www.hauntedhistorytours.com) are a little cheesy and a lot of fun, and a good way of learning about the city's supernatural side. There are all sorts of options, from vampire tours to romps through city cemeteries that run around $20.

POST

New Orleans' main post office (Map pp86–7; ☎ 589-1135; 701 Loyola Ave) is near City Hall. There are smaller branches throughout the city, including the Airport Mail Center (☎ 589-1296) in the passenger terminal; inside the World Trade Center (Map pp86–7; ☎ 524-0033; 2 Canal St); and in the CBD at Lafayette Square (Map pp86–7; ☎ 524-0491; 610 S Maestri Place). Post offices are generally open 8:30am to 4:30pm Monday to Friday and 8:30am to noon Saturday.

There are lots of independent postal shops as well, including the Royal Mail Service (Map pp70–1; ☎ 522-8523; 828 Royal St) and the French Quarter Postal Emporium (Map pp70–1; ☎ 525-6651; 1000 Bourbon St; ☻ 9am-6pm Mon-Fri, 10am-3pm Sat). These shops will send letters and packages at the same rates as the post office.

Postal Rates

Postal rates have a tendency to increase frequently, but at the time of writing the rates were 44¢ for 1st-class mail within the USA and 24¢ for postcards.

It costs 75¢ to send a 1oz letter to Canada, 79¢ to Mexico and 98¢ to other countries.

The US Postal Service (☎ 800-222-1811; www.usps .gov) also offers a Priority Mail service, which delivers your letter or package anywhere in the USA in two days or less. The cost is $4.95 for 1lb. For heavier items, rates differ according to the distance mailed. Overnight Express Mail starts at $15.

Receiving Mail

If you don't want to receive mail at your hotel, you can have mail sent to you at the main post office, marked c/o General Delivery, New Orleans, LA 70112. General Delivery is US terminology for what is known as poste restante internationally. General Delivery mail is only held for 30 days. It's not advisable to try to have mail sent to other post offices in New Orleans.

Sending Mail

If you have the correct postage, you can drop your mail into any blue mailbox. However, to send a package that weighs 1lb or more, you must take it to a post office or postal shop.

RADIO

88.3 WRBH Reading radio for the blind

90.7 WWOZ Louisiana music and community radio

91.5 WTUL Tulane Radio

93.3 WQUE Hip-hop

95.7 WKBU Classic rock

100.3 KLRZ Cajun music

SAFETY

Exercise the caution you would in any US city. The possibility of getting mugged is something to consider even in areas you'd think are safe (eg the Garden District). Solo pedestrians are targeted more often than people walking in groups, and daytime is a better time to be out on foot than nighttime. Avoid entering secluded areas such as cemeteries alone, especially in the Tremé and Bywater.

Large crowds typically make the French Quarter a secure around-the-clock realm for the visitor. However, if your hotel or vehicle is on the margins of the Quarter, you might want to take a taxi back at night. The CBD and Warehouse District have plenty of activity during weekdays, but they're relatively deserted at night and on weekends. The B&Bs along Esplanade Ridge are near enough troubled neighborhoods to call for caution in the area at night. In the Quarter, street hustlers frequently approach tourists. Walk away.

Pedestrians crossing the street do not have the right of way and motorists (unless they are from out of state) will not yield. Whether on foot or in a car, be wary before entering an intersection, as New Orleans drivers are notorious for running yellow and even red lights.

TAX & REFUNDS

New Orleans' 9% sales tax is tacked onto virtually everything, including meals, groceries and car rentals. For accommodations, room and occupancy taxes add an additional 12% to your bill plus $1 to $3 per person, depending on the size of the hotel.

Some merchants in Louisiana participate in a program called Louisiana Tax Free Shopping (☎ 568-5323; www.louisianataxfree.com). Look for the snazzy red-and-blue 'Tax Free' logo in the window or on the sign of the store. Usually these stores specialize in the kinds of impulse purchases people are likely to make while on vacation. In these stores, present a passport to verify you are not a US citizen and request a voucher as you make your purchase. Reimbursement centers are located in the Downtown Refund Center (Map pp86–7; ☎ 568-3605; Riverwalk Mall; ☺ 10am-3:30pm) and the main lobby of the Louis Armstrong Airport (☎ 467-0723; ☺ 8:30am-4:30pm Mon-Fri, 9am-1pm Sat & Sun).

TELEPHONE

New Orleans telephones are run by BellSouth. The *Yellow Pages* (www.yellowpages.com) has comprehensive business listings. The New Orleans area code is ☎ 504, which includes Thibodaux and the surrounding area. Baton Rouge and its surrounding area use the area code ☎ 225. Area code ☎ 318 applies to the northern part of the state.

When dialing another area code, you must dial ☎ 1 before the area code. For example, to call a Baton Rouge number from New Orleans, begin by dialing ☎ 1-225. At pay phones, local calls start at 50¢, but long-distance charges apply to 'nonlocal' calls even within the same area code – to Thibodaux, for example – and costs rapidly increase once you dial another area code. Hotel telephones often have heavy surcharges.

Toll-free numbers start with ☎ 1-800 or ☎ 1-888 and allow you to call free within the USA. These numbers are commonly offered by car-rental operators, large hotels and the like. (Listings in this book omit the '1,' eg ☎ 800-000-0000.) Dial ☎ 411 for local directory assistance, or ☎ 1 + area code + 555-1212 for long-distance directory information; dial ☎ 1-800-555-1212 for toll-free number information. Dial ☎ 0 for the operator.

If you're calling from abroad, the international country code for the USA (and Canada) is ☎ 1.

To make an international call from New Orleans, dial ☎ 00 + country code + area code (dropping the leading 0) + number. For calls to Canada, there's no need to dial the international access code ☎ 011. For international operator assistance, dial ☎ 00.

Cell Phones

The USA uses a variety of cell (mobile) phone systems, only one of which is compatible with systems used outside North America: the Global System for Mobile telephones (GSM), which is becoming more commonly available worldwide. Many popular phone services, including T-Mobile, Vodafone and Orange, offer GSM service. Check with your local provider to determine whether your phone will work in New Orleans.

Fax

Besides hotel fax machines, services in the French Quarter include French Quarter Postal Emporium (Map pp70–1; ☎ 525-6651; fax 525-6652; 1000 Bourbon St; ☺ 9am-6pm Mon-Fri, 10am-3pm Sat), at St Philip St. In the CBD there is a Kinko's FedEx Office Center (Map pp86–7; ☎ 581-2541; fax 525-6272; 762 St Charles Ave; ☺ 24hr).

Phonecards

Phonecards are readily sold at newsstands and pharmacies. They save you the trouble of feeding coins into pay phones, and are often more economical as well.

TIME

New Orleans Standard Time is six hours behind GMT/UTC. In US terms, that puts it one hour behind the East Coast and two hours ahead of the West Coast. In early April the clocks move ahead one hour for Daylight Saving Time; clocks move back one hour in October.

TIPPING

Tipping is not really optional. In bars and restaurants the waitstaff are paid minimal wages and rely on tips for their livelihoods. The service has to be absolutely appalling before you consider not tipping. Tip at least 15% of the bill or 20% if the service is good. You needn't tip at fast-food restaurants or self-serve cafeterias.

Taxi drivers expect a 15% tip. If you stay at a top-end hotel, tipping is so common you might get tennis elbow from reaching for your wallet. Hotel porters who carry bags a long way expect $3 to $5, or $1 per bag; smaller services (holding the taxi door open for you) might justify only $1. Valet parking is worth about $2, and is given when your car is returned to you.

TOILETS

A recording by Benny Grunch, 'Ain't No Place to Pee on Mardi Gras Day,' summarizes the situation in the French Quarter. While tour guides delight in describing the unsanitary waste-disposal practices of the old Creole days, the stench arising from back alleys is actually more recent in origin.

Public rest rooms can be found in the Jackson Brewery mall (Map pp70–1) and in the French Market (Map pp70–1). Larger hotels often have accessible rest rooms off the lobby, usually near the elevators and pay phones.

TOURIST INFORMATION

Right next to popular Jackson Sq in the heart of the Quarter, the New Orleans Welcome Center (Map pp70–1; ☎ 566-5031; 529 St Ann St; ⏱ 9am-5pm), in the lower Pontalba Building, offers maps, listings of upcoming events and a variety of brochures for sights, restaurants and hotels. The helpful staff can help you find accommodations in a pinch, answer questions and offer advice about New Orleans.

Information kiosks scattered through main tourist areas offer most of the same brochures as the Welcome Center, but their staff tend not to be as knowledgeable.

Information on Louisiana-wide tourism can be obtained through the mail from Louisiana Office of Tourism (☎ 342-8119, 800-414-8626; PO Box 94291, Baton Rouge, LA, 70804).

TRAVELERS WITH DISABILITIES

New Orleans is somewhat lax in this department. Sidewalk curbs rarely have ramps, and many historic public buildings and hotels are not equipped to meet the needs of the wheelchair bound. Modern hotels adhere to standards established by the federal Americans with Disabilities Act, with ramps, elevators and accessible bathrooms. A few of the Regional Transit Authority (RTA; ☎ 248-3900; www.norta.com) buses offer a lift service; for information about paratransit service (alternate transportation for those who can't ride regular buses), call the RTA Paratransit Customer Service on ☎ 827-7433 or visit their website. The Riverfront streetcar line features braille kiosks, platform ramps and wide doors that allow anyone to board easily. However, the St Charles Ave streetcar line has not been modified for wheelchair passengers. While these old cars continue to be used on the Canal St line, wheelchair accessibility will not be available there either.

VISAS

A passport with an official visa is required for most visitors to the USA; contact the US embassy or consulate in your home country for more information on specific requirements. Visitors between the ages of 14 and 79 have to be interviewed before a visa is granted, and all applicants must pay fees that stand at $131 (at the time of writing). You'll also have to prove you're not trying to stay in the USA permanently. The US Department of State has useful and up-to-date visa information online at http://travel.state.gov/visa.

If you're staying for 90 days or less you may qualify for the Visa Waiver Program (VWP); at the time of writing, citizens of 35 countries were eligible. The US Department of State provides useful and up-to-date online information on visa requirements and the VWP at http://travel.state.gov/visa.

Visa extensions are handled by the US Justice Department's Immigration & Naturalization Service (INS; Map pp86–7; ☎ 800-375-5283; Room T8011, 701 Loyola Ave; ⏱ 7:30am-2:15pm Mon-Fri) in the main post office.

WOMEN TRAVELERS

Intoxicated bands of men in the Quarter and along parade routes are a particular nuisance. Otherwise respectable students and professionals can be transformed by New Orleans in way not particularly flattering. Women in almost any attire are liable to receive lewd comments. More provocative outfits will lead to a continuous barrage of requests to 'show your tits.' (This occurs on any Friday or Saturday night, not just during Mardi Gras.) Many men assume that any woman wearing impressive strands of beads has acquired them by displaying herself on the street.

Any serious problems you encounter (including assault or rape) should be reported to the police (☎ 911). The YWCA offers a Rape Crisis Hotline (☎ 483-8888), as well as a Battered Women's Hotline (☎ 486-0377).

The New Orleans branch of Planned Parenthood (Map pp102–3; ☎ 897-9200; www.plannedparenthood. org; 4018 Magazine St) provides health-care services for women, including pregnancy testing and birth-control counseling.

WORK

Tourism puts butter on most people's bread in this town, and passers-through might score a low-paying job in a bar, restaurant or youth hostel. Of course, overseas visitors must have the proper work visas in order to work in the USA.

Skills in construction, electricity or plumbing are particularly in demand for the foreseeable future. Show up in town with a truck full of tools and very likely you'll find work as an independent contractor.

You probably don't need a work visa to volunteer in the rebuilding effort. Some organizations, such as Habitat For Humanity (www.habitat.org), claim to have more workers than they need, but it can't hurt to check in with them.

BEHIND THE SCENES

THIS BOOK

This 5th edition of New Orleans was written by Adam Karlin and Lisa Dunford. The Rebuilding a City chapter was written by Sean Mussenden. Earlier editions were written by Tom Downs and John T Edge. This guidebook was commissioned in Lonely Planet's Oakland office, and produced by the following:

Commissioning Editor Jennye Garibaldi

Coordinating Editor Daniel Corbett

Coordinating Cartographers Valeska Canas, Andy Rojas

Coordinating Layout Designer Carlos Solarte

Managing Editor Bruce Evans

Managing Cartographers Corey Hutchison, Alison Lyall

Managing Layout Designer Laura Jane

Assisting Editors Michelle Bennett, Victoria Harrison

Assisting Cartographer Alex Leung

Assisting Layout Designer Paul Iacono

Project Managers Eoin Dunlevy, Craig Kilburn

Thanks to Lucy Birchley, Sally Darmody, Heather Dickson, Suki Gear, Raphael Richards

Cover photographs by Lonely Planet Images: wrought-iron fence detail in Garden District, Richard Cummins

(top/back); band playing Cajun/zydeco in French Quarter Lou Jones, (bottom).

Internal photographs Cosmo Condina North America, Alamy p6 (#1). All other photographs by Lonely Planet Images: Jerry Alexander p7 (#1), p8 (#1 & #2); Olivier Cirendini p7 (#2); Richard Cummins p4 (#1); John Elk III p2, p6 (#2); Lee Foster p3; Ray Laskowitz p5 (#1 & #2); John Neubauer p4 (#2)

All images are copyright of the photographers unless otherwise indicated. Many of the images in this guide are available for licensing from Lonely Planet Images: www.lonelyplanetimages.com.

THANKS
ADAM KARLIN

Randy for the tour, Diana and John for the pad, David for being my first friend, Wil for showing off his city, Allison for help with the intro, Zach and Ted for their perspectives, Andy for giving me a place to crash, Sean F for discovering the city with me, Shane for fresh eyes, Noah for offering to sweep out my car and being a generally stand-up guy, Lisa and Sean M for their help on the city guide, Mom and Dad for the usual, Jennye for being a patient and excellent commissioning editor and New Orleans for being what it is.

LISA DUNFORD

I'd like to thank all the wonderful people in the Cajun heartland who welcomed me and invited me home,

THE LONELY PLANET STORY

Fresh from an epic journey across Europe, Asia and Australia in 1972, Tony and Maureen Wheeler sat at their kitchen table stapling together notes. The first Lonely Planet guidebook, Across Asia on the Cheap, was born.

Travelers snapped up the guides. Inspired by their success, the Wheelers began publishing books to Southeast Asia, India and beyond. Demand was prodigious, and the Wheelers expanded the business rapidly to keep up. Over the years, Lonely Planet extended its coverage to every country and into the virtual world via lonelyplanet.com and the Thorn Tree message board.

As Lonely Planet became a globally loved brand, Tony and Maureen received several offers for the company. But it wasn't until 2007 that they found a partner whom they trusted to remain true to the company's principles of traveling widely, treading lightly and giving sustainably. In October of that year, BBC Worldwide acquired a 75% share in the company, pledging to uphold Lonely Planet's commitment to independent travel, trustworthy advice and editorial independence.

Today, Lonely Planet has offices in Melbourne, London and Oakland, with over 500 staff members and 300 authors. Tony and Maureen are still actively involved with Lonely Planet. They're traveling more often than ever, and they're devoting their spare time to charitable projects. And the company is still driven by the philosophy of Across Asia on the Cheap: 'All you've got to do is decide to go and the hardest part is over. So go!'

forgiving the fact I was a Texan. Cheryl Spoor, Irish Johnson and Pamela Burnett were such a big help on the prairie. Thanks, too, to Jeff Anding, Mary Beth Romig, Marion Rundell and Jeff Richards, who were kind enough to share their expertise with me. Adam and Jennye – great working with you!

OUR READERS

Many thanks to the travelers who used the last edition and wrote to us with helpful hints, useful advice and interesting anecdotes:

Luc Assame, Jean Claude Bodard, Lisa Chan, Ashley Dyson, El Edwards, Sivan Hermon, Jillian Loveland, Deborah Luik, Heather Monell, Hawlan Ng, Dr Nikhil Pai, Bill Perry, Sue Strachan, Juliana Venning

ACKNOWLEDGMENTS

Transit map © 2009 New Orleans Regional Transit Authority. Map by Craig Dies, Let's Bus It, www .letsbusit.com

SEND US YOUR FEEDBACK

We love to hear from travelers – your comments keep us on our toes and help make our books better. Our well-traveled team reads every word on what you loved or loathed about this book. Although we cannot reply individually to postal submissions, we always guarantee that your feedback goes straight to the appropriate authors, in time for the next edition. Each person who sends us information is thanked in the next edition – and the most useful submissions are rewarded with a free book.

To send us your updates – and find out about Lonely Planet events, newsletters and travel news – visit our award-winning website: lonelyplanet.com/contact.

Note: We may edit, reproduce and incorporate your comments in Lonely Planet products such as guidebooks, websites and digital products, so let us know if you don't want your comments reproduced or your name acknowledged. For a copy of our privacy policy visit lonelyplanet.com/privacy.

Notes

Notes

Notes

Notes

INDEX

000 map pages
000 photographs

INDEX

000 map pages
000 photographs

lonelyplanet.com

GREENDEX

GOING GREEN

Lonely Planet is committed to responsible, sustainable travel. To that end, there are few destinations in the USA where your tourism dollar, well spent, has such an appreciable impact on a place's well-being as New Orleans. This is a city whose economy is, after all, primarily built on tourism. But green sensibility is not limited to the travel industry. As New Orleans rebuilds herself, she is becoming a petri dish for green construction, sustainable development and community revitalization models. As a city, she is full of heritage buildings and districts that represent a unique historical and cultural legacy. And the natural environment that ensconces her, the wetlands of the Gulf Coast, are a fragile and beautiful land- and water-scape whose preservation is wrapped up in New Orleans' survival.

By patronizing the businesses and sights listed here, we hope you can soak up the history and contribute to the rebirth of a great American city.

INDEX

MAP LEGEND

ROUTES

.... Tollway
.... Freeway
.... Primary
.... Secondary
.... Tertiary
.... Lane

.... Mall/Steps
.... Tunnel
.... Pedestrian Overpass
.... Walking Tour
.. .. .. Walking Trail

TRANSPORT

– – 🚉 – – .... Ferry
⊢–⊞–⊣ .... Rail

⚌⚌🚉⚌⚌ .... Streetcar

HYDROGRAPHY

.... River, Creek
.... Swamp

.... Water

BOUNDARIES

–⸳⸳–⸳ .... Parish

AREA FEATURES

.... Airport
.... Area of Interest
.... Building
.... Campus
+ + + Cemetery, Christian
.... Forest

.... Land
.... Mall
.... Market
.... Park
.... Sports
.... Urban

POPULATION

○ **CAPITAL (NATIONAL)**
● **Large City**
● Small City

◉ CAPITAL (STATE)
● Medium City
○ Town, Village

SYMBOLS

Information
🏦 .... Bank, ATM
✉ ...... Embassy/Consulate
✚ ...... Hospital, Medical
ℹ .... Information
@ ...... Internet Facilities
🚓 .... Police Station
✉ ...... Post Office, GPO
Sights
🕇 .... Christian
卐 .... Hindu

🔯 .... Jewish
🏛 .... Monument
🏛 ...... Museum, Gallery
● ...... Point of Interest
🏛 .... Ruin
🐦 ... Zoo, Bird Sanctuary
Shopping
🏠 .... Shopping
Eating
🍴 .... Eating

Drinking & Nightlife
🍷 .... Drinking
The Arts
🎭 .... Arts
Sleeping
🏠 .... Sleeping
Transportation
✈ ...... Airport, Airfield
🚲 ... Cycling, Bicycle Path
🅿 ...... Parking Area

Published by Lonely Planet Publications Pty Ltd
ABN 36 005 607 983

Australia Head Office, Locked Bag 1, Footscray, Victoria 3011,
☎ 03 8379 8000, fax 03 8379 8111,
talk2us@lonelyplanet.com.au

USA 150 Linden St, Oakland, CA 94607,
☎ 510 250 6400, toll free 800 275 8555,
fax 510 893 8572, info@lonelyplanet.com

UK 2nd fl, 186 City Rd, London, EC1V 2NT,
☎ 020 7106 2100, fax 020 7106 2101, go@
lonelyplanet.co.uk

© Lonely Planet 2009
Photographs © as listed (p246) 2009

Printed through Colorcraft Ltd, Hong Kong. Printed in China.

Mixed Sources
Product group from well-managed forests and other controlled sources
www.fsc.org Cert no. SGS-COC-005002
© 1996 Forest Stewardship Council

Off the
Beaten Path®

alabama

4105

3 1559 00171 7410

Help Us Keep This Guide Up to Date

Every effort has been made by the author and editors to make this guide as accurate and useful as possible. However, many changes can occur after a guide is published—establishments close, phone numbers change, hiking trails are rerouted, facilities come under new management, etc.

We would love to hear from you concerning your experiences with this guide and how you feel it could be improved and be kept up to date. While we may not be able to respond to all comments and suggestions, we'll take them to heart, and we'll make certain to share them with the author. Please send your comments and suggestions to the following address:

The Globe Pequot Press
Reader Response/Editorial Department
P.O. Box 480
Guilford, CT 06437

Or you may e-mail us at: editorial@GlobePequot.com

Thanks for your input, and happy travels!

INSIDERS' GUIDE®

OFF THE BEATEN PATH® SERIES

WITHDRAWN

Off the
Beaten Path®

SEVENTH EDITION

alabama

A GUIDE TO UNIQUE PLACES

GAY N. MARTIN

INSIDERS' GUIDE®

GUILFORD, CONNECTICUT
AN IMPRINT OF THE GLOBE PEQUOT PRESS

The prices, rates, and hours listed in this guidebook were confirmed at press time. We recommend, however, that you call establishments to obtain current information before traveling.

At press time, the 2004 hurricane season was causing massive damage to many areas in the southern coastal United States. Please check with attractions and establishments listed in this guide before making firm travel plans.

To buy books in quantity for corporate use or incentives, call **(800) 962–0973, ext. 4551,** or e-mail **premiums@GlobePequot.com.**

INSIDERS' GUIDE®

Text design by Linda Loiewski
Maps created by Equator Graphics © The Globe Pequot Press
Illustrations by Carole Drong
Spot photography throughout © Byron Jorjorian/Bruce Coleman Inc.

ISSN 1535-8291
ISBN 0-7627-3513-9

Manufactured in the United States of America
Seventh Edition/First Printing

This one's for my mother,

Edith Sorrells Newsom, who's a great traveler

and who accompanied me on many of the excursions described in this book

Florence

Huntsville

NORTHWEST
ALABAMA

NORTHEAST
ALABAMA

Birmingham

CENTRAL ALABAMA

Montgomery

SOUTHWEST
ALABAMA

SOUTHEAST
ALABAMA

Mobile

Contents

Acknowledgments

As I crisscrossed Alabama while researching this book, many people offered suggestions and provided information. I want to thank everyone who helped me with the birthing of the previous six editions. To that original list, I'd like to add the following people who assisted in the most recent delivery: Lee Sentell, Ami Simpson, Brian S. Jones, Peggy Collins, John Wild, Robyn L. Bridges, Carolyn and Dan Waterman, Peggy, Tina, and Fred Dew, Wendy and Bill James and Koa, Marge Shaw, Bill Charles, Sharon Quinn, Lisa O. Socha, Susann Hamlin, Debbie Wilson, Alison Stanfield, Pam Swanner, Patty Tucker, Chrissy Byrd, Susan Robertson, Leigh Ann Rains, Julia B. Brown, Lori Boatfield, Marla Akridge, Mayor Jim Byard Jr., Robert E. Lee, Linda and Earl Fisher, Jan and Joe Wood, James W. Parker, Mayor Al Kelley, Jeanne Hall Ashley, Robert Ratliff, Maria Traylor, Tom Barker, Al Mathis, Lin Graham, Rich Lopez, Stephanie Behrens, Laura McGill, Bebe Gauntt, Jane McClanahan, Bob Doyle, Tom Walker, Kelly Durban, Myrna Hertenstein, Georgia Turner, Doug Purcell, Deborah Gray, Marynell Ford, Janet S. Shelby, Cherie M. Wynn, Vickie Ashford, Dr. Don Dodd, Lauri Cothran, Sandy Smith, Kathy Johnson, Becky Jones, Deborah Stone, Danky and Al Blanton, Linda Vice, Kathy Danielson Williams, and Suzanne Pittinos. And a champagne toast (make that Dom Perignon, please) to Cathy Myers for her superb research assistance.

Others who contributed to this project include Joyce White, Joyce O'Brien, Robin Cooper, Gaynelle Lusk, and Carolyn Mason. I'm also grateful to writers Kathryn Tucker Windham, Jesse Culp, Mary Kay Remich, Shirley Mitchell, Joan and Neal Broerman, and the two Lynns.

Hugs and kisses go to my family and especially to Carlton Martin—my husband, best friend, navigator, and photographer.

Introduction

As a vacation destination, Alabama falls in the proverbial best-kept-secret category. With its varied and splendid geography, moderate climate, and Southern hospitality, the state makes an ideal year-round getaway. From its craggy Appalachian bluffs to sugar-sand beaches on the Gulf of Mexico, Alabama's wealth of natural beauty offers a happy (and uncrowded) vacation choice for everyone.

Some consider Alabama almost synonymous with sports and recite exploits of Bear Bryant, Joe Namath, Bo Jackson, Pat Sullivan, John Hannah, Hank Aaron, Joe Louis, Willie Mays, Jesse Owens, LeRoy "Satchel" Paige, Bobby Allison—and the list goes on. Although racing fans throng Talladega's speedway and Birmingham's Alabama Sports Hall of Fame speaks of diversity, visitors soon discover that football reigns supreme here. The first Alabama–Auburn clash dates to February 22, 1893, and loyalty lines continue to divide families, friends, and lovers. The stirring words "Roll Tide" and "War Eagle" enter the typical childhood vocabulary early on.

Thanks to the Robert Trent Jones Golf Trail (and David G. Bronner, who conceived it), Alabama recently made *Money* magazine's group of the eight best vacation spots in the world. Sharing a list with the French Alps, Baja, Martinique, Antigua, Phoenix, Alta's ski country, and Sanibel Island puts the RTJ Trail, which winds its way through Alabama, on the world map.

Unless you agree with Mark Twain that golf is a good walk ruined, you can't pass up the RTJ Trail, which will test the skills of all golfers from scratch handicappers to hopeless duffers. Beginning in the mountains and lakes of the Appalachian foothills and continuing southward to the white sands and wetlands of the Gulf Coast, this group of eight PGA tour–quality courses, ranging from thirty-six and fifty-four holes each, provides superb golfing and splendid scenery. From Huntsville's Hampton Cove, Gadsden's Silver Lakes, Birmingham's Oxmoor Valley, and Prattville's Capitol Hill to Grand National in the Auburn–Opelika area, Highland Oaks at Dothan, Cambrian Ridge at Greenville, and Magnolia Cove near Mobile, travelers can enjoy the exclusive country club experience at affordable prices. *Golf* magazine called the RTJ Trail number one in the world for value. Capitol Hill, the trail's flagship addition, allows you to pick your pleasure from among three challenging courses: the Judge, the Legislator, and the Senator. *Golf* magazine named the Senator one of the country's top new courses for 2000, and situated on its seventeenth fairway you'll find the Legends at Capitol Hill, the trail's first full-service conference resort—a perfect place to stay and play. Or you can opt for the handsome Lodge and Conference Center at Grand National. A hillside hotel/civic center will overlook the new eighteen-hole Ross Bridge Course now being built in Hoover a couple of miles from the existing fifty-four-hole course in Oxmoor Valley; the Ross Bridge Course will open in 2005. Also, in the Shoals, a thirty-six-hole RTJ golf complex awaits your pleasure. To play any or all of these public courses designed by world-famous golf architect Robert Trent Jones, call (800) 949–4444. With one phone call, you can make arrangements for tee times at any of the trail's sites plus lodging reservations.

Speaking of trails, anglers will want to follow their bliss on the new Alabama Bass Trail. Developed by the state Department of Conservation and Natural Resources and the first of its kind in the country, this trail consists of five sites showcasing major lakes across the state with plenty of outstanding bass tournaments on the agenda. And that's not all. *Audubon* magazine named the Alabama Coastal Birding Trail, which stretches through Baldwin and Mobile counties, one of the country's best viewing sites. Bird-watchers will find directional and interpretive signs all along the way.

Stars still fall on Alabama, and visitors can dip into a rich musical heritage throughout the state. Depending on your own particular penchant, you may catch a classical music concert at the Birmingham Civic Center or a swinging jazz session during Florence's yearly tribute to the "Father of the Blues," W.C. Handy. The Alabama Music Hall of Fame, near Tuscumbia, features memorabilia of Nat King Cole, Hank Williams, Sonny James, Lionel Richie, the Commodores, Emmylou Harris, Dinah Washington, the Temptations, and many other musicians with Alabama connections.

This book spotlights some of the state's special places—not only major sites such as the United States Space & Rocket Center in Huntsville but also small towns frozen in time and tucked-away treasures occasionally overlooked by the natives. In the state's northern section, Huntsville makes a handy launching pad from which travelers can easily loop both east and west to take in north Alabama's unique attractions. Heading south, the Birmingham area serves as a convenient base from which to branch out into the state's central section. From there you can sweep farther south to Montgomery to see the state capital area and southeastern section, which includes the historic Chattahoochee Trace. This account concludes with the beaches of Gulf Shores and one of the state's most beautiful cities, Mobile. In his book *A Walk Across America,* Peter Jenkins describes being captivated by Mobile, calling it a fantasy city. "Even more than by the psychedelic azaleas," he said, "I was moved by the great-grandfather live-oak trees."

Alabama's surprises start as soon as you cross the border, and the following sneak preview will give you an idea of what to expect. Huntsville, while playing a strategic role in the nation's space program, also preserves its past at

EarlyWorks and at Alabama Constitution Village, a living-history museum. Delegates drafted Alabama's first constitution here in 1819, and when you open the gate and walk through the picket fence, you may smell bread baking and see aproned guides dipping beeswax candles or carding cotton—quite a contrast to the future-focused Space & Rocket Center. By the way, if you've harbored a secret yen to taste the astronaut's life but always thought Space Camp was just for kids, you're in for another surprise: The Space & Rocket Center offers programs for all who dare to delve into space technology, from fourth graders to grandparents. You might even participate in a simulated space-shuttle mission. If you're not ready for such a challenge, you can still stop by the gift shop and sample some freeze-dried astronaut ice cream.

Heading east gets you to Scottsboro, home of the "First Monday" market, one of the South's oldest and largest "trade days." Also known for its many caves, this area attracts spelunkers from around the world. Russell Cave, located at Jackson County's northeastern tip, could be called Alabama's first welcome center. Some 9,000 years ago bands of Native Americans began occupying the large cave; archaeologists, using carbon dating, have determined it to be the oldest known site of human occupancy in the southeastern United States.

At DeSoto State Park, also in the northeast region, visitors can view Little River Canyon National Preserve, the largest and one of the deepest gorges east of the Mississippi River. Near the charming mountain hamlet of Mentone, Cloudmont Resort features a dude ranch and ski slopes (albeit with Mother Nature getting some assistance from snow machines).

Lakes Guntersville, Wheeler, and Wilson make northern Alabama a haven for water sports enthusiasts. Lake Guntersville State Park hosts an Eagle Weekend in January, a good time of the year to spot bald eagles. Many visitors report being surprised by Alabama's state parks, which offer a sampling of some of the state's most spectacular vistas, such as the newly opened and awe-inspiring Cathedral Caverns, plus a host of recreation options—and at bargain prices.

At Cullman, visitors can take a Lilliputian world tour at Ave Maria Grotto, a unique garden filled with more than 125 miniature reproductions of famous buildings. The reproductions were made by a gifted Benedictine monk named Brother Joseph Zoettl. And nearby Hanceville has become a mecca for pilgrims who want to visit the Shrine of the Most Blessed Sacrament of Our Lady of the Angels Monastery.

Another surprise for many visitors is learning that not all Alabamians backed the South during the Civil War. Sometimes staged in Winston County, an outdoor drama called *The Incident at Looney's Tavern* tells the story of hill-country people who struggled to remain independent during the conflict. In front of the county courthouse at Double Springs stands *Dual Destiny,* the statue of a soldier backed by billowing Confederate and Union flags.

In Blount County you can see three of the state's covered bridges. Master-and-slave team John Godwin and Horace King built a number of Alabama's early bridges. After gaining his freedom, King joined Godwin as a business partner, later erecting a monument in "lasting remembrance of the love and gratitude he felt for his lost friend and former master." The monument can be seen at a Phenix City cemetery.

Each summer visitors can witness the reenactment of a miracle in northwest Alabama at Ivy Green, home of America's courageous Helen Keller.

As Alabama's major metropolis, Birmingham's paths are well trampled. Still, the Magic City offers some not-to-be-missed treats, such as the historic Five Points South area with its boutiques and outdoor eateries and the new 740-acre Barber Motorsports Park near Irondale. On the somber side, the Birmingham Civil Rights Institute and nearby complex re-creates a journey through the darkness of segregation.

Farther south you'll find Montgomery, a backdrop for sweeping drama since Jefferson Davis telegraphed his "Fire on Fort Sumter" order from here and the Civil War proceeded to rip the country apart. Less than a century later, the Civil Rights Movement gained momentum in this town, paving the way for overdue national reform. The interpretative Rosa Parks Library and Museum offers an in-depth look at the Montgomery bus boycott and pays tribute to the "Mother of the Civil Rights Movement." Also located here, the Alabama Shakespeare Festival provides top dramatic entertainment.

Don't miss Selma, a quintessential Southern city, but one that preserves its drama-filled past—from Civil War to civil rights. Spring Pilgrimage events include home tours, a reenactment of the Battle of Selma, and a grand ball on Sturdivant Hall's lovely lawn. Selma also stages an annual Tale Tellin' Festival featuring Alabama's first lady of folk legends and ghost stories, Kathryn Tucker Windham (whose intriguing tales you may have heard on National Public Radio broadcasts).

Traveling down to Monroeville, the Literary Capital of Alabama, you'll see the courthouse and surrounding square where Truman Capote and Harper Lee, author of *To Kill a Mockingbird,* roamed as childhood friends.

Still farther south, the Gulf Shores and Orange Beach area, with glistening white beaches, sea oats, and sand dunes, lures many visitors. The coastal area also offers historic forts, grand mansions, a multirooted (French, British, and Spanish) heritage, and superb cuisine.

On Mobile Bay's eastern shore, a strange spectacle known as "Jubilee" sometimes surprises visitors. Spurred by unknown forces, shrimp, flounder, crab, and other marine creatures suddenly crowd the shoreline, usually several times a summer. When the cry of "Jubilee!" rings along the beach, people rush to the water's edge to fill containers with fresh seafood.

Alabama's colorful celebrations run the gamut from Mobile's Mardi Gras (which preceded New Orleans's extravaganza), Gulf Shores's National Shrimp Festival, and the Blessing of the Shrimp Fleet at Bayou LaBatre (home of Forrest Gump's successful shrimping business) to Opp's Rattlesnake Rodeo, Dothan's National Peanut Festival, and Decatur's hot-air balloon gala called the Alabama Jubilee.

When making travel plans, call ahead because dates, rates, and hours of operation change from time to time. Unless otherwise stated in this guide, all museums and attractions with admission prices of $5.00 or less per adult are labeled modest. A restaurant meal (entree without beverage) classified as economical costs less than $8.00; moderate prices range between $8.00 and $20.00; and entrees $20.00 and above are designated expensive. As for accommodations, those that cost less than $80 per day are described as standard; an overnight price between $80 and $150 is called moderate; and lodging costing more than $150 is designated deluxe.

For travel information, maps, and brochures, stop by one of the eight Alabama Welcome Centers; call (800) ALABAMA; write to Alabama Tourism and Travel, P.O. Box 4927, Montgomery 36103–4927; or visit www.tourala bama.org. To preview the state parks, log onto www.alapark.com. You can make reservations at any Alabama state park by dialing (800) ALA–PARK. So pack your bags, grab your car keys, head for the unforgettable Heart of Dixie, anticipate some surprises, and watch out for falling stars.

Fast Facts about Alabama

CLIMATE OVERVIEW

Alabama's climate falls in the temperate range, becoming mostly subtropical near the Gulf Coast. Spring's first flowers appear early, often in February. By April, average statewide temperatures reach the 60s. Summer days often fall in the hot and humid category. Fall brings changing foliage and refreshing cooler weather. Snow is such a rarity in most parts of the state that when the weather person predicts it, everyone gets excited and makes a mad dash to the grocery stores for bread and milk.

FAMOUS ALABAMIANS

Some famous Alabamians include Helen Keller, Harper Lee, Winston Groom, Fannie Flagg, the country music group Alabama, Hank Williams Sr. and Jr., Rosa Parks, Kenny Stabler, Hank Aaron, Willie Mays, and Tallulah Bankhead.

NEWSPAPERS

The state's major newspapers include *The Huntsville Times, The Birmingham News, The Montgomery Advertiser,* and the *Mobile Press Register.* Since printed papers started in the state around 1806, according to Bill Keller, former executive director of the Alabama Press Association, Alabamians have demonstrated a long-standing appreciation for newspapers. Every county in Alabama produces a newspaper. Current records show twenty-five daily newspapers, printing from five to seven days a week, and ninety-seven weekly papers, publishing from one to three times a week.

General Alabama Trivia

- In 1540 Hernando DeSoto traveled through much of what is now Alabama.
- On December 14, 1819, Alabama became the twenty-second state in the Union.
- Alabama seceded from the Union on January 11, 1861, and rejoined on June 25, 1868.
- Montgomery has served as the state capital since 1846. Former capitals included St. Stephens, Huntsville, Cahaba, and Tuscaloosa.
- In 1959 the camellia became Alabama's state flower, replacing the goldenrod, which held that honor from 1927.
- The tarpon was designated as Alabama's official saltwater fish in 1955.
- Red iron ore, scientifically known as hematite, is the state mineral.
- Distinguished educator and humanitarian Julia Tutwiler wrote the words for "Alabama," the state song.
- Alabama comprises sixty-seven counties.

Northeast Alabama

Space Capital

Traveling through this area of Alabama, with its wooded glens, rugged mountain vistas, and sparkling lakes, is almost like moving through a calendar of splendid landscapes. Keep your camera handy because you'll discover some spectacular scenery.

Entering at the state's northern border, you'll drive through the rolling Tennessee Valley to reach *Huntsville,* a handy hub whether you're heading east or west to explore north Alabama's numerous attractions.

The birthplace of America's space program, Huntsville also served as an early capital of Alabama and later grew into a cotton mill town. After Dr. Wernher von Braun and his crew of German scientists arrived in the 1950s to pioneer the space program at Redstone Arsenal, Huntsville traded its title as World Watercress Capital for World Space Capital. The decade from 1950 to 1960 saw the population in Rocket City, U.S.A., mushroom from 15,000 to 72,000. Even today, ongoing road construction cannot keep pace with the burgeoning population and traffic.

A good place to start a local tour is the *Huntsville Depot Transportation Museum* (256–564–8100) at 320 Church Street.

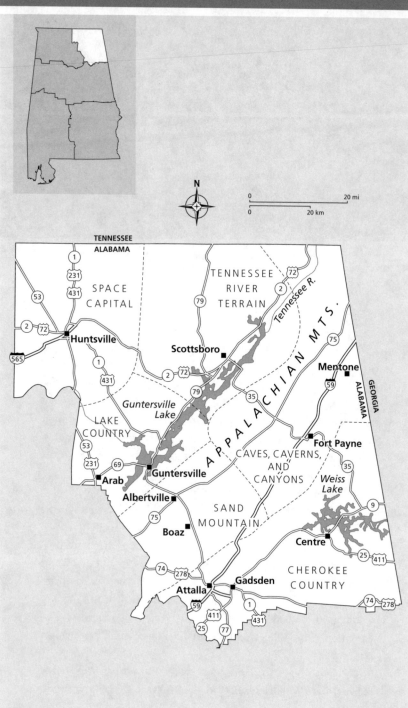

Take time to tour the authentically restored depot, a big yellow building where a robotic telegrapher, stationmaster, and engineer welcome visitors and describe railroad life in 1912. During the Civil War the depot served as a prison, and upstairs you'll see some interesting graffiti such as a rather unflattering drawing of Union officer Major Strout and an inscription that reads HAPPY NEW YEARS TO ALL IN THE YEAR OF OUR LORD 1864. The depot's hours are 9:00 A.M. to 5:00 P.M. Tuesday through Saturday. The museum is closed on major holidays. Admission is charged.

As you drive around the area, check out the Von Braun Civic Center at 700 Monroe Street. This large multipurpose complex may well be hosting a concert, sporting event, or play you'd like to take in while in town.

Continue your self-driving tour through Huntsville's Historic Twickenham District with more than sixty-five antebellum houses and churches. Architectural

Watercress Capital of the World

Huntsville acquired the title "Watercress Capital of the World" because in earlier days it produced and shipped a large volume of watercress throughout the eastern half of the country. A member of the mustard family, watercress thrives in limestone springwater and once grew prolifically in the Tennessee Valley's many limestone springs.

Huntsville's old Russell Erskine Hotel was noted for its watercress salad, and several local cookbooks feature this specialty, sometimes known simply as "cress." The *Huntsville Heritage Cookbook* contains a section devoted to watercress including the following tasty recipe, once served at a White House state banquet. Long a local favorite, this book is again in print, thanks to the Huntsville Junior League. Look for it at gift shops and bookstores throughout Huntsville, and while browsing, pick up a copy of the Junior League's award-winning *Sweet Home Alabama,* a handsome volume featuring "Food for Family and Friends from the Heart of the South."

Frozen Cheese and Cress Salad

1 teaspoon plain gelatin

⅓ cup cold water

1 cup hot water

½ teaspoon salt

8 ounces cream cheese

1 small jar pimientos, chopped

1 cup heavy cream, whipped

Soak gelatin in cold water. Add hot water and salt. Strain and set aside until barely jelled. Beat until fluffy and fold in cream cheese that has been creamed. Add pimientos and fold in cream. Mold and chill. Serve on bed of watercress.

styles represented include Federal, Greek Revival, Italianate, Palladian, Gothic Revival, and others. For a fine example of Federal architecture, tour the **Weeden House Museum** (256–536–7718) at 300 Gates Avenue. Built in 1819, the home contains period antiques and features the work of Huntsville artist and poet Maria Howard Weeden, who lived here until her death in 1905. Her impressive body of work includes book illustrations, whimsical drawings, fascinating character studies, and portraits. Except for January and February when the museum closes, hours are 11:00 A.M. to 4:00 P.M. Monday through Saturday. Modest admission.

On the square in downtown Huntsville, stop by **Harrison Brothers Hardware Store** (256–536–3631), located at 124 South Side Square. The store celebrated one hundred years on the Square in 1997. Here you can purchase marbles by the scoop, old-fashioned stick candy, cast-iron cookware, kerosene lamps, seeds, scrub boards, and other merchandise that speaks of yesteryear. Historic Huntsville Foundation volunteers ring up sales on a 1907 cash register. The interior, with pot-bellied stove, ceiling fans, rolling ladders, barrels, tools, and antique safe, looks much as it did in 1879 when the store opened for business. Hours are 9:00 A.M. to 5:00 P.M. weekdays and 10:00 A.M. to 4:00 P.M. Saturday.

Don't miss **Alabama Constitution Village** (256–564–8100) just around the corner. Entering the picket-fence gate at Franklin Street and Gates Avenue takes

GAY'S TOP PICKS IN NORTHEAST ALABAMA

Alabama Constitution Village,
Huntsville

Buck's Pocket State Park,
Grove Oak

Burritt on the Mountain,
Huntsville

Cathedral Caverns,
Grant

DeSoto State Park,
Fort Payne

EarlyWorks,
Huntsville

Lake Guntersville State Park,
Guntersville

Little River Canyon National Preserve,
Fort Payne

Noccalula Falls and Park,
Gadsden

Sequoyah Caverns,
Valley Head

Town of Mentone

U.S. Space & Rocket Center,
Huntsville

A Tribute to Everbody's Favorite Aunt

For more than half a century, the late Eunice Merrell served what many considered the best country ham and homemade biscuits in the world. Former governor Fob James declared her biscuits "the best in Alabama," and his proclamation made them the official state biscuit.

Although Eunice (better known to her customers as "Aunt" Eunice) described her diner as "just a little greasy spoon," the fame of her homemade biscuits made the *Congressional Record* in a tribute introduced by U.S. Senator Howell Heflin, who represented Alabama.

At Eunice's Country Kitchen, you often had to wait a bit for a table or even share one with someone else. Some people even kept their own favorite brand of jelly or preserves in Eunice's refrigerator, retrieving it when the hot biscuits arrived, but most folks dipped into the honey or Sand Mountain sorghum on every table.

In this small cafe that did a booming business with no advertising, it was customary to warm up your neighbors' coffee if you got up to pour yourself a refill. In fact, when prospective candidates for office visited (this was a popular stop on political campaigns), Aunt Eunice expected them to follow protocol and wait on her customers; otherwise, they did not deserve the office to which they aspired—and she told them so.

Look for an authentically replicated Eunice's Country Kitchen at the Historic Huntsville Depot. You'll see the cafe's famous "Liars' Table," with its suspended wooden sign reserving it for politicians and preachers. (During a meal, Eunice sometimes presented customers with an official "Liar's License," permitting them to prevaricate "at any time or place without notice.") Other memorabilia include favorite quotes and an extensive collection of autographed photos from governors, congressmen, actors, astronauts, sports figures, and even a president.

Aunt Eunice, we miss you.

you back to 1819, when delegates met here to draft Alabama's first constitution. Afterward, on a tour of the complex, you'll see costumed guides going about their seasonal business of preserving summer's fruits or making candles at hog-killing time.

Stop by the gift shop, with such unique items as "ugly jugs," once used as containers for harmful substances. Hours are 9:00 A.M. to 5:00 P.M. Tuesday through Saturday. The village is closed on major holidays. Admission.

Kids—both young and old—love traveling back in time to the nineteenth century and exploring *EarlyWorks,* a hands-on history museum (256–564–8100) at 404 Madison Street, where new adventures await around every corner.

Special exhibits include an amazing 16-foot-tall tale-telling tree, giant-size musical instruments, and a 46-foot keelboat. Youngsters can dress up in vintage clothing and practice tasks that children in the "olden days" performed, and toddlers can milk a "pretend" cow and gather garden vegetables. Except for major holidays, hours run from 9:00 A.M. to 5:00 P.M. Tuesday through Saturday. Admission. Special prices are available for combination tours of EarlyWorks with the historic Huntsville Depot and Alabama Constitution Village. Parking is available throughout the downtown area with handicapped parking on the Gates Avenue side. Learn more about this hands-on facility on the Internet at www.earlyworks.com.

Afterward, head south on Madison Street until you reach Governor's Drive, then turn left. Don't miss Monte Sano Mountain, which offers sweeping views of Huntsville and the surrounding Tennessee River Valley. *Burritt on the Mountain,* a living-history museum (256–536–2882), at 3101 Burritt Drive, just off Monte Sano Boulevard, features 167 wooded acres with walking trails and picnicking facilities. At this living-history site, you'll find a blacksmith shop, smokehouse, church, and some log houses depicting rural life between 1850 and 1900. An X-shaped house, built in 1937 by Dr. William Henry Burritt, serves as the park's focal point. Both a physician and gifted inventor who held twenty patents during his life, Burritt combined Classical and art deco elements when he designed this unusual home.

alabamatrivia

Alabama's Robert Trent Jones Golf Trail is the world's largest golf-course construction project.

Inside you'll see archaeological and restoration exhibits, clothing, toys, and displays on Huntsville's history. One room features the paintings of local artist Maria Howard Weeden. Special events include the Fall Sorghum and Harvest Festival and Candlelight Christmas. Admission prices are slightly higher for special events. The museum is open Tuesday through Saturday from 10:00 A.M. to 4:00 P.M. and Sunday noon to 4:00 P.M. November through March. Summer hours are Tuesday through Saturday 9:00 A.M. to 5:00 P.M. and Sunday noon to 5:00 P.M. The grounds can be visited daily from 7:00 A.M. to 5:00 P.M. October through March and 7:00 A.M. to 7:00 P.M. April through September.

Dogwood Manor (256–859–3946) at 707 Chase Road makes a lovely base for exploring the Huntsville area. Valerie and Patrick Jones own this restored Federal-style home, set on a sweeping lawn with century-old trees. The home's builder once operated a thriving nursery here and shipped his plants all over the country. Patrick, an attorney, shares history about the home and the Chase community with interested guests.

GAY'S FAVORITE ANNUAL EVENTS IN NORTHEAST ALABAMA

Art on the Lake,
Guntersville, April;
(256) 582–3612 or (800) 869–5253

Panoply, Huntsville's Festival of the Arts,
Big Spring International Park, Huntsville, last full weekend of April;
(256) 519–2787

Riverfest,
Gadsden, May;
(256) 543–3472

Stevenson Depot Days,
Stevenson, early June;
(256) 437–3012 or (800) 259–5508

Freedom Festival,
Albertville, weekend of or prior to July Fourth;
(256) 878–3821

St. William's Seafood Festival,
Guntersville, early September (Labor Day weekend);
(256) 582–3612

Big Spring Jam Music Festival,
Big Spring International Park, Huntsville, last full weekend of September;
(256) 551–2359

Depot Days Festival,
Hartselle, early October;
(256) 773–4370

Harvest Festival,
Boaz, early October;
(256) 593–8154 or (800) 746–7262

Falls Fest,
Noccalula Falls, Gadsden, October;
(256) 543–3472

Heritage Festival,
Attalla, October;
(256) 543–3472

Mentone Fall Colorfest,
Mentone, third weekend of October;
(256) 845–3957 or (888) 805–4740

Christmas on the Rocks,
Noccalula Falls, Gadsden, the day after Thanksgiving through December;
(256) 543–3472

Galaxy of Lights,
Huntsville/Madison County Botanical Garden, Thanksgiving through New Year's Eve;
(256) 830–4447

The couple reserves four charming rooms—appropriately named Dogwood, Magnolia, Azalea, and Rose—for overnight visitors and serves afternoon tea on request. Valerie, a school counselor, prepares gourmet breakfasts, complemented by her own homemade breads and muffins. She often makes apple French toast, crumpets, and English scones. Moderate rates. Visit Dogwood Manor's Web site at www.bridgenet1.com/dogwood.

Across from Dogwood Manor's driveway stands the *North Alabama Railroad Museum* (256–851–NARM) at 694 Chase Road. The restored green-and-yellow Chase Depot houses a waiting room and agent office filled with exhibits. Home of the Mercury and Chase Railroad and the country's smallest union station, the facility now features a walk-through passenger train and twenty-seven pieces of major railroading stock. Except for major holidays, the museum is open each Wednesday and Saturday from 8:30 A.M. to 2:00 P.M. April through October and offers guided tours and excursion train rides. Children enjoy watching for the concrete animals staged along the track. In addition to regular trips, a Goblin Special and Santa Trail Special are also scheduled. Call for more information on schedules, fares, and reservations, or visit the Web site at www.suncompsvc.com/narm/ for current happenings.

Tennessee River Terrain

From Huntsville take U.S. Highway 72 east to **Scottsboro,** home of **First Monday,** one of the South's oldest and largest "trade days." This outdoor market might feature anything from cast-iron skillets, church pews, and collie puppies to butter churns, gingham-checked sunbonnets, and pocketknives—all displayed around the Jackson County Courthouse Square. Lasting from morning till dark, the event dates to the mid-1800s, when people met at the courthouse square on the day Circuit Court opened to visit as well as to trade horses, mules, and other livestock. The merry mix of folks who still come to browse, banter, and barter carry on a Southern tradition, and many have honed their trading techniques to a high level of skill. Although this event takes place on the first Monday of every month (plus the Sunday preceding it), the Labor Day weekend typically proves most popular.

If you miss Scottsboro's First Monday, you can console yourself by dipping into a chocolate milk shake, ice-cream soda, or banana split at **Payne's** (256–574–2140), located at 101 East Laurel on the town square's north side. Owned by Shay and Gene Holder, this eatery occupies the site of a former drugstore dating from 1869. The interior, complete with old-fashioned soda fountain, features a black-and-white color scheme with red accents. You can perch on a bar stool, order a fountain Coke that's mixed on the spot and served in a traditional Coca-Cola glass, and munch on a hot dog with red slaw straight from the original drugstore menu. Other options include Payne's popular chicken salad and a variety of sandwiches along with homemade desserts. Hours are 11:00 A.M. to 4:00 P.M. Monday through Saturday (except on Thursday, when closing time is 3:00 P.M.). The eatery is also open 11:00 A.M. to 4:00 P.M. on the Sunday before First Monday.

To learn about the area's history, visit the ***Scottsboro-Jackson Heritage Center*** (256–259–2122), located at 208 South Houston Street. This Neoclassical-style structure, built in 1881, houses some interesting exhibits, including Native American artifacts found on land later flooded by the Tennessee Valley Authority (TVA) and rare photographic displays depicting the early days of Skyline, a unique community north of Scottsboro.

Behind the big house stands the small 1868 Jackson County Courthouse. Nearby, a pioneer village called Sage Town features a collection of authentic log structures that includes a cabin, schoolhouse, barn, and blacksmith shop, all filled with vintage items.

The museum offers a wealth of genealogical materials, says Judi Weaver, who promotes archaeological awareness in her role as director. The facility focuses on the area's history from the Paleo-Indian era through the 1930s. Special events include heritage festivals and art exhibitions. Hours are 11:00 A.M. to 4:00 P.M. Monday through Friday, or by appointment. A modest admission is charged.

If, after a plane trip, you've ever discovered yourself divorced from your bags and wondered about their final destination, it's entirely possible that your lost luggage wound up at Scottsboro's ***Unclaimed Baggage Center*** (256–259–1525), located at 509 West Willow Street (although your bags may have traveled instead to nearby Unclaimed Baggage in Decatur). At this unique outlet you can find such items as cameras, caviar, clothing, hammocks, hair dryers, jewelry, scuba gear, and ski equipment. The ever-changing merchandise from around the world also features baby strollers, books, briefcases, luggage, personal electronic devices, and high-tech equipment.

"We have to stay on top of technology to know what's coming in here," says a company executive. The diverse inventory of lost, found, and unclaimed items comes from various airlines to be sorted and offered for sale at reduced rates—50 percent or more off retail prices. In this shopping mecca, which now covers more than a city block, you can enjoy a mug of brewed Starbuck's coffee at the facility's in-house cafe, called Cups.

Business boomed here—even before Oprah spread the word on her TV show. The parking lot gets especially crowded on weekends, and car tags reveal shoppers from many states. Recent visitors also came from Ontario, Bavaria, New Zealand, South America, France, and England. Closed on Sunday, hours are 9:00 A.M. to 6:00 P.M. Monday through Friday and 8:00 A.M. to 6:00 P.M. Saturday. The Web site is www.unclaimedbaggage.com.

After sightseeing in the Scottsboro area, you can easily head south on State Route 79 toward ***Guntersville*** to take in some Marshall County attractions, or you can continue your loop northeast to Stevenson. ***Goose Pond Colony*** (256–259–2884 or 800–268–2884), a peninsula surrounded by the Tennessee River, is located 5 miles south of Scottsboro on State Route 79 at 417 Ed Hembree Drive and offers vacation cottages, picnic facilities, camping sites, swimming pool, marina and launching ramp, golf course, and nature/walking trail. Popular with both geese and golfers, the golf course is noted for its beauty and design. Named by *Golf Digest* as one of "The Places to Play," Goose Pond's course also made the top five in a previous PGA opinion poll ranking courses in the Dixie section. For more information visit www.goosepond.org.

The Docks (256–574–3071), a restaurant on the grounds behind the swimming pool, offers a variety of seafood including Cajun fare. You can dine on the deck with a fine view of the water. Some diners arrive by boat and tie up at the property's private pier. The restaurant is open from 5:00 to 10:00 P.M. Tuesday through Saturday. Prices range from moderate to expensive.

Before leaving this area, you may want to call the Scottsboro/Jackson County Chamber of Commerce (256–259–5500 or 800–259–5508) or stop by the headquarters at 407 East Willow Street to pick up brochures on various local and area attractions.

A squirrel's nest with a Web site? It's true. Way off the beaten path near Grant, you may or may not find ***The Squirrel Nest*** (256–571–0324), a restaurant at 2219 Baker Mountain Road. When owner Doris Smith transformed her secluded family home into a restaurant, she chose the name because of the setting. "We are in the woods," she says, "and surrounded by squirrels' nests."

Guests will find a comfortable, homey atmosphere with plenty of whimsical touches both inside and out. A wall-size mural depicts deer in a woodland scene. Doris does the cooking, and her daughter Carmen assists in serving. The most popular breakfast choice here is country ham with homemade biscuits, eggs, gravy, grits, and the works. Dinner entrees come with soup, salad, homemade bread, a triangle of Vidalia onion pie, and dessert. (You may want to request a box for leftovers.) Also, The Squirrel Nest houses a getaway suite complete with hot tub. Call for dinner reservations (required) and specific directions. Breakfast hours run from 6:00 to 11:00 A.M. Tuesday through Saturday. Dinner hours are 5:00 to 9:00 P.M. Thursday through Saturday. Scurry to www.thesquirrelnest.com for more information.

Tucked away in a sylvan setting about halfway between Scottsboro and Guntersville, ***Ivy Creek Inn*** (256–505–0722) awaits the traveler who wants to get in touch with nature but still enjoy creature comforts. To reach the property at 985 Carlton Road, you'll take a turn off State Route 79 North (marked by a sign) that leads down a wooded route and over a couple of single-lane bridges to the bed-and-breakfast inn, fronted by a creek. In fact, the creek's gurgling will probably be the first thing you hear upon arrival because the two resident Lassie-like collies, Lucy and Jack, don't bark—they simply wag their tails in greeting. The inn was opened in 1999 by Kathy and Hess Fridley, who fell in love with this wooded hollow while visiting and soon found themselves the owners—thanks to an auction. In addition to a large house to maintain, their property of twenty acres features an underground lake, a cave, and a waterfall, which make an enchanting backdrop for outdoor dining.

You'll see an incredible arrowhead collection amassed by Hess's father and exhibited in handmade cabinets, plus works by Colorado artist Bev Doolittle. Kathy reserves two rooms called The Country Store to showcase items hand-crafted by area artisans. Don't miss the white oak baskets created by Jesse Thomason from Blountsville. Ivy Creek offers five guest rooms plus an apart-ment, all with private baths. Breakfast arrives on lovely ivy-patterned china and might feature Kathy's delicious version of eggs Benedict or stuffed French toast with blackberries. Moderate rates. View the property at www.ivycreekn.com.

Although you might find the tiny town of Pisgah on your road map, you won't find **Gorham's Bluff** (256–451–VIEW [8439])—yet. This traditional neighborhood community (inspired by Florida's Seaside) offers travelers some stunning scenery, especially from the Overlook Pavilion, and accommodations at The Lodge. The property commands sweeping bluffside views of the Ten-nessee River. *Travel and Leisure* magazine recently chose Gorham's Bluff for inclusion in "The 30 Great U.S. Inns."

This lovely site remained undeveloped until Clara and Bill McGriff (a CPA still remembered by locals as a basketball star) started exploring their daughter

Overlook Pavilion at Gorham's Bluff

Dawn's idea of creating a brand-new, arts-oriented Appalachian town—a walking town with a strong sense of community where residents stop for front-porch chats. With each new home and resident, the McGriffs watch the family vision being translated to reality.

"There is a peace that pervades this place," says Clara, a former English teacher. "We feel it, and guests feel it." The Lodge on Gorham's Bluff gives guests ample opportunity to sample this serenity and beauty. Spacious suites, individually decorated by Clara (who also creates the beautiful floral arrangements), double-sided fireplaces, and whirlpool tubs make accommodations even more inviting.

Hiking, biking, bird-watching, rocking, reflecting, reading, and listening to classical music all rank as popular pastimes here. Dawn frequently schedules special events such as the annual Gerhart Chamber Music Festival's Concert under the Stars, the Alabama Ballet's summer residency, and storytelling and theater festivals.

Sometime during your stay, slip up to the observation deck for a panoramic overview. Many visitors want to linger at Gorham's Bluff forever. A quote from the guest book reads: "Forward our mail. We are not leaving."

Meals (enhanced by the property's own fresh herbs) feature traditional Appalachian food—served with flair. "Breakfasts, included in the rates, are huge Southern-style affairs," notes Dawn. Dinners are served with candlelight and white tablecloths as a pianist plays old and new favorites by request. By reservation only, the lodge's thirty-seat dining room offers dinner for guests and the public nightly at 7:00 P.M. Dress is casual. From Pisgah, located on Jackson County Road 58, signs point the way to Gorham's Bluff. Call for hours and specific directions or write the staff at 101 Gorham Drive/Gorham's Bluff, Pisgah 35765. Lodge rates range from moderate to deluxe. Make reservations for an evening or a weekend. You just may decide to become one of the town's new residents. For more background or a map, visit www.gorhamsbluff.com or e-mail reservations@gorhamsbluff.com.

To reach the **Stevenson Railroad Depot Museum** (256–437–3012), take US 72 and travel northwest. Near Stevenson turn at State Route 117 to go downtown. At 207 West Main Street you'll see the museum positioned between two railroad tracks. Look carefully before crossing the tracks because the Iron Horse still whizzes by. This railroad junction played a strategic role during the Civil War, and the museum director showed me an assortment of uniform buttons, coins, and other military items brought in by a resident who had dug them up nearby. The Stevenson Depot also contains displays of Native American artifacts, period costumes, early farm tools, and railroading history information.

Each June the annual Stevenson Depot Days celebration commemorates the city's past with a variety of family activities that might include an ice-cream

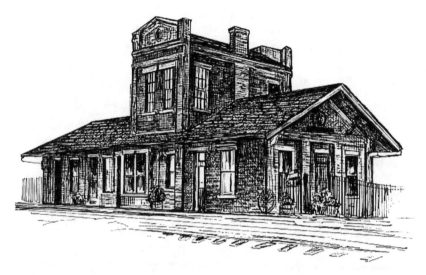

Stevenson Railroad Depot Museum

social, spelling bee, pioneer breakfast, wagon ride to the nearby Civil War fort, square dancing, tour of homes, parade, old-fashioned street dance, and fireworks. The museum is open Monday through Saturday from 8:30 A.M. to 4:30 P.M. Admission is free.

From Stevenson return to US 72 and continue to **Bridgeport,** in Alabama's northeastern corner.

Caves, Caverns, and Canyons

While exploring this region in June 1540, Spaniard Hernando DeSoto and his crew chose this area for their entry into what is now Alabama. You might like to take a driving tour of Bridgeport, once called Jonesville but renamed in the 1850s for the railroad bridge that spans the Tennessee River.

Drive through Kilpatrick Row Residential District and up bluff-based Battery Hill, the site of several Civil War battles, to see the lovely historic homes of Victorian vintage with turrets, fishscale shingles, and wraparound porches.

Russell Cave National Monument (256–495–2672), about 8 miles west of Bridgeport, is located at 3729 Jackson County Road 98. Long before DeSoto's visit, the large limestone cave served as an archaic hotel for Native Americans traveling through the area about 9,000 years ago.

The visitor center, in addition to housing a museum that displays weapons, tools, pottery, and other artifacts found in the cave, also offers several audio-visual presentations. After browsing through the museum, you can walk about

Exploring Cathedral Caverns

Both Native Americans and Confederate soldiers used these caverns as a refuge, and Disney used them as a movie setting for *Tom and Huck*. Ensconced in Marshall County's northeastern corner near the town of Grant, Cathedral Caverns (256–728–8193) opened as a state park in August 2000.

You don't have to assume a crouching position to enter because the opening to these caverns measures 125 feet wide by 25 feet high. Meandering along the lighted walkway takes you past Goliath, a massive stalagmite that appears to be a floor-to-ceiling column, and what are believed to be the world's largest stalagmite forest and frozen waterfall. Besides stalagmites and stalactites, other cave features include drapery, soda straws (capillary tubes), all the common types of shields, and "just about any formation you can expect to find in a cave," said a guide.

The deeper you go into the cave's interior, the more wondrous the surroundings. Before the grand finale, you'll enter a magnificent chamber that soars to a height of 120 feet and presumably contains the largest flowstone wall in any commercial cave. Then, to top that off, the Cathedral Room features a staggering number of fanciful, stalagmitic formations. Beyond the portion open to the public lies a magnificent crystal room with stunning calcite configurations (or so they say).

Former owner Jay Gurley, who died in 1996, dedicated much of his life and fortune to making the caverns accessible so others might share their wonder. His active involvement in developing the park spanned the period from 1952 until 1974 when he sold the property. Although the caverns were open from time to time after Gurley's tenure, they closed in 1986, and the state bought the site in 1987. Inside the cave, a plaque acknowledges Gurley's contribution and serves as a monument, as does the Jay Gurley Memorial Bridge that transports visitors across Mystery River.

The river is aptly named. "We can't see where the stream comes from or where it goes," said park manager Danny Lewis. Normally placid, the river can reach a depth of 40 feet during flooding conditions when the swirling water becomes chocolate-colored.

I first visited Cathedral Caverns with my then three-year-old daughter, and recently, the two of us returned with her three-year-old daughter, Anna Kyle. When our guide explained that this limestone cave was once part of the ocean floor, he pointed out a shark's tooth (eleven have been discovered to date) embedded in the ceiling—evidence the cave had been underwater in the distant past. "But where are the sharks?" asked Anna Kyle.

Bring a jacket (the temperature hovers at 57 to 60 degrees Fahrenheit) and jogging shoes. The 1½-mile round trip takes about an hour and fifteen minutes. Future plans for this 461-acre park include trails and camping facilities. Hours are 9:00 A.M. to 4:00 P.M. daily and to 5:00 P.M. in summer. Tours generally start at fifteen minutes after each hour. Admission.

250 yards to the cave's big opening at the base of craggy bluffs. A ranger-led tour takes you to the cave, where you can learn about how the occupants fed, clothed, and protected themselves.

One of the century's most significant archaeological finds, the relic-filled cave remained pretty much a secret until 1953 when some members of the Tennessee Archaeological Society discovered the history-rich shelter and alerted Smithsonian Institution officials, who collaborated with the National Geographic Society to conduct extensive excavations here. The National Park Service carried out more excavations in 1962. Their joint research revealed Russell Cave to be one of the longest, most complete, and well-preserved archaeological records in the eastern United States. Radioactive carbon from early campfires placed human arrival between 6500 and 6145 B.C. Remains of animal bones, tools, weapons, and pottery all helped archaeologists fit together portions of this ancient jigsaw puzzle. The evidence implies seasonal occupation, suggesting that various groups of early people wintered in Russell Cave, then moved on to hunt and live off the land during warm-weather months.

Be sure to ask a ranger about a living-history demonstration. I found it fascinating to watch a piece of flint fashioned into an arrowhead in about four minutes with the same simple tools early Native Americans used.

Except for Thanksgiving, Christmas, and New Year's Day, you can visit Russell Cave seven days a week. During daylight savings time hours are 8:30 A.M. to 5:00 P.M.; otherwise the closing time is 4:30 P.M., and there's no admission charge. For more information, write to park personnel at 3729 County Road 98, Bridgeport 35740. Explore the cave on the Internet by clicking on www.nps.gov/ruca.

A cave adventure of a different sort awaits at **Sequoyah Caverns** (256–635–0024 or 800–843–5098), located about 6 miles north of Valley Head. Returning to Stevenson, you can follow State Route 117 South to reach the caverns, well marked by signs. Travelers arriving on I–59 can take either the Hammondville–Valley Head exit or the Sulphur Springs–Ider exit to the caverns, located a few hundred yards off the interstate between these two exits.

The caverns take their name from Sequoyah (also spelled Sequoya or Sequoia), who moved to this part of Alabama as a young man. California's giant trees and Sequoia National Park were also named in honor of this Cherokee chief, who developed an alphabet for his people after being intrigued by the white man's "talking leaf." As a result the Cherokee people learned to read and write in a matter of months and soon started publishing books and newspapers in their native language.

You'll enter the caverns through the Cherokee Cooking Room, so called because of the salt troughs, cooking implements, pottery, and blackened walls found here. Wending your way through this magical world of spectacular stalactites and stalagmites in gorgeous colorations is like traveling through a giant kaleidoscope. The many reflecting pools known as "looking-glass lakes" allow you to study remote features on the multilevel ceiling that rises as high as a twelve-story building in certain portions of the caverns. A guided tour takes about an hour, and the temperature remains a constant sixty degrees Fahrenheit. Admission. From March through November the caverns are open daily from 8:30 A.M. to 5:00 P.M.; however, they are open only on Saturday and Sunday from December through February.

In *Valley Head,* only a few miles south of the caverns, you'll find *Woodhaven* (256–635–6438), a bed-and-breakfast owned by Judith and Kaare Lollik-Andersen. Located on Lowry Road and fronted by a wooden fence, the 1902 three-story white house features a wraparound porch with an inviting swing and white wicker furniture. A creek runs through the pastures of the forty-acre farm, making it a pleasant place to explore, hike, jog, or bike. Children especially enjoy helping feed the animals.

While living in south Florida, Judith and Kaare started searching out a location for a bed-and-breakfast inn because they enjoyed staying in such facilities in Europe. They wanted mountains, trees, water, and a gentle climate, "but one with seasons." Their search brought them to this part of Alabama, where the geography reminded Kaare of his native Norway, with the nearby Tennessee River a substitute for the sea.

alabamatrivia

In Valley Head's "triangle," you can delve into the mystery of a vanished village at the Ruins of Battelle. For more background on this supposedly haunted site, click on www.tourdekalb.com.

For early risers, Judith serves a pre-breakfast snack of Danish or muffins with coffee and juice. Later comes the real thing with fresh fruit, croissants or English muffins, oatmeal or cereal, and one of the house specialties: eggs (provided by the farm's own chickens) with bacon or a Norwegian dish of herring and eggs with caviar on toast. You can also expect afternoon tea and evening snacks. Moderate rates. For reservations and specific directions, call or write to Woodhaven, 390 Lowry Road, Valley Head 35989.

One block off State Route 117 in the center of Valley Head stands *Winston Place* (256–635–6381 or 888–4–WINSTON), a white-columned antebellum mansion owned by Leslie and Jim Bunch. Located 2 miles from Mentone, the property features a panoramic view of Lookout Mountain. Two levels of encircling porches with ferns, white wicker rocking chairs, and a nanny swing invite guests to relax and savor the setting. Built by William Overton Winston from Virginia, the circa-1831 home boasts a rich history. During the Civil War, Union officers occupied the home, and 30,000 soldiers camped on its grounds before leaving to fight at Chickamauga. Leslie, who shares anecdotes about her family home and its fascinating background, has amassed a collection of books and articles detailing Winston Place's role in history.

Previously selected for inclusion in *National Geographic's Small Town Getaways,* Winston Place contains lovely period antiques and lends itself well to entertaining, just as its builder intended. Original outbuildings include servants' quarters, a slanted-wall corncrib, and a smokehouse with hand-painted murals depicting the area's history.

While immersing yourself in the home's ambience, take time to see the tucked-away media room with Jim's football awards—trophies, plaques, and photos. A former Alabama football All-American (whose mastery of the game took him to three Sugar Bowls and a Liberty Bowl), Jim played under legendary coach Bear Bryant.

The couple offers five elegant suites for guests and a sumptuous breakfast, served in the dining room. Rates range from moderate to deluxe. Visit Winston Place's home in cyberspace at www.virtualcities.com/al/winstonplace.htm.

From Valley Head it's a short but scenic drive up to **Mentone,** a charming hamlet perched on the brow of Lookout Mountain at the intersection of State Route 117 and DeKalb County Route 89. Once a fashionable summer resort town that flourished through the Gay Nineties, Mentone attracted visitors from all over the country with its cool mountain temperatures, especially appealing in the days before air-conditioning.

Shops, rustic and quaint, line the single main street, but the large, rambling **Mentone Springs Hotel** (6114 State Route 117; 256–634–4040) remains the town's focal point. The three-story structure with turrets, dormers, porches, and steep-sloped roof captured my imagination the first time I saw it three decades ago. Open for bed-and-breakfast guests, the building also houses a restaurant called Caldwell's, named for the doctor who built the hotel in 1884. Rates are moderate. Go to www.mentonespringshotel.com for more information.

The name *Mentone* translates into "musical mountain spring," appropriate because the hotel's grounds once boasted two springs—Mineral Springs and Beauty Springs—which were reputed to possess "strengthening and curative properties." The hotel's early guests enjoyed nature walks, croquet, billiards, boating, and other genteel pursuits.

Although you can't join a picnicking party with a basket lunch packed by the hotel and you won't be summoned to meals by a dinner bell, you can explore the town's shops. Some of them close or limit their hours in winter, so it's best to check ahead. Also, you might inquire about the dates of upcoming festivals because Mentone stages special events throughout the year.

The downtown **Log Cabin Restaurant and Deli** (6080 State Route 117; 256–634–4560), originally a Native American trading post, serves sandwiches, salads, plate lunches, and dinner entrees with home-cooked vegetables and desserts. The eatery, where you'll find a cozy fire when temperatures drop, is open Tuesday through Sunday. Call ahead for hours. Prices range from economical to moderate. Nearby **Dessie's Kountry Chef** (5951 State Route 117; 256–634–4232), closed on Tuesday, serves evening fare along with short orders and home-style lunches. Call for hours. Prices range from economical to moderate.

While browsing for antiques and collectibles, stop by **The Hitching Post,** a complex housing several interesting shops including the antiques-filled Crow's Nest. At the Gourdie Shop you'll see Sharon Barron's unique and whimsical creations made from locally grown gourds, each signed and dated by the artist. Hours vary.

Across the road from the old hotel is St. Joseph's on the Mountain. Be sure to notice the log structure, dating to 1826, that serves as the central portion of this unusual church. North of the church on the mountain's brow, you'll find Eagle's Nest, a massive rock formation overlooking Valley Head.

After exploring the village, take a drive along the area's meandering roads. You'll see strategically placed destination markers nailed to trees and posts at junctions—these are quite helpful because the mountain terrain can prove confusing to newcomers.

Tucked away at 651 County Road 644 stands **Raven Haven** (256–634–4310), a bed-and-breakfast perched atop Lookout Mountain. Owners Eleanor and Tony Teverino welcome travelers to share their ten acres of nature and theme rooms: Queen Anne, Nautical, Casablanca, and Little Room on the Prairie—each with private bath.

"Two things that drew us here were the beauty of the place and the people," said Eleanor, who was born in Northern Ireland. "When I came to Mentone, it was very much like going back home." The Teverinos hosted recent guests from Ireland, who compared some of Mentone's narrow boulder-flanked curves to "driving on the roads right back at home."

Eleanor whisks warm and wonderful pastries from her oven and prepares a delightful breakfast daily, complete with homemade jams. Served buffet style, the menu always features a main dish, fruit, and vegetable to get your day off to a good healthy start. From Scotch eggs to fried green tomatoes to sticky buns, each morning's choices offer plenty of variety. A copy of *The Raven Haven Cookbook* makes a great souvenir. Afterward, you can trek through the woods and admire the wildflowers along the property's ¼-mile walking trail. Standard rates. For more information on this hideaway, pay a Web visit to www.bbonline.com/al/ravenhaven or www.virtualcities.com.

While driving through the area, you'll pass a number of summer camps for youngsters. In fact boyhood days spent at one such camp called Cloudmont inspired local landowner Jack Jones to pursue his unlikely dream of creating a ski resort in Alabama. After buying Cloudmont in 1947, he started developing the property as a resort and opened "the southernmost ski resort in the country" in 1970. *Cloudmont Ski and Golf Resort* (256–634–4344), about 3 miles from Mentone on DeKalb County Road 89, is marked by a large roadside sign on the left. To reach the information center, take a left onto County Road 614 for a half mile or so. Besides skiing (and yes, Mother Nature does get help from snow machines), this unique family enterprise offers golfing, hiking, fishing, and swimming for guests. Jack's son Gary and his instructors have taught thousands of people to ski. Winter season at Cloudmont usually begins around mid-December and extends through March 15. It's a good idea to call ahead and check on slope conditions. Better yet, log onto www.cloudmont.com for lodging packages, schedules, rates, and information on current activities, which include golfing, horseback riding, and more at both Cloudmont and *Shady Grove Dude Ranch.* You can write the resort at P.O. Box 435, Mentone 35984.

alabamatrivia

Alabama ranks twelfth in the nation for attracting retirees, and eighth in the nation for attracting military retirees.

Cragsmere Manna Restaurant (256–634–4677 or 256–845–2209), located about a half mile beyond the resort (at 17871 DeKalb County Road 89) in one of the area's oldest houses, offers a "country gourmet" dinner on Friday and Saturday from 5:00 to 9:00 P.M. Prices are moderate.

While in this area, don't miss the *Sallie Howard Memorial Chapel,* on County Road 165 located 6.7 miles from downtown Mentone and adjacent to DeSoto State Park. A 20-foot-tall boulder serves as the rear wall of the small church, and stones from Little River form the pulpit. Visitors often attend worship services held here each Sunday at 10:00 A.M.

To more fully explore this area's magnificent terrain, consider headquartering at *DeSoto State Park* (256–845–5380 or 800–568–8840) on County Road 89, about 7 miles from Mentone. You'll find almost 5,000 acres of breathtaking beauty and glimpses of unspoiled nature at every turn. The gorgeous scenery around here makes it hard to concentrate on driving, but if you don't, you might bash into one of the big weathered boulders that partially jut into the road.

The park extends about 40 miles along Little River, a unique waterway that runs its complete course on top of a mountain. Resort facilities include a stone lodge with large restaurant, recently renovated chalets, cabins, nature trails, playgrounds, a store, and picnic areas. Miles of hiking trails, bordered by Queen Anne's lace, blackberry vines, honeysuckle, and black-eyed Susans, beckon you to explore the terrain. The park's wheelchair-accessible boardwalk attracts families and features a covered pavilion and waterfall view. Don't miss spectacular **DeSoto Falls** (about 7 miles northeast of the park's Information Center), where water rushes over a dam to crash more than 100 feet before continuing its journey. Park superintendent Talmadge Butler has twice traveled to Washington, D.C., to accept awards for park preservation and beautification.

About 10 miles away in the park's southern section, you'll find the beginning of **Little River Canyon National Preserve,** the largest and one of the deepest chasms east of the Mississippi River. Stretching about 16 miles, the canyon drops to depths of some 700 feet. Skirting the western rim, a canyon road offers breathtaking views of rugged bluffs, waterfalls, and the rushing river. Take a look at www.desotostatepark.com.

Don't miss Fort Payne, the stomping ground of award-collecting country music group Alabama and home to the redbrick **Fort Payne Opera House** (256–845–3137 or 256–845–0419) at 510 North Gault Avenue. The building, which dates to 1889, has served as a vaudeville playhouse, a theater for silent movies, and an upholstery shop. The opera house is listed on the National Register of Historic Places and the National Register of Nineteenth Century Theatres in America. Restored in 1969, the opera house now opens for special events and performances. Tours can be arranged by appointment.

The building on the opera house's north side is home to the **DeKalb County Hosiery Museum** and the **Richard C. Hunt Reception Hall.** The hall's interesting mural, entitled *Harvest at Fort Payne,* dates back to the Great Depression when President Franklin D. Roosevelt initiated the Work Projects Administration (WPA) to aid the unemployed. Harwood Steiger, an out-of-work artist from New York, received a commission to paint murals for Southern post offices, and this is one of his creations. Before its placement here, the mural was housed in the old post office building and later the DeKalb County Courthouse. Visitors to the hosiery museum can see early mill machinery and other exhibits as well as a video providing background on the industry that played a major role in the area's history and economy. To schedule a tour, call Dale Jackson at (256) 845–4910 or Bill Cobble at (256) 845–6982. For more information contact the DeKalb County Tourist Association at (256) 845–3957.

Nearby, the Fort Payne Depot at Fifth Street Northeast houses the **Fort Payne Depot Museum** (256–845–5714). Completed in 1891, the handsome Romanesque depot of pink sandstone served as a passenger station until 1970. The museum's permanent collection includes artwork, early farm equipment, pottery, glassware, and a restored caboose containing railroad memorabilia.

You'll also see beaded moccasins, Iroquois baskets made of birch bark trimmed with porcupine quills, and Mayan and pre-Columbian artifacts dating from A.D. 400 to 800. An area resident willed to the museum her Cherokee, Hopi, Pueblo, Apache, and Seminole artifacts. Be sure to notice the collection of dioramas that were once part of a traveling medicine show and an unusual bed that belonged to local resident Granny Dollar, whose lifetime spanned more than a century. The museum is open 10:00 A.M. to 4:00 P.M. on Monday, Wednesday, and Friday. Sunday hours are 2:00 to 4:00 P.M. Admission is free, but donations are welcome.

Before leaving the "Sock Capital of the World," stop by **Big Mill Antique Mall** (256–845–3380) and browse among yesteryear's treasures. Located at 151 Eighth Street Northeast, this 1889 structure, once home to Fort Payne's first hosiery mill, now houses antiques, collectibles, reproductions, and a deli. Mall hours are 10:00 A.M. to 4:00 P.M. Monday through Saturday and 1:00 to 4:00 P.M. on Sunday.

While traveling through **Collinsville,** you might want to consider spending some time at **Trade Day,** an event that draws some 30,000 or so bargain hunters and browsers every Saturday. Spread over sixty-five acres near Collinsville on US 11 South, this weekly occasion has had a country carnival flavor since it first cranked up in 1950. Vendors start setting up their wares at the crack of dawn and stay until early afternoon. "We offer today's collectibles at yesterday's prices," says owner Charles Cook. Sightseers can munch on snacks such as boiled peanuts and corn dogs while surveying displays of wares from antiques and crafts to fresh vegetables and houseplants. Swans, ducks, rabbits, geese, goats, peacocks, hunting dogs, game cocks, and exotic pets often find new owners here. Parking costs 50 cents, but admission is free. For more information call (256) 524–2536 or (888) 524–2536.

Cherokee Country

From Collinsville it's just a short jaunt to **Leesburg** and **the secret Bed & Breakfast Lodge** (256–523–3825). Located at 2356 State Route 68 West on a mountaintop overlooking Weiss Lake, the lodge boasts a view that won't stop. "Last summer our guests saw Fourth-of-July fireworks in three cities from our rooftop pool," says Diann Cruickshank, who with husband, Carl, owns this property perched on the eastern brow of Lookout Mountain.

The view, the sunsets and sunrises, and the deer (which guests can feed) make the secret a special place. Carl cooks a delicious country breakfast, which Diann serves on a 10-foot-wide round table topped by a lazy Susan. You'll see a collection of porcelain dolls made by Diann's mother and a showcase containing Carl's interesting memorabilia. Bring your camera and prepare for surprises galore here because Diann delights in acquiring the unusual. (Not to divulge any secrets, but one surprise may leave you feeling a bit like Goldilocks.) For each guest room, the Sugar Shack, and other cottages on the grounds, Diann compiled a booklet of her engaging anecdotes along with recommended local attractions and restaurants. Movie buffs will find a video library containing more than 200 titles. Moderate rates. Visit the secret Bed & Breakfast Lodge via the Web at www.bbonline.com/al/thesecret, or send a message by e-mail to secret@tds.net.

Cherokee County, home of **Weiss Lake,** offers beautiful scenery. Add a chunk of Little River Canyon to this 30,200-acre lake bordered by 447 miles of shoreline, and you've got plenty of recreational options. Famous for its fine fishing, the Crappie Capital of the World also offers ample opportunities for catching bass and catfish. The water attracts large populations of wintering birds such as seagulls, wild ducks, and cranes.

While exploring Cherokee County's many scenic spots, don't overlook **Cornwall Furnace Park,** about 3 miles east of Cedar Bluff. To reach the park, take State Route 9 east and turn left onto Cherokee County Route 92. Then make another left onto a gravel road and follow the signs. A flight of steps leads down a steep bank (covered by lilies in spring) to the picturesque stone stack that stands about 5 feet tall—all that remains of a structure built to supply crude iron to be transformed into Confederate arms. General Sherman's forces destroyed the furnace works during the Civil War.

The well-kept grounds offer attractive picnicking facilities and a short nature trail. The park, which opens at daylight and closes at sundown, can be visited year-round. Running water is available, but there are no bathroom facilities. Admission is free.

Afterward take State Route 9 to **Centre,** about 6 miles away. Next to the courthouse stands the **Cherokee County Historical Museum** (256–927–7835), located at 101 East Main Street. This museum, formerly a department store, houses historical objects and memorabilia that characterize the area's past. You'll see a Pennsylvania Amish town buggy. Other exhibits include Bob Hope's first typewriter, Grand Ole Opry memorabilia, wagons, housewares, antique telephones, Civil War relics, early appliances, Native American artifacts, a printing press, a telephone switchboard, a doll collection, and a bale of cotton. The basement contains a blacksmith shop as well as old farm equipment such as plows, mowing machines, cotton planters, and tractors. Visitors sometimes see a quilting session in progress. Modest admission. The museum is open from 9:30 A.M. to 4:00 P.M. on Tuesday and from 8:30 A.M. to 4:00 P.M. Wednesday through Saturday.

Continue toward **Gadsden,** situated in Lookout Mountain's foothills. Turkeytown, named for Chief Little Turkey during the late 1700s, is a tiny community

Center Pieces

Members of the Cultural Arts League of Gadsden worked diligently on a cookbook called Center Pieces, which "tells the story of the Mary G. Hardin Center for Cultural Arts by using each chapter to describe a 'piece' of the whole." The handsome publication contains illustrations of creations by nationally recognized floral designer Benny Campbell, owner of Attalla Florist and Landscape.

For a tantalizing preview, try the following recipe from the appetizer section. Each time I make this treat for my guests, it gets rave reviews. Pick up a souvenir copy of the book for yourself and get some extras for gifts.

Nova Scotia Salmon Mold

1 envelope unflavored gelatin

¼ cup cold water

½ cup whipping cream

1 (8-ounce) package cream cheese, softened

1 cup sour cream

1 teaspoon Worcestershire sauce

Dash of hot sauce

1 teaspoon fresh lemon juice

2 tablespoons green onions, finely chopped

1 tablespoon fresh parsley, finely chopped

1 tablespoon prepared horseradish

8 ounces Nova Scotia salmon, chopped

1 (4-ounce) jar red caviar, drained

Sprinkle gelatin over ¼ cup cold water in a small saucepan; let stand 1 minute. Cook over low heat, stirring constantly, for 2 minutes or until gelatin dissolves. Stir in whipping cream.

Beat gelatin mixture and cream cheese at medium speed with an electric mixer for 5 minutes or until mixture is smooth. Add sour cream, Worcestershire sauce, hot sauce, and lemon juice; beat at low speed 1 minute to blend.

Fold in green onions, parsley, horseradish, and salmon. Gently fold in caviar. Pour into a lightly greased 3-quart plastic or ceramic mold. Chill 3 hours or until firm.

Unmold and serve. Yield: 20 servings.

on the Coosa River's banks near Gadsden that once served as the capital of the Cherokee nation.

Although long known as one of the state's leading industrial centers with abundant deposits of iron, manganese, coal, and limestone, Gadsden is gaining recognition for its rich Cherokee legacy. The Turkeytown Association of the

Cherokee, a nonprofit organization, works to preserve and promote the region's Native American heritage.

Downtown at Gadsden's Broad Street entrance to the Coosa River Bridge stands the statue of Emma Sansom, who, at age sixteen, helped Confederate troops find a place to ford Black Creek after Union forces crossed and burned the local bridge.

While in Gadsden, stop by the **Mary G. Hardin Center for Cultural Arts** (256–543–2787) on the corner of Fifth and Broad Streets. The complex, with a bold gold-and-black exterior in a Mondrian-like design, offers plays, concerts, lectures, classes, and art exhibits. To see the current art shows, take the escalator to the second floor. Before returning downstairs, be sure to notice the model railroad layout depicting Gadsden during the 1940s and 1950s with trains traveling past miniature reproductions of more than one hundred historical structures including the Gulf States Steel complex. The complex also houses the Courtyard Café. Modest admission. Call for information on current exhibits and hours or visit the Web site at www.culturalarts.com.

alabamatrivia

Alabama ranks among the top ten states with conditions most favorable for starting a small business.

Adjacent to the Center for Cultural Arts, the historic Kyle Building now houses the **Imagination Place Children's Museum.** Youngsters can play in a life-size tree house or a kid-size city complete with Grandma's House, a bank, grocery store, doctor's office, fire station, and other interesting sites. Hours are 9:00 A.M. to 5:00 P.M. Monday through Friday; 10:00 A.M. to 5:00 P.M. Saturday; and 1:00 to 5:00 P.M. Sunday. Admission is free for kids three and under; a modest fee is charged for others.

At **Noccalula Falls and Park** (256–549–4663), situated on Lookout Mountain Parkway (and easily reached from Interstate 59), the bronze statue of a legendary Cherokee princess stands ready to leap to her destiny in a rushing stream 90 feet below. Legend says Noccalula loved a brave of her own tribe and chose to die rather than marry the wealthier suitor selected by her father.

Explore the park's botanical gardens, especially attractive in spring with masses of azaleas in bloom. You can either walk through the park or take a mini-train ride to see the Pioneer Homestead, a village of authentic log structures including a barn, blacksmith shop, gristmill, school, and cabins moved here from various sites in Appalachia. Also here you'll find the restored Gilliland-Reese Covered Bridge.

Nearby are campgrounds, hiking trails, picnic tables, play areas, and a pool. Except for the evening light show during the annual Christmas on the Rocks, which takes place from the day after Thanksgiving through New Year's Eve, the park closes from November through February. Otherwise, the facility is open daily from 9:00 A.M. to sundown. Although the park is free, a modest admission fee is charged to see the Pioneer Homestead and Botanical Gardens. The campground number is (256) 543–7412.

If you're in the area on a weekend, you may want to schedule a jaunt to **Mountain Top Flea Market,** which is open every Sunday from 5:00 A.M. to about 3:00 or 4:00 P.M. year-round. You'll find this all-day market with some 1,500 dealers about 6 miles west of Attalla on US 278. For more information call Janie Terrell at (800) 535–2286.

Attalla, home of the world's first hydroelectric generator and birthplace of Alabama Power, lures antiques shoppers. The old Walker Drugstore in the heart of town now houses **Days Gone By** (256–538–1920) at 328 Fifth Avenue Northwest. Here, owners Judy and Royce Fant offer antiques and collectibles from twenty-two dealers. Clustered nearby are more than a dozen shops. At **The Cozy Nest** (256–570–0200), 426 Fourth Street Northwest, Vanessa Durham features full-service decorating along with a selection of antiques, primitives, and accessories for home and garden. Continuing down the street, you'll find more vintage items at **Somewhere in Time** (256–538–1899), 402 Fourth Street Northwest, and **Beulah Land Antique Mall** (256–538–1585), 216 Fourth Street Northwest. Call ahead before traveling because dealers keep their own hours, and these vary from shop to shop.

To reach Boaz, located on Sand Mountain, take US 431 north from Attalla.

Sand Mountain

A foothill of the Appalachians, Sand Mountain covers an area about 25 miles wide by 75 miles long. Atop this plateau you'll find **Boaz Shopper's Paradise**—so many stores, so little time. Ranked among America's top outlet centers, **Boaz** attracts people from across the country. Shoppers can browse through dozens of stores and specialty shops in the town's outlet centers. For discount coupons and maps, check out the Official Outlet Information office on Billy Dyar Boulevard, the Vanity Fair courtesy desk, or the Tanger Welcome Center.

Approximately 40,000 people descend on Boaz, population 8,000, for the annual Harvest Festival. The weekend celebration features an antique car show, musical entertainment, an Indian powwow, and some 200 booths brimming with handcrafted items ranging from birdhouses, cornshuck dolls, and crazy

Strange As It Sounds

Buck's Pocket State Park (256–659–2000), a secluded expanse of rugged nature that spills into three counties—DeKalb, Jackson, and Marshall—is rich in botanical beauty and local lore. Covering more than 2,000 acres of craggy canyon scenery on the western side of Sand Mountain, the park is located near Grove Oak.

For a magnificent overview of the entire canyon, head first to Point Rock, the park's highest area and a wonderful place for picnicking and hiking. According to local legend, early Native Americans took advantage of the area's geography to help them acquire their food supply by driving deer over the edge at Point Rock right into the "pocket." Both spring, with its plentiful supply of wildflowers, and fall make great times to visit.

To reach the headquarters and campground, you'll descend from Point Rock about 800 feet via a curving road to the canyon's base. The bottom line on the park's wooden sign says: HAVEN FOR DEFEATED POLITICIANS. Buck's Pocket acquired its reputation as a refuge for election losers after "Big Jim" Folsom, a former Alabama governor, lost a senate bid and announced his intention to go to Buck's Pocket, get his thoughts together, and "lick his wounds." He invited other defeated candidates to join him at this favorite retreat.

In addition to trails for hiking and rocks for climbing, recreation options include swimming and fishing at South Sauty Creek. Also, nearby Morgan's Cove offers a fishing pier and boat launching ramps. Rappelers and rock climbers should first stop by headquarters for a permit, good for a year. Write to Buck's Pocket at 393 County Road 174, Grove Oak 35975. For reservations call (800) ALA–PARK. For a guided tour call (256) 571–5445.

quilts to paintings, leather items, and furniture. Music runs the gamut from bluegrass, country, and gospel to jazz. For more information on the outlets or the festival, contact the Boaz Chamber of Commerce, P.O. Box 563, Boaz 35957, or call (256) 593–8154 or (800) 746–7262.

During your shopping spree, you might enjoy browsing among items from yesteryear at ***Adams' Antiques*** (256–593–0406) at 10310 State Route 168. Hours are 10:00 A.M. to 4:30 P.M. Tuesday through Saturday.

When you're ready for a shopping break, visit nearby ***Snead State Community College Museum.*** Snead's origins go back to 1898, when it opened as a seminary, making it the oldest school in the state's junior college system. In the Norton Building, you'll find a museum with outstanding exhibits of minerals, rocks, and fossils collected and donated by Preston Watts, an engineer and Snead Seminary graduate. In addition to the museum's natural science section with its several hands-on displays, you'll see a gospel music section featuring a vintage music printing press, recordings, hymnals dating to the 1880s, photos of gospel groups, and Sacred Harp singing memorabilia. Brought to America by the Pilgrims and Puritans, Sacred Harp singing (a unique musical form using shaped notes to represent certain sounds) all but disappeared in most areas of the country but still survives in the South.

During school sessions the museum is open on Tuesday and Wednesday 8:00 A.M. to 3:00 P.M. and on Thursday 8:00 A.M. to 2:00 P.M., or by appointment. For more information call (256) 593–5120, extension 258.

If you can't finish all your shopping in one day (and many people can't), ***Boaz Bed and Breakfast*** (256–593–8031) at 200 Thomas Avenue offers a variety of accommodations. Co-owners Faye Markham and her daughter, Margaret Casey, converted the historic Whitman-Hunt house into a haven for travelers. Built in 1924 for cotton broker Edward Fenns Whitman, the Craftsman-style two-story brick structure features a clay tile roof. In 1999 the Boaz Altrusa Club sponsored the home as a Decorator Show House.

alabamatrivia

Boaz, population 8,000, was named for a biblical character in the Book of Ruth.

Faye, a former teacher, knows that shopping takes lots of stamina, so she provides her guests with a good hearty breakfast. Her usual Sand Mountain–style breakfast features pan-fried boneless chicken breasts with gravy, hot biscuits, grits, and fresh fruits. On Sunday she serves ham and waffles. Standard rates.

If you "need a little Christmas right this very minute," search out ***Carl's Restaurant*** (256–840–5003) on the southern outskirts of Boaz at 345 Gold Kist Street. The staff often hears, "Oh, my goodness!" and "Lordy, Mercy!" from first-timers, dazzled by the clusters of Christmas ornaments interspersed with crystal chandeliers and dangling from every bit of ceiling space in every room. More decorations line the walls and fill shelves. "Some people even lose their breath," says owner Carl Vinson, who describes himself as "a big Christmas person." If you didn't feel merry upon arrival, you will before departure with this year-round decor.

Carl serves a daily special, which might feature fried chicken, meat loaf, country-fried steak, chicken and dumplings, or barbecue with macaroni and cheese, assorted vegetables, and a dessert, perhaps peach or blackberry cobbler, or you can choose salads or sandwiches. Dinner options include catfish, shrimp, and steak. The restaurant opens at 9:00 A.M. and closes at 3:00 P.M.

Tuesday and Wednesday, 8:00 P.M. Thursday, and 9:00 P.M. Friday and Saturday. Sunday hours run from 10:00 A.M. to 3:00 P.M. Economical to moderate.

Afterward continue about 5 miles north to *Albertville,* the "Heart of Sand Mountain." Albertville's *Freedom Festival,* chosen many times by the Southeast Tourism Society as one of July's Top Twenty Events, attracts a large Independence Day crowd.

For a look at some of the city's lovely historic homes, drive along East Main Street off US 431. At the street's end stands the 1891 Albertville Depot, which is listed on the National Register of Historic Places. The depot now houses a senior citizens center.

Albertville acquired its title as "Fire Hydrant Capital of the World" because the local Mueller Company turns liquefied steel into dome-topped fire hydrants and ships them to countries near and far. In front of the chamber of commerce

Albertville's Downtown Pleasures

Whether your sweet tooth yearns for a French vanilla cappuccino, Godiva chocolates, or a wedge of cheesecake, you'll find all this and more at *Main Street's Coffee, Cappuccino and Ice Cream* (256–878–1948) in downtown Albertville. What's more, you can sip your espresso or latte at a sidewalk table and watch the world go by. In fact, when I last did this, I overheard a woman at the next table say to her companion, "Kinda reminds you of Paris, doesn't it?"

Well, maybe that's a bit of a stretch, but Albertville does have a sister city by the same name in France, a fact that got some attention during the 1992 Winter Olympics when the local chamber of commerce received requests for tickets to certain events.

When Alabama's temperatures crank up to the 90s (as they are prone to do during summer), you can sip your frosty, frothy drink in the cool shop, surrounded by all manner of tempting handmade pastries, attractive gift displays, and possibly two or three tables of bridge players.

A woman who dashed in for a couple of take-away desserts wound up in a thirty-minute conversation, and that often happens here where owners Carrie and Donald Conley have created the inviting atmosphere of a neighborhood coffee house. The Conleys frequently host performing musicians, art exhibits, and special interest groups.

Located at 118 East Main Street, the business also houses a candy and gift shop. Hours run from 8:00 A.M. to 6:00 P.M. Monday through Thursday and 8:00 A.M. to 9:00 P.M. (or until everyone is served) Friday and Saturday.

building, you'll see a special nickel-plated version that marks Mueller's one-millionth locally manufactured fire hydrant.

For a sampling of some of the town's interesting stores, head to the **Little Village Shop** (256–878–6400). Located at 123 Sand Mountain Drive NW, the shop offers unique gifts, housewares, china, and Waterford crystal. Hours are 10:00 A.M. to 5:00 P.M. Monday through Saturday.

At 113 Sand Mountain Drive, you'll find **Whitten's** (256–878–3901), a clothing store that features upscale town and country fashions for women and men. Hours are 9:00 A.M. to 5:00 P.M. Monday through Saturday. The shop closes on Thursday afternoon.

When visiting a new place, some travelers like to search out a restaurant where the locals eat. Here it's **The Food Basket** (256–878–1261), located just off US 431 at 715 Sampson Circle. The Daniel family has been feeding folks in Albertville since 1959.

Noted for its country ham and homemade biscuits, the restaurant draws a big breakfast crowd. Lunch specialties include Sand Mountain fried chicken and home-style fresh vegetables. Dinners feature steaks and seafood. The restaurant's original salad dressing and sweet rolls, served at dinner, prove perennial favorites. Economical to moderate. Hours are 5:00 A.M. to 3:00 P.M. Sunday through Wednesday and 5:00 A.M. to 9:00 P.M. Thursday through Saturday.

To learn more about Alabama's rural heritage, stop by the Albertville Public Library, at 200 Jackson Street, and buy a copy of *The Good Ole Days* by Jesse Culp—broadcaster, author, speaker, syndicated columnist, and former newspaper editor. In his living-history book, Mr. Culp discusses such topics as blue back spellers, log rollings, settin' hens, funeral home fans, and cow pasture baseball, and his gift for reminiscing brings back a bit of yesteryear.

Take time to drive along some of Marshall County's rural roads. Along the way you'll notice fertile rolling farmland and chicken houses. Broilers, eggs, and turkeys produced on the state's individual farms add up to a billion-dollar poultry industry. In broiler production, Alabama ranks second in the nation.

Lake Country

While in the area, consider headquartering at **Lake Guntersville State Park** (256–571–5440 or 800–548–4553), located just off State Route 227 at 1155 Lodge Drive. Perched on Appalachian bluffs about 6 miles northeast of Guntersville, the park lodge offers panoramic views and 35 miles of hiking trails. You can roam almost 6,600 acres of woodland—much of it undisturbed—and follow paths once used by the Cherokee.

The park naturalist gives guided hiking tours on request, pointing out local flora and fauna. Deer often dash across the road in front of cars and roam the lodge's grounds. In addition to hiking, park activities include camping, canoeing, fishing, and boating. An Eagle Festival, scheduled for one weekend in January, replaces the park's former Eagle Awareness weekends. For a brochure, contact the lodge or the nature center at Lake Guntersville State Park Lodge, 190 Campground Road, Guntersville 35976, or call (256) 571–5445 or (256) 571–5444.

Resort facilities include a restaurant, a lounge, motel rooms, chalets, and campsites ranging from primitive to fully equipped and modern (that is, complete with utility hookups, tables, grills, bathhouses, hot showers, play areas, and a camp store). You'll also find tennis courts, a championship eighteen-hole golf course, a heliport, canoe and boat rentals, and 7 miles of scenic drives. Golfers should call ahead because the course will be closed for a period during its upgrading. Except for the lodge and restaurant, the park facilities will remain open to the public during its upcoming renovation, scheduled for completion by spring 2006.

Continue to nearby Guntersville Lake, a Tennessee Valley Authority (TVA) creation where sailboats and fishing vessels dot shining expanses of open water. "The most striking thing about Guntersville," says local newspaper editor Sam Harvey, "is that it's a country town with a lake all around it. Of the five approaches to Guntersville, four take you across water." With 69,100 acres of water, Guntersville bills itself as a vacationer's paradise. Truly a haven for water-sports enthusiasts, the area offers boating, swimming, skiing, and fishing. The Bass Anglers Sportsman Society calls Lake Guntersville "one of the finest sport fishing lakes in America," and the Alabama Bassmasters stage invitational tournaments here.

Drive through the downtown area and stop by Lake Guntersville Chamber of Commerce and Welcome Center (256–582–3612) which is in a house with a beckoning front porch at 200 Gunter Avenue near the big river bridge. Here you can pick up brochures on area attractions and inquire about current happenings. For instance, the local theater group The Whole Backstage mounts a mix of productions throughout the year, so check on possible performances during your visit.

Atop a hill, *Lake Guntersville Bed and Breakfast* (256–505–0133) at 2204 Scott Street offers suites with private entrances and more lovely water views from its two levels of wraparound porches. While living in Fairfield, Connecticut, former Guntersville resident Carol Dravis dreamed of returning. She got to do just that when an unexpected opportunity came along to purchase the handsome circa-1910 white brick home.

Carol picks up guests who arrive by boat and serves a bountiful break-fast—on the veranda when weather permits. Breakfast might feature her special European pancakes, beautiful and puffy with various toppings, or a sausage-and-cheese strata. Accompaniments include breakfast breads and a special mixture of fruit juices called morning sunshine. Ask about Carol's cookbook, which contains some of her guests' favorite recipes. Based on individual interests, Carol recommends local activities and provides directions to nearby walking trails and other scenic spots. In the foyer you'll see a small gift shop with works by local artists and writers.

Carol offers several special-occasion packages such as Eagle Awareness, Valentine, Anniversary, Birthday, theater, etc. One guest wrote, "How wonderful

Angels in Arab

One spring day, a friend and I drove to Guntersville for an art exhibit and lunch. Walking into Covington's restaurant, we saw two angels, dressed in flowing white tunics with gold accessories—which included halos. One of the angel-women wore gold combat boots.

We soon found out the B-Team Angels, Paula Joslin and Kay Jennings, came from nearby Arab. They were "on a quest to earn their wings by spreading happiness." Wafting a wand in our direction, the angels then glided outside, where traffic screeched to a halt.

A year later I met the B-Team Angels and learned their league had grown and their happiness ministry had expanded. Each month, for example, they surprise a local resident with an Earth Angel award, honoring people who bring happiness to others, often without recognition. On Valentine's Day the angelic band entertains at area nursing homes. They charge nothing for their programs of songs, skits, puppet shows, and birthday parties.

"We feel that sharing love with others is what life's all about," writes Kay, in her introduction to The B-Team Angels' Quest, a book filled with Paula's whimsical photo-collages featuring 700 Arab residents. (A professional artist, Paula works in all mediums and has won numerous awards in juried shows.) Proceeds from the book sales help defray costs incurred for this ministry—gifts, certificates, photography, costumes, transportation, etc. Also, the group has recently published a cookbook called *Angel Food,* featuring some heavenly recipes.

Arab resident Ralph Hammond (also Alabama Poet Laureate emeritus) describes the angels as a "wonderful group of girls, who have added a luster to Arab." So if you see an angel flitting about Arab, you know why: She's out to brighten someone's day—maybe yours. If you need to speak to a B-Team Angel or order a cookbook, call (256) 586–TIME.

Strange As It Sounds

If a boat outing fits into your travel schedule, try to catch the evening exodus of bats from **Hambrick Cave.** Some 350,000 American gray bats, a protected species, consider this cave home from late April to mid-October (although the females migrate the first of August). You'll probably join a bevy of other boaters, clustered around the water-level cave mouth at the base of a bluff, all waiting for the sunset performance as a cloud of bats swoops overhead on its nocturnal foraging flight. Going downriver toward Guntersville Dam, look for a cave (marked by a small overhead sign) on your right. Flashlights are prohibited. (For more information on this and other area bat caves, call the **Wheeler Wildlife Refuge** at 256–350–6639.)

to have found such a thoughtful, talented hostess! Your charming B&B has been a true lagniappe [a lower Alabama expression meaning something extra special], and we've discovered again the great delight of porch-sitting. Thank you for a lovely and delicious visit." Visit Lake Guntersville B&B's Web site at www.bbonline.com/al/lakeguntersville/. Standard to moderate rates.

Don't miss nearby Fant's Department Store at 355 Gunter Avenue. Still locally known as Hammer's, the rambling structure with original wooden floors offers a bargain basement and surprises galore. (You'll enjoy browsing through Hammer's stores in Albertville and Boaz, too.)

Continue to the **Basket Case** (256–582–8454) at 390 Gunter Avenue for a selection of unique gifts. Owner Debbie Newman creates gift baskets filled with items of your choice from bath products to gourmet foods such as jellies, sauces, candies, and coffees. You'll also find silver jewelry, frames, pewter trays and bowls, lamps, local pottery, and other home accessories. Hours run from 10:00 A.M. to 5:00 P.M. Monday through Saturday.

Step inside the Guntersville Post Office to see the mural that depicts De-Soto's arrival in the area. Located at the north end of the lobby, the large canvas with life-size figures of Native Americans, costumed Spanish, and spirited horses can be seen at any time.

Covington's (256–582–5377) makes a great stop for lunch. Housed in The Glover at 524 Gunter Avenue, the eatery offers tasty homemade soups, salads, sandwiches, and desserts. Try the Downtowne Delight with chicken or tuna salad, a home-baked muffin, pimento cheese on rye, and a choice of veggies or pasta salad. Economical prices. Hours run 11:00 A.M. to 2:00 P.M. Monday through Friday.

Your sightseeing excursion may take you past the **Guntersville Museum and Cultural Center** (256–571–7597) at the corner of O'Brig and Debow

Streets. The former Parish Hall of the Episcopal Church of the Epiphany now houses an art gallery and archives, with collections of documents, photos, and other items relating to the town's early days. You'll find a Tennessee Valley Authority Room, a River Room, and an Indian Room with displays of Native American projectile points and other artifacts. The museum also hosts traveling exhibits. Hours are 10:00 A.M. to 4:00 P.M. Tuesday through Friday and 1:00 to 4:00 P.M. on Saturday and Sunday. Admission is free.

Other local events include Guntersville's two-day *Art on the Lake Show,* held each April, a series of summer evening lakeside concerts on Tuesdays, and the MOVA Arts Festival featuring a songwriter competition. The latter, a fall event presented by the Mountain Valley Arts Council, also includes a juried art exhibit, children's activities, and lots of food and drink. For more information or to see a current art exhibit, stop by the Mountain Valley Arts Council (MVAC) office at 300 Gunter Avenue, or call (256) 582–1454.

On the Saturday before Labor Day, *St. William's Seafood Festival* features more than 5,000 pounds of fresh shrimp, oysters, crab, flounder, and other fish imported from coastal waters. Parish members prepare the seafood, which includes making about 400 gallons of gumbo.

For some good old-fashioned fun and a mess of "poke salat," take State Route 69 to *Arab* during the first weekend in May. When the Arab Liars' Club (the self-appointed title for a group of local men who meet daily for coffee at L Rancho Cafe) came up with the idea of the *Poke Salat Festival,* they probably did not expect it to become an annual affair with everything from street dances and craft shows to beauty contests and drama productions.

In downtown Arab, notice the weather-beaten Farmer's Exchange, a local landmark that now houses a garden center. Also, you may wish to explore the city's dozen or so antiques shops.

At the southern edge of town on Arad Thompson Road, you'll find the inviting Arab City Park with the Shoal Creek Trail, ball fields, a pool, and modern, well-equipped playground. The park is also home to several historical structures including the Hunt School, Rice Church, Elvin Light Museum, and Smith's Country Store.

Afterward head toward Huntsville to launch an exploration of Alabama's northwestern region.

Places to Stay in Northeast Alabama

ALBERTVILLE

Jameson Inn
315 Martling Road
(256) 891–2600 or
(800) 526–3766

ATTALLA

Econo Lodge
507 Cherry Street
(256) 538–9925 or
(800) 424–4777

BOAZ

Boaz Bed and Breakfast
200 Thomas Avenue
(256) 593–8031

Key West Inn
10535 State Route 168
(256) 593–0800 or
(800) 833–0555

Rodeway Inn
751 U.S. Highway 431
(256) 593–8410 or
(800) 228–2000

FORT PAYNE

DeSoto State Park
265 County Road 951
(256) 845–5380 or
(800) 568–8840

GADSDEN

Hampton Inn
129 River Road
(256) 546–2337 or
(800) HAMPTON

FOR MORE INFORMATION ABOUT NORTHEAST ALABAMA

North Alabama Tourism Association
25062 North Street,
P.O. Box 1075
Mooresville 35649
(256) 350–3500 or (800) 648–5381
Web site: www.northalabama.org
e-mail: info@northalabama.org
This organization covers sixteen north Alabama counties that are home to some one hundred attractions in a 100-mile radius.

DeKalb County Tourist Association
1503 Glenn Boulevard Southwest,
P.O. Box 681165
Fort Payne 35968
(256) 845–3957 or (888) 805–4740
Web site: www.tourdekalb.com
e-mail: pattyt@mindspring.com

Gadsden/Etowah Tourism Board, Inc.
105-B Locust Street,
P.O. Box 8269
Gadsden 35902-8269
(256) 549–0351 or (888) 565–0411
Web site: www.tourism@gadsden-etowahtourismboard.com

Huntsville/Madison County Convention & Visitors Bureau
500 Church Street,
Huntsville 35801
(256) 551–2230 or (800) SPACE–4–U
Web site: www.huntsville.org
e-mail: info@huntsville.org

Marshall County Convention & Visitors Bureau
200 Gunter Avenue,
P.O. Box 711
Guntersville 35976
(256) 582–7015 or (800) 582–6282
Web site: www.marshallcountycvb.com
e-mail: mccvb@mindspring.com

Scottsboro–Jackson County Chamber of Commerce
407 East Willow Street,
P.O. Box 973
Scottsboro 35768
(256) 259–5500 or (800) 259–5508
Web site: www.sjcchamber.org
e-mail: chamber@scottsboro.org

Holiday Inn Express
801 Cleveland Avenue
(256) 538–7861 or
(800) HOLIDAY

GUNTERSVILLE

Holiday Inn Resort Hotel
2140 Gunter Avenue
(256) 582–2220

**Lake Guntersville Bed
and Breakfast**
2204 Scott Street
(256) 505–0133

**Lake Guntersville
State Park Lodge**
1155 Lodge Drive
(256) 571–5440 or
(800) ALA–PARK

HUNTSVILLE

**Bevill Conference Center
and Hotel**
550 Sparkman Drive
(256) 721–9428 or
(888) 721–9428

Courtyard by Marriott
4804 University Drive
(256) 837–1400 or
(800) 321–2211

Dogwood Manor
707 Chase Road
(256) 859–3946

Hampton Inn
4815 University Drive
(256) 830–9400 or
(800) HAMPTON

Huntsville Hilton
401 Williams Avenue
(256) 533–1400 or
(800) 345–6565

Huntsville Marriott
#5 Tranquility Base
(256) 830–2222 or
(888) 299–5174

LEESBURG

**The secret Bed
& Breakfast Lodge**
2356 State Route 68 West
(256) 523–3825

MENTONE

Mentone Springs Hotel
6114 State Route
Highway 117
(256) 634–4040

Mountain Laurel Inn
624 Road 948
(256) 634–4673 or
(800) 889–4244

Raven Haven
651 County Road 644
(256) 634–4310

PISGAH

**The Lodge at
Gorham's Bluff**
101 Gorham Drive/
Gorham's Bluff
(256) 451–VIEW

SCOTTSBORO

Best Western
46 Micah Way,
U.S. Highway 72
(256) 259–4300 or
(800) WESTERN

Goose Pond Colony
417 Ed Hembree Drive
(256) 259–2884 or
(800) 268–2884

**Ivy Creek Inn Bed
and Breakfast**
985 Carlton Road
(256) 505-0722

Jameson Inn
208 Micah Way
U.S. Highway 72
(256) 574–6666 or
(800) 526–3766

VALLEY HEAD

Winston Place
1 block off State Route 117
(256) 635–6381 or
(888) 4–WINSTON

Woodhaven
390 Lowry Road
(256) 635–6438

Places to Eat in Northeast Alabama

ALBERTVILLE

Asia Garden Restaurant
210 State Route 75 North
(256) 891–1616

Catfish Cabin
8524 U.S. Highway 431
(256) 878–8170

The Food Basket
715 Sampson Circle
(256) 878–1261

**Giovanni's Pizza Italian
Restaurant**
711 Miller Street
(256) 878–7881

The Lumpkin House
699 North Carlisle Street
(256) 891–8900

BOAZ

Carl's Restaurant
345 Gold Kist Street
(256) 840–5003

Ryan's Family Steak House
568 U.S. Highway 431
(256) 593–1436

The Station House Grille
101 East Mann Avenue
(256) 593–6567

CENTRE

Tony's Steak Barn
804 Alexis Road
(256) 927–2844

DOUGLAS

The Old Meeting House Restaurant
Intersection of State Routes 75 and 168
(256) 840–1571

GADSDEN

The Choice
1001 Rainbow Drive
Suite 8
Gadsden Mall
(256) 546–8513

Top O' the River
1606 Rainbow Drive
(256) 547–9817

GRANT

Mi Mi's Café
On Main Street at the corner of Third Avenue
(256) 728–7483

The Squirrel Nest
2219 Baker Mountain Road
(256) 571–0324

GUNTERSVILLE

Covington's
524 Gunter Avenue
(256) 582–5377

El Camino Real
14274 U.S. Highway 431
(256) 571–9089

La Strada
12824 U.S. Highway 431
(256) 582–2250

Neena's Lakeside Grille
Inside the Holiday Inn
2140 Gunter Avenue
(256) 505–0550

Top O' the River
7004 Val Monte Drive
(256) 582–4567

HUNTSVILLE

Cafe Berlin
964 Airport Road
(256) 880–9920

Green Hills Grille
5100 Sanderson Street
(256) 837–8282

Jazz Factory
109 Northside Square
(256) 539–1919

Landry's Seafood House
5101 Governor's House Drive
(256) 864–0000

Ol' Heidelberg
6125 University Drive
(256) 922–0556

Surin of Thailand
975 Airport Road
(256) 213–9866

MADISON

Madison Street Café
101 Main Street
(256) 461–8090

MENTONE

Cragsmere Manna Restaurant
17871 DeKalb County Road 89
(256) 634–4677 or
(256) 845–2209

Dessie's Kountry Chef
5951 State Route 117
(256) 634–4232

Log Cabin Restaurant and Deli
6080 State Route 117
(256) 634–4560

PISGAH

The Lodge at Gorham's Bluff
101 Gorham Drive
(256) 451–VIEW

SCOTTSBORO

The Docks
Goose Pond Colony
417 Ed Hembree Drive
(256) 574–3071

Liberty Restaurant
907 East Willow Street
(256) 574–3455

The Lite Side
145 East Laurel Street
(256) 574–3362

Payne's
101 East Laurel Street
(256) 574–2140

Triple R Bar-B-Q
2940 Veterans Drive
(256) 574–1620

STEVENSON

Friday's
507 Second Street
(256) 437–8201

Alabama Fan Club and Museum,
101 Glen Boulevard,
Fort Payne;
(256) 845–1646 or (800) 557–8223.
This museum showcases the band's musical achievements, which are many: The group has garnered numerous awards, gold albums, and plaques for such releases as "My Home's in Alabama," "Mountain Music," and "Fallin' Again." Fans can purchase souvenirs ranging from T-shirts and jackets to photographs and mugs—and of course albums. The museum features individual sections on band members Randy Owen, Teddy Gentry, Jeff Cook, and Mark Herndon. For a little background and a Web tour, visit www.thealabamaband.com.

Huntsville Museum of Art,
300 Church Street South,
Huntsville;
(256) 535–4350.
Save time for browsing through the new $7.5-million home of the Huntsville Museum of Art, with twice as much gallery space as its former quarters in the Von Braun Civic Center. This beautiful building stands in Big Spring International Park, the heart of the city, and offers a wide range of exhibitions, art classes, and educational programs. You'll see an outstanding permanent collection with works by Picasso, Matisse, Toulouse-Lautrec, Goya, and other renowned artists as well as exhibits on loan from major institutions.

U.S. Space & Rocket Center,
Huntsville;
(256) 837–3400.
Located at One Tranquility Base on Huntsville's western side, you may feel like a character out of a science fiction movie as you wander through a world of rockets, spaceships, shuttles, nose cones, and lunar landing vehicles. Other interesting artifacts include a moon rock, Apollo 16's command module, the overpowering Saturn V moon rocket, and a SR–71 Blackbird reconnaissance plane. Don't miss the featured film presentation at the Spacedome Theater, or, for a unique adventure, sign up for Space Camp. You'll find Space Camp dates, rates, registration information, and everything else you need to know for blasting off at www.spacecamp.com.

Northwest Alabama

Tennessee Valley

Mooresville, just east of Interstate 65 at exit 2 on Interstate 565 between Huntsville and Decatur, makes a good place to start a tour of Alabama's northwest region. For information on local and area attractions, call the North Alabama Tourism Association's office at (800) 648–5381.

To best see Mooresville, a town that dates to 1818 (it's one year older than the state itself), plan to take a walking tour. Not only does everybody know everybody in this community of some twenty families, everybody knows everybody's dog. Don't be surprised if the local canines choose to accompany you on your stroll through town. Listed on the National Register of Historic Places, this charming village occupies an area of one-quarter square mile and can easily be covered in half an hour. Cedar trees and wild hydrangeas make lovely accents as you wend your way through the town. Strolling along streets lined by picket fences and fine old shade trees, you'll see a variety of vintage structures including lovely old Federal-style homes.

On Lauderdale Street you'll pass a brick church that dates to 1839 and contains its original pews. Although regular worship services no longer take place here, the historic structure is

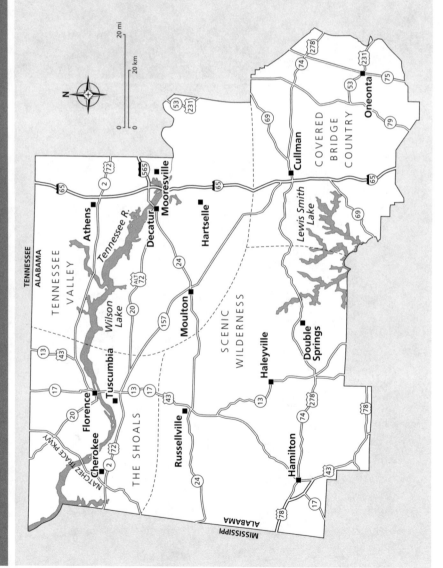

sometimes used for weddings and funerals. Notice the herringbone pattern of the brick walkway in front of the church. Mooresville's former postmistress, Barbara Coker, using many of her lunch hours, excavated through grass and layers of dirt to expose the original brickwork.

Be sure to stop by the tiny post office on the corner of Lauderdale and High Streets. Built around 1840, this small weathered poplar building, with tin roof, pegged joints, and square-head nails, contains the town's forty-eight original post boxes (first installed at the nearby Stagecoach Inn and Tavern).

The Stagecoach Inn, built sometime before 1825, once sold "supper for two bits." Across the street from the inn stands a small cottage, an example of Downing Gothic architecture. Dating to about 1890, the home was built and owned by Uncle Zack Simmons, a Black carpenter, and his wife, Aunt Mandy. Former Mooresville mayor Kathleen Lovvorn says that Aunt Mandy, famous for her jellies and pickles, often handed out homemade treats to the village youngsters.

The Hurn-Thach-Boozer-McNiell House, built around 1825 and located near the end of Market Street, once housed a tailor shop, where Andrew Johnson, who later became president, studied drafting and construction techniques under the supervision of Joseph Sloss (who specialized in making Prince Albert coats for gentlemen).

After departing Mooresville you may want to travel north to **Athens,** Limestone County's seat. Start your local tour by visiting the downtown courthouse

Turning Back the Clock to Mark Twain's Time

If you saw the Disney production *Tom and Huck,* you visited the well-preserved village of Mooresville via video. Jonathan Taylor Thomas (of TV's *Home Improvement* fame) and Brad Renfro (*The Client*) starred in this remake of a Mark Twain classic.

"The moment I saw Mooresville, I knew this was the perfect setting for Tom Sawyer," said the film's production manager, Ross Fanger, after searching for a town that fit the 1876 era of Mark Twain's novel.

For the movie, Mooresville's paved streets became dirt-covered lanes, and a Hollywood facade of nineteenth-century stores sprang up. Film crews shot some scenes along the Tennessee River and inside *Cathedral Caverns* (recently reopened to the public as a state park) in Marshall County. The caverns served as a backdrop for the novel's account of Tom and his girlfriend Becky Thatcher's lost-in-a-cave adventure.

If you missed the movie, don't despair—the film is available as a home video, and you can still visit Mooresville.

Aunt Mandy and Uncle Zack Simmons Cottage

square with its surrounding stores and stately old churches. Founded in 1818, Athens barely missed being the state's oldest incorporated town. (Nearby Mooresville won the race by only three days.) To see some of the town's antebellum and Victorian homes—many of which are identified by historic markers—drive along Beaty, Pryor, Jefferson, and Clinton Streets.

You may want to stop by the *Houston Memorial Library and Museum* (256–233–8770). Located at 101 North Houston Street, this house dates to 1835 and served as the home of George S. Houston (a former Alabama governor and United States senator) from 1845 to 1879. Exhibits include family portraits, period furniture, Native American artifacts, Civil War relics, and various items relating to local history. Each April, the library sponsors the Houston Street Fair featuring Civil War reenactments, blacksmithing demonstrations, clogging, an old-time auction, and plenty of good food. Hours are 10:00 A.M. to 5:00 P.M. Monday through Friday and 9:00 A.M. to noon Saturday.

For a toe-tapping good time, plan to take in the *Tennessee Valley Old Time Fiddlers Convention* held at Athens State College each October. Visitors converge on campus for two days of outdoor competitions featuring harmonica, banjo, fiddle, mandolin, dulcimer, and guitar playing and buck dancing sessions. For more information on local attractions and events, call (256) 232–2600.

Beaty Street takes you to Athens State College, Alabama's oldest institution of higher learning. While on this street, be sure to notice the Beaty-Mason House built in 1826, now the college president's home. Located at 302 North Beaty Street, the lovely 1840s Greek Revival *Founder's Hall* houses school offices, a library, and a chapel. This building's original portion escaped being burned by the Yankees when a letter allegedly written by President Lincoln appeared in the nick of time. On the second floor, the Altar of the New Testament features fine wood carvings in tulip poplar. Founder's Hall may be visited Monday through Friday from 8:00 A.M. to 4:30 P.M. Admission is free. For more information, call (256) 233–8100.

Before leaving Athens, plan to tour the **Donnell House.** Completed in 1851, the T-shaped home contains some period furnishings and is located at 601 South Clinton Street on the Middle School campus. A chinked log cabin kitchen with working fireplace stands nearby. *The Lure and Lore of Limestone County,* which offers an in-depth look at notable area homes is available here. Proceeds from the sales go toward the Donnell House's continuing restoration. The home is open from 2:00 to 4:00 P.M. on Monday, Wednesday, and Friday, or by appointment. For more information call (256) 232–0743 or (256) 232–7370. Modest admission.

After exploring Athens, head south to **Decatur** for another dose of history along with wildlife. Founded on the banks of the Tennessee River and originally called Rhodes Ferry, Decatur acquired its current name in 1820. At that time Congress and President James Monroe decided to honor Comm. Stephen Decatur by naming a town after him. A daring naval hero who commanded a three-ship squadron during the War of 1812, Decatur once proposed the following toast: "Our country: In her intercourse with foreign nations may she always be in the right; but our country, right or wrong."

alabamatrivia

America's first wave pool was built in 1970 at Point Mallard Park in Decatur.

You can see mallards along with blue buntings, herons, owls, woodpeckers, bald eagles, and other birds on exhibit at **Cook's Natural Science Museum** (256–350–9347), located at 412 Thirteenth Street Southeast. Hands-on exhibits and changing displays present the world of nature—from insects and seashells to reptiles and rocks. The privately owned museum features displays of iridescent butterflies and a mounted, life-size black bear dripping with honey. Hours are 9:00 A.M. to noon and 1:00 to 5:00 P.M. Monday through Saturday and 2:00 to 5:00 P.M. Sunday. Admission is free.

Nearby at 1715 Sixth Avenue Southeast, the folks who work at **Big Bob Gibson's** (256–350–6969) say they cook "the best barbecue in town." A Decatur tradition since 1925, the restaurant serves real hickory-smoked pit-barbecued pork, beef, and chicken. Barbecued potatoes (baked and topped with meat) also prove popular menu items. You can grab a bite here or get an order to go. Hours are "can to can't" (9:00 A.M. to 8:30 P.M.) seven days a week, excluding Thanksgiving, Christmas, and New Year's Day. Economical prices.

Stop by Decatur's Visitor Information Center at 719 Sixth Avenue Southeast for a pamphlet called *A Walking Tour of Historic Decatur,* which notes many of the city's late-nineteenth-century homes that can be seen in the Old Decatur and New Albany historic districts. Call (256) 350–2028 or (800) 524–6181 for more information on local attractions.

Head to the city's northern section to tour the handsome **Old State Bank** (256–350–5060), established during Andrew Jackson's presidency. Located at 925 Bank Street Northeast, Alabama's oldest bank building now serves as a museum. Upstairs you'll see the head cashier's spacious living quarters, furnished in the 1830s style.

During the Civil War this classic-style structure served as a hospital for both Union and Confederate soldiers. The bank's thick vault possibly became a shielded surgery chamber during the heat of battle. Outside, the large limestone columns, quarried at a local plantation, still retain traces of Civil War graffiti along with battle scars from musket fire. The bank was among Decatur's few buildings to survive the Civil War. Bank tours are free, and the building is open Monday through Friday from 9:30 A.M. to noon and 1:30 to 4:30 P.M., or by appointment.

To sample a good mix of shops featuring antiques, clothing, toys, and gifts, take a stroll down Bank Street. At 722 Bank Street Northeast, you'll see **Heritage House Fine Antiques** (256–351–1655). Owner Sarah Stone carries an inventory of fine French and English pieces. For a memorable dining experience, step

GAY'S TOP PICKS IN NORTHWEST ALABAMA

Alabama Music Hall of Fame,
Tuscumbia

Ave Maria Grotto,
Cullman

Bankhead National Forest,
Double Springs

Blount County Covered Bridges,
Oneonta

Dismals Canyon,
Phil Campbell

General Joe Wheeler Plantation Home,
Hillsboro

Indian Mound and Museum,
Florence

Ivy Green,
Tuscumbia

Natural Bridge,
Natural Bridge

The Shrine of the Most Blessed Sacrament of Our Lady of the Angels Monastery,
Hanceville

across the street to **Simp McGhee's** (256–353–6284), at 725 Bank Street Northeast. Named for a colorful early-twentieth-century riverboat captain, this pub-style eatery offers Simp's stuffed Gulf flounder as well as many pasta, poultry, and beef entrees. Chef Dean Moore directs culinary activities and offers seafood specialties. Dinner hours are Monday through Thursday from 5:30 to 9:00 P.M. and Friday and Saturday from 5:30 to 9:30 P.M.

Standing in Decatur's New Albany downtown area at 115 Johnston Street Southeast, you'll see the **Old Cotaco Opera House.** Often called the Old Masonic Building, the big brick structure dates to 1890. Although you won't see a touring vaudeville act here today, you'll find the complex offers other enticing treats. For instance, hungry travelers can visit **Curry's on Johnston Street** (256–350–6715), located on the building's lower level, for lunch or pick-up items. The eatery serves homemade soups, sandwiches, casseroles, fresh bread, and desserts. Moderate rates. Hours are 8:00 A.M. to 5:00 P.M. Monday through Friday and 11:00 A.M. to 2:00 P.M. Saturday.

To visit one of *The 100 Best Small Towns in America* (selected by Norman Crampton for his nationwide guide), head south for **Hartselle,** now a mecca for antiques shoppers. (For a list of the other ninety-nine towns, you'll have to buy the book.) Make your first stop the historic **Depot Building,** which houses the Hartselle Area Chamber of Commerce (256–773–4370 or 800–294–0692). On one wall you'll see a Works Progress Administration (WPA) mural painted in 1937 that illustrates the major role cotton played in the area's early economy. While here collect a map and guide to local shops. Open by 10:00 A.M., most shops close on Wednesday and Sunday. Also, some shops close on Monday.

Afterward stroll to The Emporium at Hickory Crossing (256–773–4972), located at 200 Railroad Street Southwest. This former freight building now houses some specialty shops, antiques, and arts.

Browsing along Main Street, you'll see Spinning Wheel Antiques, Sweet Pea's Antique Gallery, Country Classic Antiques, and other specialty shops, with an array of everything from bric-a-brac and potpourri to primitive antiques and quilts.

After leaving Hartselle, follow State Route 36 west, watching for the **Oakville** turn and signs directing you to *Jesse Owens Memorial Park* (256–974–3636) on County Road 203. The park's focal point is an 8-foot, one-ton bronze statue of Owens, who won four gold medals in the 1936 Olympics. Branko Medenica, a native of Germany who now lives in Birmingham, sculpted the piece, which depicts Owens running and incorporates the familiar Olympic rings. Mounted on a 6-foot granite base, the statue was unveiled in a 1996 ceremony attended by members of the athlete's family when the Olympic torch passed through Oakville en route to Atlanta's games.

The park also offers a visitor center, museum, Olympic-size track, softball field, basketball court, walking trail, picnic pavilions, and replicas of the 1936 Olympic torch and Owens's modest home. Owens, who was born in Oakville and spent his early life here, once said, "It behooves a man with God-given ability to stand 10 feet tall. You never know how many youngsters may be watching." The park is open during daylight hours, and admission is free. The museum is open from 11:00 A.M. to 4:00 P.M. Tuesday through Saturday and from 1:00 to 5:00 P.M. Sunday. Admission for museum.

Before leaving the vicinity, take time to visit the **Oakville Indian Mounds,** a park and museum (256–905–2494) at 1219 County Road 187. Located 8 miles southeast of Moulton just off State Route 157, the complex features a massive 2,000-year-old Woodland Indian Mound, a Copena Indian burial mound, and a museum modeled after a seven-sided Cherokee Council House. The museum contains a 12-foot wooden statue of Sequoyah plus thousands of artifacts—some dating back to 10,000 B.C. Generally, hours are 8:00 A.M. to 4:30 P.M. Monday through Friday and 1:00 to 4:30 P.M. Saturday and Sunday. Admission is free.

Afterward head toward **Moulton,** stopping by **Classical Fruits** (256–974–8813) at 8831 State Route 157. At this combination fruit market, restaurant, gift shop, and greenhouse, the Adair family offers a delightful selection of products made with homegrown fruits. From muscadine-hull preserve and raspberry syrup to purple basil jelly and more, you'll find unique food items and gifts.

alabamatrivia

Alabama symbols include: the yellowhammer, the state bird; the camellia, the state flower; and the Southern pine, the state tree.

Try a green apple dipped in chocolate fudge and twirled in pecans. Natalie Ann makes the fudge—and not just chocolate, either. The strawberry, maple nut, and peanut butter versions also prove popular. In season the Adairs offer peach and apple fudge. Franny packs the candy in beribboned boxes *almost* too pretty to open.

During their respective growing months, fresh strawberries, cherries, blueberries, blackberries, raspberries, plums, peaches, apples, pears, grapes, muscadines, and other fruits, vegetables, and herbs are available here. The nearby 140-acre fruit-growing operation features a wide variety of fruit cultivars.

You can opt for barbecue, which comes with a choice of three sauces, or a daily plate lunch special with fresh vegetables in season. Restaurant service starts at 11:00 A.M., but market hours are 8:00 A.M. to 8:00 P.M. except on Wednesday and Sunday, when closing time is 5:00 P.M.

Afterward continue your journey toward Moulton. Try to hit Moulton at mealtime so you can sample the terrific lemon-pepper grilled catfish fillet at

GAY'S FAVORITE ANNUAL EVENTS IN NORTHWEST ALABAMA

Bloomin' Festival at St. Bernard,
Cullman, early April;
(256) 734–0454

Alabama Jubilee Hot-Air Balloon Classic,
Point Mallard Park, Decatur,
Memorial Day weekend;
(256) 350–2028 or (800) 524–6181

Waterloo Heritage Days,
Waterloo, Memorial Day weekend;
(256) 740–4141

Helen Keller Festival,
Tuscumbia, late June;
(256) 383–4066 or (888) 329–2124

The Spirit of America Festival,
Point Mallard Park, Decatur, July 3–4;
(256) 350–2028 or (800) 524–6181

W.C. Handy Festival,
Florence, late July to early August;
(256) 766–9719

September Skirmish,
Point Mallard Park, Decatur,
Labor Day weekend;
(256) 350–2028 or (800) 524–6181

Riverfest,
Rhodes Ferry Park, mid-September;
(800) 524–6181

Oktoberfest,
Cullman, early October;
(256) 739–1258

Southern Wildlife Festival,
Decatur, October;
(255) 350–2028 or (800) 524–6181

Alabama Renaissance Faire,
Florence, fourth weekend of October;
(256) 740–4141 or (888) 356–8687

Covered Bridge Festival,
Oneonta, fourth weekend of October;
(205) 274–2153

Western Sirloin Steak House (256–974–7191), with a huge grain-bin entrance and tin walls. Located at 11383 State Route 157 (behind Winn Dixie), the restaurant also features charbroiled chicken breast and rib-eye steak at economical to moderate rates. The restaurant, which is owned by Ann and Larry Littrell and Barbara and Ray Chenault, is open Sunday through Thursday from 11:00 A.M. to 9:00 P.M. Friday and Saturday hours are 11:00 A.M. to 10:00 P.M.

At *Animal House Zoological Park* (256–974–8634), located about 8 miles northwest of Moulton near Hatton on Lawrence County Road 231 just off County Road 236, you'll find an unusual place where Dr. Doolittle would feel at home. The owners have been raising exotic and endangered animals for two decades and now care for some 400 pets, including Persian leopards, clouded leopards, black jaguars, African lions, Bengal and Siberian tigers, ligers, panthers, cougars, servals, bears, camels, llamas, Barbados sheep, antelope, capybaras, and a giraffe plus a varied collection of primates (who dine on fruit medleys that might rival a restaurant's salad creations).

You can visit the park on Saturday from 11:00 A.M. to 3:00 P.M. between June 1 and November 15. The facility closes for repairs from November 15 to March 15 and is reserved for school tours from March through June 1. Click on www.animalhouse.org for more background. Admission.

After talking to the animals, continue in the direction of ***Hillsboro*** to see "Fighting Joe" Wheeler's plantation. A Confederate cavalry commander, Wheeler later became a U.S. Army general and also served in Congress. Watch for signs directing you to the ***General Joe Wheeler Plantation Home*** (256–637–8513) at 12280 State Route 20. Turning off the highway, you'll follow a secluded drive-way lined with venerable oak trees. Open the wooden gate and thread your way through a maze of lovely old English boxwoods. On-site curator Melissa Beasley lives in the adjacent residence. Now closed for restoration, the two-and-a-half-story Wheeler home, run by the Alabama Historical Commission, contains orig-inal furniture, china, uniforms, military medals, portraits, Civil War memorabilia, books, and other family items. Wheeler's daughter, Miss Annie, who served as a nurse in Cuba and later in France during World War I, lived here until her death in 1955. Be sure not to miss the old log house and family cemetery on the grounds. The plantation grounds and outbuildings remain open for tours from 9:00 A.M. to 4:00 P.M. Thursday through Saturday and from 1:00 to 5:00 P.M. Sunday, except for major holidays. Modest admission. For more information e-mail wheplan@hiwaay.net or pay a visit to www.wheelerplantation.org.

Afterward continue west on State Route 20 about 3 miles to ***Courtland,*** named to the National Register of Historic Places for its 1818 development of the early town plan. Local architectural styles span almost two centuries. For a brochure on Courtland, which details a driving tour of the historical district, stop by Town Hall.

After exploring Courtland, continue to ***Doublehead Resort & Lodge*** (800–685–9267) for some relaxation and outdoor recreation. Located at 145 County Road 314 near Town Creek, the complex underscores a Native Ameri-can theme from its name to its design and furnishings. A split-rail fence defines pastures, and wooden poles frame the metal entrance gate with its "Welcome Friends" greeting in Cherokee characters.

The property takes its name from Doublehead, a Cherokee chief who once lived on this land. The management wants to sustain a Native American aware-ness as it continues to develop this distinctive resort. The main lodge features a 5,000-square-foot deck overlooking Wilson Lake. Hammered metal designs of free-floating feathers and an upward-pointing arrowhead frame the double hand-carved front doors. A locally found Cherokee medallion inspired the lodge's unique chandelier.

Guests occupy cedar log cabins, each with three bedrooms, two baths, and a completely equipped kitchen. (After all, Doublehead's appreciation for creature comforts is well documented.) Beds are constructed from rustic cedar posts, and Indian wall hangings echo the motif. Each cabin comes with a beckoning hammock, grill, picnic table, and private pier. Recreational activities range from fishing, boating, and hunting to horseback riding. Golfers will want to inquire about special packages with land and water shuttles to the nearby Robert Trent Jones championship golf complex now nearing completion in the Shoals. Other amenities include two tennis courts, a basketball court, and a 2½-mile walking/nature trail. The facility offers rentals for jet-skis, pontoons, canoes, and other watercraft, a sporting clays course (shooting range), and a private 1,100-acre hunting preserve. Deluxe rates.

Afterward head west toward Tuscumbia.

The Shoals

You will be transported back in time when you arrive in **_Tuscumbia._** At 300 South Dickson Street stands The Log Cabin Stagecoach Stop at Cold Water, an authentic structure from the pioneer period. Continue to Commercial Row, located on the north side of West Fifth Street between Water and Main Streets. This block of seven bordering brick buildings, dating to the 1830s, represents local antebellum commercial architecture. During the 1880s, Capt. Arthur Keller (Helen Keller's father) published his newspaper, _The North Alabamian,_ here in the corner building.

While exploring downtown, step inside the restored Palace Drugstore for a bit of nostalgia and maybe a milk shake at the 1950s soda fountain. Also, you'll want to see Spring Park's fifty-one-jet fountain with water surging to heights of more than 150 feet. On weekend evenings, you can take in a special show, choreographed to lights and music. The large fountain serves as a memorial to Princess Im-Mi-Ah-Key, wife of Chickasaw Chief Tuscumbia, for whom the town is named.

Nearby at 300 West North Commons stands **_Ivy Green,_** the birthplace of Helen Keller. After her graduation from Radcliffe College, Miss Keller worked tirelessly on behalf of the handicapped by lecturing, writing articles and books (some of which have been translated into more than fifty languages), and appealing to legislative bodies to improve conditions for those with impaired sight and hearing. Because she conquered her own handicaps and gained an international reputation for inspiring other handicapped persons to live richer lives, she became known as America's "First Lady of Courage."

Water pump at Ivy Green

Of Ivy Green Miss Keller wrote, "The Keller homestead . . . was called 'Ivy Green' because the house and surrounding trees and fences were covered with beautiful English Ivy." On the grounds you'll also see English boxwood, magnolia, mimosa, roses, and honeysuckle. The family home contains many original furnishings, photographs, letters, awards, books, and Miss Keller's braille typewriter.

Summer visitors can watch a miracle reenacted at a performance of William Gibson's drama *The Miracle Worker* staged on Ivy Green's grounds and directed by Darren Butler. The play culminates with a vivid portrayal of the poignant incident at the water pump when teacher Anne Sullivan helped the blind and deaf child break through her black void into "a wonderful world with all its sunlight and beauty."

Except for major holidays, Ivy Green is open year-round. The home can be toured Monday through Saturday from 8:30 A.M. to 4:00 P.M. and on Sunday from 1:00 to 4:00 P.M. Admission. For more information on Ivy Green, the play, or the annual ***Helen Keller Festival*** (scheduled for a weekend in late June each year), call (256) 383–4066 or (888) 329–2124.

About 3½ miles south of Tuscumbia, you'll find another interesting home, ***Belle Mont*** (256–381–5052, 256–637–8513, or 800–344–0783) on Cook's Lane. Constructed between 1828 and 1832, the U-shaped brick structure suggests the influence of Thomas Jefferson. Dr. Alexander William Mitchell, who moved here from Virginia, built this home now considered the state's finest example of Jefferson Palladian architecture. Partially furnished, most of the home's pieces date to the period between 1840 and 1860. Owned by the Alabama Historical Commission and open for tours year-round, hours run from 9:00 A.M. to

4:00 P.M. Thursday through Saturday and 1:00 to 5:00 P.M. on Sunday, or by appointment. Admission. Check out this property and other historic sites at www.preserveala.org.

At some point during your visit, you may want to learn more about this area, called **the Shoals.** Looping through north Alabama, the Tennessee River comes into its own here in the state's northwest corner. At one time navigators found the Muscle Shoals rapids too formidable to negotiate, but the Tennessee Valley Authority (TVA) solved this problem with a series of strategically placed dams. The jagged rocks that created perilous swirling currents and wrecked boats now lie "buried" far below the water's surface.

To get a good idea of the river's impact on the region, you can visit the TVA Reservation at Muscle Shoals to see **Wilson Dam.** With its north end in Lauderdale County and its south end in Lawrence County, the dam stretches almost a mile and serves as a bridge for State Route 101. Named for President Woodrow Wilson, the dam was initiated during World War I to supply power for making munitions.

Afterward follow Veteran's Drive to downtown **Florence,** which features a number of interesting attractions such as the **Indian Mound and Museum** at 1028 South Court Street near the river. The ancient mound looms to a height of 42 feet, the largest of several in the Tennessee Valley. Near the mound, called *Wawmanona* by Native Americans, stands a museum containing displays of tools, ornaments, pottery, fluted points, and other artifacts along with exhibits on the Mississippian culture's mysterious mound builders. Modest admission. Except for major holidays, the site is open Tuesday through Saturday from 10:00 A.M. to 4:00 P.M. For more information call (256) 760–6427.

Nearby, at 601 Riverview Drive, you'll find the **Frank Lloyd Wright's Rosenbaum House** (256–760–6379). Conceived by Wright in 1939 and completed in 1940, the home so reflected Wright's iconoclastic approach to organic domestic architecture that Stanley and Mildred Rosenbaum could not find a local contractor to take on this project. Along with his final plans, Wright sent an apprentice to supervise the construction of this Usonian house, now on the National Register of Historic Places.

Designed for a two-acre site overlooking the Tennessee River, the house utilizes large areas of glass to take advantage of the view and innovative radiant heating because of the proximity of Tennessee Valley Authority's low-cost electricity. "Mr. Wright wanted to use all natural materials," Mrs. Rosenbaum said, "no paint or plaster—only cypress wood, brick, glass, and concrete." After the couple's four sons arrived, Wright designed an addition—its clean lines flow naturally (and imperceptibly) from the original structure. The home is open for tours Thursday and Saturday from 10:00 A.M. to 4:00 P.M. Admission is charged.

To see the birthplace of the "Father of the Blues," head for 620 West College Street, where you'll find the **W.C. Handy Home and Museum** (256–760–6434), fronted by a fence of split rails. The hand-hewn log cabin, birthplace of William Christopher Handy, contains furnishings representative of the period around 1873. The adjoining museum features Handy's legendary trumpet and the piano on which he composed "St. Louis Blues." Handy also wrote more than 150 other musical compositions, including such standards as "Memphis Blues" and "Beale Street Blues." You'll see handwritten sheet music, photographs, correspondence, awards, and other items pertaining to Handy's life and legacy. The adjacent library houses Handy's extensive book collection and serves as a resource center for Black history and culture. The museum is open Tuesday through Saturday from 10:00 A.M. to 4:00 P.M. Modest admission.

For a week of swinging jazz, plan to visit Florence from late July to early August and take in the **W.C. Handy Music Festival.** Special events include parades, jam sessions, the "DaDooRunRun" for joggers, a picnic-jazz evening on the Tennessee River's banks, the colorful "Street Strut" led by the Grand Oobeedoo, and a concert with celebrated jazz musicians.

The Handy Festival evolved from a chance meeting in the Muscle Shoals Airport when two men struck up what turned out to be more than a casual conversation. Local veterinarian David Mussleman happened to ask Willie Ruff, a Yale music professor, about the horn he carried. This led to a discussion about native son W.C. Handy and his tremendous musical contribution—and subsequently to the annual festival held in Handy's honor. For more information call the festival office at (256) 766–7642.

While exploring Florence, you'll pass Wilson Park on the corner of Tuscaloosa Street and Wood Avenue. This setting serves as a backdrop for a number of local festivities, such as the **Alabama Renaissance Faire.** In fact, if you visit the park during this October gala, you can enjoy diversions ranging from derring-do with sword and shield to music, dance, and drama as residents bring to life some of the color, action, and excitement of the Renaissance period.

Beside the park you'll see the Kennedy-Douglass Center for the Arts at 217 East Tuscaloosa Street. This 1918 Georgian-style mansion and adjacent structures serve as a performing arts center. Stop by to view the current art exhibit and visit the gift shop.

At 316 North Court Street, you'll find **Trowbridge's** (256–764–1503), which offers sandwiches, salads, soups, chili, ice cream, and Oh My Gosh—a brownie piled high with vanilla ice cream and topped with hot caramel, whipped cream, and a cherry. The dessert gets its name from what most people say when they see it.

A mirrored soda fountain lists ice-cream flavors and drink choices. Third-generation owner Don Trowbridge credits the eatery's longevity to keeping the

Strange As It Sounds

South of Russellville and west of Phil Campbell (that's the town's name) lies a unique attraction known locally as the Dismals. Located at 901 County Road 8, **Dismals Canyon** once served as a ceremonial ground for Native Americans and a hiding place for outlaws. In addition to caves, waterfalls, craggy rock formations, rainbows, and unusual vegetation, the canyon contains phosphorescent creatures called "dismalites" that glow in the dark.

Geologists speculate that a prehistoric earthquake produced the place's chaotic geography with its many natural grottoes and bridges. This eerie but intriguing site also features both a natural arboretum and winding staircase.

After hiking through this place primeval, you may decide to take advantage of other activities—canoeing down Bear Creek, biking a 4-mile mountain trail, or swimming in Dismals Creek. For overnight visitors the site offers lodges (with fireplaces), a country store, and camping facilities. Admission. For more information call (205) 993–4559. Pay a virtual visit via www.dismalscanyon.com.

menu simple. Don's grandfather built Trowbridge's Creamery in 1918, and local farmers brought their milk and cream in to be processed. The family occupied the second floor over the ice-cream shop, and the dairy stood behind. The founder's original recipe for Orange-Pineapple Ice Cream, now shipped from New Orleans, remains a favorite with today's patrons.

A large painting on the rear wall depicts Trowbridge's interior from previous years—with almost no changes. Posters publicizing past local festivals pay tribute to Helen Keller and W.C. Handy, "Father of the Blues." Framed photos depict early Florence scenes and the construction of Wilson Dam, which originated as a World War I project to supply power for making munitions. Hours run from 9:00 A.M. to 5:30 P.M. Monday through Saturday. Economical rates.

A short distance away at 203 Hermitage Drive stands **Pope's Tavern** (256–760–6439), now a history-filled museum. Originally built as a stagecoach stopover and tavern, the attractive structure of white-painted bricks dates to 1811. Travelers on the Natchez Trace stopped here, and so did Andrew Jackson when he passed through in 1814 on his way to fight the British at the Battle of New Orleans. During the Civil War the inn served as a hospital where wounded Confederate and Union soldiers lay side by side to receive medical treatment from local doctors and the townswomen.

Inside the tavern you'll see period furnishings, kitchen utensils, tools, firearms, Civil War uniforms, photos, letters, and pioneer artifacts. Be sure to notice the worn silk Stars and Bars. This flag, hand-stitched by local ladies, traveled to Virginia with the Lauderdale Volunteers (one of northwestern

Alabama's first Confederate military units) when they left to fight in the first Battle of Manassas. Before you leave, notice the Florence Light Running Wagon, made in a local factory that at one time was the world's second-largest wagon-building operation. Modest admission. Except for major holidays, hours are 10:00 A.M. to 4:00 P.M. Tuesday through Saturday.

Nearby, at 658 North Wood Avenue in Florence's historic district, stands the *Wood Avenue Inn* (256–766–8441), a turreted, towered Victorian structure with a wraparound porch. Built in 1889, this Queen Anne–style home offers bed-and-breakfast accommodations with private bath and breakfast served in your room or suite. Standard to moderate rates.

Down the street at *The Limestone House Bed and Breakfast* (256–765–0365), located at 601 North Wood Avenue, you'll find more warm hospitality—maybe just-baked cookies on arrival and certainly a delectable breakfast (served at your convenience) in the sunroom. Henry Ford and Thomas Edison once visited this handsome 1915 Georgian Revival home, listed on the National Register of Historic Places, and you can sleep in rooms named for them.

The home makes a fitting backdrop for the extensive art collection of owners Carolyn and Dan Waterman, who have lived all over the globe and, in the process, amassed a treasure trove of artifacts such as striking sculptures and the rare African comb collection in the foyer. Visit www.thelimestonehouse.com. Moderate rates.

Scenic Wilderness

Leaving the Shoals, you might enjoy taking the *Natchez Trace Parkway.* A portion of the historic Trace cuts across this corner of Alabama through Lauderdale and Colbert Counties. Once a pioneer footpath, this route took travelers from Natchez, Mississippi, to Nashville, Tennessee. To intercept the Trace, which offers plenty of scenic stops, picnic spots, and nature trails, head northwest on State Route 20.

Exit at U.S. Highway 72 near the tiny town of *Cherokee.* At the *Wooden Nickel Restaurant* (256–359–4225), near the railroad tracks at 195 Main Street, owner Cathy Jones offers good vegetable lunches and a variety of dinner platters. Economical to moderate prices. The restaurant's hours are 6:00 A.M. to 8:00 P.M. Sunday through Thursday and until 9:00 P.M. Friday and Saturday.

Heading south to *Winfield* takes you to *White Oaks Inn* (205–487–4115 or 800–482–4115) at 300 Regal Street. At the end of a driveway flanked by stone lions, this lovely bed-and-breakfast stands on a knoll in a parklike setting. Owners Linda and Roger Sanders have achieved an open, airy look in their renovation of this 1918 home with a welcoming front porch (plus a bit of whimsy

On the Coon Dog Trail

One sunny morning in August, my mother and I set out to find the **Coon Dog Memorial Graveyard.** Our approach led up a hill, and before reaching the top, my car developed resistance symptoms. Smoke came pouring out from some private place, and the car whimpered and gave a last gasp.

Being an auto illiterate, I knew not what to do. "You don't have AAA?!" my mother said in a slightly accusatory tone. (Mothers are born saying things like "I told you so," and yes, I now have AAA and a car phone.)

We were in a wooded area, seemingly isolated, but I saw a house in the distance. A woman answered my knock and let me use her phone. As we waited on the porch for a tow truck, she told us much about the surrounding area and its abundant wildlife, even showing us several sizable snake skins. After the arrival of the tow truck, driven by a history buff, I heard even more anecdotes and collected tips on local sites to check out—thanks to a disaster in disguise and two good samaritans.

Anyway, back to Key Underwood's Coon Dog Memorial Graveyard, which is located south of Cherokee, via Colbert County Route 21. Now a park, the site contains markers and tombstones (some with epitaphs) for more than one hundred coon dogs.

The graveyard's origin dates to the death of Troop, a coonhound owned by Key Underwood. Here on September 4, 1937, Underwood and some friends buried the dog at a favorite hunting spot. An annual Labor Day celebration commemorating the anniversary of the graveyard's founding takes place in the park and features bluegrass music, buck dancing, barbecue, and even a liars' contest. Political hopefuls often show up for the festivities. Otherwise, the site projects a sense of serenity, and the surroundings look much as they did during the days when Troop picked up the scent of a coon here.

with the English telephone booth just inside the entrance). Accommodations include five rooms, each with private bath, in the main house and five cabins on the grounds. Guests can enjoy such amenities as a hot tub and pool (with robes and shower shoes provided). Standard rates. Call for reservations and specific directions.

In this area you'll find yet another fascinating attraction, **Natural Bridge** (205–486–5330). Located on US 278 about a mile west of the intersection of State Routes 5 and 13, this double-span, 60-foot-high sandstone bridge, thousands of years in the making, looms majestically in its pristine setting. Surrounding this impressive formation, presumably the longest natural bridge east of the Rockies, you'll see massive moss-covered boulders and lush vegetation. Local flora includes ferns, bigleaf magnolias, mountain laurel, and oakleaf hydrangeas. Inviting nature paths and picnic areas make this a pleasant place for an outing. Moulton photographer Charles Jordan's postcards, available in the

Meet Jerry Brown,
Ninth-Generation Potter

While exploring this region of scenic wilderness, consider a visit to **Brown's Pottery** (205–921–9483, 205–921–2597, or 800–341–4919), located at 1414 County Road 81, 3 miles south of Hamilton. Here, Jerry Brown carries on a family tradition of pottery-making that spans nine generations. In 1992 Jerry and his wife, Sandra, made a trip to Washington, D.C., where he received a National Heritage Fellowship Award, presented by President and Mrs. Bush. Jerry's work is exhibited in galleries across the country as well as the Smithsonian, where he has been invited several times to demonstrate pottery-making.

The traditional Southern folk potter has captured numerous awards at shows and festivals, and his work is sought by collectors. "Folk pottery increases in value," said Jerry, who signs and dates his pieces. In a "Quest for America's Best," QVC shopping network featured his work on national television. For this show Jerry filled an order for 1,500 pitchers, which sold out in two minutes.

One of the nation's few practicing traditional potters, Jerry remembers "playing around on the potter's wheel before I was old enough to start school." He performs his magic by combining water with local clay, which "looks almost blue. The South is known for its good clay," he added. Using a backhoe to dig the clay from a 150-year-old-pit, Jerry then turns the process over to his four-legged assistant, Blue, who does the mixing by walking circles around a mule-powered clay grinder. Jerry designed and built the brick oval kiln, in which he fires his work at temperatures that exceed 3,000 degrees Fahrenheit.

The pottery's showroom features blue-speckled pitchers, bowls, churns, candle holders, crocks, mugs, pie plates, bluebird houses, and more. Face jugs, Jerry's specialty, were historically used to hold harmful substances. Sometimes called ugly jugs, the vessels feature faces that don't win beauty contests but do earn awards and are coveted by collectors. The jugs sell for prices ranging from $30 to $200 and vary in size up to the largest, a five-gallon container.

Before leaving the pottery, I purchased several gifts. The crocks do double duty, Jerry pointed out, demonstrating how to use the container's lip to sharpen a knife. Even now as I write, I am drinking coffee from a thick mug with a blue, feathered design. (Ask Jerry to tell you the story of how a mishap with flying chicken feathers inspired one of his popular patterns.)

To view the pottery-making process as it was done in the olden days or to buy unique gifts (for yourself and others), head to Hamilton, near the Mississippi border. The Pottery's hours run from 9:00 A.M. to 5:00 P.M. Monday through Saturday.

gift shop, capture some of the site's ambience. Modest admission. The facility is open daily year-round from 8:00 A.M. till sunset.

To topple back in time a bit, drop by **Dixie Den** (205–486–8577) in nearby **Haleyville** for an authentic chocolate (or your own preference) mixed-in-a-metal-container milk shake. While slurping or sharing it, you can catch a glimpse of the town's past because black-and-white photos of the old Dixie Hotel and other bygone buildings line the walls, and you may also recognize hometown personality Pat Buttram's photo. Owners Judy and Toby Sherrill offer homemade chicken and tuna salads, soups, and sandwiches, including the Dixie Dog for big appetites (two hot dogs on a bun plus chili, kraut, and trimmings). Hours run from 10:30 A.M. to 4:00 P.M. Monday through Wednesday and to 8:00 P.M. on Thursday and Friday. On Saturday the cafe closes at 3:00 P.M. Next door in the same 1948 complex, the Dixie Theater's nostalgic lobby beckons. If the theater is closed, you might prevail upon the Sherrills to let you have a peek.

Continuing east through Winston County, you'll find the town of **Double Springs,** located in the **William B. Bankhead National Forest.** This huge forest (named for the distinguished political family of actress Tallulah Bankhead) spreads over most of Winston County and north into Lawrence County.

In front of the Winston County Courthouse at Double Springs stands *Dual Destiny,* the statue of a Civil War soldier flanked by billowing Confederate and Union flags. Contrary to common assumption, many Alabamians remained staunch Unionists during the Civil War, and "the Free State of Winston" represented such a contingent. After Alabama's secession (which passed by a narrow vote), these hill-country people, led by local teacher Christopher Sheats, took the position that if a state could secede from the Union, then a county could secede from a state.

While visiting the Free State of Winston, take time to explore some of the surrounding **Sipsey Wilderness.** With 25,988 acres, Sipsey provides plenty of off-the-beaten-path territory, including 20 miles of hiking trails.

Afterward take US 278 east and head toward Cullman.

Covered Bridge Country

To see Alabama's largest covered truss bridge, continue east from Winston County on US 278. Watch for the left turn to **Clarkson Covered Bridge** (sometimes called the Legg Bridge), located a short distance north of the highway on Cullman County Road 11. The bridge, situated in a picturesque park setting, stretches 270 feet across Crooked Creek. Supported by four large stone piers, this "town-truss" structure features latticed timbers, clapboard siding, and a roof of cedar shingles. The bridge, restored in 1975, dates to 1904.

Clarkson Covered Bridge

Once the site of a Civil War battle, the surrounding area offers picnic grounds and woodland hiking trails. During our visit my husband and I met a man who showed us a gum tree with a carving—a message left for him by a fellow Cherokee some thirty-five years earlier. The park is open year-round, and there's no admission charge.

Continuing east on US 278 takes you to **Cullman,** a city that dates to 1873 when Col. John G. Cullmann bought a large tract of land and established a colony for German immigrants here. A reproduction of the founder's Bavarian-style home (which burned in 1912) now serves as the **Cullman County Museum** (256–739–1258), located at 211 Second Avenue Northeast. The museum's eight rooms, each with a theme, preserve some of the city's German heritage and the area's history. You'll see a 7-foot wooden sculpture of a Native American warrior, china, jewelry, vintage clothing, fainting couches, early tools, a beer wagon, and other local items. Modest admission. Except for Thursday's schedule, which runs from 9:00 A.M. to noon, the museum is open Monday through Friday from 9:00 A.M. to noon and from 1:00 to 4:00 P.M., and by appointment only on Saturday. Sunday hours are 1:30 to 4:30 P.M.

For a good meal, stop by **The All Steak** (256–734–4322), located just a few blocks away on 314 Second Avenue Southwest on the fourth floor of the Cullman Savings Bank. (If it's raining, stop at the third level on the parking deck to stay under cover and take the elevator up one floor.) Contrary to its name, the restaurant serves a wide variety of entrees, including seafood and poultry. In addition to its beef specialties, the eatery is famous for homemade breads and desserts, especially the orange rolls, as well as its vegetable lunches. Prices are moderate. Hours are 6:00 A.M. to 9:00 P.M. Monday through Wednesday and 6:00 A.M. to 10:00 P.M. Thursday through Saturday. Sunday's schedule is 6:30 A.M. to 3:00 P.M.

Sample a bit of Cullman's heritage by stepping into *A Touch of German* (256–739–4592) at 218 First Avenue Southeast. Here, you'll be greeted by owner Peggy Grobe plus a flock of chirping birds popping out of their cuckoo clock homes to remind you that time is passing much too fast to browse through all the city's great shops.

Peggy stocks European and American collectibles such as handcrafted nut-crackers, music boxes, Old World Christmas ornaments, Steiff stuffed bears, table linens, laces, tapestries, blue delftware, Bavarian steins, scrumptious chocolate, Russian nested dolls, and more. You'll also find costumes—dirndls, aprons, lederhosen, and alpine hats—for Oktoberfest, which Cullman celebrates the first week in October

alabamatrivia

Cullman, known as the City of Churches, has more than 200 churches within its city limits.

each year. Hours run Monday through Saturday from 9:30 A.M. to 5:30 P.M.

Step next door for more browsing at Craig's Antiques and Gifts. Continue a few steps farther to The Duchess Bakery and pick up some doughnuts. This family-owned business at 222 First Avenue Southeast opened in 1939.

At *Southern Accents* (256–737–0554) you'll find an array of architectural antiques—everything from carved mantels, leaded-glass windows, statuary, and stately columns to chandeliers, hitching posts, molding, staircases, and claw-foot bathtubs. Housed in historic quarters at 308 Second Avenue Southeast, the inventory draws clients from across the United States. Owners Dr. Garlan Gudger and his son, Garlan Jr., search the globe for treasures from the past.

A sign near the entrance reads: YOUR HUSBAND CALLED...HE SAID TO BUY ANYTHING YOU WANT. (I especially admired a Victorian cherry parlor mantel, wearing a SOLD sign and soon to be shipped to New York.) Hours run Monday through Saturday from 10:00 A.M. to 5:00 P.M.

alabamatrivia

Cullman acquired the title "Die Deutsche Kolonie von Nord Alabama" because the town's founder, Col. John G. Cullmann, who came from Frankweiler, Germany, attracted approximately 10,000 German settlers to north Alabama.

"We will serve no swine before its time," promise Ron Dunn and Gary Wiggins, first cousins who operate *Johnny's Bar-B-Q* (256–734–8539), a family business at 1404 Fourth Street Southwest that opened in the early 1950s. Here, you can opt for a barbecue sandwich or a plate with all the fixings: coleslaw, beans, and potato salad. Other popular items include smoked chicken with white barbecue sauce, catfish, or barbecue-topped baked potatoes. "Closed on

Sunday for church and closed on Monday for rest," the restaurant's hours run Tuesday through Saturday from 10:00 A.M. to 9:00 P.M. Economical rates.

Afterward continue to 1600 Saint Bernard Drive Southeast, off US 278, on the town's east side. At *Ave Maria Grotto* (256–734–4110), on the grounds of a Benedictine monastery, visitors can take a Lilliputian world tour in a unique garden filled with more than 150 miniature reproductions of famous landmarks. Brother Joseph Zoettl, a Bavarian, who arrived at St. Bernard Abbey in 1892, constructed these reduced versions of various buildings. At age eighty the gifted monk completed his final work, the Lourdes Basilica. His architectural miniatures also include the Hanging Gardens of Babylon, ancient Jerusalem, Rome's Pantheon, and St. Peter's Basilica.

Using ingenuity and an unlikely assortment of materials, from playing marbles and fishing floats to cold-cream jars and even a discarded bird cage (for the dome of St. Peter's), along with the more standard cement, limestone, and marble, Brother Joe fashioned a small world that continues to delight travelers. Check it out at www.avemariagrotto.com. Except for Christmas and New Year's days, the grotto can be visited daily from 7:00 A.M. to 5:00 P.M. October through March, and to 7:00 P.M. April through September. Modest admission.

In south Cullman County near Hanceville, you can make a personal pilgrimage to *The Shrine of the Most Blessed Sacrament of Our Lady of the Angels Monastery.* To reach the shrine, take State Route 91 through Hanceville, watching for signs that lead to County Road 747 and then to County Road 548. A long, white-fenced approach winds through a portion of the site's 380 acres of rolling farmland. More than three years in construction, the shrine opened in December 1999, and has become a major mecca for visitors. Mother Angelica, who founded Eternal Word Television Network (EWTN), serves as Abbess here, and the monastery is home to the Poor Clare Nuns of Perpetual Adoration.

The shrine's Romanesque-Gothic style of architecture echoes Franciscan churches and monasteries of thirteenth-century Assisi. To reach the shrine, you'll cross an expansive colonaded piazza. As you approach, notice the T-shaped cross. The original top portion was struck by lightning, leaving the form of a Tau cross, the symbol that St. Francis used in signing his letters.

From inlaid Italian-marble floors and stately columns to vaulted ceiling, the awe-inspiring interior leaves no detail to chance. Made of carved cedar, the main altar is covered in gold leaf. The stained-glass windows were created in Munich, Germany, and the stonework embellishments were crafted by artisans in Spain. Other features include mosaics fashioned by Italian artisans using a four-century-old method of hand-chiseling and fitting.

Castle San Miguel stands below the piazza and houses a great hall, conference facilities, and a gift shop; hours are Monday through Saturday from 8:00 A.M. to 5:00 P.M. The shrine is open to the public from 6:00 A.M. to 6:00 P.M. daily, and the nuns' Conventual Mass takes place at 7:00 A.M. daily. To learn more about the circumstances that led to the erection of this magnificent structure in the hills of Alabama, you can attend one of the brother's commentaries, generally scheduled at 10:00 A.M. daily, depending on the crowd. For more information call (256) 352–6267 or visit www.olamshrine.com.

Continue east on US 278 until it intersects US 231, then turn south to see the *Blount County Covered Bridges.* Known as the Covered Bridge Capital of Alabama, this area features three covered bridges, all still in daily use and marked by road signs on nearby highways. If you're on a tight schedule, choose the Horton Mill Covered Bridge, probably the most picturesque of the bunch. Located about 5 miles north of Oneonta on State Route 75, the latticed structure looms some 70 feet above the Warrior River's Calvert Prong—higher above water than any other covered bridge in the United States. Adjacent to the highway there's a parking area with nearby picnic facilities and nature trails, making this a relaxing place to take a driving break.

Continuing your exploration, you'll find the county's shortest covered bridge southeast of Rosa. The 95-foot-long, tin-topped Easley Covered Bridge stands about a half-mile off Blount County Road 33 and spans Dub Branch.

Northwest of Cleveland, 1 mile off State Route 79, Swann Bridge appears rather suddenly as you're rounding a curve. The three-span bridge extends 324 feet over the Locust Fork of the Black Warrior River. You can park in a turn-off lane on the bridge's opposite side to explore the nearby terrain, where Queen Anne's lace, ferns, mountain laurel, wild hydrangeas, and muscadine vines grow. You might hear a mockingbird's serenade in the background.

Each October the *Oneonta* area stages an annual *Covered Bridge Festival* featuring bridge tours, arts and crafts exhibits, and other festivities. For additional information on the festival, award-winning Palisades Park, or other area attractions, call the Blount County/Oneonta Chamber of Commerce at (205) 274–2153.

After seeing the bridges of Blount County, you'll probably be ready for a wonderful meal, and Charlie Bottcher promises you one at *The Landmark* (205–274–2821) in Oneonta. Described by one Birmingham visitor as "a little bit of France in the middle of nowhere," the restaurant is at 601 Second Avenue East. Charlie, who's the owner/chef, creates consistently delicious combinations and demonstrates a winning way with vegetables. Be sure to note the board specials, as these change weekly.

Shrimp 'n Grits

The Landmark's chef/owner Charlie Bottcher sometimes teaches gourmet cooking classes, demonstrating culinary techniques and sharing his much-in-demand recipes. I signed up for two series of these popular sessions. My sister (who would rather grade a hundred biology exams and judge science-fair projects all day than prepare one meal) questioned my sanity: Why would anyone pay cool cash for the privilege of working in a hot restaurant kitchen? One reason: Charlie advises his students to bring good appetites, because they're required to eat all the courses prepared. It's a tough assignment, but. . . .

Charlie created the following scrumptious dish, a favorite with his patrons, and graciously granted permission to share it with my readers:

Spicy Baked Shrimp with Garlic-Cheese Grits

36 large shrimp (31/35) with tails on, peeled and butterflied

Grits:

4 cups water

½ teaspoon salt

½ teaspoon garlic, minced

1 cup quick grits

6 ounces sharp cheddar cheese, grated

In a saucepan, bring water, salt, and garlic to a boil. Add grits and stir. Turn heat to low and simmer till grits are tender and slightly thickened. Add cheese and stir until melted. Divide grits among four ramekins or individual dishes.

Dip for Shrimp:

1 cup oil

2½ tablespoons K-Paul's Redfish Seasoning

2½ tablespoons Old Bay Seasoning

2 tablespoons lemon juice

2 tablespoons Kikkoman soy sauce

4 tablespoons honey

Mix well. Dip 9 shrimp at one time to bottom of dip and transfer shrimp and lots of dip to each dish of grits. Place shrimp, alternating tails, in row over grits. Finish remaining three dishes. Bake in 400-degree oven till shrimp are firm and grits are bubbly, about 15 minutes. Serves 4.

Depending on what's fresh, good, and available, dinner selections might mean spicy Greek snapper, filet mignon in puff pastry, or blackened amberjack. Chicken Landmark, a signature dish, features a charbroiled, marinated chicken breast topped with crabmeat, charbroiled shrimp, and clam sauce. Charlie's clientele comes from a 75-mile radius. Moderate prices. Dinner is served from 4:30 to 9:00 P.M. Friday and Saturday.

Before leaving Blount County, head to **Benedikt's Restaurant** (205–274–0230), located at 4125 Blount County Road 27, about 8 miles southeast of Oneonta on Straight Mountain. Some folks just stumble on the restaurant by accident while taking a scenic drive; others make a deliberate effort, traveling regularly from Birmingham and surrounding areas to eat here. The restaurant's Sunday meal is served "buffeteria" style.

On her menu, Ruth Benedikt writes, "Ladies and Gentlemen, we are 12th generation Charlestonians: Scotch, Irish and German. Our recipes belong to our mother, aunts, grandmother and all who came before them." Ruth and her sister Joice have prepared their recipes for the public for three decades and consider themselves "among the last of the scratch cooks in the restaurant business."

Choices might include German pot roast, golden fried chicken, or ham steak along with side dishes of real mashed potatoes, mixed broccoli-cauliflower with cheese sauce, sweet tomato relish, fresh creamed corn, purple hull peas, and fried green tomatoes.

Closed Monday, the eatery is open Tuesday through Thursday from 9:00 A.M. to 3:00 P.M. and until 8:30 P.M. Friday and Saturday. Call the Benedickts for Sunday reservations; serving hours are 9:00 A.M. to 4:00 P.M. Rates are economical to moderate.

Across the road at **Capps Cove** (205–625–3039 or 800–583–4750), you'll find a country getaway with a mountain on one side and a river on the other. Located at 4126 Blount County Road 27, the complex offers bed and breakfast and much, much more. Owners Sybil and Cason Capps, native Alabamians who have lived in several states over the past fifteen years, moved here from St. Louis when Cason retired from a broadcasting career.

"We think we're unique," Sybil says, "a country village with an antiques store, barn, wedding chapel, and two old-style country cabins." Guests can enjoy a full country breakfast—smoked ham, bacon, a house specialty called "naked cowboys," grits, potatoes, the works—in the couple's lovely two-story Colonial house. Moderate rates. Visit the property at www.cappscove.com.

Continue to the state's central section. Nearby Ashville, easily reached by taking US 231 south, makes an interesting stop.

Places to Stay in Northwest Alabama

ATHENS

Country Hearth Inn
1500 U.S. Highway 72 East
(256) 232–1520 or
(888) 443–2784

CULLMAN

Hampton Inn
6100 State Route 157
(256) 739–4444 or
(800) 426–7866

DECATUR

All Suites Hotel
918 Beltline Road
(256) 355–9977

Comfort Inn & Suites
2212 Danville Road
(256) 355–1999 or
(800) 424–6423

Country Inn & Suites
807 Bank Street Northeast
(256) 355–6800

Hampton Inn
2041 Beltline Road
(256) 355–5888 or
(800) 426–7866

Holiday Inn Hotel & Suites
1101 Sixth Avenue Northeast
(256) 355–3150 or
(800) 553–3150

FLORENCE

The Limestone House
Bed and Breakfast
601 North Wood Avenue
(256) 765–0365

Wood Avenue Inn
658 North Wood Avenue
(256) 766–8441

KILLEN

Laurel Cottage
761 County Road 414
(256) 757–1635

ONEONTA

Capps Cove
4126 County Road 27
(205) 625–3039 or
(800) 583–4750

ROGERSVILLE

Joe Wheeler
State Park Lodge
4401 McLean Drive
(256) 247–5461 or
(800) 544–5639 or
(800) 252–7275

TOWN CREEK

Doublehead
Resort & Lodge
145 County Road 314
(800) 685–9267

TUSCUMBIA

Key West Inn
1800 U.S. Highway 72 West
(256) 383–0700 or
(866) 253–9937

Sharlotte's House
Bed and Breakfast
105 East North Commons
(256) 386–7269

WINFIELD

White Oaks Inn
300 Regal Street
(205) 487–4115 or
(800) 482–4115

Places to Eat in Northwest Alabama

CHEROKEE

Wooden Nickel Restaurant
195 Main Street
(near railroad tracks)
(256) 359–4225

CULLMAN

The All Steak
314 Second Avenue
Southwest
(256) 734–4322

The Creamery Restaurant
402-A Fifth Street Southwest
(256) 739–3131

Johnny's Bar-B-Q
1404 Fourth Street
Southwest
(256) 734–8539

Rumors Deli
105 First Avenue Northeast
Suite 100
(256) 737–0911

DECATUR

Big Bob Gibson's
1715 Sixth Avenue
Southeast
(256) 350–6969

Curry's on Johnston Street
115 Johnston Street
Southeast
(256) 350–6715

Simp McGhee's
725 Bank Street Northeast
(256) 353–6284

FLORENCE

Eva Marie's
106 North Court Street
(256) 760–0004

Ricatoni's Italian Grill
107 North Court Street
(256) 718–1002

Trowbridge's
316 North Court Street
(256) 764–1503

HALEYVILLE

Dixie Den
907 Twentieth Street
(205) 486–8577

MOULTON

Classical Fruits
8831 State Route 157
(256) 974–8813

Western Sirloin Steak House
11383 State Route 157
(256) 974–7191

MUSCLE SHOALS

New Orleans Transfer
1682 South Wilson
Dam Road
(256) 386–0656

FOR MORE INFORMATION ABOUT NORTHWEST ALABAMA

North Alabama Tourism Association
25062 North Street,
P.O. Box 1075
Mooresville 35649
(256) 350–3500 or (800) 648–5381
Web site: www.northalabama.org
e-mail: info@northalabama.org
This organization covers sixteen north Alabama counties that are home to some one hundred attractions in a 100-mile radius.

Colbert County Tourism & Convention Bureau
719 Highway 72 West,
P.O. Box 740425
Tuscumbia 35674
(256) 383–0783 or (800) 344–0783
Web site: www.colbertcountytourism.org
e-mail: ctourism@hiwaay.net

Cullman Area Chamber of Commerce
301 Second Avenue Southwest
P.O. Box 1104
Cullman 35056
(256) 734–0454 or (800) 313–5114
Web site: www.cullmanchamber.org
e-mail: cullman@corrcomm.net

Decatur/Morgan County Convention & Visitors Bureau
719 Sixth Avenue Southeast
P.O. Box 2349
Decatur 35602
(256) 350–2028 or (800) 524–6181
Web site: www.decaturcvb.org
e-mail: info@decaturcvb.org

Florence/Lauderdale Tourism
One Hightower Place
Florence 35630
(256) 740–4141 or (888) 356–8687
Web site: www.flo-tour.org
e-mail: dwilson@flo-tour.org

ONEONTA

Benedikt's Restaurant
4125 Blount County
County Road 27
(205) 274–0230

The Chocolate Cottage
110 Second Avenue
(205) 274–8484

The Landmark
601 Second Avenue East
(205) 274–2821

SHEFFIELD

George's Steak Pit
1206 Jackson Highway
(256) 381–1531

TUSCUMBIA

Claunch Cafe
400 South Main Street
(in Spring Park)
(256) 386–0222

MAINSTREAM ATTRACTIONS WORTH SEEING IN NORTHWEST ALABAMA

Alabama Music Hall of Fame,
617 U.S. Highway 72 West,
Tuscumbia;
(256) 381–4417 or (800) 239–2643.
You can immerse yourself in the state's musical heritage at this facility, which features exhibits, audiovisual galleries, and memorabilia related to musicians either from Alabama or associated with the state. Artists represented include Hank Williams, Elvis Presley, Emmylou Harris, the Temptations, and many others. For a little music and a Web tour of the museum, click on www.alamhof.org.

Point Mallard Park,
1800 Point Mallard Drive Southeast,
Decatur;
(256) 350–3000.
Named for nearby Wheeler National Wildlife Refuge's wintering ducks, this park for all seasons offers aquatic fun in the summer and year-round golfing on a championship course. You may even see Capt. Mike Mallard, a human-size mascot in nautical attire, wandering about. Not only does the 750-acre complex contain a wave pool, an Olympic-size diving pool, water slides, sand beach, and "Squirt Factory," but you'll also find a 173-acre campground, hiking and biking trails, and picnicking facilities here.

Central Alabama

Ridges, Springs, and Valleys

Alabama's midsection presents a pleasing pastoral landscape, a panorama of ridges, springs, and valleys. Heading south, the Birmingham area serves as a convenient base from which to branch out into the state's central region. From here, too, you can easily sweep down into Alabama's southeastern section to explore the historic **Chattahoochee Trace** as well as the state capital area.

Start your area exploration with a trip to downtown **Ashville,** home of one of St. Clair County's two courthouses (the other is in Pell City). This Neoclassical Revival structure, an enlargement of an earlier courthouse, dates from the early 1840s. Two blocks from the courthouse square, on U.S. Highway 231 at 20 Rose Lane, stands a lovely bed-and-breakfast, **Roses and Lace Country Inn** (205–594–4366). Look for a Queen Anne–style home painted a muted mauve with grape and vanilla accents. Visualize a veranda with hanging Boston ferns, swings, and wicker rocking chairs, and you'll have a good idea what to expect at this Victorian home. The roses-and-lace motif echoes from the rose garden on the side lawn to the interior's floral wallpapers, lace curtains, and selected accents.

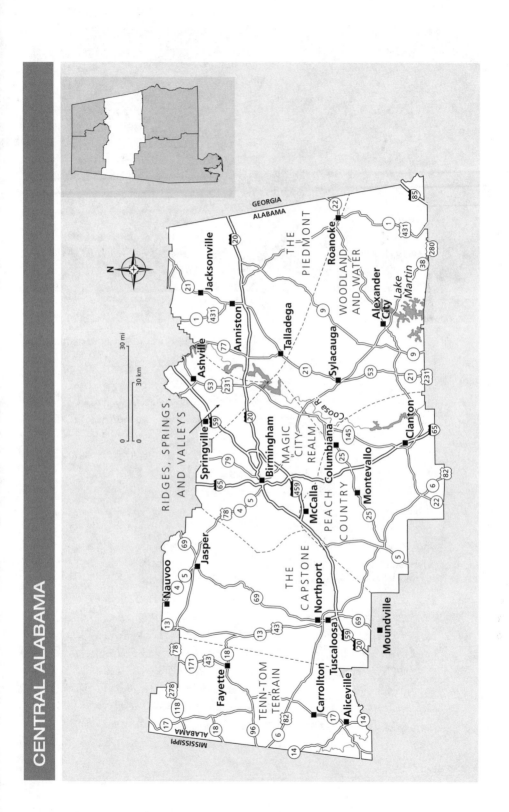

Innkeepers Wayne and Faye Payne will welcome you to this charming home. For breakfast, Faye serves homemade biscuits and jellies, bacon, sausage, country ham, and scrambled eggs. The home offers a honeymoon suite and five bedrooms with four-and-a-half baths. Standard to moderate rates.

Ask Faye to make an appointment for you to see the circa-1852 Inzer House next door, a striking, white brick structure now reincarnated as a Civil War museum. A number of black cast-iron Confederate crosses dot the grounds of nearby Ashville Cemetery.

To learn more about local history, drive out to see the *John Looney House,* one of Alabama's oldest two-story log dogtrot structures. (The term "dogtrot" refers to a central hallway connecting two rooms also known as "pens." Although covered, this passage was left open and often proved a popular napping place for the family canines, hence its name.) Located a little over 4 miles southeast of Ashville on St. Clair County Road 24, this rare example of pioneer architecture dating to about 1820 may be visited on weekends. The Paynes at Roses and Lace Country Inn will give you a current status report on this historical site. Current hours are Saturday and Sunday from 1:00 to 4:00 P.M. Modest admission.

From Ashville take State Route 23 south until you reach U.S. Highway 11 leading to **Springville,** a town that takes its name from several area springs. First called Big Springs and settled about 1817, the town became Springville with the post office's establishment in 1834; the entire downtown district is on the National Historic Register. On Main Street beside the 1892 *House of Quilts &*

GAY'S TOP PICKS IN CENTRAL ALABAMA

Aliceville Museum,
Aliceville

The American Village,
Montevallo

Anniston Museum of Natural History,
Anniston

Birmingham Civil Rights Institute,
Birmingham

DeSoto Caverns Park,
Childersburg

International Motorsports Hall of Fame,
Talladega

McWane Center,
Birmingham

Moundville Archaeological Park,
Moundville

Paul W. Bryant Museum,
Tuscaloosa

Tannehill Historical State Park,
McCalla

The Westervelt-Warner Museum of American Art,
Tuscaloosa

Antiques (205–467–6072), a natural spring flows; sometimes people stop to fill jugs with water or to pick the watercress growing here. Be sure to browse through the shop, owned by Beverly and Jack Crumpton, which contains several rooms of collectibles and unusual gifts. In addition to a large assortment of colorful handmade quilts and antique furniture, the Crumptons sell home accessories—everything from plant and magazine stands to wall hangings and letter openers. Hours are 10:00 A.M. to 4:00 P.M. Thursday through Saturday.

Take time to explore some of this state historic district's other nostalgic shops. Nearby Homestead Hollow, a fifty-five-acre pioneer homestead with a blacksmith shop, log cabin, barn, and gristmill, serves as a quaint backdrop for art-and-craft festivals throughout the year. During such events, visitors may sample sorghum and apple cider made on the premises.

The Piedmont

Located in the Appalachian foothills, Calhoun County occupies a portion of the state's Piedmont region. Start your tour in *Anniston,* an attractive, arts-oriented city that named William Shakespeare its citizen of the year in 1984—before the Alabama Shakespeare Festival left its birthplace here and moved to Montgomery.

"It's your world. Explore it!" urges the staff at the *Anniston Museum of Natural History* (256–237–6766), located a couple of miles from downtown at 800 Museum Drive. Some adventures promised by the museum's slogan include treks through jungles, deserts, and savannahs at this handsome facility surrounded by 187 acres on Anniston's northern outskirts. Entering the museum's Lagarde African Hall, you'll see a rogue elephant keeping vigil beside a towering baobab tree (the world's largest replica of an "upside-down" tree). Preserved specimens of more than a hundred creatures inhabit this African complex, most collected by Annistonian John B. Lagarde, a big-game hunter who donated his award-winning assemblage to the museum.

From antelope to zebras, all animals appear in the most realistic habitats possible. And through it all visitors see the versatility with which nature's creatures adapt to their world. Every effort has been made to achieve the effect of authenticity; for example, light in the bamboo forest filters through a type of Venetian blind to create a network of slanted rays.

Spacious corridors wind from the African depths to the Ornithology Hall with its impressive array of more than 600 specimens of North American birds, many now either extinct or on the endangered species list. Naturalist William Werner assembled this priceless bird collection more than a century ago, and several diorama groupings include nests (some with eggs) built by the birds themselves. The museum boasts one of the world's finest models of a pteranadon, a

Strange As It Sounds

Deadly beauty and intrigue await at the **Berman Museum** (256–237–6261) in Anniston's LaGarde Park. Here you'll find an arsenal of rare weapons collected from all over the world by a former secret agent. Suits of armor that now stand still once clanked as knights did battle. Beheading axes and swords from ancient China and Japan hang in silence—not divulging their roles in past dastardly deeds.

A stunning royal Persian scimitar set with 1,295 rose-cut diamonds, sixty carats of rubies, and an exquisite forty-carat emerald in a three-pound gold handle mesmerizes sightseers here just as it once did Russian audiences during the reign of Catherine the Great. Other rare items include a Greek helmet dating to 300 B.C., Jefferson Davis's traveling pistols, Adolf Hitler's silver tea service, and Napoleon Bonaparte's ivory comb and brush set. Also displayed is a saber used in the dramatic "Charge of the Light Brigade." The collection contains eighty-eight guns from the American West, Fraser's famous *End of the Trail* sculpture, and bronzes by Frederic Remington, Charles Russell, and Karl Kauba.

Army colonel Farley Lee Berman worked in counterintelligence, and he and his wife, Germaine (a Parisian with a comparable position in French Intelligence), met during World War II. Afterward they traveled the world on a decades-long quest for historical weapons and art.

Personnel from several metropolitan museums approached Berman about acquiring his collection, but he chose to donate it to the city of Anniston, saying he knew "the people of Alabama would enjoy it." Located at 840 Museum Drive next to the Museum of Natural History, the Berman Museum's hours run from 10:00 A.M. to 5:00 P.M. Monday through Saturday and 1:00 to 5:00 P.M. on Sunday. The museum closes on Monday from September through May. Modest admission.

prehistoric flying reptile with a 30-foot wingspan. In Dynamic Earth Hall, which features a life-size model of an albertosaurus, you can explore an Alabama cave complete with waterfall, stalactites, and stalagmites. The museum's newest hall, "Alabama: Sand to Cedars," features a walk through the state from seashore to mountains. NatureSpace encourages children to explore beyond backyard boundaries with a unique exhibit of natural resources.

Accredited by the American Association of Museums and a Smithsonian affiliate, the Anniston facility has received national recognition for its innovative participatory exhibits. The museum also offers rotating art exhibits, a fine gift shop, picnicking facilities, and a nature trail. The museum is open Tuesday through Saturday from 10:00 A.M. to 5:00 P.M. (plus Monday during summer) and Sunday from 1:00 to 5:00 P.M. Modest admission.

Don't miss the historic Episcopal **Church of St. Michael and All Angels** (256–237–4011) on West Eighteenth Street at Cobb Avenue. With an exterior of

Alabama stone, this 1888 Norman-Gothic structure features a magnificent marble altar backed by an alabaster reredos (ornamental screen). Bavarian woodworkers carved the church's entire ceiling by hand, and angels on corbels all face the altar at slightly different angles. Admission is free, and you can visit year-round between 9:00 A.M. and 4:00 P.M.

Take time to drive through the Tyler Hill Historic District and along tree-lined Quintard Avenue, where you'll see grand Victorian homes. At one such mansion, *The Victoria* (256–236–0503 or 800–260–8781), you can drop in for a fine meal or an overnight stay. Look for a turreted, three-story structure, painted taupe and trimmed in white with a burgundy awning covering a walkway in front, on a hill at 1600 Quintard. This 1888 home, owned by Betty and Earlon McWhorter, now serves as a country inn. Accommodations include three lovely suites—decorated in period antiques—in the main house, a guest house, and a tasteful addition containing fifty-six rooms (all with private baths) connected to the inn by covered walkways.

alabamatrivia

Alabama's name comes from a Native American tribe, the Alibamu.

The menu changes seasonally but always includes steak and fresh seafood—and by popular demand, the jumbo lump crab cakes. Appetizers might range from the chef's daily soup creation to fried green tomatoes with lime crème fraîche and tasso ham. The Victoria also offers a wide selection of wines, including its own private label. Prices are moderate to expensive.

The Victoria is open to the public for dinner from 6:00 to 9:00 P.M. Monday through Thursday and to 10:00 P.M. on Friday and Saturday. Guests can enjoy a bountiful breakfast buffet in the main house. Standard to moderate rates.

Sometime during your stay stroll down to the old carriage house on the grounds, now home of an art gallery called Wren's Nest, which has original works and limited prints by noted wildlife artist Larry K. Martin.

During your Anniston excursion, take time to explore some of the city's interesting shops such as *Noble Passage* (256–237–0266) at 903 Noble Street. Here, owner/designer Deborah McDaniel offers an array of fine furniture, Persian rugs, and accents for the home. Hours are Monday through Friday from 10:00 A.M. to 5:00 P.M.

While in the area, head to *Munford* via State Route 21 for a visit to *The Cedars Plantation* (256–761–9090), located at 590 Cheaha Road. Owners Ann and Rick Price traveled widely and called many places home, including South America, before settling on this captivating country estate. "We want to share the house and its history with others," says Ann, whose research has yielded a wealth of information about the home's builder, Joseph Camp. Purchasing the property in 1833 from area Natchez/Creek chieftains, the Reverend Camp completed the main house two years later.

Sometimes called the "Steamboat House," the raised cottage split-level design features long side porches and double front doors. Period antiques (and perhaps the Reverend Camp's spirit) fill the high-ceilinged rooms. Guests can browse through the Prices' extensive library, which includes the Reverend Camp's interesting 1882 first-person account of history in the making. A post–Civil War skirmish took place at nearby Munford, and the home's east chimney still bears scars from the fire of marching Union soldiers.

Set on a sweeping lawn with stately oak and cedar trees, the home offers a tennis court, large swimming pool, and walking trails. Pleasant pastures surround The Cedars, and Tater Creek runs through the property. Ann recommends outings to Talladega National Forest, Cheaha State Park, and other

Much Ado in Anniston

For our first anniversary, friends invited my husband and me to visit them in *Anniston* and take in some plays. At that time summer visitors to Anniston—the birthplace of the Alabama Shakespeare Festival (ASF)—could watch actors "strut and fret their hour upon the stage" in five rotating weekend productions.

Martin L. Platt came from Carnegie Mellon University to direct the community theater and soon started the festival, which attracted throngs each summer. He personally picked the performers, auditioning many of them in New York.

I remember the gorgeous costumes, noted for their quality of workmanship. In a production of *Romeo and Juliet,* for instance, the Capulets were clothed in various shades of bronze and the Montagues in lavender and rose tones, enabling the audience to easily identify members of the feuding families. Gifted ASF Guild members spent countless volunteer hours hand-sewing seed pearls on dress hems or crocheting an army's "chain" mail headgear. Other Guild members found or provided lodging for actors, stuffed envelopes, ushered playgoers, or baked cookies for "meet the cast" parties.

We enjoyed immersing ourselves in the Elizabethan era by attending "Shakespeare Sundays" at the historic Church of St. Michael and All Angels. Filled with pomp and splendor, these services featured the use of a 1559 prayer book and the talents of the festival's company.

We continued to spend each anniversary in Anniston seeing ASF productions until the festival moved to its magnificent home in Montgomery and became a year-round theater. Although we still see occasional plays (Montgomery is much farther from our home), we miss those special summers. And on each wedding anniversary, we propose a toast to Shakespeare and all the wonderful times the curtain went up in Anniston.

GAY'S FAVORITE ANNUAL EVENTS IN CENTRAL ALABAMA

Christmas Village Arts and Crafts Show,
Birmingham-Jefferson Convention Complex Exhibition Hall, Birmingham, first weekends in March and November;
(205) 836–7178 or (800) 458–8085

Sakura Festival,
Tuscaloosa, March;
(800) 538–8696

Dogwood Festival,
Aliceville, third weekend of March;
(205) 373–2363 or (888) 751–2340

Birmingham International Festival (BIF),
Birmingham, April;
(205) 252–7652 or (800) 458–8085

Bruno's Memorial Classic,
Greystone Golf Course,
Birmingham, April;
(800) 458–8085

Indian Dance & Craft Festival,
Childersburg, April and September;
(800) 933–2283

Heritage Week,
Tuscaloosa, third week in April;
(800) 538–8696

City Stages,
Linn Park, Birmingham, May;
(205) 324–6881 or (800) 458–8085

International CityFest,
Downtown Tuscaloosa, May;
(800) 538–8696

Birmingham Heritage Festival,
Civil Rights District,
Birmingham, August;
(205) 324–3333 or (800) 458–8085

Kentuck Festival of the Arts,
Kentuck Park, Northport, October;
(205) 758–1257 or (800) 538–8696

Moundville Native American Festival,
Moundville Archaeological Park, October;
(205) 371–2234, or (800) 538–8696

EA Sports 500 Weekend–NASCAR,
Talladega Superspeedway,
Talladega, October;
(256) 362–9064 or (800) 458–8085

nearby spots for nature lovers. Guests can enjoy a home-cooked breakfast in the dining room. Rates range from standard to moderate.

After basking in the country's serenity, head to nearby **Talladega** and immerse yourself in history. If you take the Jackson Trace Road, you'll follow a wagon route cut by Gen. Andrew Jackson and his Tennessee Volunteers as they marched southward through the Creek Indian nation. For a self-guided driving map of the town's historical sites, head to the chamber of commerce office just off the courthouse square in the old L&N Depot at 210 East Street. Start with the Silk Stocking District (outlined on your map), a sizable concentration of homes listed on the National Register of Historic Places. Stop by Heritage Hall, a restored 1908 Carnegie Library at 200 South Street East, for a look at its current exhibits. Afterward drive by Talladega College, established in 1867, to see Hale Woodruff's striking *Amistad* murals at Savery Library. Other points of interest include the campus chapel and Swayne Hall, the college's first building.

For a delightful history lesson in living color and a fun-filled family adventure, don't miss nearby **DeSoto Caverns Park** (256–378–7252 or 800–933–CAVE), 5 miles east of Childersburg at 5181 DeSoto Caverns Parkway. A one-hour tour presents highlights of the cave's role in history and features a spellbinding laser light and sound show in the magnificent onyx chamber, taller than a twelve-story building and bigger than a football field.

After the tour children can climb DeSoto's cave wall, wander through a lost trail maze, pan for gemstones, do battle with water balloons, and enjoy a picnic on the grounds. The facility features more than twenty attractions, and you can make arrangements to stay overnight in the cave. The park's hours run from 9:00 A.M. to 4:30 P.M. Monday through Saturday, and 12:30 to 4:30 P.M. on Sunday (or to 5:30 P.M. April through October). Admission.

Magic City Realm

Before exploring busy, bustling Birmingham, you can enjoy another back-to-nature experience at **Twin Pines Resort** (205–672–7575) near Sterrett. Although designed as a corporate retreat, travelers on holiday or opting to locate a serene weekend getaway will find a haven at 1200 Twin Pines Road, about 30 miles southeast of Birmingham.

Today's fast-paced world becomes a blur when you turn onto a road lined with nature's greenery. Large log lodges feature porches overlooking a forty-six-acre private lake, and you can opt for a room or a suite with fireplace and kitchen. Standard to moderate rates.

Outdoor recreation opportunities might focus on fishing (no license required on private property), paddleboating, canoeing, swimming, and playing volleyball, softball, tennis, or horseshoes. While exploring the jogging/walking trails, you'll discover a covered bridge and a moonshine still and, in the process, work up a good appetite for the resort's bounteous country-cooked meals. When departure time comes, you may find it hard to tear yourself away.

Another good getaway, **Oak Mountain State Park** (205–620–2524), 15 miles south of Birmingham off Interstate 65, offers canoeing, fishing, swimming, golfing, picnicking, horseback riding, and a demonstration farm. Children especially enjoy seeing the geese, peacocks, rabbits, pigs, calves, donkeys, horses, and other animals. The park, most of it in a natural state, occupies almost 10,000 acres. A drive to the top of Double Oak Mountain affords some sweeping views of the park's steep slopes and rugged terrain.

Other features include some 40 miles of hiking trails and four lakes. Don't miss the Treetop Nature Trail, where the Alabama Wildlife Rescue Service houses injured birds of prey. Climbing a boardwalk through woodsy surroundings takes you past large enclosures containing hawks, great horned owls, and other raptors. Call for park information or reservations at Oak Mountain's lakeside cabins or campground. Modest admission.

After basking in serenity you can pick up the pace with a jaunt to ***Birmingham.*** Named for the British industrial city, Birmingham acquired its nickname, Magic City, when soon after its 1871 incorporation it burgeoned into Alabama's major metropolis. No longer a fire-breathing, smoke-spewing dragon, the city projects a much-changed image—from gray smog to crisp skyline and green-bordered boulevards. As a leading medical and technological center, the city boasts an economic base broadened far beyond its mineral resources. The financial impact of the University of Alabama at Birmingham (UAB) Medical Center beefs up the local economy enormously.

As the state's biggest city, Birmingham boasts many choice restaurants. For a memorable dinner, add ***Highlands Bar & Grill*** (205–939–1400) at 2011 Eleventh Avenue South to your itinerary. Classically trained chef Frank Stitt's regional Southern creations have been dubbed "New American" cuisine, and his accolades fill walls and books. Start with an appetizer of baked grits, and select an entree ranging from beef, venison, duck, and seafood to rabbit and veal. Renowned for its crab cakes, the restaurant also serves such specialties as pan roast quail with corn pudding and grilled leg of lamb with basil aioli and ratatouille. Moderate to expensive. Dinner hours are 6:00 to 10:00 P.M. Tuesday through Thursday and to 10:30 P.M. Friday and Saturday.

alabamatrivia

Birmingham ranks as the state's largest city.

While sightseeing in the Magic City, be sure to visit towering **Vulcan,** the world's largest cast-iron statue, back in place again after some refurbishing. To reach Vulcan Park atop Red Mountain, take Twentieth Street South and watch for the sign. An observation deck affords a panoramic view of Birmingham and surrounding Jones Valley. Cast from Birmingham iron, *Vulcan* represents the mythological god of metalworking, fire, and forge. Designed for the 1904 St. Louis Exposition by Italian sculptor Giuseppe Moretti, *Vulcan* lifts his torch in tribute to the city's iron industry. At the base of the 55-foot statue, a museum presents *Vulcan's* history along with an overview of steel production.

All about Art

While in the Birmingham area, stop by **Artists Incorporated** (205–979–8990) at 3365 Morgan Drive in Vestavia Hills. Representing the work of about fifty artists, this cooperative gallery offers a feast for the eyes. Here, you'll find oils by Les Yarbrough and Troy Crisswell, fiber art by Murray Johnston, bronzes by Frank Fleming, and more. Housed in a former dairy barn, the gallery boasts the distinction of being Vestavia's oldest commercial building.

"This gallery offers a great variety of art forms in a wide range of prices," says Bill Charles, a fan and former Birmingham resident. "I'm the proud and happy owner of several works including two affordable Frank Fleming pieces, and I'm glad for the chance to have seen any number of (for me) unaffordable pieces, too. The crew here loves art and delights in sharing that love with their customers, be they buyers or browsers."

Hours are Tuesday through Saturday from 10:00 A.M. to 5:00 P.M. except on Friday, when hours extend to 8:00 P.M. A reception, featuring artists, food, wine, and sometimes music, takes place from 5:30 to 9:00 P.M. on the first Friday of every month—and you're invited.

Consider stopping by **Birmingham Botanical Gardens** (205–414–3900) at 2612 Lane Park Road, on the lower southern slope of Red Mountain. Stroll through the Japanese garden complete with a fourteenth-century teahouse reproduction. Also on the grounds, *Southern Living* magazine maintains demonstration gardens with plantings that might be duplicated at home. The museum's gift shop offers a fine selection of items, from note cards and prints to unusual plants and garden statuary—great for giving or keeping. Free admission. The gardens are open year-round, from dawn to dusk each day. The gift shop is open 10:00 A.M. to 4:00 P.M. Monday through Saturday.

The Tutwiler (205–322–2100 or 866–850–3053) at 2021 Park Place North makes a comfortable and convenient base for seeing Birmingham's attractions. The staff at this charming historic hotel will make you glad you came to the Magic City. With its rose-marble foyer, original coffered ceilings, moldings, plasterwork, and brass hardware, the hotel recaptures the elegance of another era. Your room or suite, which might come with a balcony or a marble fireplace, features high ceilings, restored woodwork, marble bathrooms, and custom-designed antique reproductions. You'll also see fresh flowers but few TVs—most are tucked away in armoires.

Built in 1913 as a prestigious apartment/hotel, the redbrick, Italianate Tutwiler recently underwent a renovation. The Tutwiler's meticulous restoration resulted in charter membership in Historic Hotels of America, a select group recognized for preserving historic architectural quality and ambience. The original Tutwiler, the hotel's namesake, made news in 1974 when it became one of the country's first structures to be leveled by "implosion" (also the inspiration for the hotel's specialty drink by the same name).

The first Tutwiler hosted such dignitaries and celebrities as Eleanor Roosevelt, President Warren G. Harding, Charles Lindbergh, Will Rogers, Nelson Eddy, Tallulah Bankhead, Rocky Marciano, and Marilyn Monroe. Carrying on tradition, the current Tutwiler counts former President George Bush, Dan Quayle, Henry Kissinger, Colin Powell, Casper Weinberger, Mick Jagger, Billy Joel, and Henry Mancini among its honored guests. As another honored guest of the Tutwiler you can enjoy such amenities as complimentary shoe shines and newspapers, airport transportation, and valet parking. Rates are moderate.

For a glimpse of the city's Iron Age, take First Avenue North over the viaduct to Thirty-second Street toward the towering smokestacks of **Sloss Furnaces** (205–324–1911). Designated a National Historic Landmark, the ironworks that served Birmingham from 1881 to 1971 now serve as a massive walk-through museum portraying the city's industrial past. Near the park gate, a visitor center features exhibits on the various aspects of combining coal, limestone, and ore at high temperatures to produce iron. In its prime, Sloss turned out 400 tons of finished pig iron a day. Hours are Tuesday through Saturday from 10:00 A.M. to 4:00 P.M. and Sunday from noon to 4:00 P.M. Admission is free.

For some down-home country cooking, head for **The Irondale Cafe** (205–956–5258)—the inspiration for the Whistle Stop Cafe in the movie *Fried Green Tomatoes.* Located at 1906 First Avenue North in the historic area of Irondale, the cafeteria offers a variety of meats and fresh vegetables including that Southern favorite, fried green tomatoes, that actress/writer Fannie Flagg put in the spotlight. Lunch hours run from 10:45 A.M. to 2:30 P.M. Sunday through Friday. Supper hours are 4:30 to 7:30 P.M. Monday through Saturday.

Solving Crimes with the Southern Sisters

Before the late Anne George wrote her critically acclaimed novel, *This One and Magic Life,* she penned award-winning poetry and became a Pulitzer Prize finalist. But her legion of mystery fans most miss the zany antics of Patricia Anne and Mary Alice, an unlikely pair of sleuths who live in Birmingham. As the "Southern Sisters" go about their crime-solving, the reader gets a light-hearted look at the local landscape and a lot of laughs. Buy a book in this series, pour yourself a tall glass of iced tea, and enjoy an easy summer afternoon.

Heading toward the Birmingham International Airport, you'll find the **Southern Museum of Flight** (205–833–8226). Look for the big McDonnell-Douglas F–4N Phantom II on the front lawn of the museum at 4343 Seventy-third Street North, 2 blocks east of the airport. Aviation buffs can spend hours here delving into the mystery and history of flying. This outstanding facility features a reproduction of a 1910 Curtis "Pusher," the second powered plane to follow on the heels of the Wright brothers' success; a 1925 crop duster that launched Delta Airlines; a dozen Cold War aircraft from the F-84 and F-86 through the A-12 Blackbird, including a MiG-15 and MiG-21; and hundreds of models that trace aviation's history. You'll see decades of memorabilia relating to Amelia Earhart, Gen. Claire Chenault's Flying Tigers, and the infamous Red Baron.

"We've doubled our collection during the last four years," said Dr. Don Dodd, the museum's assistant director. Visitors can view short movies, shown continuously, on such subjects as the Tuskegee Airmen and women in aviation as well as humorous newsreels on early attempts to fly. Take time to look through the Alabama Aviation Hall of Fame and the Air Force's Fiftieth Anniversary Collection of Aircraft Art on the second floor. The museum, which also offers an aviation reference library, is open from 9:30 A.M. to 4:30 P.M. Tuesday through Saturday and from 1:00 to 4:30 P.M. on Sunday. Modest admission.

Afterward return downtown to the Birmingham-Jefferson Civic Center for a spectator outing at the **Alabama Sports Hall of Fame** (205–323–6665). Located at 2150 Richard Arrington Jr. Boulevard, this unique two-floor facility focuses on some of the state's greatest sports figures. Walls of bronze plaques pay tribute to athletes from Olympic diving champion Jenni Chandler to Joe Louis, who boxed his way to the World Heavyweight title. You'll also see displays on such sports luminaries as John Hannah, Joe Namath, Bo Jackson, Pat Sullivan, Bart Starr, Ozzie Newsome, Hank Aaron, Willie Mays, Jesse Owens, Hubert Green, Bobby Allison, Pat Dye, and Bear Bryant. Wall cases and displays feature trophies, uniforms, photographs, and other memorabilia from the sports world.

Even though exhibits cover Hall of Fame inductees who made names for themselves in archery, auto and harness racing, golf, baseball, boxing, track, and waterskiing, the name of the game in Alabama is Football (and yes, with a capital F). A black-and-white photo exhibit, depicting unhelmeted players in skimpy uniforms, captures some historic moments during the first Alabama–Auburn clash on February 22, 1893, in Birmingham. Football fever rages in many other parts of the country, but the intensity seems several degrees higher in the South and reaches a boiling point in Alabama during the annual collegiate battle between the Crimson Tide and the War Eagles. You can visit the hall of fame Monday through Saturday from 9:00 A.M. to 5:00 P.M. and Sunday from 1:00 to 5:00 P.M. Check out www.ashof.org for more information. Admission.

Nearby at 2000 Eighth Avenue North stands the ***Birmingham Museum of Art*** (205–254–2565), noted for its excellent Wedgwood collection, the finest outside England. The museum celebrated its fiftieth anniversary in 2001. In 1991 the museum received a $50 million collection of eighteenth-century French decorative art and furniture bequeathed by Birmingham native Eugenia Woodward Hitt, who spent most of her life in Europe and New York. This magnificent assemblage of some 500 items features paintings by Fragonard, perfume fountains, silver, textiles, ceramics, signed furnishings, and porcelain from the years 1720 to 1770. Other museum treasures include the Kress collection of Renaissance paintings and the largest collection of Asian art in the South. Check with the staff regarding current offerings. Don't miss the multilevel Charles W. Ireland Sculpture Garden, which provides a splendid backdrop for outdoor exhibits. Kathy G's Terrace Cafe serves lunch from 11:00 A.M. to 2:00 P.M. Tuesday through Saturday and features a jazz brunch the first Sunday of each month. Stop by the Museum Store for an extensive selection of books, posters, jewelry, crafts, and unique gift items. Except for major holidays, the museum is open from 10:00 A.M. to 5:00 P.M. Tuesday through Saturday and noon to 5:00 P.M. Sunday. Also, on the first Thursday of each month, the museum is open until 9:00 P.M., serves dinner, and shows a film. Check on current exhibits and other happenings at www.artsBMA.org. Free admission.

Continue south on Twenty-first Street to University Boulevard and take a right to reach the ***University of Alabama at Birmingham*** campus. One of the nation's top-ranked medical centers, UAB practices a triple-thrust program of education, research, and service. Tucked in the heart of this much-trodden complex on the third floor of the Lister Hill Library Building, you'll find the ***Alabama Museum of Health Sciences*** and the ***Reynolds Historical Library*** (205–934–4475). (But you probably won't find a nearby parking place, so wear your walking shoes.) With a rare and valuable collection of medical books and manuscripts (some predate the printing press), the library houses one of the country's foremost collections of its type—on par with similar collections at Harvard, Yale, Johns Hopkins, and other prestigious institutions. Incredible as it sounds, you can read actual letters (pertaining to dental matters) handwritten by George and Martha Washington. The library also owns original correspondence of Louis Pasteur, Sir William Osler, Pierre Curie, and Florence Nightingale. These letters, of course, are safely locked up, but you can ask the curator to don white gloves and show them to you.

The library owes its existence to radiologist Lawrence Reynolds, an Alabamian who grew up in a family of physicians and devoted much of his lifetime to acquiring rare medical books and manuscripts (once spending a month's salary of $600 on a single volume). In 1958 Dr. Reynolds donated his

Christmas in Nauvoo

When Gene McDaniel planned a Christmas celebration in Nauvoo, population 249, he expected maybe 250 to 500 people. Between 2,000 to 3,000 people showed up for that first holiday festival in 1989, and that's how it's been ever since. Christmas in Nauvoo takes place the first Saturday in December with an open house at the **Old Harbin Hotel** (205–697–5652), myriad lights, attendant festivities, and parade led by Miss Alabama, who makes the hotel her overnight base.

Other special events in Nauvoo include an Antique Car and Truck Show in June and a chili dinner the last Saturday in October.

Once a booming coal mining town, Nauvoo takes its name from a Hebrew word meaning "pleasant." A railroad worker, who said the place reminded him of his hometown in Illinois, christened it Nauvoo. After two mines and a lumber mill closed in the 1950s, Nauvoo started to shrivel and dry up. The town's largest structure, the two-story brick Old Harbin Hotel, stands on the corner of McDaniel Avenue and Third Street. Built in 1923 at a cost of $24,574, the hotel boasted sixteen furnished rooms and seventy-six electric lights. The structure, which retains its original pine walls, downstairs pressed-tin ceilings, and four center rooms with skylights, was added to the Alabama Landmark Register in 1990.

Owners Gene and Earlene McDaniel, who live on the premises, have collected a variety of furnishings, antiques, and memorabilia to decorate each of the nine guest rooms individually.

"We don't advertise for customers," said Gene, a retired union coal miner and hardware store owner. "Don't expect a person on duty at the desk. Most weekends in summer, we're booked with family reunions because the whole clan can gather here." Gene, who owns several other buildings in Nauvoo, said he's had from 20,000 to 25,000 visitors at the hotel since 1989. Breakfast is included, and rates are standard.

About a mile from the hotel on the Carbon Hill and Nauvoo Road, you'll find some of the best barbecue in these parts at the **Slick Lizard Smokehouse** (205–697–5789). Named for a local mine, the eatery's walls are made of rough lumber edged with bark. Iced tea arrives in quart-size fruit jars with handles, and the decor features light fixtures made of wagon wheels. Farm implements, a wash pot, rub board, Buffalo Rock Cola signs, Alabama football memorabilia, old photos, and newspaper clippings add to the atmosphere.

The menu explains what's behind the name: "You're as slick as a lizard!" one miner said to another as they crawled out of the mine. That's how mining was done—on your belly through slick clay portals that were only about 25 inches high. This mine was located behind the present cafe in the mid-1920s.

"As the story continues, the name 'Slick Lizard' stuck with us. We were a coal-mining town, and we are very proud of our heritage and community. Welcome to Slick Lizard Smokehouse!" Owner Diane McDaniel invites you to "fill your gizzard at the Slick Lizard" on Thursday and Sunday from 10:00 A.M. to 9:00 P.M. and on Friday and Saturday from 11:00 A.M. to 10:00 P.M. Economical prices.

impressive collection of some 5,000 items (now doubled in size) to his alma mater. The library's collection features richly illustrated vellum manuscripts, rare first editions such as Vesalius's 1543 textbook on human anatomy, the earliest known treatise on wine, and a 1517 handbook of surgery (written in German instead of Latin) with extraordinary hand-executed illustrations. Another work, William Harvey's 1628 *De motu cordis,* accurately describes the body's blood circulation for the first time. Also, the library owns a comprehensive collection of primary and secondary resource material relating to Civil War medicine. Other interesting items include antique maps, a sizable collection of Nobel Prize Papers, and a set of four Chinese anatomical charts that date to 1668 and delineate the body's acupuncture points. Don't miss the display of exquisite ivory miniature mannequins (physicians' dolls used for medical instruction) dating from the seventeenth and eighteenth centuries. Another room contains displays of various medical instruments and equipment along with changing exhibits. The library and museum are open from 9:00 A.M. to 5:00 P.M. Monday through Friday, and admission is free. You can find more information at www.uab.edu/historical with links to the Reynolds Historical Library, the Alabama Museum of Health Sciences, and the UAB Archives.

Don't miss the **Birmingham Civil Rights Institute** (205–328–9696), located at 520 Sixteenth Street North. The focal point of the Civil Rights District, which also embraces historic Sixteenth Street Baptist Church and Kelly Ingram Park, the facility features innovative exhibits, which re-create in graphic fashion a sad chronology of segregation's inequities. Visitors start their journey through darkness with a film, followed by a startling entrance to the "Barriers" Gallery, where exhibits trace the struggle that led to the passage of civil rights laws. The new Richard Arrington Jr. Resource Gallery offers an interactive multimedia experience and creates a "living library" honoring persons who participated in the civil rights struggle. Video segments from the institute's Oral History Project interviews are available for learning and research. Admission. Hours are 10:00 A.M. to 5:00 P.M. Tuesday through Saturday and 1:00 to 5:00 P.M. Sunday. Visit www.bcri.org for more information.

Nearby, at 1631 Fourth Avenue North at Seventeenth Street, stands the **Alabama Jazz Hall of Fame** (205–254–2731). Housed in the art deco Carver Theatre, the museum features exhibits ranging from boogie-woogie's beginnings to the current jazz scene. Displays pay tribute to native Erskine Hawkins of "Tuxedo Junction" fame, Nat King Cole, Duke Ellington, Lionel Hampton, and other musicians with Alabama connections. Hours are 10:00 A.M. to 5:00 P.M. Tuesday through Saturday and 1:00 to 5:00 P.M. Sunday. Guided tours cost $1.00 per person, but admission is free.

While exploring the Magic City, take in nearby Homewood, where you'll find a delightful neighborhood market and cafe specializing in Mediterranean fare. **Nabeel's Cafe** (205–879–9292) at 1706 Oxmoor Road offers a menu with a global theme and a market filled with imported herbs, coffees, teas, olive oil, beans, nuts, and more. Vats of olives, bins of spices, and wedges of Greek, Italian, Bulgarian, Russian, and Lebanese cheeses tempt the shopper here.

The Krontiras family, John and Ottavia with their son Anthony, own and operate this establishment, housed in the white-painted brick building with an exterior wall mural and green canopies. The cafe evokes the intimacy of a European dining experience with a leisurely sharing of food and drink. Wine barrels and a wooden rack for wine storage along the dining room wall suggest the old country. Anthony, Nabeel's chef, focuses on family recipes and prepares food with home-cooked flavor. Nabeel's numerous awards include

Moussaka on the Menu?

True, fried chicken and barbecue star on many Alabama menus. Still, you'll find ethnic variety, too. **Nabeel's Cafe** owner John Krontiras provided the following recipe, his family's version of moussaka enhanced by bechamel sauce—a favorite with his patrons.

Moussaka

2 pounds ground beef

3 pounds eggplants, unpeeled and sliced ½ -inch thick

3 eggs

3 cups milk

½ pound kasseri cheese, grated

1 onion, sliced

1 stick cinnamon

½ cup extra virgin olive oil

2 pounds tomatoes, peeled and seeded

½ cup butter

4 tablespoons semolina (pasta flour)

salt and pepper to taste

Fry eggplants lightly and set aside Brown ground beef and set aside. Brown onion in a saucepan with oil, then add tomatoes and cinnamon. Season with salt and pepper. Stir well and turn heat off.

Heat butter in different saucepan, then add semolina and make a roux. Beat eggs with milk and pour in saucepan, stirring constantly. (Do not let boil.) When set, turn heat off and add half of cheese.

Arrange two eggplant layers in oiled 9- by 13-inch baking pan. Sprinkle with cheese and add tomatoes, removing cinnamon stick. Add all ground beef, sprinkle with more cheese, and add remaining eggplant and tomato layers. Pour sauce over mixture. Bake in 350-degree oven for about 45 minutes or until done. Serves 10.

"Birmingham's Favorite Restaurant" in a former readers' poll conducted by *Birmingham Magazine*. "We try to treat customers as if they were guests at our home," said John.

Sip some of the cafe's celebrated and refreshing mint tea and scoop up some taramasalata dip, made of red caviar and salted carp roe, with a pita wedge while you decide what to order. From homemade soups and piquant Greek salads to sandwich specialties like *fior di latte* (made with fresh mozzarella cheese, roasted peppers, and fresh basil), Nabeel's crew prepares everything fresh daily. Favorites include eggplant parmesan and a spinach pie (*spanakopita*). Made of fresh spinach and layered with phyllo, Greek feta cheese, and herbs, *spanakopita* is served with a salad and pita bread. End your meal on a sweet note with baklava, cannoli, butter cookies, or honey crescents. Hours run from 9:30 A.M. to 9:30 P.M. Monday through Saturday.

Before leaving the Birmingham area, stop by **The Bright Star** (205–424–9444) in nearby Bessemer. Housed in a tall brick building at 304 North Nineteenth Street, this restaurant beckons diners with an extensive menu prepared with Greek flair. Brothers Jimmy and Nicky Koikos continue a family culinary tradition that started in 1907.

The attractive interior features roomy brass and glass-topped booths and murals dating from 1915, painted by a European artist traveling through the area. The Bright Star offers daily luncheon specials, such as fresh trout amandine or Greek-style beef tenderloin tips with such side dish choices as fresh fried eggplant, corn on the cob, and candied yams.

For dinner start with a cup of the restaurant's scrumptious gumbo. (All fish dishes here feature fresh seafood straight from the coast.) For the main course, you might choose broiled snapper (Greek style) or the beef tenderloin. Other enticing entrees include lobster and crabmeat au gratin, a broiled seafood platter, and a tasty blackened snapper, prepared New Orleans style, with a creamy wine sauce. Top off your meal with a slice of fresh homemade pineapple-cheese or lemon icebox pie. Economical to moderate prices. Lunch hours start at 10:45 A.M. daily and end at 3:30 P.M., and dinner hours start at 4:30 P.M. and go to 9:00 P.M. except for Friday and Saturday when the closing time changes to 10:00 P.M.

The Capstone

Traveling southwest from Birmingham about 50 miles takes you to **Tuscaloosa.** On your way to "The Capstone," as the University of Alabama is often called, make a stop at the **Mercedes-Benz Visitor Center** (205–507–2266 or 888–2–TOUR–MB) in Vance, about halfway between Birmingham and Tuscaloosa. Traveling on Interstate 59, you'll see the plant on the left. Take exit 89 onto

Mercedes Drive for an up-close look at the M-class all-activity vehicle plus multimedia exhibits that span the past, present, and future of automobile technology. The company's first American manufacturing plant outside its German motherland, the operation opened in 1997. Although you cannot take tours until 2006, you can visit the museum Monday through Friday from 10:00 A.M. to 5:00 P.M. Admission is free.

After dipping into the Daimler-Benz auto history, continue your trek to Tuscaloosa. This college town, rich in tradition, served as Alabama's capital from 1826 to 1846.

Before exploring the area's many attractions, you might like to fortify yourself with a slab of ribs at **Dreamland** (205–758–8135), 2 miles from the intersection of U.S. Highway 82 and I-59, off Jug Factory Road in Jerusalem Heights. Here you don't have to agonize over what to order—the choice is ribs along with slices of white bread to sop up the sauce. You'll also get a bib that says AIN'T NOTHIN' LIKE 'EM—NOWHERE, a stack of napkins, and a wet paper towel to assist you in this gustatory project that must be performed with no inhibitions. If you want more variety in your meal, get a bag of potato chips. Beer or soft drinks, followed by toothpicks, complete the feast.

alabamatrivia

Founded in 1819 near the site of an early Indian village, Tuscaloosa occupies the highest navigable point on the Black Warrior River.

True, Dreamland stays crowded and the noise level runs high, but regulars say these things add to the place's appeal. Dreamland's hours are 10:00 A.M. to 9:00 P.M. Monday through Thursday. On Friday and Saturday the restaurant is open from 10:00 A.M. to 10:00 P.M. and Sunday from 11:00 A.M. to 9:00 P.M. Rates are economical to moderate.

Continue to nearby **Cypress Inn** (205–345–6963) at 501 Rice Mine Road North. Located on the Black Warrior's banks, this restaurant offers fresh seafood, prime steaks, and traditional Southern fare as well as a relaxing river view. House specialties include Hoppin' John (a combination of black-eyed peas, rice, scallions, and bacon), smoked chicken with white barbecue sauce, crispy fried catfish, and fresh broiled red snapper. Also popular are the homemade yeast rolls, fresh raisin-bran muffins, and peanut butter pie. The Cypress Inn serves lunch from 11:00 A.M. to 2:00 P.M. Sunday through Friday; dinner hours run from 5:00 to 9:00 P.M. Sunday through Thursday and 5:00 to 10:00 P.M. Friday and Saturday. Economical to moderate prices.

Art lovers will want to search out a rare museum near NorthRiver Lodge, at 8316 Mountbatten Road. **The Westervelt Warner Museum of American**

Art (205–343–4540) showcases Jack W. Warner's remarkable assemblage result-ing from four decades of collecting. In addition to paintings and sculpture, the collection includes American decorative arts and antiques such as furniture by Duncan Phyfe, silverware by Paul Revere, exquisite porcelain, early American firearms, and more. "Most of the furniture dates to the period between 1820 and 1840," said Warner, "and every piece is museum quality."

Here, you'll view portraits of Washington, Jefferson, and Lafayette all painted from life as you wend your way through galleries and color-coordinated suites in the Blue, Yellow, Green, and Salmon Rooms. Visitors to the Gulf States Paper offices will remember seeing some of the works previously exhibited there. Now, former CEO and chairman Warner has created a single venue as a back-drop for his extensive collection, which has been called an "unparalleled assembly of 18th, 19th and 20th century American art."

Artists represented include Andrew Wyeth, Frederic Remington, George Catlin, Mary Cassatt, and Georgia O'Keeffe. Also, you'll see works by John Singer Sargent, Winslow Homer, Albert Bierstadt, James McNeil Whistler, Childe Hassam, James Peale, Thomas Cole, Asher B. Durand, and many others.

Be sure to visit the ladies' room (if you're the right gender, that is) to see a series of etchings and other works by Mary Cassatt. The men's room decor features photographs depicting Robert E. Lee and his horse, Traveler, as well as Lee's funeral.

"I often like the little studies better than the big finished painting," said Warner, whose world-class collection can be viewed by the public noon to 5:00 P.M. Tuesday through Friday; 10:00 A.M. to 5:00 P.M. Saturday; and 10:00 A.M. to 5:00 P.M. on Sunday. Admission. For more information check out the museum's Web site at www.warnermuseum.org/contact.htm.

Afterward head for the *University of Alabama campus,* the site of a beautiful historic district as well as the home of the Crimson Tide. Since stu-dent William Gray Little organized the college's first football club in 1892, Alabama has celebrated "A Century of Champions." A good place to learn about the school's more than one-hundred-year football history is the *Paul W. Bryant Museum* (205–348–4668). To reach the museum from US 82, take the University Boulevard exit and follow the signs. If you arrive via I–59, exit onto I–359, take the Thirty-fifth Street exit to Tenth Avenue, go north to Bryant Drive, and then turn east. You'll find the museum on campus at 300 Paul W. Bryant Drive next to the Four Points Hotel Tuscaloosa-Capstone by Sheraton.

alabamatrivia

Educator Julia Tutwiler, born in 1841 in Tuscaloosa, worked to secure the admission of women to the University of Alabama.

For some background on the legendary figure called "The Bear," the man who became college football's most acclaimed coach, start your museum visit by viewing *The Bryant Legacy,* a film narrated by sports commentator Keith Jackson. While browsing among the displays, you'll see a replicated setting of Bear Bryant's office and a dazzling version of his famous hat. Sculptor Miraslav Havel translated the familiar crimson-and-white houndstooth pattern into a multifaceted Waterford crystal showpiece. A courier transported the real hat from Tuscaloosa to Ireland for its magic rendering—and back again.

Although dedicated to the memory of Bryant, who headed Alabama's football teams from 1958 to 1982, the museum also pays tribute to other coaches and players prominent in the school's history. You'll see photos, memorabilia, and audiovisual displays pertaining to such superstars as Joe Namath, Kenny Stabler, Cornelius Bennett, and Bart Starr. To supplement vintage film clips, montages, and recordings, the museum offers taped highlights of recent games.

In addition to the large exhibit hall, the museum houses a comprehensive library of media guides, game programs, photographs, books, films, scrapbooks, and other materials covering Southeastern Conference and college sports. Modest admission. Except for major holidays, hours run from 9:00 A.M. to 4:00 P.M. daily.

While exploring the campus, stop by the ***Gorgas House*** (205–348–5906) on Capstone Drive. One of four university buildings to survive the Civil War, this 1829 two-story brick Federal-style cottage with a curving cast-iron staircase originally served as a college dining hall. Inside you'll see period furnishings, an outstanding collection of Spanish Colonial silver, and memorabilia of William Crawford Gorgas, who was noted for his work in the prevention and cure of yellow fever. Modest admission. The Gorgas House is open Tuesday through Saturday from 10:00 A.M. to 4:00 P.M. Tap into gorgashouse.ua.edu for more details.

Housed at nearby Smith Hall, the ***Alabama Museum of Natural History*** (205–348–7550) features extensive fossil and mineral collections. Entering this 1909 Classical Revival building, you'll see a spacious hall and a sweeping marble staircase with iron railings. Exhibits include pottery, tools, weapons, and various artifacts from South Pacific and Central and South American cultures.

On display in the gallery upstairs, you'll find the Hodges meteorite—an outer-space missile weighing eight-and-a-half pounds that struck a Sylacauga woman in 1954. Featured fossils include mammoth, mastodon, mosasaur, and marine turtle, to name a few. You'll also see a Studebaker buggy from the 1880s and a free-standing exhibit illustrating the research methods used by Professor Eugene Allen Smith, for whom the building is named, in gathering his geological and biological collections. Except for major holidays, you can visit the museum Tuesday through Saturday from 10:00 A.M. to 4:30 P.M. Sunday hours run from 1:00 to 4:30 P.M. Modest admission. Check amnh.ua.edu for more background.

Conveniently located near the campus at 1509 University Boulevard, the **Crimson Inn** (205–758–3483 or 877–424–6622) makes a handy base for travelers. Innkeeper owners Pat and Rodney LaGrone offer Southern hospitality with a crimson glow at their Dutch Colonial home, built in 1924 by Dr. Alston Maxwell, a former physician for the college football team. In fact, you can see Bryant-Denny Stadium from the window of an upstairs guest room, named for Pat's mentor and former employer, Dr. Jewitt. A floor-to-ceiling mural in the guest parlor features the University of Alabama President's Mansion, painted by local artist Lisa Godwin.

Here, all breakfasts start with dessert—Crimson soup, made with chilled strawberries. Stuffed French toast with hot orange sauce or a hearty casserole of ham, eggs, and cheese might follow. Dessert is served each evening and might be homemade cheesecake, apple dumplings, or freshly baked cookies. Ask about Pat's mystery weekend package. Moderate rates. E-mail the bed-and-breakfast at CrimsonInnBB@comcast.net. To preview the property, log onto www.bbonline.com/al/crimsoninn/.

Downtown at 2300 University Boulevard in a building that dates to the 1890s, you'll find **DePalma's** (205–759–1879). This Italian cafe is noted for its pizzas, calzones, and dishes such as pine nut–crusted salmon, veal Marsala, or pasta DePalma—angel-hair pasta baked in a cream sauce with garlic, cheeses, and Italian herbs and topped with mushrooms, mozzarella, and a choice of ham, Italian sausage, artichokes, and more. Tiramisu ranks at the top of the dessert list, and the crew offers a great wine selection, too. In fact, the owners make regular scouting trips to Italy for their selections. Here, messages don't come *in* a bottle—but *on* a bottle—because the staff invites you to sign and date your wine label and pen an appropriate message. Then your special bottle joins a long line of others on the booth-level shelf. DePalma's is open from 11:00 A.M. to 10:00 P.M. daily. Prices are economical to moderate.

After your campus tour take time to explore Tuscaloosa (a Choctaw name that means "black warrior"). While downtown, stop by the **Battle-Friedman House** (205–758–6138), a handsome Greek Revival mansion located at 1010 Greensboro Avenue. Built in 1835, this structure now serves as a house museum and city cultural center. The home may be visited Tuesday through Saturday between 10:00 A.M. and noon and 1:00 to 4:00 P.M. and Sunday from 1:00 to 4:00 P.M. Modest admission.

Continue to 1512 Greensboro Avenue, where you'll find **The Waysider Restaurant** (205–345–8239) in a small early-twentieth-century house. Because this is *the* place for breakfast in Tuscaloosa, you may have to stand in line, so bring along a newspaper to read while you wait for a table. No wimpy affair, breakfast at The Waysider means homemade biscuits (with a deserved reputation), eggs, grits (get the cheese version), and a meat of your choice: from sugar-cured ham to grilled pork chops or steak. An order of real country-cured ham with two eggs and red-eye gravy runs in the economical range. You can also opt for pancakes.

The Waysider opens at 5:30 A.M. Tuesday through Saturday. Sunday breakfast hours run from 6:30 A.M. to 1:00 P.M. Lunch hours are 11:00 A.M. to 1:30 P.M. Tuesday through Friday.

Consider cruising the Black Warrior River aboard the **Bama Belle** (205–339–1108), a paddlewheel riverboat replica. Owners Mike and Nikki Medeiros offer scenic, dinner, and holiday cruises plus private party charters. For information on rates and the current cruise schedule, call or click on www.bama belle.com. "We're docked at #1 Greensboro Avenue in Tuscaloosa's new Riverwalk Park," said Nikki, "and the park is a great place for biking, jogging, and roller blading."

Next, head to nearby **Northport,** just a short drive across the Black Warrior River. Once called Kentuck, Northport has developed into an important craft center with a complex of studios and galleries. Each fall the **Kentuck Festival of the Arts** features more than 300 selected artists and craftspeople from all over the country. Celia O'Kelley, Steve Davis, Anden Houben, and a number of other artists maintain individual studios at **Kentuck Art Center** (205–758–1257), located at 503 Main Avenue. The gift shop, which offers photography, pottery, glass, jewelry, musical instruments, textiles, baskets, and other items, is open Monday through Friday from 9:00 A.M. to 5:00 P.M. and Saturday from 10:00 A.M. to 4:30 P.M. Call for information on the center's artists, exhibits, or Kentuck Museum's gallery.

While exploring Northport, stop by **The Globe** (205–391–0949) at 430 Main Avenue, where you'll find a menu with an international focus. As for the restaurant's name, founding partners Jeff Wilson and Gary Wise, who met during a university production of *Richard II,* chose The Globe in reference to Shakespeare's famous London theater; moreover, back in the 1820s and '30s, Northport was home to a hotel called The Globe, located nearby. Spotlighting the Bard, the decor features framed page reproductions of woodcuts from the *First Folio.* Drawings of Shakespearean characters share billing with photos of downtown Northport in earlier years.

A brisk business made it necessary to enlarge the restaurant, accomplished by knocking a hole through the wall to the adjoining structure, a former dry-goods store. Both buildings date to 1909, and an archway permits easy access between them. (Some people claim a ghost roams The Globe's premises during the wee hours.)

Jeff and his wife, Kathy, later bought Gary's interest in the business, and describe the cuisine as ranging from "traditional French to fusion." The ever-popular Athenian pasta salad consists of orzo and vegetables in a balsamic vinaigrette, topped with feta cheese, Kalamata olives, and grilled shrimp. Another favorite lunch item, The Globe's special quesadillas come in a vegetarian version or with grilled chicken, shrimp, Creole crawfish, or jumbo lump crabmeat. The menu's global influence manifests itself in such items as scallops Madrid and Jamaican jerk chicken served over a mango rum compote and topped with red onions and fresh basil mustard. Lunch hours run from 11:00 A.M. to 3:00 P.M. Tuesday through Saturday, and dinner is served from 5:00 to 10:00 P.M. Tuesday through Thursday and to 11:00 P.M. Friday and Saturday. Rates are economical to moderate.

If you have a green thumb, be sure to stop by the Potager (205–752–4761), next door at 428 Main Avenue. The shop offers everything from books and tools to gardening accessories. Zebra finches provide the chirping background music. Afterward step through the connecting door to Adams' Antiques for more browsing.

After your Northport excursion, head for Moundville, called by *National Geographic* "the Big Apple of the 14th century." To reach **Moundville Archaeological Park** (205–371–2572 or 205–371–2234), located about 15 miles south of Tuscaloosa, take State Route 69 South. Said by archaeologists to be the best-preserved prehistoric settlement east of the pueblos, Moundville is an internationally known archaeological site with more than twenty flat-topped earthen mounds, plus other less prominent ones, spread over a 317-acre setting on the Black Warrior River. For a sweeping overview of the grounds as well as a look at a re-created temple (peopled with life-size figures performing religious rites), you can climb to the top of a 60-foot ceremonial mound. At the **Jones Archaeological Museum** you'll see hundreds of Mississippian artifacts, ceremonial vessels, and tools made by the advanced group of prehistoric people who occupied this area between A.D. 1000 and 1450. One wing contains a prehistoric canoe exhibit. Don't miss the Rattlesnake disc, the most famous artifact ever found at Moundville. Although scholars disagree on the meaning of the entwined rattlesnakes on the disc, the hand with the eyelike motif in the palm is common in Mississippian art.

The park, open daily, may be visited from 8:00 A.M. to 8:00 P.M. Except for major holidays, the museum is open 9:00 A.M. to 5:00 P.M. Camping, hiking, and picnicking facilities are available. Modest admission. The annual six-day

Moundville Native American Festival, featuring southeastern Native American crafts and cultural activities, takes place during the first week in October. For more information, click on moundville.ua.edu.

Afterward return north to US 82, and travel west toward Pickensville and the Tennessee-Tombigbee (Tenn-Tom) Waterway, which offers exceptional fishing, hunting, and recreational facilities.

Tenn-Tom Terrain

Don't miss the *Tom Bevill Visitor Center* (205–373–8705) at Pickensville, ½ mile south of the junctions of State Routes 14 and 86. The white-columned Greek Revival–style mansion you see here looks as if it dates from the mid-1800s but actually was completed in 1986. Definitely not your average rest stop, this facility primarily represents a composite of three historical homes in the vicinity, and you'll see portraits of these grand mansions in the central hall. Ascend the sweeping stairway to the second floor, where various exhibits interpret the Tennessee-Tombigbee Waterway's history. A 22-foot relief map illustrates the waterway's course through several locks and dams, and a model display demonstrates the lockage process. Even better, you can climb to the roof level and perhaps watch a vessel pass through the Tom Bevill Lock and Dam. Whether or not said event happens during your visit, the splendid view from the cupola justifies the climb.

After your house tour, stop by the U.S. Snagboat *Montgomery* near the visitor center. Recently declared a National Historic Landmark, this steam-powered sternwheeler once kept Southern rivers navigable by removing tons of debris, such as fallen trees and sunken logs, that impeded river traffic. Except for some federal holidays, the center is open daily year-round.

Next, head south to *Aliceville,* home of a unique museum, a lovely bed-and-breakfast, and fine Southern fare at *Plantation House Restaurant*

Strange As It Sounds

Carrollton offers a unique site—a face imprinted on a windowpane at the *Pickens County Courthouse.* To learn the strange story behind the image of a prisoner's face preserved here since 1878 (the visage remains despite repeated scrubbings and harsher attempts at removal), step inside the courthouse and pick up a leaflet that provides some background information. You can also read an intriguing account of the mysterious face in Kathryn Tucker Windham's book *13 Alabama Ghosts and Jeffrey* (published by the University of Alabama Press in Tuscaloosa).

(205–373–8121). The eatery, located at 102 Memorial Parkway on the State Route 17 bypass across from the Piggly Wiggly supermarket, features chicken or tuna salad, vegetables, catfish, country ham, steak, and more. You'll enjoy a variety of homemade desserts at this restaurant, which dates to 1905 and is listed on the Alabama Register of Historic Landmarks and Heritage. The restaurant is closed on Monday. Lunch is served from 11:00 A.M. to 1:30 P.M. Tuesday through Saturday. Dinner hours are Thursday through Saturday from 5:00 to 9:00 P.M. Prices are moderate.

Don't miss the *Aliceville Museum* (205–373–2363), downtown at 104 Broad Street. During World War II some 6,000 German prisoners—most from Field Marshall Erwin Rommel's Afrika Korps—were interned at Camp Aliceville, site of the present-day *Sue Stabler Park* about 2 miles due west of town on State Route 17. In 1993 the city hosted its fifty-year Prisoner of War Reunion. During this three-day event, officials, residents, and visitors—including fifteen German ex-POWs and their families—gathered to dedicate the only World War II German POW museum in the United States. A fifteen-minute video, featuring first-person interviews with the camp guards and prisoners, provides background on the museum's focus. Historians will want to view a forty-five-minute video produced by the History Channel. Exhibits include drawings, paintings, sculpture, musical instruments, furniture, newspapers, photos, and other artifacts from Camp Aliceville. Museum hours are 10:00 A.M. to 4:00 P.M. Monday through Friday and 10:00 A.M. to 2:00 P.M. Saturday. Modest admission. For more information check out the museum's Web site at www.pickens.net/~museum; the e-mail address is museum@pickens.net.

You can enjoy some warm hospitality at *Myrtlewood* (205–373–2623 or 866–409–7523), a bed-and-breakfast at 602 Broad Street. Owned by Jeanne and Jerry Cockrell, this 1909 home features sun porches, stained glass, and Victorian furnishings. Be sure to notice the coffee table's display of memorabilia in a front parlor. Guests can opt for an early Continental breakfast or a full plantation breakfast in the dining room. Standard rates.

From Aliceville you can either dip southeast via State Route 14 to Eutaw (a charming town covered in the Southwest section of this book) or return east to tour Tannehill, about midway between Birmingham and Tuscaloosa.

Peach Country

To reach *Tannehill Historical State Park* (205–477–5711) near McCalla, take exit 100 off I–59 and follow the signs. This 1,500-acre wooded park spills into Tuscaloosa, Jefferson, and Bibb Counties. On the grounds you'll see the remains of the Tannehill Iron Furnaces and more than forty pioneer homes and farm outbuildings. A cotton gin, blacksmith shop, and gristmill (that grinds cornmeal one weekend a month from March to November) add to the authenticity of this mid-1800s re-creation. Exhibits at the Iron and Steel Museum of Alabama spotlight the history of technology prior to 1850. The facility offers hiking trails and camping. The park is open from 7:00 A.M. to dark year-round. Museum hours run from 8:30 A.M. to 4:30 P.M. except during daylight savings time, when they change to 9:00 A.M. to 5:00 P.M.

Afterward you might like to shift south to **Montevallo**, located in the middle of Alabama. Here the **University of Montevallo**, situated on a beautiful campus complete with brick streets, tree-lined drives, and historical buildings such as the 1823 King House and Reynolds Hall, makes a pleasant stopover. An arbor walk features thirty trees labeled by their common and scientific names. Pick up a booklet called *Guide to Campus Trees*, available on campus and at the local chamber of commerce office. The public can also attend campus concerts, plays, films, lectures, art exhibits, and sporting events; most activities are free. Call the university's information office at (205) 665–6230 to check on current happenings during the time of your visit, or stop by the Will Lyman Welcome Center (205–665–1519), located in a lovely Victorian house at 720 Oak Street.

For overnighters, the on-campus **Ramsay Conference Center** (205–665–6280) offers single rooms (without TV or phones) on a space-available basis, seven days a week during the school term, at bargain rates. A short stroll away you'll find the college dining hall with cafeteria-style meals. Pay-at-the-door prices for breakfast, lunch, and dinner are economical.

Reynolds Hall at the University of Montevallo

A Revolutionary Experience

Prepare yourself for a revolutionary experience and step into the action at *The American Village* (877–811–1776), located 4 miles off I–65 at exit 234 near Montevallo. Actually, you don't have to do much preparation if your visit coincides with that of school groups because their teachers have already primed them to participate and appreciate the exciting turn of events that brought about a struggling young nation's independence.

Authentically costumed interpreters bring to life the fervor of that time when our forebears made choices that formed the fabric of our lives today. You'll get caught up in such events as the Stamp Act Rally and interact with colonial residents expressing their growing resentment against the mother country. You'll hear Patrick Henry's fiery oratory and attend the 1787 Philadelphia Convention to form a new national government. You'll voice your opinions, vote, and maybe even sit behind the desk in the Oval Office.

The backdrop for this revolutionary experiment is a complex of various colonial buildings including the centerpiece Washington Hall, inspired by Mount Vernon, and a Williamsburg-style courthouse. But this 113-acre development is not about buildings—handsome though they are—it's about ideas. And the dreamer who envisioned this place, Tom Walker, who serves as executive director, wants citizens of today and tomorrow to realize they also have choices—just as our early leaders did. The village's mission of strengthening and renewing the foundations of American citizenship can be witnessed in action weekdays from 10:00 A.M. to 4:00 P.M. In June, the schedule changes to Tuesday through Saturday for summer. Tours start on the hour, and the day's final tour begins at 3:00 P.M. You can pay a virtual visit via www.americanvillage.com. Admission.

While in Montevallo spend some time browsing among the treasures at *The House of Serendipity.* Housed in a downtown vintage building with a pressed-tin ceiling and wraparound balcony, this unique establishment is located at 645 Main Street. Owned by Jane and Bruce McClanahan, this shop, where "the unexpected is found," features everything from antiques, greeting cards, and art supplies to Basket Case creations by basketry instructors Faye Roberts and Mimi Lawley. Jane also offers a matching service for discontinued patterns in American crystal and dinnerware. Store hours are 9:00 A.M. to 5:00 P.M. Monday through Saturday.

The *McKibbon House Bed and Breakfast Inn* (205–665–1275) at 611 East Boundary Street offers bed-and-breakfast accommodations and a beckoning front porch with comfortable swing and wicker seating. This Queen Anne Victorian, which dates to 1900, makes a lovely base while you visit local attractions in the Montevallo area. After a day of sightseeing, you can look forward to an evening treat, often the house specialty—chocolate éclairs. And of course, next morning in the dining room, a full Southern breakfast awaits. This is the kind of house with one of those inviting kitchens that seems to draw people like a magnet. Ask owners Peggy and Fred Dew and daughter Tina about their interesting experiences in this historic home, where certain lights refuse to stay turned off, a toilet flushes by magic (just like those in the airport), and you sometimes smell the aroma of coffee brewing (when none is). You can also pay a visit at www.mckibbonhouse.com, but you won't get the chocolate éclairs. Moderate rates.

Before leaving town, visit Orr Park, where you can stroll along Shoal Creek, a natural habitat for Tim Tingle's life-size wood carvings of birds, animals, and wizard faces.

Continuing south to Clanton in the heart of peach country, you'll find several places to purchase this locally grown fruit. Peach Park, for instance, features fresh peaches (in season) along with homemade peach ice cream, milk shakes, yogurt, and other delicious desserts as well as pecans and boiled peanuts.

While in the area, plan a visit to **Confederate Memorial Park** (205–755–1990), just off U.S. Highway 31 near I–65. The site of a former home for Confederate veterans and their widows, the park features a museum with historical displays, Civil War relics, flags, Confederate uniforms, and weaponry. On the grounds you'll also find two cemeteries, a chapel, the old Mountain Creek Post Office, picnic pavilions, and hiking trails. Except for Thanksgiving, Christmas, and New Year's Day, the museum is open from 9:00 A.M. to 5:00 P.M. daily with the exception of a lunch hour. The park may be visited year-round from 6:00 A.M. to dusk.

Head back north to **Calera** to see several antiques shops and the **Heart of Dixie Railroad Museum** (205–668–3435). From I–65 take exit 228 and travel 1 mile west on State Route 25, following signs to the museum. Exhibits include World War II photos, framed timetables, waiting room benches, old railroad lanterns, signal equipment, special tools used to repair steam locomotives, a caboose stove, and an arrival/departure board from the demolished Birmingham Terminal. A glass case contains dishes made by Marshall Field and Company in 1925 for the Rock Island Lines. You'll see a centralized train control board (CTC) with which one person, a railroad counterpart of the airline's air traffic controller, managed a large section of tracks and the trains that traveled it. Locomotives, guard cars (the museum owns four of only six in existence), passenger and freight cars, and the state's largest railroad crane stand outside the green depot museum. Hours are 9:00 A.M. to 4:00 P.M. Monday through Saturday. The museum sponsors train rides and special events. Call for more information on the museum and train ride schedule with excursion rates. Museum admission is free, but donations are accepted. Click on www.heartofdixie rrmuseum.org for more information.

Continue a few miles northeast via State Route 25 to **Columbiana,** where you'll discover hundreds of prized possessions from the country's *first* First Family. "People can't believe we have all these things that belonged to George Washington, and they are amazed to find such a collection here in central Alabama instead of Virginia," says Nancy Harrison, director of the **Karl C. Harrison Museum of George Washington** (205–669–8767). Housed in a newly constructed building that adjoins the Mildred B. Harrison Library's right side, the facility provides spacious quarters for the extensive collection and permits previously stored pieces to be exhibited. Located at 50 Lester Street, the museum stands behind the handsome Shelby County Courthouse.

The foyer's focal point, a commanding bust of George Washington, was created by French sculptor Jean Antoine Houdan from a life mask. Nearby, a glass case topped by a handsome pair of pink Sevres vases contains family correspondence, documents, jewelry, and a writing instrument from Washington's survey case. "One of our finest possessions is Martha's prayer book. We also have an original letter, written about a year before her death," says Harrison, whose father established the museum in 1982.

Two dining room tables feature beautiful settings with exquisite porcelain pieces and coin-silver utensils used at Mount Vernon. A prized 207-piece set of Minton porcelain is displayed on a table and buffet and also fills the shelves of a walnut cabinet signed by William Elfie.

Other treasures include family portraits, various personal items, an original 1787 Samuel Vaughn sketch of Mount Vernon's grounds, and some seventy letters and documents dating to the Revolutionary War period. You can read correspondence from James Madison, Lord Cornwallis, John Adams, Aaron Burr, and other historic figures. The collection's oldest item is the 1710 handwritten will of Col. Daniel Parke, the grandfather of Martha Washington's first husband. You'll also see an original tintype made by Civil War photographer Mathew B. Brady that depicts Robert E. Lee in uniform for the last time.

Amassed by Eliza Parke Custis Law, Martha Washington's granddaughter, the collection passed through six generations of Washington heirs down to Shelby County's Charlotte Smith Weaver. After giving her grandchildren selected items, Mrs. Weaver offered the remainder of the family collection for public preservation. Columbiana banker Karl Harrison acquired two-thirds of it for this museum, and the rest went to Mount Vernon. The Columbiana museum procured additional family pieces from the estate of George Washington's half brother, Augustin, in 1989. Except for major holidays, the museum is open 10:00 A.M. to 3:00 P.M. Monday through Friday. Admission is free.

Woodland and Water

Continue east to **Sylacauga,** sometimes called Marble City. While many cities contain marble monuments and buildings, here the entire town rests on a marble bed about 32 miles long and more than a mile wide. Sylacauga marble was used in the U.S. Supreme Court Building in Washington, D.C., Detroit's General Motors Building, and in many other distinctive edifices. "The Sylacauga area has some of the whitest marble in the world," says a local quarrying company official.

Stop by the **Isabel Anderson Comer Museum and Arts Center** (256–245–4016) at 711 Broadway Avenue North. At the museum, housed in a former library building dating from the 1930s, you'll see a big chunk of calcite quartz, unusual because it came from the middle of a local marble quarry. The museum owns several pieces by Giuseppe Moretti, the Italian sculptor who designed Birmingham's statue of *Vulcan.* Moretti came to Sylacauga in the early 1900s to open a marble quarry.

The museum's displays cover everything from beaded evening bags and Victorian hat pins to a reproduction of the Hodges meteorite that hurtled down on Sylacauga from outer space and struck a local woman in 1954. Here, you'll find a gallery of Native American artifacts, antique toys, handmade fabrics from the 1830s, and an extensive collection of photos and scrapbooks on local history. Pioneer exhibits are housed in the base-

alabamatrivia

More than two dozen albums showcase the singing talent of Sylacauga native Jim Nabors of *The Andy Griffith Show* and *Gomer Pyle, USMC* fame.

ment. One section features albums, awards, photos, costumes, and other memorabilia of native son Jim Nabors, who starred as TV's Gomer Pyle on *The Andy Griffith Show.*

The museum is open 10:00 A.M. to 5:00 P.M. Tuesday through Friday or by appointment. Although there's no admission charge, donations are accepted.

Don't leave town without treating yourself to some ice cream at **Blue Bell Creameries** (256–249–6100 or 888–573–5286) at 423 North Norton Avenue. What's your pleasure? Choices range from lemon, triple chocolate, chocolate chip, white chocolate almond, caramel pecan fudge, and banana split to pistachio almond, pecan praline and cream, cherry vanilla, and black walnut—and the list goes on. In addition to watching ice cream being made, you can relax (after you finish agonizing over which flavor to order) in the old-fashioned ice-cream parlor or browse in the Country Store. Tours, which last about forty-five minutes, take place Monday through Friday. Call ahead for information on how to schedule or join a tour. The Country Store is open from 9:00 A.M. to 5:00 P.M. Monday through Friday.

After leaving Sylacauga, follow U.S. Highway 280 southeast to ***Alexander City,*** home of the Russell Corporation. Employing about four-fifths of the local workforce, Russell outfits the sports world all the way from Little League through hundreds of college teams to most of the National Football League. This company handles every step of the process from cotton production to finished product. The sweat suit you don for your jog around the block may well have come from Alex City, as the locals call it.

The ***Russell Retail Store*** (256–500–4464), a big cheese-wedge of a building at 3562 US 280, sells sweatpants and tops, T-shirts, cardigans, and other leisure wear—maybe even your favorite team's togs. In addition to a university section (that carries mostly Atlantic Coast Conference and Southeastern Conference athletic apparel), the outlet offers casual clothing for ladies and children. Cross-Creek and HIGH Cotton lines feature an array of items in both heavyweight and lightweight knits. You may want to personalize your purchases with selected transfers—from SAVE THE EARTH to holiday and hunting themes—that can be applied by heat press in fifteen seconds.

Clothing sells here for one-third off the retail value. Also, a back room contains imperfect or discontinued items marked from one-half to two-thirds off the "designed to sell for" price. The store's hours are 9:00 A.M. to 5:30 P.M. Monday through Saturday and 1:00 to 5:00 P.M. Sunday.

While in the Alex City area, you might like to explore nearby ***Horseshoe Bend National Military Park,*** the site of the final battle of the Creek War. Located about 12 miles north of Dadeville on State Route 49, the 2,040-acre park features a visitor center with exhibits on the battle, Creek Indian culture, and frontier life.

Other local options include boating, swimming, and fishing at ***Lake Martin,*** which offers a 750-mile shoreline against a backdrop of wooded hills. This body of water spills over the southern half of Tallapoosa County and even splashes into neighboring Elmore and Coosa Counties. Depending on the season and local weather conditions, anglers haul in largemouth and striped bass, bream, bluegill, crappie, and catfish from this lake. For more outdoor recreation continue south to Elmore County.

Places to Stay in Central Alabama

ALEXANDER CITY

Holiday Inn Express
2945 U.S. Highway 280
(256) 234–5900 or
(800) HOLIDAY

Horseshoe Inn
3146 U.S. Highway 280
(256) 234–6311

Jameson Inn
4335 U.S. Highway 280
(256) 234–7099 or
(800) 526–3766

ALICEVILLE

Myrtlewood
602 Broad Street Northeast
(205) 373–2623 or
(866) 409–7523

ANNISTON

The Victoria
1600 Quintard Avenue
(256) 236–0503 or
(800) 260–8781

ASHVILLE

Roses and Lace Country Inn
20 Rose Lane
(205) 594–4366

BIRMINGHAM

Birmingham Marriott
3590 Grandview Parkway
(205) 968–3775 or
(800) 627–7468

Holiday Inn Crowne Plaza
2101 Fifth Avenue North
(205) 324–2101 or
(800) 2–CROWNE

Pickwick Hotel
1023 Twentieth
Street South
(205) 933–9555 or
(800) 255–7304

Sheraton Birmingham Hotel
2101 Richard Arrington Jr.
Boulevard North
(205) 324–5000 or
(888) 627–7095

The Tutwiler
2021 Park Place North
(205) 322–2100 or
(866) 850–3053

The Wynfrey Hotel
1000 Riverchase Galleria
(205) 987–1600 or
(800) WYNFREY

DELTA

Cheaha State Park
2141 Bunker Loop
(256) 488–5115 or
(800) 846–2654

MONTEVALLO

McKibbon House Bed & Breakfast Inn
611 East Boundary Street
(205) 665–1275

Ramsay Conference Center
University of Montevallo
(205) 665–6280

MUNFORD

The Cedars Plantation
590 Cheaha Road
(256) 761–9090

NAUVOO

Old Harbin Hotel
131 Third Street
(205) 697–5652

OXFORD

Holiday Inn Express Hotel & Suites
160 Colonial Drive
(256) 835–8768

PELHAM

Oak Mountain State Park
200 Terrace Drive
(205) 620–2524 or
(800) ALA–PARK

STERRETT

Twin Pines Resort
1200 Twin Pines Road
(205) 672–7575

SYLACAUGA

Jameson Inn
89 Gene Stewart Boulevard
(256) 245–4141 or
(800) 526–3766

TUSCALOOSA

Comfort Inn
4700 Doris Pate Drive
(205) 556–3232 or
(800) 311–3811

Courtyard by Marriott
4115 Courtney Drive
(205) 750–8384 or
(800) 321–2211

Crimson Inn
1509 University Boulevard
(205) 758–3483 or
(877) 424–6622

Four Points Hotel Tuscaloosa–Capstone by Sheraton
320 Paul Bryant Drive
(205) 752–3200 or
(800) 477–2262

VINCENT

Blue Spring Manor
2870 Shelby County Road 83
(205) 672–9955

Places to Eat in Central Alabama

ALEXANDER CITY

Cecil's Public House
243 Green Street
(256) 329–0732

Sinclair's Kowaliga
295 Kowaliga Marina Road
(334) 857–2889

ALICEVILLE

Plantation House Restaurant
102 Memorial Parkway
(205) 373–8121

ANNISTON

Betty's Bar-B-Q, Inc.
401 South Quintard Avenue
(256) 237–1411

Classic on Noble
1024 Noble Street
(256) 237–5388

Top O' the River
3330 McClellan Boulevard
(256) 238–0097

The Victoria
1600 Quintard Avenue
(256) 236–0503

ASHVILLE

Ashville House
35 Third Street
(205) 594–7046

BESSEMER

The Bright Star
304 North Nineteenth Street
(205) 424–9444

BIRMINGHAM

Bombay Cafe
2839 Seventh Avenue South
(205) 322–1930

Grammas'
2030 Little Valley Road
(205) 823–5825

Highlands Bar & Grill
2011 Eleventh Avenue South
(205) 939–1400

Hot and Hot Fish Club
2180 Eleventh Court South
(205) 933–5474

Restaurant G
Fourth Avenue North and
Nineteenth Street
(205) 323–1820

The Silvertron Cafe
3813 Clairmont Avenue
(205) 591–3707

CALERA

Zapopan Restaurant
4570 U.S. Highway 31
(205) 668–4008

HOMEWOOD

Nabeel's Cafe
1706 Oxmoor Road
(205) 879–9292

IRONDALE

The Irondale Cafe
1906 First Avenue North
(205) 956–5258

JACKSONVILLE

Old Henry Farm Restaurants (a.k.a. The Barn)
301 Henry Road Southwest
(256) 435–0673

MAYLENE

Fox Valley Restaurant
County Road 17
(205) 664–8341

MONTEVALLO

Zapopan Restaurant
4554 State Route 25
(205) 665–7404

MOUNTAIN BROOK

Chez Lulu
1909 Cahaba Road
(205) 870–7011

NAUVOO

Slick Lizard Smokehouse
Carbon Hill and
Nauvoo Road
(205) 697–5789

NORTHPORT

The Globe
430 Main Avenue
(205) 391–0949

OXFORD

China Luck
503 Quintard Drive
(256) 831–5221

SPRINGVILLE

Gulf Seafood
140 Laster Drive
(205) 467–9348

SYLACAUGA

LaCosta Mexican Restaurant
215 North Broadway Avenue
(256) 249–3360

The White Villa
300 East Third Street
(256) 249–9020

TRUSSVILLE

Chocolate Biscuit Tearoom
335 Main Street
(205) 655–0119

TUSCALOOSA

Arman's
519 Greensboro Avenue
(205) 344–5583

Cafe Venice
2321 University Boulevard
(205) 366–1209

Cypress Inn
501 Rice Mine Road North
(205) 345–6963

DePalma's
2300 University Boulevard
(205) 759–1879

Dreamland
off Jug Factory Road in
Jerusalem Heights
(205) 758–8135

Evangeline's
Galleria of Tuscaloosa
1653 McFarland
Boulevard North
(205) 752–0830

Kozy's
3510 Loop Road
(205) 556–0665

The Waysider Restaurant
1512 Greensboro Avenue
(205) 345–8239

Wings Sports Grille
500 Harper Lee Drive
(205) 556–5658

FOR MORE INFORMATION ABOUT CENTRAL ALABAMA

Alexander City Area Chamber of Commerce
120 Tallapoosa Street,
P.O. Box 926
Alexander City 35011-0926
(256) 234–3461
Web site: www.alexandercity.org
e-mail: coc@webshoppe.net

Anniston/Calhoun County Chamber of Commerce
1330 Quintard Avenue ,
P.O. Box 1087
Anniston 36202
(256) 237–3536 or (800) 489–1087
Web site: www.calhounchamber.com
e-mail: david@calhounchamber.com

Greater Birmingham Convention and Visitors Bureau
2200 Ninth Avenue North
Birmingham 35203-1100
(205) 458–8000 or (800) 458–8085
Web site: www.birminghamal.org
e-mail: info@birmingham.org

Montevallo Chamber of Commerce
720 Oak Street
Montevallo 35115
(205) 665–1519

Tuscaloosa Convention and Visitors Bureau
1305 Greensboro Avenue,
P.O. Box 3167
Tuscaloosa 35403
(205) 391–9200 or (800) 538–8696
Web site: www.tcvb.org
e-mail: tuscacvb@dbtech.net

Arlington Antebellum Home and Gardens,

331 Cotton Avenue Southwest, Birmingham;
(205) 780–5656.
This circa 1850 Greek Revival mansion contains a fine collection of period antiques.

Birmingham Zoo,

2630 Cahaba Road;
(205) 879–0408 or (205) 879–0458.
Both big and little kids enjoy outings to this facility, the home of some 900 animals from all over the globe.

International Motorsports Hall of Fame and Talladega Superspeedway,

Off Interstate 20, Talladega;
(256) 362–5002.
This unique facility, which occupies a complex of circular-shaped buildings, captures the speed of movement and thrill of competitive racing. You'll see the Budweiser Rocket Car, a missile on wheels that broke the sound barrier, and record-breaking vehicles once guided by Richard Petty, Bill Elliott, Bobby Allison, and other racing greats. Additional exhibits include vintage autos, drag racers, motorcycles, trophies, photos, and a simulator that puts you in the driver's seat. You can also tour the adjacent Talladega Superspeedway, the world's fastest speedway. For more information check out www.motorsportshalloffame.com and www.talladegasuperspeedway.com.

McWane Center,

200 Nineteenth Street North, Birmingham;
(205) 714–8300.
Definitely not off the beaten path, this science-adventure museum occupies the historic Loveman's department store building in the heart of downtown. Youngsters will especially enjoy the IMAX theater's presentations and simulated space-flight experiences offered by the Challenger Center for Space Science Education, a nonprofit organization founded by the families of the seven *Challenger* crew members who died in the tragic 1986 space shuttle explosion. The Ocean Pool, World of Water, and various interactive science exhibits all add to the excitement. Visit the museum's Web site at www.mcwane.com.

VisionLand,

Interstate 20/59 near Interstate 459, Bessemer;
(205) 481–4750.
This fun-filled family park spreads across seventy-five rolling acres in Bessemer, just southwest of Birmingham. With a theme dedicated to Birmingham's early iron and steel industry, the amusement park features multiple thrills aboard a $4.5-million wooden roller coaster, The Rampage, plus rides galore. Visit the park's Web site at www.visionlandpark.com.

Southeast Alabama

The Plains

On your way to "The Plains" (home of Auburn University) in the historic Chattahoochee Trace's upper section, you may want to swing south to *Tallassee,* just north of Interstate 85 at State Routes 14 and 229, for some home-style mouth-watering food and a yesteryear experience at *Hotel Talisi* (334–283–2769). Located at 14 Sistrunk Avenue, this 1920s hotel brims with antiques and nostalgia—from its red-carpeted lobby with ceiling fans and crystal chandeliers to the second-floor hallway's wooden "Superman" phone booth. Three baby grand pianos (including a 1924 version), three uprights, and a player spinet add to the ambience.

In the spacious upstairs hall, you'll see Western Union writing desks, interesting reading material, and an array of seating areas—great for conversation or for curling up with a mystery. Furnished in eclectic fashion with finger vases, parlor lamps, and antiques from the early 1900s, the rooms possess a uniqueness noticeably absent in today's standardized world.

Continuing the hotel's famous family-style buffet tradition, Bob Brown, Roger Gaither, and crew offer a daily feast featuring fried chicken, baked chicken with dressing, sweet potato

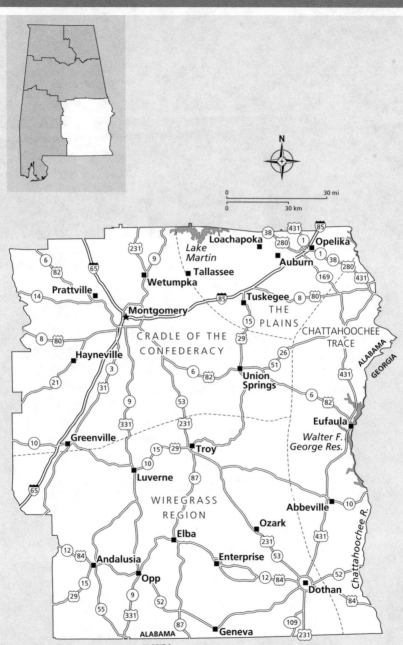

soufflé, a medley of fresh vegetables, corn bread, hush puppies, and home-made pies accompanied by piano/organ dinner music. Except for Sunday, when the feast ends at 2:50 P.M., hours are 11:00 A.M. to 7:50 P.M. daily. Stroll across the street to the hotel's under-the-stars dining oasis, a garden setting with white lights, statuary, and olive trees. Standard to moderate rates.

South of Tallassee in the Shorter area, search out the *Back Forty* (334–727–0880), a farm restaurant at 5001 County Road 30. Marjorie and Ted John-son allocated the back forty acres of their Hillcrest Farms operation to this tran-quil out-of-the-way eatery with a warm country atmosphere. Learn the legend of the hush puppy while enjoying a few with your meal of grilled or fried cat-fish or a combination platter of shrimp, frog legs, crab claws, and/or oysters. The Back Forty also serves rib-eye steaks, chicken, salads, and sandwiches plus Sunday specials. Top off your meal with cheesecake, which comes from Nota-sulga's Bulger Creek Farm. Grandma's banana pudding is another popular dessert here. Prices are economical to moderate. The restaurant opens at 5:30 P.M. on Thursday and Friday and at 4:30 P.M. on Saturday and closes at 9:00 P.M. Sunday hours run from 11:00 A.M. to 2:00 P.M.

Next, strike out east to *Tuskegee.* Stop by the *Tuskegee Human & Civil Rights Multicultural Center* (334–724–0800), which also serves as a welcome center. Located in a former bank building at 104 South Elm Street, the facility

GAY'S TOP PICKS IN SOUTHEAST ALABAMA

Alabama Shakespeare Festival,
Montgomery

First White House of the Confederacy,
Montgomery

The Jule Collins Smith Museum of Art,
Auburn

Landmark Park,
Dothan

Lovelace Athletic Museum and Hall of Honor,
Auburn

Old Alabama Town,
Montgomery

Pioneer Museum of Alabama,
Troy

Rosa Parks Library and Museum,
Montgomery

State Capitol,
Montgomery

Town of Eufaula

Tuskegee Institute National Historic Site,
Tuskegee

U.S. Army Aviation Museum,
Fort Rucker

The Intrepid Tuskegee Airmen

During the early 1940s, Moton Field served as the training grounds for the Tuskegee Airmen, who overcame formidable odds to serve their country with bravery and distinction in a segregated America. As escorts to World War II bombing missions in North Africa and Southern Europe, these African-American aviators compiled an enviable combat record and ranked among the military's best pilots. The 332nd Fighter Group never lost a bomber to enemy fighters while escorting the 15th Air Force on bombing missions. Revered by American bomber crews (who called them the "Red-tail Angels" because of their aircrafts' distinctive markings), these flying heroes also commanded the respect of the German Luftwaffe.

At the United States Air Force Academy, the **Tuskegee Airmen** statue acknowledges their extraordinary contribution: "They rose from adversity through competence, courage, commitment, and capacity to serve America on silver wings, and to set a standard few will transcend."

Lending her support to Tuskegee Institute's pilot training program, First Lady Eleanor Roosevelt visited Moton Field in March 1941. She requested to be taken on a flight by Charles Alfred "Chief" Anderson, who inspired the founding of Tuskegee's School of Aviation, and newspapers across the country carried a photo of this unprecedented event.

The Tuskegee group's achievements represent a turning point in the role of African-Americans in the U.S. military and factored into President Harry S. Truman's signing Executive Order 9981 in 1948, setting the stage for the military's desegregation and later the Civil Rights Movement.

In 1998, Congress designated the Tuskegee Airmen National Historic Site as a unit of the National Park System. Although it is still in the developmental stages, visitors can see the remaining hangar, which will later be restored to its original World War II appearance, and other structures such as the the airfield taxiway, control tower, reservoir, gasoline pits, and fuel storage facilities from that period. The modest airport terminal also features exhibits of photos that chronicle the history of Black aviation and the Tuskegee Airmen.

Located on the outskirts of Tuskegee at 1727 Airport Road, Moton Field lies just off "Chappie" James Drive. Open to the public, this small, working airfield also hosts an annual fly-in to celebrate its unique legacy. To reach the "Home of Black Aviation," take exit 38 off I-85. For more information call (334) 727–6390 or (334) 724–0922.

houses exhibits including one on the infamous Tuskegee Syphilis Study. Here, you can pick up travel information and a local walking-tour brochure. Executive director Deborah Gray will answer your questions and suggest nearby off-the-beaten-path spots to visit. Hours are Monday through Saturday from 10:00 A.M. to 3:00 P.M. Admission is free.

For a look at historic farm implements, stop by Kirk's Old Farm Museum on the downtown square at 111 Westside Street. Beyond the storefront entrance you'll find hundreds of agricultural tools and appliances used before the advent of electricity, along with merchandise from a 1902 Sears, Roebuck catalog. Admission.

Step next door to *The Country Store of Tuskegee* (334–727–7481) at 113 Westside Street (aka Commodore Square) with displays of everything from capers, sun-dried tomatoes, sandalwood soap, and lemon-pepper seasoning to antiques, Native American artifacts, memorabilia, local crafts, herbal remedies, and teas. For a great souvenir, consider buying a copy of *The African-American Heritage Cookbook* by Carolyn Quick Tillery. While here, take time to notice the architecture of the building, constructed by Tuskegee Institute students and once owned by Margaret Murray, wife of Booker T. Washington. At one time, the second floor served as a town school and library. Current owner Dr. James Tarver will share both anecdotes and antidotes with you.

You'll smell printer's ink when you walk into *Charlie Tee's* (334–724–9770) at 119 Westside Street. Former coach and owner Charles Thompson promises "the best screen printing and embroidery on earth," and you can choose a souvenir T-shirt from a selection of designs, including some featuring the famed Tuskegee Airmen. Originally the home of Brown's Dry Goods and Department Store, the building dates to the 1850s. Believed to be the state's oldest commercial building still retaining its original interior, this structure has been added to the list of Alabama's Most Endangered Historic Places. Call ahead for hours, which vary.

To keep up your energy level, stop by H. A. Vaughan Feed and Seed Company (334–727–5700) at 106 Lee Street for a bag of peanuts (warm from the oven) to munch on while exploring.

Next make your way to West Montgomery Road and the historic *Tuskegee Institute* (334–727–3200), where even peanut-butter buffs will be amazed to learn about the peanut's potential. The Carver Museum pays tribute to the creative genius of the agronomist, artist, and inventor who helped change the course of Southern agriculture. George Washington Carver's agricultural experiments with peanuts, pecans, sweet potatoes, and cotton resulted in a more educated approach to farming—not to mention hundreds of new products, many featured among the museum's exhibits. You'll also see some of Carver's artwork and a model of the first lab he used to launch research that resulted in

alabamatrivia

George Washington Carver invented peanut butter during his experiments at Tuskegee Institute.

the transformation of sweet potatoes into after-dinner mints, a coffee substitute, lemon drops, starch, synthetic ginger, tapioca, library paste, medicine, writing ink, and a multitude of other items. As for the multipurpose peanut, the legendary scientist's list of possible uses ranges from beverages, foods, cosmetics, dyes, and medicines to diesel fuel, laundry soap, and insecticide. Before you leave the museum, be sure to visit the gift section. I bought a copy of a booklet (first published in June 1925) entitled *How to Grow the Peanut and 105 Ways of Preparing It for Human Consumption,* containing recipes from peanut bisque to peanut pudding. Museum admission is free. Except for Thanksgiving, Christmas, and New Year's Day, the museum is open daily from 9:00 A.M. to 4:30 P.M.

Later take a campus stroll to see some of the handmade brick buildings, which students constructed during the institute's early years. You'll also want to tour **The Oaks,** home of Booker T. Washington, who founded Tuskegee Institute in 1881. The home is furnished as it was during the time the Washington family lived there. Be sure to notice the unique hand-carved Oriental desk in Washington's upstairs den. Admission is free. However, due to renovation, tours will be given on Tuesdays only. For the current status call (334–727–3200).

Head north to the "land where turtles live"—a former Creek Indian settlement called Loachapoka that once also thrived as a stagecoach junction. Seven miles west of Auburn on State Route 14, you'll find the **Loachapoka Historic District,** which features several structures dating from the decade 1840 to 1850. **The Lee County Historical Society Museum,** housed in the old Trade Center building, contains items ranging from a unique hand-carved cedar rocking chair and an 1840s accounting desk to an oak map case, an antique medical bag, and a punch bowl and dipper made from gourds.

Upstairs, rooms with individual themes feature vintage costumes such as an 1877 wedding dress, an exhibit on Ella Smith's Roanoke doll creations, antique quilts, and a melodeon. Other displays include military uniforms and equipment, kitchen utensils and gadgets, and an almost complete section of Auburn annuals that date to the 1890s.

On the grounds you'll see a steam-powered cotton gin, gristmill, working blacksmith shop, bandstand, doctor's buggy, and dogtrot cabin (moved here from rural Tallapoosa County and reconstructed). If you visit in October, don't miss the **Historical Fair and Ruritan's Syrup Sop** in Loachapoka. Folks at this event, harking back to yesteryear, demonstrate the entire process of converting sugar cane into syrup—from cane crushing by mule-drawn press to syrup sampling on homemade sweet potato biscuits (sometimes called "cat head biscuits" because of their large size). For information on making an

GAY'S FAVORITE ANNUAL EVENTS IN SOUTHEAST ALABAMA

Rattlesnake Rodeo,
Opp, first Saturday and Sunday
in March;
(334) 493–9559 or (800) 239–8054

Azalea-Dogwood Trail and Festival,
Dothan, late March or early April;
(334) 615–3700 or (888) 449–0212

Auburn Floral Trail,
Auburn, late March or early April;
(334) 887–8747 or (866) 880–8747

Spring Pilgrimage,
Eufaula, late March or early April;
(888) 383–2852

A-Day Football Game,
Auburn, April;
(334) 844–4040 or (800) AUB–1957

Auburn CityFest,
Auburn; April;
(866) 880–8747 or (334) 887–8747

Jubilee Cityfest,
downtown Montgomery, May;
(334) 834–7220

Alabama Highland Games,
Wynton M. Blount Cultural Park at the
Alabama Shakespeare Festival,
Montgomery, fourth Saturday in
September;
(334) 277–5021

Festival in the Park,
Oak Park, Montgomery, early October;
(334) 241–2300

**Historical Fair and Ruritan's Syrup
Sop in Loachapoka,**
Loachapoka, October;
(334) 887–8747 or (866) 880–8747

National Peanut Festival,
Dothan, November;
(334) 793–4323 or (888) 449–0212

Victorian Front Porch Christmas,
Opelika, December;
(334) 887–8747 or (866) 880–8747

appointment to see the museum, call the Auburn-Opelika Convention & Visitors Bureau at (866) 880–8747 or (334) 887–8747.

Afterward continue east to "sweet Auburn, loveliest village of the plain." This line from Oliver Goldsmith's poem "The Deserted Village" inspired the university town's name. Founded by the Alabama Methodist Conference in 1856, the school later became a land-grant institution. (Incidentally, if you enter *Auburn* by way of I-85, a trail of big orange tiger paws takes you all the way to the university campus.)

Start your tour of the ***Auburn University Historic District*** at Toomer's Corner, a busy intersection that gets layered so deeply with toilet tissue after each Tiger victory that sometimes vehicles cannot pass through for an hour or two while a celebration takes place. (Auburn is the only city in the world to have a line item in the city budget for the removal of toilet paper.) Before embarking on your campus trek, you might like to step into Toomer's Drugstore, a local landmark, to see the antique marble soda fountain and to order a lemonade.

This section of campus features several buildings that date from the 1850s to the early 1900s. You'll see the Gothic Revival University Chapel, Langdon Hall, and Samford Hall. The latter, a four-story brick structure of Italianate design, dates to 1888 and stands on the site of Old Main, a building that burned the year before.

To explore a tucked-away corner on campus, search out the Donald E. Davis Arboretum, with pavilion, lake, and some 200 labeled botanical specimens ranging from red Japanese maples and chinquapin oaks to Southern magnolias and chinaberry trees.

Don't miss the **Lovelace Athletic Museum and Hall of Honor** (334–844–4750), located at the corner of Samford and Donahue in the Athletic Complex. Honoring Auburn's athletes, the museum recognizes their sports achievements with high-tech interactive exhibits, life-size figures in talking dioramas, and a cavalcade of fascinating displays. Trip along the Tiger Trail and experience a vicarious but thrilling football victory with the crowd's roar and take a look at a replicated Toomer's Corner, triumphantly decorated with toilet paper.

Athletes represented include Heisman Trophy winner and football/baseball hero Bo Jackson, NBA star Charles Barkley, Chicago White Sox player Frank Thomas, Heisman Trophy winner/coach Pat Sullivan, and legendary coach Shug Jordan. Museum hours are 8:00 A.M. to 4:30 P.M. Monday through Friday, 9:00 A.M. to 6:00 P.M. Football Saturdays, and 9:00 A.M. to 3:00 P.M. on Football Weekend Sundays.

To visit a jewel of a museum, head to 901 South College Street. Here you'll find **The Jule Collins Smith Museum of Art** (334–844–1484) overlooking a three-acre lake. Constructed of travertine stone from Italy, the handsome new facility features eight exhibition galleries, a restaurant, a museum shop, and an auditorium. On entering, you'll see a stunning glass chandelier created for the vaulted rotunda by internationally known glass artist Dale Chihuly.

Other treasures include one of the world's largest collections of Victorian Belleek porcelain, outstanding Tibetan bronzes, and more than one hundred of Audubon's most acclaimed prints. But the big story here centers on a collection of thirty-six paintings and drawings that had remained homeless for more than half a century.

Originally assembled by the U.S. State Department in 1946, the collection features works by John Marin, Georgia O'Keeffe, Ben Shahn, Arthur Dove, Ralston Crawford, Yasuo Kuniyoski, and others. Because of its abstract nature and the political leanings of a few of the artists, the traveling exhibit met with so much criticism on the home front that it was recalled, stored, and labeled government "surplus property," thus allowing tax-supported institutions like Auburn to receive a 95 percent discount when the collection was subsequently offered at auction. An Auburn professor with foresight, Frank Applebee, spearheaded "the art bargain of the century" when he persuaded art department instructors to pool their yearly salary increase and enter the announced auction. As a result, Auburn University's Advancing American Art Collection was acquired in 1948 for an unthinkable $1,072. Experts call this body of works, now valued somewhere between $7 and $10 million, one of the most important collections of American art from the post–World War II era.

After viewing the exhibits, take time to enjoy the museum's botanical gardens with walking paths. Hours are 10:00 A.M. to 6:00 P.M. Tuesday through Saturday and noon to 5:00 P.M. on Sunday. Admission. For more information, click on www.julecollinssmithmuseum.com.

While in Auburn consider headquartering at **Crenshaw House Bed and Breakfast** (334–821–1131 or 800–950–1131), 2 blocks north of Toomer's Corner. Shaded by giant oak and pecan trees, this blue Victorian gingerbread-style house stands at 371 North College Street in Auburn's Old Main and Church Street Historic District. Owners Fran and Peppi Verma, who furnished their two-story 1890 home with lovely antiques, offer six units for overnight guests. The Vermas wanted to start a small family business and purchased the house "knowing it would lend itself well to a bed-and-breakfast facility," Fran says, adding that her husband had enjoyed bed-and-breakfast lodging while traveling in Europe. As for breakfast, guests receive a room-service menu and indicate their choices along with a serving time. The Web site is www.auburnalabama.com. Standard to moderate rates.

Also, golfers will want to check out **Auburn Links at Mill Creek** (334–887–5151), a $5-million facility that occupies 274 acres located about 3 miles south of town near the intersection of U.S. Highway 29 and I–85 at exit 51. (The eighteenth hole's sand traps form a giant tiger paw print.)

Auburn's sister city, **Opelika,** makes a good place to continue your area exploration. In Opelika's "olden days," passengers traveling through by train sometimes saw shootouts across the railroad tracks. Fortunately, today's visitors don't have to dodge stray bullets, so you can relax as you explore the Railroad Avenue Historic District.

As a result of Opelika's participation in Alabama's Main Street program (a project of the National Trust for Historic Preservation), many once-forgotten structures have been rescued and reincarnated as charming shops such as **Easterday Antiques** at 805 South Railroad Avenue. Helen Easterday, who's been called "the quintessential town person," and her husband, Kenneth, have embraced the local downtown revitalization program to the point of converting the enormous upper level of their shop into a wonderful home. Mrs. Easter-day's passion for art may be observed in the exquisite antique furnishings, paintings, and accessories displayed in her shop. For health reasons, she limits her schedule and operates by appointment only. For more information or an appointment, call (334) 749–6407.

During mid-December, the ***Victorian Front Porch Christmas*** features self-driving and walking tours through the streets of North Opelika Historic Neighborhood. This annual event has been chosen for the Southeast Tourism Society's Top 20 Events for several years and also for the American Bus Association's Top 100 Events in North America. Other awards include a Shining Example Award and *Group Leisure* magazine's Top 50 Outstanding Festivals and Events in North America. More than forty-five homes and porches serve as backdrops for unique decorations and life-size holiday figures designed by local artist Jan Jones, who maintains a studio in downtown Opelika.

After your Railroad Avenue stroll, head to ***The Museum of East Alabama*** (334–749–2751), located nearby at 121 South Ninth Street. Here you'll see a dugout canoe of white cypress that dates back as far as 3,500 B.C. Other exhibits consist of glass milk bottles, baby bonnets, Shirley Temple and Roanoke dolls, toys, collections of vintage typewriters, pianos, farm implements, war memorabilia, and surgical instruments. Other unusual exhibits include a foot X-ray machine (typical of those once used in shoe stores) and a bicycle-propelled ice-cream cart. The museum's collection also includes an early-twentieth-century kitchen and a full-size fire truck. Hours are 10:00 A.M. until 4:00 P.M. Tuesday through Friday and 2:00 to 4:00 P.M. on Saturday. Admission is free.

Looking to the right as you exit the museum, you'll see the lofty clock tower of the Lee County Courthouse, a half block away. Listed on the National Register of Historic Places, the handsome, white-columned, two-story brick structure dates to 1896 and features marble floors and decorative arched windows.

Take time to drive around a bit to see Opelika's lovely homes, which exemplify a wide range of architectural styles. Better yet, make reservations to stay in one of them—***The Heritage House Bed and Breakfast Inn*** (334–705–0485), at 714 Second Avenue. Barbara Patton, Opelika's former mayor and an advocate of historic preservation, appealed to various parties to step in and preserve this fine old 1914 Neoclassical tan brick home during the years it stood vacant. Finding no volunteers, she called a family conference to discuss its purchase. With the help of her son Richard, Barbara turned the thirteen-room home into a bed-and-breakfast. In January 2004, Carole and Steve Harrison purchased the property and continue to welcome overnight guests. See www .opelikaheritagehouse.com. Standard to moderate rates.

While in the area, golfers will enjoy playing the **Grand National,** one of Alabama's fine courses on the Robert Trent Jones Golf Trail. For more information on this award-winning course, built on 1,300 acres encompassing a 650-acre lake, call (334) 749–9042 or (800) 949–4444.

After your local tour consider an outing to a bona fide "kissin' bridge" (so called because of the privacy it afforded courting couples who once traveled through in horse-drawn buggies). One of only three such structures still left in the lower Chattahoochee Valley, the **Salem-Shotwell Covered Bridge** can be reached by traveling east for about 8.7 miles via US 280 and turning left onto Lee County Road 254 (the Wacoochee School Road). The barn-red, single-span bridge is located 1.3 miles off Lee County Road 254.

Once part of a stagecoach route, this 75-foot bridge made of heart pine features latticed trusses, a wood-shingled roof, and round wooden pegs, surprisingly still intact. A master-and-slave team, John Godwin and Horace King, introduced the "town-truss" bridge design into the Chattahoochee Valley and built many of the area's early wooden bridges. Some local sources speculate that King may have drawn the plans for the Salem-Shotwell bridge. Whether or not he did, this bridge typifies the town-truss construction for which the team gained recognition in Alabama and neighboring states. Acting on Godwin's request, the Alabama legislature granted King his freedom in 1846. The two men then became business partners, and the former slave went on to serve as a member of the Alabama House of Representatives from 1869 to 1872. After Godwin's death in 1859, King erected a marble monument that may still be seen at Godwin Cemetery in nearby Phenix City. The inscription reads: IN LASTING REMEMBRANCE OF THE LOVE AND GRATITUDE HE FELT FOR HIS LOST FRIEND AND FORMER MASTER.

Chattahoochee Trace

After touring War Eagle country, head south toward Eufaula. Along the way you'll see Pittsview (if you don't blink). Stop by the mayor's office (334–855–3568) on US 431 for a friendly chat with Frank Turner (who's the unofficial mayor) and a look at his folk art gallery. You'll find paintings by an area folk artist, signed "Mr John Henry Toney" along with his age. Frank also features the work of Butch Anthony, James (Buddy) Snipes, and other folk artists. Hours are by chance or appointment.

Afterward continue south toward **Eufaula,** sometimes called the "Natchez of Alabama." You may want to make your base at lovely **Lakepoint Resort** (334–687–8011 or 800–544–LAKE), about 7 miles north of town just off US 431.

Located on the shores of Lake Eufaula (also known as Lake George), this complex offers accommodations ranging from campsites, cabins, and cottages to resort rooms and suites along with a restaurant, coffee shop, lounge, and gift shop. Recreation options include swimming, golfing, tennis, hiking, picnicking, biking, waterskiing, and boating—not to mention fishing in a 45,200-acre lake known as the Big Bass Capital of the World. Room rates are standard.

Continue to Eufaula, a city filled with multiple versions of the perfect Southern mansion. Located on a bluff above the Chattahoochee River, Eufaula boasts the state's second-largest historic district and offers a feast for architecture aficionados. During the *Eufaula Pilgrimage,* an annual event that takes place the first full weekend in April, visitors can enjoy home tours, antiques shows, concerts, and other festivities. For more information, contact the Eufaula Heritage Association at (334) 687-3793 or go to www.eufaulapilgrimage.com.

Stop by the *Hart House* (334-687-9755) at 211 North Eufaula Avenue, an 1850 Greek Revival structure that serves as headquarters for the Historic Chattahoochee Commission. Here you can pick up visitors information about the Trace, a river corridor running through portions of Alabama and Georgia. Throughout this bi-state region, travelers will discover a wealth of historic sites, natural attractions, and recreation facilities. Except for holidays, the Hart House may be visited from 8:00 A.M. to 5:00 P.M. Monday through Friday.

Continue to *Shorter Mansion* (334-687-3793) at 340 North Eufaula Avenue. This elegant structure dates to 1884 and features seventeen Corinthian-capped columns and an elaborate frieze of molded acanthus leaves and scrolls beneath its lofty balustraded roof. Be sure to notice the front door's beveled leaded glass and the entrance hall's parquet floor and molded plaster cornices. This Neoclassical Revival mansion, furnished in fine Victorian period pieces, houses the Eufaula Historical Museum and serves as headquarters for the Eufaula Heritage Association.

One upstairs room contains portraits of six state governors who were either born in or later lived in Barbour County. Another upstairs room pays tribute to retired Adm. Thomas H. Moorer, a Eufaula native who served two terms as chairman of the Joint Chiefs of Staff. Displays include Admiral Moorer's portrait, uniform, awards, and mementos from his naval career.

You'll also see Waterford crystal and cut-glass chandeliers, antiques, Confederate relics, period wedding dresses, Alabama memorabilia, and decorative arts. You may browse through the mansion at your leisure or take a guided tour. Modest admission. Except for major holidays, the home is open Monday through Saturday from 9:00 A.M. to 4:00 P.M. and on Sunday from 1:00 to 4:00 P.M.

Before leaving Eufaula be sure to visit *Fendall Hall* (334-687-8469), at 917 West Barbour Street. Built between 1856 and 1860, the home features stenciled

Strange As It Sounds

While visiting Eufaula, don't miss Leroy Brown's marble monument—
the inscription reads:

MOST BASS ARE JUST FISH, BUT LEROY BROWN WAS SOMETHING SPECIAL.

And indeed he was. From a baby bass, Leroy ate from Tom Mann's hand. (The former owner of Tom Mann's Fish World, south of Lakepoint.) "He could jump through a hoop. I've never found another fish as intelligent," says Mann, adding that Leroy never struck a lure and even tried to keep other fish away from these enticing but deadly objects. Leroy also proved to be an exemplary father, guarding the nest until all babies hatched.

Perhaps the esteem in which the big bass was held could be measured in some degree by his final rites. Some 700 persons attended Leroy's funeral. Professional bass fishermen, outfitted in tie and black tails, served as pallbearers, and Leroy's large tackle-box coffin contained a red velvet lining. The choir sang about "big bad Leroy Brown, meanest bass in the whole damn town . . ." Leroy was survived by eight wives. Following the funeral, a grave snatcher made off with Leroy's remains and sent a ransom note demanding $10,000. After several days and no reward, the thief abandoned his quest (and Leroy's coffin), apparently concluding that this scheme was neither fruitful nor fragrant.

True, the average bass does not command such an impressive memorial, but Leroy was in a class by himself. When Tom Mann's Fish World closed, Leroy's memorial was moved from that location to Mann's front yard at 1933 North Eufaula Avenue. Ann Mann, Tom's wife, says that as long as they occupy this home, visitors will always be welcome to view the Leroy Brown memorial here.

Leroy Brown Monument

walls and ceilings painted by a nineteenth-century Italian artist, and the original decor with High Victorian colors remains relatively unchanged. Also noteworthy are the entrance hall's striking black-and-white marble floor and the home's early plumbing system, supplied by attic cisterns. Rumor has it that a ghost named Sammy makes his presence known here from time to time. Currently the house is open for tours Monday through Saturday from 10:00 A.M. to 4:00 P.M. Modest admission.

At 317 South Eufaula Avenue, you'll find **Fagin's Thieves Market** (334–687–4100), with a name inspired by Dickens's *Oliver Twist*. The Beasley family operates this business and rents space to a dozen or so antiques dealers. Browsing through various rooms, you might see children's sleighs, late 1800s cross-country skis, a red wooden rocking horse, bird cages, punch bowls, Depression glassware, books, old phonograph records, lamps, tables, cast-iron stoves, kerosene lamps, and weather vanes. Hours are 9:00 A.M. to 5:00 P.M. Monday through Saturday.

After touring this town of lovely mansions, head to **Clayton,** a small town with some unique attractions, such as the **Octagon House** at 103 North Midway Street. Listed on the National Register of Historic Places, this unusual structure is the state's sole surviving antebellum octagonal house. The ground floor served as the original kitchen (and also as the setting for a mystery, *The Rusty Key,* written by one of the home's owners). Four chimneys extending above the cupola enclose the staircase of this eight-sided structure. The first floor features four main rooms, two small rooms, and two halls that open to the surrounding porch. To arrange a tour call Sharon Martin at (334) 775–3254 or (334) 775–3490. Modest admission.

At nearby Clayton Baptist Church Cemetery (also on North Midway Street), you'll find the **Whiskey Bottle Tombstone,** once featured on *Ripley's Believe It or Not!* television show. The bottle-shaped headstone and footstone, which mark the final resting place of William T. Mullen (1834–1863), still contain their original removable stone stoppers. Such a memorial obviously tells a story, and the story behind the stone goes something like this: Mr. Mullen, a local accountant, acquired a reputation as a heavy drinker. His wife, Mary, a devout teetotaler, threatened that if he drank himself to death, she would let the world know by erecting an appropriate memorial. The Whiskey Bottle Tombstone testifies that she kept her promise.

Wiregrass Region

Continuing south along the Chattahoochee Trace takes you to **Dothan,** in the state's southeastern corner. Here, in a region called the Wiregrass, early settlers battled the odds to cultivate this large stretch of land once completely covered by clumps of stiff, dry grass growing under longleaf pines. To learn more about the Wiregrass region's roots, stop by **Landmark Park** (334–794–3452), in Dothan on US 431, about 3 miles north of Ross Clark Circle. At this living-history farmstead, you may be greeted by sheep, goats, pigs, chickens, cows, and a mule. You'll see a blacksmith shop, pioneer log cabin, smokehouse, cane-mill syrup shed, and other authentic outbuildings of an 1890s farm.

"We want to preserve the natural and cultural heritage of the Wiregrass region," says William Holman, Landmark Park's executive director, who calls the one-hundred-acre park an outdoor classroom. The cozy clapboard farmhouse looks as if its occupants just stepped out to milk the cows and may return any minute. An apron hangs on a cupboard door, and a shaving mug and brush wait beside the wash stand. Oblivious to onlookers, a cat naps on the back porch.

The park offers a full schedule of special events with demonstrations of seasonal farming activities, pioneer skills, and various crafts. In addition to the farmstead, you'll see a country store, church, one-room schoolhouse, drugstore, gazebo, interpretive center, planetarium, nature trails, boardwalks, beaver ponds, and picnic areas. Modest admission. Hours are 9:00 A.M. to 5:00 P.M. Monday through Saturday and noon to 5:00 P.M. Sunday (or 6:00 P.M. during daylight savings time).

Continue to downtown Dothan, the area's major trade center. Proclaimed "Peanut Capital of the World," this region produces one-fourth of the nation's peanuts. Each fall Dothan stages the **National Peanut Festival** with a full calendar of events, from demonstrations of square dance rounds by the Goober Gamboleers to a contest for prize-winning peanut recipes. Look for the large peanut sculptures, individually decorated and placed throughout town.

Across the street from the Civic Center, you'll see the **Wiregrass Museum of Art** (334–794–3871) at 126 Museum Avenue. This facility features a full schedule of rotating exhibits attractively displayed in two galleries flanking the entrance atrium. The museum contains a classroom/studio and a children's hands-on gallery. Youngsters will find the activity area entertaining as well as educational. The museum's hours are 10:00 A.M. to 5:00 P.M. Tuesday through Saturday and 1:00 to 5:00 P.M. Sunday. Admission is free, but donations are accepted.

First known as Poplar Head, Dothan took its present biblical name in 1885. Around that time, concerned citizens decided to tone down the town's rowdy image and hired a marshal and deputies to enforce new laws designed to terminate the saloons' regular Saturday-night brawls.

While driving around town, you'll see local history depicted in colorful murals on various city buildings. The Mule Marker in Poplar Head Park pays tribute to the animal that played a major role in the Wiregrass region's early development. Nearby at North Saint Andrews Street, you'll notice the impressive Dothan Opera House, a Neoclassical Revival structure that dates from 1915. Another downtown historic site, Porter Hardware, with its rolling ladders, still exudes the nostalgic flavor of its late-1800s origin.

While in Dothan be sure to stop by *Garland House* (334–793–2043), at 200 North Bell Street, for a delicious lunch. Try the chicken divan and peanut paradise pie. Serving hours are 11:00 A.M. to 2:00 P.M. Monday through Friday. Prices are moderate.

Afterward head to nearby Ozark, home of the Claybank Church on East Andrews Avenue just off State Route 249. This 1852 log church with hand-split board shingles and original pews is open daily during daylight hours.

You might like to continue your exploration of the Wiregrass region with a visit to *Enterprise.* If so, don't miss the *Boll Weevil Monument.* Actually, you can't miss this memorial because it stands in the middle of Main Street. And if you aren't sure you'd recognize a boll weevil (a bug about a quarter-inch long with a snout half the length of its body), just watch for a statue of a woman clad in classic drapery who stands on an ornamented pedestal and holds a magnified version of the pest high above her head. A streetside plaque explains that in 1919 the citizens of Enterprise and Coffee County erected the statue IN PROFOUND APPRECIATION OF THE BOLL WEEVIL AND WHAT IT HAS DONE AS THE HERALD OF PROSPERITY. After the boll weevil demolished two-thirds of Coffee County's cotton in 1915, local farmers started to diversify, planting other crops such as sugar cane, corn, hay, potatoes, and peanuts. Particularly suited to the Wiregrass, peanuts played a primary role in saving the local economy after the boll weevil's destruction and soon became the region's principal cash crop.

About half a block from the Boll Weevil Monument stands the venerable *Rawls Hotel* (334–308–9387) at 116 South Main Street. Listed on the National Register of Historic Places, the hotel dates to 1903 and makes a great headquarters while checking out the local sites. A hub for civic and social events until it closed in the early 1970s, the recently refurbished property once again lures travelers. In addition to several businesses, the hotel houses a fine dining restaurant, meeting rooms, Hayden's Tavern, and four handsome rooms and suites. Rates are moderate.

Boll Weevil Monument

Behind the hotel on Railroad Street, you'll find the former Enterprise Depot. In railroad's golden days, passengers simply stepped off a train here, and a short stroll took them to the Rawls. Today's visitor can browse through the depot's rooms and large freight area filled with historical artifacts. "Many of the arrow and spear points in the Indian Room were discovered by local farmers, while plowing their land," said volunteer Betty Beckson.

History buffs can dip into more local lore at Pea River Genealogical Library on Main Street. A stroll along Main Street takes you past eateries like the Magnolia Room Café and antiques shops. At Rawls Warehouse, you'll see unique gifts and may meet fourth-generation owners Amanda and Jay Beckwith. A framed 1929 newspaper ad in the store shows a Chevrolet Roadster advertised for $525. Railroad buffs and kids will want to check out Wiregrass Toys & Trains at 111 South Main Street, home to all scales of electric trains plus a selection of helicopter models.

Before or after exploring downtown, stop by the Enterprise Welcome Center and Little Red Schoolhouse (complete with pot-bellied stove and slate boards) near the U.S. Highway 84 bypass. And don't pass up Simply Southern, a log cabin complex of interesting shops at 1302 Boll Weevil Circle.

At the Boll Weevil Soap Company, you'll find Baby Cakes, High Cotton, Gardener's Love, Southern Romance, and other herbal products made by Rosemary Howell, a nurse by profession. Each month, she sells more than 1,600 pounds of soap either from the bungalow that houses her business at 1241 Shell Field Road or via the Internet at www.bwsoap.com.

Golfers will want to play Tartan Pines, a challenging eighteen-hole course on the town's west side. The facility, with a restaurant on the premises, opened in 2000 and offers club memberships but also welcomes the public.

Opp, in neighboring Covington County, hosts a unique annual event: the **Rattlesnake Rodeo.** This spring festival, scheduled the first full weekend in March, features the world's only rattlesnake race along with arts and crafts (including several made from rattlesnake skins), a buck dancing contest, and programs on rattlesnake education and safety. For specific information call (334) 493–9559. You can also write to the Opp Jaycees at P.O. Box 596, Opp 36467 or contact the chamber of commerce at (800) 239–8054.

To reach **Troy** follow State Route 87 north from Enterprise. On the southern outskirts of this town, the home of Troy State University, you'll find the **Mossy Grove School House Restaurant** (334–566–4921) just off US 231 at 1902 Elba Highway. Set among moss-draped trees, this rustic structure started out as a one-room schoolhouse in 1856. Later enlarged and renovated, the building still contains its original stage, now part of the back dining room.

Diners can order fried dill pickles to nibble on while waiting for their entrees and admire memorabilia ranging from Confederate money, swords, and a cannonball to antique tools, barrels, and even bear teeth. Also displayed here are an old-fashioned telephone, cheese cutter, barber chair, and many other items.

Popular entrees include broiled shrimp scampi, charbroiled chicken tenders, and charbroiled rib eye. All dinners include hush puppies, coleslaw or salad, wedge fries or baked potato, and white beans with a special pepper relish. Moderate prices. Hours are 5:00 to 9:00 P.M. Tuesday through Saturday.

Continuing north through Troy takes you to **Pioneer Museum of Alabama** (334–566–3597), located at 248 US 231. Situated on ten wooded acres, this fascinating folk museum contains thousands of items contributed by some 700 local residents. You'll find extensive collections, all well organized and attractively displayed. Household items range from lemon squeezers, sausage stuffers, and butter molds to cookware, fluting irons, spittoons, and an Edison phonograph with a morning glory–shaped speaker. Although the lovely period furnishings of the three Bass Rooms reflect an upper-class lifestyle, the museum's collections focus on items that played a part in the daily existence of the community's middle- and lower-class members.

Other exhibits include newspaper typesetting and printing machines, an enormous collection of farm equipment, blacksmith and carpenter shop displays, and several horse-drawn vehicles, including an antique hearse. One exhibit, "When Cotton Was King," features a mule with "a lean and hungry look." Upon seeing the sculptor's interesting armature, museum officials had the artist stop working at once to preserve the unique look of the unfinished piece. Other objects on display include a portable boll weevil catcher, a peanut sheller, and a moonshine still.

Don't miss the early-twentieth-century street setting featuring storefronts of barber and millinery shops, a bank, and offices for a dentist, doctor, and lawyer—all appropriately equipped. Save plenty of time for exploring the grounds, too. On your way to see the furnished dogtrot log cabin and nearby tenant house, you'll pass a loblolly pine known as the Moon Tree—the seed from which it grew journeyed to the moon and back with the Apollo astronauts. Before leaving the museum, stop by the country store stocked with essentials such as snuff, castor oil, patent medicines, and bone buttons. You'll also find a restored 1928 schoolhouse, a working gristmill, a corncrib made of hand-hewn logs, a covered bridge, a nature trail, and a picnic area on the grounds. Admission is modest. Except for major holidays, hours are 9:00 A.M. to 5:00 P.M. Monday through Saturday and 1:00 to 5:00 P.M. Sunday.

Cradle of the Confederacy

For a really great meal at **Red's Little School House** (334–584–7955), located at blink-and-you've-missed-it Grady, travel north from Troy on US 231, then turn onto State Route 94 in the direction of Dublin and Ramer. At the intersection of Route 94 and Gardner Road, look for a tall water tower, labeled PINE LEVEL, with a small red structure beside it. At this restaurant (housed in a former school), now owned by Jeanette and Red Deese and managed by their daughter Debbie, you'll find a buffet selection of all-you-can-eat, fresh, home-cooked vegetables such as sweet potato soufflé, fried okra, and collards. (Red grows acres and acres of vegetables each season and reaps a huge harvest.) The menu also features fried corn bread, chicken and dumplings, barbecue, and fried chicken. If you manage to save room for dessert, the choices are listed on the blackboard.

Even though the nation's presidents look sternly from their frames over the chalkboard and old maps suggest geography-test anxiety, this is a place to relax. Schoolmarm Debbie banters with the customers, who obviously enjoy both the food and the friendly surroundings. Debbie, who calls herself "a half-decent guitar player," sometimes sings for the crowd. "Everyone brags on the food, and laughs at the entertainment," she writes in the preface of her cookbook.

Debbie converted two school buses into traveling kitchens and takes her catering show on the road for large gatherings. She has cooked for four governors and one president. "I think food is the answer to everything," she says. School starts at 11:00 A.M. and ends at 9:00 P.M. Wednesday through Saturday and closes at 3:00 P.M. on Sunday. Prices are economical.

Afterward continue north on one of several roads that lead to ***Montgomery,*** about thirty minutes away. Montgomery offers a wealth of attractions appealing to all interests. In the past the city has been home to such luminaries as Tallulah Bankhead, Hank Williams, and Nat King Cole. Montgomery served as a launching ground for the Wright brothers, who gave early flying lessons here; a playground for Zelda and F. Scott Fitzgerald; and a battleground in the Civil Rights Movement.

alabamatrivia

Nat King Cole was born at the Cole-Samford House on St. John Street in Montgomery.

This city also pioneered the nation's first electric trolley system, the Lightning Route, which made its successful trial run in 1886.

Make the new ***Montgomery Area Visitor Center*** (334–262–0013) at 300 Water Street your first stop in the city. Housed in historic Union Station that dates to 1898, the center offers a handsome medley of exhibit panels on area attractions along with maps and information on accommodations, restaurants, festivals, and more. Take a virtual ten-minute city tour in the mini-theater and collect some souvenirs in the gift shop. Hours are 8:00 A.M. to 5:00 P.M. Monday through Saturday and noon to 4:00 P.M. Sunday.

Here you can also pick up a trolley map for the Lightning Route, an easy way to see the city with no parking problems. An all-day pass costs $1.00 (50 cents for seniors). Passengers can board at twenty-minute intervals along the route, and the trolleys run from 9:00 A.M. to 6:00 P.M. Monday through Saturday.

On the city's southeast side, you'll find the **Alabama Shakespeare Festival** (ASF) (334–271–5353 or 800–841–4ASF). Just off East Boulevard on Woodmere Boulevard in the Wynton M. Blount Cultural Park, ASF presents works ranging from familiar classics to world-premiere Southern Writers' Project productions. You can take in a performance of works by such writers as Sir Noel Coward, Anton Chekhov, Eugene O'Neill, George Bernard Shaw, Tennessee Williams, and, of course, the Bard. The only American theater invited to fly the same flag as that used by England's Royal Shakespeare Company, ASF attracts more than 300,000 visitors annually from all fifty states and sixty foreign countries and is the world's fifth-largest Shakespeare festival.

alabamatrivia

A life-size statue of Hank Williams stands in Montgomery's Lister Park across from the City Auditorium, where Williams's funeral service took place.

Situated in a 250-acre, landscaped, English-style park, the $21.5 million performing-arts complex houses two stages, rehearsal halls, and a snack bar along with costume, prop, and gift shops. The grounds, perfect for strolling or picnicking, feature a reflecting lake complete with gliding swans. Wend your way through Shakespeare Gardens, which features a 325-seat amphitheater against a setting that brings to life the Bard's botanical references to flowers and herbs, such as rosemary "for remembrance" (and great as a garnish for most meat dishes, too). Linger awhile and enjoy the park's various colors, textures, and smells. For information, brochures, or tickets, call or write to Alabama Shakespeare Festival, One Festival Drive, Montgomery 36117-4605. You can visit www.asf.net to check on current productions.

Before leaving the park take time to browse through the **Montgomery Museum of Fine Arts** (334–244–5700). Located at One Museum Drive, this facility features the fine Blount Collection with works representing more than 200 years of American art. Admission is free. Except for major holidays, the museum's hours are 10:00 A.M. to 5:00 P.M. Tuesday through Saturday. Thursday hours extend to 9:00 P.M. The Sunday schedule is noon to 5:00 P.M. Enjoy a lunch break in the museum at Café M, an artful bistro that serves from 11:00 A.M. to 2:00 P.M. Tuesday through Saturday. Sample the Mediterranean chicken salad and flourless fudge cake. Then save a bit of bread to toss to the ducks, who cruise by regularly with great expectations. Rates are economical to moderate.

Sometime during your Montgomery visit, consider searching out an off-the-beaten-path place called **Dawson's at Rose Hill** (334–215–7620), in the Mt. Meigs community at 11250 US 80 East. A winding tree-lined driveway leads to the restaurant, which occupies a white frame Colonial-style home on the rolling grounds of an 1814 plantation northeast of Montgomery. Originally a 4,000-acre estate, Rose Hill was built by Henry Lucas, a wealthy landowner in Montgomery County. The surrounding forty acres of rose gardens gave the estate, listed on the Alabama Historical Register, its name.

Typical dinner selections feature medallions of beef with wild rice and portobello mushrooms or sole on angel-hair pasta with lemon butter. Lunch is served from 11:30 A.M. to 2:00 P.M. Tuesday through Friday (reservations required). Dinner hours run from 5:00 to 9:00 P.M. Tuesday through Saturday. Moderate to expensive.

Back in downtown Montgomery, across the street from Cloverdale Park, stands the former home of a famous couple who personified the Jazz Age. Housed in the lower right section (Apartment B) of a circa-1910 two-story brown structure at 919 Felder Avenue, you'll find the **Scott and Zelda Fitzgerald Museum** (334–264–4222). Francis Scott Key Fitzgerald met Zelda Sayre, a native of Montgomery and daughter of an Alabama Supreme Court judge, at a local dance in 1918. The couple married in 1920, soon after Scott published his first novel, *This Side of Paradise*.

The Fitzgeralds and their daughter, Scottie, lived here from October 1931 to the spring of 1932. While here Scott worked on his novel *Tender Is the Night* and the screenplay for a Jean Harlow movie. At the same time Zelda, whose writings include a play as well as several short stories and articles, started her only novel, *Save Me the Waltz*. Beautiful, flamboyant, and driven, Zelda also excelled at painting and ballet. Unfortunately, her recurring mental collapses played havoc with the family's lives and prevented her from realizing more of her creative potential.

alabamatrivia

The Wallace Foundation in Montgomery honors Lurleen Wallace, the third woman ever elected governor of a state.

Exhibits include some of Zelda's original paintings, family photos, autographed books, letters, and other personal memorabilia. Plans were afoot to tear down this historic home until local attorney Julian McPhillips and his wife, Leslie, purchased it and set about creating this museum. In the sunroom you can watch a twenty-five-minute video that provides some glimpses into the lives of the author of *The Great Gatsby* and his talented but tormented wife. No admission is charged, but contributions are accepted. Hours are 10:00 A.M. to 2:00 P.M. Wednesday through Friday and 1:00 to 5:00 P.M. Saturday and Sunday.

Afterward head downtown to Montgomery's capitol complex, where you can easily spend a full day. If you enjoy digging into the past, you'll find this area fascinating to explore. From here Jefferson Davis telegraphed his "Fire on Fort Sumter" order, beginning the Civil War. Rising impressively above its surroundings on Dexter Avenue, the 1851 capitol reflects the period's prevailing architecture—Greek Revival. In this building Jefferson Davis took his presidential oath for the Confederacy, and a six-pointed brass star now marks the spot.

At 644 Washington Avenue, just across the street from the capitol, stands the *First White House of the Confederacy* (334–242–1861). Occupied by the Jefferson Davis family during the early days of the War Between the States, this Italianate-style home built by William Sayre dates to the early 1830s. Elegant downstairs parlors and second-floor bedrooms (including a charming nursery) contain Davis family possessions and period antiques. Other displays include Civil War relics, letters, and glass-cased documents. Hours are 8:00 A.M. to 4:30 P.M. Monday through Friday. Admission is free.

Next door to the Davis home, you'll find a treasure-filled museum, the Alabama Department of Archives and History. This building houses an enormous manuscript collection and exhibits spanning the gap from the Stone Age to the Space Age.

A short jaunt takes you to the *Dexter Avenue King Memorial Baptist Church* (334–263–3970). Located at 454 Dexter Avenue, the church became a National Historical Landmark in 1974. It was at this church, pastored by Dr. Martin Luther King Jr., that the Montgomery bus boycott was organized on December 2, 1955, launching the American Civil Rights Movement.

A forty-five-minute tour covers the church's early history as well as the more recent role it played as a rallying place for civil rights activists. On the ground floor, a six-section folk mural illustrates major events from Dr. King's life. Call for tour times. Modest admission.

Nearby, in front of the Southern Poverty Law Center at 400 Washington Avenue, stands the *Civil Rights Memorial.* Designed by Maya Lin, who also served as the architect for the Vietnam Memorial in Washington, D.C., this black granite memorial documents major events in the struggle for civil rights.

Don't miss the *Rosa Parks Library and Museum* (334–241–8615 or 888–357–8843, extension 661), a state-of-the-art facility at 252 Montgomery Street. This site marks the spot where Mrs. Parks was arrested in 1955 and offers an in-depth look at the event that launched the Montgomery bus boycott. A project of Troy State University Montgomery, the interpretative museum opened in December 2000 and features original exhibits, including historical papers from that era and a replica of the public bus, complete with a unique treatment of the scene in which Mrs. Rosa Parks played her significant role in shaping history to become "Mother of the Civil Rights Movement." Admission. Museum hours run from 9:00 A.M. to 5:00 P.M. Monday through Friday and from 9:00 A.M. to 3:00 P.M. on Saturday. For more background on this pivotal event in the city's (and nation's) civil rights heritage, visit www.tsum.edu.

Also downtown, at 301 Columbus Street, you can step back into the nineteenth century at **Old Alabama Town** (334–240–4500 or 888–240–1850). This fascinating concentration of historically restored buildings provides glimpses of city and country living in the nineteenth and early twentieth centuries. Start your tour at the Loeb Center, where you can also visit the museum store. Continue your excursion into the past at Lucas Tavern and other buildings in this history-filled complex. You'll see an 1850s dogtrot house (a dogtrot is a form of Southern architecture that features an open central hall connecting two rooms, sometimes called pens). Other stops include such buildings as a grange hall, carriage house, grocery store, church, country doctor's office, and a one-room schoolhouse—complete with *McGuffey's Readers* and slates.

You'll also see the nearby Rose-Morris House, where you can enjoy music on the dogtrot, and the **Ordeman House,** a handsome townhouse with elegant furnishings and backyard dependencies. Guided tours here take place at 11:30 A.M. and 1:30 P.M. Monday through Friday. Admission. Except for major holidays, the center's hours are 9:00 A.M. to 3:00 P.M. Monday through Saturday. Check out www.oldalabamatown. com to learn more.

"Your Cheatin' Heart" immediately brings Hank Williams to mind for all country music lovers, and fans from throughout the world travel to Montgomery to pay tribute at his grave site. Set in Oakwood Cemetery, the marble memorial is sculpted in the shape of two large music notes and a cowboy hat. You can also see a life-size bronze statue of the musician in Lister Hill plaza, across from City Hall.

Ordeman House

Stop by 118 Commerce Street for an in-depth look at the legacy of Alabama-born Hank Williams. Paying tribute to the memory of this country music legend, the **Hank Williams Museum** (334–262–3600) contains recordings, albums, musical instruments, clothing, a saddle with silver trim, family photos, and other personal items. The museum's focal point is the baby-blue 1952 Cadillac convertible in which the singer/songwriter died while being driven to his scheduled performance in Canton, Ohio, on January 1, 1953. Other exhibits showcase memorabilia of family members and associates. A carved Kowliga, like the wooden Indian that inspired Williams's song, "Kowaliga" and created by the Wood Chippers (with a time investment of 559 hours), looms 8½ feet tall. Museum hours are 9:00 A.M. to 6:00 P.M. Monday through Saturday and 1:00 to 4:00 P.M. on Sunday. Admission. Tap into www .hank50.com for more details and some toe-tapping music.

alabamatrivia

Life magazine ranked Hank Williams as Number One in the "100 Most Important People in Country Music."

Across the street at 551 Clay Street, you'll find a warm welcome at **Red Bluff Cottage** (334–264–0056 or 888–551–CLAY), a perfect place to headquarter in Alabama's capital city. In fact, the upstairs porch of this raised cottage offers fine views of the state capitol and the Alabama River. Bonnie and Barry Ponstein, who purchased the inn from previous owners Anne and Mark Waldo, share the cooking and dispense Southern hospitality—Alabama style. "We have a good time down here," says Barry, quoting his three rules: No smoking, no pets, and no grumpy people. Pay a virtual visit via www.RedBluffCottage.com. Moderate rates.

After exploring the capital of the Old South, head north to **Wetumpka,** a charming town with a unique setting. Not only situated on the Coosa River's banks, Wetumpka also sits in the bowl of a 4-mile-wide crater created by the impact of a meteorite about eighty-three million years ago. Head first to the Wetumpka Area Chamber of Commerce (334–567–4811), located at 110 East Bridge Street in the heart of downtown. While collecting travel information at the chamber office, housed in a former bank building that dates to 1905, notice the original brass chandelier with a Greek key design that repeats the ceiling motif. "Wetumpka comes from an Indian word that means 'tumbling waters,'" said executive director Jan Wood.

alabamatrivia

Wetumpka sits on the western brim of a 4-mile-wide crater created by a meteorite some 83 million years ago.

Spanning the Coosa River, you'll see the town's focal point, a picturesque arched bridge built in 1937. Named for a former governor, the Bibb Graves Bridge allegedly is the only one south of the Mason/Dixon Line suspended by reinforced concrete. After crossing the bridge, notice the historic First Presbyterian Church, organized in 1834. It was here that soldiers in the Wetumpka Light Guard gathered on April 16, 1861, before leaving to confront their destinies in the Civil War.

If you saw the movie *Big Fish,* filmed in and around Montgomery and starring Jessica Lange, Albert Finney, Ewan McGregor, and Danny DeVito, then the town might look vaguely familiar although the film crew made several exterior changes. To view Wetumpka from another perspective, consider cruising down the river on an authentic sternwheeler, the **Betsy Ann *Riverboat.*** The boat is currently docked downtown at Crommelin's Landing in Gold Star Park, but the crew makes Montgomery its home base. For information on rates and cruise schedules, call (334) 265–7739 or click on www.betsyannriverboat.com.

Before leaving town, be sure to visit ***Our Place Café*** (334–567–8778) for a delectable dinner. Located at 809 Company Street, the restaurant occupies a brick building once owned by the Graham family. Back in the 1930s, the structure housed a grocery store with an apartment above and later served as an office for the family's wholesale gasoline business.

Owners David and Mona Funderburk offer casual elegance in dining and an ambience-filled restaurant with seating on two levels. Try the signature crab cakes, served with a special dill sauce, or the evening special. David describes his cuisine as "more Creole than Cajun," and his menu features six seafood selections nightly as well as steaks. The restaurant opens at 4:30 P.M. Tuesday through Saturday. Prices are moderate.

Save time to explore nearby ***Fort Toulouse–Jackson Park*** (334–567–3002). To reach the park, the site of two forts from different centuries, take US 231 North and watch for the turnoff sign across from the Food World supermarket. Continue 2.4 miles down this road to the main gate. After entering the park you'll see the visitor center on the left. Inside, displays of artifacts unearthed in archaeological digs, from brass uniform buttons and silver earrings to French wine bottles and cannonballs, provide background on the site's history.

The original 1717 French fortress, named for Count Toulouse (son of Louis XIV), served as a trading post where Native Americans exchanged furs and deerskins for European goods. This French outpost also helped keep the British at bay. Gen. Andrew Jackson's forces later built a larger nineteenth-century counterpart while fighting the Creek Indians. From here Old Hickory plotted his campaign against the British and Spanish that ended with the Battle of New Orleans.

The Elms

While driving around the Millbrook area in Elmore County north of Montgomery, search out *The Elms* (334–290–ELMS) with a backdrop of camellias, roses, spirea, wisteria, and magnolias. Located at 360 Lindsey Road in Coosada, the historic home once served as the centerpiece of a cotton plantation that covered 16,000 acres. Here you'll be greeted by owner Jeanne Hall Ashley and Boomer, a friendly bearded collie. "One thing that's so special about this property," said Jeanne, "is that we have the original pioneer home, the second home, a cemetery, and early family correspondence."

Built for Absalom and Emma Bolling Hall Jackson in 1836, the handsome two-story home with Greek Revival architectural influences contains "antiques, family portraits, memorabilia, and maybe a ghost or two," said Jeanne. Mary Louisa Crenshaw Hall, Jeanne's great-grandmother, gave Millbrook its name.

Although she grew up in Colorado, Jeanne spent her childhood summers in Alabama with her grandmother here at The Elms and gladly shares some of the area's rich history and fascinating anecdotes with visitors. Now on a mission to rescue The Elms as well as nearby Ellerslie (built in 1818 and the area's oldest home), Jeanne left northern Virginia and a career as an aviation disaster planning consultant to preserve these ancestral treasures. Presently, she offers house tours but is considering opening The Elms as a bed-and-breakfast in the future. Call ahead for an appointment. Admission.

Fort Toulouse and Fort Jackson living-history programs, staged monthly on the park's grounds, permit visitors to dip a bit deeper into the forts' earlier days. "We usually have something going on here three out of four weekends," said site director James Parker.

This 164-acre park also offers a picnic area, campground, and launching ramp. Another attraction is the thirty-acre arboretum with walkway, foot-bridges, and study decks. Nearby, the Coosa and Tallapoosa Rivers—with their cache of bass, bream, catfish, and crappie—beckon anglers. (A state fishing license is required.) Modest admission. Except for major holidays, the park is open from sunup to sundown year-round, and the visitor center hours run from 8:00 A.M. to 5:00 P.M. daily. For more information visit www.preserveala.org.

After your park outing follow State Route 14 west to *Prattville.* Daniel Pratt, for whom the town was named, came here from New Hampshire in the 1830s and established an industrial center—still the site for the manufacture of cotton gins. A drive through *Old Prattvillage* takes you past a section of restored nineteenth-century buildings. For a driving tour map, which highlights about forty homes in the historic district along with area churches and industrial sites, stop by the chamber of commerce at 1002 East Main Street or City Hall at 101 West Main Street.

Better yet, a walking tour of the village lets you get up close and personal. At Prattvillage Gardens you'll see a small 1800s plantation chapel surrounded by a profusion of plants and a butterfly walk. Open the gate and stroll past theme gardens devoted to herbs, perennials, and old-fashioned favorites like hollyhocks, dianthus, and oak-leaf hydrangeas.

Stop by the ***Prattaugan Museum*** (334–361–0961), which houses the Heritage Center. Located at 102 East Main Street, this circa 1848 home show-cases antiques, exhibits on area history, Indian artifacts, and genealogical records. In the backyard, notice the artesian well with a dipper hanging nearby. Prattville acquired its "Fountain City" title because it boasts a number of arte-sian wells. Except for city holidays, hours are Monday through Friday from 10:00 A.M. to 4:00 P.M. Admission is free, and donations are accepted.

Heritage Park, which features a three-tiered fountain, overlooks the town's focal point, Daniel Pratt's big brick gin factory. From this scenic spot, you can watch water spilling over the dam into Autauga Creek. A short stroll takes you to Tichnor Street Antiques & Interiors with a large selection of inter-esting pieces. Don't miss Prejean House Antiques with English imports in the rear section.

Wander along historic West Main Street past Red Arrow Hardware with its nostalgic inventory and The Elephant Walk, which houses a boutique and gar-den cafe. Across the street, you can browse through Stained Glass Emporium and see all sorts of timepieces awaiting repair at The Village Clocksmith. Check out A Carousel of Shops with an impressive inventory of "antiques, boutiques, and uniques."

Nature lovers will enjoy trekking through Wilderness Park on Upper Kingston Road. Located inside the city limits, the park could be a world away—in central China by the looks of it. Instead of a typical Southern forest's foliage, the paved half-mile path leads through a thick stand of towering bamboo.

alabamatrivia

Alabama's forest acreage ranks as third largest in the nation and second largest in the South.

While exploring Prattville, if you happen to spot a car with a sign that says "FOLLOW ME TO ***CHOCODELPHIA,***" then by all means, do so. Otherwise, head to Pratt's Mill Shopping Center at 2096 State Route 14 East, where the staff produces things celestial and chocolate—milk chocolate, white chocolate, and dark choco-late, the favorite of chocoholics. Assortments of hand-dipped candies fill glass cases, and a candy-making demonstration will soon have your mouth watering.

To order a selection of your favorite chocolates, call Chocodelphia (334–361–2106 or 877–246–2633) or visit on the Web at www.chocodelphia.com.

For some scrumptious Southern cooking, make reservations (required) at *The Guest House* (334–365–7532) at 209 Doster Street. With the motto "If you leave here hungry, it's your own fault," you can guess what's in store: turkey and dressing, roast beef with rice and gravy, ham with raisin sauce, oven-roasted chicken, squash croquettes, sweet potato casserole, baked pineapple, curried fruit, and more. The dessert tray features an alluring array of cheese-cakes, meringues, and pies. Heaping dishes of food are passed around the table, family-style. In 1990, Linda and Doug Blackwell took over this business, which Miss Floy Burton founded and operated for almost four decades. For some recipes straight from The Guest House kitchen, pick up a cookbook called *Miss Floy's Finest*.

Search out nearby *Buena Vista* (334–365–3690 or 334–361–0961), an early plantation home, located on Autauga County Road 4 between US 31 and State Route 14. Fronted by four Ionic columns and constructed of heart pine, the Greek Revival–style structure stands on a sweeping lawn studded with camellias and magnolias. A striking circular staircase spirals from the large entrance hall to the third-floor banquet room. Originally built in the Federal style and known as Montgomery House, the home is listed on the National Register of Historic Places. Some historians claim the house dates to 1822, but other sources say circa 1830 would be more accurate. You'll see some period furnishings and a beautiful white quilt stitched in patterns that repeat the home's architectural accents. Created by Flavin Glover, a contemporary quilter based in Auburn, the Buena Vista quilt was featured in an issue of *Decorating and Crafts* magazine. Owned by a local corporation and operated by the Autauga County Heritage Association, Buena Vista is open to the public for tours on Tuesday between 10:00 A.M. and 2:00 P.M. or by appointment. Admission is free, but donations are accepted.

Head to *Lowndesboro,* south of Prattville. This small town, founded by cotton planters in the 1830s, contains some thirty surviving antebellum structures. If you'd like to visit *Marengo* (334–278–4442 or 334–272–8508), an 1835 plantation home with an interesting history, take US 80 west. At the flashing caution light 13 miles past Dannelly Field Airport, turn right and travel 1.3 miles. You'll find Marengo on the left. Owned by the Lowndesboro Landmarks Foundation, this historic home serves as an intimate restaurant for dinner parties. Operated by Art Moody along with his son Mark, who lives on the premises and performs the duties of chef, the facility opens when a minimum of thirty guests make a dinner party reservation. Once that quota is reached, individual diners are accepted by reservation.

Guests arrive around 6:00 P.M. for appetizers, drinks, socializing, and a tour of the historic home. When the dinner bell rings about an hour later, Mark serves a multicourse dinner starting with homemade soup that's followed by a seasonal salad and a palate-cleansing sorbet. The entree might be a chargrilled tenderloin filet, beef kabobs, or Cornish hen with homemade rolls, vegetables, and dessert. After dinner Art tells guests about Marengo's history and shares some intriguing ghost stories. Call for reservations and rates.

Want to visit the best little town in Alabama? Then head about 40 miles (or minutes) south of Montgomery, take the Greenville exit 130 off I–65, and turn left. Ditto if you're looking for the best small town in America.

It's true—**Greenville,** with a population of some 8,000—outscored every other U.S. city with fewer than 100,000 residents in a national home towns index that measures the power of place using statistical data compiled by academic researchers.

Known as "Camellia City," Greenville promises plenty for flower lovers, history buffs, and golfers. Founded in 1820, the town boasts lovely homes, churches, and public buildings, many on the Register of Historic Places. Cambrian Ridge, one of the award-winning courses on the Robert Trent Jones Golf Trail, beckons only minutes away with the famed RTJ course, Capitol Hill, in easy driving distance.

Stop by the Greenville Area Chamber of Commerce (334–382–3251 or 800–959–0717) housed in the old CSX depot on Bolling Street to pick up a brochure called *Historic Main Street Greenville,* which details a self-guided tour of the town's interesting sites. Shady streets, brick paving, and gas lights make Commerce Street an attractive place to stroll.

"People are walking downtown as part of their exercise program—you'd be amazed at the number of people downtown in the evenings," says Nancy Idland, executive director of Greenville's Main Street Program, which promotes downtown revitalization.

A jaunt takes you past a local landmark, the ***Ritz Theatre.*** Dating to 1935, the former movie house built in the then-popular art deco style later fell into disrepair. Now rescued and restored, the Ritz serves as the venue for a variety of productions from theater to music and dance. Other sites of interest include Greenville's circa-1936 City Hall, a WPA project and the city's best example of Colonial Revival civic architecture. Continue your stroll through Confederate Park, established in1897. With a fountain as its centerpiece, this block-size space is sometimes the setting for evening concerts.

You'll see several handsome churches such as First Presbyterian, Greenville's oldest brick church. Search out the Pioneer Cemetery with its ornate cast-iron fence and elaborate monuments. Unusual cast-iron covers, an invention patented in 1874 by Greenville native Joseph R. Abrams, top several graves, and others are covered with giant cockleshells, a Victorian custom. Many of the area's early settlers, including Capt. William Butler for whom the county is named, are buried here.

Spend some time browsing through some of Greenville's one-of-a-kind boutiques and gift shops such as The Pineapple at 132 West Commerce Street, which offers unusual flags and banners, photo frames, hand-decorated clothing, and collectibles. In a beautifully restored building at 112 West Commerce, Thomas Sanderson showcases antiques and accessories and provides decorator services for interiors from Gulf Coast condos to Atlanta townhouses. Grayson's in Greenville at 850 Fort Dale Road specializes in antiques, accent pieces, and gifts, and High Cotton Gallery at 900 Fort Dale Road features accessories, books, clothing, gifts, and antiques.

With a wooded recreation area plus playgrounds and pavilions for picnickers, **Sherling Lake** about 4 miles west of Greenville via exit 130 off I–65, offers plenty of recreation options, including camping and fishing. August visitors can take in the annual Watermelon Jubilee with arts, crafts, food, and fun.

From Greenville, a short drive south takes you to Georgiana and the **Hank Williams, Sr., Boyhood Home and Museum** (334–376–2396). Located at 127 Rose Street, the home contains six rooms filled with walls of family photos, original posters, albums, 78 rpm recordings, a church pew, piano, and 1923 Victrola. Fans from all over the world donated many of the items on display. Draperies, custom made for the musician's Nashville home, feature an overall design of lyrics and music from "Your Cheatin' Heart." Hours are 10:00 A.M. to 5:00 P.M. Monday through Saturday and 1:00 to 5:00 P.M. on Sunday. Modest admission. During the first Friday and Saturday in June, Georgiana hosts an annual Hank Williams Day Celebration with country music concerts, food concessions, and street dances.

Places to Stay in Southeast Alabama

AUBURN/OPELIKA

Auburn University
Hotel and Dixon
Conference Center
241 South College Street
(334) 821–8200 or
(800) 228–2876

Chewacla State Park
124 Shell Toomer Parkway
(334) 887–5621 or
(800) ALA–PARK

Crenshaw House
Bed and Breakfast
371 North College Street
(334) 821–1131 or
(800) 950–1131

The Heritage House Bed
and Breakfast Inn
714 Second Avenue
(334) 705–0485

Hilton Garden Inn
2555 Hilton Garden Drive
(334) 502–3500 or
(800) HILTONS

The Lodge and Conference
Center at Grand National
3700 Sunbelt Parkway
(334) 741–9292 or
(866) 846–4655

DOTHAN

Best Western Dothan Inn & Suites
3285 Montgomery Highway
(334) 793–4376 or
(800) 528–1234

Comfort Inn
3593 Ross Clark Circle
Northwest
(334) 793–9090 or
(800) 474–7298

Courtyard by Marriott
3040 Ross Clark Circle
(334) 671–3000 or
(800) 321–2211

Holiday Inn South
2195 Ross Clark Circle
(334) 794–8711 or
(800) 777–6611

ENTERPRISE

Rawls Hotel
116 South Main Street
(334) 308–9387

EUFAULA

Comfort Suites
12 Paul Lee Parkway
(334) 616–0114

Jameson Inn
136 Towne Center Boulevard
(334) 687–7747 or
(800) 541–3268

Lakepoint Resort
U.S. Highway 431 North
(334) 687–8011 or
(800) 544–LAKE

GREENVILLE

Jameson Inn
71 Jameson Lane
(334) 382–6300 or
(800) 526–3766

MONTGOMERY

Embassy Suites
300 Tallapoosa Street
(334) 269–5055 or
(800) 362–2779

Fairfield Inn
5601 Carmichael Road
(334) 270–0007 or
(800) 228–2800

Holiday Inn East
1185 Eastern Boulevard
(334) 272–0370 or
(800) HOLIDAY

MAINSTREAM ATTRACTIONS WORTH SEEING IN SOUTHEAST ALABAMA

Montgomery Zoo,
2301 Coliseum Parkway,
Montgomery;
(334) 240–4900.
Observe more than 800 animals from five continents in the zoo's naturalistic settings and take a train ride around the park.Relocated from its former home in Opelika and housed next to the zoo, the Mann Museum allows you to get acquainted with bears, wolves, moose, and more mounted specimens of North American wildlife, all presented in realistic settings. The natural history museum's life-size exhibits numbered more than 300 at last count. Both attractions are open from 9:00 A.M. to 5:00 P.M. daily. Admission.

U.S. Army Aviation Museum,
Andrews Avenue and Novosel Street,
Fort Rucker;
(334) 255–3036, (334) 598–2508, or
(888) 276–9286.

This museum is in Fort Rucker, a training base for military helicopter pilots located 5 miles west of Ozark. Covering the complete history of Army Aviation, this complex contains one of the world's largest collections of helicopters. Exhibits include maps and photos of Army Aviation's role in the Louisiana Maneuvers through Operation Desert Storm, a full-scale model of the Wright B Flyer, and unusual pieces such as a Sopwith Camel and a Nieuport 28. You can even walk through a Chinook (CH-47-A) and view today's high-tech Apache combat helicopter. The Army Aviation Museum is free and open to the public from 9:00 A.M. to 4:00 P.M. Monday through Saturday and from noon to 4:00 P.M. on Sunday. Visit the museum's Web site at www.armyavnmuseum.org.

Quality Inn
5175 Carmichael Road
(334) 277–1919

Red Bluff Cottage
551 Clay Street
(334) 264–0056 or
(888) 551–CLAY

Studio Plus
5115 Carmichael Road
(334) 273–0075

Wingate Inn
2060 Eastern Boulevard
(334) 244–7880

PRATTVILLE

The Legends at Capitol Hill
2500 Legends Circle
(888) 250–3767 or
(334) 290–1235

TALLASSEE

Hotel Talisi
14 Sistrunk Avenue
(334) 283–2769

Places to Eat in Southeast Alabama

AUBURN/OPELIKA

Auburn City Limits
2450 State Route 14 West
(334) 821–3330

Hamilton's
174 East Magnolia Avenue
(334) 887–8780

The Lodge and Conference Center at Grand National
3700 Sunbelt Parkway
(334) 741–9292

Mellow Mushroom
128 North College Street
(334) 887–6356

Warehouse Bistro
105 Rocket Avenue
(334) 745–6353

DOTHAN

Garland House
200 North Bell Street
(334) 793–2043

Hunt's Steak, Seafood, and Oyster Bar
177 Campbellton Highway
(334) 794–5193

Old Mexico
2920 Ross Clark Circle
(334) 712–1434

The Old Mill Restaurant
2557 Murphy Mill Road
(334) 794–8530

ENTERPRISE

Carlisle's on Main
401 South Main Street
(334) 347–8108

Cutt's
417 East Lee
(334) 347–1110

Rawls Hotel
116 South Main Street
(334) 308–9387

EUFAULA

Airport Restaurant
1720 North Eufaula Avenue
(334) 687–3132

Cajun Corner
114 North Eufaula Avenue
(334) 616–0816

Chewalla
1015 Cotton Avenue
(334) 687–8858

Dakota Coffee
101 North Eufaula Avenue
(334) 688–0330

Lakepoint Resort
104 Lake Point Drive
(334) 687–8011

Old Mexico
114 North Eufaula Avenue
(334) 687–7770

GRADY

Red's Little School House
20 Gardner Road
(334) 584–7955

GREENVILLE

Bates' House of Turkey
1001 Fort Dale Road
(334) 382–6123

LOWNDESBORO

Marengo
100 North Broad Street
(334) 278–4442 or
(334) 272–8508

MILLBROOK

Fantail Restaurant
2060 Downing
(334) 285–7255

Miss Mary's Restaurant
3580 Main Street
(334) 285–1466

Smokehouse Barbecue
2461 Main Street
(334) 285–0006

MONTGOMERY

Dawson's at Rose Hill
11250 U.S. Highway 80 East
(334) 215–7620

Gracie's English Tearoom
1734 Mulberry Street
(334) 240–2444

**Jimmy's Uptown Grille &
Backdoor Bistro**
540 Clay Street
(334) 265–8187

Lek's Railroad Thai
Union Station,
300 B Water Street
(334) 269–0708

Leslie Bailey's Silver Spoon
222 North McDonough
Street
(334) 264–1116

Martha's Place
458 Sayre Street
(334) 263–9135

**Montgomery Brewing
Company**
12 West Jefferson Street
(334) 834–BREW

Sahara Restaurant, Inc.
511 East Edgemont Avenue
(334) 262–1215

FOR MORE INFORMATION ABOUT SOUTHEAST ALABAMA

**Auburn/Opelika Convention &
Visitors Bureau**
714 East Glenn Avenue
Auburn 36831-2216
(334) 887–8747 or (866) 880–8747
Web site: www.aocvb.com
e-mail: elbridges@aocvb.com

**Dothan Area Convention &
Visitors Bureau**
3311 Ross Clark Circle Northwest
P.O. Box 8765
Dothan 36304
(334) 794–6622 or (888) 449–0212
Web site: www.dothanalcvb.com
e-mail: dothancvb@mail.ala.net

Enterprise Chamber of Commerce
553 Glover Avenue
P. O. Box 310577
Enterprise 36331-0577
(334) 347–0581 or (800) 235–4730
Web site: www.enterprisealabama.com
e-mail: chamber@entercomp.com

**Eufaula/Barbour County
Chamber of Commerce**
333 East Broad Street
P.O. Box 697
Eufaula 36072
(334) 687–6664 or (800) 524–7529
Web site: www.eufaula-barbourchamber
.com
e-mail: ebcchamber@bellsouth.net

Historic Chattahoochee Commission
P.O. Box 33
Eufaula 36072-0033
(334) 687–9755
Web site: www.hcc-al-ga.org
e-mail: hcc@alalinc.net

**Montgomery Convention &
Visitors Bureau**
300 Water Street
P.O. Box 79
Montgomery 36101
(334) 261–1100
Web site: www.visitingmontgomery.com
e-mail: tourism@montgomery
chamber.com

**Tuskegee Area Chamber of
Commerce**
121 South Main Street
Tuskegee 36083
(334) 727–6619
Web site:
www.tuskegeeareachamber.com
e-mail: tachwa@earthlink.net

Sinclair's
1051 East Fairview Avenue
(334) 834–7462

Vintage Year, Inc.
405 Cloverdale Road
(334) 264–8463

PRATTVILLE

The Guest House
209 Doster Street
(334) 365–7532
(reservations only)

The Legends at
Capitol Hill
2500 Legends Circle
(334) 290–1235 or
(888) 250–3767

SHORTER

Back Forty
5001 County Road 30
(334) 727–0880

TALLASSEE

Hotel Talisi Restaurant
14 Sistrunk Avenue
(334) 283–2769

TROY

Mossy Grove School
House Restaurant
1902 Elba Highway
(334) 566–4921

WETUMPKA

Our Place Café
809 Company Street
(334) 567–8778

Southwest Alabama

Black Belt

Alabama's Black Belt, so called because of a strip of dark, rich soil that stretches across part of the state's south-central section, covers 4,300 square miles. This fertile farmland became the setting for a host of plantations prior to the Civil War, and you'll see many antebellum structures throughout the area. From **Selma,** which retains a lingering flavor of the Old South's cotton-rich aristocratic past, you can easily make a loop of several small Black Belt towns with their treasure troves of architecture. Situated on a bluff above the Alabama River, Selma served as a major munitions depot, making battleships as well as cannonballs, rifles, and ammunition for the Confederate cause.

Soon after arriving in Selma, make a point to stop by the ***Crossroads Visitor Information Center*** (334–875–7485), conveniently located at 2207 Broad Street. Between George "Cap" Swift and his back-up volunteer, Allen Gaston, you can count on getting your local questions answered and collect plenty of literature on city and area attractions. The facility houses a Book Nook with publications by Alabama authors, a variety of gift items, driving-tour brochures, and more. Hours run from 8:00 A.M. to 8:00 P.M. daily.

SOUTHWEST ALABAMA

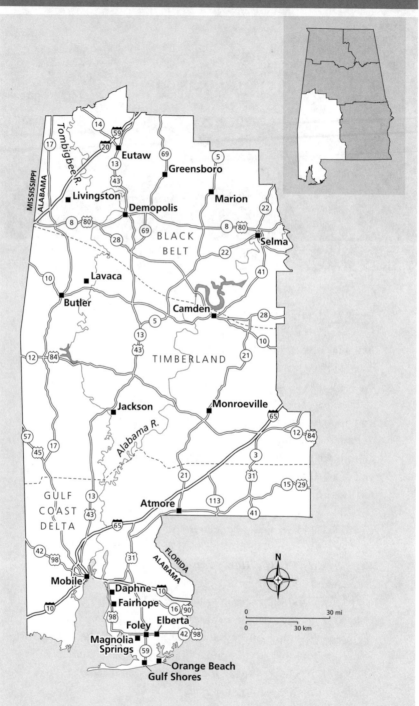

MISSISSIPPI
ALABAMA

Tombigbee R.

14
59
20
17
Eutaw
13
69
Greensboro
5
43
Livingston
Demopolis
Marion
22
8 80
8 80
28
BLACK
69
BELT
Selma
22
41
10
Lavaca
5
Butler
13
Camden
28
12 84
43
10
TIMBERLAND
21
Jackson
Monroeville
65
57
12 84
45 17
3
21
31
GULF
COAST
15 29
DELTA
13
Atmore
113
43
41
65

FLORIDA
ALABAMA

42
31
98
Mobile
Daphne
10
10
Fairhope
16 90
98
Foley
Elberta
42 98
Magnolia
Springs
59
Orange Beach
Gulf Shores

Alabama R.

N

0   30 mi
0   30 km

U.S. Highway 80 west from Montgomery to Selma leads across the *Edmund Pettus Bridge,* a landmark that figured prominently in the civil rights struggle. In 1965 marchers followed Martin Luther King Jr. across this bridge on their trek to Montgomery during voting-rights demonstrations.

Located near the bridge, the *National Voting Rights Museum* (334–418–0800) at 1012 Water Avenue presents a visual history of the Selma-to-Montgomery march and related events. Upon entering, viewers see themselves reflected in a mirrored "I Was There" wall with a display of cards recording first-hand observations by individuals. A series of rooms focus on reconstruction, suffrage, and other aspects of the voting-rights struggle. A large window, etched with the names Andrew Young, Martin Luther King Jr., Thurgood Marshall, Dick Gregory, and other museum Hall of Fame inductees, provides a fitting vantage point for viewing the historic Pettus Bridge. Hours are 9:00 A.M. to 5:00 P.M. Tuesday through Friday, 10:00 A.M. to 3:00 P.M. Saturday, and Sunday by appointment. Admission.

Take time to stroll along historic Water Avenue, a restored nineteenth-century riverfront warehouse district with brick streets, arcades, and parks overlooking the river. Nearby, at 1124 Water Avenue, you'll find a mini-mall with an eatery and several interesting shops.

Settle into a room at the newly restored *St. James Hotel* (334–872–3234) and map out your Selma itinerary. One of the country's few remaining antebellum riverfront hotels, the St. James occupies a corner at 1200 Water Avenue. Lacy iron grillwork traces the balconies of the camel-colored structure, which surrounds a courtyard with fountain. The original 1837 hotel served passengers from paddle wheelers and steamboats that plied the Alabama River and also

GAY'S TOP PICKS IN SOUTHWEST ALABAMA

Battleship U.S.S. *Alabama,*
Mobile Bay

Bellingrath Gardens and Home,
Theodore

Fort Morgan,
Mobile Bay

Gulf Coast beaches

Mobile's historic districts

Mobile Museum of Art,
Mobile

Old Cahawba Archaeological Park,
Cahaba

Town of Demopolis

Town of Fairhope

Town of Marion

Town of Selma

those from the nearby railroad station. Jesse and Frank James (under assumed names) once stayed at the St. James.

Many of the rooms' balconies overlook the historic Edmund Pettus Bridge. Furnished with antebellum and Victorian pieces, the hotel boasts a ballroom; elegant guest rooms and suites; a Drinking Room with handsome, marble-topped mahogany bar; and a white-tablecloth dining room. Moderate.

At the **Bridgetenders House** (2 Lafayette Park, off Washington Street; 334–875–5517), a cottage that dates to 1884, you can sit on the porch in the shadow of the Edmund Pettus Bridge, sip cider, and contemplate Selma's history. Television camera crews stationed themselves here, plugging into the house's electrical outlets while reporting on the Selma-to-Montgomery march.

To welcome travelers, owners Kathi and George Needham offer two guest suites with kitchens, bedrooms, and sitting rooms and provide a continental breakfast with plenty of snacks and goodies plus a selection of historic photos, periodicals, and background materials as a frame of reference for this unique site. You can e-mail the property at Bridgtendr@aol.com. Rates are standard.

During your waterfront excursion, saunter into **Major Grumbles** (334–872–2006), a restaurant named for a local character in Selma's storybook of history. You'll find this eatery at 1 Grumbles Alley, a few steps from the Bridgetenders House. Be sure to notice the restaurant's two original black iron gates (believed to be slave doors) that weigh about 400 pounds each. And don't get the wrong idea from the century-old skeleton, attired in a Confederate uniform, seated on the stair landing—starving is not something you have to worry about here.

Everything served here, including the bread for sandwiches and the dressings for salads, is made from scratch. Some customers claim Major Grumbles serves the best Reuben sandwiches they ever ate. You might instead opt for the restaurant's justly famous marinated chicken-breast sandwich or hearty red bean and rice soup. Dinner entrees include such items as baked shrimp stuffed with crabmeat dressing and a variety of steak cuts. Economical to moderate prices. Restaurant hours are 11:00 A.M. to 3:00 P.M. on Monday and 11:00 A.M. to 10:00 P.M. Tuesday through Saturday.

To dip into more of the city's interesting history, stop by the handsome **Old Depot Museum** (334–874–2197), located on the corner of Martin Luther King Street and Water Avenue. Built in 1891 by the Louisville and Nashville Railroad, this arched and turreted two-story redbrick structure stands on the site of the Confederate Naval Foundry, which Union troops destroyed during the Battle of Selma in 1865. The museum houses everything from a 1908 portrait camera used by psychic Edgar Cayce (who once lived in Selma and operated a photography studio here) to Victorian hair combs, plantation records, quilts, Confederate bills, cannonballs, early medical equipment, and antique tools.

GAY'S FAVORITE ANNUAL EVENTS IN SOUTHWEST ALABAMA

Mardi Gras,
Mobile, February;
(800) 5MOBILE

Arts & Crafts Festival,
Fairhope, March;
(251) 621–8222

Azalea Trail Run and Festival,
Mobile, March;
(800) 5MOBILE

Festival of Flowers,
Mobile, March;
(877) 777–0529 or (800) 5MOBILE

Historic Selma Pilgrimage,
Selma, March;
(800) 45–SELMA

The Original German Sausage Festival,
Elberta, last Saturday in March
and October;
(251) 986–5805

Crawfish Festival,
Faunsdale, Second weekend in April;
(334) 628–3240

Blessing of the Fleet,
Bayou La Batre, May;
(251) 824–2415

To Kill a Mockingbird,
Monroeville, first three weekends in May;
(251) 575–7433

Alabama Deep Sea Fishing Rodeo,
Dauphin Island, July;
(800) 5MOBILE

Alabama Tale Tellin' Festival,
Selma, second weekend in October;
(800) 45–SELMA

Bayfest Music Festival,
Mobile, first weekend in October;
(251) 470–7730

Fishing Rodeo,
Orange Beach, October;
(251) 974–1510

National Shrimp Festival,
Gulf Shores, October;
(251) 968–6904 or (800) 745–SAND

Riverfront Market,
Selma, second Saturday of October;
(800) 45SELMA

Frank Brown International Songwriters Festival,
Gulf Shores, November;
www.fbisf.com

Pow Wow,
Atmore, November;
(251) 368–9136

Heritage Harbor Days,
Foley, November;
(251) 943–1200

Magic Christmas in Lights,
Bellingrath Gardens & Home,
late November through December;
(251) 973–2217

Christmas on the River,
Demopolis, December;
(334) 289–0270

In the Black Heritage Wing, you'll see sculpture by Earl Hopkins, nationally recognized for his wood carvings and leather crafts. Hopkins, who uses exotic woods in his creations, worked at Colonial Williamsburg before retiring to his native Selma. A not-to-be-missed rare display of photographs, made between 1895 and 1905 by Selmian Mary Morgan Keipp, depicts daily life on a Black Belt plantation. Curator Jean Martin calls this wonderful series "one of the finest and most complete collections of photos covering that period in history."

Behind the museum you'll see a Firehouse Museum plus a boxcar, caboose, and old farm equipment. Monday through Saturday the museum is open from 10:00 A.M. to 4:00 P.M. or by appointment. Modest admission.

Nearby at 410 Martin Luther King Street, stands **Brown Chapel African Methodist Episcopal Church,** another significant structure in Selma's history. This 1908 Byzantine-style building served as headquarters for the civil rights activists who played a pivotal role in bringing about the passage of the National Voting Rights Act during the turbulent decade of the 1960s. Visitors may take a self-guided walking tour of the surrounding historic area.

Sometime during your local tour, be sure to stop at 109 Union Street to tour the white-columned, three-story, brick **Joseph T. Smitherman Historic Building** (334–874–2174), named in honor of Selma's former mayor, who played an active role in historic preservation. Crowning Alabama Avenue, this impressive building opened its doors in 1848 as the Central Masonic Institute and later served as a hospital for wounded Confederates (escaping the fate of many Selma buildings when Union general John Harrison Wilson's raiders, disobeying orders, embarked on a wholesale campaign of wanton destruction in April 1865). The building later served as a courthouse, military school, and private hospital. Inside you'll see a large collection of Civil War relics, Confederate money, medical artifacts, and period furnishings from the mid-1800s. Hours are 9:00 A.M. to 4:00 P.M. Tuesday through Saturday or by appointment. Modest admission.

On a drive through the Old Town Historic District, you'll see block after block of antebellum and Victorian architecture. The **Historic Selma Pilgrimage** provides visitors with opportunities to tour many of the city's outstanding homes each spring (see http://pilgrimage.selmaalabama.com for more information). A reenactment of the Battle of Selma is another popular springtime event.

For a memento of your visit, consider purchasing a cookbook called *Tastes of Olde Selma,* available in several places throughout the city. Compiled by Selma's Olde Towne Association, the book contains line drawings and brief histories of many of the town's significant structures along with a selection of wonderful recipes. The front cover features a color illustration of **Sturdivant Hall** (334–872–5626), a Neoclassical mansion located at 713 Mabry Street. Designed by Thomas Helm Lee (Robert E. Lee's cousin), this magnificent home that took three years to build boasts elaborate ceilings and decorative moldings with a motif of intertwined grape leaves and vines. You'll also see a spiral staircase, marble mantels, and servant pulls—each with a different tone. Other treasures include period furnishings, portraits, silver, crystal, china, and a rare French-made George Washington commemorative clock of ormolu and gold—one of only seven in existence.

Coral vines climb the home's back walls, and mock lemons perfume the air. You may be presented with a sprig or cutting of lavender, mint, or sage from the mansion's herb garden outside the backyard kitchen. The home's formal gardens, which feature a variety of native flowers, shrubs, and trees, serve as a lovely backdrop for the pilgrimage's annual grand ball. Except for major holidays, Sunday, and Monday, Sturdivant Hall is open from 10:00 A.M. to 4:00 P.M. Admission.

By the way, some Selmians say the ghost of John McGee Parkman, one of Sturdivant Hall's former owners, roams the mansion. You may or may not see house ghosts here, but you can certainly find several in Sturdivant Hall's gift shop—sandwiched between the covers of some of Kathryn Tucker Windham's books, such as *13 Alabama Ghosts and Jeffrey* or *Jeffrey's Latest 13.* For a souvenir or gift, you might like to buy *Alabama—One Big Front Porch,* an engrossing collection of stories compiled by Mrs. Windham. To hear her in person—along with other famous Southern storytellers—plan your visit to coincide with the **Alabama Tale Tellin' Festival,** an annual fall event staged in Selma. (In

alabamatrivia

Currency issued in Louisiana before the Civil War ($10 notes bearing the word *dix,* French for the number ten) led to the South being called "Dixie Land" and gave Alabama her nickname, "Heart of Dixie."

great demand as a speaker, Alabama's famous First Lady of Folk Tales and Ghost Stories travels frequently, so if you see someone behind the wheel of a Dodge Spirit with a license plate that reads JEFFREY, be sure to wave.)

Driving along Dallas Avenue (which becomes State Route 22), you'll pass the **Old Live Oak Cemetery,** filled with ancient trees festooned by Spanish moss. During spring, dogwoods and azaleas make this site even more spectacular. A number of Confederate graves and unique monuments may be seen here, including the mausoleum of William Rufus King, who named Selma and planned its layout. King, on the Democratic ticket with Franklin Pierce, died shortly after being elected vice president of the United States.

For dinner strike out for the **Tally-Ho Restaurant** (334–872–1390), located at 507 Mangum Avenue, just off Summerfield Road in the northern section of town. Owner Bob Kelley's entrees run the gamut from seafood and chicken to London broil and prime rib au jus. A blackboard features daily specials, which might include grilled pork chops with rosemary sauce. (The rosemary, thyme, and other herbs used in several dishes come from the restaurant's herb garden on the grounds.) Homemade zucchini muffins accompany entrees. For dessert try the chocolate cheesecake or amaretto soufflé. The restaurant's hours are 5:00 to 10:00 P.M. Monday through Saturday. Prices are moderate.

During your Selma visit, swing southwest about 9 miles on State Route 22 toward **Cahaba** (Cahawba is the historical spelling). Watch for a sign that says TO CAHABA, then turn left and travel 3½ miles. When you reach a dead end, turn left again and continue 3 miles to **Old Cahawba Archaeological Park** (334–872–8058), the site of Alabama's first permanent state capital. Here, near the place where the Cahaba and Alabama Rivers merge, once stood a thriving town. Today's visitors will have to use some imagination to visualize the remaining ruins as grand mansions that surrounded a copper-domed capitol, completed in 1820. A large stone monument and interpretive signs in conjunction with old street markers, brick columns, cemeteries, and domestic plants growing wild offer the few clues that this off-the-beaten-path spot once flourished as a political, commercial, and cultural center. You'll also see an artesian well (where watercress grows), the source of water for the elaborate gardens surrounding the Perine family mansion, which once stood nearby.

The visitor and education centers provide information on Cahaba's glory days. In 1825 legislators voted to move Alabama's capital to Tuscaloosa. While local lore holds that frequent flooding caused Cahaba to lose its position as the state's seat of government, evidence suggests that sectional politics probably played a larger role. Gradually Cahaba became a ghost town, and by 1900 most of its buildings had disappeared. The park offers a handicapped accessible nature trail. Except for major holidays, the park is open daily from 9:00 A.M. to 5:00 P.M. Admission is free.

Afterward follow US 80 west from Selma until you reach Dallas County Road 45; then turn north to **Marion,** one of Alabama's oldest towns and a leading cultural center for planter society. The city is home to both Judson College and Marion Military Institute. The latter's chapel, Old South Hall, and Lovelace House on campus served as hospitals during the Civil War. The graves of more than a hundred Southern and Union soldiers were later relocated from campus to Confederate Rest, a cemetery behind St. Wilfrid's Episcopal Church. The Old Marion City Hall (moved to MMI's campus from the downtown square) houses the Alabama Military Hall of Honor. For an appointment to see the exhibits, call (334) 683–2346.

Downtown you'll see several historical churches and the handsome Perry County Courthouse dating from the early 1850s. Be sure to drive down Green Street, the setting for a number of antebellum residences, including the Lea-Griffith Home (circa 1830), where Texas hero Sam Houston married Margaret Lea (their marriage license is recorded in the courthouse). With some 200 sites (in a wide variety of architectural styles) listed on the National Register of Historic Places, Marion promises plenty to see.

During your Marion excursion take a stroll across the Judson College campus and stop by the *Alabama Women's Hall of Fame,* which occupies the first floor of Bean Hall. Formerly the school's library, this Carnegie-built structure stands on the corner of Bibb and East Lafayette Streets. Bronze plaques pay tribute to Helen Keller, Julia Tutwiler, Lurleen Burns Wallace, Tallulah Bankhead, Zelda Sayre Fitzgerald, her daughter Frances Scott Fitzgerald Smith, and many other women of achievement with Alabama connections. Former first ladies Barbara Bush and Rosalynn Carter have spoken at past induction ceremonies. Except for major holidays, hours are 8:00 A.M. to 5:00 P.M. Monday through Friday. For a tour call (334) 683–5184. Admission is free.

At 303 and 305 West Lafayette Street, you'll find *Myrtle Hill* (334–683–9095), which consists of neighboring antebellum homes surrounded by twelve acres of Victorian gardens. Elegantly furnished with period antiques, the homes offer spacious accommodations for bed-and-breakfast guests and the option of a Continental or plantation breakfast. Owners Wanda and Gerald Lewis sometimes treat guests to ghost-story and folk-tale sessions. Moderate rates.

The Gateway Inn (334–683–2582), located at 1615 State Route 5 South, offers a hearty noon buffet or sandwiches (available for take-out) Monday through Friday from 11:45 A.M. to 1:30 P.M. The restaurant also opens for dinner from 5:00 to 10:00 P.M. Friday and Saturday. Save room for the luscious homemade lemon icebox pie. Prices are economical to moderate.

Marion's early-twentieth-century train depot serves as a visitor center complete with walking trail along the former railroad tracks. For more information on Marion, call the chamber of commerce at (334) 683–9622 or stop by 1200 Washington Street.

After exploring Marion follow State Route 14 west to Alabama's Catfish Capital, *Greensboro.* Because this Black Belt town managed to escape the Civil War's ravages, a large number of its antebellum homes and churches have been preserved. In fact the entire downtown district, featuring some 150 nineteenth-century structures, is on the National Register of Historic Places. More than sixty of the town's homes predate the Civil War. Be sure to drive along Main, Tuscaloosa, and South Streets, all of which offer interesting architecture. At Market and South Streets, you'll see the Noel-Ramsey House. Built between 1819 and 1821, this is the only remaining residence of French settlers from nearby Demopolis's Vine and Olive Colony (see page 147).

Don't miss *Magnolia Grove* (334–624–8618), a two-story Greek Revival house built around 1840 by a wealthy cotton planter, Col. Isaac Croom. Located at 1002 Hobson Street, the home stands among lovely magnolia trees and landscaped gardens on a twelve-acre setting. Magnolia Grove was also the home of Croom's nephew, Rear Adm. Richmond Pearson Hobson, recently inducted into the Alabama Men's Hall of Fame. A naval hero in the Spanish-American War,

Hobson later served in Congress and introduced legislation (the Hobson Amendment) that became the basis for the Constitution's prohibition amendment. My guide explained that this amendment, generally understood to refer only to alcohol, was also directed at drug control because, prior to aspirin's advent, the use of potent pain relievers such as morphine and opium commonly led to addiction. The Museum Room contains memorabilia from Hobson's military and political careers.

The house also features family portraits, heirlooms, and furnishings from the 1830s to the early 1900s. You'll see an 1866 piano, a Persian rug from the late 1800s, a chaperon's bench, and antique quilts. Outbuildings include a kitchen, slave cottage, and a structure that probably served as a classroom or library and office. Modest admission. Hours are 10:00 A.M. to 4:00 P.M. Tuesday through Saturday. The grounds may be visited from noon to 4:00 P.M. on Sunday.

From Greensboro head south on State Route 25 toward *Faunsdale*—population ninety-eight. Housed in an 1890s mercantile building on the town's main street, *Ca-John's Faunsdale Bar & Grill* (334–628–3240) serves great steaks and seafood, and owner John (Ca-John) Broussard, originally from Louisiana, offers a variety of crawfish specialties in season. The food speaks for itself, attracting diners from distant towns. Windows sport red-and-white checkered cafe curtains. A pot-bellied stove and fireplace add to the ambience. Saturday night patrons can enjoy live music until the wee hours. Hours are 5:00 to 10:00 P.M. Thursday and Friday and 11:00 A.M. to 11:00 P.M. on Saturday. From Faunsdale return to US 80 and head west toward Demopolis.

alabamatrivia

An immense 1833 meteor shower inspired the song, "Stars Fell on Alabama."

Sometime during your visit to the area, make an outing to *Prairieville,* the site of *St. Andrews Episcopal Church.* Located a short distance off US 80, this red Carpenter Gothic structure dates from 1853 and is a National Historic Landmark. Nearby you'll see a picturesque old cemetery, where many of this area's early settlers are buried.

Peter Lee and Joe Glasgow, master carpenters and slaves of Capt. Henry A. Tayloe, supervised a crew of slaves belonging to church members in the construction of this edifice, built to serve settlers from the Atlantic seaboard.

Craftspeople created the mellowed appearance of interior wood walls by applying a brew made from the stems of tobacco plants. Pokeberry weeds provided color for some portions of the lovely stained-glass windows. Ragweed, chewed and molded, forms the decorative relief letters of a biblical quotation near the altar. Be sure to notice the pipe organ (which still plays) and the choir

St. Andrews Episcopal Church

gallery. Closed as a regular parish in 1927, the church hosts a special service the first Sunday in October followed by a picnic dinner on the grounds. Group tours can be arranged by appointment; call (334) 289–3363.

Traveling 9 miles west on US 80 takes you to **Gaineswood** (334–289–4846), a gorgeous cream-colored mansion with white-columned porticos. Once the centerpiece of a huge plantation, the home now stands in the suburbs of the town of **Demopolis** at 805 South Cedar Avenue. Gen. Nathan Bryan Whitfield, a gifted inventor, musician, artist, and architect, started construction on the house in 1843. He spent almost two decades planning and building this elegant Greek Revival home and continued to refine it until the Civil War's outbreak.

Stepping into the columned ballroom, you'll see yourself reflected thirteen times in the vis-à-vis mirrors. Be sure to notice the glass-ceiling domes and the elaborate friezes and medallions. The home contains its original furnishings, family portraits, and accessories. Don't miss the flutina (invented by Whitfield), a one-of-a-kind musical instrument that sounds something like a riverboat calliope.

In many ways Gaineswood reminded me of Thomas Jefferson's splendid Monticello, and my guide said visitors often make that observation. Except for major holidays, Gaineswood is open Tuesday through Saturday from 9:00 A.M. to 4:00 P.M. Tours are on the hour with other times by appointment. Admission.

Continue to downtown Demopolis, "the City of the People," a town with an interesting origin that goes back to 1817 when 400 aristocrats, fleeing France after Napoleon's exile, landed here at the white limestone bluffs overlooking the Tombigbee River. They acquired a large tract of land along the river and set about establishing the **Vine and Olive Colony**. The agricultural experiment, however, yielded little more than frustration for the colonists, who lacked essential farming skills and found the local climate and soil unsuitable for cultivating their imported grape vines and olive trees.

You'll see a display on this early colony in the French Room at **Bluff Hall** (334–289–9644). Located at 407 North Commissioners Avenue next to the Civic Center, this 1832 brick home takes its name from its position overlooking the Tombigbee River. Originally built in the Federal style, the home took on a Greek Revival appearance after later additions. Furnishings are Empire and mid-Victorian.

As you start upstairs notice the newel post's amity button, symbolizing a state of harmony between the owner and builder. In addition to documents, crystal, silver spoons, cannonballs, portraits, and other memorabilia of the Vine and Olive Colony, you'll see a room filled with period costumes, such as an 1831 wedding dress. Bluff Hall is noted for its extensive collection of vintage clothing.

The kitchen's interesting gadgets range from an egg tin, sausage stuffer, and fluting iron to the "humane" rat trap on the hearth. Adjacent to the home, the Canebrake Craft Corner offers a choice selection of items including posters depicting a European artist's imaginative conception of the early Vine and Olive Colony, handmade split-oak baskets, and eye-catching pottery by Susan Brown Freeman. Bluff Hall is owned and operated by the Marengo County Historical Society. (The county's name was inspired by Napoleon's victory at the Battle of Marengo in northern Italy.) Except for major holidays, Bluff Hall is open Tuesday through Saturday from 10:00 A.M. to 5:00 P.M. and on Sunday from 2:00 to 5:00 P.M. During January and February, the home closes at 4:00 P.M. Admission.

Dip into more history at **Laird Cottage** (334–289–0282), which also houses the Geneva Mercer Museum and the Marengo County Historical Society headquarters. Located at 311 North Walnut, the circa-1870 home reflects a Greek Revival–Italianate style of architecture. Here you'll see works by Mercer, a gifted Marengo County artist and sculptor, who studied and worked with Giuseppe Moretti, the Italian sculptor who designed Birmingham's statue of Vulcan. Call for hours or an appointment. Admission is free.

While sightseeing stop by the Demopolis yacht basin on US 43 for a meal at **New Orleans Bar & Grill** (334–289–2668). If you sit near a window, you can still see a portion of the white chalk bluffs where the French Bonapartists landed. (This landmark is less prominent since the Demopolis Lock and Dam raised the river level by 40 feet in 1954.)

Here you can meet and eat with "the boat people," members of the city's maritime community who live aboard their yachts and play active roles in the town's civic and social life. The restaurant serves a variety of sandwiches, salads, and dinner entrees. Try the steak salad. Hours are 11:00 A.M. till 10:00 P.M.

Monday through Saturday. Prices are moderate. When you leave, take along some bread to feed the fish and turtles that congregate below the boardwalk—they expect it.

Demopolis offers more than mansions and water recreation. You'll find plenty of interesting places to shop, too. Downtown, at 109 West Washington Street, The Mustard Seed offers fine gifts, china, crystal, housewares, collectibles, dolls, and toys. Maison de Briques, a flower and gift shop at 102 US 80 East, stocks a variety of decorative items.

Local festivals include a July the Fourth celebration, Freedom on the River at City Landing, and December's *Christmas on the River,* which features a weeklong festival of parades, tours, and events culminating in an extravaganza of decorated, lighted boats gliding down the Tombigbee River. For more information on these or other special events, including productions by the Canebrake Players (a local theater group) or on other area attractions, call (334) 289–0270.

Traveling north takes you to *Eutaw,* a charming hamlet situated around a courthouse square that dates from 1838. The town boasts fifty-three antebellum structures, with many on the National Register of Historic Places. Head first to the visitor information center, located in the Vaughn-Morrow House at 310 Main Street, where you'll find information on both Eutaw and Greene County. If the museum is not open, look for a telephone contact number posted on the porch.

Beside the visitor center stands the First Presbyterian Church. Organized in 1824 as Mesopotamia Presbyterian Church, the congregation's current home dates from 1851. This white-steepled structure looks as if it belongs on a Christmas card (without the snow, of course—a rare commodity in most of Alabama). Original whale-oil lamps, stored for a time in the slave gallery, have been wired for electricity and again grace the church's interior. For a tour, inquire at the church office in the adjacent Educational Building.

Nearby, on the corner of Main Street and Eutaw Avenue, stands St. Stephen's Episcopal Church. The handsome brick structure features a hand-carved lectern, an elegant white marble baptismal font, and beautiful stained-glass windows. To see the lovely interior, check with the church office.

Don't miss *Kirkwood Mansion* (205–372–2694) at the intersection of State Route 14 and Kirkwood Drive. Topped by a belvedere, this impressive 1860 American Greek Revival home features eight massive Ionic columns, Carrara marble mantels, and Waterford crystal chandeliers. Owners Danky and Al Blanton have furnished the home with museum-quality antiques. Built by Foster Mark Kirksey, the mansion was on the verge of completion when the Civil War brought construction to a halt. After a century of neglect, the house was rescued by Mary and Roy Swayze, who moved here from Virginia and set about transforming Kirkwood. In 1982 Nancy Reagan, on behalf of the National Trust

Kirkwood Mansion

for Historic Preservation, presented the Swayzes with the National Honor Award in recognition of their outstanding restoration. Call for a mansion tour between the hours of 9:00 A.M. and 5:00 P.M. Monday through Saturday and 1:00 to 5:00 P.M. Sunday. Admission.

Overnight visitors can make reservations at **Oakmont Bed & Breakfast** (205–372–2326), owned by Deborah and Scott Stone. Situated on a grassy knoll at 119 Pickens Street and framed by wisteria, azaleas, camellias, and magnolias, Oakmont stands three stories tall with a widow's walk roof railing. Deborah said she had never heard of Eutaw (population 2,000) until a few years ago. Returning home to Madison, Mississippi, after a visit to Atlanta, she exited the interstate on a whim when her mother noticed a small Historic Homes sign. After discovering a lovely columned Greek Revival home for sale, Deborah called her husband, and the couple soon became the new owners. They completed a restoration of the circa-1908 home and in January 2002 opened it for bed-and-breakfast guests.

Deborah serves as the Greene County Historic Society's president and spearheads the annual Eutaw Pilgrimage, an October event that showcases the town's architectural treasures. She shares insider tips on what to see and do in Eutaw and the surrounding area. Guests can anticipate a Southern gourmet breakfast that starts with fresh fruits and juice as a prelude to bacon, cheese-topped baked tomatoes, and French toast with pecans or an equally enticing menu. Standard rates. Preview the property at www.oakmont.biz.

After exploring Eutaw head west to **Gainesville,** a delightful piece of the past populated by 307 people. Most places like this charming town have vanished from today's landscape. Here you'll see historic cemeteries and churches like the First Presbyterian Church, which dates from 1837 and has been rescued from flames on three occasions—once with a hand-to-hand bucket brigade. Interior features include whale-oil lamps, box pews, the altar's original chairs, and a bell with a tone enhanced by 500 melted silver dollars. Because several denominations share this church (one per Sunday), attendees label themselves "Metho-bap-terians." Other sites of interest include the 1872 Methodist Church; St. Alban's Episcopal Church, founded in 1879; and the Confederate Cemetery. For more local information stop by one of the downtown stores.

Afterward continue south to nearby *Livingston.* The town was named for Edward Livingston, who served as Andrew Jackson's secretary of state.

On your way into town, stop by Sumter County's *Alamuchee Covered Bridge,* across from the Baptist Student Union on the campus of Livingston State University. Capt. W.A.C. Jones of Livingston designed and built this 1861 structure, one of the South's oldest covered bridges. Made of hand-hewn heart pine held together by large wooden pegs, the bridge originally spanned the Sucarnochee River, south of town. In 1924 the bridge was taken down and reconstructed across a creek on the old Bellamy-Livingston Road, where it remained in use until 1958. The bridge was moved to its present location and restored in 1971. You might enjoy seeing more of the campus, which also boasts two lakes.

Downtown you'll see a lovely square surrounding the impressive domed Sumter County Courthouse (circa 1900). This area remained Choctaw country until 1830, when the United States acquired it in the Treaty of Dancing Rabbit Creek.

Local businesswomen Mary Tartt, Molly Dorman, and Louise Boyd find that *The Dancing Rabbit* (205–652–6252) is a good name for their shop near the courthouse square. Located at 307 Monroe Street, the charming store features silver, crystal, antique linens, wicker items, china, Christmas ornaments, and other collectibles along with a variety of rabbits (but not the real live kind). Hours are 10:00 A.M. to 5:30 P.M. Tuesday through Friday and 10:00 A.M. to 4:00 P.M. Saturday.

Head to *York,* about 11 miles southwest of Livingston. In this small town near the Mississippi border, you'll find a wonderful art museum inside *The Coleman Center* (205–392–2005 or 205–392–2004), at 630 Avenue A. The museum, a library, genealogical room, and a cultural center occupy an early-twentieth-century general store. On an exterior wall of the building, a repainted vintage ad shows silent film star Clara Bow promoting an early brand of gasoline. You'll enter The Coleman Center through a courtyard on the opposite side.

Director Kaye Kiker, an artist specializing in stained glass, describes the four-building complex as a community effort and the only facility of its kind in Sumter County. Local citizens contributed the land, building, services, and funds for the center. Tut Altman Riddick (who grew up in York but now lives in

Mobile) and her husband, Harry, were early promoters of this project, and their outstanding contemporary art collection may be seen at the museum. In addition to its permanent collection, which includes an original etching by Renoir, prints, paintings, pottery, and other items, the museum features traveling exhibits. The facility closes each day from noon to 1:00 P.M. and also on Thursday and Saturday afternoons. Otherwise, hours are 9:00 A.M. to 4:30 P.M. or by appointment. The museum closes on Sunday. Admission is free.

Timberland

Timber is big business in this part of the state, and hunting and fishing are popular pastimes. If you're in the mood for a feast, head for **Ezell's Fish Camp** (205–654–2205) near **Lavaca.** This out-of-the-way restaurant is definitely worth adding some extra miles to your trip. In fact, some customers fly in, and an Ezell's staffer meets them at the airport. The restaurant also gets a lot of river traffic and often provides transportation into town for boating customers who need motel lodging.

To reach the restaurant from Lavaca, take State Route 10 east toward Nanafalia and turn left just before reaching the big bridge. Located on the west bank of the Tombigbee River, this family operation is the granddaddy of "catfish cabins" you might see while driving through the state. Following family precedent, each of the Ezells' three children went into the restaurant business.

As you arrive, you'll see a large rustic structure with a roof of wooden shingles. The restaurant started out as a Civil War–era dogtrot cabin, and the Ezells added more rooms for their brisk business. The rambling structure now seats 400 people. Mounted deer and moose heads line the walls. (Mr. Ezell, an avid angler, hunter, and trapper, used to ship his furs to New York's garment district.)

The back porch, a favorite spot for eating, overlooks the river. Start with an appetizer of onion rings, crab claws, or fried dill pickles. In addition to catfish, the restaurant serves seafood specialties such as shrimp and oysters. Entrees come with slaw, potatoes, and hush puppies. Moderate prices. Open seven days a week, Ezell's has flexible hours, but the typical schedule is 11:00 A.M. to 9:00 P.M. Sunday through Thursday and to 10:00 P.M. Friday and Saturday.

Traveling south from Lavaca takes you through large expanses of timberland. Forestry and related industries play major roles in the area's economy. Clarke County holds the title of Forestry Capital of Alabama, and Fulton, a small town south of Thomasville, pays tribute to this important industry by hosting a **Sawmill Days** celebration each fall.

If you visit **Camden** during the Wilcox Historical Society's biennial (slated for odd-numbered years) Fall Tour of Homes, you can survey some of the area's antebellum structures. The stately Wilcox Female Institute, which dates from 1850, serves as tour headquarters. Located at 301 Broad Street, the former school (open by appointment) houses a small museum of local history.

For a Southern taste treat, make reservations at the **Gaines Ridge Dinner Club** (334–682–9707), located about 2 miles east of Camden on State Route 10. Housed in Betty Gaines Kennedy's two-story circa-1830 family home, the restaurant seats about one hundred guests in five dining rooms. From shrimp bisque to spinach salad and steak or seafood, everything on the menu is well prepared and tasty. (Ask Betty about the home's ghosts.) Prices fall in the economical to moderate range, and hours are 5:30 to 9:00 P.M. Wednesday through Saturday.

alabamatrivia

Several Alabama cities offer Saturday walking tours. Check these out at www.walkingtour.com.

Wilcox County, which promises good fishing, attracts out-of-state deer and turkey hunters, and many make their headquarters at nearby **Roland Cooper State Park.** If you're in the area during harvest season, consider purchasing some fresh-shelled pecans from Joe C. Williams. To order the local product, write P.O. Box 640, Camden 36726; or call (334) 682–4559. For more information on Camden and the surrounding area, call the Wilcox Development Council at (334) 682–4929.

Traveling south from Camden on State Route 265 takes you by **Rikard's Mill,** just north of Beatrice. Stop by to browse through the Covered Bridge Gift Shop and watch the old-fashioned water-powered gristmill in operation. You'll also find a restored blacksmith shop and hiking trails. Modest admission. For seasonal hours, April through mid-December, call (251) 789–2781 or (251) 575–7433.

Continue south to **Monroeville** (where Alabama authors Truman Capote and Harper Lee played as children) for a stop at the **Old Monroe County Courthouse.** This 1903 three-story brick structure served as a model for the courthouse in the film *To Kill a Mockingbird,* based on Harper Lee's Pulitzer Prize–winning novel (and starring Gregory Peck in the role of Atticus Finch). During my visit, I entered the courthouse and asked to see Atticus Finch. While applauding myself on being so imaginative, I learned that "everyone wants to meet Atticus Finch."

During the first three weekends in May, visitors can watch the stage version of *To Kill a Mockingbird* in a bona fide courtroom setting. Produced by the Monroe County Heritage Museum under the direction of Kathy McCoy, who heads up the museum staff, the local stage adaptation boasts the authenticity of the story's actual location plus cultural awareness and genuine Southern accents.

Monroeville—Literary Capital of Alabama

In recognition of the exceptional literary heritage of **Monroeville** and Monroe County, the Alabama legislature designated this region the Literary Capital of Alabama in a 1997 joint resolution. Author of "A Christmas Memory," *In Cold Blood, Breakfast at Tiffany's,* and other classics, Truman Capote spent idyllic hours roaming the town as a youngster along with friend Harper Lee, who penned the Pulitzer Prize–winning novel, *To Kill a Mockingbird.* Other writers who have called Monroeville home include nationally syndicated columnist Cynthia Tucker and novelist Mark Childress. The small town of Monroeville, which packs a rich literary history, hosts an Alabama Writers Symposium the first weekend in May. For more information on this event, contact the Alabama Southern Community College at P.O. Box 2000, Monroeville 36461; or call (251) 575–3165, extension 223.

As guests of the government of Israel in 1996, the talented performers (and only amateur group ever invited to participate) presented this classic drama on stage in Jerusalem at the International Cultural Festival. In September 1998 the production traveled to England and was staged at the Hull Theater. In June 2000 the local production traveled to Washington, D.C., for performances at the Kennedy Center for Performing Arts. For more information visit the Web site at www.tokillamockingbird.com, or call or visit the *Old Courthouse Museum* (251–575–7433), which also features changing exhibits related to Monroe County's past and a gift shop with works by area artists. The museum is located at 31 North Alabama Avenue; admission is free. Hours run from 8:00 A.M. to noon and 1:00 to 4:00 P.M. Monday through Friday and 10:00 A.M. to 2:00 P.M. on Saturday.

While downtown, stop by Finishing Touches at 107 East Claiborne Street on the square's south side. You'll enjoy browsing through this shop with lovely handmade items, antiques, kitchen accessories, gifts, clothing for children and ladies, customized baskets, and books. Other interesting shops include On the Square, Magnolia Cottage, and Williams Drug Store, where you can hear some tall tales. Monroeville also offers some great outlet shopping at Vanity Fair.

Before leaving the area, you might want to visit the *River Heritage Museum,* housed in the old Corps of Engineers building at the Claiborne Lock & Dam. The surrounding region is a great place for camping and fishing, too. Located about 18 miles from the square in downtown Monroeville, the museum can be reached by taking State Route 41 to County Road 17 and then following the signs to the Claiborne Lock & Dam. The museum's exhibits feature fossils,

Native American artifacts, and steamboat relics. With seasonal hours, the museum is open April through October. Hours run from 9:00 A.M. to 4:00 P.M. Friday and Saturday; admission is free. For more information call (251) 575–7433.

Gulf Coast Delta

After your timberland excursion head south to Escambia County, where traveling pilgrims can spend an authentic Thanksgiving Day with the Poarch Band of Creek Indians at their annual Pow Wow. Tribal members welcome friends, relatives, and visitors to help them celebrate the Thanksgiving holidays on the **Poarch Creek Reservation,** 8 miles northwest of Atmore at 5811 Jack Springs Road. Festivities include exhibition dancing by tribes from throughout the country, a greased pig chase, turkey shoot, and much more. You can feast on roasted corn, Indian fry bread, ham, fried chicken, or traditional turkey and dressing. Booths feature beadwork, basketry, silver work, and other Native American crafts. Take a lawn chair, camera, and your appetite. Modest admission. For more information on this two-day event, call (251) 368–9136.

Continue southwest toward the Eastern Shore and stop by Malbis, 12 miles east of Mobile on US 90. On Baldwin County Road 27, you'll find the **Malbis Greek Orthodox Church.** This magnificent neo-Byzantine–style structure, built at a cost of more than $1 million, was dedicated to the memory of Jason Malbis. A former monk who emigrated from Greece in 1906, Malbis traveled through thirty-six states before selecting this Baldwin County site to establish Malbis Plantation (virtually a self-supporting colony that grew to cover 2,000 acres).

The marble in this edifice came from the same Greek quarries used to build Athens's ancient Parthenon. The majestic interior features a dark-blue 75-foot domed ceiling, stained-glass windows, mosaics, and murals. Greek artists spent eight months completing the paintings that extend from the cathedral's entrance to its altar. The church is open daily, and admission is free. Hours run from 10:00 A.M. to 4:00 P.M. For more information call (251) 626–3050.

Next swing westward to Daphne, perched on Mobile Bay's Eastern Shore, where you might hear someone shout "Jubilee!" When you do, people will grab buckets and rush to the water's edge for flounder, shrimp, and crabs—theirs for the scooping. Although not unique to the area, this "shoreward migration of bottom-living organisms"—to put it in technical terms—surprises most visitors. This natural phenomenon might occur several times a summer, usually during the wee morning hours. Some natives claim they can predict an approaching jubilee by watching weather conditions and studying certain indicators in the moon, tide, and winds.

After exploring Daphne continue south to *Fairhope,* a charming flower-filled town founded about 1894 on the "single tax" concept of economist Henry George, who considered land the source of all wealth. The Fairhope Single Tax Colony still functions today, one of the country's few model communities operating on George's taxation theories. A percentage of the town's property is held by the Fairhope Single Tax Colony office, and a resident can lease his or her land for ninety-nine years (or perpetuity). The resident pays a single annual tax on the land only—not on improvements—and this yearly payment covers school district, city, county, and state taxes as well as community services.

Save plenty of time for browsing through Fairhope's downtown area, where baskets of cascading blossoms adorn every street corner. You'll see art galleries, eateries, boutiques, and shops offering everything from antiques, toys, and clothing to crafts and nautical gear. Located at the foot of Fairhope Avenue, the attractive Fairhope Pier attracts strollers and joggers.

The *Church Street Inn* (251–928–5144 or 866–928–8976) makes a lovely and convenient base for travelers. Located at 51 South Church Street, the white stucco-and-brick home contains five generations of family photos and antiques. Visitors can relax on the front porch and watch passersby (who often wave

Strange As It Sounds

Whether or not you hear the cry of "Jubilee!" during your visit to the Eastern Shore of Mobile Bay, you can see this strange spectacle depicted in a photo display at *Manci's Antique Club* (251–626– 9917) in downtown Daphne. Located at the corner of Daphne and Bellrose Avenues, this combination bar/museum (originally opened as a gas station in 1924 by Frank Manci, converted to its current status in 1947 by Arthur Manci, and now operated by a third-generation family member, Alex Manci) houses a rickshaw, oxen yokes, and Victrolas. You'll also see collections of antique tools, cowbells, political campaign buttons, and Native American artifacts. The club boasts the biggest assemblage of Jim Beam decanters outside the distillery's own collection. Claiming the title "Bloody Mary Capital of the Eastern Shore," the house serves its specialty garnished with a pickled string bean. A sign over the bar promises FREE BEER TOMORROW.

Those who visit the ladies' room at Manci's will see the wooden figure of a man—dressed only in a fig leaf. The observant will notice the fig leaf is hinged, and the curious might go even further. Unrestrained curiosity can soon turn to horror, however, because a blaring alarm alerts all within hearing distance that one possesses an inquisitive nature. One then must make the uncomfortable choice of exiting—red-faced—to the merriment of Manci's patrons or occupying the ladies' room till closing time. Manci's hours are 10:00 A.M. to 10:00 P.M. Monday through Thursday, and on Friday and Saturday the club stays open until—.

Eat Their Words

Want to sample Fannie Flagg's own fried green tomatoes? Or Winston Grooms's gumbo? Or Pat and Sandra Conroy's dinner party mini-crab casseroles? Then contact the Eastern Shore Literacy Council (251–990–8300) of Fairhope for a copy of *Eat Their Words: Southern Writers, Readers and Recipes.* To order this entertaining 450-page cookbook containing anecdotes and recipes contributed by Dave Barry, Rick Bragg, Barbara Bush, Laura Bush, Kathryn Tucker Windham, and other celebrities, send $20 per book (which includes shipping) to:

Eastern Shore Literacy Council
409 North Section Street, Suite C
Fairhope, AL 36532

(All proceeds benefit the Eastern Shore Literacy Council, a United Way agency.)

hello) or retreat to the back-garden courtyard. The living room's window seat makes a cozy spot for reading about local history. Guests may help themselves to ice cream when hunger pangs strike and enjoy an ample serve-yourself Continental breakfast when they choose. Moderate rates.

Hosts Becky and Bill Jones also welcome visitors to **Bay Breeze Guest House** on historic Mobile Bay, where they can watch the glorious sunsets, go beachcombing or fishing, and feed the resident ducks. Ask Becky, a former biology teacher, about the local jubilee phenomenon. From May through September, guests can enjoy breakfast served on Bay Breeze's pier. Moderate rates. For reservations at either property, call (251) 928–5144 or (866) 928–8976.

Before leaving Fairhope, stop by the Eastern Shore Art Center, at 401 Oak Street, to see its current exhibits. You might also enjoy visiting a unique museum on Faulkner State Community College's Fairhope campus that houses memorabilia from the early days of the **Marietta L. Johnson School of Organic Education** (251–990–8601). Counselor Clarence Darrow, who summered in Fairhope, lectured at this nontraditional school, which was noted for its progressive curriculum promoting creativity. The museum occupies the west wing of the historic Bell Building at 10 South School Street. Hours are 2:00 to 4:00 P.M. Tuesday through Friday or by appointment. Admission is free.

South of Fairhope at Point Clear (designated "Punta Clara" on sixteenth-century maps of Spanish explorers), you'll find **Grand Hotel Marriott Resort, Golf Club & Spa** (251–928–9201 or 800–228–9290) on scenic US 98. This legendary resort on Mobile Bay offers facilities spreading over 550 lovely acres studded with moss-festooned oaks more than 300 years old. The locale has long attracted generations of wealthy Southern families—the site's first resort dates from the mid-1800s. Today's guests continue to enjoy "the Grand's" traditions, such as afternoon tea in the wood-paneled lobby.

The hotel's restaurants offer delightful dining options. Recreation choices range from golf, boating, tennis, swimming, and fishing to croquet. With its new world-class spa and other additions, the Grand is even grander. See for yourself at www.marriottgrand.com. Call for a rate schedule on current package offerings or reservations.

Be sure to visit a candy shop called **Punta Clara Kitchen** (251–928–8477), located in an 1897 gingerbread house 1 mile south of the Grand Hotel. Here you can sample confections from pecan butter crunch and divinity to chocolate-covered bourbon balls and buckeyes (balls of creamy peanut-butter confections hand-dipped in chocolate). The shop also sells jellies, recipe books, pickles, and preserves. Before leaving, take a few minutes to look around this historic home, furnished as it was during the late 1800s. Hours are 9:00 A.M. to 5:00 P.M. Monday through Saturday and 12:30 to 5:00 P.M. Sunday.

Ready for an anti-stress kind of place? Then head for nearby **Magnolia Springs,** where you can unwind in a serene setting of dappled sunlight and live oaks. In its heyday as a resort area during the early part of the 1900s, Magnolia Springs lured visitors with twice-a-day train service from Chicago, St. Louis, and Cincinnati. "Many a consumptive, rheumatic, nervous, worn-out and over-worked person whose case was thought hopeless by the physicians has found health and a new lease on life by spending a few months at Magnolia Springs," states an early promotional pamphlet.

Once known as the Sunnyside Hotel, the **Magnolia Springs Bed and Breakfast** (251–965–7321 or 800–965–7321) at 14469 Oak Street exudes a friendly aura with its welcoming wraparound porch accented by a swing, white wicker furniture, rocking chairs, and ferns. One of the county's three remaining hotels from the resort era, the historic structure is painted a buttery yellow with white trim. Committed to providing warm hospitality, owner David Worthington welcomes guests to his 1867 home, nourishes them with a delicious breakfast, and recommends local excursions. If you go cruising down the river, you'll see mailboxes at the water's edge. Magnolia Springs's first postmaster launched a mail service by water in 1915, and many residents still get their mail delivered by boat. "It's one of only a few places in the country with a water mail route," says David.

You may have seen Magnolia Springs Bed and Breakfast featured on Bob Vila's *Restore America,* a home-and-garden TV program, in *Southern Living* magazine, or maybe on a past Alabama Public Television special. E-mail David at info@magnoliasprings.com. For a virtual tour and more information, log onto www.magnoliasprings.com. Moderate rates.

A short stroll down tree-lined Oak Street takes you to **Moore Brothers Village Market,** a great place to catch up on local news. The market houses a bakery, deli, butcher shop, gourmet foods, and plenty of nostalgia. You can enjoy lunch or dinner Monday through Saturday at **Jesse's Restaurant** (251–965–3827), also on the premises.

The original Moore Bros. Gen'l Merchandise opened in 1922 and remained a family business until it closed in 1993. Then, in 1997, Charlie Houser (who spent childhood days here) returned and purchased the neighborhood store and adjacent post office. With the help of an architect and contractor, he connected and rejuvenated the two buildings to implement his image of the perfect neighborhood gathering place.

Paintings depicting local scenes, old photos, and news articles line the walls of the restaurant and also the entryway, where an antique pie safe displays freshly made pastries. Nearby, you can check your weight on the penny scales. If you find yourself penniless, there's usually a spare coin on top of the machine. By the way, it's best to weigh *before* dining at Jesse's, where the evening special might mean prime rib, shrimp scampi, or whiskey steak. Other popular entrees include crab cakes, Cajun fettuccine, stuffed flounder, and chicken Pontalba. Moderate prices.

Across the road from Jesse's stands Magnolia Springs Park, which showcases one of the town's springs and makes an inviting shady retreat.

After basking in Magnolia Springs's serenity, head for **Foley,** situated around the intersection of US 98 and State Route 59. The town offers not only factory-outlet shopping but a host of attractions such as antiques malls, arts centers, and charming eateries.

Start your tour at 111 West Laurel Avenue with the **Baldwin Museum of Art** and the **Holmes Medical Museum** (251–970–1818 or 251–943–1818), housed in a building that dates to the early 1900s. After viewing the current downstairs art exhibits, climb to the second floor for a close-up look at instruments and memorabilia from medicine's earlier years. Once a hospital for Baldwin County residents, the rooms contain an operating suite complete with table, bone-breaking apparatus, Kelly pad, ether container, and attendant tubes. Also on display are X-ray equipment and medical cabinets filled with delivery forceps, tonsil guillotine and snare, and other instruments. In addition to patient quarters, you can inspect a room devoted to quackery paraphernalia—a color spectrum device for treating everything from headaches to kidney infections, barber bowl for bleeding patients, and diagrammed phrenology skull. Hours are 10:00 A.M. to 4:00 P.M. Monday through Friday. Admission is free.

Continue to the **Performing Arts Center** (251–943–4381) at 119 West Laurel Avenue. Step inside the lobby of the former Foley Hotel, which dates to 1928, for a look at exhibits of juried fine art, and browse back through the dining room filled with more art and crafts by area artists. Notice the extensive pottery selection featuring a variety of techniques. The facility sponsors a sales gallery (a great place to buy unique gifts) as well as cultural events and art classes. Staffed by an all-volunteer organization, the center's hours run from 10:00 A.M. to 4:00 P.M. Monday through Friday and 11:00 A.M. to 2:00 P.M. on Saturday.

Take a break next door at **Stacey Rexall Drugs** (251–943–7191), with its "Old Tyme Soda Fountain." In this delightful pharmacy at 121 West Laurel Avenue, you can savor a banana split, slurp on an ice-cream soda, cherry Coke, or chocolate milk shake, and listen to old favorites from the jukebox or player piano while watching a toy train make its rounds above the soda fountain. A penny scale reveals your weight and fate. Owners Kathi (the "druggist") and John J. Henderson (the "fizzician"), with the help of Adam (the soda jerk), will treat you to an old-fashioned good time. Hours run from 8:00 A.M. to 6:00 P.M. Monday through Friday and 9:00 A.M. to 5:00 P.M. on Saturday. Economical rates.

Continuing to the next block, you'll find **The Gift Horse** (251–943–3663 or 800–FOLEYAL), located at 209 West Laurel Avenue. Beyond the restaurant's leaded-glass doors, you'll see a grand banquet table with a buffet of salads, vegetables, meats, breads, and desserts. House specialties include fried biscuits, spinach soufflé, mystery crab-shrimp salad, and the restaurant's famous apple cheese—all prepared from owner Jackie O. McLeod's recipes. Lunch is served from 11:00 A.M. to 4:15 P.M. Monday through Saturday. Dinner hours run from 4:30 to 9:00 P.M. Monday through Saturday, and Sunday hours run from 11:00 A.M. to 8:00 P.M. Rates are moderate. Jackie's cookbook, available in the gift shop, makes a great souvenir and divulges some of her culinary secrets. While in Foley you may want to visit The Gift Horse Antique Centre, too.

Follow US 98 east to Elberta. During the first half of the century, this fertile area attracted families from central, northern, and southern Europe, as well as Quebec. At Elberta's **German Sausage Festivals,** staged in March and October, descendants of early settlers dress in native attire to perform Old World dances. Call (251) 986–5805 for more information.

To learn more about the ethnic diversity and lifestyles of the county's early settlers, stop by the **Baldwin County Heritage Museum** (251–986–8375), ½ mile east of Elberta on US 98. In front of the five-acre wooded setting called "Frieden Im Wald," you'll see a working windmill and several outdoor agricultural exhibits.

Displays inside the museum feature the Kee tool collection and vintage farm equipment, a printing press, and an interior section of a post office from Josephine, Alabama. Household items include an Edison phonograph, antique sewing machines, stoves, cooking utensils, and washing machines. Also on display are old-fashioned school desks, folk sculpture, and a moonshine still. The museum is staffed entirely by volunteers, many of them snowbirds from Minnesota, Wisconsin, Michigan, New York, and other northern states, who contribute their time and skills to restoring artifacts and putting old machinery in running order again. Modest admission. Hours are 10:00 A.M. to 4:00 P.M. Wednesday through Saturday, with a special program offered at 2:00 P.M. on the second Sunday of each month. Weekday tours can be arranged by appointment.

At 12695 County Road 95 in Elberta, you can study carnivorous plants like Venus's-flytrap, pitcher plants, and other unusual botanical specimens at ***Biophilia Nature Center.*** "Different kinds of wildlife can be seen in season," said Carol Lovell-Saas, who promotes environmental education and takes you on a walk through her "open book of nature" that spreads across twenty acres. Tours offer a mini-course in butterfly gardening for the South and the Midwest and include free pamphlets on each plus literature on ecogardening.

From spring through early winter, several kinds of showy native butterflies are raised indoors and outdoors, allowing visitors to observe all stages from egg to adult. You'll see forest wildflower meadows and swamps, now being restored with 300 native species, and can stop by a plant nursery and bookstore on the premises. Contact Carol at (251) 987–1200 for specific directions and hours. Check her Web site at www.Biophilia.net.

Afterward make your way back to Foley, then follow State Route 59 south to the glistening white sands of ***Gulf Shores.*** Although a Diners' Club publication once conferred highest honors on the stretch of shoreline along the Florida panhandle between Destin and Panama City, calling it "the world's most perfect beach," fewer people know about the other end of the Southern Riviera—Alabama's toehold on the Gulf of Mexico. In fact, the relatively new town of Gulf Shores did not appear on Alabama's official highway map until the sixties. But a retreat offering sugar-sand beaches and a balmy climate cannot remain a secret forever, and this 32-mile crescent known as Pleasure Island (once a peninsula) now attracts vacationers from across the country.

Some one hundred charter boats dock at nearby ***Orange Beach*** marinas, offering outings from sunset cruises to fishing excursions. Surrounding waters feature world-class fishing throughout the year. (For information about state fishing licenses, call 334–242–3829 or 888–848–6887, or check out www.outdoor alabama.com.)

To see some secluded portions of the area, sign up for a barefoot cruise aboard the **Daedalus** with Captain Barry Brothers. Based at 5749 Bay La Launch, you'll find the 50-foot sailboat at Bear Point Marina in Orange Beach. Because the big vessel performs in shallow water, passengers can visit hidden bayous and bays and even venture onto an uninhabited beach. Also, you'll

Flora-Bama—Home of the Annual Mullet Toss

Jimmy Buffett used to come here and jam. John Grisham wrote about it in a novel. It's the area's hottest hangout—the *Flora-Bama,* boasting an identity all its own. Located ten minutes from Gulf Shores on the Alabama/Florida line, the place bills itself as "one of the nation's last great roadhouse watering holes."

"You never know what'll be going on here," says a local. The crowd is mixed, and so is the music—everything from country to rock and roll—and mostly original music. Flora-Bama offers entertainment every day of the year and attracts throngs including now-and-future-famous musicians and songwriters.

Regulars claim good music is the big draw here. You might happen on a folk singer holding court or six bands on three stages in different sections nightly (in season). They swap sets, so it's possible to hear up to twelve bands in one evening. Several Nashville regulars perform and record at Flora-Bama.

The party heats up after five, and the parking lot gets full fast. Though success often invites duplication, Flora-Bama's idiosyncratic style and haphazard floor plan make cloning a remote possibility. Beyond the storefront package shop through room after rambling room, one ultimately finds a large deck overlooking the Gulf of Mexico. Here's the best vantage point for watching the annual Interstate Mullet Toss, held the last weekend in April. (What's a mullet toss? An event on the beach where people vie for the dubious distinction of pitching a dead fish the greatest distance—from Florida to Alabama.)

If your April calendar is too full to fit in the Mullet Toss, there's always next January 1 and the Polar Bear Dip. After testing the Gulf of Mexico's cold waters, you can warm up with a serving of black-eyed peas—the traditional Southern dish declared to bring good luck throughout the year. (The luck intensifies if you consume collards or other greens, and adding hog jowl almost guarantees more luck than you can stand.)

Otherwise you can meander around, buy souvenirs, consume beverages, visit the Beach Oyster Bar, eat crab claws or Royal Reds (the very best of steamed shrimp), purchase lottery tickets, or converse with other patrons. The person standing next to you might have a total of five dollars in his jeans pocket or five million on his net worth statement.

Located at 17401 Perdido Key Drive, with a Pensacola zip, Flora-Bama (251–980–5119 or 850–492–3048) opens daily at 9:00 A.M. and shuts down in the wee hours.

enjoy watching cavorting dolphins, ospreys, blue herons, and other wildlife. To book your passage call (251) 987–1228 or click on www.sailthedaedalus.com for more information.

While exploring Orange Beach, once home to myriad orange trees, search out *Bayside Grill* (251–981–4899) at Sportsman Marina. Located at 27842

Canal Road, the eatery promises lunch, dinner, and sunsets on the deck. Owner Greg Bushmohle features Creole and Caribbean cuisine in a casual setting. Ask about the fresh catch of the day with several choices, grilled to perfection, and served with Cuban yellow rice and steamed fresh vegetables. (During my visit, cobia, a migratory fish that passes through the area during certain months— April and May are the best times to catch it—was on the menu.) Moderate prices. Hours are 11:00 A.M. to 9:00 P.M. Monday through Thursday and 11:00 A.M. to 10:00 P.M. on weekends except Sunday, when brunch is served from 11:00 A.M. to 2:00 P.M.

During the second weekend of October, seafood lovers flock to *Gulf Shores's National Shrimp Festival.* Speaking of shrimp, this is the place to walk into a seafood outlet, just after the fleet has docked, and buy your dinner fresh from coastal waters. Many area fish markets will ice-pack local seafood for travel.

The tiny fishing village of *Bon Secour,* located west of State Route 59 between Foley and Gulf Shores, is home to several shrimp-packing operations. At some of these, you can crunch your way through oyster shells to watch the unloading process and buy the day's freshest catch directly off the boat. Look for signs along Baldwin County Road 10 that lead to several of these markets with their colorful shrimp boats on the Bon Secour River.

During the late 1700s French settlers staked a claim here, naming the area Bon Secour for "Safe Harbour." While driving around, notice the lovely little church, Our Lady of Bon Secour, framed with Spanish moss in its tree-shaded setting.

Several area eateries will cook your catch. Mike Spence, owner of *Fish Camp Restaurant* (251–968–CAMP) at 4297 Baldwin County Road 6, offers a "You hook 'em and we cook 'em!" option. Try the bottomless house-salad, garlic bread, and corn fritters with a Caribbean-style seafood and pasta dish or a house specialty like sautéed scallops or crawfish tails. Open daily at 11:00 A.M., the restaurant's hours are flexible, but usually the staff serves till 9:00 P.M. every night except Friday and Saturday, when closing time is 10:00 P.M. Moderate prices. Call for specific directions.

After dipping into the Gulf of Mexico's foaming waves and basking in the sunshine, you may want to sally forth to other points of interest, such as historic *Fort Morgan* (251–540–7127). Located

alabamatrivia

Isabella de Soto planted America's first fig trees, which came over from Spain, at Fort Morgan.

at the end of a scenic drive 22 miles west of Gulf Shores on State Route 180, the fort—built to guard Mobile Bay—played a major role during the Civil War. At

A Sunken Treasure— Discovered by Mistake

Once upon a time, a Spanish ship named *El Cazador* went sailing on the Gulf of Mexico. The ship, loaded with a fortune in minted silver coins, never reached its destination—New Orleans. Then on an ordinary fishing trip in August 1993, Jerry Murphy, captain of a fishing vessel named *Mistake,* brought up his nets to find—not butterfish—but ballast and clusters of encrusted coins. He'd discovered "the wreck that changed the world." This significant find prompted Murphy to call his uncle, Jim Reahard, who soon set wheels in motion by claiming the wreck (located outside state and federal boundaries) and forming the Grumpy Partnership.

After hearing this engrossing story about a museum where visitors could see, touch, and purchase silver coins dating back to 1783, I set out for Grand Bay near the Mississippi border. And, sure enough—treasure! I saw the anchor, ship's bell, gold and silver coins, sword handles, jewelry, china, silverware, brass buttons, and other artifacts recovered from the Spanish brigantine of war.

Jim brought me a cup of coffee, and his wife, Myrna, showed me displays of photographs documenting the recovery. The Reahards spend much of their time these days dealing with matters from research to reclaiming the treasure. Their daughter, Debbie Hale, works as preservationist. Through a painstaking process she transforms clumps of corroded coins into shiny polished pieces of eight and reales.

Working with the Spanish archives in Seville, Jim started fitting the puzzle together. He explained that the El Cazador sailed from Veracruz, Mexico, on January 11, 1784, bound for New Orleans in Spanish-owned Louisiana with silver to bolster the sagging economy. "We don't know why the ship sank," Jim says. "We can only speculate." The silver's loss drained a declining economy even more, and Spain's North American grip gradually weakened, forcing the Spanish king to sell his holdings to Napoleon.

I found both a treasure and a fascinating history lesson at **El Cazador Museum** (251–865–0128), housed in a former bank building at 10329 Freeland Avenue. Museum hours run from 10:00 A.M. to 4:00 P.M. Thursday through Saturday. Admission is free.

To peep into the museum's treasure trove, visit its Web site at www.elcazador.com.

the Battle of Mobile Bay on August 5, 1864, "torpedoes" (underwater mines) were strung across the channel to stop the Union fleet from entering. This strategy failed when Adm. David Farragut issued his famous command: "Damn the torpedoes—full speed ahead!"

Today's visitors can explore vaulted corridors and peer into dark rooms of this historic fort, named in honor of Revolutionary War hero Gen. Daniel Morgan. Designed by Simon Bernard, a French engineer and former aide-de-camp to Napoleon, the five-pointed star structure pays tribute to the craftsmanship of men who labored from 1819 to 1834. As technology changed, the original fort continued to be modified and upgraded, says curator Mike Bailey. In the museum, exhibits cover military history from the fort's early days through World War II. Except for major holidays, the museum is open daily from 9:00 A.M. to 5:00 P.M., and the fort is open from 8:00 A.M. to 6:00 P.M. in winter and 7:00 P.M. during summer months. Modest admission.

After seeing Fort Morgan you may want to board the Mobile Bay Ferry for a visit to Fort Gaines on Dauphin Island. The ferry transports passengers and vehicles between the two forts at ninety-minute intervals. Call (251) 540–7787 for specific times and current rates.

Don't miss nearby **Bellingrath Gardens and Home** (251–973–2217 or 800–247–8420), located at Theodore about 20 miles southwest of Mobile. Once a simple fishing camp, the sixty-five-acre wonderland lures visitors year-round. Because of south Alabama's climate, you can expect gorgeous displays of blossoms here, whatever the season. You can also wend your way along the Nature Boardwalk and take a river cruise while visiting. Upon arrival you'll receive a map illustrating the layout of the six gardens linked by bridges, walkways, streams, lakes, and lily-filled ponds. (Be sure to wear your walking shoes.)

After exploring the gardens you may want to tour the former home of Bessie and Walter Bellingrath (he was an early Coca-Cola executive). The house contains outstanding collections of Dresden china, Meissen figurines, and antique furnishings. The world's largest public exhibit of porcelain sculptures by Edward Marshall Boehm is on display in the visitors lounge. Separate admission fees for gardens and home. The gardens are open daily from 8:00 A.M. to 5:00 P.M. To tiptoe through the tulips or see what else might be in bloom via the Internet, click on www.Bellingrath.org.

Save plenty of time for **Mobile**, a city famous for its magnificent live oaks, some reputed to be more than 400 years old. Trimmed in silvery Spanish moss, the enormous trees spread their branching canopies over city streets. Always magical, Mobile is especially so during spring, when masses of azaleas explode into vibrant pinks, reds, and magentas, making the Church Street area, DeTonti Square, Oakleigh Garden, Spring Hill, and other historic districts more beautiful than ever. March is the month to view the azaleas at their vibrant peak. During the

alabamatrivia

Mobile is Alabama's oldest city.

annual **Azalea Trail Festival**, you can follow the signs along a 37-mile route that winds past lovely homes ranging in style from Greek Revival and Italianate to Southern Creole. (Mobile's own "Creole cottage," adapted for the local clime, evolved from the French Colonial form.)

Cruising on the Cotton Blossom

Discover Mobile from a different perspective by taking an excursion on the **Cotton Blossom** *Riverboat,* docked near the Conference Center at 1 South Water Street. You'll get a close-up view of Mobile's bustling harbor scene while relaxing aboard this authentic 1928 stern-wheeler, one of only four boats in the nation to be listed on the National Register of Historic Places. To make reservations for a sunset dinner, or a historical, environmental, or holiday cruise, call (251) 438–3060. For a different sort of aquatic adventure, ask about a pontoon outing on the **Delta Explorer,** docked at 3809 Battleship Parkway on Scenic Causeway US 90/98. This eco-tour boat navigates the Mobile-Tensas Delta, one of the state's ten natural wonders, and lets you delve into an expansive wetland habitat teeming with wildlife.

Be sure to stop by the official welcome center, **Fort Condé,** (251–208–7304) at 150 Royal Street, for some background on Alabama's oldest city. Mobile has been governed by France, England, Spain, the Republic of Alabama, the Confederate States of America, and the United States. Built in 1711, Fort Condé was once home base for the sprawling French Louisiana territory, and a re-created version now serves as a living-history museum. Soldiers in period French uniforms greet visitors, guiding them through the complex with its thick walls and low-slung doors. A succession of exhibits and dioramas tell the city's story, and part of that story is the birth of Mardi Gras—Mobilians celebrated America's first Mardi Gras in 1703. Today's Mardi Gras festivities, which extend over a two-month period, feature more than twenty-five spectacular parades and magnificent balls. Hours are 8:00 A.M. to 5:00 P.M. daily, and admission is free.

Near the fort you'll see **Roussos** (251–433–3322) at 166 South Royal Street. Although celebrated for its fresh seafood, Roussos offers a variety of menu items including Greek salads, chicken, and steak. You might start with gumbo (made from a secret Creole recipe used by Mr. George when he started the business three decades ago) and then order the sautéed crabmeat. Hours are 11:00 A.M. to 10:00 P.M. Monday through Saturday. Prices are moderate to expensive.

Nearby you'll find the **Malaga Inn** (251–438–4701 or 800–235–1586) at 359 Church Street. A charming place to make your base, this quaint hotel started out as twin townhouses in 1862—the families of sisters shared a patio between their mirror-image houses. In 1967 the historic structures were joined by a connector and converted into a hotel.

Individually decorated rooms and suites are furnished with antiques or nostalgic reproductions. You'll enjoy relaxing in the inn's garden courtyard with its flowing fountain, umbrella-topped tables, and surrounding galleries of ornamental ironwork. The inn serves a deluxe Continental breakfast, and evening cocktails are available. Rates range from standard to moderate.

Several mansions, including the **Richards-DAR House** (251–208–7320), open their doors to the public not only during spring tours but throughout the year. Located at 256 North Joachim Street in DeTonti Square, this 1860 Italianate antebellum home is noted for its "frozen lace" ironwork that decorates the facade in an elaborate pattern. Be sure to notice the etched ruby Bohemian glass framing the entrance. Other fine features include a suspended staircase, Carrara marble mantels, and striking brass and crystal chandeliers signed by Cornelius. In the rear wing you'll find a gift shop. Except for major holidays, the home, operated by the Daughters of the American Revolution, is open from 11:00 A.M. to 3:30 P.M. Monday through Friday, 10:00 A.M. to 4:00 P.M. Saturday, and 1:00 to 4:00 P.M. Sunday. Admission.

You may also want to tour the Oakleigh Historic Complex in its serene oak-shaded setting at 350 Oakleigh Place. The guides dress in authentic costumes of the 1830s to conduct tours through an 1833 antebellum house/museum filled with early Victorian, Empire, and Regency furnishings.

To dip into more of the city's past, make reservations at the **The Kate Shepard House Bed and Breakfast** (251–479–7080) in the heart of historic Dauphin Way. Located at 1552 Monterey Place, this handsome Queen Anne Victorian home is listed on the National Register of Historic Places. Built by C. M. Shepard in 1897, it was designed by well-known architect George Franklin Barber.

"Guests can pull into the driveway and park under the porte cochere," says Wendy James, who with husband Bill owns the home. "We have a dog that will bark loudly when you arrive, but will be your best friend in minutes." The couple, who lived in Hawaii for almost fifteen years, searched the southeast for the perfect historic house and setting to establish their long-planned bed-and-breakfast. Captivating Mobile and this lovely home, surrounded by century-old magnolia trees, won their hearts. Along with eleven fireplaces, four original

Richards-DAR House

Indulge Your Sweet Tooth at Three Georges

Long a local tradition, **Three Georges** (251–433–6725) at 226 Dauphin Street has been tempting Mobilians and lucky visitors with luscious hand-dipped chocolates, heavenly hash, pralines, divinity, and many varieties of fudge—from buttermilk to Mardi Gras. George Pappas, George Sparr, and George Coudopolos founded this enterprise, the city's oldest candy company, in 1917. Marble-based cases and original glass candy jars hold a rainbow assortment of jelly beans and rock candy. Current owner George—oops—Scott Gonzales shared this recipe for his ever-popular buttermilk fudge (my favorite).

Buttermilk Fudge

1 cup buttermilk

½ cup margarine

3 tablespoons light corn syrup

1 teaspoon baking soda

2 cups sugar

1 teaspoon vanilla

2 cups pecans, chopped (optional)

Butter 9-inch square pan and set aside. In saucepan, combine buttermilk, margarine, corn syrup, baking soda, and sugar. Cook on medium-high heat, stirring occasionally until mixture boils. Scrape down sides of pan if sugar crystals form. Cook to 236 degrees (soft ball). Remove from heat and let stand until mixture cools to 210 degrees. Add vanilla and pecans. Stir until mixture becomes creamy. Pour into pan and refrigerate until firm (about 3 hours). Cut into squares.

stained glass windows, and beautiful woodwork, the home came with a surprise—an attic full of treasures. Wendy shares stories regarding this *lagniappe* (something extra) with her guests.

Shepard's daughters, Kate and Isabel, operated a private boarding and day school here during the early 1900s. Wendy, who continues to research the home's history, filled several glass-front cases with school memorabilia and framed several photos from that era. Moderate rates. For more information, click on www.bbonline.com/al/kateshepard.

No visit to the Port City would be complete without scaling the decks of the **Battleship U.S.S. Alabama** (800 GANGWAY), moored in Mobile Bay. This renowned vessel played the role of the U.S.S. *Missouri* in the movie *Under Siege,* starring Steven Seagal.

Now the focal point of the 155-acre park on Battleship Parkway just off the Interstate 10 causeway, the U.S.S. *Alabama* served in every major engagement in the Pacific during World War II, apparently leading a charmed life through-out her thirty-seven months of active duty. She earned not only nine battle stars but also the nickname "Lucky A" (from her crew of 2,500) because she emerged unscathed from the heat of each battle.

You can explore below and upper decks and roam through the captain's cabin, officers' staterooms, messing and berthing spaces, and crew's galley. Authentic touches include calendar girl pinups and background music, with such singers as Bing Crosby and Frank Sinatra crooning songs popular during the 1940s.

Anchored beside the battleship, the U.S.S. *Drum* gives visitors a chance to thread their way through a submarine and marvel at how a crew of seventy-two men could live, run their ship, and fire torpedoes while confined to such tight quarters. You'll also see the U.S.S. *Alabama* Battleship Memorial Park's Aircraft Exhibit Pavilion.

Open every day except Christmas, the park can be visited from 8:00 A.M. until 6:00 P.M. Admission is charged. To visit the battleship via the Internet, check out www.ussalabama.com.

Places to Stay in Southwest Alabama

CAMDEN

Roland Cooper State Park
285 Deer Run Drive
(334) 682–4838

EUTAW

Oakmont Bed & Breakfast
119 Pickens Street
(205) 372–2326

FAIRHOPE

Bay Breeze Guest House
742 South Mobile Street
(251) 928–5144 or
(866) 928–8976

Church Street Inn
51 South Church Street
(251) 928–5144 or
(866) 928–8976

GULF SHORES/ ORANGE BEACH

The Beach Club
925 Beach Club Trail
(251) 540–2500 or
(888) 260–7263

The Beach House
9218 Dacus Lane
(251) 540–7039 or
(800) 659–6004

Island House Hotel
26650 Perdido Beach Boulevard
(251) 981–6100 or
(800) 264–2642

Meyer Real Estate (for resort rentals)
1585 Gulf Shores Parkway
(251) 968–7516 or
1–800–487–5959

Perdido Beach Resort
27200 Perdido Beach Boulevard
(251) 981–9811 or
(800) 634–8001

MAGNOLIA SPRINGS

Magnolia Springs Bed and Breakfast
14469 Oak Street
(251) 965–7321 or
(800) 965–7321

MARION

The Gateway Inn
1615 State Route 5 South
(334) 683–9166

Myrtle Hill
303 and 305 West Lafayette Street
(334) 683–9095

MOBILE

Adam's Mark Hotel
64 South Water Street
(251) 438–4000 or
(800) 444–ADAM

The Kate Shepard House Bed and Breakfast
1552 Monterey Place
(251) 479–7080

Lafayette Plaza Hotel
301 Government Street
(251) 694–0100 or
(800) 692–6662

Malaga Inn
359 Church Street
(251) 438–4701 or
(800) 235–1586

Mauvila Mansion
1306 Dauphin Street
(251) 432–2492 or
(866) 432–4600

**Radisson Admiral
Semmes Hotel**
251 Government Street
(251) 432–8000 or
(800) 333–3333

MONROEVILLE

Best Western Inn
4419 South Alabama Avenue
(251) 575–9999 or
(800) WESTERN

Holiday Inn Express
120 State Route 21 South
(251) 743–3333 or
(800) HOLIDAY

POINT CLEAR

**Grand Hotel Marriott
Resort, Golf Club & Spa**
One Grand Boulevard
(251) 928–9201 or
(800) 544–9933

SELMA

Bridgetenders House
2 Lafayette Park
(334) 875–5517

Hampton Inn
2200 West Highland Avenue
(334) 876–9995 or
(800) 726–7866

MAINSTREAM ATTRACTIONS WORTH SEEING IN SOUTHWEST ALABAMA

The Gulf Coast Exploreum, Science Center, and IMAX Theater,
65 Government Street at exit 26B
off I–10, Mobile,
features fascinating exhibits from the world of science, and that's not all. The facility hosted a rare exhibit in 2002—*Rockefeller: 300 Years of American Art,* on loan from the Fine Arts Museum of San Francisco during Mobile's year-long 300th birthday party. For more information call (251) 208–6873 or (877) 625–4FUN or visit www.exploreum.net.

Adjacent to The Gulf Coast Exploreum, at 111 South Royal Street, **The Museum of Mobile** offers a treasure-trove in a National Historic Landmark building that dates to 1857 and occupies a portion of the Southern Market/Old City Hall. The Changing Exhibit Gallery has featured the intriguing (especially to Civil War buffs) *CSS Alabama: The Untold Story and Fun and Finery—Costumes of Mobile's Mardi Gras,* featuring some royal regalia never shown before.
Check out www.museumofmobile.com or call (251) 208–7569.

In 2002, the city of Mobile celebrated its 300th birthday with a host of activities such as the blockbuster exhibit, *Picturing French Style: Three Hundred Years of Art and Fashion,* at the stunning new **Mobile Museum of Art.** Established in 1964, the museum moved from its former quarters on Civic Center Drive to its present setting at 4850 Museum Drive in Langan Park. The grand lobby's commanding glass entrance hall overlooks a lake and makes the outdoors seem part of a sweeping landscape. The handsome building is home to a permanent collection of more than 6,000 works of art, which span 2,000 years of cultural history, and is particularly strong in American paintings of the 1930s and 1940s plus works by Southern artists, art of the French Barbizon School, and contemporary American crafts. For more information click on www.mobilemuseumofart.com or call the museum at (251) 208–5200.

St. James Hotel
1200 Water Avenue
(334) 872–3234

Places to Eat in Southwest Alabama

CAMDEN

Gaines Ridge Dinner Club
933 State Route 10 East
(334) 682–9707

CODEN

Mary's Place
5075 State Route 188
(251) 873–4514

DAPHNE

Guido's Italian Restaurant
1709 Main Street
(251) 626–6082

DEMOPOLIS

Ellis V
708 U.S. Highway 80 East
(334) 289–3446

Foscue House
21333 U.S. Highway 80
West
(334) 289–2221

New Orleans Bar & Grill
Demopolis Yacht Basin
(334) 289–2668

The Red Barn
901 U.S. Highway 80 East
(334) 289–0595

EUTAW

The Cotton Patch
Union Road
(205) 372–4235

Main Street Eatery and Deli
208 Main Street
(205) 372–0209

FAIRHOPE

Gambino's
18 Laurel Avenue
(251) 928–5444

The Royal Oak
14 North Church Street
(251) 928–1714

FAUNSDALE

**Ca-John's Faunsdale
Bar & Grill**
35558 State Route 25
(334) 628–3240

FOLEY

The Gift Horse
209 West Laurel Avenue
(251) 943–3663 or
(800) FOLEYAL

GULF SHORES/ ORANGE BEACH

Bayside Grill
27842 Canal Road
(251) 981–4899

**Calypso Fish Grille
& Market**
27075 Marina Road
(251) 981–1415

Fish Camp Restaurant
4297 Baldwin County
State Route 6
(251) 968–CAMP

**Fort Morgan Marina
Restaurant**
1577 State Route 180 West
(251) 540–HOOK

Gulf Bay Seafood Grill
24705 Canal Road
(251) 974–5090

Lulu's at Homeport Marina
Under W.C. Holmes Bridge
Intracoastal Waterway
(251) 967–LULU

Mango's on the Island
Orange Beach Marina
27075 Marina Road
(251) 981–1416

LAVACA

Ezell's Fish Camp
166 Lotts Berry Road
(205) 654–2205

MAGNOLIA SPRINGS

Jesse's Restaurant
14770 Oak Street
(251) 965–3827

MARION

The Gateway Inn
1615 State Route 5 South
(334) 683–2582

MOBILE

The Pillars
1757 Government Street
(251) 471–3411

Loretta's
19 South Conception Street
(251) 432–2200

Nan Seas
4170 Bay Front Road
(251) 479–9132

Roussos
166 South Royal Street
(251) 433–3322

Spot of Tea
310 Dauphin Street
(251) 433–9009

The Tiny Diny
2159 Halls Mill Road
(251) 473–9453

SELMA

Major Grumbles
1 Grumbles Alley
(334) 872–2006

Tally-Ho Restaurant
509 Mangum Avenue
(334) 872–1390

FOR MORE INFORMATION ABOUT SOUTHWEST ALABAMA

Alabama Gulf Coast Convention & Visitors Bureau
23685 Perdido Beach Boulevard
Orange Beach 36561 OR
P.O. Box 457
Gulf Shores 36547
(251) 974–1510 or (800) 982–8562
Web site: www.gulfshores.com
e-mail: info@gulfshores.com

Demopolis Area Chamber of Commerce
102 East Washington Street
P.O. Box 667
Demopolis 36732
(334) 289–0270
Web site: www.demopolischamber.com

Eastern Shore Chamber of Commerce
327 Fairhope Avenue
Fairhope 36532
(251) 928–6387

Foley Convention & Visitors Bureau
109 West Laurel Avenue
Foley 36535
(251) 943–1200
Web site: www.foleycvb.com
e-mail: foleycvb@gulftel.com

Gulf Shores Welcome Center
3150 Gulf Shores Parkway
(State Route 59 South)
Gulf Shores 36542
(251) 968–7511 or (800) 745–SAND
www.gulfshores.com

Mobile Bay Convention & Visitors Bureau
One South Water Street
P.O. Box 204
Mobile 36601-0204
(251) 208–2000 or (800) 5MOBILE
Web site: www.mobile.org
e-mail: mbcvb@mobile.org

Monroeville Area Chamber of Commerce
36 North Alabama Avenue
P.O. Box 214
Monroeville 36461
(251) 743–2879
Web site: www.monroecountyal.com
e-mail: info@monroecountyal.com

Orange Beach Welcome Center
23685 Perdido Beach Boulevard
Orange Beach 36561
(251) 974–1510
Web site: www.orangebeach.com

Selma/Dallas County
Chamber of Commerce
912 Selma Avenue
P.O. Box 467
Selma 36702
(334) 875–7241 or (800) 45–SELMA
Web site: www.SelmaAlabama.com
e-mail: info@SelmaAlabama.com

Index

About the Author

Gay N. Martin, who lives in Alabama, enjoys writing about travel in the Southeast. Her articles and travel pieces have appeared in *Modern Bride*, the *Boston Herald, Kiwanis*, the *Atlanta Journal-Constitution*, the London *Free Press*, the *San Antonio Express-News*, the *Seattle Post-Intelligencer, Far East Traveler*, the *Birmingham News*, the *Times-Picayune*, the *Grand Rapids Press*, and other publications. She has won numerous writing awards for fiction and nonfiction in state, regional, and national competitions. She is also the author of Globe Pequot's *Louisiana Off the Beaten Path* and *Alabama's Historic Restaurants and Their Recipes*, published by John F. Blair.

Before embarking on her writing career, Martin taught high school for eleven years, served as resource coordinator of her school's program for gifted and talented students, and sponsored the school newspaper. She is a member of the Society of American Travel Writers and International Food, Wine, and Travel Writers Association. Visit her Web site at www.gnmartintravels.com.